The Russian Peasantry
1600–1930

C000220148

The Russian Peasantry
1600–1930

The World the Peasants Made

David Moon

LONGMAN
London and New York

Addison Wesley Longman Limited
Edinburgh Gate,
Harlow, Essex CM20 2JE, United Kingdom
and Associated Companies throughout the world.

Published in the United States of America by Addison Wesley Longman, New York.

© Addison Wesley Longman Limited 1999

First published 1999

ISBN 0-582-09508-5 CSD
ISBN 0-582-09507-7 PPR

Visit Addison Wesley Longman on the World Wide Web at http://www.awl-he.com

British Library Cataloguing in Publication Data

A catalogue entry for this title is available from the British Library

Library of Congress Cataloging-in-Publication Data

Moon, David, 1959–
    The Russian peasantry : the world the peasants made / David Moon.
      p. cm.
    Includes bibliographical references and index.
    ISBN 0–582–09507–7 (pbk). — ISBN 0–582–09508–5 (hbk)
    1. Peasantry—Russia. 2. Russia—Social conditions. I. Title.
HD1536.R9M66 1999
305.5′633′0947—dc21   98–51943
                                                         CIP

Set by 35 in 10/12pt Bembo
Printed in Singapore (KKP)

Contents

List of tables, maps and figures

Acknowledgements

While working on this book I have incurred many debts which it is a pleasure to acknowledge. Financial support has been provided by the Research Committee, Small Grants Committee, Staff Travel Fund and Department of History of the University of Newcastle upon Tyne, and by the British Academy. I have received much assistance from the staffs of the Robinson Library at the University of Newcastle, the Main and Alexander Baykov Libraries at the University of Birmingham, the British Library (at Bloomsbury, St Pancras and Boston Spa), and the Russian National Library (formerly the Saltykov–Shchedrin State Public Library) and the Russian State Historical Archive (RGIA, formerly TsGIA SSSR) in St Petersburg. I am especially grateful to the staff of the Inter-Library Loans Desk at the Robinson Library, who have set the highest standards of efficiency, courtesy and good humour while processing several hundred requests.

Preliminary versions of the outline and some of the ideas in this book first saw light in a lecture course entitled 'The Russian Peasantry from Serfdom to the Collective Farm', which I taught at the University of Texas at Austin in the spring semester of 1989. I am grateful to the History Department for giving me the opportunity to teach the course, and to the students, whose interest persuaded me the project was worth returning to and pursuing in more depth when time permitted.

More recently, while writing this book, I have had the good fortune to present papers on aspects of the subject at seminars and conferences at the following (British) universities: Birmingham (Centre for Russian and East European Studies); Cambridge (including twice at the annual conference of the British Association for Slavonic and East European Studies); Essex (Department of History); London (School of Slavonic and East European Studies); and St Andrews (Department of Modern History). I should like to thank my hosts on these occasions, and all who contributed to the discussions and asked probing questions. I have endeavoured to respond in this book to some of the questions I was unable to answer at the time.

A number of these papers and other pieces of work towards this book have appeared as articles. None is reproduced in its entirety, but revised versions of some sections or passages do appear. I am grateful to the editors and publishers of the following journals for permitting me to use adaptations of previously published material: *Europe–Asia Studies*, Carfax Publishing Ltd, Abingdon

OX14 3UE ('Estimating the peasant population of late Imperial Russia from the 1897 census', vol. 48 [1996], pp. 141–153); *Historical Journal*, Cambridge University Press ('Peasant migration and the settlement of Russia's frontiers, 1550–1897', vol. 30 [1997], pp. 859–893); *European History Quarterly*, SAGE Publications Ltd, London EC2A 4PU ('Reassessing Russian serfdom', vol. 26 [1996], pp. 483–526); *Continuity and Change*, Cambridge University Press ('Women in rural Russia from the tenth to the twentieth centuries' [review article], vol. 12 [1997], pp. 129–138); *Revolutionary Russia*, Frank Cass Publishers, Ilford IG2 7HH ('Peasants into Russian citizens? A comparative perspective', vol. 9 [1996], pp. 43–81, and 'Peasant rebels under Stalin' [review article], vol. 11 [1998], pp. 74–78). I have also reused a few sentences from other review articles and book reviews which appeared in *Historical Journal, European History Quarterly* and *Revolutionary Russia*. I should also like to thank Professor Peter Czap and Cambridge University Press for permitting me to reproduce the diagrams in Figure 5.1.
I have received a great deal of advice from many specialists on Russian history, peasant societies and other aspects of social history. A full list would be very long and implicate too many people. To all I am very grateful. I have already expressed my thanks to some in the articles cited above, but would like to single out here those scholars who were kind enough to read and comment on earlier drafts of parts of this book (in some cases in the capacity of formal discussants): Paul Dukes, Peter Gatrell, Carol Leonard, Ed Melton, R. I. Moore, Judith Pallot, Maureen Perrie and David Saunders. None necessarily agrees with what I have written in this book, and sole responsibility for any errors and shortcomings lies with the author. I should also like to express my gratitude to Andrew MacLennan of Addison Wesley Longman for his encouragement and patience.
On a personal level, I am very grateful for the support I have received from my parents, sisters Pauline and Angela, brother-in-law Alan, and, especially, from Alison, to whom this book is dedicated.

David Moon
Newcastle upon Tyne
August 1998

Author's note

I have endeavoured to find satisfactory English translations or equivalents for Russian historical terms. In several cases the original Russian terms are given in brackets in the text on their first appearance in each chapter, e.g. labour services (*barshchina*). A Glossary of terms, both Russian and English, is provided on pp. 378–80.

The notes contain references to many of the main sources for each point. Space did not permit the citation of all works consulted. Books and articles are cited in full on first appearance, and thereafter in the form: author, short title. The Index of authors cited will enable readers to find the full references. The titles of frequently cited journals and collections of essays have been abbreviated (see the list of abbreviations on the following pages). At the end of the book is a brief, highly selective Guide to further reading, in which preference is given to recent works in English.

All Russian words in the text and notes have been transliterated according to the British Standard system. All dates before February 1918 are given according to the Julian calendar, which had been in use in Russia since 1 January 1700, and thereafter according to the Gregorian calendar.

Abbreviations used in notes

LCPCR	Bartlett, R. P. (ed.), *Land Commune and Peasant Community in Russia: Communal Forms in Imperial and Early Soviet Society* (Basingstoke and London, 1990)
MGSR	*Materialy dlya geografii i statistiki Rossii, sobrannye ofitserami General'nogo Shtaba* (multi-volume [by province or region], St Petersburg, 1860–68)
NCMH	*New Cambridge Modern History*, 14 vols (Cambridge, 1957–79)
NGM	*National Geographic Magazine*
OI	*Otechestvennaya istoriya* (from 1992)
P & P	*Past and Present*
PECPER	Kingston-Mann, E. and Mixter, T. (eds), *Peasant Economy, Culture, and Politics of European Russia, 1800–1921* (Princeton, NJ, 1991)
PS	*Peasant Studies*
PSN	*Peasant Studies Newsletter*
REcH	*Research in Economic History*
RevR	*Revolutionary Russia*
RH	*Russian History*
RHMC	*Revue d'Histoire Moderne et Contemporaine*
RPW	Farnsworth, B. and Viola, L. (eds), *Russian Peasant Women* (Oxford, 1992)
RR	*Russian Review*
SEER	*Slavonic and East European Review*
SR	*Slavic Review*
SS	*Soviet Studies* (to 1992, followed by *EAS*)
SSH	*Soviet Studies in History* (to 1992)
VI	*Voprosy Istorii*
VMU (I)	*Vestnik Moskovskogo Universiteta. Seriya 8. Istoriya*
VR	Dzhivelegov, A. K. *et al.* (eds), *Velikaya Reforma: Russkoe Obshchestvo i Krest'yanskii Vopros v Proshlom i Nastoyashchem. Yubileinoe izdanie*, 6 vols (Moscow, 1911)
WRP	Eklof, B. and Frank, S. P. (eds), *The World of the Russian Peasant: Post-Emancipation Culture and Society* (Boston, MA, and London, 1990)

COLLECTIONS OF RUSSIAN LAWS

PSZ	*Polnoe sobranie zakonov Rossiiskoi imperii*, 1st series, 45 vols (St Petersburg, 1830); 2nd series, 55 vols (St Petersburg, 1830–84)
SZ	*Svod zakonov Rossiiskoi Imperii*, 1st edn (St Petersburg, 1832)

Abbreviations used in notes

Introduction

The Russian peasantry made up the overwhelming majority of the population of Russia between 1600 and 1930. Throughout this period, 80–90 per cent of Russians were peasants.[1] In this respect, tsarist and early Soviet Russia were similar to other pre-industrial societies, and societies in the early stages of industrialisation, in early modern Europe and 'less developed' regions of Asia, Africa and South and Central America until the late twentieth century. In England in 1500, around 80 per cent of the population worked in agriculture. In China as recently as the 1980s, 74 per cent of the labour force farmed the land. The low and uncertain levels of agricultural productivity in most pre-industrial societies meant that only small minorities of their populations, typically 10–20 per cent, could give up farming for other economic activities, or live off the labour of others as privileged elites.

In stark contrast, in many industrialised or 'developed' societies in the second half of the twentieth century, only around 10–20 per cent of the labour force worked in agriculture. In the Soviet Union on the eve of its collapse in 1991, the proportion was 20 per cent, most of whom were no longer peasants in the strict sense of the term, but workers on collective and state farms (*kolkhozy* and *sovkhozy*). The proportion of the population of England that farmed the land had fallen to 20 per cent by 1850. In the UK and USA in the late twentieth century, only 3–4 per cent of the labour force were engaged in farming. Many people who worked on the land in the developed world in the twentieth century, especially in Britain and North America, were not peasants, but farmers who ran agricultural businesses with the aim of making profits, and farm workers who were employed in return for wages.

The dramatic transformations of many societies, which began in north-west Europe two or three centuries ago, came about partly as a consequence of massive increases in agricultural productivity. These were a result of several factors, including the introduction of 'improved' methods of cultivation that made more intensive use of the land, new and more productive varieties of crops and breeds of livestock and, more recently, mechanisation and the use of chemical fertilisers, pesticides and herbicides. The subsidies national

---

1 See Moon, D., 'Estimating the peasant population of late imperial Russia from the 1897 census', *EAS*, vol. 48 (1996), pp. 141–53; Wheatcroft, S. G. and Davies, R. W., 'Population', in Davies, R. W., Harrison, M. and Wheatcroft, S. G. (eds), *The Economic Transformation of the Soviet Union, 1913–1945* (Cambridge, 1994), pp. 59, 65; and Ch. 1.

1

governments and supra-national organisations such as the European Union paid to farmers greatly reduced the uncertainties of making a living from the land and the vagaries of the market. The enormous capacity of industry to generate wealth and the growth in world trade enabled whole countries to rely heavily on imported food and to specialise in other areas of economic activity.[2]

These are only some of the developments which transformed, and continue to transform, many areas of life at a pace previously unknown in human history. The information and communication revolutions of the late twentieth century mean that books such as this may soon seem as outmoded as the wooden ploughs still used by many Russian peasants in the 1920s did to the Communist Party officials who sought to transform rural Russia. In order to try to understand peasant societies, in Russia and elsewhere, therefore, it is necessary to think away the radical changes that shaped the 'modern' world. It is even more important to guard against notions that change, or rather incremental change in the sense of development, has been constant in human societies, and that the past is not just different from the present, but also 'backward'. This is not to argue that Russian peasants between 1600 and 1930 did not know change; they certainly did, but until the late nineteenth century the changes they took part in and experienced need to be considered in ways appropriate to societies before the transformations associated with industrialisation.[3]

Most peasantries, throughout the world, faced similar problems in their struggles to create viable ways of life and maintain their livelihoods.[4] They had to support themselves mainly from the land and usually with the labour only of members of their households, some livestock, simple implements, seed set aside from the last harvest, and the experiences accumulated and passed down by previous generations. Moreover, all peasantries were oppressed and exploited by the ruling and landowning elites of the wider societies of which they were parts. As well as the forms and levels of exploitation, peasant societies had to contend with the opportunities and constraints provided by the natural environments they lived in, and the sizes of their populations, especially in relation to the amounts of land available for them to cultivate. For the most part, peasants had only limited control over these factors.

Peasant societies developed various strategies to deal with these problems. They did so both by themselves and in conjunction with elites. Peasantries evolved ways of farming the land, and have created economies based on varying balances between agricultural and other productive and income-generating activities. They developed ways of organising their households and communities

---

2 See Crone, P., *Pre-industrial Societies* (Oxford, 1989), pp. 13–16; Keyfitz, N. and Flieger, W., *World Population Growth and Aging: Demographic Trends in the Late Twentieth Century* (Chicago and London, 1990), pp. 345, 351, 437, 449, 581, 537; Overton, M., *Agricultural Revolution in England* (Cambridge, 1996), pp. 8, 81–2, 137–8; Rösener, W., *The Peasantry of Europe* (Oxford, 1994), esp. pp. 188–214. On definitions of peasants, see Ch. 1.
3 See Burke, P., 'Introduction: Concepts of continuity and change in history', in *NCMH*, vol. 13, pp. 1–14; *id.*, *Popular Culture in Early Modern Europe* (London, 1978), pp. [xi–xiii].
4 For general works on peasantries, see Guide to further reading.

to manage their resources, principally labour and land. Households and communities encouraged certain patterns of marriage and reproductive behaviour. Peasant societies developed practices regulating the ways land and other property were distributed between households and bequeathed to subsequent generations. Peasantries evolved political processes to address disagreements within their communities, and between peasant communities and outside elites. Peasant societies produced rich, usually oral, cultures, in which they tried to explain, record and pass on to later generations their knowledge of the human and natural worlds they lived in, and the strategies they developed to cope with them. These strategies, enshrined in peasant cultures, served as norms of their ways of life. Their main aim, and the key to making sense of them, was to ensure the livelihoods of peasant households and communities in the present and continued existence in the future.

Much of the scholarly literature on peasant societies has stressed the subordination of individuals to the subsistence needs of their households and communities. But the practices and customs of peasant life cannot be reduced solely to a struggle for survival. Peasants were not pre-programmed with certain instincts designed to give them the best chance of living and reproducing. All attempts to understand peasant societies must also take account of the human dimension: the needs, aspirations and desires of individual peasants.[5]

THE SCOPE OF THE BOOK

This book considers the problems Russian peasants faced, the factors influencing their lives, the strategies they developed to ensure their livelihoods, and the parts played by peasant households, village communities, and individual peasants, female and male, young and old, poor and rich, between the early seventeenth and early twentieth centuries.

By 'Russian' peasants is meant those belonging to the ethnic group sometimes called 'Great Russian' to distinguish it from the other eastern Slavs (Belorussians and Ukrainians). The geographical area covered by this book is that part of the Russian state, including Siberia, where the large majority of 'ethnic Russian' peasants lived throughout the period under consideration. This vast and environmentally diverse realm coincided roughly with the tsarist state in the late seventeenth century (excluding left-bank Ukraine incorporated after 1654), the Russian Soviet Federative Socialist Republic (RSFSR) between 1921 and the demise of the Soviet Union in 1991, and the present-day Russian Federation. For sake of convenience, and with apologies to the many non-Russians who have lived there, I have called this area 'Russia'. (See Ch. 1.) The significant populations of non-Russian peasants who lived in 'Russia' have not been covered in detail, nor have the large non-Russian peasant populations of the western borderlands of the tsarist Russian and Soviet

5 See Glickman, R., '"Unusual circumstances" in the peasant village', *RH*, vol. 23 (1996), pp. 215–29.

states, for example Ukrainians and Belorussians. Throughout the book, however, some comparisons are made between Russian peasants and non-Russian peasants living under Russian rule, and between Russian peasants and peasants (and other peoples) elsewhere in the world.

The dates in the title of this book, 1600–1930, give only a general indication of the period covered. The main focus is on the period from the early eighteenth century to the 1860s: the high point of serfdom, under which very roughly half the peasantry was bound to the estates of noble landowners. At the start of this period, Peter the Great (1682–1725) reinforced the hierarchical social structure of Russia, which was based on the oppression and exploitation of all peasants. Peter introduced or reformed the main obligations the state demanded from peasants, chiefly taxes and recruits. Peasant households and communities adapted the strategies they used to support themselves to take account of the Petrine reforms. In the second half of the nineteenth century, many of the ways peasants were exploited were done away with or reformed by tsar Alexander II (1855–81) and his successors. Serfdom was abolished in 1861, and the systems of taxation and recruitment radically altered in the 1860s–80s.

This book also covers, in less detail, the periods immediately before 1700 and after 1861. The century or so prior to 1700 is of particular importance as this was the period when significant numbers of Russian peasants began to migrate from the forest-heartland of Russia to the steppes and to Siberia. The enserfment of the Russian peasantry began in earnest in the late sixteenth century, and was consolidated in law in 1649. The decades after 1861 are also very important. The reforms of the 1860s–80s were part of broader social, economic and cultural changes as tsarist Russia began to embark on 'modernisation', including industrialisation and urbanisation. In the long term, these developments threatened the continued existence of the Russian peasantry. In the short term, however, many Russian peasants took part in and adapted to these changes. Peasants also participated in the revolutions of 1905–07 and 1917–21. The Russian Empire collapsed in February and March 1917. The Bolshevik Party (renamed Communist in 1918), led by Lenin, seized power in October 1917, and went on to found the Soviet Union. The Russian peasantry's ways of life persisted until the late 1920s, but little survived Stalin's forced collectivisation of agriculture launched in 1929–30.

LITERATURE AND SOURCES

This book is based largely on the enormous secondary literature on the Russian peasantry. Much of this body of work can be divided into three strands. The first is the work of pre-revolutionary Russian historians. They began seriously to research and write the history of the Russian peasantry in the second half of the nineteenth century as a counterbalance to the predominance of the 'statist' school in Russian historical scholarship. The most important student of the peasantry in this period was Vasilii Semevskii. In an article published in 1881, he asked: 'Is it not time to write the history of the peasants in Russia?'. He clearly felt that it *was* time, spent much of the rest of his life doing so, and died at his desk in the library of the Academy of Sciences in 1916. His extensive works have retained their importance.[6]

At around the same time as Semevskii and others were starting to write the history of the Russian peasantry, many statisticians, geographers and ethnographers were collecting and publishing statistical data and descriptive material on the contemporary Russian peasantry. Some of these specialists were employed by the central government or the local councils (*zemstva*) set up after 1864, or worked under the auspices of the Imperial Russian Geographical Society. Much writing on the peasantry by Russian intellectuals in the late nineteenth century reflected the sympathy of the Populist movement towards the mass of the rural population. A number of educated Russians idealised the peasantry. Some even saw peasant institutions and ways of life as models for a future socialist society in Russia.[7] Alexander Engel'gardt, an academic chemist who was exiled from St Petersburg to his estate in Smolensk province in 1870, had a more matter-of-fact approach to the peasants he lived among and knew at first hand. In the words of Catherine Frierson, he 'believed that there was a reason for every aspect of village culture, and he took up the challenge of identifying and displaying those reasons to his urban readers'.[8]

Other Russian intellectuals were hostile to the peasantry. In the late nineteenth and early twentieth centuries, Lenin and other Marxists denigrated the peasantry as an outmoded 'class', which was splitting into conflicting classes and destined to disappear with 'the development of capitalism in Russia'. Lenin's writings presaged the second strand in the literature on the Russian peasantry: the work of Soviet historians after 1917. Some historians who had begun their careers before 1917, for example Semevskii's student I. I. Ignatovich, continued to write under the Soviet regime. But survivors from before 1917 and historians trained after the revolution were obliged to work mostly on 'good' Marxist–Leninist topics, such as the 'feudal' economy, exploitation, 'class struggle', and the transition from the 'feudal' to the 'capitalist' 'modes of production'.

The restrictions on historians were greatest during the Stalin years (*c.* 1929–53). Nevertheless, many Soviet historians published work on the peasantry

6 See Petrovich, M. B., 'The peasant in nineteenth-century historiography', in Vucinich, W. S. (ed.), *The Peasant in Nineteenth-Century Russia* (Stanford, CA, 1968), pp. 191–230; *id.*, 'V. I. Semevskii (1848–1916): Russian social historian', in Curtiss, J. S. (ed.), *Essays in Russian and Soviet History in Honor of Geroid Tanquary Robinson* (New York, 1962), pp. 63–84; Baluev, B. P., 'Iskrennii i pravdivyi drug naroda: Vasilii Ivanovich Semevskii', in Sakharov, A. N. (ed.), *Istoriki Rossii: XVIII–nachalo XX v.* (Moscow, 1996), pp. 446–85.
7 See Worobec, C. D., *Peasant Russia: Family and Community in the Post-Emancipation Period* (Princeton, NJ, 1991), pp. 225–31; Frierson, C. A., *Peasant Icons: Representations of Rural People in Late Nineteenth-Century Russia* (New York and Oxford, 1993); Fanger, D., 'The peasant in literature', in Vucinich, *Peasant*, pp. 231–62; Lincoln, W. B., *Petr Petrovich Semenov-Tian-Shanskii* (Newtonville, MA, 1980), esp. pp. 49–72.
8 Frierson, C. A., 'Forced hunger and rational restraint in the Russian peasant diet: One populist's vision', in Glants, M. and Toomre, J. (eds), *Food in Russian History and Culture* (Bloomington, IN, 1997), p. 54. See also [Engel'gardt, A. N.], *Letters from the Countryside, 1872–1887*, edited and translated by C. A. Frierson (New York and Oxford, 1993).

which, although often lacking a satisfactory analytical framework, contained a wealth of empirical data mined from a variety of archival sources. The 'thaw' inaugurated by Khrushchev after 1956 led to a distinct improvement in much work by Soviet historians, including that on peasants. A number of historians conducted interesting debates, albeit within the confines of the official interpretations of history. It is significant that historians who worked away from the centre of power in Moscow in more outlying areas of the Soviet Union, such as northern Russia, the Urals and Siberia, produced particularly valuable work on peasants in their regions. Since the relaxation of Communist party control in the late 1980s, and the end of party rule and collapse of the Soviet Union in 1991, many Russian historians have endeavoured to find new perspectives for their work.[9]

Specialists on the Russian peasantry can disregard some of the cruder, and occasionally misleading, works by a number of Soviet historians. Some have openly admitted the limitations of their work. The authors of the volume on the period covered by this book in a multi-volume history of the Russian peasantry, which appeared belatedly in 1993, wrote disarmingly in their introduction:

> The authorial collective and editorial college . . . acknowledge that . . . this work has not kept pace with our swiftly changing lives, [and] changing opinions on certain problems in the history of the fatherland. We hope that the reader will not complain about this, especially because at the present time it is still not possible to talk about new large works on agrarian history which will take account of the developing trends in academic life.[10]

Nevertheless, for the foreseeable future, historians of the Russian peasantry will need to continue reading and engaging with the substantial body of higher quality work produced by Soviet scholars (including that by some of the contributors to the volume just mentioned), while bearing in the mind the circumstances in which it was written.

The intellectual conformity enforced by the Communist Party had detrimental effects on other academic disciplines and their practitioners. Most notable was the fate of the agricultural economist Alexander Chayanov (1888–1937). His original and still influential works on the peasant economy, which stressed the central role of peasant households, contradicted the writings of Lenin and the Party's policy of collectivising agriculture. For much of the 1920s, Chayanov and his colleagues were attacked by Marxist agronomists as 'anti-Marxists' and 'neo-Populists'. The attacks reached a climax at the 1st

9 See Kingston-Mann, E., *Lenin and the Problem of Marxist Peasant Revolution* (New York and Oxford, 1983); Baron, S., 'The transition from feudalism to capitalism in Russia', *AHR*, vol. 77 (1972), pp. 715–29; Channon, J., 'New insights into rural Russia – east and west', *EHQ*, vol. 17 (1987), pp. 493–504; Davies, R. W., *Soviet History in the Yeltsin Era* (Basingstoke and London, 1997).

10 Buganov, V. I. *et al.* (eds), *Istoriya krest'yanstva SSSR/Rossii s drevneishikh vremen do Velikoi Oktyabr'skoi sotsialisticheskoi revolyutsii/1917 g.* (Moscow, 1987–), vol. 3; Preobrazhenskii, A. A. (ed.), *Krest'yanstvo perioda pozdnego feodalizma (seredina XVII v.–1861 g.)* (Moscow, 1993), p. 13.

All-Union Conference of Marxist-Agronomists in December 1929, at which Chayanov was singled out for criticism by Stalin. The timing was deliberate. It coincided with Stalin's decision to launch all-out collectivisation. Chayanov was arrested in July 1930, charged with 'counter-revolutionary conspiracy', and imprisoned. He was released in 1934, but exiled to Alma Ata, Kazakhstan, in Soviet central Asia, where he was permitted to work in agricultural institutes. In 1937 he was re-arrested and executed.[11]

The third strand in the literature on the Russian peasantry is the work of Western specialists. Western Europeans began to take a serious interest in the Russian peasantry in the nineteenth century. The German Baron August von Haxthausen (1792–1866) and the Briton Sir Donald MacKenzie Wallace (1841–1919) travelled extensively in Russia in the 1840s and 1870s respectively. Wallace lived there for six years, and spent several years in a village in the north-western province of Novgorod. Both men wrote influential books in which they devoted a lot of space to rural Russia and the peasantry.[12] Wallace believed the interest was mutual. He described how, on steamers on the river Volga,

> one meets with curious travelling companions. The majority of the passengers are probably Russian peasants, who are always ready to chat freely without demanding formal introduction, and to relate to a new acquaintance the simple story of their lives. Often I have thus whiled away the weary hours both pleasantly and profitably, and have always been impressed with the peasant's homely common sense, good-natured kindliness, half-fatalistic resignation, and strong desire to learn something about foreign countries.[13]

Much of the work by Western scholars on the Russian peasantry published in the first two-thirds of the twentieth century followed in the tradition of pre-revolutionary Russian scholarship. Indeed, some of the works published in the West in the middle decades of the century were written by Russian emigres, for example George Pavlovsky and Sergei Puskarev. Most Western specialists writing before the 1970s had to rely mainly on printed sources and secondary works by pre-revolutionary and Soviet scholars. These limitations did not prevent some Western historians, such as Geroid Tanquary Robinson, Donald Treadgold, R. E. F. Smith and Michael Confino, from producing important works.[14] The standard English-language history of the Russian peasantry dates from this period: Jerome Blum's magisterial *Lord and Peasant in Russia from the Ninth to the Nineteenth Century* (Princeton, NJ, 1961).

11 See Kerblay, B., 'A. V. Chayanov: Life, career, works', in [Chayanov, A. V.], *The Theory of Peasant Economy*, 2nd edn, D. Thorner, B. Kerblay and R. E. F. Smith (eds) (Manchester, 1986), pp. xxv–lxxv; Wehner, M., 'The soft line on agriculture: The case of *Narkomzem* and its specialists, 1921–27', in Pallot, J. (ed.), *Transforming Peasants: Society, State and the Peasantry, 1861–1930* (Basingstoke and London, 1998), pp. 210–37.
12 Haxthausen, A. von, *Studies on the Interior of Russia*, S. F. Starr (ed.), E. L. M. Schmidt (trans.) (Chicago, 1972); Wallace, D. M., *Russia*, 1st edn, 2 vols (London, Paris and New York, 1877) (see also *Dictionary of National Biography*).
13 Wallace, *Russia*, vol. 1, p. 8.
14 Works by these scholars are cited at the appropriate points; see Index of authors cited.

The 1960s and 70s saw major changes in Western historical writing on the Russian peasantry. It became much easier for Western scholars to gain access to libraries and archives in the Soviet Union. And a younger generation of Western historians of Russia began to pay attention to social history in place of the concerns of many of the older generation with high politics, foreign policy and intellectuals. Initially, most Western social historians worked on the urban working classes, but some looked beyond the towns and cities to rural Russia and peasant society. Recent Western specialists of the Russian peasantry have paid increasing attention to culture and gender, as well as the society, economy and politics of rural life. Much of the growing body of work on the Russian peasantry produced in the West since the 1960s, however, has concentrated on the period between 1861 and the 1930s.[15]

Some American historians have produced invaluable 'micro-studies' of peasant communities, based on the records of individual estates under serfdom. The estate of Mishino, in Ryazan' province in the Central Black Earth region,[16] has been the subject of a series of articles by Peter Czap. Petrovskoe, a village in Tambov province in the same region, was the focus of a monograph by Steven Hoch. In both communities, peasants engaged mainly in agriculture and were obliged to perform labour services (*barshchina*) for their landowners. Rodney Bohac studied the estate of Manuilovskoe, in Tver' province in the Central Non-Black Earth region. The peasants' main economic activity was agriculture, but they also engaged in handicrafts, trade and migrant wage labour. They paid dues (*obrok*) to their landowner. (Manuilovskoe, Mishino and Petrovskoe were all the property of the Gagarin family.) The villages of Mstera, in Vladimir province, and Baki, in Kostroma province, both in the Central Non-Black Earth region, have been examined by Edgar Melton. In both villages agriculture was of secondary importance. The peasants' main activity in Mstera was icon painting, and in Baki, the timber trade. Their landowners demanded dues. These micro-studies, and others by Western, Russian and Soviet scholars, will be referred to throughout this book.

OUTLINE AND AIMS OF THE BOOK

The largest part of this book is divided into eight thematic chapters, each of which covers the period from the early seventeenth to the turn of the twentieth centuries. The first three chapters address demographic, ecological and political factors affecting the Russian peasantry: the size and growth of the population; the natural environments they encountered in the regions they lived in and migrated to; and the forms and levels of exploitation they were subjected to by the ruling and landowning elites. The most important factor affecting the history of the Russian peasantry, however, was the actions of the peasants themselves in making the world they lived in. Thus, the next four

15 See Guide to further reading.
16 On regions, see Ch. 2.

chapters consider the main strategies Russian peasants developed to ensure their livelihoods by looking in turn at production, agricultural and otherwise; households, especially their role in controlling their labour resources; village communes, in particular their function in managing their land; and protest against elites. The eighth chapter assesses levels and trends in peasant consumption, or living standards, in the context of these factors and strategies. Continuity in Russian peasant society throughout the period from the early seventeenth to the early twentieth centuries is discussed in Chapter 9, which also serves as a conclusion to the preceding eight chapters. Change in the twentieth century, especially the collectivisation of agriculture launched in 1929–30, is the subject of the final chapter.

There are many problems in organising the chapters of a book by theme. Some subjects are relevant to more than one theme, creating a problem of repetition. I can only ask the forbearance of readers for repetitions that occur in this book. It is difficult to decide, moreover, which themes merit a chapter to themselves. The absence of a chapter on culture is in no way intended to indicate that an appreciation of the role of culture is not important to an understanding of the history of the Russian peasantry. I felt it better, however, to discuss various aspects of culture in the relevant chapters. For example, rituals accompanying the agricultural year are included in the chapter on production, ceremonies of family life in the chapter on households, while ways peasants hoped elites would behave, as reflected in folklore, are discussed in the chapter on protest. Some general remarks on culture are made in Chapter 9.[17]

It is also difficult to decide the order in which to discuss the themes. The sequence of the thematic chapters in this book is at least the third variant I considered in aiming to organise the material in a coherent manner. The order of the themes could be taken to imply distinctions between causes and effects, which are difficult if not impossible to determine. In any case, trying to make such distinctions conceals more complex and important interrelationships. Readers who are not happy with the order of the chapters or the implications for the argument can, of course, read the thematic chapters in whatever order they wish. The thematic chapters can also be read independently for purposes of comparison with similar aspects of the history of other societies.

The aims of this book are threefold. The first is to produce a synthesis based on my reading of what I hope is a reasonably representative selection of work from the three strands in the vast scholarly literature on the Russian peasantry. In identifying and discussing some of the broad contours of peasant life, I have aimed to supplement Blum's coverage of this period in *Lord and Peasant in Russia* by paying particular attention to work published since he was writing and to themes which had been the subject of relatively little work at that time, in particular the inner workings of households and communities and the importance of gender.

17 For an introduction to Russian peasant culture, see Gromyko, M. M., 'Kul'tura russkogo krest'yanstva XVIII–XIX vekov kak predmet istoricheskogo issledovaniya', *IS* (1987), no. 3, pp. 39–60.

The second aim is to draw attention to the history of the Russian peasantry in the very important period between the early eighteenth century and 1861, which has suffered from the same relative neglect as other aspects of the history of imperial Russia. I hope also to have provided a long-term context for the large and growing literature on the peasantry in late tsarist and early Soviet Russia (1861–1930s), in the hope of encouraging scholars working on that period to consider their findings in the light of the history of the peasantry in the epoch before 1861. It is not an aim of this book to discuss in detail the major developments of the twentieth century, such as the rural revolutions of 1905–07 and 1917–21, Stolypin's land reforms of 1906–11, the collectivisation of agriculture that began in 1929–30, and the subsequent decline of Russian peasant society. These are considered in the final two chapters, but are to be covered in much greater depth in a companion volume by another author.

The third and main aim of this book is to cut through the disparaging images and stereotypes of Russian peasants constructed by many educated outsiders, including contemporary officials and intellectuals as well as some historians. I hope to have gained some insights into the strategies developed by peasant households and communities, both among themselves and in interaction with the ruling and landowning elites, by trying to understand these strategies from the peasants' point of view and on their terms. In these ways and from this perspective, this book will try to explain the endurance of the world the peasants made between the early seventeenth and early twentieth centuries.

CHAPTER 1

Population

Peasants made up the vast majority of the population of Russia throughout the period covered by this book. The numbers of Russian peasants, moreover, grew considerably between the early seventeenth and early twentieth centuries. This chapter starts by examining the peasant population of the Russian Empire at the end of the nineteenth century. Particular attention is paid to the different ways peasants have been defined and the composition of the peasantry. The chapter goes on to consider the reasons for the massive increase in the Russian peasant population over the preceding three centuries. Like most pre-industrial populations, Russian peasants lived in an uncertain world of high and unpredictable mortality. The lives of the very young and old were particularly precarious. The Russian peasantry also had very high birth rates, which in the medium and long terms more than compensated for the high death rates. The growth in the numbers of peasants, especially in relation to the amounts of land available for cultivation, were important factors affecting many aspects of the Russian peasantry's ways of life.

THE PEASANT POPULATION OF THE RUSSIAN EMPIRE IN 1897

On 28 January 1897 the first, and only, general census of the population of the Russian Empire was held. In rural areas, enumerators visited every household in each village in the districts assigned to them. Most were clergymen, teachers, estate stewards and clerks. Only a few were peasants. The majority of enumerators had received secondary education, and some had been to university. When they crossed the thresholds of the peasants' houses, however, the enumerators entered a different world. Sometimes they had to wait while the peasants drove the chickens and other domestic animals out. Other peasants were less scrupulous, and invited them to join the livestock that were sharing their homes for the winter. Once inside, many experienced great discomfort from either the unbearable cold or the intense heat and sometimes blinding smoke from the peasants' stoves. An enumerator in Tver' province reported that he had to write on benches, or 'on rocking and cluttered tables, kneeling down, in an atmosphere at times simply . . . stupefying with stench . . .'.[1]

---

1 See Plyushchevskii-Plyushchik, Ya. A., 'Otchet upolnomochennogo po Vysochaishemu poveleniyu dlya ob'' edineniya deistviya mestnykh uchrezhdenii po Pervoi Vseobshchei Perepisi Naseleniya 28 yanvarya 1897 goda v Tverskoi, Yaroslavskoi i Kostromskoi guberniyakh', *Vremennik Tsentral'nogo Statisticheskogo Komiteta, Ministerstva Vnutrennikh Del*, no. 45 (1898), p. 93.

The census form asked various questions about each member of the household, including name, 'social estate' (*soslovie*), primary and secondary occupations, native language, place of birth, registration (*pripiska*) and residence, age, sex, marital status, relationship to the head of household, religion, education and literacy. The census was conducted in accordance with contemporary international statistical practices. Although the data it produced have come in for some criticism, there is no doubt that, in the words of a recent authority, it is a 'unique source on the peasantry of Russia'. The 1897 census provides a 'snapshot' of the Russian peasantry at the end of the main period covered by this book.[2]

Defining and counting peasants

The 1897 census counted 96.9 million peasants in the Russian Empire as a whole, out of a total population of 125.6 million, a proportion of 77.1 per cent. While these figures are useful yardsticks, they pose three problems. First, the precise number of peasants depends on how they are defined. Second, these 96.9 million included peasants from many ethnic groups in addition to the Russian peasants who are the main subjects of this book. Finally, in order to make meaningful comparisons with the peasant population in the centuries before 1897, we need figures based on similar definitions, and have to take account of Russian territorial expansion.

The compilers of the 1897 census used the term 'peasant' to describe members of a legally defined, hereditary and subordinate social estate of rural inhabitants. The population of the Russian Empire was divided into a hierarchy of social estates, the origins of which predate the seventeenth century. At the top of the hierarchy were the privileged social estates of the nobility, clergy and (after 1775) the merchantry. Collectively, they made up under 2.5 per cent of the population in 1897. At the bottom of the hierarchy were the enormous peasantry (*krest'yanstvo*) and smaller townspeople (*meshchanstvo*), who together comprised almost 88 per cent of the total population of the empire at the end of the nineteenth century. Until the 1870s and 80s these two subordinate social estates had alone born the brunt of the twin burdens imposed on the mass of the population by Peter the Great in the early eighteenth century: annual levies of recruits into the lower ranks of the Russian army from 1705, and the poll tax, which was collected for the first time in 1724. Moreover, for around two and a half centuries prior to 1861, nobles effectively owned very roughly half the peasantry as serfs. Before 1762–64, the Russian Orthodox Church had also enjoyed this privilege. The distinct and inferior legal status of the peasant estate survived the reforms that began in the 1860s. Serfdom was

2 Litvak, K. B., 'Perepis' naseleniya 1897 goda o krest'yanstve Rossii', *IS* (1990), no. 1, pp. 114–26 (quotation); Shanin, T., *Russia as a 'Developing Society'* (Basingstoke and London, 1986), pp. 57–65. Summaries of the census data were published as: Troinitskii, N. A. (ed.), *Obshchii svod po imperii rezul'tatov razrabotki dannykh pervoi vseobshchei perepisi naseleniya, proizvedennoi 28 Yanvarya 1897 goda*, 2 vols (St Petersburg, 1905).

abolished in 1861, men of all social estates were made liable to conscription in 1874, and the poll tax was phased out after 1883. Nevertheless, the peasant estate continued to have its own, separate systems of local administration and justice, its members were still liable to corporal punishment, and still provided most of the recruits for the army and a large part of tax revenues. Peasants were grossly under-represented, moreover, on the elected local councils (*zemstva*) set up after 1864, and in the four State Dumas elected at national level between 1905 and 1917.[3]

The definition of peasants used in the 1897 census was peculiar to Russian law in the eighteenth and nineteenth centuries. Anthropologists and some historians have defined peasants differently. Not all specialists agree, but many of their definitions share several features. Peasants are politically and socially dominated and economically exploited by elite members of the larger societies of which they are a part, for example by nobles, churches and rulers. Peasants live in rural areas and support themselves chiefly, but not exclusively, by subsistence agriculture. They have access to plots of land, which they farm with their own manual labour, draught animals and fairly simple equipment. Production for the market and use of hired labourers are of secondary importance. The basic units of peasant life are households, which are grouped into village communities. Specialists have also identified peasant cultures, which are predominantly oral, in contrast to the largely literate cultures of elites.

Specialists have disagreed whether definitions of peasants should include people on the margins of peasant society. Most agree that hunters and gatherers, whose ways of life predate the invention of agriculture, and nomadic and semi-nomadic pastoralists, who move around with herds of livestock in search of pasture, are different from peasants. Specialists have debated whether to include the following marginal groups: small-scale commercial farmers who put the largest part of their produce on the market and/or rely on hired labour; agricultural labourers who do not cultivate a plot of land for themselves; and rural artisans, traders, carters, foresters and people engaged mainly in fishing who earn the largest part of their livelihood outside settled agriculture. Even if we exclude all these marginal people, there is still great diversity between peasant societies in different regions and countries, and inside peasantries, between villages and households within villages. Another problem is posed by changes over time, in particular those associated with 'modernisation', such as improvements in transport, the expansion of markets, industrialisation, urbanisation, the growth of literacy and formal schooling, and changes in people's senses of identity, both as individuals and as members of larger,

---

3 On the legal definition of peasants, see *SZ*, 1st edn (St Petersburg, 1832), book IV, *Zakony o Sostoyaniyakh*, esp. pp. 121–225, arts 386–712; Bauer, H., Kappeler, A. and Roth, B. (eds), *Die Nationalitäten des Russischen Reiches in der Volkszählung von 1897*, 2 vols (Stuttgart, 1991), vol. 1, pp. 377–429; Frank, S. P., 'Emancipation and the birch: The perpetuation of corporal punishment in rural Russia 1861–1907', *JGO*, vol. 45 (1997), pp. 401–16. On social estates, see Freeze, G. L., 'The *Soslovie* (Estate) paradigm and Russian social history', *AHR*, vol. 91 (1986), pp. 11–36. The proportions of the population in each estate in 1897 are taken from Troinitskii, *Obshchii svod*, vol. 1, p. xii. See also Ch. 3.

national communities. Nevertheless, many specialists have agreed that it is possible to define distinct groups of people as peasants.[4]

The definition of peasants in Russian law coincided with specialists' definitions on only two points: exploitation by elites and residence in rural areas. Membership of the legally defined peasant estate in Russia was determined mainly by heredity rather than way of life. People whose lives changed radically did not always transfer to other social estates. The number of members of the peasant estate in 1897 whose ways of life differed from specialists' definitions of peasants can be estimated from the census data. Since specialists' definitions are of necessity blurred at the edges, any estimates can be regarded only as guides. The peasant estate in 1897 included 6.5 million people who had left their home villages for towns and cities, many of whom had given up agriculture as their main occupation; 1 million men who were serving in the armed forces;[5] and around 100,000 people who had received secondary or higher education and been socialised into the elite culture. Thus, around 7.5 million members of the peasant estate in 1897 fell outside the peasantry as defined by specialists.

On the other hand, some members of other social estates supported themselves largely by farming and differed little from their peasant neighbours. The most numerous were around half of the townspeople, many non-Slav subjects of the empire who were classified as 'aliens' (*inorodtsy*) and, by the late nineteenth century, large numbers of cossacks. In total they came to around 13 million people. If the non-peasants (according to specialists' definitions) who were members of the peasant estate are excluded, and peasants (also according to specialists' definitions) who were members of other social estates are included, the peasant population of the Russian Empire in 1897 can be estimated at 102.5 million, or 81.5 per cent of the total population.[6]

A third way to estimate the peasant population of the Russian Empire from the 1897 census is to ignore the figures on social estates altogether, and to rely instead on the data on occupations. 'Arable farming (*zemledelie*) in general' was by far the largest occupational category in the census data. Over 87 million people in 16.7 million households, almost 70 per cent of the population, were engaged in 'arable farming in general' as their primary occupation or were the dependants of people who were. These figures included around 2 million hired agricultural labourers, but excluded about 600,000 people,

4 For examples of the large literature on defining peasants, see Shanin, T. (ed.), *Peasants and Peasant Societies: Selected Readings*, 2nd edn (Harmondsworth, 1988), esp. pp. 1–11. On the impact of 'modernisation', see Ch. 9. See also general works on peasants listed under Introduction in Guide to further reading.
5 After 1867 soldiers from the peasantry retained their legal status as peasants during their military service. Before 1867 the lower ranks of the armed forces had been, in effect, a social estate in its own right. *SZ*, 1 (1832), book IV, *Zakony o Sostoyaniyakh*, pp. 82, 129, 140, arts 271, 402, 438; *PSZ*, 2, vol. XLII, p. 998, no. 44745, I, 1–2 (25 June 1867). See also Wirtschafter, E. K., *From Serf to Russian Soldier* (Princeton, NJ, 1990).
6 Moon, 'Estimating', pp. 142–5. See also Slocum, J. W., 'Who, and when, were the *inorodtsy*? The evolution of the category of "aliens" in imperial Russia', *RR*, vol. 57 (1998), pp. 173–90. On cossacks, see below.

including dependants, whose main occupations were more specialised forms of crop cultivation that must have been market orientated, for example market gardening and growing flax and hemp. In addition, over 4.5 million people, including family members, were engaged primarily in 'animal husbandry' (*zhivotnovodstvo*). The majority, around 3.6 million, were not peasants, however, but nomadic or semi-nomadic pastoralists. Most nomads lived in central Asia, nearly 3 million being Turkic-speaking Kazakhs, and smaller numbers lived in Siberia. Excluding nomads, there were approximately 900,000 people engaged in settled animal husbandry. The combined total of people and their dependants who gave agriculture ('arable farming in general' and settled 'animal husbandry') as their principal occupation in the 1897 census, almost all of whom would have been inside specialists' definitions of peasants according to narrow occupational criteria, was 88.6 million, or 70.5 per cent of the total population.

The villages of the Russian Empire also contained people who had primary occupations other than agriculture, but were close to the peasantry in other respects, and supplemented their incomes by working a plot of land or keeping a few animals. Including family members, the numbers of rural artisans (or cottage workers) and rural traders can be estimated at around 4.2 million and 1.5 million respectively, rural carters can be estimated at 168,000, and a further 800,000 people were engaged in forestry or fishing: a total of 6.6 million people on the margins of the peasantry. Together with those engaged in agriculture as their main occupation, we arrive at a figure of 95.2 million (75.8 per cent of the population) for the peasant population of the Russian Empire in 1897 according to a broader occupational definition.[7]

Thus, the three ways of defining peasants used here to estimate the size of the peasant population of the Russian Empire from the 1897 census (the peasant estate, a combination of social estates and other criteria, and broad occupational criteria) all produce roughly similar figures (see Table 1.1).

Ethnic Russian peasants

The estimates for the numbers of peasants produced so far are for all ethnic groups in the Russian Empire. By the end of the nineteenth century, the tsar ruled a vast multi-ethnic, Eurasian empire that extended from St Petersburg on the Baltic Sea to Vladivostok on the Sea of Japan, and from the Arctic Ocean to the border of Afghanistan in central Asia. As well as Russians, the tsar's subjects included Poles and Chukchi, Finns and Chechens, and scores of other peoples.

The numbers and proportions of the population classified as peasants varied greatly between ethnic groups. Russians were the largest group inside the peasantry, making up just under half the total for the empire as a whole. From data in the 1897 census on native language and social estate, and after

7 Moon, 'Estimating', pp. 145–8.

TABLE 1.1
THE PEASANT POPULATION OF THE RUSSIAN EMPIRE IN 1897

	Numbers (millions)	Per cent total population
1. Peasant estate	96.9	77.1%
2. Social estates and other criteria	102.5	81.5%
3. Occupations:		
'Arable farming in general'	87.7	69.8%
Settled animal husbandry	0.9	0.7%
Sub-total agriculture	88.6	70.5%
Marginal occupations (rural artisans, traders, etc.)	6.6	5.3%
Total	95.2	75.8%

Sources: Calculated from Troinitskii, *Obshchii svod*, vol. 1, pp. xiii, 161–2, 193–4; vol. 2, pp. 256, 264–88, 334–51.

discounting some members of other ethnic groups who had been assimilated to the Russian-speaking majority, the number of ethnic Russian peasants can be estimated at 43.2 million. This was 83.7 per cent of ethnic Russians of all social estates. The next largest groups inside the peasantry were the empire's other main Slav peoples (Ukrainians, Belorussians and Poles), and Finnic, Turkic and Baltic peoples. Russians were also the largest ethnic group among the population of the empire engaged in agriculture. The number of Russians who relied on arable farming as their main occupation (after adjustment to take account of assimilation) was 39.2 million, or 76 per cent of the ethnic Russian population. The inclusion of people whose primary occupations were rural crafts and trades, who were on the margins of the peasantry, bring this figure to around 42 million, near to the 43.2 million ethnic Russian members of the peasant estate.[8] Thus, both ways of estimating the numbers of ethnic Russian peasants in 1897 – by social estate and native language, and occupation and mother tongue – produce similar figures. (See Table 1.2.)

Peasant identity

All the definitions of peasants discussed so far have been those of non-peasants: the Russian authorities and academic specialists. Russian peasants had their own ways of thinking about themselves. It is likely that they thought

8 Moon, 'Estimating', pp. 148–51; Troinitskii, *Obshchii svod*, vol. 2, pp. i–ii, 2, 326. See also Bruk, S. I. and Kabuzan, V. M., 'Dinamika i etnicheskii sostav naseleniya Rossii v epokhu imperializma (konets XIX v.–1917 g.)', *IS* (1980), no. 3, pp. 90–1.

TABLE 1.2

ETHNIC RUSSIAN PEASANTS AND PEASANTS IN RUSSIA IN 1897

	Numbers (millions)	Per cent total population
1. Ethnic Russian peasants (social estate)	43.2	83.7%
2. Ethnic Russian peasants (broad occupational criteria)	42.0	81.4%
3. Peasants in Russia (social estate)	53.4	86.0%
4. Peasants in Russia (broad occupational criteria)	50.0	80.5%

Sources: Calculated from Troinitskii, *Obshchii svod*, vol. 1, pp. 165–71; vol. 2, pp. 302–26.

in terms of various identities, negative and positive, narrow and broad. Some aspects of peasants' self-perceptions were in relation to non-peasants. Peasants had a strong sense of who was not a peasant. 'Outsiders' who differed markedly in their social statuses, occupations and cultures usually provoked suspicion, if not hostility. Peasants identified with their families and village communities, and also with people in their villages of the same generation and gender. Some thought in geographical terms, and had a sense of identity with their villages, districts and provinces. Such identities were especially keen among peasants who travelled away from their native places. Most Russian peasants seem to have identified with the tsar. But peasant 'monarchism' was ambiguous and, during the February revolution of 1917, non-existent. It is unlikely, however, that in the period covered by this book many peasants had a concept of a 'Russian peasantry', or a modern sense of nationality or citizenship.[9]

Another focus of identity was religion. The majority of Russian peasants were members of the Orthodox branch of the Christian church. Indeed, from around the fourteenth century, the standard Russian word for 'peasant' was *krest'yanin*, which originally meant someone who had been christened. In the medieval period, when many Russian peasants came into contact with Finnic, Turkic and Mongol peoples, one of the things that distinguished them from these peoples of other faiths was their Christian religion. Difference of religion was one of the things that distinguished Russian peasant migrants from peoples they encountered in later centuries (see Ch. 2). The word *krest'yanin*

9 See Shanin, T., *The Awkward Class: Political Sociology of Peasantry in a Developing Society: Russia 1910–1925* (Oxford, 1972), pp. 177–9, 192–7; Moon, D., 'Peasants into Russian citizens? A comparative perspective', *RevR*, vol. 9 (1996), pp. 43–81; Figes, O., 'The Russian revolution of 1917 and its language in the village', *RR*, vol. 56 (1997), pp. 323–45. See also Ch. 9.

was formal. The words adult peasants used to describe themselves in everyday life were *muzhiki* (literally 'little men') and *baby* (married women). When employed by elite outsiders, however, these words had a pejorative sense that reflected the subordinate status of peasants in Russian society.[10] The different layers and imprecision in Russian peasants' self-identities mean that the numbers of people conforming to them cannot be quantified; nor would there be any point in trying to do so. It is important, however, to bear in mind the various ways Russian peasants thought of themselves when considering how they related to each other, and to other people, including nobles and state officials, with whom they came into contact and interacted.

The peasant population in Russia

The Russian Empire in 1897 was much larger than the Russian state had been in the seventeenth century because of the conquest of large territories along its borders in Europe and Asia over the intervening period. Most, but by no means all, non-Russian and non-peasant inhabitants of the empire lived in the borderlands. The proportions of both Russians and peasants and, in particular, the Russian peasants who are the main subjects of this book, are higher if we strip away most of the lands annexed after the mid-seventeenth century. In 1897, most Russian peasants still lived inside the borders of what had been the realm of the Muscovite tsars a little over two centuries earlier. This was the territory of the Russian state after the conquest of Siberia and the 'recovery' of Smolensk from Poland in 1667, but excluding left-bank Ukraine, which had transferred its allegiance to Moscow in 1654, and prior to the era of imperial expansion that began in the reign of Peter the Great, and led to the annexation over the eighteenth and nineteenth centuries of the Baltic region, Lithuania, Belorussia, Poland, right-bank Ukraine, Bessarabia, the steppes to the north of the Black Sea (New Russia or southern Ukraine), the Crimea, the Caucasus, central Asia and the Pacific far east. The territory of the pre-Petrine Russian state was also, but for a few important later additions, that of the Russian Republic (RSFSR) in the Soviet Union, and the Russian Federation that emerged as the successor state when the Soviet Union broke up in 1991. This territory thus has considerable ethnic, historical and political importance.[11]

This territory also has great practical significance for tracing trends in the growth of the peasant population of Russia between the late seventeenth and

10 See Blum, *Lord and Peasant*, p. 106; Dal', V. I., *Tolkovyi slovar' zhivogo Velikorusskogo yazyka*, 4 vols (Moscow, 1989–91) (reprint of 1955 edn, based on 2nd edn of 1880–82), vol. 2, pp. 191–3; vol. 4, p. 565; vol. 2, p. 357; vol. 1, p. 32. *Krest'yanin* was derived from the word for 'cross' (*krest*), not Christ (*Khristos*). The idea that the English word 'peasant' came from the Latin *paganus*, in the sense of 'heathen', because rural people in the later Roman Empire retained their traditional beliefs long after the conversion of the urban population, is a false etymology: see *Oxford English Dictionary*, 2nd edn, entries under 'pagan' and 'peasant'.
11 See Kappeler, A., *Russland as Vielevölkerreich: Entstehung, Geschichte, Zerfall* (Munich, 1992); Sumner, B. H., *Survey of Russian History* (London, 1944), pp. 10–16. The 'later additions' include the imperial capital of St Petersburg, the Kuban'/Krasnodar region and Dagestan in the north Caucasus, the southern Altai region, Tuva on the Mongolian border, and the Pacific far east.

the end of the nineteenth centuries. In order to identify trends in peasant population growth that do not simply reflect territorial expansion, we need figures for the numbers of peasants in a fixed territory. The realm of the tsars in the late seventeenth century was roughly that covered by the first poll tax census of 1719–21. The census counted the taxable male population within the borders of much of the Russian state at that time. The census included St Petersburg and its environs, but excluded the rest of the newly conquered Baltic region, left-bank Ukraine and the Don Cossack territory. For the purposes of this book, however, I have added the Don Cossack territory to that covered by the first poll tax census because it was settled by large numbers of Russian peasants in the eighteenth and nineteenth centuries. For sake of convenience, this territory will be referred to as 'Russia'.[12]

Members of the peasant estate living in 'Russia' in 1897 numbered 53.4 million, or 86 per cent of the total population of Russia. In the same territory, 46.6 million people, or 75.2 per cent of the population, relied on arable farming as their main occupation. The inclusion of people on the margins of the peasantry brings this figure for the peasant population by a broader occupational definition in Russia in 1897 to around 50 million.[13] (See Table 1.2.) These figures are rather higher than the estimate of 43.2 million ethnic Russian peasants. After allowing for the roughly 4 million Russian peasants who lived outside Russia (see Ch. 2), the difference, 6.2 million, was the approximate number of non-Russian peasants who lived inside the borders of Russia. They included some Finnish peasants in the vicinity of St Petersburg, Belorussian peasants who lived around Smolensk, and larger numbers of Ukrainian peasants who lived in Voronezh and Kursk provinces, the Don territory and the north Caucasus. There were also sizable populations of Finno-Ugrian-speaking Mordvinian, Mari and Udmurt peasants, Turkic-speaking Chuvash, Tatar and Bashkir peasants, and German colonists in the Volga basin and southern Urals. Most other non-Russians inside these borders (especially Siberia) were classified as aliens, many of whom were nomads. Many of the Ukrainians and all the Germans had migrated to Russia after the mid-seventeenth century. The lands of most of the other non-Russian peoples, however, had been annexed to the Russian state before the 1650s.[14]

Thus, the estimates for the peasant population of the Russian Empire as a whole, in Russia, and for ethnic Russian peasants are similar whichever way

---

12 On the territory covered by the first poll tax census, see Kabuzan, V. M., *Izmeneniya v razmeshchenii naseleniya Rossii v XVIII-pervoi polovine XIX v. (Po materialam revizii)* (Moscow, 1971), pp. 3, 59–63; id., *Narody Rossii v XVIII v.: Chislennost' i etnicheskii sostav* (Moscow, 1990), pp. 11, 57. Slobodskaya Ukraina (Khar'kov province from 1835) was separate from that part of Ukraine which came under Russian rule after 1654, but was also excluded from the first poll tax census. See also Introduction.

13 Calculated from Troinitskii, *Obshchii svod*, vol. 1, pp. 165–71; vol. 2, pp. 302–23. For a list of the provinces included in the calculation, see Moon, D., 'Peasant migration and the settlement of Russia's frontiers, 1550–1897', *HJ*, vol. 4 (1997), p. 865 n. 8.

14 Troinitskii, *Obshchii svod*, vol. 2, pp. ix–xxiv; Bruk, S. I. and Kabuzan, V. M., 'Etnicheskii sostav naseleniya Rossii (1719–1917 gg.)', *Sovetskaya etnografiya* (1980), no. 6, pp. 24–5, 32–4; Kabuzan, *Narody Rossii v XVIII v.* See also Ch. 2.

they are estimated from the 1897 census data. This suggests that most members of the peasant estate, as defined in Russian law, met specialists' definitions of peasants; that most peasants, according to specialists' criteria, were members of the peasant estate; and that the exceptions roughly cancelled each other out. Figures on the size of the peasant estate can, therefore, serve as approximations for the numbers of peasants according to specialists' definitions. This is important because the published data on the population of the Russian state before 1897 are nowhere near as detailed as those in the 1897 census. The discrepancy between the estimates of the numbers of peasants who lived in Russia and of ethnic Russian peasants in 1897 is rather greater than the deviations between those of the numbers of peasants according to different definitions. Nevertheless, the limitations in the data for the earlier period mean that, for purposes of comparison over time, we will have to use figures for the numbers of peasants in the territory of 'Russia', rather than among ethnic Russians.

THE PEASANT POPULATION IN RUSSIA, 1600–1917

The main sources for the population of the Russian state in the two centuries or so before 1897 are the ten poll tax censuses or revisions (*revizii*) held between 1719–21 and 1857–58 and the household tax census of 1678. The poll tax censuses were much less comprehensive than the 1897 census. Their main purpose was to count the male members ('male souls') in the social estates of peasants and townspeople in order to calculate how much tax they had to pay. Some poll tax censuses did little more than this. Even less complete was the household tax census of 1678, which, as the name suggests, counted only the number of households in order to assess the taxes they owed. The male population can be estimated from the returns of this census by multiplying the number of households by four.[15] The size of the peasant estate in Russia was much larger in 1897 than it had been in 1678. The number of male peasants in Russia increased from 4.3 million in 1678 to almost 16 million in 1857 and, more rapidly, to 25.9 million in 1897. (See Table 1.3.) Assuming the numbers of men and women were similar,[16] the peasant population grew from just under 9 million in 1678 to around 32 million in 1857 and 52 million in 1897.

Figures for the peasant population in Russia are harder to come by for the period before 1678. Censuses held before 1678 were even less complete than subsequent counts, and have survived only in parts. Estimates of the total population of Russia at the end of the sixteenth century (inside a slightly smaller territory) vary between 2.5–2.9 million and 11 million, but a figure of

15 On the poll tax censuses, see Kabuzan, V. M., *Narodonaselenie Rossii v XVIII-pervoi polovine XIX v.* (Moscow, 1963); on the household tax census of 1678, see Vodarskii, Ya. E., *Naselenie Rossii v kontse XVII–nachale XVIII v.* (Moscow, 1977).
16 In fact, there were slightly more women than men.

TABLE 1.3

THE PEASANT POPULATION OF RUSSIA, 1600–1917[1]

Year	Peasant estate (males)[2]	Total population (males)[3]	Per cent peasants
1600	3,150,000	3,500,000	[90.00%]
1678	4,300,000	4,800,000	89.58%
1719	5,722,332	6,345,132	90.18%
1744	6,697,410	7,399,546	90.51%
1762	7,971,843	8,507,901	93.70%
1782	9,654,921	10,570,270	91.34%
1795	10,438,318	11,502,043	90.75%
1811	11,968,416	13,183,793	90.78%
1815	11,786,493	13,565,821	86.88%
1833	13,944,824	16,303,966	85.53%
1850	15,403,787	18,288,299	84.23%
1857	15,991,396	19,113,102	83.67%
1897	25,866,082	30,074,926	86.01%
1914–17	45,811,641	53,269,350	[86.00%]

[1] All figures for Russia = territory of first poll tax census 1719 + Don region.
[2] Peasant estate before 1867 excludes peasants conscripted into armed forces; peasant estate in 1897 includes peasants serving in armed forces.
[3] Total population before 1897 excludes armed forces; total population in 1897 includes armed forces stationed in Russia.

Sources: Vodarskii, *Naselenie Rossii za 400 let*, p. 27 (1600); Vodarskii, *Naselenie Rossii v kontse XVII v.*, pp. 134, 192 (1678); Kabuzan, *Izmeneniya*, pp. 59–181 (1719–1858) (including corrections in Kahan, *Plow*, p. 8); Troinitskii, *Obshchii svod*, vol. 1, pp. 165–71 (1897); Bruk and Kabuzan, 'Etnicheskii sostav', pp. 24–5 (1914–17).

7 million seems plausible.[17] Assuming 90 per cent were peasants, then 6.3 million (3.15 million men) can serve as an approximation for the total number of Russian peasants in 1600. There are far more, and more accurate, data for the other end of the period under consideration. Following the census of 1897, incomplete censuses were held in 1916 and 1917. The total population in the territory of the first poll tax census (but excluding the Don Cossack territory) in 1914–17 has been calculated at 106.5 million. If we assume that the peasant estate made up the same proportion as in 1897 (86 per cent), then the total number of peasants in Russia in 1917 was around 91.6 million. Several million, however, were serving in the army in the First World War, or had moved to urban areas and worked in factories but had not changed their social estate.[18]

17 See Kastanov, S. M., 'Zu einigen Besonderheiten der Bevölkerungssituation Russlands im 16. Jahrhundert', *JGO*, vol. 43 (1995), pp. 321–46 (low); Dunning, C., 'Does Jack Goldstone's model of early modern state crises apply to Russia?', *CSSH*, vol. 39 (1997), p. 584 (high); Vodarskii, Ya. E., *Naselenie Rossii za 400 let (XVI–nachalo XX v.)* (Moscow, 1973), pp. 23–7 (in between).
18 Bruk and Kabuzan, 'Etnicheskii sostav', pp. 24–5 (they put the number of ethnic Russians in 1914–17 at 76.7 million); Moon, 'Citizens', pp. 46, 55–60.

Before the reforms of the 1860s, the authorities divided the Russian peasantry into different categories depending on the owners of the land they lived on. Between the 1760s and the 1860s the main categories were the seigniorial peasantry (or serfs) who lived on nobles' estates, the state peasantry who lived on land belonging to the state, and the appanage peasantry whose land was the property of the imperial family. Until they were taken over by the state in 1762–64, significant numbers of peasants lived on church land. (See Ch. 3.) In this and the following chapter, however, all data on the peasant population are for all categories combined.

A comparison of figures from the 12 censuses held between 1678 and 1897 also shows that the average proportion of members of the peasant estate in the total population of Russia fell slightly from 89.6 per cent to 86 per cent over the whole period, but more markedly from 93.7 per cent to 83.7 per cent between 1762 and 1857 (see Table 1.3). This decline was due mostly to transfers from the peasant estate to other social estates.[19] The large numbers of peasants who were conscripted into the pre-reform army in most years from 1705 to 1867 ceased to count as members of their original social estate. Their wives and any children born subsequently were also excluded from the peasant estate. The slight increase in the proportion of peasants between 1857 and 1897 was due largely to the fact that after 1867 peasants serving in the armed forces retained their peasant status.[20] Some peasants were lost to the peasantry because they transferred to the urban estates. Relatively small but significant numbers re-registered as townspeople or merchants after settling in towns. Thousands of peasants were converted to townspeople or merchants by decree when their villages were reclassified as towns for administrative purposes after the provincial reform of 1775.[21] In addition, many of the peasants who fled to the frontiers throughout the period managed to register as cossacks. On several occasions, moreover, the state augmented cossack hosts by resettling Russian and Ukrainian peasants and reclassifying them as cossacks.[22]

More important than the small decrease in the proportion of peasants in the total population of Russia, however, was the enormous increase in their absolute numbers over the entire period covered by this book. This was despite the fact that transfers from the peasant estate were not matched by similar

19 On the decline in the size of the enserfed peasantry in the first half of the nineteenth century, which has been the subject of rather more discussion, see Ch. 3.
20 On the legal status of recruits, see above, note 5. On the numbers of peasants conscripted, see Ch. 3. I have counted state peasants in the 'military settlements' in the first half of the nineteenth century as 'peasants', not 'military settlers'. See Kabuzan, *Izmeneniya*, p. 181.
21 See Kabuzan, V. M., 'Krepostnoe krest'yanstvo Rossii v XVIII-50-kh godakh XIX v.: Chislennost', sostav i razmeshchenie', *IS* (1982), no. 3, p. 77; *id.*, 'Gosudarstvennye krest'yane Rossii v XVIII-50-kh godakh XIX veka: Chislennost', sostav i razmeshchenie', *IS* (1988), no. 1, p. 83; Rieber, A. J., *Merchants and Entrepreneurs in Imperial Russia* (Chapel Hill, NC, 1982), p. 50; Hittle, M., *The Service City: State and Townsmen in Russia, 1600–1800* (Cambridge, MA, and London, 1979), pp. 208–10. On the legal procedure, see *SZ*, 1 (1832), *Zakony o Sostoyaniyakh*, pp. 76, 78–83, 148–50, 152, arts 248, 254–72, 465–72, 481–2; *Polozhenie o sel'skom sostoyanii. Osoboe prilozhenie k tomu IX Zakonov o Sostoyaniyakh* (St Petersburg, 1876), pp. 116–17, arts 172–9.
22 See *MGSR*, Krasnov, N., *Zemlya Voiska Donskogo* (St Petersburg, 1863), pp. 10–13, 192–4. See also Chs 2 and 7.

numbers moving in the other direction. Moreover, there was net emigration by peasants from Russia. Immigration by Ukrainian peasants in the seventeenth and eighteenth centuries and by German colonists in the late eighteenth and early nineteenth centuries was more than cancelled out by large-scale migration by Russian peasants, beyond Russia, to the borderlands of the empire in the late nineteenth century.[23] The growth in the peasant population of Russia was thus due entirely to natural increase. The numbers grew because, in most years, more peasants were born than died.

Demographic historians have developed sophisticated techniques to analyse population data, and have considered many factors, including biological, environmental, nutritional, economic, cultural and others, in explaining population changes. Largely as a result of constraints on research in the Soviet Union, serious study of Russian demographic history is still in its infancy. Nevertheless, it is possible to discuss trends in the main indicators: rates of birth, death, and population growth.

Birth rates

Birth rates in Russia were very high. Data from parish records on the Orthodox population of the European part of the Russian Empire[24] indicate an average annual birth rate of 44.3 per thousand in the first half of the nineteenth century, fluctuating between 40 per thousand in 1811–20 and 49.7 per thousand in the 1840s. Figures from the same sources for the second half of the century suggest that the average birth rate was both higher, around 50 per thousand, and less subject to variation. All figures based on parish records need to be treated with caution. Until the 1850s, the parish clergy were lax in reporting births, especially of girls. The apparent increase in the second half of the century may simply reflect more complete reporting. Birth rates among the peasantry may have been higher than among the total population. Steven Hoch calculated that in the village of Petrovskoe, in Tambov province, from 1754 to 1827, there were an average of 52.6 births per thousand peasants each year. In the second half of the nineteenth century, birth rates among the Russian peasantry exceeded 50 per thousand.[25]

23 See Vodarskii, *Naselenie Rossii za 400 let*, pp. 54–5; Kabuzan, *Narody Rossii v XVIII v.*, pp. 89–248. On migration, see Ch. 2.
24 Because of the relative shortage of reliable published data on the peasant population of Russia as a whole before the late nineteenth century, in the following section I have sometimes relied on figures on larger populations in which Russian peasants made up the majority. The Orthodox population of the European part of the empire included Ukrainians, Belorussians, Moldavians and some Finnic peoples as well as Russians. I have also used figures on the total or rural populations of Russia or the European part of the empire. In addition to Russians and the other Orthodox peoples, these included Baltic and some Turkic peoples. The demographic behaviour of Ukrainian and Belorussian peasants was similar to that of Russian peasants.
25 See Rashin, A. G., *Naselenie Rossii za 100 let (1811–1913)* (Moscow, 1956), pp. 38–9, 154, 165–6; Gatrell, P., *The Tsarist Economy, 1850–1917* (London, 1986), p. 244 n. 3; Mironov, B. N., 'Traditsionnoe demograficheskoe povedenie krest'yan v XIX–nachale XX v.', in Vishnevskii, A. G. (ed.), *Brachnost', rozhdaemost', smertnost' v Rossii i v SSSR* (Moscow, 1977), p. 90; Hoch, S. L., *Serfdom and Social Control in Russia: Petrovskoe, A Village in Tambov* (Chicago and London,

Russian peasants had some control over the numbers of children they had. The birth rate was high because, for a variety of reasons, peasant marriage customs were designed to maximise fertility. Virtually all Russian peasants married and, especially the women, married young. For most of the period between the early seventeenth and late nineteenth centuries, peasant women usually entered wedlock in their late teens. Towards the end of the nineteenth century the average age at which peasant women married increased slightly, but only to around 21. Separation and divorce were rare. Most marriages lasted until one partner died, and most young widows remarried. The average length of marriages of women aged 15 to 49 among the rural population of the European part of the empire in 1897 was 25.8 years. This meant, on average, women marrying at 20 could expect to remain married until they were 45. Since Russian peasant women were usually sexually mature by the time they were 15–17 years old and reached the menopause between the ages of 42 and 47, most were married for nearly all their child-bearing years. Peasant women did not practise contraception or abortion. Consequently, they gave birth to many children. In Petrovskoe between 1813 and 1827, the average peasant woman living through her child-bearing years gave birth to seven children. Statistics collected by *zemstvo* doctors in the late nineteenth century suggest that, on average, peasant women had seven to nine children.[26]

There were regional variations in fertility that reflected slight variations in the mean ages at which female peasants married. Birth rates were a little higher in the fertile, agricultural provinces of south–central and south-east Russia than in the central and northern provinces. In the period 1861–1913, the range was from 58.2 births per thousand in Orenburg province, in the Southern Urals region in the extreme south-east, to 35.2 in St Petersburg province in the north-west. All but four provinces (St Petersburg, Yaroslavl', Novgorod and Moscow) had birth rates in excess of 45 per thousand.[27] There were also seasonal variations in birth rates. In rural Russia in the late nineteenth century, the numbers of births peaked in the late summer and autumn, and were lowest in the spring and in December. This indicates that conceptions were highest during the lull in agricultural labour in the winter months and the winter festivals of Christmas and Shrovetide. The numbers of conceptions were lowest during the peak period of labour in the fields, in which women

1986), p. 72; Coale, A., Anderson, B. A. and Härm, E., *Human Fertility in Russia since the Nineteenth Century* (Princeton, NJ, 1979), pp. 10–12, 20–1, 54. On the accuracy of parish records, see Freeze, G. L., *The Russian Levites: Parish Clergy in Eighteenth Century Russia* (Cambridge, MA, and London, 1977), pp. 30–3; Hoch, S. L., 'Famine, disease, and mortality patterns in the parish of Borshevka, 1830–1912', *Population Studies*, vol. 52, no. 3 (1998).

26 See Mironov, 'Traditsionnoe', pp. 91, 94–6; Hoch, *Serfdom*, p. 73; *id.*, '"On good numbers and bad": Malthus, population trends and peasant standard of living in late imperial Russia', *SR*, vol. 53 (1994), p. 69; Tol'ts, M. S., 'Brachnost' naseleniya Rossii v kontse XIX–nachale XX v.' in Vishnevskii, *Brachnost'*, pp. 141–51; Vishnevskii, A. G., 'Rannie etapy stanovleniya novogo tipa rozhdaemosti v Rossii', *ibid.*, pp. 118–19. On marriage, see also Ch. 5.

27 Rashin, *Naselenie*, pp. 165–6. See also Engel, B. A., *Between the Fields and the City: Women, Work and Family in Russia 1861–1914* (Cambridge, 1994), p. 47; Vishnevskii, 'Rannie etapy', pp. 122–3.

took part, in the summer. The trough in the numbers of births in December may reflect the Orthodox Church's ban on sexual intercourse during Lent.[28]

Death rates

The very high birth rates among the peasant population have to be set against, and were partly a reaction to, the high death rates. In contrast to birth rates, Russian peasants were unable to exert much control over mortality. Moreover, a number of their customary practices had the unintended effect of increasing their susceptibility to disease, and thus contributed to high death rates.

An alarmingly large proportion of peasant children died in infancy or early childhood. Between 25 and 30 per cent of all infants born in the European provinces of the empire in the last third of the nineteenth century died before they were a year old: an infant mortality rate of 250–300 per thousand live births. Almost half of all children, moreover, did not survive until their fifth birthday. The death rate among infants and children under five seems to have been at a similar level in the rest of the nineteenth century and, in all likelihood, in earlier times. This grim phenomenon can be explained partly by the prevalence of diarrhoeal and infectious diseases. Newborn babies were at risk because of some of the practices of traditional midwives. High infant mortality was also a result of peasant women's unhygienic child-care practices. For example, they gave babies unsterile rags bound around chewed bread as pacifiers (*soski*). From a very early age, mothers fed their babies solid food as well as breast-feeding them. Unknown to the women, the pacifiers and solid food were major sources of germs and disease. Overcrowded housing further increased infant and childhood susceptibility to infection. The numbers of infant deaths were exacerbated by mothers rolling over and smothering their babies in bed. In some cases this was carelessness, but in others it may have been a form of infanticide to kill unwanted babies. Peasants sometimes practised selective rearing, favouring healthy babies over sickly ones and boys over girls.[29]

Death rates were very high among peasants of all ages. Data for all the European provinces of the empire for the four decades after 1860 reveal an average annual death rate of around 36 per 1,000. This figure conceals higher levels of mortality among Russians since it includes other ethnic groups which

28 Kaiser, D. H., 'The seasonality of family life in early modern Russia', *FOG*, vol. 46 (1992), pp. 22–30. On the calendar of agricultural labour and its relationship with the church calendar, see Chs 4 and 9.

29 See Rashin, *Naselenie*, pp. 192–5; Chertova, G. I., 'Smertnost' naseleniya Rossii v XIX v. po issledovaniyam sovremennikov', in Vishnevskii, *Brachnost'*, p. 162; Frieden, N. M., 'Child care: Medical reform in a traditionalist culture', in Ransel, D. L. (ed.), *The Family in Imperial Russia: New Lines of Historical Research* (Urbana, Chicago and London, 1978), pp. 236–8, 246–8; Ramer, S. C., 'Childbirth and culture: Midwifery in the nineteenth-century Russian countryside', in *RPW*, pp. 107–20; Ransel, D. L., 'Infant-care cultures in the Russian empire', in Clements, B. E. *et al.* (eds), *Russia's Women: Accommodation, Resistance, Transformation* (Berkeley, Los Angeles and Oxford, 1991), pp. 113–23; Hoch, 'Famine'; Semyonova-Tian-Shanskaia, O., *Village Life in Late Tsarist Russia*, D. L. Ransel (ed.) (Bloomington, IN, 1993), pp. 7–15, 95–6.

had lower death rates. Death rates among Russians before the 1860s may have been higher, because this average includes the late nineteenth century when mortality levels were starting to fall. Fewer estimates for overall mortality exist for the period before 1860. Hoch calculated that in Petrovskoe in the early nineteenth century the annual average death rate was at least 38 per 1,000.[30]

Estimates of life expectancy at birth provide a useful indication of mortality. Between the mid-eighteenth and mid-nineteenth centuries, newborn Russians could expect to live only until they were around 24 years old. Life expectancy at birth in Petrovskoe in the 1850s was 24.8 years for female peasants and 29.8 years for male peasants. The lower figure for women is because of deaths in childbirth. Life expectancy at birth was low because of the extremely high rates of infant and child mortality. Russians, including peasants, who reached their teens, however, could expect to live until their 50s or 60s.[31] Expected life spans in rural Russia had increased slightly by the late nineteenth century (see below, p. 32).

The high death rates among the Russian population, especially the very young and old who were most vulnerable, were largely caused by gastrointestinal diseases such as diarrhoea and dysentery, and infectious diseases such as influenza, measles, smallpox, syphilis and typhus. These were widespread, and sometimes endemic, among the peasantry as a result of environmental factors and the poor sanitation and crowded housing common in Russian villages. Two lethal fungal diseases acquired from eating mouldy rye (ergotism and alimentary toxic aleikiia), contributed to high death rates. Since rye was the staple diet of many peasants, and cold winters caused grain in storage to become contaminated, the diseases were common in rural Russia.[32]

There were distinct seasonal variations in the timing of deaths. Although Russians died throughout the year, more died in the spring and early summer. The depleting supplies of food as the previous year's harvest became more distant may have been a factor. The warm summer months, moreover, were conducive to the spread of infectious diseases.[33] There were also variations in

30 See Chertova, 'Smertnost'', pp. 154–61, 164; Rashin, *Naselenie*, pp. 38–41, 153–4, 184–6, 192, 201–5; Mironov, 'Traditsionnoe', p. 90; Blum, A. and Troitskaja, I., 'La mortalité en Russie aux XVIIIe et XIXe siècles: Estimations locales à partir des *Revizzi*', *Population*, vol. 51 (1996), pp. 303–28; Hoch, *Serfdom*, p. 73. Death rates of 25–28 per 1,000 for the Orthodox population in the early nineteenth century (e.g. Rashin, *Naselenie*, p. 38; Mironov, 'Traditsionnoe', p. 90) are suspiciously low, probably as a result of under-counting by parish priests, and can be discounted. See above, p. 23.
31 Blum and Troitskaja, 'La mortalité', p. 314; Dulov, A. V., *Geograficheskaya sreda i istoriya Rossii: konets XV–seredina XIX v.* (Moscow, 1983), p. 149; Hoch, *Serfdom*, pp. 67–8; Chertova, 'Smertnost'', p. 166.
32 Rashin, *Naselenie*, pp. 207–14; Hoch, *Serfdom*, pp. 51–56; *id.*, 'Famine'; Dulov, *Geograficheskaya*, pp. 21–4; Kahan, A., *The Plow, the Hammer and the Knout: An Economic History of Eighteenth-Century Russia* (Chicago and London, 1985), pp. 12–15; Worobec, C. D., 'Contemporary historians on the Muscovite peasantry', *CSP*, vol. 23 (1981), pp. 323–5; Engelstein, L., 'Morality and the wooden spoon: Russian doctors view syphilis, social class, and sexual behaviour, 1890–1905', *Representations*, vol. 14 (Spring 1986), pp. 169–208; Matossian, M. K., 'Climate, crops, and natural increase in rural Russia, 1861–1913', *SR*, vol. 45 (1986), pp. 457–69.
33 Kaiser, 'Seasonality', pp. 39–49, 50; Blum and Troitskaja, 'La mortalité', p. 320. See also Ch. 8.

death rates from year to year. The high mortality in 'normal' years was exacerbated by periodic 'spikes of mortality' during occasional demographic crises caused by famines, epidemics and wars (see below, pp. 28–34).

Rates of population increase to 1857

The peasant population of Russia increased throughout the period from the early seventeenth to the mid-nineteenth centuries because, although death rates were very high, on average birth rates were even higher. In order to get a balanced picture of growth rates due to natural increase, which takes account of the transfers from the peasantry to other estates and migration by Russian peasants to the borderlands beyond the territory of Russia, average annual rates of increase can be considered for three populations: the peasant estate in Russia; the total population in Russia; and ethnic Russians in the empire as a whole (see Table 1.4). The average rates of growth per annum over the period 1678 (or 1719) to 1857 are similar for all three populations, between 0.74 and 0.82 per cent. Growth rates were below average in the late seventeenth and first half of the eighteenth centuries and between 1833 and 1857. The rate of increase was above average for most of the second half of the eighteenth century and, with the exception of the blip between 1811 and 1815, in the first three decades of the nineteenth century. The general trend in the growth

TABLE 1.4

RATES OF POPULATION INCREASE, 1678–1897

Years	Interval in years	Peasant estate in Russia[1]	Total population in Russia[1]	Years	Interval in years	Ethnic Russians in empire[1]
1678–1719	41	0.70%	0.68%			
1719–44	25	0.63%	0.62%	1719–82	63	0.77%
1744–62	18	0.97%	0.78%			
1762–82	20	0.96%	1.09%			
1782–95	13	0.60%	0.65%	1782–95	13	0.82%
1795–1811	16	0.86%	0.86%	1795–1834	39	0.91%
1811–15	4	−0.42%	0.72%			
1815–33	18	0.94%	1.03%			
1833–50	17	0.59%	0.68%	1834–58	24	0.82%
1850–57	7	0.54%	0.63%			
1678–1857	179	0.74%	0.77%	1719–1858	139	0.82%
1857–1897	40	1.21%	1.14%	1858–1897	39	1.21%

[1]Average rate of increase per annum.

Sources: Peasant estate and total population in Russia calculated from data in Table 1.3; ethnic Russians calculated from Bruk and Kabuzan, 'Dinamika', p. 14.

of the peasant population in Russia from the early seventeenth to the mid-nineteenth centuries seems to have been one of high but fluctuating rates of increase, with an acceleration from the mid-eighteenth century.[34]

The impact of demographic crises to 1857

The fluctuations in the rates of increase in the relatively short intervals between censuses may be explained partly by the number and extent of demographic crises. In his famous essay published in 1798, the English clergyman Thomas Malthus argued that demographic crises were 'positive checks' on population growth which indicated that the size of a population was approaching the upper limit the land could support. The Malthusian model was soon rendered obsolete in nineteenth-century England by economic development. However, most pre-industrial societies, including Russia in the period under consideration, were periodically hit by famines, epidemics and wars that often led to declines in the total population or lower rates of growth in the short term. Whether demographic crises had long-term significance for rates of population growth, however, is open to question.[35]

Although peasants tried to reduce the risk and impact of crop failures, Russia suffered from fairly frequent bad harvests. Serious harvest failures or successive poor harvests in particular regions could lead to famines, because grain reserves were often insufficient, and because Russia's endemic transport problems meant it was difficult and expensive to move food to areas where crops had failed. Throughout the period there were regular, localised poor harvests. There were also famines on a nationwide scale. Estimates of deaths in the famine of 1601–03 are as high as one-third of the total population. In the early eighteenth century, large parts of Russia were hit by famine in 1722 and 1733–34. The second half of the eighteenth century and first two decades of the nineteenth century, however, witnessed a temporary respite from large-scale famines. Bad harvests and food shortages returned in the 1820s. The worst occurred in 1822, 1832–33, 1839–40, 1848 and 1855. Lack of detailed figures makes it difficult to estimate famine deaths in these years. It was not always clear, moreover, how many deaths were a direct result of food shortages. A relatively small proportion were due to starvation. Many more malnourished people died from illnesses. Subsistence crises had an additional impact on official data on the peasant population since many peasants left their homes in search of food, and some avoided registering at the following poll tax censuses.[36]

34 See Czap, P., 'Russian history from a demographic perspective', in Kosinski, L. A. (ed.), *Demographic Developments in Eastern Europe* (New York and London, 1977), p. 124.
35 See Wrigley, E. A., *Population and History* (London, 1969), pp. 32–5, 62–76; Le Roy Ladurie, E., 'Peasants', in *NCMH*, vol. 13, pp. 126–34.
36 See Kabuzan, *Izmeneniya*, pp. 6–8; Kahan, A., 'Natural calamities and their effect on the food supply in Russia', *JGO*, vol. 16 (1968), pp. 353–77; Dunning, 'Does', p. 573; Moon, D., *Russian Peasants and Tsarist Legislation on the Eve of Reform: Interaction between Peasants and Officialdom, 1825–1855* (Basingstoke and London, 1992), pp. 41–6. See also Arnold, *Famine: Social Crisis and Historical Change* (Oxford, 1988), pp. 91–5; Chs 4 and 8.

The idea that periodic famines were a major cause of crisis mortality in rural Russia has recently been challenged. In a sophisticated study of mortality patterns in the parish of Borshevka, in Tambov province, between 1830 and 1912, Hoch has demonstrated that there was little correlation between crisis mortality and shortages of food. Far more important, he argued, were repeated epidemics of acute infectious diseases, including smallpox, scarlet fever and measles, which are 'minimally associated' with nutrition, but spread rapidly among the rural population as a result of the overcrowded housing and climatic factors.[37]

The most serious epidemic illnesses to strike Russia were bubonic plague and cholera. There was no effective treatment for these diseases before the twentieth century, and most people who fell ill died. Plague broke out in parts of southern Russia in 1690, 1727–28 and 1738–39. Following three decades free from major outbreaks, the pestilence returned to southern, central and northwest Russia in 1770–72. Around 120,000 people died of plague in the empire as a whole in 1770–72. Most deaths occurred in the cities, especially Moscow, but many of the urban dead were peasant migrants from the surrounding countryside. The epidemic of 1770–72 was the last serious plague outbreak in Russia, and there were no epidemics of other diseases on a similar scale in the late eighteenth and early nineteenth centuries. At the end of the 1820s, however, plague was replaced by a new scourge, cholera. There were three great cholera epidemics in mid-nineteenth century Russia: in 1831, 1848 and 1855. The worst single year was 1848, when almost 700,000 people died of cholera in the European provinces of the empire. On occasions, for example in 1848 and 1855, famines and epidemics struck simultaneously. This was not coincidental. Poor nourishment weakened people's resistance to some diseases. Moreover, refugees from areas hit by famine or epidemics spread illnesses to healthy people in the areas they fled to.[38]

The peasant population was also affected by disasters which were more directly man-made than famines and epidemics. Between 1600 and 1856, Russia fought many wars with its neighbours, especially Turkey, and was involved in a number of general European conflicts. Russian military victories pushed the borders of the empire well beyond those of the Muscovite tsars, but imperial expansion was achieved at great cost. Large numbers of Russian soldiers were killed on the battlefield or died of wounds. Even greater numbers died from disease in the insanitary conditions which prevailed in military camps and hospitals. Total deaths in the Russian armed forces in wartime between 1700 and 1856 were around 1.75 million men. About 680,000 of these died over

37 Hoch, 'Famine'.
38 See Kabuzan, *Izmeneniya*, pp. 7–12; Kahan, *Plow*, pp. 12–15; id., *Russian Economic History: The Nineteenth Century* (Chicago and London, 1989), pp. 138–9; Rashin, *Naselenie*, pp. 35–7, 208; Alexander, J. T., *Bubonic Plague in Early Modern Russia: Public Health and Urban Disaster* (Baltimore, MD, and London, 1980), pp. 16–29, 257–8, 263, 73–5, 233–7; McGrew, R. E., *Russia and the Cholera 1823–1832* (Madison and Milwaukee, WI, 1965). See also Wheatcroft, S. G., 'The 1891–92 famine in Russia', in Edmondson, L. and Waldron, P. (eds), *Economy and Society in Russia and the Soviet Union, 1860–1930* (Basingstoke and London, 1992), p. 59.

the course of the eighteenth century. Over a million men died in wartime between 1801 and 1856, more than half during the Napoleonic Wars in the early nineteenth century. A further half million soldiers died in wartime between the 1820s and 1856, of whom 153,000 perished during the Crimean War of 1853–56. The vast majority of those who died had been drafted into the army from the Russian peasantry.

Deaths in wartime did not have such a direct impact on the Russian peasant population as famines and epidemics. Indeed, the exclusion of peasant-soldiers and the armed forces from the figures on the peasant and total populations in Table 1.3 makes it impossible to trace the direct effect of war deaths. From the point of view of assessing the impact of deaths in war on the peasant population, however, the important point is the extent to which the army made up for heavy losses by raising extra recruits from the peasantry. High levels of conscription had a dramatic impact on the peasant population in the last stage of the Napoleonic Wars and during the Crimean War. Between 1811 and 1814, an estimated 436,000 men were drafted from the peasant estate in Russia into the regular army, around 3.6 per cent of the male peasant population. This was a major cause of the fall in the absolute number of peasants in Russia between the censuses of 1811 and 1815. During the Crimean War, the peasantry in Russia provided roughly 470,000 recruits, almost 4 per cent of the male peasant population. This contributed to the slower rate of population growth in these years (see Table 1.4).[39]

Wars affected the civilian peasant population in other ways. Most of Russia's wars were fought in the borderlands of the empire or abroad, but Napoleon's invasion in 1812 caused devastation and death in a broad swath of central Russia. Moreover, soldiers returning from wars, especially from Turkey, often brought back illnesses. Civilian refugees from the fighting also spread diseases. The epidemics of plague and cholera in 1738–39, 1770–72, 1831 and 1855 all occurred during or just after wars with Turkey. Official figures on the population were also affected by wars because some refugees avoided registering at subsequent poll tax censuses.[40]

During all demographic crises resulting from famines, epidemics and wars, more people than usual died or were lost from the peasantry through migration or conscription. The impact of crises on population growth was compounded by the fact that fewer people were born. Birth rates fell for a number of reasons. Marriages were postponed or cancelled, sometimes because one of the prospective partners had died, fled or been conscripted. Women were less inclined to engage in sexual relations and conceive if they were malnourished or ill, if their partners had died, or if large numbers of men had been drafted into the army. In years of acute crises more people died than were born.

39 See Kabuzan, *Izmeneniya*, p. 13; Kahan, *Plow*, pp. 7–11; Rashin, *Naselenie*, pp. 36–7; Urlanis, B. Ts., *Voiny i narodonaselenie Evropy* (Moscow, 1960), pp. 340–70, 472. On the impact of conscription, and the sources of the data in the text, see Ch. 3.
40 See Kabuzan, *Izmeneniya*, p. 13; Kahan, *Plow*, p. 15; Alexander, *Bubonic*, pp. 16, 25, 101–7.

Examples of deaths exceeding births occurred during the plague epidemic in Moscow province in 1771, and as a consequence of the combination of bad harvests and cholera epidemics in at least five Russian provinces in 1848 and two in 1855.[41]

Demographic crises thus caused sudden increases in the numbers of deaths and decreases in the numbers of births. As a result, short-term rates of population increase fluctuated much more dramatically than growth rates averaged out over the intervals of several years between censuses (see Table 1.4). But the frequency of crises may have contributed to the variations in the rates of population growth over these intervals. The mostly impressionistic evidence presented in this section suggests that there were more, and more serious, crises in the first half of the eighteenth century, the short period between 1811 and 1815, and the second third of the nineteenth century. These were also the times when the rate of population growth was lower than the average for the whole period between 1678 and 1857. Recently, however, some demographic historians of north-west Europe have cautioned against linking evidence of crisis mortality with long-term trends in death rates and population change.[42]

Despite the undeniable short-term impact of demographic crises, the Russian peasant population recovered fairly quickly. In the aftermath of calamities, death rates fell as many of the weakest people, especially the very young and old, had died during the crises. In many cases, moreover, they had probably died only a few years sooner than they would have done in any case. The numbers of marriages increased after crises as weddings which had been postponed or cancelled were rearranged. Following spates of weddings, and as people recovered from the impact of famine and disease, birth rates rose. The populations that survived demographic crises were thus healthier, had higher proportions of young adults and, consequently had lower death rates and higher birth rates. The recovery of the Russian peasant population after crises can be illustrated by a couple of examples. The population of Moscow province made up for the losses from the plague epidemic of 1770–72 within a decade, although part of the increase in the city's population was due to immigration. The population also recovered quickly from the impact of the bad harvest and cholera epidemic in 1855 and the simultaneous increase in conscription during the Crimean War. In Simbirsk province, for example, there were twice as many weddings in 1856 as in 1855. Regular, short-lived, demographic crises from which populations recovered rapidly were common in pre-industrial societies.

41 See Alexander, *Bubonic*, p. 258; Kabuzan, *Narodonaselenie*, p. 80; *MGSR*, Baranovich, M., *Ryazanskaya guberniya* (St Petersburg, 1860), p. 130; Laptev, M., *Kazanskaya guberniya* (St Petersburg, 1861), pp. 166–73; Mikhalevich, V., *Voronezhskaya guberniya* (St Petersburg, 1862), pp. 106–13; Tsebrikov, *Smolenskaya guberniya* (St Petersburg, 1862), pp. 139–47; Poprotskii, M., *Kaluzhskaya guberniya* (St Petersburg, 1864), vol. 1, pp. 330–59; Lipinskii, *Simbirskaya guberniya* (St Petersburg, 1868), vol. 1, pp. 279–81.
42 See Kabuzan, *Izmeneniya*, pp. 6–14; Kahan, *Russian*, pp. 137–8; Houston, R. A., *The Population History of Britain and Ireland 1500–1750* (Basingstoke and London, 1992), p. 49.

The result was a cyclical pattern in population increase, with waves of 'baby booms' following crises echoing through the population.[43]

This cyclical pattern was reflected in the average growth rates of the population calculated from the poll tax censuses in the first half of the nineteenth century. The censuses of 1815, 1850 and 1857 were held after major demographic crises, and the losses sustained are reflected in the low growth rates calculated by comparing the returns of these censuses with the previous ones. The tax census of 1833 was also held just after a crisis, but the losses from the cholera epidemic and famine which preceded the census may not have wiped out all the gains from the population boom that probably followed the Napoleonic Wars. This explains why the rate of population increase between 1815 and 1833 was higher than average. While the rates of increase calculated between years immediately after crises show the impact of crises on the population, they may distort the actual medium- and long-term trends. This makes comparisons between growth rates in the first and second halves of the nineteenth century problematic.[44]

Rates of population increase after 1857

There is, nevertheless, little doubt that the peasant population of Russia grew faster in the second half of the nineteenth century than in the preceding two and a half centuries. Data on the peasant estate and the total population of Russia, and the numbers of ethnic Russians in the empire as a whole, show average annual growth rates of 1.14–1.21 per cent between 1857 and 1897. These are far higher than the rates of 0.74–0.82 per cent between 1678/1719 and 1857 (see Table 1.4). The high rate of population increase continued until the outbreak of the First World War in 1914. Following the pattern in northwest Europe, the main reason for the faster rate of population increase in Russia in the second half of the nineteenth century was that the death rate began to fall, slowly at first, while the birth rate remained high. An indication of the decline in death rate in Russia is that by 1897, life expectancy at birth had risen from around 25–29 earlier in the century to 30.1 for men and 31.9 for women.[45]

The slow decline in Russian death rates after the mid-nineteenth century has been explained in a number of ways. It is likely that, as in other European

43 See Alexander, *Bubonic*, pp. 258–60; Czap, P., 'The perennial multiple family household, Mishino, Russia 1782–1858', *JFamH*, vol. 7 (1982), pp. 5–26, pp. 9–10; Hoch, *Serfdom*, pp. 51, 56, 75–7; *MGSR*, Lipinskii, *Simbirskaya guberniya* (St Petersburg, 1868), vol. 1, pp. 279–81. See also Dupâquier, J., 'Population', in *NCMH*, vol. 13, pp. 85–6, 93, 96–7; Wrigley, *Population*, pp. 62–9, 113.
44 See Hoch, S. L. and Augustine, W. R., 'The tax censuses and the decline of the serf population in imperial Russia, 1833–1858', *SR*, vol. 38 (1979), pp. 422–3; Hoch, 'On good numbers', p. 58.
45 See Gatrell, *Tsarist Economy*, pp. 50–1; Chertova, 'Smertnost'', pp. 162–4, 166; Kabuzan, *Izmeneniya*, pp. 10–15; Bruk, S. I. and Kabuzan, V. M., 'Dinamika chislennosti i rasselenie Russkogo etnosa (1678–1917 gg.)', *Sovetskaya etnografiya* (1982), no. 4, pp. 14–16; Mironov, 'Traditsionnoe', pp. 102–3; Rashin, *Naseleniya*, pp. 37–42, 154, 205.

countries in the eighteenth and nineteenth centuries, part of the decline was due to a reduction in the number of demographic crises. In the last four decades of the nineteenth century the death rate in the European provinces of the empire exceeded 40 per thousand (compared with an average of 36 per thousand) in only three years, 1872, 1882 and 1892. These were a result of harvest failures of 1882 and 1891 and cholera epidemics of 1871–72 and 1892. Bad harvests and epidemics had been more frequent, and more severe, before 1860. More Russians died of cholera in the epidemics of 1831, 1848 and 1855 than in the whole of the last four decades of the nineteenth century.

The only major demographic crisis to strike the Russian peasantry in the late nineteenth century was the famine and cholera epidemic of 1891–92. Excess mortality during the crisis has been estimated at 500,000. Deaths exceeded births in no fewer than 15 Russian provinces. In the European part of the empire as a whole, the rate of population increase fell to only 0.5 per cent. The crisis of 1891–92 shocked contemporaries, especially critics of the tsarist regime. Yet, in spite of the scale of the human tragedy, the impact on the population was less than that of the crises of the first half of the century. Government relief measures mitigated some of the effects of the famine, if not the cholera, and the population made good the considerable losses within a few years.[46] There were also fewer wars after 1857. From the end of the Crimean War in 1856 to the outbreak of the Russo-Japanese War in 1904, Russia was involved in only one major war, the Russo-Turkish War of 1877–78, although the Russian army was heavily involved in the conquest of central Asia. Between 1857 and 1897, 116,000 Russian soldiers died on active service. This was well below the average numbers of war deaths in similar periods between 1700 and 1856. The reforms of the 1860s and 1870s, moreover, reduced the impact of conscription on the peasant population in Russia.[47] But the First World War of 1914–18 cost the lives of around 1.8 million Russian soldiers, in addition to over 5 million taken prisoner or missing.[48] This proved a foretaste of the catastrophic man-made demographic crises of the Soviet period (see Ch. 9).

The reduction in the number and magnitude of demographic crises in rural Russia between the mid-nineteenth and early twentieth centuries contributed to the new pattern of higher, and steadier, rates of growth among the peasant population. The reduction in 'crisis mortality' only partly explains the higher rate of population increase. Some demographic historians of north-west Europe have argued that changes in 'background mortality' were more important than declines in 'crisis mortality' in bringing down overall death rates. This seems also to have been the case in Russia.

46 See Rashin, *Naselenie*, pp. 155–9, 208, 220; Robbins, R. G., *Famine in Russia, 1891–1892: The Imperial Government Responds to a Crisis* (New York and London, 1975); Simms, J. Y., 'The economic impact of the Russian famine of 1891–92', *SEER*, vol. 60 (1982), pp. 63–74; Wheatcroft, '1891–92 famine', pp. 44–64. See also Ch. 3.
47 See Gatrell, *Tsarist Economy*, p. 60; Kahan, *Russian*, pp. 139–40; Urlanis, *Voiny*, pp. 356, 362; Schofield, R. and Reher, D., 'The decline of mortality in Europe', in Schofield, R. *et al.* (eds), *The Decline of Mortality in Europe* (Oxford, 1991), pp. 1–3. On conscription, see Ch. 3.
48 Wheatcroft and Davies, 'Population', p. 46.

A variety of factors led to the start of the fall in mortality in 'normal years' in late nineteenth-century Russia. Some historians have stressed the import-ance of improvements in public health provision, for example better sanita-tion and water supplies, and in the availability of 'modern' medical care. It is unlikely, however, that these had much impact in most of rural Russia before the twentieth century. Other scholars have emphasised the role of improved availability of food. There is increasing evidence that, contrary to the older view of the 'hungry village' in late tsarist Russia, average peasant living stand-ards were improving. Not only were there fewer serious bad harvests, but the construction of railways meant it was easier to move grain to deficit areas, reducing the risk of localised famines. Moreover, nutritional standards were improving as the amounts of food produced, and consumed, increased faster than the population. A more reliable supply of more food meant a healthier population, reduced susceptibility to infectious diseases, and a lower death rate.

Peasant living standards in Russia in the late nineteenth and first years of the twentieth centuries have been the subject of much debate between historians in recent years. Moreover, the interrelationships between economic growth, improved living standards, better nutrition and population increase are highly complex. In any case, there is still much research to be done on the reasons for the start of the decline in death rates in rural Russia before the overall picture becomes clearer. Particular attention will need to be paid to variations between different regions, urban and rural areas, and differences inside the peasantry.[49]

* * *

In order to put Russia's largely peasant population in the period between the early seventeenth and early twentieth centuries into perspective, the basic demographic indicators can be compared with those of other societies at other times. The crude rates of birth, death and, especially, infant mortality in rural Russia in the period under consideration were much higher, and life expect-ancy much lower, than in the developed regions of the world (including the Soviet Union) in the late twentieth century. In these respects, the rural Rus-sian population also differed, but not to the same degree, from the populations of many north-west European countries in the eighteenth and nineteenth cen-turies. The biggest contrast was in birth rates. The levels of fertility in rural Russia before the twentieth century were extremely high by the standards of other societies. Average annual birth rates over 45 per thousand are uncom-mon, and the 50 per thousand attained by the Russian peasantry is around the

49 See Patterson, K. D., 'Mortality in late tsarist Russia: A reconnaissance', *Social History of Medicine*, vol. 8 (1995), pp. 179–210; Ramer, S. C., 'Traditional healers and peasant culture in Russia, 1861–1917', *PECPER*, p. 209; Gregory, P. R., 'Grain marketings and peasant consump-tion in Russia, 1885–1913', *EEH*, vol. 17 (1980), pp. 135–64; Hoch, 'On good numbers', esp. pp. 67–70. *Cf.* Robinson, G. T., *Rural Russia under the Old Regime* (Berkeley and Los Angeles, 1960) (1st edn, 1932), pp. 94–116. See also Ch. 8.

maximum possible, except in societies with unusually large numbers of young women. Unlike the Russian peasantry's practice of early, universal marriage, most societies in early modern north-west Europe deliberately limited the number of births by delaying marriage and restricting the numbers of people who married (see Ch. 6). The basic demographic indicators of the Russian population in the nineteenth century were closer to those of contemporary eastern Europe and of less developed countries of Asia, Africa, and South and Central America in the first half of the twentieth century.

The average rate of increase in the population of late nineteenth-century Russia, around 1.2 per cent per annum, is high by any standards. Higher rates of population growth have been achieved only in countries experiencing mass immigration, such as the USA at the same time, and in less developed and developing countries in the late twentieth century, where *natural* growth rates have exceeded 2 per cent a year.

The growth of the Russian population throughout the entire period under consideration was part of the increase in the European population as a whole that began in the eighteenth century. In much of north-west Europe in the nineteenth century, however, high rates of natural population increase began to slow as death rates, and then birth rates, began to fall. This was the start of 'demographic transition' towards much lower rates of death, birth, and natural increase. This transition has been connected with the broader transformation, or 'modernisation', of societies that began in north-west Europe and North America in the eighteenth and nineteenth centuries. In the long term, these changes spelled the end of peasantries' numerical predominance in the societies they lived in, and of peasant societies themselves. In rural Russia at the time of the 1897 census, however, such changes were only just beginning. Indeed, the rate of population growth among the Russian peasantry was still increasing. Although death rates had started to decline, birth rates were still very high and showed few signs of starting to fall. Rural Russia did not experience 'demographic transition' until the twentieth century.[50]

CONCLUSION

The most striking features of the Russian peasant population over the period covered by this book were that peasants made up by far the largest part of the total population of Russia, and that the number of peasants increased considerably. Although peasants were largely responsible for the growth in their numbers by favouring a marriage pattern that ensured high birth rates, at least in part they were reacting to high rates of death, including infant mortality, over which they were not able to exert much control. It is extremely unlikely,

---

50 See Anderson, M., *Population Change in North-Western Europe, 1750–1850* (Basingstoke and London, 1988), pp. 29–36; Keyfitz and Flieger, *World Population*, pp. 106–7; Vallin, J., 'Mortality in Europe from 1720 to 1914: Long-term trends and changes in patterns by age and sex', in Schofield, *Decline*, pp. 50–2; Heer, D. M., 'The demographic transition in the Russian empire and the Soviet Union', *JSocH*, vol. 1 (1968), pp. 193–240.

moreover, that Russian peasants were consciously trying to increase the total numbers of peasants throughout Russia. Rather, they were concerned to ensure adequate supplies of labour in their households and communities (see Chs 5 and 6). The growth in the size of the peasant population of Russia, and peasants' numerical predominance in the total population, were, in turn, important factors which had an impact on many of the ways peasants organised their lives.

In contrast to the populations of contemporary north-west Europe, most Russian peasants did not try to limit their birth rates, did not give up agriculture for industry, or migrate permanently to urban areas. Instead, most maintained their traditional marriage pattern and stayed on the land. From the late sixteenth century, however, large numbers of Russian peasants migrated from the heartland to more outlying regions of the expanding Russian state, where they encountered a variety of environmental conditions and peoples with ways of life and cultures that differed greatly from those they were familiar with.

CHAPTER 2

Environment

Environmental factors had a significant impact on the ways Russian peasants ran their lives. At the start of the seventeenth century, most Russian peasants eked out a living from the relatively infertile soils and in the harsh climate of the forested zone of central and northern Russia that lay to the north of the Oka river. This was the forest-heartland of Russian peasant settlement. In the late sixteenth century, however, some Russian peasants had moved south and east, across the Oka river, out of the forest, and on to the steppes. This was the start of a massive population movement. Over the following centuries, millions of peasants migrated to the steppe zone. In comparison with the forest-heartland, the soils of the steppes were more fertile and the climate less severe. Prior to Russian conquest and peasant settlement, the steppes had been the preserve of nomadic pastoralists, and had formed part of the vast Eurasian empire of the Mongols. Other Russian peasants migrated east from the forest-heartland, over the Ural mountains, to the immense forested land of Siberia.

This chapter examines the environmental conditions and native inhabitants of the regions Russian peasants lived in and migrated to. It goes on to discuss the reasons why peasants moved, and traces trends in the numbers and directions of migration. The final parts consider the impact of the interactions between peasant-migrants, natural environments and native peoples on the ways of life of the Russian peasantry.

NATURAL ENVIRONMENTS, NATIVE PEOPLES, RUSSIAN CONQUEST

Most of the European part of Russia and western Siberia is a vast plain. With the exception of the Ural Mountains, the customary border between Europe and Asia, the only mountain ranges are along the periphery: the Caucasus to the south, the Altai in south–central Siberia, and the mountains of eastern Siberia. The plain is drained by broad, slow-flowing rivers: among the most important west of the Urals are the Oka, which is a tributary of the mighty Volga, and the Don, and in Siberia, the Ob, Yenisei and Lena.[1] As well as similarities, there are also differences in the environment of Russia. Donald MacKenzie Wallace wrote:

1 See Christian, D., 'Inner Eurasia as unit of history', *Journal of World History*, vol. 5 (1994), pp. 175–9; Tochenov, V. V. *et al.* (eds), *Atlas SSSR* (Moscow, 1985), pp. 14–15.

If it were possible to get a bird's eye view of European Russia, the spectator would perceive that the country is composed of two halves, widely different from each other in character. The northern half is a land of forest and morass, plentifully supplied with water in the form of rivers, lakes, and marshes, and the southern half is . . . an immense expanse of rich arable land, broken up by occasional patches of sand or forest.[2]

The territory of Russia (see Ch. 1) can be divided into three zones that reflect the natural environments and Russian expansion: the forest-heartland to the north; the steppes to the south-east; and Siberia to the east. These zones can be further divided into a number of regions. (See Maps 2.1–2.3.)[3]

The forest-heartland

The first zone, the forest-heartland of central and northern Russia, lies to the north of the Oka river, to the west of the Ural Mountains, and to the east of the Baltic region, Lithuania and Belorussia. Apart from a belt of sparsely populated tundra north of the Arctic circle, most of the zone was originally cloaked by forest: coniferous forest to the north, and mixed coniferous and broadleaved woodland to the south. The mixed forest forms a wedge shape, pointing east as far as the Urals, and includes the city of Moscow. Over the centuries, however, large areas of forest were cleared by peasants to prepare the land for cultivation.

The belt of coniferous forest of northern Russia forms part of the vast northern, or boreal, forest which almost circumnavigates the globe. It stretches westwards into Scandinavia, and eastwards across Siberia, the Bering Straits, and the northern part of America to the Atlantic seaboard. In Russia, the coniferous forest is dominated by evergreen pine, fir, larch and spruce trees. The soils are mostly poor *podzols*, which are acidic and contain a lot of clay. Large parts of the land are marshy. In the southern part of the coniferous forest, the variety of trees is increased by hardier broadleaved trees, especially birch, aspen and alder, and the soils are more fertile.

The mixed coniferous and broadleaved woodland in central Russia is also part of a much larger forest, which continues on the eastern and western shores of the Baltic Sea. The southern part of the wedge joins the European wildwood that once covered most of the continent. In addition to the trees in the south of the coniferous forest, the mixed forest of central Russia contains a greater variety of broadleaved trees such as oak, maple, elm and lime. In much of the

2 Wallace, *Russia*, vol. 1, p. 42. See also Pallot, J. and Shaw, D. J. B., *Landscape and Settlement in Romanov Russia, 1613–1917* (Oxford, 1990), pp. 5–6.
3 On the regionalisation scheme, see Moon, 'Peasant migration', pp. 865–7, esp. n. 10. I have followed Kabuzan (*Izmeneniya*, p. 4) in using the provincial boundaries of 1806, but have included Smolensk province in the Central Non-Black Earth region and the Don Cossack territory in a combined Lower-Volga and Don region. The borders of the regions do not coincide exactly with environmental belts. See Semenov, V. P. (ed.), *Rossiya: Polnoe geograficheskoe opisanie nashego otechestva*, 11 vols (St Petersburg, 1899–1914), vol. 1, *Moskovskaya promyshlennaya oblast' i Verkhnee Povol'zhe* (St Petersburg, 1899), p. vii n. 1.

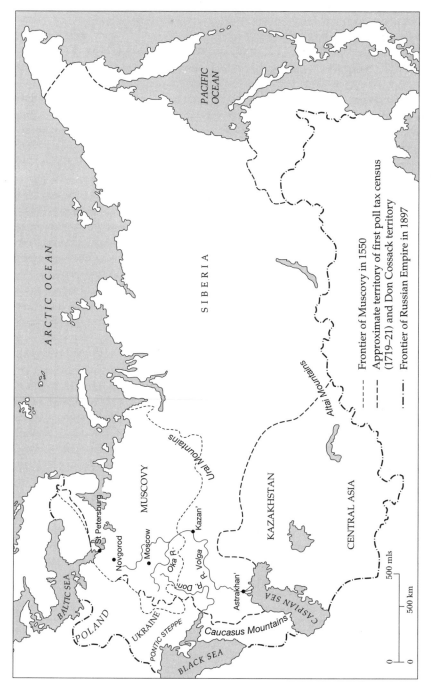

Map 2.1 Russia's political frontiers, 1550–1897 (from Moon, 'Peasant migration', *Historical Journal*, vol. 40 (1997), p. 860; reproduced with permission of Cambridge University Press)

Legend:

- - - - - Frontier of Muscovy in 1550

– – – – – Approximate territory of first poll tax census (1719–21) and Don Cossack territory

–·–·–·– Frontier of Russian Empire in 1897

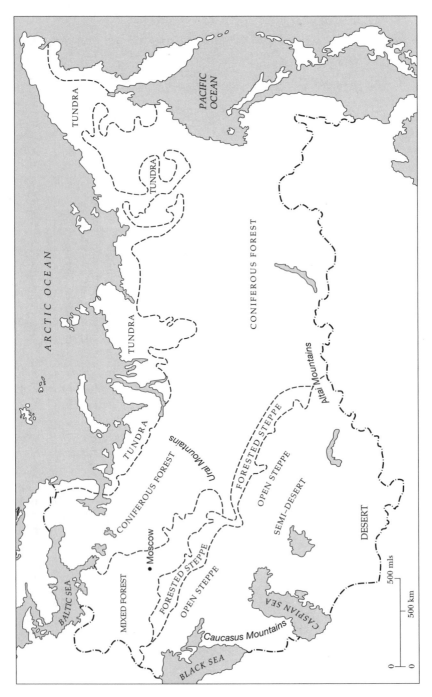

Map 2.2 Environmental belts (from Moon, 'Peasant migration', *Historical Journal*, vol. 40 (1997), p. 875, based on Pallot and Shaw, *Landscape*, Figure 1; reproduced with permission of Cambridge University Press)

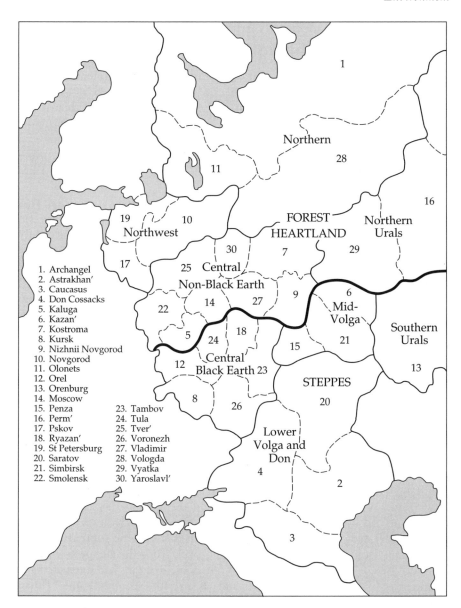

1. Archangel
2. Astrakhan'
3. Caucasus
4. Don Cossacks
5. Kaluga
6. Kazan'
7. Kostroma
8. Kursk
9. Nizhnii Novgorod
10. Novgorod
11. Olonets
12. Orel
13. Orenburg
14. Moscow
15. Penza
16. Perm'
17. Pskov
18. Ryazan'
19. St Petersburg
20. Saratov
21. Simbirsk
22. Smolensk
23. Tambov
24. Tula
25. Tver'
26. Voronezh
27. Vladimir
28. Vologda
29. Vyatka
30. Yaroslavl'

Map 2.3   Regions of European Russia (after Moon, 'Peasant migration', *Historical Journal*, vol. 40 (1997), p. 866)

mixed forest, the soil is moderately fertile, loamy *podzol*. In many places, however, it is interspersed with sand and clay. In the north-west there are several large lakes, for example Ladoga and Onega, and sizable areas of bog, but in the south-east and around Vladimir and Suzdal' there are stretches of more fertile, grey forest soil. The whole of the forest-heartland played host to a rich and varied wildlife before hunting, trapping and the decimation of their forest habitats greatly reduced their numbers. The forests had contained substantial populations of larger mammals such as bison, elk, deer, bears, wolves and wild boar; smaller, fur-bearing animals, for example foxes, hares, squirrels, mink and sable; and gamebirds, wildfowl and birds of prey. The rivers and lakes were full of fish.

The climate of most of the forest-heartland (except the Arctic tundra) is temperate and continental: the summers are fairly warm, but there are big differences between summer and winter. In most of the zone, the mean July temperatures range from 60° to 68° Fahrenheit (16°–20° Celsius), but in January the average is much lower, between 3° and 18°F (–16° and –8°C). The summers are cooler and the winters even more severe in the extreme north-east. Throughout the forest-heartland, the winters are not only cold but also long. In the northern coniferous forest belt, snow lies on the ground for at least five months a year, and there are fewer than four months without frost. Further south, in the mixed forest, the frost-free period is a few weeks longer. Thus, the growing season in the forest-heartland was confined to less than half the year. Peasant farming was not constrained by lack of moisture, however, as central and northern Russia receives between 18 and 24 inches (450–600 mm) rainfall a year.[4]

The forest zone to the north of the Oka river was the heartland of Russian peasant settlement at the start of the period covered by this book. The forest-heartland was also approximately the territory of the Grand Duchy of Muscovy in the late fifteenth century, after the annexation of the other Russian principalities of the Volga–Oka mesopotamia and the extensive northern lands of Novgorod.[5] A few centuries earlier, however, the inhabitants of much of this forest zone had been various Finnic peoples. By the sixteenth century, most had been defeated, assimilated or pushed north-east into the coniferous forest by Russians, some of whom were moving back from the steppe frontier to the south (see below, p. 45). Over these centuries, Russians had interacted and intermarried with the Finnic peoples and, as a result, acquired some of their cultural and physical characteristics.[6]

4 See Dulov, *Geograficheskaya*, pp. 5–10; Tochenov, *Atlas*, pp. 98–103, 104–5, 108–9; Semenov, P., *Geografichesko-statisticheskii slovar' Rossiiskoi imperii*, 5 vols (St Petersburg, 1863–85) (entries under relevant provinces); Sparks, J., *Realms of the Russian Bear: A Natural History of Russia and the Central Asian Republics* (London, 1992), pp. 22–31, 154–239.
5 Crummey, R. O., *The Formation of Muscovy, 1304–1613* (London, 1987), pp. 87–93; Gilbert, M., *Atlas of Russian History* (London, 1972), p. 25.
6 Forsyth, J., *A History of the Peoples of Siberia: Russia's North Asian Colony, 1581–1990* (Cambridge, 1992), pp. 2–7; Martin, J., 'Russian expansion in the far north: X to mid-XVI century', in Rywkin, M. (ed.), *Russian Colonial Expansion to 1917* (London and New York, 1988), pp. 23–43.

The forest-heartland can be divided into four regions. The largest part of the mixed forest and the more fertile central–southern part of the coniferous forest make up the first and most important: the Central Non-Black Earth region (Moscow, Vladimir, Nizhnii Novgorod, Kostroma, Yaroslavl', Tver', Kaluga and Smolensk provinces). Straddling the border of the mixed and coniferous forests in the west is the North-western region (St Petersburg, Pskov and Novgorod provinces). Most of the coniferous forest, with the exception of the southern parts, but together with the Arctic tundra, form the Northern region (Archangel, Vologda and Olonets provinces). The fourth forested region is the Northern Urals (Perm' and Vyatka provinces) in the north-east, which contains both coniferous and mixed forest. (See Maps 2.2–2.3.)

Until the late eighteenth century, most Russians lived in the forest rather than on the steppe. This is reflected in Russian culture. The Russian language has over 100 words for varieties of forest ecosystems. In the dictionary of the Russian language compiled by Vladimir Dal' in the second half of the nineteenth century, the entry for 'forest' (*les*) is four times as long as that for 'steppe' (*step'*). Prominent among the nature spirits of Russian folk beliefs, which predated Christianity, was the forest spirit (*leshchii*), whom peasants believed to be the evil-natured or capricious master of the woodland. Ethnographers collected numerous tales and superstitions about forest spirits, but far fewer about the field spirit (*polevoi*) or its southern cousin, the steppe spirit (*stepovoi*).[7]

The steppes

To the south of the Oka river lie the steppes. They fall into two natural belts: the transitional forested steppe in the north, and the open steppe grasslands in the south and east. The steppes of Russia to the west of the Urals are part of the vast Eurasian steppes, which extend from Hungary and Ukraine in central and eastern Europe into Russia, and then across southern Siberia and northern central Asia into Mongolia. The great expanses of the Eurasian steppes resemble the prairies or great plains of North America, the pampas of South America, and the veldt of southern Africa.

In the European part of Russia, the transitional forested steppe originally contained areas of broadleaved woodland alternating with stretches of open grassland. The native flora and fauna of the woodlands were similar to those of the forested regions to the north, until peasants cleared many of the trees to prepare the land for farming. Before peasants ploughed up stretches of grassland, they had been covered with dense high grasses, flowering herbs and thickets of bushes. Further south and east, the areas of woodland become

7 See Klyuchevskii, V. O., *Russkaya istoriya: Polnii kurs lektsii v trekh knigakh*, 3 vols (Moscow, 1993): vol. 1, pp. 52–4, 267; French, R. A., 'Russians and the forest', in Bater, J. H. and French, R. A. (eds), *Studies in Russian Historical Geography*, 2 vols (London, 1983), vol. 1, pp. 23–4; Dal', *Tolkovyi slovar'*, vol. 2, pp. 279–80; vol. 4, pp. 322–3; Ivanits, L. J., *Russian Folk Belief* (Armonk, NY, 1989), pp. 64–82, 178–89.

scarcer, except in valleys and ravines, and the forested steppe shades into the open steppe: a seemingly endless sea of grass dominated by big skies. The open steppe of Russia to the west of the Urals encompassed the lower Don and Volga river basins, and reached as far south as the northern shores of the Black and Caspian Seas and the foothills of the Caucasus Mountains.

The soils of the steppes are much more fertile than those of the forest-heartland. In the north of the forested steppe, grey forest earth predominates. In the central and southern parts of the forested steppe and most of the open steppe, however, is the famous black earth (*chernozem*), rich in humus and very fertile, which lured millions of Russian peasants out of the forest. To the south and east of the open steppe, along the lower reaches of the river Volga, the black earth gives way to poorer, chestnut soils, which become lighter and more sandy and saline on the arid steppe to the north of the Caspian Sea. Before the arrival of large numbers of peasants, the grasslands had been inhabited by wild horses and asses, wild goats, deer, camels, antelopes, including the strange saiga with their inflatable nostrils, as well as rodents, such as marmots, and many lizards and birds. With the spread of peasant agriculture to the open steppes, many of the wildlife moved south and east to more arid steppe and deserts, or suffered catastrophic collapses in their numbers.

Compared with the forest-heartland, the climate of the steppe zone is less severe. The summers are a little warmer, and the winters are shorter, but still very cold. More importantly, however, the rainfall is lower. The mean July temperature in most of the steppe zone ranges from 68° to 75°F (20°–24°C). The summers are hotter in the south-east of the open steppe belt. Throughout the steppe zone, the mean temperature in January is between 7° and 23°F (−14° and −5°C). There are over five months a year without frost on the forested steppe, and slightly longer on the open steppe. Only along the northern shores of the Black and Caspian Seas and in the north Caucasus are there over six months a year without frost. The amount of rain in Russia decreases from the north-west to the south-east. In the forested steppe, the annual average is 14–22 inches (350–550 mm), but in most of the open steppe, only 12–16 inches (300–400 mm). Further south-east, on the Caspian steppe, the average is even lower. The rainfall in the steppe zone is not only fairly low, it is also unreliable: droughts were a frequent cause of crop failures.[8]

The steppe zone can be divided into four regions. The forested steppe comprises two regions. In south–central Russia is the Central Black Earth region (Ryazan', Tula, Orel, Kursk, Voronezh and Tambov provinces). To the east is the Mid-Volga region (Kazan', Penza and Simbirsk provinces). Both regions also include areas of mixed forest with grey forest soils in the north, and open steppe in the south and east. Most of the Russian open steppe comprises the Lower-Volga and Don region (Saratov and Astrakhan' provinces and the Don

8 See Dulov, *Geografcheskaya*, pp. 10–11; Tochenov, *Atlas*, pp. 98–103, 104–5, 108–9; Pallot and Shaw, *Landscape*, pp. 58–63; Semenov, *Geografchesko-statisticheskii slovar'* (entries for relevant provinces); Sparks, *Realms*, pp. 110–53. See also McNeill, W. H., *Europe's Steppe Frontier, 1500–1800* (Chicago and London, 1964), pp. 2–3.

Cossack and Caucasus territories). The fourth steppe region is the Southern Urals (the large province of Orenburg), which includes the eastern parts of the open steppe, together with the remainder of the forested steppe and mixed forest belts and, in the mountains, a narrow strip of coniferous forest. (See Maps 2.2–2.3.)

Very few Russian peasants lived in the steppe zone before the late sixteenth century. The main reason for this was that most of the zone lay along and beyond the hazardous open frontier between the forest and steppe. For centuries, while the peasants had lived in the forest, the Eurasian steppes had been the domain of nomadic pastoralists. The last and most powerful of the nomad empires was the Mongol Empire founded by Genghis Khan in the early thirteenth century. In the late 1230s, a large army of nomadic horsemen led by Batu Khan swept across the steppes from Mongolia and conquered much of Russia. The Mongols set up the Golden Horde as the westernmost division of their vast empire. Although the Mongols ruled Russia indirectly, the peasants were pushed back deeper into the forest. The transitional forested steppe belt became a sparsely populated no-man's land between the peasants of the forest and the nomads of the steppe.

The tide turned in favour of the emerging Russian state, with its largely peasant population, in the late fifteenth century. By the middle of the century, the Golden Horde had split into the Tatar Khanates of Kazan' and Astrakhan' on the middle and lower Volga, the Crimea to the north of the Black Sea, and Siberia across the Urals. The Russians finally threw off the 'Mongol Yoke' in 1480, and went on the offensive. In the 1550s, tsar Ivan the Terrible (1533–84) conquered Kazan' and Astrakhan'. Critical factors in Ivan's victory were the firepower of his infantry and artillery, which proved more than a match for the superior horsemanship of the Tatars, and the ability of the Russian state to mobilise its resources. Ivan's victories over the khanates of the Volga, but not the Crimea, began the process of Russian annexation of the steppes. By the end of the sixteenth century, Russia controlled the full length of the river Volga and most of the forested steppe. The fertile lands beyond the Oka river were thus opened to peasant colonisation and the spread of settled agriculture in place of nomadic pastoralism.[9]

Peasant agriculture was not completely new to the steppes. Not all the inhabitants of the Khanates were pastoralists. Although the nomadic nobility considered crop cultivation to be beneath them, some of the lower orders grew grain. Moreover, many of the indigenous peoples of the forested part of the Khanate of Kazan', in the mid-Volga basin, were sedentary farmers, for example the Mordvinians, Mari and Chuvash, as well as many Tatars.[10]

---

9 Christian, 'Inner Eurasia', pp. 193–207; Huttenbach, H. R., 'Muscovy's conquest of Muslim Kazan and Astrakhan, 1552–56. The conquest of the Volga: prelude to empire', in Rywkin, *Russian*, pp. 45–69; Zagorodovskii, V. P., *Istoriya vkhozhdeniya Tentral'nogo Chernozem'ya v sostav Rossiiskogo gosudarstva v XVI v.* (Voronezh, 1991), pp. 5–8, 31–5.
10 See Gorskaya, N. A. (ed.), *Krest'yanstvo v period rannego i razvitogo feodalizma* (Moscow, 1990), pp. 462–8; Kabuzan, *Narody Rossii v XVIII v.*, pp. 104–5.

The land to the south and east of the steppe frontier was known as the 'wild field' (*dikoe pol'e*). The Russian steppe frontier and the 'wild field' in the sixteenth and seventeenth centuries have been compared with the American frontier and the 'wild west' in the eighteenth and nineteenth centuries. Like the native Americans of the great plains, the indigenous peoples of the steppes opposed expansion by European agriculturalists onto their traditional lands. On Russia's steppe frontier, resistance continued long after Ivan the Terrible's victories in the 1550s. The strongest opposition came from the Crimean Tatars, who were provided with firearms by their Ottoman overlords. The Russians did not conquer and annex the Crimea until the late eighteenth century. For much of the intervening period, Crimean Tatars and other nomads raided Russian settlements. They burnt buildings, destroyed crops, drove away live-stock, and seized prisoners to be sold as slaves. On occasions they reached deep into Russia. Crimean Tatars sacked and burned Moscow in 1571. Nomadic raids were not just expressions of hostility towards Russian colonisation, but an integral part of the economy and culture of the nomadic societies of the Eurasian steppes. Relations between steppe nomads and Russian peasants were not always antagonistic. The pastoral economy of the nomads and the agricul-tural economy of the peasants were complementary, and there was some trade between them.

After the victories of the 1550s, the Russian state took measures to sub-jugate the native inhabitants of the steppes, and to secure the fertile land for Russian peasant settlement. The state joined in and manipulated the constantly shifting alliances and rivalries between the various steppe peoples, periodically allying with the Kalmyks against the Bashkirs, Kazakhs and rebellious cos-sacks. The state constructed a series of fortified lines along its steppe frontier to protect Russian settlers and the heartland of Russia from nomadic raids. The most important were the Belgorod and Simbirsk lines, which were built in the first half of the seventeenth century. They stretched from the border with Polish Ukraine in the west to the left bank of the Volga in the east, and secured the forested steppe. These and later fortified lines served as bases for further expansion to the open steppes.[11]

The most serious resistance, besides that of the Crimean Tatars, came from the Bashkirs of the southern Urals and the peoples of the north Caucasus, for example the Chechens. These Islamic peoples declared *jihads* (holy wars) against Russian incursion on to their lands. The Bashkirs rebelled at regular intervals between the late sixteenth and late eighteenth centuries, and took part in the Pugachev revolt by cossacks, peasants and other Russians in 1773–74. The peoples of the north Caucasus fought a long guerilla war against the regular Russian army that lasted from the late eighteenth century to the 1860s. In the long run, however, the native inhabitants of the steppes proved no match for the expanding Russian state and its growing peasant population. The Russian

11 See Hellie, R., *Enserfment and Military Change in Muscovy* (Chicago and London, 1971), pp. 28–31; Khodarkovsky, M., *Where Two Worlds Met: The Russian State and the Kalmyk Nomads, 1600–1771* (Ithaca, NY, 1992), pp. 30–1, 50–7, 74–213; Pallot and Shaw, *Landscape*, pp. 14–20.

conquest and settlement of the steppes were decisive events in the history of the Russian state and the Russian peasantry.[12]

Siberia

East of the Ural Mountains lies the third main zone of Russian peasant settlement: Siberia. In keeping with its popular image, the natural environment of much of Siberia is extremely harsh. A broad belt in the north is covered by tundra. Dense, coniferous forest, or *taiga*, shrouds most of the rest of Siberia. The soils of the *taiga* are not very fertile, but the forest was the home of a wealth of fur-bearing animals that attracted hunters and trappers from west of the Urals. In contrast to the inhospitable tundra and evergreen forest is a narrow strip of forested steppe with fertile black earth which stretches from the southern end of the Urals, across the most southerly part of western Siberia, as far as the Altai Mountains. The forested steppe of southern Siberia shades into the more arid, open steppe of Kazakhstan and central Asia. The climate of Siberia is harsher and more extreme than that of the European part of Russia. The average summer temperature in most of Siberia is similar to that of Russia west of the Urals, but the winters are even colder and longer. The mean temperature in January is below $-4°F$ $(-20°C)$ and can fall much lower, especially in the north and east. In the northern part of western Siberia and most of central and eastern Siberia, the subsoil is permanently frozen (permafrost). The rainfall is high in the mountains of central and eastern Siberia, but the fertile strip of southern Siberia receives an average of under 16 inches (400 mm) a year.[13]

The Russian conquest of Siberia began in the late sixteenth century, in the wake of Ivan the Terrible's victories over the Khanates of Kazan' and Astrakhan'. In 1581 or 1582, the cossack Yermak Timofeevich and his men crossed the Urals in defence of the commercial interests of a Russian trading family, the Stroganovs. Yermak and his band defeated the Tatar Khanate of Siberia. The Khanate covered only a small part of western Siberia. Yet, by the mid-seventeenth century, Russian fur trappers and traders had travelled 3,000 miles through the *taiga* to the shores of the Pacific Ocean. On the way, they set up a series of forts and trading posts.

On the eve of Russian conquest, the Siberian forest had a significant, if thinly spread, population of many ethnic groups. Most relied on nomadic reindeer herding, hunting and fishing. They put up serious resistance, but their bows and arrows and spears were no match for the Russians' firearms. The Russians also inadvertently brought with them another weapon: diseases such as

---

12 See Donnelly, A., 'The mobile steppe frontier: The Russian conquest and colonization of Bashkiria and Kazakhstan to 1850', in Rywkin, *Russian*, pp. 189–202; Atkin, M., 'Russian expansion in the Caucasus to 1813', *ibid.*, pp. 154–67; Brooks, E. W., 'Nicholas I as reformer: Russian attempts to conquer the Caucasus, 1825–1855', in Banac, I. *et al.* (eds), *Nation and Ideology* (New York, 1981), pp. 227–63. On the Pugachev revolt, see Ch. 7.
13 Dulov, *Geograficheskaya*, pp. 11–12; Tochenov, *Atlas*, pp. 98–103, 104–5, 108–9.

smallpox, measles, typhus and syphilis. Since these diseases were previously unknown in Siberia, the indigenous population had no resistance to them, and consequently fell ill and died in tragically large numbers. A much greater obstacle to Russian expansion into Siberia was presented by the Turkic and Mongol nomadic peoples (including Tatars, Kazakhs, Buryats and Dzhungars) who lived on the steppe to the south of the forest. The Russian authorities built further lines of fortifications from the southern end of the Urals to the Altai Mountains, along the boundary of the forest and steppe. Further east, China posed an even more formidable barrier to Russian expansion. Russian settlers had to abandon the Amur' river basin after Russia was forced to acknowledge Chinese rule over the region, under the terms of the Treaty of Nerchinsk, in 1689.

Russian peasants began to settle in western Siberia in the seventeenth century. Peasant farming provided some of the food needed by the growing numbers of Russian fur trappers, traders, soldiers and officials. Many of the early migrants came from the Northern and Northern Urals regions, and settled directly across the Urals from their homelands. The majority of peasant-migrants to Siberia settled further south, in the narrow, fertile strip of forested steppe. Peasant-migrants moved eastwards, more slowly than the trappers and traders, in a series of short stages, establishing islands of peasant settlement in the Yenisei and Lena river basins.[14]

* * *

Many writers have commented on the relative poverty of the natural environment of Russia relative to other parts of the world. Some have gone on to argue that the environment had a profound impact on Russian history. Large parts of northern and central Russia and Siberia have relatively infertile soils. The black earth of the steppes, however, is among the most fertile in the world. But the climate of most of Russia, including the black earth regions, is colder and drier, and has greater variations in temperature from summer to winter and greater fluctuations in rainfall, than much of the rest of Europe, Asia and North America. The more extreme climate is a consequence of Russia's northerly location, the distance of most of Russia from the sea, and the unbroken topography of the Russian plain. The contrast with the climates of Britain, with its very moderate weather, and the USA are enormous. The temperature range around Moscow, in central Russia, is similar to that in the northernmost part of the mid-west of the USA. The rainfall of the drier southern and eastern steppe regions of Russia is comparable with that of the more arid, western half of the USA. The climate of Siberia is similar to, but more extreme

---

14 See Forsyth, *History*, pp. 1–151; Stebelsky, I., 'The frontier in central Asia', in Bater and French, *Studies*, vol. 1, pp. 144–53; Crosby, A. J., *Ecological Imperialism: The Biological Expansion of Europe, 900–1900* (Cambridge, 1986), pp. 36–40; Vodarskii, *Naselenie Rossii za 400 let*, pp. 48–51, 147.

than, Canada's.[15] Nevertheless, the Russian peasantry succeeded in supporting their growing numbers by migrating to, settling and cultivating vast areas of the forest-heartland, the steppes, Siberia and, towards the end of the period under consideration, parts of the Russian Empire's non-Russian borderlands further south and east.

CAUSES AND TYPES OF PEASANT MIGRATION

It has sometimes been claimed that a constant desire to move off in search of new land was an innate characteristic of the Russian peasantry. Some pre-revolutionary Russian historians wrote about the 'wanderlust (*brodyachii instinkt*) of the Russian people' and, rather ominously, 'the natural striving of the Slavonic race to the east'. The German Baron von Haxthausen had similar views. Others have argued against this rather simplistic idea. Sergei Aksakov, in his fictionalised account of his family's life written in the 1840s, described the great reluctance of his grandfather's peasants to move from their village in Simbirsk province, in the Mid-Volga region, to a new estate, 200 miles to the east, in Bashkir territory in the Southern Urals region. Although Aksakov was writing a work of fiction, and was a Slavophile who venerated the Russian peasantry, there are grounds to accept his view. There is evidence from proverbs and folk tales that Russian peasants felt deep attachment to their native soil. It would have been extremely impractical, moreover, for peasant farmers to abandon their homesteads, move, and rebuild them regularly. The sedentary life of peasant farmers can be contrasted with the nomadic life of the pastoral peoples of the steppes, for example some Bashkirs, who needed to move constantly with their herds of livestock in search of pasture. These genuine nomads lived in felt tents (*gers*) which, unlike peasants' wooden houses, were designed to be taken down, moved and re-erected every few months.[16]

The large numbers of Russian peasants who left their homes and migrated further afield did so for more pragmatic reasons than an innate desire to wander. The dramatic increase in the Russian peasant population, from under 9 million men and women in 1678 to over 50 million in 1897 (see Table 1.3), put growing pressure on the land available for cultivation in the traditional areas of peasant settlement, and was an important factor behind migration from the forest-heartland. The rapid population growth in the late nineteenth century led to growing 'land hunger' in the European part of Russia, especially

---

15 See Bassin, M., 'Turner, Solov'ev, and the "frontier hypothesis": The nationalist significance of open spaces', *JMH*, vol. 65 (1993), pp. 473–511; Blum, *Lord and Peasant*, pp. 9–10; Christian, 'Inner Eurasia', pp. 179–84; Milov, L. V., 'Prirodno-klimaticheskii faktor i osobennosti rossiiskogo istoricheskogo protsessa', *VI* (1992), no. 4–5, pp. 37–56; Pipes, R., *Russia under the Old Regime* (London, 1974), p. 2.
16 See Yakimenko, N. A., 'Agrarnye migratsii v Rossii (1861–1917 gg.)', *VI* (1983), no. 3, p. 17 (quotations); Haxthausen, *Studies*, p. 285; Aksakov, S., *A Russian Gentleman*, trans. J. D. Duff (Oxford, 1982), pp. 8–9. See also Blum, *Lord and Peasant*, pp. 112–13, 155; Hellie, *Enserfment*, pp. 94, 318 n. 21; Moon, *Russian Peasants*, pp. 34–5, 191. I have not translated '*brodyachii*' as 'nomad' to avoid confusion with pastoral nomadism.

the Central Black Earth and Volga regions, and was a major reason why ever-larger numbers of peasants migrated in this period. Analysis of migration based on the 1897 census has shown a trend for peasant migrants to Siberia and Asiatic Russia to come from provinces with high rates of natural population increase.[17] Land shortages were also a reason behind periodic actions by the government in the nineteenth century to encourage peasant resettlement.[18]

The relationship between population growth and migration was more complex than the notion that the increasing numbers of peasants led to land shortages which forced impoverished peasants to move to the frontier. Russian peasants began to leave the forest-heartland in large numbers in the late sixteenth century. Although there is evidence that the population of Russia was increasing over the sixteenth century, the population density of the heartland remained very low, and there was still plenty of land available for settlement and cultivation. Large-scale migration in this period, moreover, led to deserted villages, abandoned fields and the depopulation of parts of the heartland.[19]

The idea that Russian peasants were suffering from declining living standards in the late nineteenth century, and that this was a major cause of migration, has come under attack in recent years. Steven Hoch probably went too far, however, in arguing that no Russian provinces suffered from overpopulation in this period.[20] Peasant-migrants to Siberia at the end of the nineteenth century often gave the reason for their departure as 'lack of land'. Nevertheless, many moved because they wanted to continue their traditional methods of farming on the vast acres of uncultivated land available in Siberia. Migrating to Siberia was easier than going to the expense of renting additional land at home or changing to more complicated and demanding intensive farming techniques.[21]

Most Russian peasants for most of the period covered by this book preferred extensification of agricultural production, by cultivating more land, to intensification, by changing their methods of farming. As the population of individual households and villages increased, some peasants left their households and villages to form new ones, often only a short distance away, and brought more land into cultivation. These new settlements then grew in size and divided, thus giving birth to still more new communities. R. E. F. Smith presented an image of farm households as cells which 'replicated themselves', 'amoeba fashion', and colonised the vast Russian plain.[22] The relationship

17 Robinson, *Rural Russia*, pp. 109–10; Anderson, B. A., *Internal Migration During Modernization in Late Nineteenth-Century Russia* (Princeton, NJ, 1980), pp. 129–30, 139–40, 152, 191–2.
18 See Sunderland, W., 'Peasants on the move: State peasant resettlement in imperial Russia, 1805–1830s', *RR*, vol. 52 (1993), pp. 473–4; Druzhinin, N. M., *Gosudarstvennye krest'yane i reforma P. D. Kiseleva*, 2 vols (Moscow and Leningrad, 1946–58): vol. 1, pp. 89–92; Gorlanov, L. R., *Udel'nye krest'yane Rossii 1797–1865 gg.* (Smolensk, 1986), p. 19; Marks, S. G., *Road to Power: The Trans-Siberian Railroad and the Colonization of Asian Russia, 1850–1917* (Ithaca, NY, 1991), pp. 143, 156.
19 See Blum, *Lord and Peasant*, pp. 120–2, 152–4; Pipes, *Russia*, p. 84.
20 Hoch, 'On good numbers', p. 55. See also Ch. 8.
21 Treadgold, D. W., *The Great Siberian Migration: Government and Peasant in Resettlement from Emancipation to the First World War* (Princeton, NJ, 1957), pp. 62–3, 239. See also Ch. 4.
22 Smith, R. E. F., *Peasant Farming in Muscovy* (Cambridge, 1977), pp. 9, 226.

between growing numbers of peasants and migration is complicated further, since the populations of areas being settled had faster rates of natural increase (see below, pp. 58–9).

Environmental factors were also significant in peasant migration. The eminent pre-revolutionary Russian historians Vasilii Klyuchevskii and Sergei Solov'ev emphasised the role of the environment in Russian history. They argued that the uninterrupted lowlands and empty spaces of the vast Russian plain, with its network of navigable rivers, conditioned the expansion of the Russian state and ensured that the Russian population moved across the plain.[23] Another, more important environmental factor in peasant migration was regional variation in soil fertility. The main trend in the direction of migration was away from the less fertile regions of the forest-heartland, towards the more fertile, black earth regions of the steppes. But, this changed in the late nineteenth century. The majority of migrants to Siberia came not from the infertile northern regions, but from the fertile and densely settled provinces of the Central Black Earth and Volga regions of Russia, and from equally fertile, but also heavily populated Ukraine. In the same period, peasant-migrants from non-black earth provinces were more likely to move to the cities, especially St Petersburg and Moscow, than to the agricultural frontier in Siberia.[24] Like population growth, therefore, environmental factors played a part in peasant migration, but were not the decisive influences. For these, we need to turn to the roles of the Russian state and the peasant-migrants themselves.

There were two main types of peasant-settlers in the outlying regions: those who had moved, or had been moved, as a result of state policy; and those who had migrated voluntarily. The Russian state pursued a deliberate policy of organising resettlement or encouraging its subjects to colonise the territories along its frontiers. State settlement policy followed a fairly standard pattern, which was repeated over the centuries and in the various regions that were annexed along Russia's southern and eastern borders.

First, the state sent militarised settlers to serve on the fortified lines and in the garrison towns it built to defend its frontiers from nomadic raids. Military settlers came from a variety of backgrounds, including gentry, townspeople, soldiers, cossacks and peasants. Many were granted land in payment for their service. Once the frontier had been secured, some military settlers moved on to the new frontier, further south and east, while others stayed behind and formed the nucleus of the Russian civilian population.[25] Once areas behind the frontiers were secure, the state granted land to noble landowners, or permitted them to buy land, in what had become the old borderlands. The state encouraged the landowners to populate their new estates by moving peasants from

23 Bassin, 'Turner', pp. 493–9; Klyuchevskii, *Russkaya istoriya*, vol. 1, pp. 19–20.
24 See Anderson, *Internal*, pp. 109, 118–19, 146–9; Tikhonov, B. V., *Pereseleniya v Rossii vo vtoroi polovine XIX v.* (Moscow, 1978), pp. 149, 159–62; Treadgold, *Great*, pp. 88–92.
25 See Gorskaya, *Krest'yanstvo*, pp. 398–421; Hellie, *Enserfment*, pp. 53, 128–9, 174–80, 212–15; Pallot and Shaw, *Landscape*, pp. 14–26, 33–46, 58–62; Shaw, D. J. B., 'Southern frontiers of Muscovy, 1550–1700', in Bater and French, *Studies*, vol. 1, pp. 117–39.

their existing domains in the central regions. In this way, noble landowner-ship and serfdom spread from the forest-heartland to the Central Black Earth and Mid-Volga regions, and later the Lower Volga and Don and Southern Urals regions. The state also made grants of land in border areas to Russian Orthodox monasteries, which settled them by transferring peasants from their parent monasteries in central Russia. Monastic settlement was most wide-spread in the Mid-Volga region in the seventeenth century.[26]

The state also tried to persuade settlers from the lower orders to move to the borderlands, independent of noble and monastic landowners. The author-ities offered land, grants and loans, and temporary exemptions from taxes and conscription to state peasants, cossacks, religious dissenters, retired soldiers, foreigners and even vagrants, including fugitives from serfdom. Large num-bers of Russian peasants responded, and moved off to the outlying regions. The number of foreign settlers in Russia was fairly small. In the late eighteenth century, around 30,000 Germans settled in Saratov province in response to invitations from Catherine the Great. Larger numbers of foreigners settled in southern Ukraine.[27]

On occasions, when the state was unable to attract sufficient settlers, it used compulsion to move people to the borderlands. For example, there was some compulsory resettlement to the south of the Central Black Earth region in the mid-seventeenth and early eighteenth centuries. Forced settlement met with mixed success. Many reluctant migrants later returned home.[28] The most extensive use of compulsion was the policy of exiling criminals, vagrants and other undesirables to Siberia. Although historians have paid most attention to political exiles, the vast majority were peasants. The exile system did not make a very significant contribution to the settlement of Siberia. Most exiles were men, many were old, the death rate was high, and some were later allowed to return home. Only a small proportion settled permanently in Siberia and had families. At the end of the nineteenth century, exiles made up only 5 per cent of Siberia's population.[29]

A much greater contribution to the settlement of Siberia was made by the state policy of promoting peasant migration in the late nineteenth century.

26 See Pallot and Shaw, *Landscape*, pp. 25–6, 35–45; Shaw, 'Southern frontiers', pp. 122–3, 133–8; Donnelly, 'Mobile', pp. 189–97, 201–2; Hart, J. G., 'From frontier outpost to provincial cap-ital: Saratov, 1590–1860', in Seregny, S. J. and Wade, R. A. (eds), *Politics and Society in Provincial Russia: Saratov, 1590–1917* (Columbus, OH, 1989), pp. 10–27; Gorskaya, *Krest'yanstvo*, p. 406; Tarasov, Yu. M., *Russkaya krest'yanskaya kolonizatsiya Yuzhnogo Urala* (Moscow, 1984), pp. 34–55, 61–2, 127. See also Ch. 3.
27 See Stebelsky, 'Frontier', p. 148; Tarasov, *Russkaya*, pp. 35–6, 89; Sunderland, 'Peasants', pp. 472–85; Moon, *Russian Peasants*, pp. 23–61; Bartlett, R. P., *Human Capital: The Settlement of Foreigners in Russia, 1762–1804* (Cambridge, 1979), pp. 118–24.
28 See Pallot and Shaw, *Landscape*, pp. 28, 43; Gorskaya, *Krest'yanstvo*, p. 407; Donnelly, 'Mobile', pp. 197, 202.
29 Anuchin, E. N., 'Issledovaniya o protsente soslannykh v Sibir' v period 1827–1846 g.', *Zapiski Imperatorskogo Russkogo Geograficheskogo obshchestva po otdeleniyu statistiki*, vol. 3 (1873), pp. 8, 65–73; Vodarskii, *Naselenie Rossii za 400 let*, p. 102; Wood, A., 'Russia's "Wild East": exile, vagrancy and crime in nineteenth-century Siberia', in *id.* (ed.), *The History of Siberia: From Russian Conquest to Revolution* (London and New York, 1991), pp. 117–18.

This was the most extensive state scheme for resettling peasants in outlying regions of Russia before the twentieth century. Colonising Siberia was one of the reasons for building the Trans-Siberian railway. After 1881, the state offered subsidised fares to peasant-migrants, provided them material assistance, loans and tax exemptions, and surveyed and prepared land and some basic infrastructure in the areas being settled. In practice, however, not all migrants received the promised help. Nevertheless, the opening of parts of the railway in the 1890s led to a massive increase in the numbers of peasant-migrants to Siberia.[30]

By no means all settlement of Russia's borderlands was organised or promoted by the state. Many peasants moved of their own accord, for their own reasons, and often illegally. The first Slavs to settle on the steppes after the Mongol invasion did so before the conquests of Kazan' and Astrakhan' in the 1550s, and in advance of the fortified lines. These were the first communities of cossacks, made up mostly of Russian and Ukrainian fugitives from the Muscovite and Polish states who intermarried with local Tatars. From the early sixteenth century, cossacks lived along the middle and lower reaches of the Don and the Volga rivers and, further west, the river Dnepr. They acted as irregular border guards, and received subsidies from the Muscovite tsars and Polish kings. Some cossacks moved further south and east, staying ahead of the fortified lines and state settlements. New communities were founded on the Yaik river in the Southern Urals region and in the north Caucasus. Although the Russian state sometimes augmented cossack hosts by resettling peasants, and later created new hosts along new frontiers, the main source of additional cossacks continued to be fugitive peasants.[31]

Another important group who settled in the Russian borderlands of their own accord was Ukrainian peasants. Many moved east from their traditional areas of settlement in the Dnepr basin in the seventeenth and eighteenth centuries. Most settled on vacant lands to the south of the Belgorod line in Slobodskaya Ukraine and the southern parts of the Russian provinces of Kursk and Voronezh in the Central Black Earth region. In the eighteenth and nineteenth centuries, Ukrainians made up around 10 per cent of the population of the region. Significant numbers of Ukrainians moved further east, to the Don Cossack territory and to Saratov province on the lower Volga. Many Ukrainian settlers in Russia were later enserfed, but most maintained their identity, language and culture.[32]

30 Marks, *Road*, pp. 141–5, 153–69, 220–2; Treadgold, *Great*, pp. 32–5, 67–81, 107–49.
31 See Shaw, 'Southern frontiers', pp. 121, 129–31; Pronshtein, A. P. (ed.), *Don i stepnoe Predkavkaz'e: XVIII-pervaya polovina XIX v. Zaselenie i khozyaistvo* (Rostov na Donu, 1977), pp. 31–64; *MGSR*, Krasnov, *Zemlya Voiska Donskogo*, pp. 10–13, 192–4; Semenov, *Rossiya*, vol. 14, *Novorossiya i Krym* (St Petersburg, 1910), pp. 190–7; Longworth, P., *The Cossacks* (London, 1969), pp. 18–20, 127–8, 224–42. Many rank-and-file cossacks differed little from peasants in the late nineteenth century, but cossacks were distinct from peasants in many respects in the preceding centuries. See Chs 1 and 7.
32 See Kabuzan, *Narody Rossii v XVIII v.*, pp. 84–5, 95–6, 134–5, 138–9, 204, 209; Pallot and Shaw, *Landscape*, pp. 63–6; Semenov, *Rossiya*, vol. 6, *Srednee i Nizhnee Povol'zhe i Zavol'zhe* (St Petersburg, 1910), p. 158; vol. 14, *Novorossiya*, p. 185. (Slobodskaya Ukraine was renamed Khar'kov province in 1835.)

Most importantly, throughout the period from the mid-sixteenth century, untold numbers of Russian peasants migrated voluntarily, and illegally, from the central regions of Russia to more outlying areas. Most were fugitives from the growing oppression and exploitation by the Russian state and noble land-owners. Peasants also fled from bad harvests, famines and epidemics. If peasants were pushed into fleeing the central regions by oppression, exploitation and natural disasters, they were pulled towards the borderlands by the possibility of greater freedom, more land, better conditions, and the chance of being able to take advantage of some of the privileges the state offered to migrants in some frontier areas.[33]

Historians have contrasted the two types of settlement, state and voluntary, legal and illegal, and considered which made the greater contribution to the settlement of Russia's southern and eastern borderlands. Many pre-revolutionary Russian historians and Western historians stressed the importance of state-sponsored settlement. Most Soviet historians and other Western historians have been at least as keen to emphasise the leading role of voluntary migration.[34] However, many recent historians of peasant migration in Russia have argued that it is not appropriate to distinguish between state and voluntary settlement. Rather, it was the combination of actions by the state and peasant-settlers, to varying degrees in different places and times, and the constant interaction between them that best explains how Russia's outlying regions were settled by Russian peasants between the late sixteenth and late nineteenth centuries. Willard Sunderland's conclusions on state peasant resettlement in the early nineteenth century are perhaps valid for the whole period. He argued that by looking beyond the 'official dimension' of the resettlement policy 'we discover a different, much more dynamic world in which state policy interacted with timetables, arrangements and initiatives established by the peasant settlers themselves'.[35]

TRENDS IN PEASANT MIGRATION, 1678–1897

In 1678, at the time of the household tax census, most Russian peasants still lived in the forest-heartland. The patterns of peasant settlement changed considerably over the following two centuries as a result of mass migration to the south and east, first to the forested steppe and, from the eighteenth

---

33 On exploitation, see Ch. 3; on flight, see Ch. 7; and on bad harvests and epidemics, see Coquin, F.-X., 'Faim et migrations paysannes en Russie au XIXe siècle', *RHMC* (1964), vol. 2, pp. 127–44.
34 Compare Sumner, *Survey*, pp. 47–8; Donnelly, 'Mobile', pp. 197, 202; Marx, *Road*, pp. 141, 153–6; and Bruk, S. I. and Kabuzan, V. M., 'Migratsiya naseleniya v Rossii v XVIII–nachale XX v.: (Chislennost', struktura, geografiya)', *IS* (1984), no. 4, pp. 41–2; Tarasov, *Russkaya*, pp. 88–89, 171; Vodarskii, *Naselenie Rossii v kontse XVII*, p. 197; Treadgold, *Great*, p. 9. See also Coquin, F.-X., *La Sibérie: Peuplement et Immigration Paysanne au XIX Siècle* (Paris, 1969), pp. 722–3, 741; Bagalei, D. I., *Ocherki iz istorii kolonizatsii i byta stepnoi okrainy moskovskogo gosudarstva* (Moscow, 1887), pp. xv–xvi, 131–2, 569–71.
35 Sunderland, 'Peasants', p. 484. See also Gorskaya, *Krest'yanstvo*, p. 405; Shaw, 'Southern frontiers', pp. 118, 139.

TABLE 2.1

PEASANT SETTLEMENT BY REGION, 1678–1897 (MALES, NUMBERS)

	1678[1]	1719	1762	1811	1857	1897
Forest-heartland						
Mixed forest:						
Central NBE	1,852,000	2,346,177	2,776,051	3,513,327	3,838,852	5,097,216
North-western	271,000	418,671	598,052	807,598	888,094	1,897,390
Conif. forest:						
Northern	478,000	325,723	396,513	484,015	625,566	910,146
North Urals	—[2]	265,810	588,780	1,008,772	1,717,238	2,757,237
Total	2,601,000	3,356,381	4,359,396	5,813,712	7,069,750	10,661,989
Steppes						
Forested steppe:						
Central BE	850,000	1,446,904	2,029,777	3,303,690	4,159,932	5,777,960
Mid-Volga	221,000	727,268	861,820	1,314,702	1,802,482	2,625,958
Open steppe:						
L. Volga & Don	—[3]	1,684	221,753	601,609	1,183,363	2,750,973
South Urals	—[3]	16,181	143,047	334,334	661,774	2,100,152
Total	1,071,000	2,192,037	3,256,397	5,554,335	7,807,551	13,255,043
Siberia	49,000	173,912	356,050	600,368	1,114,090	1,949,050
Total (Russia)	3,721,000	5,722,330	7,971,843	11,968,415	15,991,391	25,866,082

[1] Totals for 1678 are incomplete.
[2] North Urals included in Northern for 1678.
[3] L. Volga and Don and South Urals virtually unsettled by Russian peasants in 17th century.

Sources: Kabuzan, *Izmeneniya*, pp. 59–175; Vodarskii, *Naselenie Rossii v kontse XVII v.*, p. 152; Troinitskii, *Obshchii svod*, vol. 1, pp. 165, 167, 169, 171 (Table VII); Troinitskii, *Pervaya vseobshchaya perepis' naseleniya Rossiiskoi imperii 1897 g.* (St Petersburg, 1899–1905), vol. 12 (Don), pp. 48–9; vol. 28 (Orenburg), pp. 26–7; vol. 36 (Samara), pp. 34–5; vol. 38 (Saratov), pp. 48–9; vol. 39 (Simbirsk), pp. 32–3. Where necessary 1897 census data for provinces revised to take account of border changes since 1806: see Den', V. E., *Naseleniya Rossii po V revizii*, vol. 1 (St Petersburg, 1902), pp. 163–83.

century, to the open steppe. The proportion of the Russian peasantry living in the four regions of the forest-heartland declined steadily from almost 70 per cent in 1678 to 41 per cent by the time of the 1897 census. Over the same period, the percentage of the Russian peasantry which lived in the four steppe regions increased from 29 per cent in 1678 to 51 per cent in 1897. The peasant population of the steppes surpassed that of the forest-heartland in the early nineteenth century. Over the whole period, moreover, a steady stream of peasant-migrants crossed the Urals and settled in Siberia. The proportion of the Russian peasantry living in Siberia increased from 1.3 per cent in 1678 to 7.5 per cent in 1897. (See Tables 2.1–2.2.) S. I. Bruk and V. M. Kabuzan estimated that, from the 1670s to 1896, in the whole Russian Empire, almost ten million people migrated to the outlying regions, well over a third of whom moved between 1871 and 1896.[36]

36 Bruk and Kabuzan, 'Migratsiya', p. 52.

TABLE 2.2

PEASANT SETTLEMENT BY REGION, 1678–1897 (PERCENTAGES)

	1678[1]	1719	1762	1811	1857	1897
Forest-heartland						
Mixed forest:						
Central NBE	49.77%	41.00%	34.82%	29.35%	24.01%	19.71%
North-western	7.28%	7.32%	7.50%	6.75%	5.55%	7.34%
Conif. forest:						
Northern	12.85%	5.69%	4.97%	4.04%	3.91%	3.52%
North Urals	—[2]	4.65%	7.39%	8.43%	10.74%	10.66%
Total	69.90%	58.66%	54.68%	48.57%	44.21%	41.23%
Steppes						
Forested steppe:						
Central BE	22.84%	25.29%	25.46%	27.60%	26.01%	22.34%
Mid-Volga	5.94%	12.71%	10.81%	10.98%	11.27%	10.15%
Open steppe:						
L. Volga & Don	—[3]	0.03%	2.78%	5.03%	7.40%	10.64%
South Urals	—[3]	0.28%	1.79%	2.79%	4.14%	8.12%
Total	28.78%	38.31%	40.84%	46.40%	48.82%	51.25%
Siberia	1.32%	3.04%	4.47%	5.02%	6.97%	7.54%
Total (Russia)	100.00%	100.01%	99.99%	99.99%	100.00%	100.02%

[1] Totals for 1678 are incomplete.
[2] North Urals included in Northern for 1678.
[3] L. Volga and Don and South Urals virtually unsettled by Russian peasants in 17th century.

Sources: See Table 2.1.

There were more specific patterns of peasant migration, including movement between regions within the larger zones, and between provinces inside regions. In the forest-heartland, peasants moved from the Central Non-Black Earth and Northern regions to the Northern Urals region and to the North-western region, in particular to St Petersburg. The new capital city was a magnet to migrants from the rest of the North-western region and other parts of the forest-heartland after its foundation by Peter the Great in 1703. From the late nineteenth century, the growth of industry in the city, and consequent demand for labour, drew many peasant-migrants. Moscow also attracted migrants from the villages throughout the period under consideration.[37] (See Tables 2.1–2.2.)

There were significant movements of peasants inside the steppe regions, as well as migration to the steppes from the forest-heartland. Peasants moved

37 Kabuzan, *Izmeneniya*, pp. 16–22, 27–8, 43–8; *id.*, *Narody Rossii v XVIII v.*, pp. 64, 78–90, 97–100, 123, 130–1, 203; Vodarskii, *Naselenie Rossii za 400 let*, pp. 86–90, 131–2, 136–8; Anderson, *Internal*. On migrant labour, see Ch. 4.

from the forested steppe towards the open steppe in the extreme south and east of the Central Black Earth and Mid-Volga regions. From the early nineteenth century, however, both regions ceased to be net recipients of migrants, and began to experience net emigration as more peasants moved further south and east to the open steppe of the Lower Volga and Don and the Southern Urals regions. Russian peasant colonisation of the open steppe had begun in the eighteenth century, and continued throughout the following century. By 1897, a little under 20 per cent of the Russian peasantry lived in the two regions. In the mid-eighteenth century, the biggest influx of migrants was experienced by Saratov province on the lower Volga. From the 1780s, the north Caucasus became one of the major destinations of peasant-migrants.[38] (See Tables 2.1–2.2.)

Russian peasant settlement of the steppes took a long time. Many peasant-migrants moved only relatively short distances. Migrants often travelled to the nearest available free land inside their home provinces or in neighbouring provinces. Peasant-settlers had to overcome the hostility of many of the native inhabitants of the steppes. Moreover, peasants who were used to living in the forest had to adapt to the very different environmental conditions of the steppes, especially the treeless, open plains.[39] Nevertheless, by the late nineteenth century, the steppes had been transformed from the sparsely populated 'wild field' of the sixteenth and seventeenth centuries into a densely populated territory with little vacant land left for settlement. In the late nineteenth century, moreover, all four steppe regions were experiencing net emigration. In the nineteenth century, especially after the 1880s, many peasant-migrants moved further than most of their predecessors. Between 1867 and 1897 over a million people, including many Ukrainians, moved from the European part of the Russian Empire to Siberia.[40]

Until the mid-nineteenth century, most Russian peasants lived in Russia (as defined in Ch. 1). By the second half of the nineteenth century, however, the Russian Empire had expanded far beyond the territory of the Muscovite tsars, and increasing numbers of Russian peasants were migrating further afield to the empire's non-Russian borderlands. Most moved south and east, to left-bank Ukraine, southern Ukraine and the Kuban' territory in the north Caucasus, all of which had been added to the empire by the end of the eighteenth century. Peasants also moved to parts of Transcaucasia, central Asia and the Pacific far east, most of which were annexed in the nineteenth century.

38 Bruk and Kabuzan, 'Migratsiya', pp. 44–53; Vodarskii, *Naselenie Rossii za 400 let*, pp. 86–7, 93–5, 131–2, 141–2; Kabuzan, *Narody Rossii v XVIII v.*, pp. 82–3, 94–6, 103, 119–25, 197–202; *id.*, *Naselenie Severnogo Kavkaza v XIX–XX vv: Etnostatisticheskoe issledovanie* (St Petersburg, 1996), pp. 27–101; Tarasov, *Russkaya*, pp. 34–55, 88–122.
39 See Gorskaya, *Krest'yanstvo*, pp. 407, 411; Hellie, *Enserfment*, p. 129; Pallot and Shaw, *Landscape*, pp. 7–8, 17; Tarasov, *Russkaya*, pp. 54–5, 88; Vodarskii, *Naselenie Rossii v kontse XVII*, p. 157. See also Ch. 4.
40 Vodarskii, *Naselenie Rossii za 400 let*, pp. 130–2, 139–41, 146–7; Tarasov, *Russkaya*, p. 172; Goryushkin, L., 'Migration, settlement and the rural economy of Siberia, 1861–1914', in Wood, *History*, pp. 140–1.

The total number of Russian peasants, both men and women, who lived in the southern and eastern non-Russian borderlands in 1897 can be estimated at around 3 million, about 6 per cent of the number of peasants that lived in Russia proper. Few Russian peasants moved to the empire's non-Russian borderlands in the west (the Baltic region, Lithuania, Belorussia, Poland, right-bank Ukraine and Bessarabia) since these regions already had their own indigenous peasant populations, and had little land available for settlement.[41] Migration by Russian peasants to the non-Russian borderlands was only partly cancelled out by the large numbers of Ukrainian peasants and smaller numbers of German settlers who moved to the Central Black Earth and Lower Volga and Don regions of Russia and Siberia.[42]

Russian peasant colonisation of the steppes, Siberia and the south-eastern non-Russian borderlands was a very slow process. The nomadic horsemen of Batu Khan's army rode from central Asia to the forest-heartland of Russia in only a few months in the 1230s. From the 1550s, however, three centuries elapsed before several generations of Russian peasant-migrants, most travelling on carts and river barges laden with their belongings, had completed a similar journey in the opposite direction. Only in the second half of the nineteenth century did the construction of railways ease the problems for peasant-migrants travelling long distances. In 1888, the editor of the journal of the Ministry of Transport enthused that once the Trans-Siberian railway was completed 'the ancient routes of the Huns and Mongols to Europe will be opened anew, but this time not for them; along these paths steam engines and railroad cars will whistle and dart, bringing life and culture to the land of bears, sable, and gold!'. The Trans-Siberian railway also brought with it hundreds of thousands of peasant-migrants.[43]

Immigration accounted for only part of the increase in the Russian peasant population of the steppes, Siberia and the non-Russian borderlands. The rates of *natural* increase, the difference between births and deaths, were higher than in the forest-heartland. Ya. E. Vodarskii estimated that around one-third of the total increase in the population of the southern and eastern regions was due to immigration, while the remaining two-thirds was a result of natural growth. In the second half of the nineteenth century, birth rates in the steppe zone and Siberia were above the Russian average. The explanation for the higher rates of natural population growth in regions receiving large numbers of migrants may be quite straightforward. A lot of the migrants were healthy young people who moved to new regions, set up homesteads, and then started families. They left behind older, weaker people who had passed their fertile years and were likely to die sooner. The populations of regions which were being settled grew more quickly, therefore, because they were younger, and

41 For sources of data in estimates, see Moon, 'Peasant migration', p. 868.
42 See Vodarskii, *Naselenie Rossii za 400 let*, pp. 54–5; Kabuzan, *Narody Rossii v XVIII v.*, pp. 89–248.
43 Marks, *Road*, pp. 22–4, 80 (quotation from p. 80); Treadgold, *Great*, pp. 95–8.

thus had higher birth rates and lower death rates than the populations of the older regions of settlement. According to data for 1897, moreover, rural women in the steppe regions were marginally more fertile than those in the forest-heartland. Jacques Dupâquier concluded that in eastern Europe 'population growth was at the same time the cause and the consequence of territorial expansion'.[44]

Over the two centuries after 1678, continual migration to the steppes and Siberia led to a shift in the centre of gravity of Russian peasant settlement from the forest-heartland to the forested steppe. From the late seventeenth to the mid-nineteenth centuries, at least two-thirds or more of the Russian peasantry lived in the two regions of the mixed forest (the Central Non-Black Earth and North-western regions) and the two regions of the forested steppe (the Central Black Earth and Mid-Volga regions). These four central regions, which straddled the Oka river and the old steppe frontier, were the main regions of Russian peasant settlement for most of the period covered by this book. Throughout the period, and especially in the nineteenth century, growing numbers of peasants moved further south and east, to the open steppe (the Lower Volga and Don and Southern Urals regions), Siberia, and further afield to the southern and eastern non-Russian borderlands. (See Tables 2.1–2.2.) Peasant migration, especially to Siberia and other parts of Asiatic Russia, continued at an even greater rate in the early twentieth century.[45]

THE CONSEQUENCES OF PEASANT MIGRATION

Besides the change in the centre of gravity of Russian peasant settlement, there were other consequences of peasant migration. Throughout the regions they settled in, Russian peasants encountered the indigenous populations and natural environments. All three were changed in the processes of interaction that followed.

Peasants and native peoples

Russian peasant-migrants adapted some aspects of their ways of life and adopted some new practices as a result of contact with native peoples. The size and location of villages in the steppe regions were influenced by the needs of defence against nomadic raiders. Thus, settlers lived in larger villages than in the forest-heartland, and took advantage of high river banks with commanding views, or concealed their settlements in patches of dense woodland.

44 See Vodarskii, *Naselenie Rossii v kontse XVII*, pp. 153–6; Rashin, *Naselenie*, pp. 165–6, 216–19, 231; Coale, *Human Fertility*, pp. 20–1; Dupaquier, 'Population', pp. 100–102.
45 Borodkin, L. I. and Maksimov, S. V., 'Krest'yanskie migratsii v Rossii/SSSR v pervoi chetverti XX v.', *OI* (1993), no. 5, pp. 124–43.

In addition, new settlers learned from and adopted farming methods and other practices from native peoples and more long-standing Russian inhabitants (*starozhily*).[46]

In most regions, some Russian settlers intermarried with members of the local populations. Ethnic mixing between settlers and the indigenous Finnic and Tatar peoples left marked traces in the physical appearance of the Russian population of the Mid-Volga and Urals regions. Intermarriage was also common in Siberia. A few settlers, especially in remote parts, 'went native'. Some children of mixed marriages became partly 'Buryatised' or 'Yakutised'. In northern Siberia, Russian settlers living among the Khantys and Nentsy adopted the local custom of eating raw meat and the Shamanist religion. These were exceptional cases. Only a minority of Russian settlers assimilated to the local populations. In spite of their interaction with local peoples, most Russian peasant-settlers retained the essentials of their ways of life. In some regions, Russian settlers and native peoples lived alongside each other in separate communities until pressure on resources led to conflict.[47]

At the heart of most conflicts was land. Disputes over land reflected the contrast between the settled, agricultural way of life of the incoming peasants and the nomadic pastoralist and hunting economies of many native peoples. The different ways of life entailed very different ways of using land and concepts of land ownership. The Russian state assumed that most land in conquered regions was state property, and disposed of the land as it saw fit. It expropriated nomads' pastures and handed them out to Russian nobles and settlers, or simply permitted Russians to take land for themselves. In many regions, incoming Russians bargained with native people for land. Many deals were one-sided as a lot of native peoples had little concept of buying or renting land, scant understanding of its value to the Russians or what they intended to do with it.[48]

Some peasant-settlers took over and cultivated land with little regard to who owned it or its customary use. In many cases this meant ploughing up pastures while nomads were grazing their herds elsewhere. Some native people appealed to the Russian government, with mixed success, in their struggle to retain their land. To take just one of countless examples, a dispute between a Bashkir village and a neighbouring Russian state peasant settlement in Orenburg province, in the Southern Urals region, dragged on in the courts for most of the first half of the nineteenth century. In 1842 the Bashkirs complained that, after allowing the peasants to cultivate part of their land in 1804, they were

46 See Pallot and Shaw, *Landscape*, pp. 18–19; Barrett, T. M., 'Lines of uncertainty: The frontiers of the north Caucasus', *SR*, vol. 54 (1995), pp. 584; Goryushkin, 'Migration', pp. 142, 145–7, 155–6. See also Ch. 4.
47 See Semenov, *Rossiya*, vol. 6, *Srednee i Nizhnee Povol'zhe*, p. 157; Forsyth, *History*, pp. 67–9, 78, 143, 155, 163, 198–9; Minenko, N. A., *Russkaya krest'yanskaya sem'ya v Zapadnoi Sibiri (XVIII-pervoi polovine XIX v.)* (Novosibirsk, 1979), p. 192; Treadgold, *Great*, pp. 241–3; Sunderland, W., 'Russians into Yakuts? "Going native" and problems of Russian national identity in the Siberian north, 1870s–1914', *SR*, vol. 55 (1996), pp. 806–25.
48 See Donnelly, 'Mobile', pp. 197, 201; Forsyth, *History*, pp. 64, 157–9, 172, 181–6.

gradually taking over the rest of it with the support of local Russian officials. The Bashkirs appealed to the Russian authorities to order the peasants to stop seizing their land because they feared that they would soon be left with insufficient to support themselves and their cattle.[49] In spite of their complaints, native peoples throughout the borderlands of the expanding Russian state lost large amounts of land to Russian landowners and settlers.

The Russian state permitted members of indigenous populations to keep some land, but on its terms. From the eighteenth century, the state pursued a deliberate policy of sedentarising nomads. Since nomadic pastoralism made far more extensive use of land than settled farming, the state restricted nomadism to make land available for peasant-settlers. Once they had lost much of their land, nomads were no longer able to support themselves by herding livestock. Many tried to live by growing crops or working as labourers, or faced destitution. In some parts of the steppes and Siberia, indigenous peoples were swamped by incoming peasants. Some peoples rebelled in vain attempts to stop the flood of migrants from taking their land and undermining their ways of life. Others migrated themselves, further south and east, to escape the incoming tide of peasants. Of those people who stayed in their homelands, some assimilated to Russian life and culture. Others, especially Islamic peoples, retained their ethnic identities, if not all of their land.

Peasants and the environment

Russian peasants also interacted with the environments of the regions they settled in. Over the centuries when most Russian peasants lived in the forest-heartland, they learned to support themselves by growing cereals and keeping livestock. Because of the relatively infertile soil, many peasants supplemented their incomes with handicrafts, trade and other non-agricultural activities. In the process of making a living from the land, peasants chopped down millions of acres of trees to convert forest into arable land, meadows and pasture, and to provide timber for construction and craft production.[50]

This pattern of peasants adapting to the environment and altering it to suit the needs of their productive activities was repeated in the steppe regions, Siberia and further afield. Since most peasant-migrants aimed to continue farming, they settled in areas where the conditions were suitable. Peasants did not, therefore, settle in large numbers in central, eastern and northern Siberia, where the permafrost made crop cultivation extremely difficult, or in the central Asian deserts beyond the open steppe. Peasant-migrants frequently settled in areas with similar environments to their homelands. Migrants from the forested steppe in European Russia often made new homes in the continuation of the belt east of the Urals. Many peasants who settled on the arid open steppe of

49 *RGIA, f.* 1380, *op.* 1, 1842, *d.* 68, esp. ll.4–5 *ob.* The outcome of the case is unknown. See also Wallace, *Russia*, vol. 2, pp. 45–9.
50 See French, 'Russians', pp. 27–30, 38–41; Pallot and Shaw, *Landscape*, pp. 6–7. See also Ch. 4.

northern Kazakhstan in the late nineteenth century came from the open steppes of southern Russia and Ukraine.[51]

Some peasant-settlers did have to change their practices to adjust to different natural conditions. Villages tended to be larger in the drier steppe regions than in the forest-heartland, not just for the sake of security among hostile native peoples, but also because there were fewer sources of water to settle by. On the treeless steppe, peasant-settlers learned to build houses out of clay or bricks rather than wood. Peasant-settlers adapted and sometimes changed their farming methods, including their implements and crops. As a result of initial problems in ploughing the heavy soil of the steppes, some Russian settlers devoted more time to raising livestock than to growing grain. By the nineteenth century, however, many peasant-settlers had successfully adapted their farming methods to suit the environmental conditions on the steppes, Siberia and other outlying regions.[52]

Russian peasants developed and adapted their practices and customs in response to the environmental conditions they encountered. But, in spite of the process of interaction, many of the essentials of the ways of life of the Russian peasantry were retained. Peasants changed the environment rather more than it altered them. In the forest-heartland and forested steppe, the biggest impact peasants had on the environment was the destruction of vast areas of forest. Deforestation was greatest in the most densely populated regions, and the amounts of woodland destroyed increased considerably over the nineteenth century as the population grew more quickly. In most provinces of central Russia, both north and south of the Oka river, the area of land covered by forest fell by between a half and two-thirds over the eighteenth and nineteenth centuries. The open steppe regions lost much of what little woodland they had. Deforestation destroyed the habitats of forest wildlife, some of which came close to extinction.[53]

The arrival of peasant agriculture had a serious impact on the environment of the steppes. The natural grasses and scrub of the open steppe were burnt by settlers as they prepared the land for ploughing. The area of steppe land cleared and ploughed up increased with the rising tides of peasant migration and population increase. The loss of the natural grass covering, and the small areas of woodland, were very harmful. By the nineteenth century, in large parts of the steppe regions, overcropping, overgrazing and the use of marginal lands had led to widespread soil erosion, resulting in the loss of more and more of the valuable, fertile, black earth which had attracted peasant migrants

51 See Forsyth, *History*, pp. 100–1; Goryushkin, 'Migration', pp. 141–2; Treadgold, *Great*, p. 241; Stebelsky, 'Frontier', p. 158.
52 See Gorskaya, *Krest'yanstvo*, pp. 409–13; Deal, Z. J., *Serf and State Peasant Agriculture: Kharkov Province 1842–1861* (New York, 1981), pp. 331–3, 395; Barrett, 'Lines', esp. p. 584; Matossian, M., 'The peasant way of life', in Vucinich, *Peasant*, pp. 1–8; Pallot and Shaw, *Landscape*, p. 8; Goryushkin, 'Migration', pp. 144–50. See also Ch. 4.
53 See French, 'Russians', pp. 30–41; Semenov, *Rossiya*, vol. 2, *Sredne-Russkaya chernozemnaya oblast'* (St Petersburg, 1902), pp. 64–8, 77–8; vol. 14, *Novorossiya*, p. 72.

to the steppes in the first place. Moreover, it became increasingly clear that deforestation and ploughing up the land had had a harmful effect on the climate of the steppe regions, making it drier and more extreme, and the rainfall less reliable. These climatic changes all had harmful consequences for agriculture.[54]

In Siberia, peasant-settlers also had a harmful impact on the natural environment. If the damage was less than in the European part of Russia, it was only because the number of settlers relative to the enormous area of land was much lower. The spread of peasant agriculture across the southern part of Siberia was achieved at the cost of large areas of forest, the animal life it supported, and the livelihoods of many of the native peoples who lived off its resources.[55]

In most regions where Russian peasants settled, the activities of the native peoples were more appropriate and less harmful to the environment. That conditions on the open steppe are better suited to nomadic pastoralism than to settled agriculture is demonstrated by the fact that this had been the dominant way of life for thousands of years before the arrival of large numbers of peasants in the eighteenth century.[56]

*   *   *

The Russian conquest and peasant settlement of the steppes was part of a larger process of the spread of peasant agriculture to 'Europe's steppe frontier' – the region between the Russian, Austrian and Turkish Empires – from the sixteenth to the nineteenth centuries. Settlement of sparsely populated lands which had previously been the domain of nomadic pastoralists and others also took place at the far eastern end of Eurasia, where Chinese peasants were settling China's steppe frontier. In the late nineteenth century, Chinese settlement of the right bank of the Amur' river in Manchuria mirrored, and met, Russian settlement of the left bank of the river in its newly acquired Pacific far east.[57] At the Atlantic end of Eurasia there were no nomads to be displaced, and little land left to be settled. Some western European states created large overseas empires. There are obvious parallels between Russia's conquest and peopling of the steppes, Siberia and other parts of 'Asiatic Russia' and the acquisition and settlement by western Europeans of their colonies. A common parallel is the USA's expansion and colonisation of its frontiers. The motives for all these expansions of states and migrations by agricultural peoples were

---

54 See Stebelsky, I., 'Agriculture and soil erosion in the European forest–steppe', in Bater and French, *Studies*, vol. 1, pp. 45–61; Semenov, *Rossiya*, vol. 2, *Sredne-Russkaya*, pp. 50–1, 113; vol. 14, *Novorossiya*, pp. 72–3. See also Ch. 4.
55 See Forsyth, *History*, pp. 43, 64, 101, 159, 163, 191, 218.
56 See Christian, 'Inner Eurasia', pp. 193–9; Khodarkovsky, *Where*, pp. 17–22; Forsyth, *History*, p. 19.
57 See McNeill, *Europe's Steppe Frontier*; T. J. Barfield, *The Perilous Frontier: Nomadic Empires and China, 221 BC to AD 1757* (Oxford, 1989); Lattimore, O., *Inner Asian Frontiers of China* (New York, 1940).

similar, all had harmful consequences for indigenous peoples and environments, but all were changed in the process.[58]

CONCLUSION

The distinction made at the start of this chapter between the forest-heartland, the steppes, and Siberia remains important for the entire period between the early seventeenth and early twentieth centuries. It needs to be supplemented, however, by another distinction: between the four central regions of Russia (the Central Non-Black Earth and North-western regions of the mixed forest belt, and the Central Black Earth and Mid-Volga regions of the forested steppe) and the more outlying regions (the Northern and Northern Urals regions of the coniferous forest in the north, the Lower-Volga and Don and Southern Urals regions of the open steppe to the south-east, as well as Siberia, and the non-Russian borderlands annexed after the mid-seventeenth century). As a result of the territorial expansion of the Russian state and mass peasant migration from the late sixteenth century, the centre of gravity of Russian peasant settlement moved south and east from the forest-heartland to the forested steppe. For most of the period covered by this book, a substantial majority of Russian peasants lived in the four central regions. Moreover, increasing numbers of Russian peasants moved further south and east to the open steppe, Siberia, and the non-Russian borderlands. Both distinctions (forest-heartland/steppes/Siberia and the central/more outlying regions) will be referred to throughout the rest of this book.

While the environmental conditions and indigenous populations of all these regions had an impact on Russian peasant-migrants, it was the peasants who had the greater influence. At the centre of the interactions between settlers and native peoples and peasants and the environment were struggles to control and exploit the natural resources, especially land. With some changes to adapt to new conditions, Russian peasants expanded their economy, based largely but not solely on arable farming, from the forest-heartland to the steppes, parts of Siberia and beyond. Large-scale migration was, thus, one of the ways in which the Russian peasantry was able to support its growing numbers.

Russian peasant settlement of the borderlands and the Russian state's expansion of its southern and eastern frontiers were interdependent. Peasant-settlers, whose main concerns were their families and farms, were no match militarily for the mobile nomadic horsemen who had dominated the steppes before the peasants arrived. Peasant-settlers on the open steppes had left behind the forests that had afforded some protection from nomadic raiders. The settlers needed the military might of the Russian state to defeat and displace the nomads. It was the state which organised the construction of the fortified lines and towns, and which mobilised the men to defend them. The turn of the tide between

---

58 See Bassin, 'Turner', pp. 476–509; Forsyth, *History*, pp. 1, 43, 110–11; Marks, *Road*, pp. 141, 160, 169, 220–6; Pallot and Shaw, *Landscape*, pp. 21–2, 30.

the Russian state, with its largely peasant population, and its nomadic neighbours was due also to the superior firepower of the Russian army. The state
went on to play an important part in curtailing nomadic pastoralism to release
land for peasants to settle. From the state's point of view, the additional tax
revenues generated by the peasant-settlers who cultivated the rich black earth
of the steppes, and the larger tax-paying population which could be supported
by expanding its frontiers, made the conquest, defence and agricultural settlement of the steppes a worthwhile proposition. In order to conquer and secure
the stèppe regions, however, the state needed to exploit the resources of its
realms, among the most important of which was the peasantry.[59]

59 See Bagalei, *Ocherki*, pp. 10–11, 253–69, 569; McNeill, *Europe's Steppe Frontier*, pp. 6–14,
126–31, 182–202.

CHAPTER 3

Exploitation

According to R. E. F. Smith and Rodney Hilton, 'Serfdom is the legal expression of one of the means by which the ruling groups in a peasant society make sure that they get as big a share as they can of the product of peasant labour.'[1] In Russia, where serfdom developed over the late sixteenth and early seventeenth centuries and lasted until 1861, peasants living on nobles' estates were exploited by their owners, who demanded obligations in the form of labour or dues. Large numbers of other Russian peasants lived on lands belonging to the state, the Russian Orthodox Church (until 1762–64), and the tsar's family (the court). These landowners exploited the peasants on their domains. In addition, the state obliged all Russian peasants to pay taxes and send recruits to the army. Exploitation was thus at the heart of the hierarchical social structure. The main uses to which the tsars put the resources they extracted from the peasantry were the defence, expansion and colonisation of their realms.

Serfdom and the other means by which the 'ruling groups' exploited the peasantry were superimposed on a peasant society and economy which already existed. The ruling and landowning elites were not primarily responsible for creating the main productive units in Russia's rural economy, nor for taking the basic economic decisions about production. The impact of exploitation on the peasants' ways of life will be considered in subsequent chapters. The main subjects of this chapter are the forms and levels of exploitation.

ENSERFMENT

It is important to distinguish between 'peasants' and 'serfs'. 'Peasants' were all members of a subordinate stratum of rural society (see Ch. 1). The term 'serf' is narrower, and describes a distinct category of peasants. Serfs, or 'seigniorial peasants', were peasants who were legally bound to a plot of land and to the person of the landowner, were subject to his or her administrative and judicial authority, and who passed their servile status on to their children.

In Russia, peasants who lived on noble landowners' estates had been free tenant farmers until the mid-sixteenth century. Their right to leave their landowners had been guaranteed in the law codes of 1497 and 1550, but it was limited to two weeks a year after the end of the agricultural season, around St George's day on 26 November (the second feast day for St George in the

1 Smith, R. E. F., *The Enserfment of the Russian Peasantry* (Cambridge, 1968), p. 3.

Orthodox calendar). A century later, terms of the law code (*Sobornoe ulozhenie*) of 1649 laid down that peasants, landless labourers (*bobyli*), and their children were not only tied to the land, but permanently liable to be returned to their previous homes and owners if they fled. In other words, they were bound to the land in perpetuity. Noble landowners acquired more rights over their peasants. By the early eighteenth century, they were allowed to move them from one estate to another, convert them to domestic serfs, and buy and sell them with or without the land. Above all, landowners were able to demand obligations from their peasants.[2]

The Russian state retained some limited authority over peasants who were enserfed to noble landowners. This is important as it is one of the main distinctions between serfs and slaves. In slave-holding societies, slaves were not considered to be subjects or citizens of the state, but the personal property of their owners. Slavery (*kholopstvo*) had a long history in Russia, lasting until 1723 (see below, p. 98). Russian slaves worked as agricultural labourers, domestic servants, in skilled occupations and administrative posts on estates, and served with their masters in the army. In the sixteenth and seventeenth centuries, slaves made up around 10 per cent of the Russian population.[3]

Historians have put forward differing interpretations to explain how and why a large part of the Russian peasantry became enserfed to noble landowners between the late sixteenth and mid-seventeenth centuries. Some have tried to explain the process by the relative scarcities of land and labour. In sixteenth- and seventeenth-century Russia, there was an abundance of land but a shortage of people to cultivate it. Since labour, not land, was the scarce resource, the chief problem for the 'ruling groups' in trying to exploit the resources of the state through agriculture was not ownership of land but control over the peasantry. The problem of labour scarcity was exacerbated by the massive depopulation of parts of the forest-heartland in the late sixteenth century (see Ch. 2). Although the shortage of labour relative to land was an important precondition for the emergence of unfree labour in Russia, it was not in itself a cause of serfdom.[4]

The enserfment of a substantial part of the Russian peasantry required the active role of outside forces to compel peasants to remain where they were and hand over part of the product of their labour. Some scholars, for example Klyuchevskii, argued that noble landowners played this role. Writing in the 1880s, he argued that landowners deliberately created and then took advantage of peasant indebtedness. They lent money to peasants who settled on their estates to help set them up and to assist them in times of hardship. They then compelled peasants who owed them money to work for them to pay the

2 See Blum, *Lord and Peasant*, pp. 6–8, 247–8, 262–7, 423–4, 463; Hellie, *Enserfment*, pp. 15, 86–7, 137.
3 See Hellie, R., *Slavery in Russia 1450–1725* (Chicago and London, 1982), pp. 467–502, 689; Blum, *Lord and Peasant*, pp. 259, 270–3; Kolchin, P., *Unfree Labor: American Slavery and Russian Serfdom* (Cambridge, MA, and London, 1987), pp. 41–6.
4 See Domar, E. D., 'The causes of slavery or serfdom: A hypothesis', *JEcH*, vol. 30 (1970), pp. 18–32.

interest and repay the loans. Some landowners made the terms so difficult that many peasants could never repay what they owed, but fell deeper into debt. Thus, they became indentured labourers and lost the right of departure. Decrees of 1586 and 1597 reinforced landowners' control over indentured labourers. The argument that peasant indebtedness played a large part in enserfment has been criticised. Richard Hellie questioned the extent of indebtedness, whether it increased over the sixteenth century, the power landowners had over debtor-peasants, and the similarity between the status of indentured labourers and serfs.[5]

Documents have come to light since the 1880s which suggest it was the state that played the largest role in the enserfment of the peasantry. The most important new documents are texts of, or references to, legislative acts of the late sixteenth century which gradually restricted and then abolished the peasants' right of movement around St George's day. The discoveries included references to 'forbidden years', starting in the 1580s, when peasants' right of movement was temporarily prohibited in some areas. Moreover, in the 1950s, V. I. Koretskii came across references in texts of court cases on birch bark to a decree of 1592/93 banning peasant movement altogether throughout Russia. These discoveries, and decrees which were already known, filled the gap between the law code of 1550, which allowed peasants to move once a year, and that of 1649, which permanently bound them to the land.[6]

According to this interpretation, the Russian state took a series of steps to bind peasants to the land at times of crisis in order to ensure the loyalty of the gentry cavalrymen (*pomeshchiki*) who made up the backbone of the Russian army in the sixteenth and early seventeenth centuries. Since the state lacked the money to pay the cavalrymen, it gave them tracts of land in return for service. They held the land on condition that they continued to serve. From 1556, moreover, boyars (aristocrats), who had previously held their extensive estates in unconditional, hereditary tenure, also held their lands on condition that they served the state. It was straightforward for the state to pay its servitors with land, since it was plentiful in Russia; the scarce resource was labour. As the gentry's grants of land were worthless without people to cultivate them, the state enacted a series of measures to bind peasants to their land.

The need to keep peasants on the estates of the gentry cavalrymen became urgent in the late sixteenth and early seventeenth centuries. Thousands of peasants left gentry estates in the forest-heartland for the more fertile steppes (see Ch. 2). Peasants also left gentry land for the larger estates of boyars and monasteries, who were able to offer peasants better terms, including lower obligations and aid in times of dearth. Some wealthy landowners kidnapped peasants from poorer gentry. Boyars and larger monasteries could rely on their

5 Klyuchevskii, V. O., 'Proiskhozhdenie krepostnogo prava v Rossii', in *Sochineniya*, vol. 8 (Moscow, 1990), pp. 120–93; *id.*, *Russkaya istoriya*, vol. 2, pp. 25–62; Hellie, *Enserfment*, pp. 5–7.
6 See Hellie, *Enserfment*, pp. 77–147; Koretskii, V. I., *Zakreposhchenie krest'yan i klassovaya bor'ba v Rossii vo vtoroi polovine XVI v.* (Moscow, 1970), esp. pp. 122–33. See also Moon, D., 'Reassessing Russian serfdom', *EHQ*, vol. 26 (1996), pp. 515–16 n. 2.

own resources to retain, and increase, their labour forces. The gentry were in a much weaker position, and turned to the state. They petitioned successive tsars to take action to stem the loss of their peasants. These petitions led to the decrees that, in stages, bound peasants to the land. From the 1590s to the 1640s, landowners had to recover fugitive or kidnapped peasants within a certain time limit, which was gradually raised from five to fifteen years. This loophole was closed in 1649 by the abolition of the time limit. The state backed up the decrees by organising search parties to seek out and return fugitives.

The state had other reasons to restrict peasants' mobility. It was easier to collect taxes from them if they stayed in one place. For this reason, the provisions of the 1649 law code binding peasants to the land applied also to peasants who lived on state, church and court lands. Between the late sixteenth and mid-seventeenth centuries, regardless of who owned the land they lived on, most Russian peasants in the central regions (and, later, some more outlying regions) experienced a similar decline in their status.[7]

It has been argued that the poverty of the environment of the forest-heartland, in particular the low fertility of much of the land, meant that the Russian state needed to make maximum use of its comparatively scarce resources if it was to support military forces capable of competing successfully with its better-endowed neighbours. Serfdom and the other means by which the state extracted a large part of the product of the labour from its mainly peasant population met this need. Together with all landowners, moreover, the state was concerned to maintain internal security against the threat of peasant revolts. Serfdom and restrictions on all peasant movement were ways to keep peasants under control.[8]

By the early eighteenth century, the measures binding peasants to the land had led to the division of the Russian peasantry into categories according to the owners of the land they lived on. The main categories were: seigniorial (*pomeshchich'i*) peasants, or 'serfs', who lived on the estates of nobles; state (*kazennye, gosudarstvennye*) peasants, whose land was state property; church (*tserkovnye, ekonomicheskie*) peasants, who lived on lands belonging to the Russian Orthodox Church; and the smaller numbers whose landowners were members of the tsar's family, known as court (*dvortsovye*) peasants until 1797, and thereafter as appanage (*udel'nye*) peasants.[9]

The emergence of servile labour was not restricted to Russia. While serfdom had largely died out in north-west Europe by the sixteenth century, in

7 See Blum, *Lord and Peasant*, pp. 188–98, 213–14, 268–70; Gorskaya, *Krest'yanstvo*, pp. 220–1, 372–3; Hellie, *Enserfment*, pp. 119, 145.
8 See Christian, 'Inner Eurasia', pp. 201–7; Pipes, *Russia*, pp. 1–24, 85–105.
9 See *SZ*, 1st edn (St Petersburg, 1832), book IV, *Zakony o Sostoyaniyakh*, pp. 121–5, arts 386–90. I have followed Blum in preferring the term 'seigniorial peasants' to 'serfs'. Some historians have applied the term 'serfs' ('krepostnye') to church and court peasants (e.g. Madariaga, I. de, *Russia in the Age of Catherine the Great* (London, 1981), p. 93; Vodarskii, *Naselenie Rossii za 400 let*, pp. 30, 57–9). Kahan used the term 'serf' to include state peasants (*Plow*, p. 23). The important point is that all were *peasants*; the owner of the land they lived on was only one of several factors that influenced their lives.

addition to Russia it also developed in large areas of eastern and central Europe, including right-bank Ukraine, Belorussia, Lithuania and the Baltic provinces of Estonia, Livonia and Kurland, which were annexed by the Russian Empire in the eighteenth century. At roughly the same time, moreover, slavery was introduced to Europe's American colonies.[10]

PEASANTS' OBLIGATIONS TO LANDOWNERS AND THE STATE (TO 1860s)

The enserfment of a large part of the Russian peasantry and similar restrictions on the rest of the peasantry greatly facilitated the exploitation of the mass of the rural population by the ruling and landowning elites. The main forms of exploitation lasted until the reforms of the 1860s–80s.

Seigniorial peasants' obligations to landowners: forms

Many seigniorial peasants were liable to one of two main forms of obligations to their landowners: labour services (*barshchina*) or dues in cash or kind (*obrok*). Some had to serve both. In addition, many landowners compelled their peasants to supply them with specified amounts of meat, fowl, grain, fruit and vegetables, other goods, such as firewood and cloth, and minor services including repair work on their estates. Landowners who did not live on their estates often required their peasants to transport the supplies to their residences. There were considerable variations in the forms and levels of seigniorial peasants' obligations because they were set by thousands of different landowners.

Landowners who demanded labour services set aside part of their estates as demesne for their own production, and handed over the rest of the land to the peasants to cultivate for themselves. Originally, most of the labour on demesnes had been carried out by slaves. From the late sixteenth century, however, landowners began to demand labour services from the peasants on their estates. Some of the produce of the demesne was for landowners' own consumption, but many put part on the market. On estates where landowners demanded dues rather than labour, they handed over most of the land to the peasants, who then cultivated it to support themselves and their landowners. In the sixteenth century, a sizable part of many peasants' dues were payable in kind, for example agricultural and handicraft produce. Most dues in kind were converted to cash over the seventeenth and eighteenth centuries.[11]

The form of obligations landowners demanded depended on a number of factors. Labour services were more common in the fertile black earth

10 See Blum, J., 'The rise of serfdom in Eastern Europe', *AHR*, vol. 62 (1957), pp. 807–36; Kolchin, *Unfree Labor*, pp. 1–31.
11 See Blum, *Lord and Peasant*, pp. 220–8, 444–55; Rubinshtein, N. L., *Sel'skoe khozyaistvo Rossii vo vtoroi polovine XVIII v.* (Moscow, 1957), pp. 79–91; Ignatovich, I. I., *Pomeshchich'i krest'yane nakanune osvobozhdeniya*, 3rd edn (Leningrad, 1925), pp. 106–13, 130–7; Hellie, *Slavery*, pp. 495–502.

provinces, where agriculture was the main economic activity. In seven black earth provinces in the late eighteenth century, according to data computed by V. I. Semevskii from the 'General Land Survey' (*General'noe mezhevanie*), 74 per cent of seigniorial peasants worked labour services and 26 per cent paid dues. In the less fertile forest-heartland, where many peasants engaged in handicrafts, trade and wage labour as well as farming, dues were more common. In 13 non-black earth provinces, *obrok* prevailed over *barshchina* by 55 per cent to 45 per cent. This regional distinction based on soil fertility and peasants' economic activities should not be overstated. Landowners also took account of access to markets. In the forest-heartland, large proportions of peasants on estates near large cities, especially Moscow and St Petersburg, and in the vicinity of transport routes to the Baltic ports were required to work on their landowners' demesnes to produce grain for sale. In the more fertile Central Black Earth and Mid-Volga regions, high proportions of peasants on estates near the Oka and Volga rivers, which were important trading arteries, were required to perform labour services for the same reason. But in more remote parts of the black earth regions, for example Voronezh province, many landowners demanded dues.

The proportions of seigniorial peasants required to perform labour services or pay dues changed over time. From the late sixteenth to the late eighteenth centuries, growing numbers of landowners demanded *barshchina*. By the late eighteenth century, in the 20 provinces examined by Semevskii, 56 per cent of seigniorial peasants performed *barshchina*, while 44 per cent paid *obrok*. From the end of the eighteenth century, however, the trend was in the other direction, towards *obrok*. The trend was most marked in the Central Non-Black Earth region, where dues were already the main seigniorial obligation. The proportions of seigniorial peasants paying dues also grew in the north-west of the Central Black Earth region, but remained well below half. On the other hand, the proportions of peasants required to perform labour services grew in the mainly agricultural Mid-Volga region and in the south-east of the Central Black Earth region, including Voronezh province. The proportion of seigniorial peasants required both to pay dues and to perform labour services increased over time. By the 1850s, around a quarter of seigniorial peasants in some provinces had 'mixed obligations'. This trend has caused problems in estimating the numbers of peasants on either *obrok* or *barshchina*. In contrast to Russia, almost all seigniorial peasants in the empire's western borderlands (especially Ukraine, Belorussia and Lithuania) performed labour services.[12]

---

12 See Blum, *Lord and Peasant*, pp. 224–5, 394–401; Smith, *Peasant Farming*, pp. 108, 130–2; Tikhonov, Yu. A., *Pomeshchich'i krest'yane v Rossii: Feodal'naya renta v XVII–nachale XVIII v.* (Moscow, 1974), p. 292; Rubinshtein, *Sel'skoe*, pp. 92–127; Semevskii, V. I., *Krest'yane v tsarstvovanie Imperatoritsy Ekateriny II*, 2 vols (St Petersburg, 1901–03), vol. 1, pp. 47–51; Ignatovich, *Pomeshchich'i*, pp. 71–84; Koval'chenko, I. D., *Russkoe krepostnoe krest'yanstvo v pervoi polovine XIX v.* (Moscow, 1967), pp. 58–64; Fedorov, V. A., *Pomeshchich'i krest'yane tsentral'no-promyshlennogo raiona Rossii: kontsa XVIII–pervoi poloviny XIX v.* (Moscow, 1974), pp. 225–6, 247; Litvak, B. G., *Russkaya derevnya v reforme 1861 goda: chernozemnyi tsentr, 1861–1895 gg.* (Moscow, 1972), pp. 58–60.

*Labour services (*barshchina*): levels*

The level of labour services can be measured either by the amount of demesne land peasants cultivated or by the number of days a week they worked for their landowners. However they are measured, the average levels increased over time. Yu. A. Tikhonov examined the records of 365 estates, mostly in the Central Non-Black Earth region of the forest-heartland, from the seventeenth and first quarter of the eighteenth centuries. He calculated that the average amount of demesne cultivated by each male peasant who performed *barshchina* increased from 0.4 *desyatiny* to 0.8 *desyatiny* (just over 2 acres) during this period. (Working 0.8 *desyatiny* would have taken a little under two days a week.)[13] The level of labour services demanded by landowners grew over the eighteenth century. Information gathered by the Free Economic Society in the 1760s and in the General Land Survey of the late eighteenth century indicates that the average amount of demesne that male peasants were required to cultivate was around 1.5 *desyatiny* in the Central Black Earth region and 1 *desyatina* in the Central Non-Black Earth region. Measured the other way, average *barshchina* was increasing towards three days a week. This was the norm by the end of the eighteenth century.[14]

In the first half of the nineteenth century, seigniorial peasants' labour services were higher still. On the basis of estate records, data from provincial governors' reports and material gathered by local agricultural societies, both Steven Hoch and Soviet historian I. D. Koval'chenko argued that the average total area of land male peasants were required to cultivate in the Central Black Earth region in the mid-nineteenth century was around 2 *desyatiny*. This took around four days a week. The 'Descriptions of Seigniorial Estates' (*Opisaniya pomeshchich'ikh imenii*) – which were compiled by landowners in 1858–59 on the eve of the abolition of serfdom – also contain information on labour services. The majority of landowners in the Central Non-Black Earth region who demanded *barshchina* reported that they required three days' labour a week. Around a quarter of landowners in some provinces admitted demanding four days a week.[15] If an intensification of labour services did occur over the first half of the nineteenth century, it did not necessarily mean peasants were working more days a week. Many peasants were compelled to work harder by the spread of the task system. Rather than being told to work on the demesne for so many days a week, which was an invitation to work as

---

13 Tikhonov, *Pomeshchich'i*, pp. 292–6. See also Blum, *Lord and Peasant*, pp. 225–8; Shapiro, A. L., *Russkoe krest'yanstvo pered zakreposhcheniem (XIV–XVI vv.)* (Leningrad, 1987), pp. 81–90; Smith, *Peasant Farming*, pp. 108, 130–2, 226, 238.
14 Semevskii, *Krest'yane*, vol. 1, pp. 61–70; Rubinshtein, *Sel'skoe*, pp. 160–6; Koval'chenko, *Russkoe*, p. 276.
15 Hoch, *Serfdom*, pp. 23–4, 118–19 (I have computed Hoch's figures on *barshchina* per labour team [*tyaglo*] to per male soul by dividing by 2.5 [there were 4.6–5.5 peasants per team: *ibid.*, p. 41]); Koval'chenko, *Russkoe*, pp. 105–6, 155, 275–81; Krutikov, V. I. and Fedorov, V. A., 'Opisaniya pomeshchich'ikh imenii 1858–1859 gg. kak istochnik po istorii pomeshchich'ego khozyaistva i krest'yanstva nakanune reformy 1861 g. (Po materialam Tul'skoi i Moskovskoi gubernii)', *EAIVE 1970 g.* (Riga, 1977), p. 144; Fedorov, *Pomeshchich'i*, p. 227.

slowly as they could get away with, peasants were assigned certain tasks to complete, for example an area of land to be ploughed or so many sheaves to be reaped. The faster the peasants worked on the demesne, the more time they had to farm their own land.[16] Some landowners demanded additional days of *barshchina* in the summer, when haymaking, harvesting and other tasks put enormous demands on peasants' labour resources. Some made excessive demands, forcing their peasants to work on the demesne for five or six days a week, leaving them only night-time, Sundays and holidays to cultivate their own land.[17]

There were regional variations in the levels of labour services. *Barshchina* was lower in outlying areas than in the central regions. In the late sixteenth century, for example, landowners in the recently conquered Mid-Volga region demanded about half as much labour from their peasants as those in the forest-heartland. As late as the 1760s, landowners in the North-western region required their peasants to work only two days a week, in case higher demands persuaded them to flee across the nearby border with Poland. The Russian annexation of north-east Poland (western Belorussia) in 1772 reduced the need to moderate their demands. Some landowners in the south-eastern steppe regions demanded lower obligations for this reason into the nineteenth century.[18]

The logical extension of *barshchina* was for landowners to take all the arable land away from their peasants, and compel them to work full-time on their estates, run on plantation lines, in return for monthly rations. This system, known as *mesyachina*, was rare, and in the mid-nineteenth century involved only a few hundred Russian peasants.[19] Some landowners required their peasants to work in manufactories, which processed food, distilled vodka, and produced potash, cloth and other goods for sale. Such peasants had to work at least as hard as those who toiled on their owners' land.[20]

Some Soviet historians, for example Koval'chenko, argued that by the first half of the nineteenth century, the average level of seigniorial labour services had increased to such an extent that it was undermining the peasant economy. He probably overstated the case. Another Soviet historian, B. G. Litvak, showed that in the Central Black Earth region, where labour services were highest, most peasant households had enough labour resources to cultivate their own land as well as their share of the demesne, because they could call

16 Koval'chenko, *Russkoe*, pp. 155, 275; Ignatovich, *Pomeshchich'i*, pp. 162–3. For evidence that seigniorial peasants were working harder, see Deal, *Serf*, pp. 394–9; Mironov, B. N., 'When and why was the Russian peasantry emancipated?', in Bush, M. L. (ed.), *Serfdom and Slavery: Studies in Legal Bondage* (London and New York, 1996), pp. 326–8; Leonard, C., 'Landlords and the *Mir*: Transaction costs and economic development in pre-emancipation Russia (Iaroslav Guberniia)', in *LCPCR*, pp. 133–4.
17 Semevskii, *Krest'yane*, vol. 1, pp. 64–6; Blum, *Lord and Peasant*, pp. 444–7; Rubinshtein, *Sel'skoe*, pp. 161–5; Ignatovich, *Pomeshchich'i*, pp. 34–5, 175–6.
18 Hellie, *Enserfment*, p. 318, n. 16; Semevskii, *Krest'yane*, vol. 1, p. 63.
19 Fedorov, *Pomeshchich'i*, pp. 228–30; Litvak, *Russkaya*, pp. 49–50, 147.
20 See Blum, *Lord and Peasant*, pp. 318–20.

on youths and older peasants who were not required to work as many days' *barshchina* as young adult and middle-aged peasants.[21]

Thus, the levels of labour services demanded by noble landowners increased over the whole period of serfdom, and were higher in the central regions than in more outlying areas. In the late eighteenth and first half of the nineteenth centuries, on average, at least a third of the total production of enserfed peasants who were compelled to perform labour services was taken away from them by their landowners.

Dues (obrok): levels

The average level of *obrok* rates, in nominal monetary terms, also increased over time. Before assessing the actual impact of cash *obrok*, however, it is necessary to consider changes in the real value of the rouble as a result of depreciation and inflation. Tsars frequently debased the currency to pay for their wars. Among the most expensive were the Thirteen Years' War with Poland (1654–67), the Great Northern War with Sweden (1700–21), and the Seven Years' War (1756–62). At various times, silver coins were replaced by copper, and the metal content reduced. In 1769, during the Russo-Turkish War (1768–74), paper roubles (assignats) were issued in tandem with silver roubles. They held their value until the 1790s, but fell sharply as more were issued to pay for Russia's involvement in the wars with France. By 1800 the paper money was worth around two-thirds of its nominal value and, by the end of the Napoleonic Wars in 1815, less than a quarter. In 1839–41 the currency was stabilised. The exchange rate was set at 1 paper rouble to 0.286 silver roubles (3.5 paper roubles = 1 silver rouble). The stable currency did not survive the expense of the Crimean War (1853–56), and the new paper 'credit roubles' lost some of their value. The depreciation of the rouble gave unscrupulous landowners and traders opportunities to deceive peasants into paying more. For much of the early nineteenth century, the 'popular rate' was 1 paper rouble to 0.25 silver roubles: a bad deal for peasants paying in silver for dues or goods priced in paper.[22] The purchasing power of the rouble also fell as a result of inflation. Boris Mironov traced changes in average grain prices in the Russian Empire between the mid-sixteenth and early twentieth centuries. Although there were significant regional and short-term variations, he showed that there were periods of inflation in the mid-seventeenth and the third quarter of the nineteenth centuries. The most striking trend, however, was a 'price revolution' over the eighteenth century, when grain prices increased sixfold, measured in grams of silver, and elevenfold in nominal terms. The

---

21 Compare Koval'chenko, *Russkoe*, pp. 280–1, and Litvak, *Russkaya*, pp. 139–44, 149–50. See also Semevskii, *Krest'yane*, vol. 1, pp. 68–70; Fedorov, *Pomeshchich'i*, p. 227; Hoch, *Serfdom*, pp. 23–4, 118–19.

22 See Tikhonov, *Pomeshchich'i*, pp. 296–9; Kahan, *Plow*, pp. 239, 321–2, 339; Domar, E., 'Kahan on Russian economic history', *JEcH*, vol. 47 (1987), p. 771; Pintner, W. M., *Russian Economic Policy under Nicholas I* (Ithaca, NY, 1967), pp. 184–220, 256–63; Hoch, S. L., 'The banking crisis, peasant reform, and economic development in Russia, 1857–1861', *AHR*, vol. 96 (1991), pp. 799–800. See also Blum, *Lord and Peasant*, pp. 222–3, 304–7, 450–1.

prices of manufactured goods rose more slowly. To the extent that peasants raised the money to pay their cash dues by selling agricultural or handicraft production, and that the amounts of money they received increased faster than their dues, then the level of these dues, in real terms, fell.[23]

In the Central Non-Black Earth region over the seventeenth and first quarter of the eighteenth centuries, average annual nominal rates of seigniorial *obrok* per peasant household increased. But average rates per male peasant[24] fell slightly after 1680, due partly to the increase in average household size in this period (see Ch. 5). When allowance has been made for depreciation and inflation, however, in real terms, *obrok* rates per household and per male peasant remained roughly constant until 1679, but over the next half-century both declined, the latter by 50 per cent. Mironov estimated that the real level of *obrok*, in cash and kind, fell by a third in the first two decades of the eighteenth century. In the second half of the eighteenth century, however, there were rapid increases in both the nominal and real levels. Average rates per male peasant grew from around 1.50 roubles in the 1760s to about 5 (paper) roubles in the 1790s. Additional dues in kind were worth around half monetary dues. Real levels of *obrok* increased nearly four times between the 1720s and 1770s, before falling back to 70 per cent above their 1700 level by 1800.[25]

Average nominal rates of *obrok* demanded by landowners continued to increase in the first half of the nineteenth century. But historians have disagreed over the real level of seigniorial peasants' dues, and the proportion of their incomes they took up. Koval'chenko and L. V. Milov presented data from the 'Descriptions of Seigniorial Estates' (drawn up by landowners in 1858–59) to show that average *obrok* rates per male peasant were around 10.5 silver roubles in the Non-Black Earth regions, where many households had non-agricultural sources of income, and 9.5 silver roubles in the chiefly agricultural Black Earth regions. They compared these figures with data for the late eighteenth century. After making allowance for the depreciation of the currency by converting paper roubles into silver roubles, and for inflation by converting silver roubles into measures of grain, they argued that *obrok* rates had doubled or trebled between the end of the eighteenth century and the 1850s. Not only were landowners insisting on higher dues, the two historians asserted, but they were demanding higher proportions of their peasants' incomes. Based on a sample of four provinces in the central regions, they argued that, by the

23 Mironov, B. N., 'Consequences of the price revolution in eighteenth-century Russia', *EcHR*, vol. 45 (1992), pp. 457–78.
24 For purposes of comparison, most historians estimate average *obrok* per male peasant. Most landowners and communes, however, assigned dues to households based on the number of labour teams (*tyagla*) they contained. See Chs 5 and 6.
25 Tikhonov, *Pomeshchich'i*, pp. 296–300; Semevskii, *Krest'yane*, vol. 1, pp. 51–5, 593–5; Mironov, 'Consequences', p. 468. For slightly different views, see Blum, *Lord and Peasant*, pp. 221–4, 448–51; Kahan, A., 'The costs of "westernization" in Russia: The gentry and the economy in the eighteenth century', *SR*, vol. 25 (1966), p. 51 (Kahan excluded dues in kind). Rubinshtein denied that rising prices eased the burden of *obrok* in the late eighteenth century: *Sel'skoe*, pp. 156–60.

1850s, *obrok* payments were taking 30–38 per cent of peasants' earnings, compared with 18–21 per cent in the 1790s.

These conclusions were challenged by other Soviet historians, who argued that Koval'chenko and Milov had overstated the levels of *obrok* and understated peasants' incomes. Litvak disputed his two colleagues' figures on *obrok* in the late 1850s. He argued that their main sources, the 'Descriptions of Seigniorial Estates', were inaccurate, since the landowners who compiled them had deliberately exaggerated their *obrok* rates in the hope of getting higher compensation when serfdom was abolished. Instead, he examined the 'Regulatory Charters' (*Ustavnye gramoty*), which were drawn up by landowners immediately after the abolition of serfdom in 1861, but were subject to the peasants' approval under the supervision of officials. He claimed that data in the charters were more accurate, and estimated that average *obrok* rates in the Central Black Earth region were lower than Koval'chenko and Milov's estimate, at around 8 silver roubles per male soul. 'Revisionist' Soviet scholars also challenged their two colleagues' conclusion that landowners were increasing their demands for *obrok* more quickly than peasants were able to increase their incomes. They paid particular attention to the growth in peasants' earnings from handicrafts and trade, especially in the Central Non-Black Earth region, and argued that the average proportion of peasants' incomes taken up by *obrok* in the 1850s varied from 22 to 30 per cent. This was a little more than at the end of the eighteenth century, but lower than Koval'chenko and Milov's estimates.[26]

Levels of *obrok* also varied by region. Owners of estates in sparsely populated borderlands demanded lower rates than landowners in the central regions. For example, landowners in Kursk province in the south of the Central Black Earth region in the early eighteenth century offered short-term immunities to settlers followed by light obligations. There were similar cases in the Don Cossack territory 100 years later. The aim was to encourage more peasants to settle on their estates, and to discourage their existing peasants from leaving to seek lighter burdens further afield.[27]

The rates of *obrok* set by landowners are not an accurate guide to actual levels of exploitation. There were differences between what landowners demanded and what they received. Many peasants ran up arrears. Some peasants did not pay in full because they were too poor, or after bad harvests. To cite

26 See Koval'chenko, I. D. and Milov, L. V., 'Ob intensivnosti obrochnoi ekspluatatsii krest'yan tsentral'noi Rossii v kontse XVIII–pervoi polovine XIX v.', *IS* (1966), no. 4, pp. 55–80; *id.*, 'Eshche raz o metodike izucheniya intensivnosti ekspluatatsii obrochnogo krest'yanstva. (Otvet P. G. Ryndzyunskomu)', *IS* (1967), no. 2, pp. 223–30; Koval'chenko, *Russkoe*, pp. 21–38, 142–54, 281–96; Ryndzyunskii, P. G., 'Ob opredelenii intensivnosti obrochnoi ekspluatatsii krest'yan Tsentral'noi Rossii v kontse XVIII–pervoi polovine XIX v. (O stat'e I. D. Koval'chenko i L. V. Milova)', *IS* (1966), no. 6, pp. 44–64; *id.*, *Utverzhdenie kapitalizma v Rossii 1850–1880 gg.* (Moscow, 1978), pp. 55–8; Litvak, *Russkaya*, pp. 30–42, 70–5, 115–27, 148–9; Fedorov, *Pomeshchich'i*, pp. 13–18, 231–45. See also Blum, *Lord and Peasant*, pp. 451–2.
27 Gorskaya, *Krest'yanstvo*, pp. 407; Melton, H. E., *Serfdom and the Peasant Economy in Russia: 1780–1861*, unpublished PhD dissertation (Columbia University, 1983), pp. 55–7; Ignatovich, I. I., *Krest'yanskoe dvizhenie na Donu v 1820 g.* (Moscow, 1937), p. 17; Rubinshtein, *Sel'skoe*, pp. 156–9.

just one of numerous examples, after the harvest failure in 1822, the peasants on the Musin-Pushkins' estates in Yaroslavl' province had arrears amounting to 60 per cent of their total annual dues. Rich peasants also ran up arrears, suggesting that many tried to get away with paying as little as possible. Shortfalls in peasants' payments have to be taken into account when assessing levels of exploitation.[28]

Thus, average nominal rates of seigniorial *obrok* per male peasant increased over the whole period of serfdom, with the exception of the late seventeenth and early eighteenth centuries (the reign of Peter the Great). After making allowance for changes in the value of the rouble, however, real levels of *obrok* fell substantially during Peter's reign, but more than recovered the lost ground in the middle decades of the eighteenth century. Average real levels of *obrok* probably did increase in the last six decades of serfdom, but not by as much as Koval'chenko and Milov claimed. For most of the period, *obrok* took up a large part of peasants' incomes, but many were able to earn more to cover part or all of the higher rates. Many peasants also reduced the burden of their *obrok* by not paying the full rates. Nevertheless, in the last century of serfdom, many landowners were able to extract up to a third of their peasants' incomes in dues.

Domestic serfs

On most seigniorial estates, a proportion of the peasants were domestic serfs (*dvorovye lyudi*). Aside from the impact of their owners' demands on the domestic serfs themselves, if landowners had large numbers of such people, they were a burden on the other peasants as they had to support them and pay their taxes. The conversion of field serfs into domestic serfs could also be burdensome if it significantly reduced the labour capacity of peasant communities and households. In fact, the negative impact of this category of serfs has been exaggerated. Although some were unproductive domestic servants (including the famous serf actors and musicians) or worked in estate administrations, many worked as blacksmiths and in other skilled occupations. Domestic serfs performed many of the functions that had been carried out by domestic slaves prior to the end of slavery in 1723 (see above, p. 67). Many domestic serfs had kitchen gardens, where they grew some of their own food. In addition, most were the children of domestic serfs, rather than peasants taken from their households. Contrary to the long-accepted notion, there was no big increase in the numbers of domestic serfs in Russia in the 1850s as a result of landowners taking over their land in anticipation of the end of serfdom.[29]

State, church and court/appanage peasants' obligations

The other categories of peasants owed obligations to the owners of the land they lived on. The state, in its capacity as landowner, demanded obligations

28 Fedorov, *Pomeshchich'i*, pp. 242–5. See also Ch. 7.
29 Hoch, *Serfdom*, pp. 17–21; Litvak, *Russkaya*, pp. 44–50, 147–8. *Cf.* Blum, *Lord and Peasant*, pp. 455–60.

from peasants on state domains. Originally, these took the forms of a variety of dues and labour services. In 1723 Peter the Great replaced them with dues in cash (also called *obrok*). Peter intended them to be the equivalent of seigniorial peasants' obligations. In fact it was rather lower. The state peasants' *obrok* was initially set at 40 kopeks per male soul (100 kopeks = 1 rouble). The nominal rate was increased to 55 kopeks in 1755, 1 rouble in 1761, 2 roubles in 1768, and 3 (paper) roubles in 1783. It was raised again in 1798, but an attempt was made to take account of peasants' incomes. Each province was allocated to one of four bands depending on its prosperity. *Obrok* was then levied at four different rates, ranging from 3.5 to 5 paper roubles. In 1810–12, the rates were increased to between 7.5 and 10 paper roubles (or 2.15–2.86 silver roubles after 1839). As part of his reforms of the state peasantry in the 1840s (see below, pp. 107–8), P. D. Kiselev refined the system of setting *obrok* rates in conformance with peasants' ability to pay, but was not able to complete the change. In 1859 his successor increased nominal rates of *obrok* by up to 13 per cent.

Some Soviet historians, for example N. M. Druzhinin, argued that the increases in the nominal levels of the state peasants' *obrok* led to an intensification in the degree of exploitation. Once allowance has been made for depreciation, inflation and increases in state peasants' incomes, however, the overall picture is not as bleak. Over the eighteenth century, state peasants' *obrok* increased at around twice the rate of inflation, but more slowly than seigniorial peasants' dues. Throughout the period from 1723 to 1861, state peasants' dues were well below the mean level of seigniorial *obrok*.[30]

Back in the early eighteenth century, Peter the Great had made further impositions on the state peasantry. Some of the labour force for his construction projects, including his new capital city of St Petersburg, was made up of state peasants drafted in from the surrounding areas. Peter used forced peasant labour to build his navy, and extended the use of forced labour to industry. He assigned thousands of state peasants to factories, metallurgical plants, munitions works and mines. They became known as ascribed (*pripisnye*) peasants. Many worked in the Urals regions which were rich in minerals but sparsely populated. In addition, between 1721 and 1762, merchants were allowed to buy peasants to work in factories. These workers were known as 'possessional' serfs. Although many received wages and had plots of land, the degree of exploitation of all peasants who worked in industry was at least as high as that of the mass of the agricultural peasantry.[31]

---

30 Compare Druzhinin, *Gosudarstvennye*, vol. 1, pp. 46–51; Neupokoev, V. I., *Gosudarstvennye povinnosti krest'yan Evropeiskoi Rossii v kontse XVIII–nachale XIX v.* (Moscow, 1987), pp. 89–163, and Blum, *Lord and Peasant*, pp. 485–8; Crisp, O., *Studies in the Russian Economy before 1914* (London, 1976), pp. 79–80, 88–90; Pintner, *Russian*, pp. 163–70.
31 Blum, *Lord and Peasant*, pp. 308–9, 320–1, 485–91; Kahan, *Plow*, pp. 138–44; Kopanev, A. I. (ed.), *Istoriya krest'yanstva Severo-Zapada Rossii: period feodalizma* (St Petersburg, 1994), pp. 168–9, 177–81; Neupokoev, *Gosudarstvennye*, pp. 89–95; Esper, T., 'The condition of the serf workers in Russia's metallurgical industry, 1800–1861', *JMH*, vol. 50 (1978), pp. 660–79; *id.*, 'The incomes of Russian serf ironworkers in the nineteenth century', *P & P*, no. 93 (1981), pp. 137–59.

Church and court peasants had obligations to their landowners. The Russian Orthodox Church and its monasteries depended on the incomes from their estates. Large monasteries, such as the Trinity–St Sergei monastery northeast of Moscow, were among the wealthiest landowners in Russia. Church peasants were burdened with obligations in kind, labour and cash. Although the church authorities did not have such extensive legal powers over their peasants as secular landowners, they had a reputation as demanding masters. Until 1762, the forms and levels of church peasants' obligations depended on the will of the monasteries and churchmen who owned them. Likewise, court peasants owed a variety of obligations to the tsar's family but, during the eighteenth century, labour services were replaced by cash *obrok*. Obligations tended to be lighter on monastery and court lands in frontier regions than in the central regions.[32]

In one of a number of radical measures in his brief reign, Peter III secularised the church's land and peasants in 1762. All the peasants' obligations to their former ecclesiastical landowners were commuted to a flat-rate *obrok* of 1 rouble per male soul, to be paid to the state. Peter III was overthrown in June 1762 by his wife, Catherine the Great (1762–96). She cancelled his decree, and introduced her own in 1764, which raised the former church peasants' *obrok* to 1.5 roubles per male soul.[33] In 1768 the former church and court peasants' *obrok* rates were set at the same level as that of the state peasants, at 2 roubles per male soul. They were increased together for most of the rest of the eighteenth century. Thereafter, the former church peasants were treated as part of the state peasantry. The court peasants, renamed appanage (*udel'nye*) peasants in 1797, were treated differently. Their obligations were reformed in 1797 and 1829 with the aim of bringing them into line with their incomes. The main result, however, was to increase their dues. Like state peasants' dues, the church and court/appanage peasants' dues were below the average level of those of the seigniorial peasants. Nevertheless, non-seigniorial peasants also ran up arrears.[34]

All peasants' obligations to the state

On top of obligations to their landowners, peasants of all categories had to pay taxes to the state treasury and supply conscripts to the armed forces.

Direct taxes

Until the mid-seventeenth century, the main direct tax paid by the peasantry was a land tax, which was assessed according to the quantity and quality of land each household farmed. An advantage of the land tax, from the standpoint

32 Blum, *Lord and Peasant*, pp. 207–9, 213–14, 218; Gorskaya, *Krest'yanstvo*, pp. 406–7; Preobrazhenskii, *Krest'yanstvo*, pp. 154–8; Shapiro, *Russkoe krest'yanstvo*, pp. 78–95, 107.
33 Leonard, C. S., *Reform and Regicide: The Reign of Peter III of Russia* (Bloomington, IN, 1993), pp. 73–89; Madariaga, *Russia*, pp. 113–19, 125–7.
34 See Blum, *Lord and Peasant*, pp. 493–7; Gorlanov, *Udel'nye*, pp. 4–8, 11, 18–19, 21, 24, 29, 73–9; Neupokoev, *Gosudarstvennye*, pp. 91, 94; Pintner, *Russian*, pp. 75, 158–9, 166–7.

of the peasants, was that it took account of their ability to pay. A disadvantage, from the point of view of the treasury, was that peasants reduced their tax liability by cultivating less land, or by concealing some of it from the authorities. In order to remove this disadvantage and raise more revenue, the state altered the main direct tax twice over the rest of the seventeenth century. In 1645–47, the treasury changed the unit of assessment to a combination of land and a flat rate for each household. This was a transitional measure. In 1679, after the household tax census, taxes were levied at a set amount per household, regardless of the quantity and quality of its land, its incomes from other sources, or the number of peasants it contained. The treasury raised more revenue by imposing additional taxes for specific purposes. Peter the Great financed his wars, especially the Great Northern War, by levying several additional taxes to pay for his army and navy. He also resorted to extraordinary taxes, most famously his 'beard tax'. Peasants were not liable to be taxed on their beards if they stayed in their villages, but on entering and leaving a town, for example to go to a market, they had to pay a kopek for the privilege of being unshaven.[35]

Towards the end of the Great Northern War, Peter tried to put state revenues on a more stable footing. Most, but not all, of the additional and extraordinary taxes were cancelled, and the unit of assessment of the main direct tax was changed again. A flaw in the household tax, from the treasury's point of view, was that households reduced their tax liability by combining into larger households or not splitting into smaller ones (see Ch. 5). Partly to remove this loophole, the treasury decided to levy direct taxes at a flat rate per head of the male population of the lower orders, chiefly the peasantry and townspeople. In 1718 Peter ordered a census to be taken. It was begun in 1719 and largely completed by 1724, when the poll (or soul) tax was collected for the first time.[36]

At first the poll tax was not levied in some of the non-Russian borderlands of the state. In addition, Ukrainian peasants who had settled in the Central Black Earth and Lower Volga and Don regions of Russia, and many native peoples of the Northern, Urals and Volga regions and Siberia, were exempt from the poll tax, but paid other taxes and forms of tribute. The poll tax was not extended to Ukrainian peasants in Russian provinces, and to left-bank Ukraine and other western borderlands, until 1783 and later. Moreover, the authorities regularly offered temporary immunities from the poll tax in order to attract settlers to some frontier areas.

The poll tax was very long-lasting. It was reassessed on the basis of new censuses ('revisions') held at irregular intervals between 1719 and 1857, and survived until the 1880s. The only sections of the population not liable to the

35 See Blum, *Lord and Peasant*, pp. 228–35; LeDonne, J. P., *Absolutism and Ruling Class: The Formation of the Russian Political Order, 1700–1825* (New York and Oxford, 1991), pp. 258–9; Shapiro, A. L., *Agrarnaya istoriya Severo-Zapada Rossii XVII v.: (naseleniya, zemlevladenie, zemlepol'zovanie)* (Leningrad, 1989), pp. 180–3.
36 Milyukov, P. N., *Gosudarstvennoe khozyaistvo Rossii v pervoi chetverti XVIII stoletiya i reforma Petra Velikogo*, 2nd edn (St Petersburg, 1905), pp. 471–80; Anisimov, E. V., *Podatnaya reforma Petra I: Vvedenie podushnoi podati v Rossii 1719–1728 gg.* (Leningrad, 1982).

poll tax, regardless of which part of the empire they lived in, were the privileged nobility and clergy. Merchants were exempted in 1775. Immunity from the poll tax was thus an important distinction between the elites and the mass of the 'tax-paying' population.[37]

Back in 1724, the poll tax was initially set at 74 kopeks per male soul. Peter intended the new tax to increase state revenue without overburdening the tax-paying population. Historians have long maintained, however, that the poll tax greatly intensified the load of direct taxes on the peasantry. The prerevolutionary historian Pavel Milyukov calculated that the total expected yield of the poll tax in 1724 was 4,614,638 roubles, compared with an expected annual yield from the old direct taxes in the period immediately before 1724 of 1,778,533 roubles. In other words, the poll tax should have raised 260 per cent more than the direct taxes it replaced. After taking account of the decline of the real value of the rouble, Milyukov estimated that the total expected yield from *all* taxes (direct and indirect) increased threefold between 1680 and 1724 (roughly Peter's reign).

Milyukov's conclusions have been challenged. Soviet historian E. V. Anisimov approached the question from the point of view of individual taxpayers, rather than total yields, and estimated that the immediate increase in direct taxation per male soul was only 16 per cent. But, if the additional direct taxes that were still collected in 1724 are included, then the immediate increase amounted to 64 per cent. He agreed with Milyukov, however, that over the whole of Peter's reign the total burden of taxation increased threefold. A more revisionist argument was presented by Arcadius Kahan. He argued that state demands on the population peaked during the difficult wartime years of 1705–15. In assessing the impact of the poll tax, he took account of the additional taxes levied before 1724, and the fact that the total revenue raised by the poll tax must be divided by the larger number of people liable to pay it than by the number subject to the old household tax. He reached the 'very iconoclastic conclusion' that 'the introduction of the poll tax *reduced* the tax burden on the Russian peasantry from the high level of the taxation in money and kind . . . during the [Great] Northern War'. Mironov, who does not seem to have taken full account of the additional taxes, accepted that the introduction of the poll tax led to an immediate 260 per cent increase in the direct tax burden, but argued that the rapid price rises over the first quarter of the eighteenth century meant that, on average, the real burden of direct taxes simply returned to the level it had been in 1700.[38]

Another way of trying to assess the burden of the poll tax is to look at the difference between the revenue the treasury expected and the sum it actually

---

37 See LeDonne, *Absolutism*, pp. 259–62. See also *PSZ*, 1, vol. XXI, pp. 907–12, no. 15724 (3 May 1783); vol. XXIV, pp. 845–6, no. 18277 (18 December 1798); Belyavskii, M. T., *Krest'yanskii vopros v Rossii nakanune vosstaniya E. I. Pugacheva* (Moscow, 1965), pp. 46–7; Moon, *Russian Peasants*, p. 53.
38 See Milyukov, *Gosudarstvennoe*, pp. 478–9, 486, 489–91; Anisimov, *Podatnaya*, pp. 274–82; Kahan, *Plow*, pp. 328–32 (quotation, p. 332, my emphasis, DM); Mironov, 'Consequences' (1992), pp. 468–9.

received. Only 3,338,678 of the 4,614,638 roubles the treasury expected were collected in 1724. The shortfall was a result of a number of factors. There was an inevitable delay in tax receipts reaching St Petersburg, and unscrupulous officials took a cut of the revenues they collected. In addition, some peasants simply managed to avoid paying. Others were unable to pay because of poor harvests and epidemics over the preceding three years. However, even if some peasants managed to cushion the immediate effect of the poll tax by not paying it in full, most had made up their arrears by 1727.

All these arguments should be treated as hypotheses as we cannot be certain of the accuracy and significance of the data. Officials at the time were not always fully aware of how much money was coming into the treasury, and subsequent historians have admitted difficulty in finding information on all the various taxes and the revenue raised. The reign of Peter the Great was a time of considerable changes, reforms and upheavals as well as long and costly wars. In addition, the value of the currency changed markedly as a result of debasement and inflation. Despite some conclusions to the contrary, common sense suggests that Peter's wars and reforms must have been very expensive, and it is likely that most of the cost fell on the shoulders of the Russian peasantry.[39]

Peter's widow and successor, Catherine I (1725–27), reduced the poll tax slightly to 70 kopeks per male soul in 1725. It remained at this level until 1794, when the nominal rate was raised to 1 (paper) rouble. Thereafter, the cost of Russia's involvement in the wars with France and the declining value of the paper rouble compelled the treasury to increase the nominal rate regularly. It was raised to 1.26 paper roubles in 1798, 2 paper roubles in 1810, 3 paper roubles in 1812, 3.30 paper roubles in 1816 (or 95 silver kopeks from 1839), and 1 silver rouble in 1861. There is little doubt about trends in the level of the poll tax in real terms after 1725. Mironov showed that the real level of the tax remained fairly constant between 1730 and 1759, but fell by over two-thirds over the last decades of the eighteenth century. In spite of the regular increases during the Napoleonic Wars, the level of the poll tax in real terms struggled to maintain its lower value of the 1790s. In the decades after 1815, it held this level and increased slightly, but fell back as prices began to rise in the 1850s. State revenue also suffered as a result of the growing arrears as some peasants failed to meet their poll tax payments in full and on time.[40]

Conscription

Probably the most onerous obligation peasants owed to the state was conscription into the armed forces. In the first half of the seventeenth century, some peasants were inducted into the army and, on the steppe frontier, whole

39 See Milyukov, *Gosudarstvennoe*, pp. 483, 486, 489–91; Anisimov, *Podatnaya*, pp. 264–7; Kahan, *Plow*, p. 331.
40 Neupokoev, *Gosudarstvennye*, pp. 22–35; Mironov, 'Consequences', p. 468. Blum (*Lord and Peasant*, pp. 464–5) anticipated Mironov's findings. Neupokoev (*op. cit.*, p. 35) unconvincingly argued that the poll tax did increase in real terms.

villages were converted into soldiers. Regular conscription of peasants into the lower ranks of the army began during the Thirteen Years' War with Poland (1654–67). In most years during the war, one recruit was taken from every 20–25 households. Most served as infantrymen in 'new formation' regiments. The number of men under arms was cut back at the end of the war, and many peasant-soldiers were discharged and sent home.[41]

Peter the Great reintroduced annual levies of recruits into the lower ranks. His measures established new principles. In 1699, on the eve of the Great Northern War, he introduced military service for life. Many of the early recruits were slaves, but the brunt of conscription came to be borne by the peasantry. In 1705 Peter ordered a general levy of recruits to be raised throughout Russia at a rate of one man for every 20 households from the lower orders. The 1705 levy set a pattern. Recruits were raised in this manner almost every year for the rest of Peter's reign, and in most years for the next century and a half. There were only a few changes to Peter's system. In 1793 the term of service was reduced from life to 25 years. From the 1830s some soldiers with 20 years' service were allowed home on 'indefinite leave', but were liable to be called up in wartime. In essence, however, Peter's system lasted until the reforms of the 1860s–70s.[42]

Many Russian noblemen also served in the armed forces. Indeed, noblemen were obliged to serve the state in the army or the bureaucracy until Peter III, in another radical measure in his short reign, abolished compulsory noble state service in 1762. Both before and after 1762, however, noble service in the army was organised separately from the conscription of peasants and townsmen. Most nobles, moreover, served as officers. Although, in principle, a soldier of peasant origins could earn promotion to officer and, thus, noble status, this was unusual in practice. Liability to conscription into the lower ranks of the armed forces was another factor defining the subordinate position of the mass of the population.[43]

Conscription was a constant drain on the Russian peasantry. In the first two decades of the eighteenth century, around 300,000 men, mostly peasants, were drafted into Peter the Great's army. Between 1720 and 1867, a total of 7.25 million men were conscripted in the empire as a whole. If we assume that before 1782 all recruits came from Russia proper, and that after 1782, when conscription was extended to some of the non-Russian borderlands, men were recruited in equal proportions from all regions, then at least 4.8 million of the 7.25 million recruits came from the peasant population of Russia: an average of 32,500 a year. The numbers recruited were greatest during the major wars of the nineteenth century, especially at the height of the Napoleonic Wars

41 Davies, B., 'Village into garrison: The militarized peasant communities of southern Muscovy', *RR*, vol. 52 (1992), pp. 481–501; Hellie, *Enserfment*, pp. 226–34; Keep, J. L. H., *Soldiers of the Tsar: Army and Society in Russia, 1462–1874* (Oxford, 1985), pp. 80–7.
42 Fuller, W. C., *Strategy and Power in Russia, 1600–1914* (New York, 1992), pp. 45–50; Keep, *Soldiers*, pp. 103–7, 144–7, 161, 325–8, 333–4, 374–8.
43 Keep, *Soldiers*, pp. 118–29, 345; Leonard, *Reform*, pp. 40–72; Curtiss, J. S., *The Russian Army under Nicholas I* (Durham, NC, 1965), pp. 176–90, 233.

in 1812–14 and during the Crimean War in 1853–56. This estimate probably understates the real impact of conscription on the Russian peasantry. The populations of the non-Russian borderlands got off relatively lightly (except for Jews), and settlers in some frontier areas enjoyed temporary immunities.[44]

Most of the men conscripted into the army were lost forever from the peasant estate. Until 1867 recruits (and their wives and any children born subsequently) ceased to be counted in tax censuses as members of their original social estates. After the end of lifetime service in 1793, retired soldiers were legally classified as 'raznochintsy' ('people of various ranks'). Some retired soldiers of peasant origin returned to the villages, but many had become so cut off from village life that they settled in towns. The impact of conscription on the peasant population was exacerbated by the fact that most recruits were healthy young men, who would otherwise have stayed at home, worked on the land, and fathered children who would have counted as peasants.[45] Conscription was a major cause of the decline in the size of the peasant estate relative to the total population between 1719 and 1857 (see Table 1.3). The continual loss of young men to the army had a substantial impact on the labour resources of peasant households and communities (see Chs 5 and 6).

In 1719 Peter the Great had introduced internal passports to keep track of people liable to conscription and, after 1724, the poll tax. Peasants and townspeople were not allowed to leave their places of residence, as recorded in the tax census, without a passport or other papers. Peasants were thus bound to land twice over: by the decrees culminating in the 1649 law code and by the internal passport system. The state backed up the second ban on movement by additional measures to find fugitives and, in vain, to prevent future illegal movement. Internal passports were also a source of revenue as people who needed permission to move had to pay for them. The passport system, like the poll tax and conscription, was thus another boundary between the mass of the tax-paying population, mostly peasants, and the privileged elites.[46]

Indirect taxes

The state also extracted revenue from the peasantry by indirect taxes, which were easier to collect and harder to avoid. The state established monopolies on certain goods, in particular salt and vodka, which enabled it to make profits

44 On the numbers conscripted, see Beskrovnyi, L. G., *Russkaya armiya i flot v XVIII v.* (Moscow, 1973), pp. 26–9, 33–7, 294–7; *id.*, *Russkaya armiya i flot v XIX v.* (Moscow, 1958), pp. 71–9, 86. I have assumed that 95% of recruits were peasants. For 1782–94, I have estimated that 74% of recruits came from 'Russia' (the territory of the first poll tax census and the Don) and, after 1795, 62%. (These were the proportions of the total population liable to conscription who lived in 'Russia'.) See also Pintner, W. M., 'The burden of defense in imperial Russia, 1725–1914', *RR*, vol. 43 (1984), pp. 231–59.
45 See Keep, *Soldiers*, pp. 148, 327, 330; Wirtschafter, *From Serf*, pp. 3–25, 32–40, 156 n. 45, 164 n. 3; *id.*, 'Social misfits: Veterans and soldiers' families in servile Russia', *Journal of Military History*, vol. 59 (1995), pp. 215–36. See also Ch. 1.
46 See Matthews, M., *The Passport Society: Controlling Movement in Russia and the USSR* (Boulder, CO, 1993), pp. 1–8; Kozlova, N. V., *Pobegi krest'yan v Rossii v pervoi treti XVIII v.* (Moscow, 1983), pp. 128–40.

through the sale of these goods at artificially high prices. In practice, the state sold the right to trade in these goods in a franchise system known as 'tax farming'. The tax farmers, usually merchants and nobles, paid a fixed sum to the treasury, and kept the rest of their income as profits. Since salt and vodka were goods of mass consumption, tax farming was primarily a system for exploiting the peasantry. Some outlying regions, in particular the 'privileged' western borderlands and cossack territories, were exempt from the monopolies.

The state set up the monopoly of the wholesale trade in salt in 1705. It was especially burdensome for peasants as salt was a necessity: it was the main preservative for meat and vegetables, and an essential dietary supplement. In the mid-eighteenth century the salt monopoly generated about 10 per cent of state income. At the same time average peasant spending on salt made up around 10 per cent of their total expenditure, and was between 15 and 45 per cent of their poll tax payments. In 1762 Catherine the Great ordered the first of a series of reductions in salt prices. Thereafter, the importance of salt as a source of state revenue and a burden on the peasantry fell. Free trade in salt was authorised in 1812, but it was still subject to excise duties.

A more important source of state revenue, which predated and outlived the salt monopoly, was the monopoly in the Russian provinces of the empire of the production and sale of distilled alcoholic drinks, including vodka. For much of the period, the right to distil spirits was restricted to nobles, who sold most of their output to the state for a profit. The state then sold the spirits, and the right to retail trade, in 'tax farms', mostly to merchants. The system was reformed and vodka prices raised in the mid-eighteenth century. The drink tax farms were a heavy burden on peasants, because vodka was central to most of the rituals of their social and cultural lives. In the peasants' 'traditional drinking culture', it would have been inconceivable to celebrate the end of the harvest, a wedding or a religious holiday without the communal consumption of copious quantities of hard liquor. Between the mid-eighteenth century and 1863, when drink tax farms were abolished, they contributed an average of 33 per cent of state revenue. In the late eighteenth century, peasants spent an average of 2 paper roubles a year on vodka, around twice their poll tax payments. Peasants were well aware that the state monopoly on vodka was exploitation, and they reviled tavern keepers as robbers. David Christian concluded: 'It was the state's thirst for revenue as much as the peasants' thirst for forgetfulness that made vodka so important at both the national and local levels of Russian life.'[47]

Other obligations

Peasants also had obligations to the state in kind and labour. A particularly onerous duty was providing quarters for the army. From 1721 until well into

47 See Christian, D., *'Living Water': Vodka and Russian Society on the Eve of Emancipation* (Oxford, 1990), pp. 1–251; Smith, R. E. F. and Christian, D., *Bread and Salt: A Social and Economic History of Food and Drink in Russia* (Cambridge, 1984), pp. 27, 72, 78–92, 133–49, 186–7, 217–23, 290–335 (quotation, pp. 300–1). See also LeDonne, *Absolutism*, pp. 263–7; Kahan, *Plow*, pp. 322–8, 347.

the nineteenth century, much of the Russian army was billed in peasants' houses for several months a year.[48] The obligation to provide billets for soldiers was taken further in Novgorod province and Ukraine in the early nineteenth century. In order to reduce the cost of maintaining the massive standing army in peacetime, regiments were sent to live permanently in some state peasant villages, which were designated as 'military settlements'. Although the peasants in the settlements were freed from the poll tax and, initially, conscription, they were placed under military discipline. The settlements were plagued with problems and erupted in revolt in 1831. They were reorganised, but lasted until the 1850s.[49]

Peasants also had obligations to the local authorities. They were required to construct and maintain roads and bridges, and to supply horses and carts to transport officials, the mail, troops and prisoners. These obligations were greatest for peasants who lived along major communication routes, for example the road from Moscow to St Petersburg, and for peasants living near supply routes to the front in wartime. Landowners tried to ensure that state peasants, not their own peasants, bore the brunt of these obligations.[50]

Village communes levied dues on peasant households to cover their costs, including the expense of administering the villages on behalf of their landowners (see Ch. 6). Peasants were also obliged to maintain their parish churches and clergy. Many communes provided parish clergy with land and helped them farm it. Peasants had to pay fees to priests for celebrating the rites that marked important family events, especially christenings, marriages and funerals. To the extent that peasants were paying for rites that were required by the Orthodox Church, and that they were subsidising priests who also had secular duties imposed on them by the authorities, the peasants' obligations to their parish churches and clergy can be seen as exploitation. In any case, there was constant friction between peasants and clergy over fees.[51]

* * *

All these obligations to the central and local authorities, village communes and parish clergy amounted to a substantial burden on the peasantry, and one which may have been increasing in the first half of the nineteenth century. In the Central Non-Black Earth region in this period, seigniorial peasants' total state and communal obligations were around half to two-thirds of their dues to their landowners.[52]

* * *

48 Keep, *Soldiers*, pp. 133–5; Wirtschafter, *From Serf*, pp. 81–5.
49 See Keep, *Soldiers*, pp. 275–307.
50 Neupokoev, *Gosudarstvennye*, pp. 164–92; Druzhinin, *Gosudarstvennye*, vol. 1, pp. 338–41.
51 See Freeze, *Russian Levites*, pp. 125–36; id., *The Parish Clergy in Nineteenth Century Russia* (Princeton, NJ, 1983), pp. 51–101.
52 Fedorov, *Pomeshchich'i*, p. 249.

Between the mid-seventeenth and mid-nineteenth centuries, including obligations to their landowners and the state, seigniorial peasants had higher obligations than other categories of peasants. The amounts extracted from seigniorial peasants by landowners and the state respectively changed over time. During the seventeenth century and the reign of Peter the Great, the state extracted more from them than did their landowners. The increase in direct taxation at the height of the Great Northern War severely restricted the amounts of money and labour landowners could get from their peasants. This is probably the main reason for the fall in seigniorial peasants' *obrok* in Peter's reign. After 1725 the situation was reversed. Landowners increased their demands for *obrok* and *barshchina* more quickly than the state raised the poll tax. In real terms, the burden of the poll tax fell, while that of seigniorial *obrok* rose. In the first half of the nineteenth century, the poll tax was around 1 silver rouble per male soul, while average rates of seigniorial *obrok* approached 10 silver roubles. The state partly made up the loss of revenue from seigniorial peasants by increasing its demands on the state peasants. Their *obrok* also increased faster than the poll tax, but not as quickly as seigniorial peasants' dues. The state also compensated for the decline in the share of seigniorial peasants' production it received through direct taxes by increasing revenue from indirect taxes.

Exploitation of the peasantry was highest in the central regions of Russia, which were the heartland of serfdom and state control. Exploitation by landowners and the state was less severe in more outlying regions, especially in frontier areas that were being settled. The obligations demanded from peasants in the borderlands grew with the expansion of seigniorial landownership, serfdom and state authority from the centre. By the nineteenth century, borderlands where peasants enjoyed lighter obligations were a very long way from the heartland of the state and peasant settlement. The levels of exploitation in the old borderlands, moreover, were similar to those in the central regions.

It is difficult to make general conclusions about trends in the overall levels of exploitation of the Russian peasantry as a whole. In the short and medium terms, the levels of obligations rose and fell in response to the needs of the ruling and landowning elites. The most important factor was warfare. The twin burdens of taxes and conscripts were especially high during Russia's regular, long and costly wars, but lower in peacetime. From the peasants' point of view, obligations were not necessarily most burdensome when they were highest, but when they were most out of proportion with their production and incomes. Fairly light obligations were very onerous in years of dearth, while heavy demands may not have threatened subsistence in years of plenty.

In the long term, levels of obligations that landowners and the state demanded, and the proportion they extracted from what peasants produced and earned, grew over the sixteenth, seventeenth and first half of the eighteenth centuries. This was a direct result of the development of serfdom and the growing power of the state. It is possible that the overall level of exploitation of the peasantry reached a plateau in the reign of Peter the Great and the middle decades of the eighteenth century. This was the period when the Russian Empire consolidated its position as a major European power, with its large and expensive armed forces, which were manned and paid for mostly by the peasants. It is often argued that exploitation of the seigniorial peasantry peaked in Catherine the Great's reign. From the late eighteenth to the mid-nineteenth centuries, the growth in exploitation as a proportion of the peasantry's production may have levelled off, albeit at a high level. The extent by which the amounts extracted increased after the mid-eighteenth century was at least partly compensated for by growth and development in the peasant economy (see Ch. 4). In the last century of serfdom, it can tentatively be concluded that Russian peasants were compelled to hand over to the ruling and landowning elites around half of the product of their labour.[53]

SEIGNIORIAL AND STATE 'OBLIGATIONS' TO PEASANTS (TO 1860s)

Most historians have focused on Russian peasants' obligations to the state and landowners. As in other pre-industrial societies, however, the relationship between peasants and the landowning and ruling elites was reciprocal. Peasants had obligations to elites, but elites made some efforts to ensure that they were able to meet the burdens imposed on them, and to 'protect' them from threats to their subsistence. To argue that landowners and the state had 'obligations' to peasants in Russia is not the same as arguing that the relationship between them was equal, nor that what peasants received was of equivalent value to what they were compelled to hand over. They were not. The balance of exchange was weighted heavily in favour of the elites. But out of self-interest, if not respect for the few laws that protected peasants' rights or humanitarian concern, many landowners and officials did not set out to extract as much as they could without regard for the impact they were having on the peasantry's productive capacity and subsistence. Elites also offered 'protection' in response to demands made by the peasants who depended on them.[54]

The Russian state did not introduce major reforms of the means by which peasants were exploited until the mid-nineteenth century, but began to take an active interest in 'protecting' peasants' welfare at least a century and a half

---

53 See Blum, *Lord and Peasant*, pp. 228–30; Smith, *Peasant Farming*, pp. 232–8; Tikhonov, *Pomeshchich'i*, pp. 301–4; Kahan, *Plow*, pp. 343–7; Mironov, 'Consequences', pp. 467–72. In contrast to my conclusion, Blum suggested that the peasantry's total burden 'may ... have decreased in the last decades of serfdom' (*Lord and Peasant*, p. 471), while Koval'chenko asserted that it rose (*Russkoe*, pp. 296–7). Shapiro estimated that total peasant obligations in the 1590s averaged around half the total product of their labour (*Russkoe krest'yanstvo*, p. 107), but expenditure on defence was very high at this time: Dunning, 'Does', pp. 578–9, 588. For European comparisons, see Blum, J., *The End of the Old Order in Rural Europe* (Princeton, NJ, 1978), pp. 73–9.
54 See Moon, 'Reassessing', pp. 500–6. See also Thompson, E. P., 'The moral economy of the English crowd in the eighteenth century', in *id.*, *Customs in Common* (London, 1991), pp. 185–258; Scott, J. C., *The Moral Economy of the Peasant: Rebellion and Subsistence in South East Asia* (New Haven, CT, and London, 1976), esp. pp. 7, 157–92. See also Ch. 7.

earlier. Peter the Great's introduction of conscription and the poll tax increased the state's concern for its peasants. In 1724, despite the impact of his demands on the peasantry, Peter wrote: 'The husbandmen are the arteries of the state which is nourished by them as the body is fed by the arteries. For this reason they must be cared for and not burdened to excess but rather protected against all assault and damage.'[55] Similar concerns were articulated by several eighteenth-century government advisers and officials. For example, in the 1750s, Count Peter Shuvalov noted that the 'basic resource' in Russia was the poll-tax-paying population, because it provided recruits for the army, the material means to support the armed services, the government, nobility and clergy, and the labour force for industry, agriculture and transport. Thus, he argued, the 'well-being of this basic resource . . . ought to be the center of attention for government policy, and anything that would lead to its diminution . . . ought to be avoided.'[56] At around the same time, some 'enlightened' landowners started to redefine their relationship with their peasants 'in moral as well as economic terms'. Their main motive, like that of the state, was to secure their incomes from their estates.[57]

Whatever their motives, tsars, officials and landowners presented their concern for the welfare of the peasantry in the language of paternalism. Most tsars' accession and coronation proclamations, which were read out all over Russia, were conscious attempts to create and support an image of the benevolent, paternal '*batyushka*' ('little father') tsar, who cared for his subjects like his children. The empresses of the eighteenth century used maternal imagery. Some landowners, especially absentee magnates, strove to create a similar image for themselves.[58]

The ruling and landowning elites 'protected' the welfare of the Russian peasantry in a number of ways, the most important being granting them allotments of land, offering some relief in years of famine or hardship, and taking some measures against excessive exploitation and cruel treatment.

Land allotments

The state and most landowners made sure that the majority of peasants under their jurisdiction had access to land to farm to enable them to meet their

55 Quoted in Bartlett, R. P., 'Defences of serfdom in eighteenth-century Russia', in Di Salvo, M. and Hughes, L. (eds), *A Window on Russia* (Rome, 1996), p. 67.
56 Kahan, *Plow*, pp. 327, 377 n. 6. See also Shmidt, S. O., 'Proekt P. I. Shuvalova 1754 g. "O raznykh gosudarstvennoi pol'zy sposobakh"', *IA* (1962), no. 6, pp. 100–18; Smith and Christian, *Bread*, pp. 194–5, 227.
57 Melton, E., 'Enlightened seigniorialism and its dilemmas in serf Russia, 1750–1830', *JMH*, vol. 62 (1990), pp. 679, 690, 708.
58 See Cherniavsky, M., *Tsar and People: Studies in Russian Myths* (New Haven, CT, 1961), pp. 44–99; Wortman, R., *Scenarios of Power: Myth and Ceremony in Russian Monarchy*, vol. 1 (Princeton, NJ, 1995), pp. 62–4, 114–16, 217, 229–31, 305, 318; Roosevelt, P., *Life on the Russian Country Estate* (New Haven, CT, and London, 1995), pp. 173–91, 233–42. In contrast, Kolchin argued that paternalism was common in the *ante bellum* American south, but largely absent in servile Russia: *Unfree Labor*, pp. 58–9, 144, 148–9.

obligations and to support themselves. Indeed, landowners granted peasants land in return for their obligations. Russian peasants may have been banned from moving by decrees of 1592/93, 1649 and 1719–24 but, as Hoch has argued, if peasants' main aim was to ensure their subsistence, then 'being tied to the land is a much undervalued notion; for in Russia . . . being a peasant (with few exceptions) implied an entitlement to land'.[59]

The evidence bears this out. The decrees binding peasants to the land were followed by grants of land to rural inhabitants who had previously had access to little or no land. Until the late seventeenth century, there were substantial numbers of landless labourers (*bobyli*), who owed only light obligations to their landowners. Over the late seventeenth and early eighteenth centuries, however, they largely disappeared as landowners and village communes allotted them shares of the village arable land. They were motivated by the intention of making them liable to shares of the villages' obligations. An allotment of land was a burden as well as a boon: peasants who held land had obligations in return. With the growth in exploitation by landowners and the state, some peasants tried to reduce their burden by giving up part of their land. Landowners saw the advantage in ensuring that all able-bodied inhabitants of their estates had full allotments of land and, in return, full shares of the obligations. Communes also realised the advantage of sharing out the land and obligations between all their members.[60]

The 'few exceptions' to the entitlement of peasants to land were partly a result of rights accrued by landowners after 1649. They acquired the rights to convert landed peasants to domestic serfs and to buy and sell peasants without land. Moreover, the state deprived some peasants of land by sending them to work on construction projects and in mines and factories (see above). Overall, however, the numbers who lost their land in these ways were very small.

The state tried to restrict the exceptions. Starting with Peter the Great, tsars regularly, if not very successfully, tried to limit or end the sale of peasants separately from the land. State instructions for the General Land Survey in the mid-eighteenth century laid down, and protected, norms for state peasants' land holdings. In 1762, when Peter III secularised the church's land and peasants, he granted the former church peasants the titles to their land. They lost them in 1764, however, when Catherine the Great transferred full ownership to the state, and granted the peasants only use rights in return for their dues. It was not until 1801 that Russian state and appanage peasants were permitted in law to have full rights of land ownership. The reforms of the appanage and state peasants in the 1820s–40s included provisions to try to ensure peasants had sufficient land. Some noble landowners, moreover, instructed their estate managers to allocate adequate amounts of land to peasants. Nevertheless, in

59 Hoch, S., 'The serf economy and the social order in Russia', in Bush, *Serfdom and Slavery*, p. 312.
60 See Shapiro, A. L., 'Perekhod ot povytnoi k povechnoi sisteme oblozheniya krest'yan vladel'cheskimi povinnostyami', *EAIVE 1960 g.* (Kiev, 1962), pp. 207–17. See also Blum, *Lord and Peasant*, pp. 240–2; and Chs 6 and 8.

1814 and 1827, tsars Alexander I (1801–25) and Nicholas I (1825–55) saw fit to issue decrees stating that landowners were not permitted to sell or mortgage land on their estates if it would mean that their peasants were left with less than 4.5 *desyatiny* (about 12 acres) per soul. In 1848, seigniorial peasants were allowed to own land in their own right.[61]

There was a big difference between policy or pious wishes by rulers, officials or landowners and the actual situation in the villages. The gap between them, however, does not seem to have been as great as might have been expected.

In spite of wide variations in soil fertility, especially between non-black earth and black earth regions, in the crops peasants grew, the techniques they employed and the yields they attained, it is possible to produce general figures on how much land peasants needed to subsist. R. E. F. Smith estimated that an average household of five to six peasants in the forest-heartland in the period before the mid-seventeenth century had between 9 and 15 *desyatiny* of arable and meadow land. Assuming that meadow comprised one-third of the holding, each household had 6–10 *desyatiny* of arable, roughly 2–3 *desyatiny* per male peasant. Given prevailing yields and access to forest, this was sufficient to support a family and the draught animals they needed to cultivate the land. Smith's estimates are similar to those for later periods that peasants needed 2.5 *desyatiny* of arable per male soul in non-black earth regions and 2 *desyatiny* in black earth regions.[62]

In most of Russia in the sixteenth and seventeenth centuries, there was an abundance of land and a shortage of labour. At the same time, the amount of land available for peasants to farm was increasing with the expansion of the Russian state and peasant settlement of the steppes (see Ch. 2). It is likely, therefore, that most peasant households had enough land in this period, and that the size of their allotments was limited more by the amount they could cultivate than by restrictions by landowners and the state. It was only in the eighteenth century that population growth began to put pressure on the land, leading to slight falls in average allotment sizes, especially in the central regions. From data in the General Land Survey of the late eighteenth century, Semevskii estimated that the average allotment of arable land for each male peasant was between 2.5 and 3.8 *desyatiny* in the non-black earth provinces, and between 3.5 and 4.4 *desyatiny* in the black earth provinces (where population densities were lower). His estimates overstated the size of peasants' allotments, however, because they included the total areas of land available, rather than the plots peasants actually farmed. Nevertheless, Kahan concluded that, in the eighteenth century: 'There was no scarcity of land in general or even within particular regions.'[63]

61 Blum, *Lord and Peasant*, pp. 424–8, 532, 539; Semevskii, V. I., *Krest'yanskii vopros v Rossii v XVIII i pervoi polovine XIX v.*, 2 vols (St Petersburg, 1888), vol. 1, p. 247; vol. 2, pp. 533, 566–70; Bartlett, 'Defences', p. 68; Leonard, *Reform*, p. 82.
62 Smith, *Peasant Farming*, pp. 84–94. See also Hoch, *Serfdom*, pp. 23–4; Ignatovich, *Pomeshchich'i*, pp. 100–2; Koval'chenko, *Russkoe*, pp. 263–4; Chayanov, *Theory*, pp. 159–66.
63 Semevskii, *Krest'yane*, vol. 1, pp. 20–32; Kahan, *Plow*, p. 45. See also Blum, *Lord and Peasant*, pp. 527–9; Rubinshtein, *Sel'skoe*, pp. 205–37.

Between the late eighteenth and mid-nineteenth centuries, there is little doubt that there was a decline in the average amounts of arable land available to peasants to cultivate to support themselves. The growing size of the population put increasing pressure on the land. This was most marked in the more densely populated central regions. Many historians, especially Soviet specialists, went to great lengths to try to demonstrate that a large part of the fall in the average size of seigniorial peasants' allotments of arable land in the last decades of serfdom was due to landowners taking land away from them to expand their demesnes, which they cultivated using increased labour obligations. Koval'chenko compared data on peasant land allotments from the General Land Survey of the late eighteenth century with figures from the 'Descriptions of Seigniorial Estates' of 1858–59, which he adjusted slightly to allow for their downward bias. He concluded that there had been an overall fall in this period in the amount of land per capita among seigniorial peasants who performed labour services of 9–17 per cent in the Central Non-Black Earth region and 16–24 per cent in the Central Black Earth region.

These findings have been challenged by scholars who have relied on more accurate data from the 'Regulatory Charters' produced just after 1861. Fedorov estimated that the trend over the first half of the nineteenth century towards smaller average land allotments among seigniorial peasants who performed labour services in the Central Non-Black Earth region was less marked than in other regions. He stated that cases of landowners taking land from their peasants were not widespread, since it was not in their interests to undermine the peasant economy. Litvak found significant decreases in the average allotments of *barshchina* peasants in the Central Black Earth region between the late eighteenth and mid-nineteenth centuries. Since the decreases were less than the increases in population, however, he concluded that there could not have been widespread landowner incursions on peasant land.[64]

Historians have also disagreed whether seigniorial peasants who were obliged to work on their landowners' demesne had sufficient arable land to ensure their subsistence on the eve of the end of serfdom. Koval'chenko claimed that seigniorial peasants' allotments of arable land were declining towards subsistence levels in the central regions by the 1850s. He reckoned that most *barshchina* peasants on larger estates had between 2.1 and 2.5 *desyatiny* of arable land per male soul, but that over 10 per cent had under 1.5 *desyatiny*, less than they needed to support themselves. Again, Koval'chenko's conclusions and sources have been disputed. Fedorov discovered that, compared with the 'Charters', the 'Descriptions' understated the size of peasants' arable land allotments by between 23 and 77 per cent in the Central Non-Black Earth region. Litvak calculated that the average allotment of arable among peasants serving *barshchina* in the Central Black Earth region was 3 *desyatiny* per male soul. No *barshchina* peasants had under 2 *desyatiny* per male soul; 62 per cent had between 2 and

64 Compare Koval'chenko, *Russkoe*, pp. 259–74, and Fedorov, *Pomeshchich'i*, pp. 27–9, 50; Litvak, *Russkaya*, pp. 73–5, 150–1. See also Blum, *Lord and Peasant*, pp. 224–5, 447; Ignatovich, *Pomeshchich'i*, pp. 94–106. On the sources, see above, pp. 72, 75–6.

3 *desyatiny*; and 38 per cent had over 3 *desyatiny*. Records of magnates' estates support the higher figures for the Central Black Earth region.[65]

The reason for concentrating on the land allotments of seigniorial peasants who served labour obligations and who lived in the central regions in the last few decades of serfdom is that, of all the main groups of Russian peasants in the period before the 1860s (apart from the 'exceptions' mentioned above), this group had the smallest allotments of land. Seigniorial peasants who paid *obrok* generally had larger amounts of land.[66] So did state and appanage peasants. Moreover, during the reforms of the 1820s–40s, some state and appanage peasants who had insufficient land were granted more.[67] Many peasants of all categories who lived in less densely populated 'old' borderlands, including seigniorial peasants in the south-east of the Central Black Earth region in the early nineteenth century, had land allotments that were more than adequate for their needs.[68] Most peasants in more outlying regions, as well as all peasants throughout Russia in the earlier part of the period, also had sufficient land.

All figures on the sizes of land allotments need to be treated with caution. In addition to the problems of the reliability and comparability of the data, figures for average allotments conceal variations between villages, and between households within villages. Moreover, the raw data do not make sufficient allowance for variations in soil fertility, or differences and changes in land use. In the earlier part of the period under consideration and in the borderlands, when and where land was plentiful, peasants used methods of cultivation that required larger areas than the more intensive systems used in the central regions from the sixteenth and seventeenth centuries. Some peasants, moreover, used part of their land for intensive production of cash crops, for example flax and hemp. Furthermore, most of the figures discussed in this section are for arable land only. Peasants also needed access to meadows, pastures, woodland and water. And farming was not peasants' sole means of support; some needed little land as they engaged mainly in handicrafts, trade and wage labour.[69]

From the late seventeenth and early eighteenth centuries until the reforms of the 1860s, the vast majority of Russian peasants had access to land to cultivate, and only a few had insufficient to support themselves. This was in contrast to many other parts of Europe, including Ukraine, where large numbers of rural inhabitants were landless labourers and smallholders who, to a large extent, depended for their livelihoods on the uncertainty of finding employment on another person's land or in someone else's household.[70]

---

65 Compare Koval'chenko, *Russkoe*, pp. 261–71, and Fedorov, *Pomeshchich'i*, pp. 25–6; Litvak, *Russkaya*, pp. 70–3, 87, 142–4; Hoch, *Serfdom*, pp. 23–8.
66 Litvak, *Russkaya*, pp. 70–3, 87.
67 Adams, B. F., 'The reforms of P. D. Kiselev and the history of N. M. Druzhinin', *CASS*, vol. 19 (1985), pp. 35–8; Gorlanov, *Udel'nye*, pp. 42–7.
68 See Rubinshtein, *Sel'skoe*, pp. 209–10; Hoch, *Serfdom*, pp. 5–6, 27–8.
69 See Blum, *Lord and Peasant*, p. 528; Fedorov, *Pomeshchich'i*, pp. 25–6, 32–49; Rubinshtein, *Sel'skoe*, pp. 38–49. See also Chs 4 and 8.
70 See Blum, *End*, pp. 108–13; Rösener, *Peasantry*, pp. 121, 153–6, 181–3.

Famine relief

The Russian state and some landowners offered peasants a measure of protection against hunger if the harvest failed. They were acting out of self-interest, since starving peasants could not pay taxes, serve in the army, or perform seigniorial obligations, and were likely to flee famine-stricken areas, rise in revolt, or die, unless they were given aid. In the terrible famine years of 1601–03 tsar Boris Godunov gave out money to the starving. Thousands of hungry people, including peasants, descended on Moscow. Boris also tried to alleviate hardship by intervening in the market. He took action against 'hoarders' and 'speculators', and compelled people with supplies of grain and bread to sell them at fixed, moderate prices. The state authorities took similar action during other lean and famine years in the seventeenth and early eighteenth centuries. The poor harvests of 1721–24 forced Peter the Great to take measures, including creating reserve granaries, to provide for the hungry. The state postponed or reduced its demands for taxes and recruits in times of economic and demographic crises that threatened peasants' subsistence on many occasions in the eighteenth and nineteenth centuries, for example during the bad harvests of 1832–33 and 1848, Napoleon's invasion in 1812, and the Crimean War of 1853–56.[71]

Some landowners, especially rich magnates, were prepared to accept, or had little choice but to go along with, reduced or postponed payments of peasants' dues in time of hardship. When necessary, some landowners offered material assistance to their peasants with loans of grain for consumption or seed. In difficult times in the late sixteenth and early seventeenth centuries, it was not unknown for peasants to acquiesce in servile status by settling on the estates of wealthy landowners in the hope of 'protection' against the threat of famine. In the seventeenth century, even rapacious magnates such as Boris Morozov were flexible in their demands, and aided peasants on their estates who were in need. Over the following two centuries other landowners assisted their peasants in times of hardship.[72]

Not all landowners were willing or able to look after their peasants when harvests failed. As a result, the state took action to compel them. The principle that landowners had to assist their peasants in the event of harvest failure was established in law in 1734. The fact that it had to be repeated at regular intervals suggests that many did not obey it. A succession of bad harvests in the early nineteenth century forced the government to introduce new measures, in 1822 and 1834, which shared responsibility for famine relief between

71 Smith and Christian, *Bread*, pp. 109–11; Robbins, *Famine*, pp. 16–17; Semevskii, *Krest'yane*, vol. 1, pp. 263–6; Hoch and Augustine, 'Tax censuses', p. 423; Keep, *Soldiers*, pp. 374–5. On attitudes to charity, see Lindenmeyr, A., *Poverty is Not a Vice: Charity, Society, and the State in Imperial Russia* (Princeton, NJ, 1996).
72 Hellie, *Enserfment*, pp. 93–4, 106, 113, 132; Crummey, R. O., *Aristocrats and Servitors: The Boyar Elite in Russia 1613–1689* (Princeton, NJ, 1983), p. 126; Ryabkov, G. T., 'Tormozyashchee vliyanie krepostnogo prava na rasslonie krest'yan v Smolenskoi votchinakh Baryshnikovykh v pervoi polovine XIX v.', *EAIVE 1960 g.* (Kiev, 1962), p. 357. Some landowners assisted poor peasants at other times: *ibid.*

the state and landowners, and legislated for the obligatory creation of reserve granaries at provincial and village levels. The granaries were to be stocked by the peasants, who were thus obliged to hand over part of their harvest as insurance against future shortages. The central government was prepared to lend grain and money when local reserves were exhausted and, in more serious famines, to give out aid in the form of grants. The authorities sometimes set up public works in areas hit by harvest failures to make work and money available to the local population.[73]

The measures had some effect during the famine that hit large parts of central and southern Russia and Ukraine in 1833–34. On the estate of Petrovskoe in Tambov province, the estate manager doled out monthly grain rations from estate granaries to the peasants. The famine was one of the worst of the century, and the reserves were not sufficient to avert a crisis. Other estate owners were even less able to assist their peasants. Many landowners in neighbouring Voronezh province petitioned the state for assistance. In response, the state made substantial aid available to all stricken regions. By the end of 1833, almost 22 million paper roubles had been released from central and provincial government resources to alleviate the looming disaster.[74]

Thus, the Russian state was prepared to intervene in the economy in times of dearth. State aid for peasants suffering from the consequences of harvest failures was limited more by lack of resources, and by suspicions that landowners were shirking their obligations, than by ideology. For example, in 1834, the Committee of Ministers rejected an appeal for more aid from landowner S. A. Goryainov of Voronezh province on the grounds that it did not 'believe that [he] . . . had exhausted all means of feeding the peasants', and that the state was 'not able to feed an entire region'. It may be significant that the committee did not say it was not the state's *responsibility* to assist famine-stricken regions.[75]

The periodic willingness of the ruling and landowning elites in Russia to take active, if not always effective, measures to assist peasants in times of hardship was similar to the conduct of elites in other pre-industrial societies as diverse as imperial China and early modern England. E. P. Thompson characterised this as 'the paternalist model of the manufacturing and marketing process', and coined the term 'moral economy'. He contrasted it with the '*laissez faire*' attitude widespread in north-west Europe from the late eighteenth century and, later, in some of its overseas colonies, including French Indo-China and British India.[76]

---

73 Semevskii, *Krest'yane*, vol. 1, pp. 263–71; Kahan, *Russian*, pp. 115–22. On famine relief measures enacted as part of the appanage and state peasant reforms in the 1820s–40s, see Gorlanov, *Udel'nye*, pp. 22–3; Druzhinin, *Gosudarstvennye*, vol. 1, pp. 526–30, 541, 551; vol. 2, pp. 46–51, 223–33.
74 Hoch, *Serfdom*, pp. 52–6; Moon, *Russian Peasants*, pp. 41–4.
75 *RGIA*, *f.* 1287, *op.* 2, *d.* 151, *ll.* 181–3 *ob*; Seredonin, S. M., *Istoricheskii obzor deyatel'nosti Komiteta ministrov*, 3 vols (St Petersburg, 1902), vol. 2, pt 1, p. 186.
76 Thompson, 'Moral economy', p. 193. See also Arnold, *Famine*, pp. 99–115; Scott, *Moral Economy*, pp. 44–55; Hardiman, D., 'Usury, dearth and famine in western India', *P & P*, no. 152 (1996), pp. 113–16.

Protection against excessive exploitation and cruelty

The tsarist government also offered seigniorial peasants some protection against their landowners. In 1719 Peter the Great, and subsequently most of his successors, instructed landowners not to reduce their peasants to ruin by demanding unreasonable obligations or subjecting them to cruel treatment. In the eighteenth century, only exceptionally cruel landowners were taken to task. The best-known case is the infamous Darya Saltykova, who tortured and murdered dozens of her peasants in the 1750s and 60s. She was deprived of her noble status and confined to a convent. Other abuses, for example the sexual exploitation of female peasants by noblemen, were common and continued unchecked. The very tentative attempts by the state in the eighteenth century to prevent landowners from mistreating their serfs also have to be seen in the context of the simultaneous increases in seigniorial authority. Decrees of 1760 and 1765 allowed serf owners to banish recalcitrant and troublesome peasants to Siberia or to the Admiralty for hard labour, and a decree of 1767 repeated the ban in the 1649 law code on seigniorial peasants submitting collective complaints about their owners directly to the ruler.[77]

A step in the other direction was taken in 1797, when tsar Paul (1796–1801) issued a proclamation repeating the prohibition in the 1649 law code on landowners requiring their peasants to work on Sundays, and recommending that peasants should work three days a week on the landowners' land, and three days on their own land. This was later interpreted by a number of officials, in particular Michael Speranskii (and several historians), as a tentative attempt to regulate serfdom by restricting labour services. Some steps were taken to enforce it in the nineteenth century.[78]

The ultimate sanction for landowners who mistreated or made excessive demands on their peasants was for their estates to be taken away from them, and managed by members of their families or trustees appointed by the local nobility. The authorities became increasingly concerned that 'abuses of seigniorial authority' jeopardised peasants' ability to meet their obligations to the state, and might provoke serious unrest. The threat of taking landowners' estates into trusteeship (*opeka*) was given greater force by Catherine the Great in 1775, and the procedure was tightened up in the early nineteenth century. In the reign of Nicholas I, significant numbers of estates were taken into trusteeship. Between 1834 and 1845 alone, nearly 3,000 landowners were tried for mistreating their peasants, of whom 630 were convicted. The state's efforts to protect peasants (and its revenues) from the excesses of seigniorial power were

---

77 Semevskii, *Krest'yane*, vol. 1, pp. 213–28; Blum, *Lord and Peasant*, pp. 426–41. For a defence of Catherine the Great's policy on serfdom, see Madariaga, I. de, 'Catherine II and the serfs: A reconsideration of some problems', *SEER*, vol. 52 (1974), pp. 34–62.
78 Okun', S. B. and Paina, E. S., 'Ukaz ot 5 aprelya 1797 goda i ego evolyutsiya', in Nosov, N. E. (ed.), *Issledovaniya po otechestvennomu istochnikovedeniyu* (Leningrad, 1964), pp. 283–99. *Cf.* Blum, *Lord and Peasant*, p. 445.

not very successful, however, since their enforcement depended largely on the noble-dominated provincial authorities.[79]

The tentative measures taken by the Russian state to intervene in landowner–peasant relations in the Russian part of the empire can be contrasted with its greater willingness to act in the non-Russian western borderlands. Of the 630 landowners convicted for mistreating their peasants in 1834–45, 269 were from right-bank Ukraine. In 1847–48, moreover, the Russian authorities tried to regulate serfdom in the region by imposing on landowners written 'inventories', which fixed peasants' seigniorial obligations. The main reason for the state's actions was not concern for the peasants' welfare, however, but that some local landowners had taken part in the Polish revolt of 1830–31.[80] Elsewhere in eastern and central Europe, beyond the Russian Empire's western border, rulers also tried to restrict the exploitation of peasants by landowners. In the late nineteenth century, even the British rulers in India moved away from their earlier '*laissez faire*' policy to landlord–tenant relations and famine relief.[81]

The seriousness with which some state officials and peasants treated the elites' 'obligations' to peasants can be illustrated by an episode in 1819 on the estate of Zhukovo in Smolensk province. The owner (and future Decembrist rebel) Ivan Yakushkin offered to free his peasants and rent them land. The peasants rejected his plan. Addressing Yakushkin as '*batyushka*' ('little father'), they replied that they preferred to carry on 'in the old way', adding 'we are yours, but the land is ours'. The Minister of Internal Affairs, Victor Kochubei, also turned down the scheme, on the grounds that it might encourage other landowners to rid themselves of their obligations to their serfs.[82]

CATEGORIES OF PEASANTS

The Russian peasantry was divided into categories according to the owners of the land they lived on: seigniorial peasants (or serfs); state peasants; church peasants (until 1762–64); and the court/appanage peasants (see above). Actions by the state and landowners in establishing control over groups of peasants had led to the creation of the categories in the first place, and were largely responsible for subsequent changes in their sizes and geographical distribution prior to their merger following the reforms of the 1860s.

79 See Blum, *Lord and Peasant*, pp. 422–46; Ignatovich, *Pomeshchich'i*, pp. 35–6, 41–2, 45–7, 58–68; Mironov, B. N., 'Local government in Russia in the first half of the nineteenth century', *JGO*, vol. 42 (1994), p. 193.
80 See Beauvois, D., *Le Noble, le Serf et le Révizor: la Noblesse Polonaise entre le Tsarisme et les Masses Ukrainiennes (1831–1863)* (Montreux and Paris, 1985). See also, below, p. 108.
81 Blum, *End*, pp. 205–9; Hardiman, D., *Peasant Resistance in India, 1858–1914* (Delhi, 1993), pp. 20–3.
82 Yakushkin, I. D., *Zapiski*, 3rd edn (St Petersburg, 1905), pp. 26–35.

Numbers

State measures to increase the numbers of people liable to direct taxation in the late seventeenth and early eighteenth centuries led to the addition of two groups to the peasant estate as a whole, and to the seigniorial and state peasants in particular. Agricultural slaves who lived in their own houses became liable to the household tax in 1679. All slaves, including those who lived in their owners' households, were added to the poll tax census in 1723. By making slaves liable to taxation, the state extended its jurisdiction to them, thereby abolishing slavery in Russia. There was no longer any legal distinction between slaves and seigniorial peasants, and former slaves were merged with the seigniorial peasantry.[83] The military settlers who had served on the steppe frontier in the sixteenth and seventeenth centuries (see Ch. 2) ranked below the gentry cavalrymen in the Muscovite social hierarchy. Their status declined as their military significance fell after the consolidation of the frontier in the mid-seventeenth century. They were made liable to the household tax in 1679, and were counted in the poll tax census and made liable to the new tax in 1719. At the same time they were renamed 'single homesteaders' (*odnodvortsy*), and became part of the newly created 'state peasantry'. In spite of their demotion, they kept the right to own a few serfs and to buy and sell land. Although many aspired unsuccessfully to noble status, the *odnodvortsy* had ended up on the wrong side of the border between the tax-paying masses and the privileged elite.[84]

The categories of peasants continued to change in size between the 1720s and 1860s. Seigniorial and state peasants were the largest categories. At the time of the first poll tax census of 1719–21, they comprised 55.8 and 21.5 per cent respectively of the peasant estate in Russia, while church and court peasants made up 13.8 and 8.9 per cent. In 1719–21 seigniorial peasants outnumbered state peasants by over 2.5:1. By 1857–58, however, there were more state than seigniorial peasants, and the former made up over half the total peasant estate. The numbers of court/appanage peasants grew slowest of all, and declined as a proportion of the peasant estate to only 5.9 per cent in 1857 (see Tables 3.1–3.2).[85]

The main reason for these changes was that many peasants transferred to different categories. The numbers and percentages of court peasants declined steadily over the eighteenth century. Successive rulers gave out large tracts of court land and peasants to their favourites, high officials and generals. As a result, tens of thousands of court peasants were converted to seigniorial peasants. Catherine the Great was notorious for rewarding her supporters with

83 Anisimov, E. V., 'Changes in the social structure of Russian society at the end of the 17th and the beginning of the 18th century: The final page in the history of Russian slavery', *SSH* (Summer 1989), pp. 33–58; Hellie, *Slavery*, pp. 697–9.
84 Esper, T., 'The odnodvortsy and the Russian nobility', *SEER*, vol. 45 (1967), pp. 124–7; Pallot and Shaw, *Landscape*, pp. 33–54.
85 All figures are for the regions covered by the first poll tax census of 1719–21 and the Don Cossack territory (see Ch. 1).

TABLE 3.1

CATEGORIES OF PEASANTS, 1719–1857 (MALES, NUMBERS)[1]

Year	Serf ps[2]	State ps[3]	Church ps[4]	Court ps[5]	Total ps
1719	3,193,085	1,227,965	791,798	509,484	5,722,332
1744	3,781,097	1,588,559	898,471	429,283	6,697,410
1762	4,422,021	2,029,585	1,026,930	493,307	7,971,843
1782	5,132,366	3,921,101		601,454	9,654,921
1795	5,686,223	4,257,833		494,262	10,438,318
1811	6,276,781	5,116,044		575,591	11,968,416
1815	6,011,990	5,018,708		755,795	11,786,493
1833	6,719,251	6,349,107		876,466	13,944,824
1850	6,704,655	7,832,693		866,439	15,403,787
1857	6,691,555	8,357,007		942,834	15,991,396

[1] Russia (territory of first poll tax census + Don). For 1833 and 1857, no separate figures were available for the Don and Black Sea (Kuban) Cossack regions. The latter was assumed to be 20% of the total (as in 1815) and subtracted to produce an estimate for the numbers of peasants in the Don Cossack region, to include in the above figures. The Kuban region is outside the territory of Russia (see Ch. 1).
[2] Serf ps = *pomeshchich'i*.
[3] State ps = *gosudarstvennye*.
[4] Church ps = *tserkovnye* (1719–44), *ekonomicheskie* (1762–1811), part of state ps (1815+).
[5] Court ps = *dvortsovye* (1719–95), *udel'nye* (appange) (1795–1857).

Source: Kabuzan, *Izmeneniya*, pp. 59–181.

TABLE 3.2

CATEGORIES OF PEASANTS, 1719–1857 (PERCENTAGES)

Year	Serf ps	State ps	Church ps	Court ps	Total ps
1719	55.80%	21.46%	13.84%	8.90%	100.00%
1744	56.46%	23.72%	13.42%	6.41%	100.00%
1762	55.47%	25.46%	12.88%	6.19%	100.00%
1782	53.16%	40.61%		6.23%	100.00%
1795	54.47%	40.79%		4.74%	100.00%
1811	52.44%	42.75%		4.81%	100.00%
1815	51.01%	42.58%		6.41%	100.00%
1833	48.18%	45.53%		6.29%	100.00%
1850	43.53%	50.85%		5.62%	100.00%
1857	41.84%	52.26%		5.90%	100.00%

Notes and sources: See Table 3.1.

populated estates. She gave out around 60,000 court peasants of both sexes in the first decade of her reign, and even larger numbers after 1772. These later gifts had little impact on the numbers of court peasants in the Russian provinces of the empire, however, because most lived on land annexed during the partitions of Poland of 1772–95. Catherine's son Paul continued the custom of handing out large numbers of court/appanage and state peasants to his supporters. Alexander I and Nicholas I put a stop to the practice. This partly explains the growth in the numbers of appanage peasants in the first half of the nineteenth century. Moreover, Alexander I converted some state peasants into appanage peasants.[86] The numbers of court and state peasants had also been depleted in the seventeenth and eighteenth centuries by nobles seizing court and state lands, and registering the peasants on them as their serfs. Over 800,000 free men were registered as seigniorial peasants in this manner in the first two tax censuses of 1719 and 1744. Over a third of all noble land recorded and given legal recognition by the General Land Survey in the late eighteenth century had been expropriated from the state or court.[87]

The biggest single change came in 1762–64, when Peter III and Catherine the Great secularised the church's land and peasants, converting the million male church peasants and their families to state peasants. The two rulers had similar motives. Secularisation was part of the anti-clerical spirit of the Enlightenment, which influenced Peter and Catherine. Both were concerned to put an end to mismanagement and abuses on church property, which had led to peasant disorders. Most important was the need for money. In 1762 the treasury was desperately short of money following the Seven Years' War. Secularisation completed moves by the state to get control over the church's landed wealth that can be traced back to the end of the fifteenth century.[88]

The most well-known change in the sizes of the categories of peasants was the decline in the relative, and later absolute, size of the seigniorial peasantry and increase in the numbers of state peasants in the first half of the nineteenth century. Many Soviet historians argued that the seigniorial peasantry was 'dying out', because exploitation on noble estates was so great that it was causing lower birth rates and higher death rates. This view has been challenged. Many historians now accept that the fall in the numbers of seigniorial peasants was a result of transfers to other categories, in particular the state peasantry. Under the provisions of several laws in the first half of the nineteenth century, noble landowners freed tens of thousands of seigniorial peasants, who became state peasants (see below, pp. 108–9). The departments in charge of the state and appanage peasants bought several noble estates, thus converting their inhabitants to state and appanage peasants. Further losses from the seigniorial peasantry were caused by landowners and courts exiling peasants to Siberia, and as a result of illegal migration by seigniorial peasants to the borderlands, where many registered as state peasants, townspeople or cossacks. The most important reason why the proportion of seigniorial peasants fell, while that of state peasants rose, was that the tens of thousands of seigniorial peasants who

86 Blum, *Lord and Peasant*, pp. 355–8; Kakhk, Yu. Yu., *Krest'yanstvo Evropy v period razlozheniya feodalizma* (Moscow, 1986), pp. 318–20; Madariaga, 'Catherine II', pp. 55–61; Vodarskii, Ya. E., *Dvoryanskoe zemlevladenie v Rossii v XVII-pervoi polovine XIX v.* (Moscow, 1988), pp. 228–9.
87 See Hellie, *Enserfment*, p. 253; Vodarskii, *Dvoryanskoe*, pp. 227, 236–7.
88 Leonard, *Reform*, pp. 73–89; Madariaga, *Russia*, pp. 113–19, 125–7.

were drafted into the army every year ceased to count as seigniorial peasants. Conscripts from the enserfed peasantry who survived military service, moreover, were not permitted to return to their previous servile status. Some, however, registered as state peasants. While conditions on nobles' estates may not have affected the numbers of seigniorial peasants, Bruce Adams has suggested that the grants of land made to some state peasants during Kiselev's reforms in the 1830s–40s may have contributed to growing prosperity, and higher rates of population growth, among the state peasantry.[89]

For a variety of reasons, therefore, the main trends in the changes in the proportions of the total peasant estate in each category were the growth in the relative size of the state peasantry throughout the eighteenth and first half of the nineteenth centuries, the disappearance of the church peasantry in 1762–64, and the gradual decline in the proportion of seigniorial peasants from around 1800.

Regional distribution

The four main categories of peasants were distributed in different proportions between the regions of Russia. The distribution reflected the process of enserfment, the geographical origins of the peasants who made up the categories, and the settlement of the expanding state.[90]

Seigniorial peasants made up the majority of the peasantry in the Central Non-Black Earth, Central Black Earth and North-western regions throughout the period between the mid-seventeenth century and 1861. Until the early nineteenth century, moreover, over 80 per cent of all Russian seigniorial peasants lived in these three central regions. Enserfed peasants were concentrated in central Russia because this was where the lands the Muscovite tsars had given out to the gentry cavalrymen, and many boyars' estates, had been located. It was to these lands that peasants had been bound by the decrees which had enserfed a large part of the Russian peasantry. As the steppe frontier moved further south and east the state gave out more land to the gentry in these newly acquired regions. The peasants who lived, or settled, on these lands became seigniorial peasants. In this way, serfdom spread deeper into the Central Black Earth and Mid-Volga regions from the end of the sixteenth century and, later, to the open steppe regions. There were very few seigniorial peasants in the northern regions. The tsars did not give out much land to gentry cavalrymen in these regions because of the distance from the usual theatres of military action (the western border and the steppe frontier). The absence of seigniorial peasants in Siberia can also be explained in this way. The introduction

89 See Hoch and Augustine, 'Tax censuses'; Ryndzyunskii, P. G., 'K izucheniyu dinamiki chislennosti krepostnogo naseleniya v doreformennoi Rossii', *IS* (1983), no. 1, pp. 209–12; Ryanskii, L. M., 'Dvizhenie krepostnogo naselenie v period krizisa feodalisma v rossii', *IS* (1991), no. 2, pp. 142–50; Adams, 'Reforms', pp. 37–8. *Cf.* Kabuzan, 'Krepostnoe', pp. 67–85.
90 For an overview, see Semevskii, *Krest'yane*, vol. 1, pp. iii–vii.

TABLE 3.3

REGIONAL DISTRIBUTION OF PEASANTRY BY CATEGORY, 1678-1857 (MALES, NUMBERS)

	Category	1678[3]	1719	1762	1811	1857
Forest-heartland						
Central NBE	Serf	1,160,000	1,627,015	1,974,977	2,534,565	2,535,125
	State	0	6,080	59,761	704,822	1,108,740
	Church[1]	371,000	452,373	528,012		
	Court[2]	321,000	260,709	213,301	213,940	194,987
	All	1,852,000	2,346,177	2,776,051	3,453,327	3,838,852
North-western	Serf	170,000	254,253	397,903	521,240	506,227
	State	0	5,920	5,934	226,100	257,809
	Church[1]	76,000	92,656	144,321		
	Court[2]	25,000	65,842	49,894	60,458	124,058
	All	271,000	418,671	598,052	807,798	888,094
Northern	Serf	107,000	68,818	83,285	99,853	108,359
	State	273,000	161,612	216,899	335,850	453,619
	Church[1]	74,000	49,581	63,110		
	Court[2]	24,000	45,712	33,219	48,312	63,588
	All	478,000	325,723	396,513	484,015	625,566
North Urals	Serf		46,433	98,488	242,931	205,088
	State		201,185	396,635	710,548	1,413,181
	Church[1]		16,096	63,962		
	Court[2]		2,096	29,695	55,293	98,969
	All		265,810	588,780	1,008,772	1,717,238
Steppes						
Central BE	Serf	529,000	893,133	1,340,501	1,929,603	2,117,852
	State	158,000	342,579	463,223	1,295,993	2,005,224
	Church[1]	71,000	119,611	123,344		
	Court[2]	92,000	91,581	102,709	78,095	36,856
	All	850,000	1,446,904	2,029,777	3,303,691	4,159,932
Mid-Volga	Serf	98,000	297,352	361,986	549,386	628,037
	State	51,000	336,414	392,530	686,960	836,160
	Church[1]	28,000	53,480	60,312		
	Court[2]	44,000	40,022	46,992	78,356	338,285
	All	221,000	727,268	861,820	1,314,702	1,802,482
L. Volga & Don	Serf		1,195	127,862	337,697	469,639
	State		489	55,883	240,280	667,750
	Church[1]		0	25,940		
	Court[2]		0	12,068	23,632	45,979
	All		1,684	221,753	601,609	1,183,368
South Urals	Serf		789	34,932	58,941	119,534
	State		11,644	99,043	257,888	502,128
	Church[1]		226	3,638		
	Court[2]		3,522	5,429	17,505	40,112
	All		16,181	143,042	334,334	661,774

TABLE 3.3 *cont'd*

	Category	1678[3]	1719	1762	1811	1857
Siberia	Serf	0	4,097	2,087	2,765	1,694
	State	45,000	162,042	339,672	597,603	1,112,396
	Church[1]	4,000	7,775	14,291		
	Court[2]	0	0	0	0	0
	All	49,000	173,914	356,050	600,368	1,114,090
Totals[4]		3,721,000	5,722,332	7,971,838	11,908,616	15,991,396

[1] Church peasants were part of state peasantry after 1762–64.
[2] Court peasants were known as appanage peasants after 1797.
[3] Figures for 1678 not strictly comparable with those for 1719; figures for Northern and North Urals regions combined in 1678.
[4] For total numbers of peasants in each category in given years, see Table 3.1.

Sources: Vodarskii, *Naselenie Rossii v kontse XVII*, p. 151; Kabuzan, *Izmeneniya*, pp. 59–175.

of restrictions on peasant movement in some border regions, for example the Don Cossack territory, north Caucasus and southern Ukraine in 1796, enabled landowners to enserf some formerly free peasants. However, noble estates inhabited by seigniorial peasants never became as widespread in these outlying areas. It is also notable that seigniorial land and peasants were most widespread in central regions, where conditions were best suited to agriculture, rather than the less fertile north and Siberia.[91] (See Tables 3.3–3.5.)

State peasants made up the majority of the peasant population of the Northern, Northern Urals, Mid-Volga and Southern Urals regions and Siberia throughout the period from the late seventeenth to the mid-nineteenth centuries. Until the 1760s, over 70 per cent of all Russian state peasants lived in these more outlying regions. By the 1850s, moreover, the proportion of state peasants had overtaken that of seigniorial peasants in the Lower Volga and Don region, and had almost caught up in the Central Black Earth region (see Tables 3.3–3.5). The concentration of state peasants on the periphery can be explained by the origins of this category. The state peasantry was formed on the introduction of the poll tax by the merger of several groups. The largest was the 'black-ploughing' peasants who lived in the northern regions on 'black' lands with no immediate landowner that ultimately belonged to the state. (The state had long since handed out 'black' lands in other regions to private landowners.) Most of the *odnodvortsy* lived along the old steppe frontier in the Central Black Earth and Mid-Volga regions. The overwhelming majority of peasant settlers in Siberia were classified as state peasants. The last main group that made up the state peasantry were non-Russian peoples of the Volga basin,

91 See Hellie, *Enserfment*, p. 27; Koretskii, V. I., *Formirovanie krepostnogo prava i pervaya krest'yanskaya voina v Rossii* (Moscow, 1975), pp. 83–116; Vodarskii, *Naselenie Rossii v kontse XVII*, p. 93; Druzhinina, E. I., *Yuzhnaya Ukraina v 1800–1825 gg.* (Moscow, 1970), pp. 84–5; Semevskii, *Krest'yanskii vopros*, vol. 2, pp. 544–7; Kolchin, *Unfree Labor*, pp. 27–30.

TABLE 3.4

	Category	1678[3]	1719	1762	1811	1857
Forest-heartland						
Central NBE	Serf	56.20%	50.95%	44.66%	40.38%	37.89%
	State	0.00%	0.50%	2.94%	13.94%	13.27%
	Church[1]	59.46%	57.13%	51.42%		
	Court[2]	63.44%	51.17%	43.24%	37.17%	20.68%
	All	49.77%	41.00%	34.82%	29.00%	24.01%
North-western	Serf	8.24%	7.96%	9.00%	8.30%	7.57%
	State	0.00%	0.48%	0.29%	4.47%	3.08%
	Church[1]	12.18%	11.70%	14.05%		
	Court[2]	4.94%	12.92%	10.11%	10.50%	13.16%
	All	7.28%	7.32%	7.50%	6.78%	5.55%
Northern	Serf	5.18%	2.16%	1.88%	1.59%	1.62%
	State	51.80%	13.16%	10.69%	6.64%	5.43%
	Church[1]	11.86%	6.26%	6.15%		
	Court[2]	4.74%	8.97%	6.73%	8.39%	6.74%
	All	12.85%	5.69%	4.97%	4.06%	3.91%
North Urals	Serf		1.45%	2.23%	3.87%	3.06%
	State		61.38%	19.54%	14.05%	16.91%
	Church[1]		2.03%	6.23%		
	Court[2]		0.41%	6.02%	9.61%	10.50%
	All		4.65%	7.39%	8.47%	10.74%
Steppes						
Central BE	Serf	25.63%	27.97%	30.31%	30.74%	31.65%
	State	29.98%	27.90%	22.82%	25.63%	23.99%
	Church[1]	11.38%	15.11%	12.01%		
	Court[2]	18.18%	17.98%	20.82%	13.57%	3.91%
	All	22.84%	25.29%	25.46%	27.74%	26.01%
Mid-Volga	Serf	4.75%	9.31%	8.19%	8.75%	9.39%
	State	9.68%	27.40%	19.34%	13.59%	10.01%
	Church[1]	4.49%	6.75%	5.87%		
	Court[2]	8.70%	7.86%	9.53%	13.61%	35.88%
	All	5.94%	12.71%	10.81%	11.04%	11.27%
L. Volga & Don	Serf		0.04%	2.89%	5.38%	7.02%
	State		0.04%	2.75%	4.75%	7.99%
	Church[1]		0.00%	2.53%		
	Court[2]		0.00%	2.45%	4.11%	4.88%
	All		0.03%	2.78%	5.05%	7.40%
South Urals	Serf		0.02%	0.79%	0.94%	1.79%
	State		0.95%	4.88%	5.10%	6.01%
	Church[1]		0.03%	0.35%		
	Court[2]		0.69%	1.10%	3.04%	4.25%
	All		0.28%	1.79%	2.81%	4.14%
Siberia	Serf	0.00%	0.13%	0.05%	0.04%	0.03%
	State	8.54%	13.20%	16.74%	11.82%	13.31%
	Church[1]	0.64%	0.98%	1.39%		
	Court[2]	0.00%	0.00%	0.00%	0.00%	0.00%
	All	1.32%	3.04%	4.47%	5.04%	6.97%
Totals[4]		100.00%	100.01%	99.99%	99.99%	100.00%

Notes and sources: See Table 3.3.

TABLE 3.5

DISTRIBUTION OF PEASANTRY BY CATEGORY IN EACH REGION (PERCENTAGES)

	Category	1678[3]	1719	1762	1811	1857
Forest-heartland						
Central NBE	Serf	62.63%	69.35%	71.14%	73.39%	66.04%
	State	0.00%	0.26%	2.15%	20.41%	28.88%
	Church[1]	20.03%	19.28%	19.02%		
	Court[2]	17.33%	11.11%	7.68%	6.20%	5.08%
	All	100.00%	100.00%	100.00%	100.00%	100.00%
North-western	Serf	62.73%	60.73%	66.53%	64.53%	57.00%
	State	0.00%	1.41%	0.99%	27.99%	29.03%
	Church[1]	28.04%	22.13%	24.13%	0.00%	
	Court[2]	9.23%	15.73%	8.34%	7.48%	13.97%
	All	100.00%	100.00%	100.00%	100.00%	100.00%
Northern	Serf	22.38%	21.13%	21.00%	20.63%	17.32%
	State	57.11%	49.62%	54.70%	69.39%	72.51%
	Church[1]	15.48%	15.22%	15.92%	0.00%	0.00%
	Court[2]	5.02%	14.03%	8.38%	9.98%	10.16%
	All	100.00%	100.00%	100.00%	100.00%	100.00%
North Urals	Serf		17.47%	16.73%	24.08%	11.94%
	State		75.69%	67.37%	70.44%	82.29%
	Church[1]		6.06%	10.86%	0.00%	0.00%
	Court[2]		0.79%	5.04%	5.48%	5.76%
	All		100.00%	100.00%	100.00%	100.00%
Steppes						
Central BE	Serf	62.24%	61.73%	66.04%	58.41%	50.91%
	State	18.59%	23.68%	22.82%	39.23%	48.20%
	Church[1]	8.35%	8.27%	6.08%	0.00%	0.00%
	Court[2]	10.82%	6.33%	5.06%	2.36%	0.89%
	All	100.00%	100.00%	100.00%	100.00%	100.00%
Mid-Volga	Serf	44.34%	40.89%	42.00%	41.79%	34.84%
	State	23.08%	46.26%	45.55%	52.25%	46.39%
	Church[1]	12.67%	7.35%	7.00%	0.00%	0.00%
	Court[2]	19.91%	5.50%	5.45%	5.96%	18.77%
	All	100.00%	100.00%	100.00%	100.00%	100.00%
L. Volga & Don	Serf		70.96%	57.66%	56.13%	39.69%
	State		29.04%	25.20%	39.94%	56.43%
	Church[1]		0.00%	11.70%	0.00%	0.00%
	Court[2]		0.00%	5.44%	3.93%	3.89%
	All		100.00%	100.00%	100.00%	100.00%
South Urals	Serf		4.88%	24.42%	17.63%	18.06%
	State		71.96%	69.24%	77.13%	75.88%
	Church[1]		1.40%	2.54%	0.00%	0.00%
	Court[2]		21.77%	3.80%	5.24%	6.06%
	All		100.00%	100.00%	100.00%	100.00%
Siberia	Serf	0.00%	2.36%	0.59%	0.46%	0.15%
	State	91.84%	93.17%	95.40%	99.54%	99.85%
	Church[1]	8.16%	4.47%	4.01%	0.00%	0.00%
	Court[2]	0.00%	0.00%	0.00%	0.00%	0.00%
	All	100.00%	100.00%	100.00%	100.00%	100.00%

Notes and sources: See Table 3.3.

including Tatars, Chuvash, Mordvinians, Mari and Bashkirs, and some native Siberians, whose lands had been annexed by Russia in the sixteenth century.[92] The state peasantry became more evenly spread after the addition in 1762–64 of the church peasants, whose regional distribution was similar to that of the seigniorial peasantry. Over 75 per cent of church peasants lived in the central regions. Nevertheless, the pattern of seigniorial peasants predominating in the centre and state peasants in more outlying regions continued in the nineteenth century. It was reinforced by the resettlement of many state peasants in the Lower Volga and Don region in the first half of the century.[93] (See Tables 3.3–3.5.)

The regional distribution of court peasants in the late seventeenth and early eighteenth centuries was also similar to that of the seigniorial peasants. The estates of the tsars and their families, like those of the nobles and the church, were mostly in the central regions. The proportions of court peasants in these regions fell over the eighteenth century as the tsars handed out court lands and peasants to nobles. The regional distribution of the appanage peasantry (as the court peasantry was known after 1797) also changed as a result of exchanges of land and peasants between the Appanage Department and the Finance Ministry, which was responsible for the state peasantry. At the start of the nineteenth century, the Appanage Department swapped most of its peasants in the Baltic provinces for state peasants in the Central Black Earth region. The biggest change was the 'Simbirsk exchange' of 1835. The Appanage Department exchanged around 200,000 male appanage peasants and their families, who lived on overcrowded estates in the central regions and in Belorussia, for a similar number of state peasants, who had around four times as much land, in Simbirsk province. As a result, in the 1850s, over a third of all appanage peasants lived in the Mid-Volga region.[94] (See Tables 3.3–3.5.)

THE REFORMS OF THE MID- AND LATE NINETEENTH CENTURY

The various measures taken by the state over the eighteenth and early nineteenth centuries to try to ensure peasants had access to sufficient land, to assist them if harvests failed, and to protect seigniorial peasants from excessive exploitation and cruelty were precursors to more substantial reforms in the mid- and late nineteenth century. The most important was the abolition of serfdom in 1861. There were also reforms of the other categories of peasants, and major changes in recruitment and taxation. Many of the earlier measures had been motivated by the desire to ensure that peasants had the wherewithal to meet their obligations and did not threaten the social order. In other words,

---

92 Blum, *Lord and Peasant*, pp. 475–85; Pallot and Shaw, *Landscape*, pp. 33–5; Vodarskii, *Naselenie Rossii v kontse XVII*, pp. 102–4; *id.*, *Dvoryanskoe*, p. 3; see also Ch. 2.
93 Druzhinin, *Gosudarstvennye*, vol. 1, pp. 89–95; vol. 2, pp. 189–93; Vodarskii, Ya. E., *Vladeniya i krepostnye krest'yane russkoi tserkvi v kontse XVII v.* (Moscow, 1988), pp. 137–8.
94 Gorlanov, *Udel'nye*, pp. 26, 30–1.

they aimed to shore up the existing hierarchical and exploitative system. While these were still factors behind the more wide-ranging reforms that began in the 1850s, these reforms had the additional, long-term objective of creating a new social, economic and political order in a reformed Russia.

Reforms of the appanage and state peasants (1820s–40s)

The reforms of the two main categories of non-seigniorial peasants in the 1820s–40s were a halfway house between bolstering the old social order and preparing for more radical changes. In the 1820s and 1830s L. A. Perovskii reformed the appanage peasantry. He aimed to improve their condition in order to increase the revenue raised from them, but without overburdening them. Since 1797 appanage peasants' dues (*obrok*) to the Appanage Department had been assessed according to the quality of their land in an attempt to take account of their incomes. This system was made more effective in 1829 (see above, p. 79). Perovskii encouraged 'improvements' in farming methods (see Ch. 4). He introduced communal cultivation of part of villages' land to stock reserve granaries in case of bad harvests. He tackled the problem of land shortages by swapping overcrowded appanage estates in the central provinces for less crowded state lands in the Mid-Volga region (see above, p. 106). Perovskii's reforms had mixed results, and aroused suspicion among the peasants, but served as models for P. D. Kiselev's reforms of the state peasantry.[95]

Kiselev was put in charge of the state peasantry in 1837, and appointed to head the new Ministry of State Domains in 1838. He ordered a general survey into the condition of the state peasantry. It produced a picture of maladministration and abuses, which were detrimental both to the welfare of the state peasants and to the state's revenues from its lands. The Ministry of Finance, which had previously been responsible for the state peasants, had treated them solely as sources of income with little regard for their condition.

Kiselev set up a new administrative structure, extending from the ministry in St Petersburg, to agencies in each province, and three lower tiers, which supervised state peasant self-government at the lowest levels of township (*volost'*) and village (see Ch. 5). The new minister attempted to appoint and reward educated, competent officials, and to deal with corruption and abuses. Kiselev took steps to make sure that state peasants had the means to support themselves and pay their dues. Large amounts of land were granted to those with insufficient land. Some peasants in overcrowded provinces were resettled in less densely populated areas. Kiselev also aimed to improve the welfare of the state peasantry more generally. Primary education and medical and veterinary services were made available in a few areas. Famine relief measures were improved by the creation of a new system of reserve granaries and funds, to be maintained by the peasants. Attempts were made to encourage peasants

---

95 Gorlanov, *Udel'nye*, pp. 21–9, 73–9; Pintner, *Russian*, pp. 73–5, 117–19.

to 'improve' their farming techniques (see Ch. 4). The reforms also aimed to bring the state peasants' obligations (*obrok*) to the state more into line with their ability to pay by reforming the system set up in 1798, which took account of the fertility of peasants' land and their incomes from non-agricultural activities (see above, p. 78). The introduction of a lottery system for selecting recruits made the burdensome conscription obligation fairer and, in theory, stopped the practice of sending the dregs of rural society to the army.

Historians are divided on the outcome of Kiselev's reforms. Druzhinin argued that they failed, left the state peasants worse off, and provoked unrest as peasants resisted official meddling in their lives. Western historians have been less critical, and concluded that the reforms were a qualified success. They have argued that exploitation and abuses were reduced, that land shortages were partly remedied, that the condition of the state peasantry improved and, as the reformers intended, the state's income from its peasants increased. Kiselev and Nicholas I hoped that the reforms of the state peasantry would serve as models for noble landowners to copy on their estates. Although this was in vain, Kiselev's reforms should be seen, as he intended, as the start of a general reform of the entire peasantry in Russia.[96]

The abolition of serfdom

In the first half of the nineteenth century major reforms of serfdom were carried out in parts of the empire's non-Russian western borderlands. Following a number of lesser measures, serfdom was abolished in the Baltic provinces of Estonia, Kurland and Livonia in 1816–19. The freed serfs were not granted land, however, and further laws had to be enacted to ensure they had access to land. An attempt to regulate serfdom through written estate 'inventories' was implemented in right-bank Ukraine in 1847–48. The 'inventories' fixed peasants' land allotments and recorded in detail all their seigniorial obligations. The results were mixed.[97]

In contrast to the reforms of serfdom in the western borderlands and of the appanage and state peasants, reforms of serfdom in the empire as a whole (including Russia) were tentative and limited. Alexander I's law on 'free farmers' of 1803 allowed landowners, if they so wished, to conclude agreements with their peasants to grant them personal freedom and sell them land. Only around 100,000 male seigniorial peasants had bought land and freedom under the terms of the law by 1855. Nicholas I convened ten secret committees to discuss 'the peasant question'. Apart from the reforms of the non-seigniorial peasantry and the 'inventory reform', the committees' legislative output was meagre. The 1842 decree on 'obligated peasants' was a step backwards. It permitted landowners, who chose to, to conclude contracts with their peasants to fix the size of their land allotments and the obligations they owed in return.

96 Compare Druzhinin, *Gosudarstvennye*, and Pintner, *Russian*, pp. 153–81; Crisp, *Studies*, pp. 79–92; Adams, 'Reforms'.
97 See Blum, *End*, pp. 228–35.

The landowners were freed from the duty to provide for them in times of dearth, but retained administrative and judicial authority and full ownership of the land. Only 27,000 male peasants had been converted to 'obligated peasants' by 1858. A decree of 1847 allowed peasants who lived on estates sold at public auction (to repay the owners' debts) the right to buy those estates, but only if they could match the highest bid within 30 days. Peasants who could raise the money received both the land and their freedom. Only 964 did so. The right to buy was made conditional on the debtor-landowner's agreement in 1849.

All these measures, and the greater efforts to prevent and prosecute 'abuses of seigniorial authority', demonstrate that, by the early nineteenth century, Russia's rulers recognised the importance of enacting major reforms of the existing structures of rural life. The modest and largely voluntary decrees concerning serfdom in Russia suggest that both Alexander I and Nicholas I were very reluctant to impose a major reform of serfdom on the Russian nobility.[98]

Historians have put forward a range of reasons to explain why Russia's rulers had become persuaded that serfdom needed to be done away with.[99] Many echo the contemporary arguments of proponents of abolition in the bureaucracy and intelligentsia. Some officials and economists argued in favour of abolition in the belief that free labour was more efficient than forced labour. An exaggerated fear of peasant rebellions undoubtedly affected the authorities' mood, but may also have made them reluctant to enact a major reform in case it sparked off a massive revolt. Publicists and writers, for example Alexander Herzen and Ivan Turgenev, drew attention to moral objections to human bondage. By the mid-nineteenth century, moreover, Russian serfdom was becoming an ever more obvious anachronism. The eradication of servile labour elsewhere in eastern and central Europe had begun in the late eighteenth century, and had been given greater impetus by Napoleon and the 1848 revolutions.

There were more specific reasons to abolish serfdom in Russia. The practice of paying nobles in land for serving the state had been ended by Peter the Great in 1714, and compulsory noble state service had been abolished by Peter III in 1762. Thus, the original reason for introducing and enforcing serfdom in the sixteenth and seventeenth centuries had disappeared. As service in the officer corps of the armed forces and in the bureaucracy became more professionalised, and as the state established a greater presence at the local level following the provincial reform of 1775, the next logical step was to remove the intermediary of the nobles between the state and the enserfed peasants, thereby converting the seigniorial peasants to state peasants in the same way that the church peasants had been taken over by the state in 1762–64. In the 1840s and 50s, moreover, a number of 'enlightened bureaucrats' came to occupy

98 See Semevskii, *Krest'yanskii vopros*, vol. 1, pp. 252–81; vol. 2, pp. 1–254, 529–70; Moon, *Russian Peasants*, pp. 62–112.
99 See Blum, *Lord and Peasant*, pp. 536–78, 612–18.

important positions in the government apparatus. These men possessed the ability and will to draw up and enact the abolition of serfdom.[100]

Many historians agree that Russia's defeat in the Crimean War in 1856 was at least the catalyst for reform. Russia's vast army of peasant-conscripts had failed against the more advanced and better-equipped armies of Britain, France and Turkey. Alfred Rieber made a strong case that serfdom was abolished as the necessary precursor to reforming the Russian army along western European lines. One of the 'enlightened bureaucrats', Dmitrii Milyutin, argued that the creation of a modern army, with large trained reserves which could be called up in wartime, was incompatible with the continued existence of serfdom. Since seigniorial peasants and their families were freed when they were inducted into the army, if larger numbers were conscripted for shorter terms before being sent home as reservists, then serfdom would disappear by default in two or three generations. And sending peasant-reservists with military training back to the villages was deemed very risky in view of official concerns about peasant disorders.[101]

Alexander II (1855–81) began to consider reforming serfdom at the start of his reign, but it was not until 1861 that the reform was implemented. Conservative officials and landowners tried to stall the reform process, or to make sure that if reform had to come, it would be on favourable terms, allowing them to retain much of their land, and granting them substantial compensation for the loss of their peasants. These aims were reflected in the inaccurate data on the sizes of peasants' obligations and land allotments which landowners presented in the 'Descriptions of Seigniorial Estates' they compiled in 1858–59 (see above, pp. 75–6). Alexander II received crucial support from his aunt Elena Pavlovna, his brother Konstantin Nikolaevich, the 'enlightened bureaucrats', in particular Nicholas Milyutin, and the senior statesman Yakov Rostovtsev. They had learned the lesson of the landless abolition of serfdom in the Baltic provinces, and made sure that the freed serfs in the rest of the empire were guaranteed access to arable land, and the opportunity to buy it.[102]

Alexander II ratified the statutes abolishing serfdom on 19 February 1861 and promulgated them on 5 March. The statutes laid down a gradual, three-stage process for the abolition of serfdom and the transition to a new agrarian order in which the 'peasants who have emerged from servile dependence' would eventually become the full owners of allotments of arable land.[103] The first stage began on 5 March 1861. All former seigniorial peasants entered a two-year 'transitional period'. At once, all seigniorial peasants became legally free. Everything else remained unchanged while preparations were made for

---

100 See Lincoln, W. B., *In the Vanguard of Reform: Russia's Enlightened Bureaucrats, 1825–1861* (DeKalb, IL, 1982).
101 See Rieber, A. J. (ed.), *The Politics of Autocracy: Letters of Alexander II to Prince A. I. Bariatinskii* (Paris and The Hague, 1966), pp. 17–29.
102 For a fine discussion of the 'Politics of Emancipation', see Saunders, D., *Russia in the Age of Reaction and Reform, 1801–1881* (London and New York, 1992), pp. 214–38.
103 For summaries, see Robinson, *Rural Russia*, pp. 64–85; Moon, D., 'The emancipation of the serfs in Russia: The serfs' perspective', *Modern History Review*, vol. 4, no. 1 (1992), pp. 31–3.

the second stage, 'temporary obligation'. During this stage, the sizes of the freed serfs' land allotments and the obligations they owed landowners in return were set according to principles laid down by the statutes and recorded in 'Regulatory Charters' (see above, p. 76). These were drawn up for each estate by the landowners. But, unlike the earlier 'Descriptions', the 'Charters' were subject to the peasants' approval under the supervision of officials known as 'peace mediators'. The period of 'temporary obligation' ended when the land-owner chose to initiate the third and final stage, the 'redemption operation', during which the peasants bought ('redeemed') their allotments of arable land. The government advanced most of the price set for the land to the landowners in long-term bonds. The peasants then began to repay the money to the state, with interest, in instalments ('redemption payments') spread over 49 years. In 1881 transfer to redemption was made compulsory for the 15 per cent of former serfs still 'temporarily obligated' to their landowners.

Much of the administrative and judicial authority which landowners had previously held over their peasants was handed over to reconstituted village communes or 'village societies' (*sel'skie obshchestva*) and new township (*volost'*) organisations (see Ch. 6). These bodies were responsible for making sure that peasants fulfilled their obligations to the state, including the redemption payments. The legislation also introduced peasant *volost'* courts.[104] Noble author-ity over the former seigniorial peasants was not totally removed. Officials from the local nobility and provincial government supervised the new institu-tions of peasant self-government. Many of the restrictions on the peasants under serfdom continued. Peasants were still bound to the land, and needed their communes' permission to move. Thus, the abolition of serfdom of 1861 did not restore peasants' freedom of movement.

Nor did the abolition of serfdom put an end to the exploitation of the former seigniorial peasants. Many lost part of the land they had cultivated for themselves under serfdom. Overall, the former seigniorial peasants lost as much as a fifth of their arable land. This average conceals many variations. The most striking were regional. In the infertile northern regions, freed peas-ants gained land, while in the fertile black earth regions they lost land. Many landowners kept the best land for themselves, and much of the meadow, pas-ture and woodland, which gave them leverage over the peasants as they needed access to these lands.[105] Moreover, most peasants had to pay more than the free-market price for the land. It is likely that peasants were overcharged by 90 per cent in non-black earth provinces and 20 per cent in black earth prov-inces. The higher price included hidden compensation for landowners for the loss of their seigniorial obligations as well as part of their land. The price

104 See Czap, P., 'Peasant-class courts and peasant customary justice in Russia, 1861–1912', *JSocH*, vol. 1 (1967), pp. 149–79.
105 See Robinson, *Rural Russia*, pp. 82, 87–8; Zaionchkovskii, P. A., *Provedenie v zhizn' krest'yanskoi reformy 1861 g.* (Moscow, 1958), p. 180. For regional studies, see Litvak, *Russkaya*, pp. 152–96; Kashchenko, S. G., *Reforma 19 fevralya 1861 g. na severo-zapade Rossii* (Moscow, 1995).

was higher in non-black earth regions because the peasants' obligations, often based on earnings from non-agricultural activities, were of greater value to their former owners than the relatively infertile land. In the black earth regions, however, the fertile land was of more value. Many peasants found the redemption payments burdensome and fell behind. The government periodically wrote off part of the arrears and rescheduled the rest. The payments were finally cancelled with effect from 1 January 1907.[106]

The terms of the abolition of serfdom in Russia were less favourable to the peasants than those in most of the empire's western borderlands (right-bank Ukraine, Belorussia and Lithuania). The Russian government changed the statutes of 1861 in these regions to allow the peasants to redeem more land at less cost. The aim was to punish their mostly Polish landowners for their part in the Polish revolt of 1863. This was a special case. The terms of abolition in Russia proper were comparable with most similar reforms elsewhere in eastern and central Europe in the first half of the nineteenth century. But they were rather more favourable to the freed bondsmen and women than the terms of the abolition of slavery in the southern states of the USA in 1865, which did not ensure the freed slaves had access to land.[107]

Further reforms of the appanage and state peasants (1860s)

Terms similar to those of the abolition of serfdom were extended to the appanage and state peasants. The appanage peasants were granted personal freedom in 1858, but reform did not begin in earnest until 1863. The decree of 26 June 1863 laid down that the size of appanage peasants' land allotments and the dues they paid in return were to be recorded in 'regulatory charters' by local officials of the Appanage Department and checked by the peace mediators. Once the charters were complete, the appanage peasants started to 'redeem' their land in 1865 in a process set to last 49 years.

The state peasants were already personally free. Decrees of 18 January and 24 November 1866 granted them security of tenure and controlled the dues they owed the state for the use of the land. Their land allotments and dues were to be recorded in charters (*vladennye zapisi*) by local officials of the Ministry of State Domains. The decrees of 1866 left the former state peasants in a similar position to that of 'temporary obligation' for the freed seigniorial peasants. Not until 1886 were the state peasants' dues converted to 'redemption payments', which were to be spread over 44 years. At the same time, these payments were increased to cover the loss of income caused by the simultaneous abolition of the poll tax (see below).

106 See Domar, E. D., 'Were Russian serfs overcharged for their land by the 1861 emancipation?' in *AOCI*, pp. 429–39; Gregory, P. R., *Before Command: An Economic History of Russia from Emancipation to the First Five-Year Plan* (Princeton, NJ, 1994), pp. 52–3. See also Hoch, 'On good numbers', pp. 42–8, 71–2.
107 See Blum, *End*, pp. 383–400; Kieniewicz, S., *The Emancipation of the Polish Peasantry* (Chicago and London, 1969), pp. 155–71; Kolchin, P., 'Some controversial questions concerning 19th-century emancipation from slavery and serfdom', in Bush, *Slavery and Serfdom*, pp. 42–67.

The reforms of the appanage and state peasants abolished the systems of local administration set up by the earlier reforms, and replaced them with the two-tier system based on villages and townships introduced on former seigniorial estates in 1861. As a result of all the reforms of the 1860s, the three main categories of peasants were abolished and merged into one. While the new legal status of most Russian peasants was similar, the former appanage and state peasants were allowed to redeem more land at a lower price. Their outstanding redemption payments were also written off with effect from 1 January 1907.[108]

Reforms of conscription and taxation (1860s–80s)

Although a strong case can be made that one of the main reasons for abolishing serfdom was as a prerequisite to reforming conscription, 13 years separated the two reforms. There were some lesser changes to military service in the aftermath of the Crimean War. The full term of service was reduced from 25 to 15 years in 1859, and the term of active service cut to ten years, followed by five years in the reserve, in 1868. The big change came in 1874. Under Dmitrii Milyutin's military service reform, the nobles' exemption from conscription was ended. All male subjects of the empire, regardless of their social estate, were made eligible for military service in the ranks when they reached the age of 20. After some 20-year-olds had been ruled out on health grounds or because they were only sons or sole breadwinners, those who were to serve were decided by lot. A quarter of the age cohort was called up each year. The full term of service was left at 15 years, but the term of active service was reduced to six years, followed by nine years in the reserve. Men with formal education were entitled to shorter terms of active service. At the top of the scale, university graduates served for only six months, while at the other end, men with primary education served for four years. This was a concession to the nobility, who resented their sons having to serve alongside ill-educated peasants, but was also an inducement to peasants to send their sons to school. After 1874, peasants continued to provide most of the recruits. Nevertheless, the reform did reduce the impact of conscription on the peasantry. Many more soldiers of peasant origin survived the much-reduced term of active service, and many returned to their villages.[109]

The other main burden on the lower orders introduced by Peter the Great, the poll tax, was also abolished. Some minor adjustments were made in the 1860s, but it was not until the end of the 1870s that the government moved towards a major reform in the wake of the cost of the recent Russo-Turkish

108 On the appanage peasant reform, see Gorlanov, *Udel'nye*, pp. 91–101. On the state peasant reform, see Druzhinin, *Gosudarstvennye*, vol. 2, pp. 566–70; Zaionchkovskii, P. A., 'Podgotovka i prinyatie zakona 24 noyabrya 1866 g. o gosudarstvennykh krest'yanakh', *IS* (1958), no. 4, pp. 103–13. See also Robinson, *Rural Russia*, pp. 89–92.
109 *PSZ*, 2, vol. XLII, p. 417, no. 44508 (1 May 1867); pp. 998–9, no. 44745, I, 1–6 (25 June 1867); vol. XLIX, pt. 1, pp. 1–29, nos 52982–3 (1 January 1874); Keep, *Soldiers*, pp. 375–8.

War, and increasing arrears. Finance minister N. Kh. Bunge phased out the poll tax in the European part of the empire between 1883 and 1887. It was abolished in Siberia in 1899. To make up for the lost revenues, the former state peasants' dues were increased under the guise of converting them to redemption payments (see above). In addition, new taxes were introduced on private businesses, existing taxes on urban property were raised, and indirect taxes were increased on consumer goods, including kerosene, matches, tea, sugar, tobacco and, above all, vodka.[110]

Indirect taxation had already been reformed in 1863. In that year the drink tax farm was abolished, and replaced by excise duties on distillers and licence fees for wholesale and retail traders. Retail prices for vodka fell after 1863, leading to a temporary fall in state receipts. But prices rose and revenues returned to and then exceeded previous levels as the state raised the excise duty. The introduction of a new state monopoly in 1894 further increased state income from drink. The main losers from the 1863 reform were the noble-distillers and merchant-tax farmers who had benefited from the old system by cheating their customers and syphoning off revenues that should have gone to the state. But taxes on vodka, regardless of how they were organised, continued to be a burden on consumers, including the peasantry.[111]

The end of two of Peter the Great's main methods of exploiting the lower orders, conscription and the poll tax, together with the move towards indirect and business taxes, greatly reduced the need for another Petrine innovation: internal passports, which had been introduced to control the movement of the peasants and townsmen liable to military service and the poll tax. The passport system was relaxed in 1895. But it was not until 1906 that Russian peasants finally recovered the right of freedom of movement they had lost over 300 years earlier in the 1580s and 1590s.[112]

'Exploitation' and 'protection' after the 1860s

The overall effect of the reforms of the 1860s–80s on the exploitation of the Russian peasantry has been the subject of controversy, and is part of wider debates over peasant living standards in late tsarist Russia (see Ch. 8). The standard view of Soviet historians, shared by many Western historians until the late 1970s, was that the abolition of serfdom and reforms of the other categories shouldered peasants with very heavy burdens of redemption payments. The freed serfs, moreover, received less land than they needed. The resulting 'land hunger' was worsened by the rapidly growing population. The

110 Anan'ich, N. I., 'K istorii otmeny podushnoi podati v Rossii', *IZ*, vol. 94 (1974), pp. 183–212; Bowman, L., 'Russia's first income taxes: The effects of modernized taxes on commerce and industry, 1885–1914', *SR*, vol. 52 (1993), pp. 256–82. The salt tax had been abolished in 1880.
111 Christian, *'Living Water'*, pp. 353–81.
112 Anan'ich, B. V., 'Iz istorii zakonodatel'stva o krest'yanakh (vtoraya polovina XIX v.)', in Mavrodin, V. V. (ed.), *Voprosy istorii Rossii: XIX–nachala XX v.* (Leningrad, 1983), pp. 34–45; Crisp, O., 'Peasant land tenure and civil rights implications before 1906', in Crisp, O. and Edmondson, L. (eds), *Civil Rights in Imperial Russia* (Oxford, 1989), pp. 55–7.

move from direct taxes to taxes on goods of mass consumption was seen as a major hardship for peasants. However, the state's demands on the peasantry may have been falling after the reforms of the 1860s–80s. It has been calculated that, among peasants in the European part of the empire in 1901, indirect and direct taxes (including redemption payments) took up 18 per cent of their gross income from agriculture. Rents and interest to the Peasant Land Bank (see below) took up a further 11 per cent. If income from non-agricultural sources is included, however, the proportion of peasants' total incomes taken up by payments to the state was roughly 20 per cent. Average figures for a large area for only one year can serve as only a very general guide. Nevertheless, they suggest that the proportion of Russian peasants' output and incomes that was being taken away from them had fallen substantially since the reforms. Moreover, the extent to which payments for renting and buying land can be considered 'exploitation' is questionable.[113]

In the decades after 1861, some tsarist bureaucrats had tried to take further steps in the direction of a new social and economic order. Finance Minister Bunge presented his tax reforms of the 1880s as a move away from the old system, under which the main burden of taxation was imposed on the lower orders while elites were exempt from taxation, and as a move towards a new system in which everyone paid taxes.[114] This 'all-estate' principle had already been adopted by Dmitrii Milyutin in his military service reform of 1874.

Did these changes mean the end of the old reciprocal relationship, whereby the state and elites, at least in principle, offered 'protection' to the peasantry in return for obligations? The rhetoric of paternalism continued. 'Enlightened bureaucrats' who advocated moving from a 'particularistic society of [social] estates' to a 'national state governing a civil society' were out of step with more conservative nobles, officials, and the last tsars.[115] Nicholas II (1894–1917), in his heart, would probably have preferred to rule at an earlier time when the paternalist ideal of the '*batyushka*' tsar, which he shared in principle if not in practice, may have been more appropriate.

To some extent the 'protection' offered by the state and elites continued after the reforms. Historians have rightly focused on the land that freed peasants lost after 1861. It is important to remember, however, that the terms of the reform were designed to ensure that peasants had access to land, and would eventually become its full owners. The authors of the reform cannot be held responsible for the banking crisis of the late 1850s, which limited the amount of land the state could include in the redemption process,[116] nor for failing to anticipate the rapid growth in the rural population that put such pressure on the land. Moreover, the government took some measures to alleviate growing

113 Anfimov, A. M., *Ekonomicheskoe polozhenie i klassovaya bor'ba krest'yan Evropeiskoi Rossii, 1881–1904 gg.* (Moscow, 1984), pp. 110–11.
114 Anan'ich, 'K istorii', p. 203.
115 Wcislo, F. W., *Reforming Rural Russia: State, Local Society, and National Politics, 1855–1914* (Princeton, NJ, 1990) (quotation from p. xii).
116 See Hoch, 'Banking crisis'.

'land hunger'. In 1883, it set up the Peasant Land Bank, which enabled peasants to rent and buy millions of *desyatiny* of land.[117] From the 1890s the state subsidised peasant resettlement in Siberia (see Ch. 2). Stolypin's land reforms of 1906–11 took a different line. Instead of making more land available for all peasants, some were encouraged to consolidate their land outside their village communes (see Chs 6 and 9). Overall, however, the tsarist government's land policies were too cautious, and did not solve the problems facing Russia's peasants.

The nobility's legal obligation to provide for their peasants in times of dearth ended in 1861. Thereafter, the burden of famine relief was shared between village communes, the district and provincial councils (*zemstva*) set up after 1864, and the central authorities. The central government took measures to alleviate the impact of the major famine in 1891–92. While it did not succeed in preventing a massive human disaster, its efforts were probably more effective than those of the British in India at the same time.[118] The tsarist government's attempts to assist famine victims stand out in stark contrast, however, to those of the Soviet government, whose policies were a major cause of the famines of 1921–22, 1932–33 and 1946–47 (see Ch. 10).

CONCLUSION

Throughout the tsarist period, the ruling and landowning elites in Russia exploited the peasants, taking away from them a large part of the product of their labour. From the late sixteenth and early seventeenth centuries until 1861, the social hierarchy that placed nobles at the top and peasants at the bottom was bolstered by serfdom. Peter the Great's reforms of conscription and taxation in the early eighteenth century reinforced the division of Russian society into an elite, privileged minority and the tax-paying masses. In spite of the reforms of the nineteenth century, Russian peasants remained at the bottom of the hierarchy, were still tainted with legal and social disabilities, and were still exploited.

Some tentative conclusions can be made on trends in the levels of exploitation. The degree of exploitation varied between the different categories of peasants before the reforms of the 1860s, and between the former members of the defunct categories after the 1860s. It was the seigniorial, and former seigniorial, peasants who bore the highest burdens. There were also regional differences. Exploitation was highest in the central regions of Russia, but the lighter burdens in the old borderlands gradually disappeared with the expansion of state and landowner power in the train of peasant migration. There were also changes over time. In the short term, the state's demands were higher in wartime and lower in peacetime. In the longer term, the proportion of the

117 Vasudevan, H. S., 'Peasant land and peasant society in late imperial Russia', *HJ*, vol. 31 (1988), pp. 212–16.
118 Matsuzato, K., 'Sel'skaya khlebo-zapasnaya sistema v Rossii 1864–1917 gg.', *OI* (1995), no. 3, pp. 185–97. For comparisons, see Robbins, *Famine*, pp. 15–16, 168, 171–2.

peasantry's output extracted by the ruling and landowning elites grew from the mid-sixteenth to the mid-eighteenth centuries, although the relative shares taken by nobles and the state changed. The state took the lion's share during the reign of Peter the Great. The level of exploitation seems to have peaked between the mid-eighteenth and mid-nineteenth centuries, when the state and landowners together extracted around half the product of the peasantry's labour. The level of exploitation declined after the 1860s.

In return for the obligations they demanded from the peasants, the state and landowners had some 'obligations' *to* the peasants. They provided them with land, and took some measures to assist them in the event of hardship and to protect them from excessive exploitation. The idea of 'protection' survived the reforms of the 1860s. To the extent that the ruling landowning elites met these 'obligations', they were acting in their own interests. It was not to their advantage to reduce 'their' peasants to ruin, or to provoke disorders. Nevertheless, the balance of exchange was unequal, and heavily weighted against the peasants.

The forms and levels of exploitation, together with the growing population and environmental conditions discussed in the previous two chapters, profoundly affected the ways of life of Russia's peasants. Nevertheless, generations of peasants were able to support their increasing numbers by developing strategies, sometimes in conjunction with the elites, to ensure their livelihoods. The main strategies involved production, principally but not solely agriculture; the ways households managed their labour resources; the practices village communes developed to share out their obligations and, especially, their land between households; and the ways peasants tried to extract concessions from the landowning and ruling elites by protest and accommodation. These strategies are the subjects of the next four chapters.

CHAPTER 4

Production

Serfdom and the other means by which the ruling and landowning elites exploited the Russian peasantry were superimposed on an existing peasant economy that was based mainly, but not solely, on agriculture. With the partial exception of labour services (*barshchina*) on landowners' demesnes, the forms of exploitation were not ways of organising production. Russian landowners did not run their estates like slave plantations. Instead, Russian landowners and the state allowed peasants considerable leeway in organising production. Throughout the period under consideration, right up to the end of the 1920s, the landscape of rural Russia was a patchwork of thousands upon thousands of peasant households grouped in village communities. In the early twentieth century, the agricultural economist Alexander Chayanov stressed the importance of the peasant 'family farm' ('*khozyaistvuyushchaya sem'ya*') as the basic unit of production (and consumption) in rural Russia.[1]

The main economic decisions about what, how, and how much to produce were, thus, taken mainly by peasants in their households and communities. In making these decisions, peasant households and village communes took account of external factors, especially the local population densities, the opportunities and constraints provided by the environmental conditions, and the forms and levels of obligations demanded from them. They also took account of internal factors, in particular the resources they possessed, principally labour and land. Chayanov argued that peasant households' primary consideration was the need to produce enough to ensure their subsistence, and that production for the market was of far less importance. A number of specialists on peasants have contrasted the profit motive in capitalist economies with a 'subsistence ethic' and aversion to risk in pre- or non-capitalist peasant economies.[2]

This chapter considers the various productive (and other income-generating) activities Russian peasants engaged in, both agricultural and non-agricultural. Particular attention is paid to the ways they organised their economic pursuits, the role of culture in recording and passing on the strategies they devised, and the levels of output they attained.

1 Chayanov, *Theory*.
2 For a concise survey of the theoretical literature, see Ellis, F., *Peasant Economics: Farm Households and Agrarian Development*, 2nd edn (Cambridge, 1993).

118

PEASANT HOUSEHOLDS AS UNITS OF PRODUCTION

The main units of production in the rural economy were individual peasant households. Their chief resources were the labour of household members and their land. Also important were their farmstead buildings, implements, draught animals and other livestock, supplies of seed, and the tools and raw materials they used in handicraft production. Although peasants did not think in terms of economic theory, most of these were capital items that entailed a degree of investment for the future rather than consumption in the present. In most of their productive activities, peasants relied heavily, but not blindly, on knowledge that had been accumulated by their forebears and passed down from generation to generation.

Many Russian peasants, especially in the central regions between the late seventeenth and late nineteenth centuries, lived in large, multi-generational households. The oldest generation did little or no work. Children were required to help out as soon as they were able. The main labour resources, however, were one or more teams (*tyagla*) of able-bodied, adult men and women, usually married couples. Marriage was vitally important in Russian peasant society because it created units of production as well as human reproduction. According to custom, peasants divided their tasks between men and women. Men did most of the labour in the fields, especially ploughing and sowing, looked after the horses, and did construction work. Women were responsible for looking after the children, domestic chores, tending kitchen gardens and some of the livestock, but were also expected to work in the fields in the summer. This division of labour was determined largely by culture (i.e. gender), rather than biology (i.e. sex). There was a certain symbolism in the tasks men performed. Ploughing and sowing conformed to their perceived roles as providers for their families, and the male function in sexual intercourse. Although men tended to do the most physically arduous work, most women were perfectly capable of doing 'men's work'. When necessary, moreover, if many men were away as migrant labourers or had been conscripted into the army, women carried out most or all of the tasks usually performed by men. But Russian peasant men rarely, if ever, did 'women's work'.[3]

Peasant households needed access to different types of land to support a balanced economy based mainly on farming. They required the plots on which they built their houses and farm buildings, and laid out kitchen gardens where they grew vegetables and kept small livestock. They needed pasture where they grazed larger animals, and meadows or hayfields where they mowed hay for fodder. Woodland was important as a source of firewood and timber as well as fruit, berries, mushrooms and game. Peasants used clearances in woods for pasture and mowing hay. Streams, rivers, ponds and lakes were essential

3 See Glickman, R., 'Peasant women and their work', in *RPW*, pp. 54–72; Engel, *Between*, pp. 14, 34–46; Meyer, A. G., 'The impact of World War I on Russian women's lives', in Clements, *Russia's Women*, pp. 216–18; Ellis, *Peasant Economics*, pp. 169–80. See also Ch. 5.

119

as sources of water, and also of fish. Most importantly, households needed arable land where they grew the cereal crops that were the staples of their diet.

Customs relating to land tenure changed over time, and varied between regions and different categories of peasants. In many villages, households held their house and garden plots in individual tenure, and had rights of access to pasture, meadows, woodland and water resources held jointly by the village communes. Before the eighteenth century, and in some outlying regions as late as the nineteenth century, many households held their plots of arable land in individual tenure. In large parts of Russia in the eighteenth and nineteenth centuries, however, especially the central regions, many households were assigned strips of arable in the village fields by their communes, but held them subject to periodic repartitions. Communes aimed to maintain a balance between the size of households' land allotments and their labour capacity. This was the famous Russian peasant custom of communal and repartitional land tenure (see Ch. 6).

On seigniorial estates under serfdom many landowners set aside part of the arable land as demesne for their own production. Strips of demesne and peasant land were usually intermingled in the open fields. In addition, many estate owners controlled access to pasture, woodland and meadows, and demanded additional obligations from the peasants in return for allowing them to use these resources. Many peasant households supplemented their allotments of communal arable land and rights of access to other land by renting or buying more land. Peasants bought and sold land long before they were permitted to do so by law in 1801 and 1848 (see Ch. 3).[4]

AGRICULTURE

Agriculture was the main source of livelihood for most Russian peasant households. The natural environment of Russia provided both opportunities and limitations for peasant farmers. The Russian plain, including southern Siberia, contained extensive areas of land suitable for cultivation and pasture, in particular the band of fertile black earth. But the long and harsh winters reduced the growing season in much of Russia to well under half the year, and meant that animals had to be kept indoors for several months each year. It was a tragedy for the Russian peasantry that large parts of Russia suffer from shortages of either heat or moisture, or both. In the European part of Russia, the available heat increases from the north-west to the south-east, whereas the reverse is true for moisture. In the damp north-west, moreover, the soil is fairly poor, while the fertile black earth of the open steppe in the south-east is cursed with low and unreliable rainfall. Adequate and reliable heat and moisture coincide with fertile soils only in the forested steppe, which included most of the Central Black Earth and Mid-Volga regions. The precipitation in much of Russia is not only comparatively low, but concentrated in the

4 See Smith, *Peasant Farming*, pp. 7–95; Hoch, *Serfdom*, pp. 44–5, 48–9, 56–7.

winter, and in the mid- to late summer when it threatens to prevent grain from ripening. Overall, the environmental conditions in large parts of Russia approached the margins for peasant farming. (See Ch. 2.) Nevertheless, Russian peasants learned to cope with all but the most extreme regional variants and periodic fluctuations in the natural conditions. Moreover, they sanctified the land as 'Moist Mother Earth' in a pagan, folk belief that predated and survived the conversion of Rus' to Orthodox Christianity in the tenth century. The extent to which peasants venerated the land is suggested by the fact that they ratified oaths by swallowing mouthfuls of soil.[5]

Grain cultivation

The main form of agriculture practised by Russian peasants was cultivating grain. In the eighteenth and nineteenth centuries, over 90 per cent of the arable land in Russia was used for grain, and about 40 per cent of that was sown with rye. Rye was the main cereal as it was best suited to the environmental conditions of much of Russia. Next in importance was oats. In parts of the Northern region and Siberia, with their very short growing season, barley was grown because it was more resistant to frost and ripened quickly. In the black earth regions, with their longer frost-free period and more fertile soil, wheat became more important over the eighteenth and nineteenth centuries. Peasants also grew smaller quantities of buckwheat and millet.[6]

In the medieval era, the abundance of land relative to the population meant that it was appropriate for peasants to employ tillage systems which made extensive use of the land. In the forested regions, peasants used the 'slash-and-burn' system. They felled the trees from a stretch of land, hauled away any logs that could be used for building, and burnt the rest to produce a fertile mixture of ash and soil. The clearances were usually ploughed and harrowed to prepare them for sowing. Peasants grew crops in the fields they had hewn from the forest for a few years, until the soil became exhausted and crop yields began to fall. The land was then left fallow and allowed to revert to forest. Meanwhile, the peasants had cleared other plots to farm. Clearances were cultivated for as few as two or as many as ten or more years, while the fallow period could last as long as 30 years. Slash-and-burn farming had once been common throughout the forest-heartland but, by the seventeenth and eighteenth centuries, it was confined mostly to the coniferous forest belt in the north and Siberia. The system was still used in some northern areas at the turn of the twentieth century.[7]

5 Ivanits, *Russian Folk Belief*, pp. 12–16.
6 Smith, *Peasant Farming*, pp. 33–5; Smith and Christian, *Bread*, pp. 255–7; Okladnikov, A. P. (ed.), *Krest'yanstvo Sibiri v epokhu feodalizma* (Novosibirsk, 1982), p. 61; Saburova, L. M. and Toren, M. D., 'Sistemy zemledeliya i sel'skokhozyaistvennye kul'tury u russkikh krest'yan v seredine XIX–nachale XX v.', in Kushner, P. I. (ed.), *Russkie: istoriko–etnograficheskii atlas: Zemledelie. Krest'yanskoe zhilishche. Krest'yanskaya odezhda. (Seredina XIX–nachalo XX v.)* (Moscow, 1967), pp. 23–8.
7 Pallot and Shaw, *Landscape*, pp. 112–14; Smith, R. E. F., *The Origins of Farming in Russia* (Paris and The Hague, 1959), pp. 51–74; Okladnikov, *Krest'yanstvo Sibiri*, pp. 57–61, 182–8.

The equivalent long-fallow system in the steppe regions was 'field-grass husbandry'. Peasants cleared the natural vegetation from areas of steppe, ploughed them up, and cultivated them for a few years. They then let the fields return to grassland, and farmed other areas of steppe which they had cleared. 'Field-grass husbandry' was widespread in parts of the steppe regions until the late eighteenth century, and continued to be used in outlying areas of the Lower Volga and Don and Southern Urals regions of the open steppe in the nineteenth century. In more arid areas along the lower Volga and in the north Caucasus, Russian settlers learned to irrigate the land from indigenous peoples.[8] Peasant-settlers in Siberia adapted the tillage systems they had used in their previous homes, and developed new ones appropriate to local conditions. One of the most widespread was a hybrid long-fallow, short-fallow system, which was still used in some sparsely populated areas in the nineteenth century.[9]

Peasants in the more fertile and heavily populated southern parts of the forest-heartland began to adopt new ways of cereal farming, which made less extensive use of the land than the long-fallow systems, as far back as the late medieval period. Quite common were two-field systems, in which each field was cultivated in alternate years, while the other was left fallow. The most important change began in the fifteenth century. Some large landowners, both noble and ecclesiastical, consolidated their arable land into three fields, and adopted a three-course crop rotation. Many peasant communities followed suit, sometimes on the instructions of their landowners. Peasants were under pressure to increase the productivity of their land in order to meet the increasing demands made by their landowners and the state, and to support the growing population. The connection between population growth and more intensive forms of cultivation was one of interaction: an increase in productivity enabled peasants to support larger numbers, as well as larger numbers compelling them to alter the ways they farmed.

The 'three-field system' became prevalent in the Central Non-Black Earth and North-western regions in the sixteenth and seventeenth centuries. With the expansion of peasant settlement, the growth of the population in areas being settled, and the extension of serfdom and other forms of exploitation, the three-field system spread into the Central Black Earth and Mid-Volga regions of the forested steppe and, in the eighteenth and the nineteenth centuries, further south and east to parts of the open steppe regions and Siberia.[10]

---

8 Pallot and Shaw, *Landscape*, pp. 69, 95, 112–14; Barrett, 'Lines', p. 584; Kogitin, V. V., 'Sistemy zemledeliya u russkogo naseleniya nizhnego povolzh'ya vtoroi poloviny XVIII–nachalo XX v.', in Seleznev, A. G. and Tomilov, N. A. (eds), *Material'naya kul'tura narodov Rossii* (Novosibirsk, 1995), pp. 117–20.

9 Okladnikov, *Krest'yanstvo Sibiri*, pp. 57–61, 182–7.

10 See Confino, M., *Systèmes Agraires et Progrès Agricole: l'Assolement Triennal en Russie aux XVIIIe–XIXe Siècles* (Paris and The Hague, 1969), pp. 27–40; French, R. A., 'The introduction of the three-field agricultural system', in Bater and French, *Studies*, vol. 1, pp. 65–81; Smith, *Peasant Farming*, pp. 27–33, 115, 123–9; Kogitin, 'Sistemy', pp. 113–16; Okladnikov, *Krest'yanstvo Sibiri*, pp. 57–9, 179, 182–7.

Under the three-field system,[11] the arable land surrounding a village was divided into three open fields, each consisting of strips held by individual peasant households and sometimes also the landowner. Under the direction of the village commune (see Ch. 6), one field was used for growing the winter crop, another was sown with the spring crop, and the third left fallow to allow the soil to recover its fertility. The crops were rotated the following year. The first field was sown with the spring crop, the second left fallow, and the winter crop grown in the third. The next year, the crops were rotated again, establishing a three-year cycle in each field of winter crop, spring crop, fallow that carried on for year after year, decade after decade.

The three-field system was one of the major determinants of the rhythm of agricultural labour. With the arrival of the spring in March and April, the men ploughed up their strips in the field in which the spring crop was to be sown. In the forest-heartland, most used the traditional, wooden plough (*sokha*).[12] This was a simple implement, usually without wheels, which was pulled by one or two horses. The early wooden ploughs used in slash-and-burn farming did little more than scratch the surface. Later variants had iron tips, and could cut and turn the light soils of the forest-heartland. New types of plough, such as the *kosulya*, which had larger ploughshares and mouldboards, were developed in areas with denser soils. Traditional wooden ploughs were of less use in the black earth regions, as the soil was heavier than in the forest-heartland, and virgin black earth was bound together by the matted roots of the steppe grasses. Peasant-settlers adapted their wooden ploughs and *kosuli* to the new soil conditions. Many Russian peasants in the steppe regions began to use the heavier, iron-shod 'true plough' (*plug*) used by Ukrainian settlers, who had experience of cultivating black earth in their homeland in the Dnieper basin. In the south-east of the steppe zone, some Russian peasants adopted the Tatar *saban*. Most ploughs used on the steppes needed more draught power than the lighter wooden ploughs, and were usually pulled by teams of oxen, which were hardier than horses.

The main tasks in the arable fields were marked by rituals and ceremonies, which evolved together with peasants' agricultural techniques.[13] The rituals and ceremonies served the practical purpose of coordinating the work of individual households on their strips in the communal fields. This was essential under the three-field system. They were also part of wider agricultural ceremonies through which peasants hoped to ensure the fertility of the soil, ward

11 The following section is based largely on Confino, *Systèmes*, pp. 59–88; Kahan, *Plow*, pp. 47–8; Saburova and Toren, 'Sistemy', pp. 17–32; Smith, *Peasant Farming*, pp. 11–26, 33–9, 43–4.
12 On all implements, see Smith, *Peasant Farming*, pp. 10–53, 223; Naidich, D. V., 'Pakhotnye i razrykhlyayushchie orudiya', in Kushner, *Russkie*, pp. 33–59; Toren, M. D., 'Sposoby uborki khlebov', *ibid.*, pp. 60–84; Naidich, 'Orudiya i sposoby molt'by i veyaniya', *ibid.*, pp. 85–98; Saburova, L. M., 'Sel'skokhozyaistvennye postroiki dlya obrabotki i khraneniya zerna', *ibid.*, pp. 99–128.
13 On these rituals, from ploughing to harvesting, see Gromyko, M. M., *Traditsionnye normy povedeniya i formy obshcheniya russkikh krest'yan XIX v.* (Moscow, 1986), pp. 117–25; Ivanits, *Russian Folk Belief*, pp. 12, 25. On agricultural rituals in Britain (for comparison) see Hutton, R., *The Stations of the Sun: A History of the Ritual Year in Britain* (Oxford, 1996). See also Ch. 9.

off the risk of crop failure, and guarantee a bountiful harvest by appealing to supernatural forces. The rituals connected with particular tasks varied from district to district, and many were recorded in writing for the first time only in the late nineteenth century. The start of ploughing in the spring was accompanied by several practices. In parts of Kaluga province, for example, the men set off for the field with a loaf of bread, an icon, and one of the horses which they had already harnessed to a plough. On arrival, one man who had been chosen beforehand bowed down to the ground three times before the icon and to each of the four sides of the field. He then ploughed a single furrow across the strips of all the households. Only after this ritual did all the men begin to plough their strips.

The spring sowing began in May in the forest-heartland, and in April further south. Guided by proverbs such as 'sow in mud and you will be a prince',[14] peasants chose the best time for sowing. The main spring crops were oats in most of the forest-heartland, barley in the northern regions and, increasingly, wheat in the black earth provinces. The sowers put a certain amount of seed into sacks or baskets hung around their necks. They then walked through the ploughed strips and, with their right hands, broadcast seed to their right and left, ensuring it was evenly spread. Sowing was carried out by the men. This was considered very important and ordained by God. Many peasants believed that women were not to take part in sowing, and that their presence in the fields when sowing began could threaten the harvest. The sowers selected one of their number to begin. In many areas, village priests conducted special ceremonies in the fields. In parts of Kaluga province, the clergy led a service and procession involving loaves of bread, icons, holy water, and a handful of seed taken from all the households in the village.

Peasants worked the sown seed into the soil with horse-drawn harrows, which also removed weeds, broke up clods, and mixed in any manure which had been applied. The earliest harrows had been simply sections of tree trunks with the stubs of the branches still attached. Later harrows were wooden frames with wooden or metal spikes affixed. Harrowing, like ploughing and sowing, was the responsibility of the men. By the spring, the winter crop – which had been sown in one of the other fields the previous summer – had begun to sprout. The winter cereal in most of Russia was rye. In some communities, peasants were so anxious to seek divine intervention that they had special services held in the rye field twice: when it was sown in the summer, and when it began to sprout the following spring. Peasants also sought the help of St Nicholas 'the Wonderworker', who, among his many other duties in Orthodox Russia, was the patron of arable fields.

With or without supernatural help, the peasants' crops usually grew to maturity and ripened. In much of the forest-heartland, the winter rye was ready to be harvested in late July, and the spring cereals in early August. To the south, in the black earth regions, the crops ripened sooner under the hotter sun, and

14 Wallace, *Russia*, vol. 1, p. 146.

were gathered in a little earlier. Both men and women took part in harvesting. The winter crop was often reaped by women, bent double, using short-handled sickles with serrated edges. The spring crop was harvested mainly by men, usually also with sickles, but long-handled scythes with smooth-edged blades were used in some areas (see below, pp. 129–30).

The harvest was the culmination of all the peasants' work in their arable fields over the preceding months, and was of central importance to their livelihoods. A good harvest ensured their subsistence and even prosperity; a bad harvest could lead to disaster. Harvesting was accompanied by various rituals. In a typical example, the villagers decided the day when harvesting would begin, and chose a woman to reap the first sheaves. The woman selected was usually an old widow renowned for her peaceful and virtuous life. On the evening of the appointed day, she lit a candle in front of the icons in her house, bowed down several times before it, and then set off for the fields. She tried to avoid being seen to escape the 'evil eye'. On arrival in the field, she bowed down again, reaped three sheaves, and bound them together in the form of the Orthodox cross. She then returned home, prayed, and extinguished the candle. The rest of the villagers began to harvest their strips the following day. If the community decided there was no woman of sufficient virtue to start the harvest, all the peasants began reaping together. The first and last sheaves were treated specially. Grain from the first sheaf was blessed by the priest in the village church, and mixed with the seed to be sown for the next year's harvest. Peasants brought the last sheaf back to their houses, adorned it with flowers, ribbons or women's clothing, and put it in a place of honour, either by the door or in the icon corner. A small area of the field was left unharvested. Women bound a patch of uncut grain with ribbons or towels into a circle, and placed in the middle some bread and salt (the traditional symbol of hospitality). The rituals surrounding reaping were intended to seek supernatural assistance to ensure plentiful harvests.

The reason women took part in harvesting in the fields, which were usually a 'male domain', was the pressing need for labour at the height of field work in the summer. While the women were bringing in the winter rye, the men were busy ploughing and harrowing the fallow field. In the forest-heartland, with its less fertile soils, they usually applied manure to the fallow, but the use of organic fertiliser was less common in the fertile black earth regions. The men sowed the newly prepared fallow field with seed which had been threshed from that year's harvest. Winter rye was sown in August in the forest-heartland and the northern part of the steppe regions, and a little later further south. All these tasks had to be completed before frosts began, and the onset of winter put an end to the agricultural season. The celebration of the harvest, involving a church service as well as feasting and drinking, was one of the most joyous times in Russian peasant villages (see Ch. 9).

During the harvest, the peasants carried the sheaves from the fields to the threshing floor. Harvested grain was often dried in kilns to prevent it from rotting. Over the winter months, the peasants threshed and winnowed the harvested grain to remove the ears from the stalks, and to separate the grain from the chaff. These tasks were shared between men and women. In some villages, peasants threshed by beating the sheaves with wooden flails; in others they hit them against a rail mounted horizontally. If labour was short, peasants used livestock to trample on the sheaves to remove the ears of grain. Peasants winnowed the ears with sieves, or used wooden shovels to throw them into the air and let the wind blow away the chaff. The final stage in preparing grain was milling it into flour or grits. Some households had their own hand-operated millstones, but many villages had water or wind-powered mills operated by specialist millers.

The three-field system was the archetypal method of grain cultivation in much of Russia, especially the central regions, for most of the period under consideration. In many Russian villages the three-field system ended only with the collectivisation of agriculture in 1929–30 (see Ch. 10). Similar tillage systems had been common in large parts of medieval and early modern Europe, until the open fields were enclosed, and many farmers adopted more complex crop rotations that made more intensive use of the land. These changes were part of the 'agricultural revolution', which began in north-west Europe in the seventeenth and eighteenth centuries, before spreading slowly to other parts of the continent.[15]

Backwardness or prudence?

It has long been common to castigate Russian peasant agriculture, especially grain cultivation, as backward and inefficient. The persistence of strip farming, the three-field system, and the wooden plough have become symbols of this alleged backwardness. Some contemporaries, for example members of the Free Economic Society (founded in 1765) and the few 'improving' landowners and 'enlightened bureaucrats', criticised the low technical level and poor productivity of peasant farming. This negative evaluation has been taken up by many historians. Jerome Blum attributed the 'backwardness' of Russian peasant agriculture to the 'disadvantages of soil and climate', the negligent attitude of most noble landowners, and the 'incredibly bad condition of the empire's communications system', which made it difficult and expensive to transport produce to market and, therefore, acted as a disincentive to 'agricultural progress'. He asserted that the peasants' techniques of tillage and agricultural implements were 'virtually unchanged' since 'the middle ages', and argued that strip farming and the three-field system were 'wasteful' because of the amount of land that had to be set aside for boundaries between strips and paths across the fields, and because one-third of the arable land was left fallow. He also attacked the practice of communal and repartitional land tenure as a disincentive to individual initiative and innovation. Similar criticisms of the peasantry's customary methods of cereal farming were made by many Soviet historians.

15 See Overton, *Agricultural Revolution*; Rösener, *Peasantry*, pp. 21–3, 53–6, 158–9, 189.

Many contemporary critics and Western historians were influenced by classical and neo-classical economics, which set great store by individual enterprise, maximisation of profits, and 'progress'. Blum's perspective is clear from his remark that his book 'is also meant to be a study in the history of human freedom'. Soviet historians wrote from the viewpoint of Marxist–Leninist ideology, which was also interested primarily in 'progress', and portrayed 'feudalism' as an obsolete 'mode of production', which hindered any further development in the techniques and implements used in production.[16]

These writers had their own agendas, and very different criteria from those of the peasants who actually farmed the land. In 1882, Alexander Engel'gardt (the Populist–chemist who lived in exile on his estate in Smolensk province) attacked a writer who had implied condescendingly that Russian peasants were stupid because they did not understand 'Ville fertilizers and German agronomy'. Engel'gardt replied: 'The muzhik [peasant] may not have read the popular pamphlets from which you have taken your wisdom, but he understands farming and the land rather more than you do. And that is understandable: the muzhik does not live on a salary, but from Mother Earth.'[17]

While a number of the criticisms of Blum and others have some validity, it is important to try to understand Russian peasants' 'traditional' agriculture from their point of view. From this perspective, the peasants' tillage systems and technology appear to be carefully thought out and in keeping with the resources available to them, and the demographic and environmental conditions and the exploitative social structure they lived in. Moreover, peasants' main aim was subsistence rather than profit.

Russian peasants had no need to make more intensive use of land as long as there was sufficient to continue with their customary methods. Land was not a scarce resource in most of Russia until the late eighteenth and early nineteenth centuries. Therefore, the three-field system was entirely appropriate. It is often forgotten, moreover, that the three-field system was relatively 'advanced' in its day, and made more intensive use of land than the long fallow and two-field systems it replaced.

The practice of leaving a field fallow was not wasteful. On the contrary, it was an effective way of looking after the soil, especially since most Russian peasants had only limited resources. A fallow period allowed the soil to regain its fertility by absorbing nitrogen from the air and, in non-black earth regions, organic matter from the manure that was spread on the field. Fallowing also enabled peasants to control weeds by ploughing and harrowing the field several times. This would not have been possible if it had been under crops. Furthermore, leaving land fallow improves moisture retention. Moreover, the fallow was not always unproductive. Although initially it was kept clear

---

16 Blum, *Lord and Peasant*, pp. 4, 326–9, 337; Koval'chenko, *Russkoe*, pp. 73–6, 302–5, 329–30. See also Kingston-Mann, E., 'In the light and shadow of the West: The impact of Western economics in pre-emancipation Russia', *CSSH*, vol. 33 (1991), pp. 86–105; Ellis, *Peasant Economics*, pp. 17–60. On the alleged disadvantages of communal and repartitional land tenure, see Ch. 6.
17 Engelgardt, *Letters*, p. 236.

of all vegetation, in the eighteenth and nineteenth centuries many peasant communities allowed natural vegetation to grow in the fallow, and used it as pasture for their livestock, which then, conveniently, deposited manure where it was needed. The reason peasants did not use manure to fertilise arable land in black earth regions was not ignorance, but because experience had taught them that grain grown in manured black earth tended to be 'leggy' and easily blown over. In these regions, peasants used manure to fertilise the plots where they grew hemp (see below, p. 143), as it exhausted the soil faster than grain. They also used dried manure as fuel, since the scarcity of woodland in steppe regions meant that firewood was in short supply.[18]

The long-fallow systems used in earlier times, and later in some outlying regions, were appropriate in circumstances where there was an abundance of land and a shortage of labour. Extensive tillage systems have often been used by farmers when land is plentiful, for example by American farmers in parts of the mid-west into the twentieth century. In contrast, the 'advanced' crop rotations without fallow, which were introduced during the 'agricultural revolution', were first developed in the Low Countries and eastern England, where land was at such a premium that it was reclaimed from the sea or the fens in expensive drainage schemes.[19]

The simple implements used by most Russian peasants can be looked at in a similar light.[20] Their implements, especially the much-derided wooden ploughs, were appropriate to the types of soil in the forest-heartland, the crops peasants grew, and the draught animals they owned. The shallow furrows cut through the light forest soils by wooden ploughs were perfectly adequate for sowing the rye and oats that were the main crops. The light wooden ploughs could be pulled by the scrawny but hardy horses that were able to survive the rigours of the Russian climate. In pre-Petrine Russia, most horses were only 12–14 hands (the size of modern ponies). In emergencies, wooden ploughs could even be pulled by women.[21] More 'advanced' steel ploughs cut deeper furrows which were not necessary for rye and oats. These ploughs required larger and stronger draught animals, which needed more fodder than most peasants had available. As already noted, when peasants migrated to the black earth regions, they adapted their wooden ploughs or used heavier ploughs, where necessary pulled by teams of oxen rather than horses, to cut and turn the heavier soils. Households without enough oxen pooled their animals. In drier parts of the steppe regions, wooden ploughs could have an advantage over more modern ploughs because the shallower furrows they cut helped the soil retain precious moisture. At the time of the collectivisation, and partial

---

18 See Shapiro, *Agrarnaya istoriya . . . XVII v.*, p. 179; Pallot and Shaw, *Landscape*, pp. 113–15; Deal, *Serf*, pp. 65–70; Simms, J. Y., 'The crop failure of 1891: Soil exhaustion, technological backwardness, and Russia's "agrarian crisis"', *SR*, vol. 41 (1982), pp. 248–9.
19 See Overton, *Agricultural Revolution*, pp. 16–17, 89–90; Rösener, *Peasantry*, pp. 22, 127–9, 134–7; Klinkenborg, V., 'A Farming Revolution', *NGM*, vol. 188, no. 6 (1995), p. 80.
20 In addition to works cited in note 12, see Confino, *Systèmes*, pp. 110–15, 230–3; Pallot and Shaw, *Landscape*, p. 72; Pintner, *Russian*, pp. 115–19; Rubinshtein, *Sel'skoe*, pp. 349–52.
21 Meyer, 'Impact', pp. 216–17.

mechanisation, of agriculture in 1929–30, the following ditty circulated among some peasants: 'The tractor ploughs deeply. / The land dries up. / Soon all the collective farmers / will die of starvation.'[22]

Most of the Russian peasants' traditional implements, including wooden ploughs, had the important advantages of reliability and simplicity. They could be made and repaired with the relatively low levels of skill which could be attained by many peasants or village craftsmen, out of raw materials, chiefly wood, which were readily available. Many of the more 'advanced' implements and machinery developed in north-west Europe during the eighteenth and nineteenth centuries were inappropriate in the conditions of Russian agriculture and, in any case, required resources and skills that most Russian peasants did not have.

Russian peasants' farming systems and implements have often been compared unfavourably with the crop rotations and machinery employed by the German farmers who settled in the Volga basin and southern Ukraine in the eighteenth and nineteenth centuries. But many German settlers were more innovative and productive than their Russian neighbours, because they had the money to hire labourers and to buy and maintain more and stronger draught animals, and because they were better endowed with land by the Russian government. Most Russian peasants lacked the resources, not the ability or the initiative, to emulate the German settlers.[23]

There were many cases of Russian peasants resisting attempts to compel them to change the ways they farmed. Donald MacKenzie Wallace related a tale about a landowner who, in the last years of serfdom, tried to 'improve' the level of farming on his estate by importing from England 'a threshing machine, ploughs, harrows, and other implements of the newest model'. When he explained the advantages of the machinery to the peasants, most remained silent. In the landowner's absence they spoke more freely: 'These may be all very well for the Germans, but they won't do for us. How are our little horses going to drag these big ploughs and harrows? And as for that (the threshing machine), it's of no use.' The peasants 'unanimously decided that no good would come of the new-fangled inventions'. Their misgivings turned out to be correct. Their horses were not strong enough to pull the ploughs and harrows. Suspiciously, the threshing machine broke the first time it was used. The landowner could not afford to buy larger horses or lighter machinery, and there was no engineer in the area who could repair the threshing machine. The implements were put away and, as they had undoubtedly intended, the peasants reverted to their old ones.[24]

When interventionist state authorities tried to 'improve' peasant agriculture, they often met with a similar response. In 1721 Peter the Great ordered that peasants in fertile parts of Russia be trained in the use of scythes, in place

22 Viola, L., *Peasant Rebels under Stalin: Collectivization and the Culture of Peasant Resistance* (New York and Oxford, 1996), p. 63.
23 See Pallot and Shaw, *Landscape*, pp. 80–111.
24 Wallace, *Russia*, vol. 1, pp. 58–9, 382–6. (Russians called all western Europeans 'Germans'.)

of their customary sickles, for harvesting grain. Peter knew that peasants in the newly conquered Baltic provinces and in Prussia used scythes and, therefore, he believed them to be more efficient. Ninety-two Baltic peasants were dispatched as instructors, large numbers of long and straight-shafted 'Lithuanian' scythes were made, and thousands of Russian peasants were taught how to use them. Nevertheless, most Russian peasants continued to reap cereal crops, especially winter rye, with sickles throughout the eighteenth and nineteenth centuries. The reasons were straightforward. It was not difficult to harvest the peasants' small strips of land with sickles. It was hard to use scythes on the uneven or stony terrain which was quite common in the forest-heartland, or to reap crops which had fallen down after wind and rain. And, when peasants first tried to use scythes, ears of grain showered on to the ground and were lost.[25] The central authorities made further attempts to encourage 'improvements' in agriculture during the reforms of the appanage and state peasants in the 1820s–40s. Agricultural colleges, model farms, shows and exhibitions were set up to train some peasants in the use of new rotations, crops and implements, and to demonstrate the advantages to others. Shortages of money and trained agronomists hindered progress, and most peasants were indifferent. When the authorities attempted to impose changes by decree, for example compulsory sowing of potatoes in arable fields, they succeeded only in provoking disorders.[26]

Russian peasants were not blindly hostile to all 'improvements', however, and their agricultural methods were not static. The ways Russian peasants grew grain certainly changed later, and more slowly, than in north-west Europe. But Russian peasant farmers were prepared to adopt innovations cautiously, if they felt they would serve their objectives. The transition to the three-field system in the central regions of Russia in the sixteenth and seventeenth centuries, its subsequent spread to some outlying regions, the ways peasant-migrants adapted their techniques and implements to their new environments, and adopted new methods, all testify that Russian peasants were prepared to change the ways they farmed when they believed it necessary.

Peasant communities in the central regions of Russia made some changes to their farming techniques in the eighteenth and nineteenth centuries. Many began to plough and harrow the arable fields two or three times to keep weeds under control and prepare the land better for sowing. In areas where manure was in short supply, peasants tried other fertilisers, for example potash and marl. In some villages peasants began to plant non-grain crops, such as peas and beans, in the arable fields in variations of the three-course rotation. There were a few examples in the late eighteenth century, which would have gladdened the hearts of agricultural 'improvers', of peasants planting turnips and fodder grasses in the fallow fields. This important practice of cultivating root vegetables and other fodder crops in fields previously left fallow was later

25 Toren, 'Sposoby', pp. 66–7. On the potential advantages of sickles, see Overton, *Agricultural Revolution*, pp. 122–4.
26 Pintner, *Russian*, pp. 174–8. See also Ch. 3.

adopted more widely. The government's attempts to 'raise' the level of farming on appanage and state lands in the 1820s–40s were not totally without result. By 1859 about 11 per cent of appanage peasants used new implements, including light, iron ploughs. The pace of change quickened in the late nineteenth century in response to the rapid population growth and greater opportunities to sell grain on the market. Some villages adopted four-field rotations including clover, improved their arable land by drainage and irrigation, and reclaimed waste land.[27]

The 'improvement' of Russian peasant agriculture in the nineteenth century should not be overstated. The introduction of more complex crop rotations, new crops and implements, and more commercially orientated farming were most common in the outlying regions of the Russian Empire, including the open steppes of southern Russia and Ukraine, and the western borderlands. 'Progressive' agriculture was less common on peasant land than on large estates run by landowners who took up commercial farming after 1861. Most peasants, especially in central Russia, persisted with their traditional ways, geared mainly towards subsistence, into the twentieth century.[28]

Most Russian peasant households for much of the period did not aim to grow as much grain as they could to sell it for profit, because limitations in the market for agricultural produce greatly reduced the incentive to devote the necessary time, effort and resources to produce more than they needed. A major problem was the poor transport network in Russia. Until the late nineteenth century, producing grain mainly for the market made much sense only in the hinterland of large cities, especially Moscow and St Petersburg, and in the vicinity of rivers which served as transport arteries, in particular the Volga and its tributaries. Peasants sold an increasing, but still small, part of their grain harvests over the eighteenth and nineteenth centuries. The percentage of the total Russian grain harvest, net of seed, which was put on the market has been estimated at around 9–10 per cent in the mid-eighteenth century, 18–20 per cent a century later, but still only around 25 per cent at the end of the nineteenth century. For much of the period under consideration, moreover, most of the grain on the market was probably supplied not by peasants from the harvests on their land, but by landowners from the produce of their demesnes. Before the 1860s, most peasant-produced grain on the market came from the plots of peasants who paid cash dues (*obrok*) to their landowners or

<hr>

27 Rubinshtein, *Sel'skoe*, pp. 267–8, 317–19, 343–53; Pallot and Shaw, *Landscape*, pp. 97–9, 292 n. 7, 116–21; Nifontov, A. S., *Zernovoe proizvodstvo Rossii vo vtoroi polovine XIX v.* (Moscow, 1974), pp. 200–19, 258–61; Gorlanov, *Udel'nye*, p. 50; Kingston-Mann, E., 'Peasant communes and economic innovation', in *PECPER*, pp. 36–42; Zyryanov, P. N., *Krest'yanskaya obshchina evropeiskoi Rossii, 1907–1914 gg.* (Moscow, 1992), pp. 56–62, 220–3. On a few 'improving' landowners, see Blum, *Lord and Peasant*, pp. 404–13, 492, 498. For an argument that communes did not impede development, see Ch. 6.
28 See Gatrell, *Tsarist Economy*, pp. 104–5, 119–28; Frierson, L. G., 'Bukkers, plows and lobogreikas: Peasant acquisition of agricultural implements in Russia before 1900', *RR*, vol. 53 (1994), pp. 399–418; Munting, R., 'Mechanization and dualism in Russian agriculture', *JEEH*, vol. 8 (1979), pp. 743–60; Pallot, J., 'Agrarian modernization on peasant family farms in the era of capitalism', in Bater and French, *Studies*, vol. 1, pp. 423–49.

the state. Only in the late nineteenth century did peasants supply the largest part of the grain on the Russian market. It should be noted, however, that grain cultivation was probably the least market-orientated branch of peasant agriculture.[29]

The majority of Russian peasant households, throughout the period under consideration, grew grain mainly for subsistence. It is likely that the main objective of most households was not to maximise production, moreover, but to minimise the risk of harvest failures, which could lead to food shortages and famine. Subsistence-orientated and risk-averse farming among the Russian peasantry can be contrasted with the development of output- and profit-maximising commercial cereal production in parts of contemporary north-west Europe. But the attitudes of Russian peasants were common among peasants in pre-industrial Europe and elsewhere in the world. Discussing the attitudes of south-east Asian peasants to farming staple crops in the twentieth century, James Scott wrote:

> The fear of food shortages has, in most precapitalist peasant societies, given rise to . . . a "subsistence ethic." This ethic, which Southeast Asian peasants shared with their counterparts in nineteenth-century France, Russia, and Italy, was a consequence of living so close to the margin . . . The family's problem . . . was to produce enough rice [or grain] to feed the household, buy a few necessities . . . , and meet the irreducible claims of outsiders. The amount of rice [or grain] a family could produce was partly in the hands of fate, but the local tradition of seed varieties, planting techniques, and timing was designed over centuries of trial and error to produce the most stable and reliable yield possible under the circumstances.[30]

'Risk aversion', or a 'safety-first' principle, can be seen to lie behind many of the Russian peasantry's traditional agricultural methods, in particular individual peasant households farming a number of strips of arable land spread around the open fields. There is little doubt that, on average, farming scattered strips was less productive than cultivating the same area of land in consolidated holdings. D. McCloskey has estimated that, in pre-industrial England, the harvest from open fields farmed in strips was around 10–13 per cent lower than from enclosed fields covering the same acreages. Nevertheless, McCloskey argued very strongly that strip farming made good sense. Harvests could vary quite dramatically in different areas of the open fields. Soil quality and fertility were not uniform. Some parts might be more clayey, sandy or stony and, hence, less productive than others. Micro-climates could vary around the village land, as some sections were likely to be more sheltered or exposed than others. Accidents or other incidents did not affect all areas equally. Livestock might trample a corner of one field; birds or insects might gorge themselves

29 Kahan, *Plow*, pp. 57–9; Nifontov, *Zernovoe*, pp. 126–37; Gregory, 'Grain marketings', pp. 147–51. See also Smith, *Peasant Farming*, pp. 152–7, 223, 225; Rubinshtein, *Sel'skoe*, pp. 199–201, 242, 250–67, 315–16. *Cf.* Preobrazhenskii, *Krest'yanstvo*, pp. 97–99, 333–7.
30 Scott, *Moral Economy*, pp. 3–5.

in another. Therefore, it was possible that a household with all its arable land consolidated in one plot might harvest far less than its neighbour with a single plot in another area. In the worst case, a household could lose most or all of its harvest. If all the households in a village farmed a number of strips scattered around open fields, however, then the risks were shared out. The loss of crops in one or two strips could be cancelled out by better yields in others. The Russian practice of periodic redistribution of strips was a further development of the risk aversion inherent in strip farming (see Ch. 6).

Strip farming in open fields was common throughout pre-industrial Europe and less developed parts of the world. Farmers who employed the practice in the twentieth century insisted that risk aversion was their motive. The logic is the same as that of investors who put together diversified portfolios of shares in different companies and in a number of markets. McCloskey's conclusion on strip farming in pre-industrial England is likely also to be valid for Russia: 'The inefficiencies of the open fields ... were payments on an insurance premium in a milieu in which agricultural yields were low and unpredictable and the costs of a shortfall – at best crushing debt or malnutrition and its associated diseases, at worst starvation – were high.'[31]

In the last analysis, strip farming, the three-field system, wooden ploughs, and the traditional crops were tried and trusted. Russian peasants knew from generations of experience that, in most years, their customary techniques guaranteed a reasonable harvest that would meet their needs and support their ways of life. Only in the late nineteenth century did some peasants begin to question the efficacy of their customary methods and, tentatively, to make changes.

Many peasants in much of Russia for most of the period from the seventeenth to the late nineteenth centuries were committed to their customary methods of growing grain and very suspicious of innovations. This is evidence not of ignorance or innate hostility to change, but of common sense and pragmatism. Russian peasants opposed attempts to introduce changes because they lacked the necessary resources, had insufficient draught power, and believed many proposed 'improvements' were unsuitable to Russian conditions, and likely to fail. Russian peasants were also suspicious that changes imposed from outside would mean that they would have to work harder, while any resulting increases in production would be taken away from them by their landowners or the state. On the other hand, Russian peasants' traditional agriculture was in keeping with the population densities and environmental conditions of the regions they lived in, and with their main objective of growing enough to feed themselves, and a small surplus to sell to earn money to buy a few necessities and meet their cash obligations.[32]

31 McCloskey, D. N., 'English open fields as behaviour towards risk', *REcH*, vol. 1 (1976), pp. 124–70 (quotation from pp. 125–6); *id.*, 'The prudent peasant: New findings on open fields', *JEcH*, vol. 51 (1991), pp. 343–55.
32 See Confino, M., *Domaines et Seigneurs en Russie vers la Fin du XVIIIe Siècle* (Paris, 1963), pp. 136–83; *id.*, *Systèmes*, pp. 225–62; Martin, J., '"Backwardness" in Russian peasant culture', in Baron, S. and Kollman, N. S. (eds), *Religion and Culture in Early Modern Russia and Ukraine* (DeKalb, IL, 1997), pp. 19–33.

Crop yields and grain production

The most appropriate way to assess the expedience of Russian peasants' customary ways of growing crops is to examine whether they did indeed produce sufficient to meet their needs. Many historians have agreed that the average grain yields attained by traditional peasant farming in Russia were very low. R. E. F. Smith concluded that average yields of winter rye and spring oats, expressed as a ratio between the amounts of seed sown and grain harvested, were around 1:3 in the forest-heartland before the mid-seventeenth century. Figures calculated from the annual reports of provincial governors from the late eighteenth century to the 1860s indicate that average yields for winter and spring cereals combined in Russia as a whole were about 1:3–3.5. These figures have been cited by most Soviet historians, for example Koval'chenko and A. S. Nifontov, and many Western specialists, including Blum and Arcadius Kahan. A yield of 1:3 did not mean that peasants had three times as much grain as they sowed for consumption or sale, because one-third of the harvest had to be set aside for seed. Net yields of 1:2–2.5 were a meagre return for the peasants' efforts.[33] Gross average yields for cereal production of 1:3–3.5 were low by the standards of pre-industrial Europe. They were similar to those attained by farmers in Britain and France in the twelfth and thirteenth centuries, around half the average yields in much of north-west Europe in the sixteenth and seventeenth centuries, and only a third of the productivity of cereal farming in England, Holland and Ireland in the second half of the eighteenth century.[34]

However, data on average Russian grain yields in the eighteenth and first half of the nineteenth centuries from sources other than governors' reports suggest that a figure of 1:3–3.5 may be too low, especially for the fertile Central Black Earth region where environmental conditions were well suited to grain cultivation. N. L. Rubinshtein cited figures on yields in the late eighteenth century, including those collected by the Free Economic Society, which are higher than those reported by governors. Yields recorded in estate records are sometimes above those reported by the governors of the provinces in which they were situated. For example, Steven Hoch calculated average yields of between 1:4.8 and 1:6.2 for different cereals over the first half of the nineteenth century from data in the estate records of Petrovskoe, Tambov province, in the Central Black Earth region. Koval'chenko noted the high yields in the records of estates, including Petrovskoe, but did not comment on the disparity between them and the lower figures he took from governors' reports.

The figures in the governors' reports may be inaccurate. They were based on test threshings of grain gathered in parts of fields. The local officials who carried out the tests were notoriously inefficient and corrupt, and both peasants and landowners were concerned that reports of high yields might encourage

33 Smith, *Peasant Farming*, pp. 86–7; Koval'chenko, *Russkoe*, p. 77; Nifontov, *Zernovoe*, pp. 71–6, 122; Blum, *Lord and Peasant*, pp. 329–30; Kahan, *Plow*, pp. 45, 48–50, 66.
34 See Braudel, F., *Capitalism and Material Life, 1400–1800*, M. Kochan (trans.) (London, 1973), p. 81.

the state to raise taxes or the army to increase requisitions in wartime. It is likely that they directed the officials to areas where the crops had grown badly in order to mask the real levels of productivity. Siberian peasants even managed to conceal entire fields from local officials. The army general staff, which carried out its own surveys of the provinces, repeatedly questioned the low yields reported by governors. Even some governors doubted the veracity of their figures. In his annual report for 1853, the governor of the black earth province of Voronezh admitted that his data on crop yields were not 'absolutely reliable'. In addition, given the perennially low output of Soviet collective farms, some Soviet historians may have understated the productivity of pre-revolutionary agriculture to show Soviet farming in better light. Hoch asserted that 'the belief that Russia suffered from relatively low agricultural productivity, with average yields of 3.5 . . . is quite simply incorrect', and that: 'For Russia as a whole, government figures consistently underestimated yields by as much as 30 per cent.' While Hoch may have overstated the case, the view that Russian grain yields were very low in the late eighteenth century and first half of the nineteenth century, especially in the black earth provinces, may well be in need of revision.[35]

Regardless of average levels of productivity of Russian peasant grain cultivation, the most striking trend was the sizable short-term fluctuations. Peasants often achieved very high yields when they cultivated land for the first time. Yields of 1:10 or higher were obtained on virgin soil throughout Russia. In exceptionally good years, high yields were sometimes reported in both black earth and non-black earth provinces. On the other hand, in bad years, peasants obtained very low yields, sometimes harvesting less grain than they had sown.[36]

Most short-term fluctuations were part of the cycle of good and bad harvests that has afflicted all agricultural societies. The chief determinants of Russian grain production were not the peasants' crop rotations and implements, nor, as Soviet historians asserted, a 'crisis of the feudal-serf system' in the first half of the nineteenth century, but environmental factors, especially the weather. Since conditions approached the margins for grain cultivation in much of Russia, even slight variations could be disastrous. When the harsh winters lasted longer than usual, late frosts seriously damaged the crops. Too little rain or drought in the spring and early summer prevented the crops from growing. But too much rain in the mid- to late summer stopped grain from ripening. In the steppe regions, dry scorching summer winds, hailstorms, and swarms of

---

35 Rubinshtein, *Sel'skoe*, pp. 353–63; Hoch, *Serfdom*, pp. 28–36; Koval'chenko, I. D., *Krest'yane i krepostnoe khozyaistvo ryazanskoi i tambovskoi gubernii v pervoi polovine XIX v.* (Moscow, 1959), pp. 82–8; Okladnikov, *Krest'yanstvo Sibiri*, p. 189; Druzhinin, *Gosudarstvennye*, vol. 1, pp. 401, 408. The governor of Voronezh's comment is in *RGIA, f.* 1281, *op.* 5, 1854, *d.* 31a, *l.* 100. On the sources, see also Litvak, B. G., *Ocherki istochnikovedeniya massovoi dokumentatsii XIX–nachala XX v.* (Moscow, 1979), pp. 125–44; Nifontov, *Zernovoe*, pp. 15–81. N.B. Caution is needed when comparing data on yields calculated in different ways.
36 See Koretskii, *Formirovanie*, pp. 93–4; Pallot and Shaw, *Landscape*, pp. 71–2; Smith, *Peasant Farming*, p. 86.

locusts sometimes destroyed whole fields of grain. It is perhaps not surprising that Russian peasants were reluctant to adopt innovations in case they made their situation even more precarious.

Many bad harvests were local, but the worst hit larger areas. Harvest failures plagued Russia throughout the period covered by this book. At the very start of the seventeenth century Russia was hit by one of the most devastating in its history. In the summer of 1601, it rained ceaselessly in some areas, and crops became so sodden that they did not ripen. Peasants simply left them in the fields to rot. The winter began early in 1601, and lasted long into the spring of 1602, when late frosts killed large acreages of winter rye when it was in flower. The harvest was poor again in 1603, because peasants were short of seed. Towards the end of the period under consideration, in 1891, a vast area of the black earth regions was struck by another devastating crop failure caused by the lethal combination of severe frosts followed by drought in the spring and summer.

There were certain periods between 1603 and 1891 when crop failures were more common than average. There were a large number of bad harvests between the mid-seventeenth and mid-eighteenth centuries. Another period characterised by frequent crop failures was the 1820s–50s. There are a number of probable causes for the recurrent poor harvests in these periods. Analysis of tree rings has shown that between the mid-sixteenth and mid-eighteenth centuries, like the rest of Europe, Russia was affected by the downturn in the climate known as the 'little ice age'. Long, severe winters had a particularly adverse affect on agricultural productivity in Russia in much of this period, although there was some respite in the first half of the seventeenth century. In the early nineteenth century a number of protracted winters and summers which were either cold and wet or very dry hit agricultural production in much of Russia.

From the late eighteenth century, the spread of arable farming onto the open steppe led to an increase in the degree of short-term fluctuations in the harvest (see Table 4.1). There were some very large harvests in good years, but also some very bad harvests. Several harvest failures in the nineteenth century, including those of 1822, 1832–33, 1848, 1855 and 1891, were especially bad in the open steppe regions. The main reason was the low and unreliable rainfall in the south-east. In addition, as peasants cleared ever-larger areas of steppe of its natural vegetation, including the small patches of woodland, and converted wild grassland into cultivated fields, the modification of the environment led to a change in the climate. In his study of the Ukrainian province of Khar'kov (adjoining the Central Black Earth region of Russia), Zack Deal has shown that winters became colder and summers hotter and drier as a direct consequence of peasant farming. The change increased the chance of bad harvests.[37]

37 See Smith and Christian, *Bread*, pp. 110, 339–42; Nifontov, *Zernovoe*, pp. 140–5, 267–8; Rubinshtein, *Sel'skoe*, pp. 363–71; Simms, 'Crop failure', pp. 236–50. On climate, see Borisenkov, E. P., 'Documentary evidence from the USSR', in Bradley, R. S. and Jones, P. D. (eds), *Climate*

TABLE 4.1

HARVEST FLUCTUATIONS IN FOREST AND STEPPE ZONES (DATA FOR 1857–66, 1870–76, 1883–89)

Zone	Good harvests[1]	Average harvests[2]	Poor harvests[3]	Bad harvests[4]
Forest (non-black earth)	22%	56%	21%	4%
Steppe (black earth)	38%	28%	22%	12%
Total	30%	42%	22%	8%

[1] Good harvests = over 10% above mean.
[2] Average harvests = within 10% of mean.
[3] Poor harvests = 10–66% below mean.
[4] Bad harvests = more than 66% below mean.

Source: Adapted from Smith and Christian, *Bread*, p. 343.

In spite of the periodic harvest failures, over the long term the average size of Russian harvests increased. One of the more pessimistic Soviet historians, Koval'chenko, was prepared to accept that total grain (and potato) output increased over the first half of the nineteenth century, but argued that it did not keep pace with population growth.[38] Blum was more optimistic. He stated: 'Because of the vast area devoted to cereals, Russia produced more grain per capita than did any other European land.' He noted the view of some contemporary observers that 'Russia suffered from chronic overproduction of grain during the first half of the nineteenth century', but that others argued that the surpluses in good years were needed to cover shortfalls in bad years.[39]

More reliable figures on grain yields and output are available for the late nineteenth century. There is little doubt that average yields rose in the last third of the century. According to governors' reports, the average seed/harvest ratios for rye cultivation in the European part of the Russian Empire increased from 1:4 in the 1870s to 1:5.1 in the 1890s, while the average yields of wheat rose from 1:3.3 to 1:5.3 in the same period. Yields were higher in the more fertile black earth regions. (See Table 4.2.) Both Soviet and Western scholars have produced data that show not only a steadily rising trend in the output of grain (and potatoes), but also that output grew more quickly than the population. Late nineteenth-century Russia produced more grain per head of population than the average in Europe as a whole. The increases in the average size of the harvest were caused partly by the higher average grain

---

Since AD 1500 (London and New York, 1992), pp. 171–5; Graybill, D. A. and Shiyatov, S. G., 'Dendroclimatic evidence from the northern Soviet Union', in *ibid.*, p. 409; Deal, *Serf*, pp. 325–72. See also Chs 1, 2 and 8.
38 Koval'chenko, *Russkoe*, pp. 77–9, 301–5, 386. See also Nifontov, *Zernovoe*, p. 138. Some peasants began to grow potatoes in place of part of their grain crop in the nineteenth century. See below, pp. 142–3.
39 Blum, *Lord and Peasant*, pp. 331–3.

TABLE 4.2

GRAIN YIELDS (1870s–1890s) EXPRESSED AS SEED : HARVEST RATIOS

Region	Rye			Wheat			Oats		
	1870s	1880s	1890s	1870s	1880s	1890s	1870s	1880s	1890s
Non-Black Earth	1:3.4	1:3.9	1:4.5	1:3.4[1]	1:3.7[1]	1:4.6[1]	1:3.0	1:3.0	1:3.4
Black Earth	1:4.4	1:4.9	1:5.5	1:3.3	1:4.6	1:5.3	1:3.7	1:3.9	1:4.2
Total	1:4.0	1:4.5	1:5.1	1:3.3	1:4.5	1:5.3	1:3.4	1:3.5	1:3.8

[1] Very little wheat was grown in non-black earth regions.

Source: Nifontov, *Zernovoe proizvodstvo*, p. 276.

yields. These, in turn, were a result of the improvement in the climate following the end of the 'little ice age', the expansion of arable farming in the fertile open steppe regions, and some intensification of production, including the spread of the three-field system to some outlying areas where long-fallow systems had persisted, as well as the adoption of more intensive methods of cultivation by some farmers in the central regions.[40]

The traditional Russian peasant solution to the problem of raising grain output to keep pace with increases in the population and in the demands of the landowning and ruling elites was not to hope for better weather or adopt new farming methods, but to expand the area of land under cultivation, while continuing with the customary tillage systems, i.e. extensification rather than intensification of production. This was a major factor behind peasant migration to the borderlands, especially to the more fertile black earth regions (see Ch. 2). The total area of arable land in Russia and the male peasant population both roughly doubled over the eighteenth century. Assuming that average levels of grain consumption and exploitation *per capita* remained relatively unchanged, and that average grain yields were stable throughout the eighteenth century, then this would suggest that the increase in grain output was almost entirely due to extensification. The expansion of arable land began to lag behind the growth in the number of peasants in the nineteenth century.[41] Again, assuming relatively unchanged average levels of consumption and exploitation *per capita*, then this would suggest that average grain yields were increasing.

Part of any shortfall in the late nineteenth century may have been made up for by potatoes, which were more productive per acre than cereals (see below, p. 143). Moreover, some grain was imported from Ukraine after railway

40 See Nifontov, *Zernovoe*, pp. 155, 183, 198, 266–8, 275–7, 316; Gregory, 'Grain marketings'; Borisenkov, 'Documentary', pp. 173–5; Graybill and Shiyatov, 'Dendroclimatic', p. 409.
41 Mironov, 'Consequences', p. 462. Data on land use in Tsvetkov, M. A., *Izmeneniya lesistosti Evropeiskoi Rossii s kontsa XVII stoletiya po 1914 g.* (Moscow, 1957), pp. 110–17, can be compared with figures on population in Ch. 1.

construction had partly overcome the transport problems. But, the grain trade between Ukraine and Russia had never been large and, from the late eighteenth century, most surplus Ukrainian grain was exported via the Black Sea ports.[42]

The picture was not as rosy as it might seem. Aggregate figures on increasing grain output conceal regions and households that were not doing as well. The increase in the amount of arable land was achieved partly by bringing virgin land into cultivation, but also at the expense of pastures and meadows. Large areas of land were ploughed up to grow grain, mostly for human consumption, rather than to produce fodder for animals. To some extent, this was a sustainable shift from animal husbandry to cereal cultivation. But in parts of the densely populated central regions it was taken too far, leading to shortages of draught animals to pull the ploughs and of manure to enrich the soil. Some peasant communities reduced the area of fallow, or sowed crops without a regular rotation in 'degenerate systems'. In parts of the central regions, the land was becoming exhausted, and soil erosion was a serious problem. As a result of all these factors, the crop yields attained by peasants in some central areas were beginning to decline at the end of the nineteenth century.[43]

Animal husbandry

Although grain cultivation was the most important sector of Russian peasant agriculture, the majority of peasant households also engaged in animal husbandry.[44] The two main forms of agriculture were closely linked and interdependent: animals provided the draught power to pull the implements used to cultivate the arable fields, and manure for use as organic fertiliser. Peasants also raised livestock for meat, dairy produce, hides and wool. Cattle were very common throughout Russia and Siberia; peasants also kept sheep, especially in the steppe regions, and pigs, chickens and geese. Men and women shared responsibility for looking after the livestock. Women tended the small domestic livestock and the cows, while men looked after the draught animals. Most households raised livestock for their own needs, but in some areas, for example near towns and cities, peasants engaged in market-orientated meat and dairy production.

The pattern of work in tending livestock was seasonal. In the spring, once the grass had started to grow, peasants allowed their horses, cows and sheep to leave the stalls where they had spent the winter to graze on pasture, in

---

42 See Koropeckyj, I. S. (ed.), *Ukrainian Economic History* (Cambridge, MA, 1991), pp. 173, 210, 227, 312, 320.
43 Smith and Christian, *Bread*, p. 262; Pavlovsky, G., *Agricultural Russia on the Eve of Revolution* (London, 1930), pp. 50, 85–6, 303–6; Stebelsky, 'Agriculture'; Pallot and Shaw, *Landscape*, pp. 118–19.
44 The following section is based largely on Blum, *Lord and Peasant*, pp. 340–2; Smith, *Peasant Farming*, pp. 41–6, 209–11; Pallot and Shaw, *Landscape*, pp. 7–8, 20, 69–70, 73, 113; Rubinshtein, *Sel'skoe*, pp. 280–94, 322–4; Hoch, *Serfdom*, pp. 44–7; Fedorov, *Pomeshchich'i*, pp. 59–62, 73–5; Okladnikov, *Krest'yanstvo Sibiri*, pp. 66–7, 198–203; Pavlovsky, *Agricultural*, pp. 299–318.

woodland and the fallow field. The customary day for letting livestock outside was the first of the two St George's days in the Orthodox calendar, 23 April. In the Northern region and parts of Siberia, where winter lasted longer, the first of the two St Nicholas's days, 9 May, served this purpose. Since most pasture was held in common, it was important that all households started pasturing their animals outside on the same day, and that none pre-empted their neighbours at the expense of the young shoots of grass.

Taking the animals outside in the spring was accompanied by various rituals.[45] Peasants used switches of pussy willow, which had been blessed in their churches on Palm Sunday, to drive their livestock to the pasture. The priest held a special service and blessed the animals by sprinkling them with holy water. The day was marked by communal celebrations and feasting. Peasants also sought supernatural protection for their livestock on two feast days in the summer. Saint Ilya (Elijah) was a patron saint of cattle. On his feast day, 20 July, peasants attended church services and held feasts. Saints Flor and Laur were patron saints of horses, and their feast day, 18 August, was also marked by services and rituals to invoke their protection. Peasants sought extra help from St George and St Nicholas. These patron saints were probably Christianised versions of old pagan gods of livestock.

In the late summer, after the harvest had been gathered in, peasants let their animals feed on the stubble in the open fields. Most livestock spent the long winter months in barns or other outbuildings. Livestock were kept indoors for six months of the year in northern Russia. During the winter, animals lived on the straw and chaff left over after threshing, and some animals were fed oats and turnips, but the most important fodder crop was hay. Hayfields or meadows were thus a vitally important part of the village land. In much of Russia, peasants began haymaking on the day after the feast of St Peter, 29 June. Mowing the hay with scythes was mainly the men's responsibility, but women also helped. The need for fodder was so great that grass was mown along river banks and in woods. Peasants gathered hay into stacks or stored it in haylofts until it was needed in the winter.

As a result of the long winters spent indoors living on fodder, Russian peasants' livestock were often small and thin. Wallace, who spent some time in a village in Novgorod province in the North-western region, noted:

> The cattle . . . are never very fat, but [when they are brought out for the first time at the end of April] . . . their appearance is truly lamentable. During the winter they have been cooped up in small unventilated cowhouses, and fed almost exclusively on straw [?]; now, when they are released from their imprisonment, they look like the ghosts of their former emaciated selves. All are lean and weak, many are lame, and some cannot rise to their feet without assistance.[46]

45 On rituals connected with livestock and haymaking, see Gromyko, *Traditsionnye*, pp. 120–3; Ivanits, *Russian Folk Belief*, pp. 8–9, 24–30; Matossian, 'Peasant', pp. 35–7.
46 Wallace, *Russia*, vol. 1, pp. 145–6.

Cows fared badly because peasants kept the best fodder, including most of the oats, for their draught animals, usually horses, which needed to be fit for the spring ploughing. If supplies of fodder ran short by the end of the winter, it was the horses which got the largest share of what remained. Livestock were affected by the periodic harvest failures. In bad years, peasants had little option but to slaughter and eat their animals to save fodder and avoid starving, or to sell them to buy food. In addition, livestock were regularly hit by epidemic diseases.

Raising livestock was secondary to arable farming in most of Russia, especially the central provinces, but was more important in outlying regions. In some peripheral areas, the natural conditions were better suited to livestock husbandry than cereal farming. In the Northern region and parts of Siberia, the short growing season and infertile soil were unfavourable to arable farming but more compatible with rearing animals. In the steppe regions, the initial problems peasant-migrants experienced in ploughing the heavy black earth with their wooden ploughs slowed the development of arable farming, and meant that, initially, animal husbandry was more important. Throughout the outlying regions, with their lower human population densities, there was an abundance of land for pasture and hay. In the Northern region and parts of Siberia, peasants grazed their livestock in the forests. The vast areas of grassland in the open steppe regions, including the southernmost part of Siberia, provided excellent pastures for large herds of cattle and sheep. The long-fallow farming systems which were widespread in parts of the northern and open steppe regions and Siberia until relatively late in the period under consideration enabled peasant households to combine extensive animal husbandry and arable farming. Herding had been the principal occupation of the nomadic pastoralists who had lived on the steppes before the peasants' arrival, and had played a large part in the livelihood of the cossacks, who had been among the pioneers of Slavonic settlement of the steppes (see Ch. 2).

Over time, the importance of animal husbandry relative to grain cultivation declined in most of Russia, first in the central regions, and later in outlying areas. The spread of the more intensive three-field system from the centre to the periphery led to a reduction in the area of meadows and pastures, as many were ploughed up and turned over to cereal cultivation. By the mid-eighteenth century, many peasant households in the Central Non-Black Earth region and in the north and west of the Central Black Earth region had access to more arable land than hayfields and pasture. In the south-east of the Central Black Earth region, for example southern Tambov, Voronezh and Kursk provinces, raising livestock remained a very important part of the peasant economy into the first half of the nineteenth century. By the 1880s, however, there was far more arable land than meadows and pastures throughout most of the central regions. Only in parts of the North-western, Northern and Northern Urals regions, and in the south and east of the open steppe regions, was there more meadow and pasture land than arable land. Moreover, the loss of hayfields and grazing land in the more central regions was only partly offset by the new practice of growing fodder crops in fields previously left fallow.[47]

One of the main reasons for the shift from raising livestock to cultivating cereals was population increase. Growing grain for people to eat makes much more efficient use of land than animal husbandry, as there is one less link in the food chain. When grass or oats are grown to feed animals, only a small proportion of the calories from the fodder crops are converted into animal flesh or milk for human consumption. Cereals produce as much as ten times as many calories from the same area of land than animal husbandry and, therefore, can support a much larger human population.[48] This was part of the explanation for the 'triumph' of settled peasant farming over nomadic pastoralism on the steppes (see Ch. 2).

Several historians have argued that there was a decline in the average numbers of animals kept by peasant households over the nineteenth century, especially in the Central Black Earth region. Soviet scholars saw the apparent decline in the first half of the century as further evidence for a 'crisis' in the 'feudal-serf economy' before 1861, and for the immiseration of the mass of the peasantry in the late nineteenth century. It has proved extremely difficult to produce accurate and meaningful data on peasant livestock holdings *per capita*, and there is no consensus whether they were increasing or decreasing in the nineteenth century. If there was a decline overall, it probably reflected the gradual change in many regions away from livestock husbandry in favour of cereal cultivation.[49]

Vegetables, fruit and other crops

In addition to grain cultivation and animal husbandry, most peasant households also grew vegetables, fruit and other crops. The most common vegetables were cabbage, cucumber, onions, garlic, carrots, beetroots, turnips, radishes, peas and beans. Many households had orchards or a few apple trees. Melons were common in southern Russia. Vegetables were grown mainly in kitchen gardens, which were cultivated by the women. In some villages, root vegetables and pulses were incorporated into the crop rotations in the arable fields. Most households grew vegetables and fruit for their own consumption, both human and animal, but in the hinterland of large towns and cities, many households grew larger quantities for sale.[50]

Potatoes spread slowly to Russia from central Europe, via the Baltic provinces, Belorussia and Ukraine, in the nineteenth century. At first many Russian peasants were suspicious. Peasants rioted when the Appanage Department

47 For data on land use, see Tsvetkov, *Izmeneniya*, pp. 110–17.
48 Smith and Christian, *Bread*, p. 262.
49 See Koval'chenko, *Russkoe*, pp. 298–300; Anfimov, A. M., *Krest'yanskoe khozyaistvo evropeiskoi Rossii, 1881–1904* (Moscow, 1980), pp. 212–13; Wheatcroft, S. G., 'Crises and the condition of the peasantry in late imperial Russia', in *PECPER*, pp. 142–4.
50 See Smith, *Peasant Farming*, p. 39; Rubinshtein, *Sel'skoe*, pp. 267–9; Hoch, *Serfdom*, pp. 48–9; Fedorov, *Pomeshchich'i*, pp. 66–9, 72–3.

and Ministry of State Domains tried to compel them to grow potatoes in the 1830s–40s. Peasants were unwilling to plant this unknown root vegetable in part of their arable land, in place of tried and trusted cereals, as they did not know from their own experience whether it would prosper. Peasants' concerns were heightened when some initial attempts to sow potatoes failed. Cultivating potatoes was also unpopular because they required more work than growing grain. The forcible introduction of potatoes provoked other worries. Some state peasants feared the measure was a precursor to their conversion to appanage or seigniorial peasants. Religious dissenters identified the humble potato as the 'devil's apple', and refused to have anything to do with it. Peasants' resistance to potatoes began to melt away as they became more accustomed to them. In the 1840s and 50s, when there was a succession of poor grain harvests, many peasants began to see the value of the potato as insurance against hunger. Furthermore, although potatoes are less nutritious than cereals pound for pound, their chief advantage is that the same area of land planted with potatoes yields around three times more calories than if it is sown with grain. The area of land under potatoes grew quickly from the mid-nineteenth century, and potato production increased faster than grain output. Consequently, potatoes made an important contribution to supporting the rapidly growing rural population in late nineteenth- and early twentieth-century Russia.[51]

Peasant households grew other crops in parts of their kitchen gardens or arable land. Flax and hemp were grown for their seeds and fibres. Flax was grown throughout the non-black earth regions, while hemp was more common in western Russia and the black earth regions. Peasants grew hops, sunflowers and tobacco in areas where the conditions were appropriate. Peasants grew these 'industrial crops' as cash crops as well as for domestic consumption.[52]

HANDICRAFTS, TRADE AND WAGE LABOUR

Agriculture was the main productive activity of most Russian peasant households, but many also allocated resources, time and energy to other endeavours. Handicrafts, trade and wage labour, including migrant labour, were important secondary occupations for many households, and were the main pursuits for some.[53] Households produced goods they needed if they were

51 See Smith and Christian, *Bread*, pp. 199–200, 278–84; Pintner, *Russian*, pp. 176–8; Fedorov, *Pomeshchich'i*, pp. 58–9, 69–71; Nifontov, *Zernovoe*, pp. 120, 163–4, 183, 187, 224–5, 229.
52 See Smith, *Peasant Farming*, p. 40; Rubinshtein, *Sel'skoe*, pp. 270–8; Melton, *Serfdom*, pp. 147–82; Fedorov, *Pomeshchich'i*, pp. 63–6, 71–2.
53 The following section is based largely on Fedorov, *Pomeshchich'i*, pp. 82–197; Melton, E., 'Proto-industrialization, serf agriculture and agrarian social structure: Two estates in nineteenth-century Russia', *P & P*, no. 115 (1987), pp. 73–87; Pallot and Shaw, *Landscape*, pp. 216–40; Rudolph, R. L., 'Agricultural structure and proto-industrialization in Russia: Economic development with unfree labour', *JEcH*, vol. 45 (1985), pp. 47–69. See also Blum, *Lord and Peasant*, pp. 293–325; Smith, *Peasant Farming*, pp. 47–56; Rubinshtein, *Sel'skoe*, pp. 247–9, 295–309; Okladnikov, *Krest'yanstvo Sibiri*, pp. 67–77, 203–10; Hilton, A., *Russian Folk Art* (Bloomington, IN, 1995). (Although trade and some wage labour were not productive activities, it is convenient to discuss them in this chapter.)

not readily available at local markets, or if they could not afford to buy them. In the late nineteenth century, when the numbers of peasants involved in non-agricultural pursuits was higher than in the preceding period, members of over half of all peasant households in Russia were engaged in some form of 'off-farm' work.[54]

Non-agricultural activities were more common in the forest-heartland, where 80–90 per cent of peasant households were involved to some degree in the late nineteenth century,[55] than in the black earth regions, where farming remained predominant throughout the period under consideration. This regional specialisation can be explained partly by the differences in soil fertility. In addition, the short agricultural year in the forest-heartland left over half the year free for other activities. The big cities of the forest-heartland, especially Moscow and St Petersburg, provided large urban markets for peasant handicraft and agricultural production, and attracted many traders and migrant workers from the surrounding areas. Non-agricultural activities were also fairly common in the black earth regions, which had more fertile soil and a longer growing season, but were further from the main cities. Households with large families or insufficient land engaged in crafts, trade and wage labour to make use of extra hands that were not needed for farming. Rural underemployment and land hunger became serious problems in the Central Black Earth region in the late nineteenth century. Regardless of the regions they lived in, households engaged in crafts, trade and wage labour in order to earn the money they needed to pay their taxes and other dues, and to purchase items they needed but could not make for themselves. Diversifying into non-agricultural activities was also a form of risk aversion: if the harvest failed, households still had incomes from other sources.

Peasant households engaged in a very wide variety of handicrafts. Many dated back to the sixteenth and seventeenth centuries or earlier, but most developed and became more widespread from the mid-eighteenth century. Some handicrafts involved processing agricultural produce, for example milling grain; brewing beer and (illegal) distilling; making butter and other dairy produce; rendering tallow from animal fat for soap and candles; tanning hides, and using the leather to make footwear, harnesses and other goods; making sheepskin coats; extracting vegetable oil from flax, hemp and sunflower seeds; spinning yarn from flax and hemp fibres and fleeces; weaving linen, canvas and woollen cloth; and making rope, sacks, clothes, hats and felt boots.

The vast forests of central and northern Russia and Siberia provided a wealth of raw materials for other handicrafts. Lumbering was a major occupation for many peasants in densely wooded areas of the forest-heartland. Peasants used timber for building, and for making an assortment of things ranging from carts, sledges, boats and agricultural implements to barrels, bowls and wooden

54 Merl, S., 'Socio-economic differentiation of the peasantry', in Davies, R. W. (ed.), *From Tsarism to the New Economic Policy* (Basingstoke and London, 1990), p. 61.
55 *ibid.*

spoons. The inner bark from trees (bast) was used to make footwear and baskets and, in earlier times, had been used in place of paper. Wood was also the raw material for making potash, for soap and fertiliser, and for producing pitch, which was used in construction and boat building. Many villages had a smithy where peasant craftsmen made ploughshares, blades for sickles and scythes, and heads for axes. Pottery, especially making household crockery, was also widespread. In regions where timber was in short supply, peasants made bricks for construction. Peasant craftsmen and women also produced less prosaic items, for example cheap icons for peasants to hang in the icon or 'red' corners of their houses. Aside from handicrafts, other common non-agricultural activities included hunting, trapping and fishing. In Siberia, some peasants dug up frozen mammoths, removed their tusks, and sold the ivory.

Many peasants produced handicrafts on a small scale as a cottage industry (*kustarnaya promyshlennost'*) inside their households, using the labour of family members and raw materials which they had grown or gathered locally. Peasants sold some of their wares at local markets and fairs. The handicraft activities of many households were dependent on other people for supplies of raw materials and markets for the finished products in a 'putting out' system. For example, many of the domestic weavers in the Central Non-Black Earth region in the nineteenth century relied on mills and middlemen to supply them with yarn, and on merchants, middlemen and owners of dyeworks to buy the cloth they made. Middlemen and merchants tried to establish control over peasant-craftsmen and women. They sold them raw materials on credit, and then bought their produce for low prices. Other middlemen paid peasants in kind, with boxes of vodka, kerosene, matches, tea, soap and other consumer goods. The rise of cotton textiles in place of linen in the nineteenth century increased the dependence of peasant textile workers on middlemen and the market, because their basic raw material, cotton instead of flax, could not be grown locally but had to be imported.

In contrast to the small scale of cottage industries and the 'putting out' system, some rich peasants ran large-scale manufacturing operations. They employed other peasants as wage labourers, and had some control over the markets for their produce. Whole settlements and districts, mainly in the Central Non-Black Earth region, specialised in making particular goods. Ivanovo, in Vladimir province, became a major centre of textile production in the eighteenth and nineteenth centuries. It was often referred to as the 'Russian Manchester'. In 1857 Ivanovo contained 135 mills and factories, with 10,300 workers, and an annual output worth 5.8 million roubles. In neighbouring Nizhnii Novgorod province, the villages of Pavlovo and Vorsma and the surrounding settlements specialised in metal working. Peasant workshops made metal parts for agricultural implements and scissors, locks, cutlery and other goods. Pavlovo was also known by the name of an English industrial city: the 'Russian Sheffield'. In Mstera, Palekh and Kholui, Vladimir province, icon painting had been the main occupation of the local peasants since the seventeenth century. The villages had been the property of a monastery (before it was acquired by the Panin family), and the monks had taught the peasants their skills.

Many industrial villages were on the estates of magnates. Both Ivanovo and Pavlovo were owned by the Sheremetevs. Other manufacturing centres belonged to the Panins, Golitsyns and other prominent nobles. These wealthy landowners actively encouraged their peasants' enterprise. They assisted their 'serf-entrepreneurs' by supplying them with raw materials from their estates, allowing them to hire other seigniorial peasants as workers, and helping them keep their labour forces under control. Magnates also aided their industrious peasants by making capital and credit available, and securing commercial privileges for them. Nobles who encouraged their peasants' enterprises were motivated by self-interest. They demanded a substantial share of their profits in seigniorial obligations, or considerable sums to free them from serfdom.

In industrial villages, handicrafts became the main economic activity of many peasant households, and farming was relegated to secondary importance or abandoned altogether. In Pavlovo, for example, only ten households out of over 1,000 still engaged in arable farming in 1849, but most probably still grew some vegetables and kept a few livestock. The peasants of Pavlovo and other industrial villages rented their arable land to peasants from neighbouring villages, or hired peasants to cultivate it. Some activities, for example spinning and weaving, were often considered 'women's work', and others, such as metal working, were usually carried out by men. These distinctions began to break down in the late nineteenth century. Some women withdrew from farm work altogether, and concentrated on handicrafts. The greater symmetry between women's and men's work in cottage industry did not mean equality. Women were usually paid less than men, and were sometimes prevented from using new machinery.[56]

Trade and commerce were also important activities in the peasant economy.[57] Many peasants made a living buying and selling the agricultural and handicraft produce of other peasants, and supplying villages with a variety of necessities and a few luxuries. Trading peasants were most common in the Central Non-Black Earth and North-western regions of the forest-heartland because the opportunities for trade were greatest. The extent of cottage industry and manufacturing, for example in Ivanovo and Pavlovo, meant that many peasant households had manufactured goods to sell, and needed to purchase raw materials for their handicrafts and food to eat. Moscow, St Petersburg and other large towns in these regions provided bigger markets where trading peasants could sell foodstuffs and craft production. One of the major centres of trade was the great annual fair at Nizhnii Novgorod, which was situated in

56 See Glickman, 'Peasant women', pp. 58–69; Pallot, J., 'Women's domestic industries in Moscow province, 1880–1900', in Clements, *Russia's Women*, pp. 163–84.
57 The following section is based largely on Tarlovskaya, V. P., *Torgovlya Rossii perioda pozdnego feodalizma: Torgovye krest'yane vo vtoroi polovine XVII–nachale XVIII v.* (Moscow, 1988); Rieber, *Merchants*, pp. 45–52; Fedorov, *Pomeshchich'i*, pp. 67–9, 124–7, 134–5.

the east of the Central Non-Black Earth region at the confluence of the Volga and Oka rivers.[58]

The major transport routes, especially navigable rivers, of the Central Non-Black Earth region enabled peasant-traders and merchants to deal in goods from further afield, and those destined for more distant markets. Transport arteries also provided commercial opportunities for peasant-traders in other regions. Merchants in the Mid- and Lower-Volga regions shipped grain up the Volga and its tributaries to Nizhnii Novgorod, Moscow and, via canals, St Petersburg. The grain was then sold to urban populations and rural craftsmen and tradesmen. Rivers were the main arteries for the timber trade, which was widespread in the north of the forest-heartland. Peasant timber merchants in Baki, Kostroma province, hired their neighbours to work as lumberjacks to fell trees and float the logs down the Vetluga and Volga rivers for sale in Kazan' and as far south as Saratov and Astrakhan'.[59] Rivers were not suitable for transporting all bulky goods. From the early eighteenth century, drovers brought herds of cattle to central Russia overland from the south of the Central Black Earth region.[60]

There were wide variations in the scale of trading peasants' commercial operations. Some peasants supplemented their incomes by buying up their neighbours' surplus agricultural and craft produce, and then selling it, together with their own households' output, to merchants and middlemen, and at local markets and fairs. The Nizhnii Novgorod fair served as a centre for the activities of thousands of itinerant peasant traders or pedlars, for whom petty trade was their main source of income. They met up every summer at the fair to buy new supplies of goods to sell, and to settle accounts from the previous summer's fair. Most pedlars bought up inexpensive manufactured goods, including cotton yarn and cloth, pins and needles, knives and scissors, cheap icons and a host of other items. They then spent the next ten or eleven months travelling around villages in large parts of Russia selling their wares. Some pedlars travelled on foot and carried their goods in boxes. Other peasants had larger-scale trading operations. They owned carts or trains of wagons, and had sufficient capital to buy up more supplies. As well as selling goods, some peasant traders also bought up peasant handicraft produce, and acted as middlemen between peasant producers and their sources of raw materials and markets. From the mid-eighteenth century trading peasants increasingly took over large areas of commerce from the traditional Russian merchantry. The owners of wealthy serf-traders protected them against competition from merchants. It was not until 1824, however, that trading peasants were granted the same commercial rights in law as the merchantry.

58 See Fitzpatrick, A. L., *The Great Russian Fair: Nizhnii Novgorod, 1840–90* (Basingstoke and London, 1990).
59 Melton, E, 'Household economies and communal conflicts on a Russian serf estate, 1800–1817', *JSocH*, vol. 26 (1993), p. 565.
60 Smith and Christian, *Bread*, p. 194.

The numbers of trading peasants increased over the eighteenth and nineteenth centuries, not just because they were squeezing out merchants from some areas of commerce, but because opportunities for trade were growing. As more peasant households and villages in the forest-heartland devoted a greater part of their resources and time to non-agricultural activities, demand for raw materials and foodstuffs increased, together with the supply of manufactured goods. The developing regional specialisation between the forest-heartland and the still largely agricultural black earth regions led to the growth of inter-regional trade.

A few peasants became wealthy businessmen. A good example is Nikita Demidov, who was born a state peasant in 1656 in Tula in the Central Black Earth region. He founded industrial enterprises in the Urals, and employed thousands of workers. His munitions works supplied Peter the Great's army, and he was ennobled by Peter in 1720. A number of the serf mill-owners in Ivanovo became extremely rich. I. I. Grachev, who established the first linen mill in the town in 1748, became a successful entrepreneur. In 1795 he purchased his freedom from Count Sheremetev for 130,000 roubles. Other serf-entrepreneurs in Ivanovo followed suit. Some allegedly paid up to a million roubles for their freedom. There were several wealthy peasant-manufacturers in the Pavlovo–Vorsma metal-working region in the mid-nineteenth century. The largest business was that of I. G. Zav'yalov. He owned five workshops, which employed 100 hired workers, and 'put out' work to nearly 500 peasant-craftsmen. Zav'yalov's business specialised in surgical instruments, which were reputed to be 'no worse than English instruments', and had an annual turnover of 100,000 silver roubles. One of the largest textile businesses in Moscow at the end of the nineteenth century was the Morozov company, which employed 22,000 workers and had a turnover of 32 million roubles a year. It had been founded a century earlier by Savva Morozov, who was born a seigniorial peasant in 1770 and had bought his freedom in 1823.[61]

Although handicrafts and trade became more important over the eighteenth and nineteenth centuries, especially in the non-black earth regions, they did not challenge the predominance of agriculture in the peasant economy of Russia as a whole. Although most peasant households had some members involved in non-agricultural activities at the end of the nineteenth century, it can be estimated from the 1897 census that only around 6 per cent of the peasantry of the entire Russian Empire relied on craft production and commerce as their principal sources of income.[62]

While the vast majority of Russian peasants engaged in farming and handicrafts in their own households and villages, a small proportion worked as wage

---

61 See Blum, *Lord and Peasant*, pp. 299–300, 472–4; Fedorov, *Pomeshchich'i*, pp. 137–9; Rosovsky, H., 'The serf entrepreneur in Russia', *EEH*, 1st series, vol. 6 (1954), pp. 207–33; debate between Rosovsky and P. Gutman, *EEH*, vol. 7 (1954), pp. 48–54; Hudson, H. D., *The Rise of the Demidov Family and the Russian Iron Industry in the Eighteenth Century* (Newtonville, MA, 1986), esp. pp. 35–46.
62 Moon, 'Estimating', pp. 146–7.

labourers outside their households.[63] Some continued to live in their households, but worked for fellow villagers. Richer households who engaged in handicrafts and trade hired poorer neighbours to cultivate their land and to work in their workshops and trading operations. Under serfdom, only a few landowners employed labourers to work on their estates as most preferred to use the labour services (*barshchina*) of their own peasants. After 1861, however, landowners and some wealthy peasants began to employ labourers to farm their land. The total numbers of permanent agricultural labourers, however, remained low.[64]

Growing numbers of peasants worked far from their home villages as migrant wage labourers (*otkhodniki*). Many peasants left their homes to seek work during the slack season in the agricultural calendar in the autumn and winter, and returned home in the summer to help with haymaking and harvesting. Others stayed away for the whole year or longer. Migrant wage labour was most common in the Central Non-Black Earth and North-western regions. A smaller proportion of peasants in the black earth regions left their homes in search of work. Migrant labourers worked in a wide variety of occupations, for example as domestic servants, cab drivers, traders and building workers in St Petersburg, Moscow and other cities; as barge haulers (*burlaki*) along major rivers, in particular the Volga; as factory and mill hands in manufacturing areas in the forest-heartland; and as miners, especially in the Urals, Siberia and south-east Ukraine. Many worked as seasonal agricultural labourers. The demand for farm workers was greatest in the sparsely populated but fertile open steppe regions of the Lower Volga and Don basins and southern Ukraine, where large-scale commercial farming developed in the nineteenth century. Migrant labourers from the same area tended to specialise in particular jobs. For example, most of the masons and carpenters in St Petersburg and Moscow came from Vladimir and Yaroslavl' provinces; and in some villages in Mozhaisk and Vereya districts of Moscow province, many boys were sent to Moscow to work as tailors. Most migrant labourers were men, but in the late nineteenth century, larger numbers of peasant women left their villages to work in towns and cities.

Peasants who wished to leave their villages to work needed written permission from their landowners, local officials or village communes, who thus had the authority to regulate or prevent migrant labour. Under serfdom, many landowners allowed some peasants to leave in search of wage labour, and demanded parts of their wages as seigniorial obligations. In the early nineteenth century, Prince Gagarin assigned some of the peasants on his Manuilovkoe estate in Tver' province to work on other Gagarin estates, and others to work

---

63 The following section is based largely on Blum, *Lord and Peasant*, pp. 321–4, 452–3; Fedorov, *Pomeshchich'i*, pp. 75–80, 134–9, 187–8, 198–224; Gatrell, *Tsarist Economy*, pp. 84–97; Kahan, *Plow*, pp. 144–9, 284–5, 290–2; Plyushchevskii, B. G., *Krest'yanskie otzhozhie promysly na territorii evropeiskoi Rossii v poslednie predreformennye desyatiletiya (1830–1850 gg.)*, unpublished doctoral dissertation (Leningrad, 1974).
64 Moon, 'Estimating', p. 147. See also Ch. 8.

in St Petersburg. The migrant workers in the capital were supervised by foremen, who negotiated contracts with employers and sent their wages to an estate official. Many landowners were more flexible and allowed peasants to organise their own work. The end of serfdom in 1861 and the reforms of the other categories of peasants did not end restrictions on peasant mobility, but passed them to communes. Many encouraged migrant labour, since the workers' wages contributed to the upkeep of their households, and to their shares of the communes' taxes and redemption payments.[65]

The numbers of peasants who left their villages for wage labour increased steadily during the eighteenth century, and more quickly in the following century. The number of boatmen on Russia's rivers and canals, around 80 per cent of whom were peasants, increased from 60,000 to 220,000 over the eighteenth century. The numbers of hired factory workers in the Russian Empire, many of whom were peasants, grew from under 20,000 in 1767, to over 60,000 in 1804 and, dramatically, to 862,000 by 1860. In the 1850s around 25 per cent of men in the Central Non-Black Earth region left home to work. At the same time, three million peasants in the European part of the Empire worked away from their homes with permission, and a further 300,000–500,000 did so without authorisation. The numbers of migrant labourers grew most rapidly in the late nineteenth century. Nearly seven million passports were issued every year in the 1890s. The pressure of rapid population increase and greater opportunities for work in Russia's industrialising cities contributed to a growing exodus from the villages. As a proportion of the total peasant population, however, the numbers of migrant workers were still a small minority at the end of the nineteenth century. Moreover, most retained links with their villages. They sent money back to support their families, went home in the summer to work in the fields, and many returned for good after a few years. The small proportion that remained in towns and cities joined the emerging urban working classes.[66]

ECONOMIC GROWTH AND DEVELOPMENT IN PEASANT RUSSIA

The Russian peasant economy was not stagnant in the period under consideration. In spite of the environmental constraints, the level of exploitation, and the weakness of the market, the peasant economy gradually developed from one based largely on agriculture and geared almost entirely towards subsistence into a more diversified economy with greater, but still limited, links with the market.[67] Economic growth and development were caused by a

65 See Prokof'eva, L. S., *Krest'yanskaya obshchina v Rossii vo vtoroi polovine XVIII-pervoi polovine XIX v. (na materialakh votchin Sheremetevykh)* (Leningrad, 1981), pp. 179–84; Bohac, R. D., 'Agricultural structure and the origins of migration in central Russia, 1810–1850', in *AOCI*, pp. 374–80; Burds, J., 'The social control of peasant labor in Russia, 1861–1905', in *PECPER*, pp. 52–100.
66 See Blum, *Lord and Peasant*, p. 324; Kahan, *Plow*, pp. 290–1; Fedorov, *Pomeshchich'i*, pp. 198–207; Plyushchevskii, *Krest'yanskie*, pp. 248–61; Gatrell, *Tsarist Economy*, pp. 84–5. See also Ch. 9.
67 For a positive assessment of economic growth in eighteenth-century Russia, see Blanchard, I., *Russia's 'Age of Silver': Precious-Metal Production and Economic Growth in the Eighteenth Century* (London and New York, 1989), pp. 215–83. See also Kahan, *Plow*, esp. pp. 364–7.

number of factors. The peasant population grew throughout the period, with the rate of growth increasing in the mid-eighteenth century, and especially after the 1850s. The result was more labourers to work on the land and in other activities, but also more mouths to feed. Population growth was both a cause and a consequence of growth and development in the rural economy. Until the nineteenth century, population growth was compensated for by an increase in the area of land under cultivation. The expansion of arable farming from the forest-heartland to the more fertile forested steppe and, from the second half of the eighteenth century, to the open steppe made major contributions to the long-term upward trend in both agricultural productivity and output. There were some changes in techniques, especially in the late nineteenth century, but intensification was less important than extensification.

Many peasant households diversified their activities into handicrafts, trade and wage labour. Some historians have linked the development of cottage industry and industrial villages in Russia with broader debates about the role of 'proto-industrialisation' in the origins of industrialisation and capitalism in Europe as a whole. There were a number of differences between the experiences of eastern and western Europe. In Russia, many peasant households divided their resources between both agricultural and non-agricultural activities, in part as a means of reducing risk, rather than specialising in one or the other. The continued location of much of Russian industrial production in rural rather than urban areas, especially in the less fertile forest-heartland, continued until the late nineteenth century. Regardless of their main economic activities, therefore, most Russian peasants remained on the land, instead of moving permanently to towns and cities.[68]

Over the period under consideration, Russian peasant households put an increasing part of their agricultural and handicraft production on the market, and many grew some crops and made some goods specifically for sale. But, for most households, limitations in the market meant that commercial production remained very much secondary to production for subsistence. Market-orientated activities were important only among peasants who lived near large towns and along major transport routes. In spite of the weaknesses in the market, however, regional specialisation did develop in Russia and became more pronounced from the mid-eighteenth century. A growing number of peasant households in the forest-heartland devoted more of their resources to non-agricultural activities. In contrast, in the more fertile steppe regions, farming remained predominant. By the end of the eighteenth century, the forest-heartland no longer produced enough to feed itself, and relied on shipments of grain and other foodstuffs from the steppe regions. To facilitate the growing inter-regional trade in handicraft and agricultural produce, more peasants engaged in commerce, and the number of periodic fairs where goods were traded grew rapidly. Historians have debated the degree and timing of the

68 See Melton, 'Proto-industrialization'; Rudolph, R. L., 'Family structure and proto-industrialization in Russia', *JEcH*, vol. 40 (1980), pp. 111–18.

emergence of a regional division of labour and an 'all-Russian market'.[69] Suffice to say here that their origins preceded the construction of an extensive railway network in the second half of the nineteenth century. But, before then, the development of an integrated Russian market was hindered by the problems and cost of moving bulky goods, especially grain and livestock, long distances.

Peasant households in Russia were also inhibited from adopting more intensive forms of production or maximising their output because, prior to the reforms of the 1860s, they knew that most of any extra output was likely to be expropriated by the landowning and ruling elites. Many historians have argued that serfdom presented a serious barrier to economic development in Russia. Most Soviet historians asserted that, by the mid-nineteenth century, the productivity of 'feudal' agriculture was declining, and that further economic development was incompatible with the continued existence of unfree labour. These factors, they argued, contributed to a 'crisis of the feudal-serf economy', which inevitably culminated in the end of serfdom in 1861. This, in turn, led to the less restrained development of 'capitalism'. Soviet historians were influenced by Lenin's book, *The Development of Capitalism in Russia*, first published in 1899. Lenin analysed data collected by some *zemstvo* statisticians, and argued that 'capitalist relations of production' were increasingly penetrating the rural economy, and leading to the emergence of a stratum of rich peasants, who strove to increase their production for the market by relying increasingly on the hired labour of poorer peasants.[70]

The case for a sharp break in Russian economic development in the reform era of the 1860s–80s has been overstated. The evidence in this chapter suggests that serfdom, peasant household economies and village communes were compatible with a degree of economic development and commercialisation. Economic historians have argued, moreover, that servile estates were profitable for their owners right down to 1861.[71] There is no doubt that the Russian economy as a whole was developing slowly in the first half of the nineteenth century, nor that it was lagging behind some north-west European economies. Russian relative economic backwardness was not a consequence of serfdom, however, but of such factors as transport problems and the weakness of domestic demand. Olga Crisp concluded: 'Serfdom was a symptom not the cause' of the slowness of Russia's economic growth until the 1850s.'[72] Peter Gatrell has convincingly argued that there was continuity in Russian economic development before and after the 'great reforms'. The acceleration of development and industrialisation in the late nineteenth century was caused

69 See Koval'chenko, I. D. and Milov, L. V., *Vserossiiskii agrarnyi rynok XVIII–nachalo XX v.* (Moscow, 1974); Mironov, B. N., *Vnutrennii rynok Rossii vo vtoroi polovine XVIII–pervoi polovine XIX v.* (Leningrad, 1981); Pallot and Shaw, *Landscape*, pp. 193–215.

70 See Lenin, V. I., 'The development of capitalism in Russia', in *Collected Works*, 4th edn, 45 vols (Moscow and London, 1960–80), vol. 3, pp. 70–187, 252–330. See also Ch. 8.

71 Domar, E. D. and Machina, M. J., 'On the profitability of Russian serfdom', *JEcH*, vol. 44 (1984), pp. 919–55.

72 Crisp, *Studies* (quotation from p. 95).

partly by increases in state intervention, foreign investment and domestic demand, but was also building on foundations laid earlier.[73] In spite of the faster pace of change in the late nineteenth century, however, peasant agriculture remained by far the largest sector of the Russian economy. Many of the workers in the new, urban industries, moreover, were transient migrants from the villages.

Turning from the macro-level of national and regional economies in the long term to the micro-level of peasant households in the short and medium term, a number of factors can be identified which influenced individual households' decisions concerning their productive activities. Local environmental conditions, especially soil fertility, the length of the growing season, and the amount and reliability of rainfall all played a large part in peasants' decisions on the most appropriate balance between their productive activities, both agricultural and non-agricultural. The largely seasonal nature of most agricultural work affected the timing of all economic pursuits. Social customs prescribed a division of labour by gender within households, but women did 'men's work' when necessary.

Peasant households' decision making was also influenced by changes over time. Most Russian peasants would have been unaware of many of the long-term trends detected later by economic historians, although most would have been all too well aware of the increasing pressure on the land caused by the growing population, especially in the late nineteenth century. The trends that would have been most apparent to Russian peasants before the mid-nineteenth century were of short- or medium-term duration, and were haphazard or cyclical rather than incremental in direction. Very important were the unpredictable, year-by-year fluctuations in the size of the harvest. The pressing need to reduce the risk of bad harvests prompted the majority of peasant households throughout the period to adopt risk-averse strategies, for example relying on tried and trusted techniques and crops, and diversifying their activities rather than concentrating solely on farming.

Another change over time which influenced peasants' decision making was the numbers of people in their households, and the ratio between 'consumers' and 'workers' (or the 'dependency ratio'). Consumers were all the household members, including those who were not able to take part in productive activities but still consumed part of their output, in particular the old and infirm and young children. Workers, or producers, were the able-bodied youths and adults who produced all, and consumed part, of their households' output. The ratio between consumers and workers changed over time as children grew up and became workers, as older peasants died, and as mature adults reached old age. (The resulting 'household life cycles' are discussed in Chapter 5.)

In the 1910s and 1920s Chayanov put forward his 'theory of peasant economy'. His work, like Lenin's, was based on analysis of data collected by

73 Gatrell, P., 'The meaning of the great reforms in Russian economic history', in Eklof, B. *et al.* (eds), *Russia's Great Reforms, 1855–1881* (Bloomington, IN, 1994), pp. 84–101.

zemstva statisticians over the previous few decades, but his conclusions conflicted with both Marxist and neo-classical economic principles. Chayanov argued that the more consumers there were to every worker in a peasant household (or the higher the consumer/worker ratio), the longer and harder the workers had to work to satisfy its consumption needs. Households weighed the utility of increasing output beyond their consumption and other basic needs against the increase in 'drudgery' and loss of 'leisure' that would be entailed. Chayanov argued that peasants were averse to the drudgery of agricultural labour, and valued leisure over increased production. According to his theory, therefore, once workers in a peasant household had produced sufficient to satisfy its needs, they stopped working. Chayanov's theory (which was more complex and had wider implications than this summary suggests) has been criticised, especially for its neglect of the fact that some peasant households hired labourers to supplement the work of their own members. It has also been argued that the theory is not supported by evidence for the time when Chayanov was writing, but that it may be valid for the earlier period, which is the main concern of this book. Most importantly, Chayanov stressed the need to take into account that the economic behaviour of most peasant households was influenced by the fact that they consumed, rather than sold, a large part of what they produced.[74]

CONCLUSION

Russian peasant households and village communities used the degrees of leeway they were allowed by the landowning and ruling elites to develop strategies in the area of production. Most households devoted a large part of their resources to agriculture, but supplemented it with some non-agricultural activities. The largest part of peasant households' production was for their own use, and to meet their obligations to the landowners and the state. Only a small part was for sale. At the heart of the economy of many peasant households in Russia was grain cultivation under the three-field system of crop rotation in open fields surrounding their villages. These strategies had their origins in the rural economy of medieval Russia, but began to develop more fully in the southern part of the forest-heartland in the sixteenth and seventeenth centuries, especially, but by no means solely, among peasants living on the estates of noble and ecclesiastical landowners. The practices of these peasants then spread gradually to peasants in the northern part of the steppe zone, and then further afield, and to peasants of other categories, especially state peasants. These strategies, especially the three-field system, were most fully developed among peasants in the central regions in the eighteenth and first half of the nineteenth centuries. After the mid-nineteenth century, peasants

74 See Chayanov, *Theory*. For critical analyses of Chayanov's theory, see Harrison, M., 'Chayanov and the economics of the Russian peasantry', *JPS*, vol. 2 (1975), pp. 389–417; *id.*, 'The peasant mode of production in the work of A. V. Chayanov', *JPS*, vol. 4 (1977), pp. 323–36. On the implications of Chayanov's (and Lenin's) theories for consumption, see Ch. 8.

adapted their productive practices, and adopted new ones, slowly, as and when necessary to ensure their subsistence and livelihoods.

The most important events in the calendar of agricultural work were accompanied by rituals and festivals. Many reflected the ways in which peasants, with their largely pre-scientific understanding of nature, sought the help of supernatural powers (both Christian and pagan) in the hope of ensuring the fertility of the soil, protection against crop failures and livestock diseases, and abundant harvests. The rituals and ceremonies were also ways of recording the timing of the key points in the calendar of work, and making sure that all households followed the same routine on communal land. Since Russian peasants lived in a largely oral culture, rituals and ceremonies were an important way of passing on their customary practices from one generation to the next. Last but not least, the ceremonies and festivals were a major part of the social and cultural life of peasant communities. Village culture, like the peasants' productive strategies, was not set in stone, but changed when peasants changed their practices.

The Russian peasant economy was, thus, more flexible and viable than has often been assumed and, throughout the entire period from the early seventeenth to the early twentieth centuries, was capable of adapting to changing circumstances. Nevertheless, many peasant households perpetuated 'traditional' farming methods and took other decisions that, from the perspectives of neoclassical and Marxist economics, may seem unwise, illogical and 'backward'. The main objective of most Russian peasant households, however, was to ensure their subsistence by minimising the risk of failure, with the catastrophic consequences it would bring, while avoiding the drudgery of unnecessary labour. They were influenced in the ways they tried to achieve their goal of subsistence by the impact of the growing peasant population, and the environmental conditions and exploitative social system they lived in. In these contexts, therefore, the decisions taken by Russian peasant households and village communes on their productive activities were both prudent and rational.

Peasant households and village communes, in particular the strategies they developed to manage their labour and land resources, are the subjects of the next two chapters.

CHAPTER 5

Households

At the heart of Russian peasant life were the households that constituted the basic units of economic and social organisation. The Russian peasant household was a dwelling place (*dvor*), an economic unit (*khozyaistvo*), and a family (*semeistvo/sem'ya*). It was a unit of production and consumption as well as human reproduction. The modern notion of the ideal family as a hub of affection in the privacy of the home was partly, but not totally, absent. The head of the household or patriarch (*bol'shak*), usually the eldest male, wielded considerable authority over the other members. Women headed households only in exceptional circumstances. Under the head's direction, the needs of the household as a whole took precedence over those of individuals. The members worked to produce and earn sufficient to support their households and meet its obligations to the landowning and ruling elites. In addition, the married couple or couples tried to make sure there would be enough children who would grow up to provide labourers for the household economy, support their parents in old age and, in time, take over from the previous generation.[1]

This chapter examines the strategies peasants developed to organise their labour resources in their households in order to maintain them in the present and ensure their continued existence in the future. Particular attention is paid to household structures and life cycles. The most important determinants of these were the marriage pattern and the customs governing the partition of larger households into smaller units. The practices of family life were enshrined in various rituals and ceremonies, and were enforced by the older generation. Age and gender were important determinants of the positions and roles of individuals in their households.

HOUSEHOLD STRUCTURES

Some family historians have focused on the structures of households at particular points in time. I have greatly simplified their typologies and terminologies, and have divided the most common household structures among the Russian peasantry into two main types: the 'simple household', which comprised a 'nuclear family' of a husband and wife and their young, unmarried children; and the 'complex household', which contained an 'extended family' of two

---

1 See Chayanov, *Theory*, pp. 53–5; Smith, *Peasant Farming*, pp. 7–9, 80–95; Shanin, *Awkward*, pp. 28–32; Dal', *Tolkovyi slovar'*, vol. 1, p. 422; vol. 4, pp. 173, 557. See also Chs 4 and 8.

or more related married couples, or a married couple with their children and one or more other relatives. Most complex households were 'paternal' (parents and married sons), or 'fraternal' (married brothers). Structures should not be confused with sizes. A simple household could be large if a couple had many children; while a complex household could be small if a couple had only one or two children and lived with one elderly, widowed parent. Nevertheless, complex households were usually larger than simple ones.[2]

Simple households prevailed in most of pre-industrial north-west Europe, but nuclear families often lived under the same roof as servants to whom they were not related. In contrast, in much of southern and eastern Europe, complex households containing wider kin but no live-in servants predominated. The most famous example was the large South Slav *zadruga*, which usually included several related nuclear families. The large, complex households of southern and eastern Europe in many ways resembled household structures in India, China and elsewhere outside Europe and North America.[3]

Until comparatively recently, many specialists believed that, until the end of the nineteenth century, most Russian peasants had always lived in large, complex households containing more than one married couple and three or even four generations. It was also widely accepted that such households were the descendants of the big, patriarchal family-communes, similar to the *zadruga*, which were thought to have been the basic units of medieval Slavonic society. This view was based, to some extent, on 'soft', descriptive data, including ethnographic studies such as the influential work of Aleksandra Efimenko published in the 1870s–80s.[4] At the end of the nineteenth century, some Russian intellectuals noted, with a mixture of concern and nostalgia, what they saw as the gradual demise of the 'old, large, Great Russian patriarchal family' as it broke up into smaller units.[5]

More recently, some American historians have found 'hard' evidence for the widespread existence of large, complex households among Russian peasants in 'household inventories' in estate records. In 1982, Peter Czap concluded that there were 'significant grounds ... for arguing that the large multi-generational [i.e. complex] family/household was the predominant form of domestic group among [seigniorial peasants] throughout large areas of Russia in the eighteenth and first half of the nineteenth centuries'.[6] In contrast, several

2 For more sophisticated typologies, see Laslett, P., *Household and Family in Past Time* (Cambridge, 1972), pp. 28–32; Hajnal, J., 'Two kinds of pre-industrial household formation system', in Wall, R. (ed.), *Family Forms in Historic Europe* (Cambridge, 1983), pp. 65–104. N.B. Different historians have used different terms to describe similar structures, or similar terms to describe different structures.
3 See Wall, 'Introduction', in *id.*, *Family*, pp. 1–63; Hammel, E. A., 'The zadruga as process', in Laslett, *Household*, pp. 335–73.
4 See Efimenko, A. Ya., *Issledovaniya narodnoi zhizni*, vol. 1 (Moscow, 1884), pp. 51–68, 206–7, 217–22. See also Blum, *Lord and Peasant*, pp. 24–6; Robinson, *Rural Russia*, pp. 10–11, 273; Chistov, K. V., 'Severnorusskie prichtaniya kak istochnik dlya izucheniya krest'yanskoi sem'i XIX v.', in Putilov, B. N. (ed.), *Fol'klor i Etnografiya* (Leningrad, 1977), pp. 131–43.
5 Semenov, *Rossiya*, vol. 1, *Moskovskaya*, p. 104.
6 Czap, 'Perennial', p. 6. See also the work of Bohac and Hoch cited below.

Soviet historians argued that many Russian peasants lived in small, simple households, similar to those in north-west Europe. They also relied on 'hard' data, taken from tax registers, censuses, parish registers and estate records. V. A. Aleksandrov asserted, also in 1982, that 'accumulated data . . . testify that the nuclear family [i.e. simple household] was the foundation of the family system among the rural Russian population everywhere . . . from the sixteenth to the middle of the nineteenth [centuries]'. Aleksandrov did not deny the existence of larger households with complex structures, but argued that those in which married sons lived with their parents or married brothers lived together were 'exceptions', 'secondary formations' that were outgrowths of nuclear families that had not yet divided into simple households.[7]

Although Czap was writing about only one category of peasants (seigniorial) over a shorter time period, we face a dilemma in trying to reconcile his careful conclusion with the more sweeping statement made by Aleksandrov. However, the growing body of scholarship on Russian peasant households has made it possible to trace changes in household structures over time and regional variations, and to move beyond these to suggest explanations for Czap's and Aleksandrov's conflicting views.

A large proportion of Russian peasant households were small in size and simple in structure until the mid-seventeenth century. Analysis of tax registers (*pistsovye knigi*) has shown that, between the late fifteenth and early seventeenth centuries, the average peasant household in the North-western region contained five or six people (men and women), and that a substantial proportion comprised only a married couple and their unmarried children. This conclusion is valid for the whole forest-heartland.[8] (See Table 5.1.)

In the mid-seventeenth century, however, peasant households began to increase in size. Estimates based on the 1678 household tax census show that the average number of peasants in households in the forest-heartland and Siberia had increased to between six and eight, while in the Central Black Earth region, mean household size approached nine people. The trend continued after 1678. Between 1680 and 1725, the average number of peasants in households in the Central Non-Black Earth region increased to 9.2. The growth in size was caused by an increase in the proportion of complex households. A comparison of church peasant households in Vologda province, in the Northern region, in 1678 and 1717 revealed that the percentage of simple households fell from 80 to 55 per cent, while that of complex households rose from 20 to 45 per cent. Half these complex households in 1717 consisted of co-resident married brothers. Similar trends towards higher proportions of

7 Aleksandrov, V. A., 'Typology of the Russian peasant family in the feudal epoch', *SSH*, vol. 21, no. 2 (1982), p. 48.

8 Shapiro, A L, *Agrarnaya istoriya severo-zapada Rossii: vtoraya polovina XV–nachalo XVI v.* (Leningrad, 1971), pp. 17–20, 363; *id.*, *Agrarnaya istoriya . . . XVII v.*, p. 56. See also Aleksandrov, V. A., *Obychnoe pravo krepostnoi derevni Rossii: XVIII–nachalo XIX v.* (Moscow, 1984), pp. 50–3; Smith, *Peasant Farming*, pp. 80–3; Hellie, *Slavery*, pp. 418–19.

TABLE 5.1

AVERAGE SIZE OF PEASANT HOUSEHOLDS BY REGION (EARLY 17TH TO LATE 19TH
CENTURIES)

Region	1620s–40s	1678	1710	1858	1897
Forest-heartland					
Central NBE	5.00–6.00	7.30	7.40	6.80	5.50
North-western	5.40	7.20		6.80	6.10
Northern & N. Urals	5.50	6.70	6.80	7.40	5.50
Total	5.00–6.00				5.60
Steppes					
Central BE		8.90	7.80–9.20	10.20	6.30
Mid-Volga		6.40	6.60	8.20	5.60
L. Volga & Don					5.80
S. Urals					5.70
Total					6.00
Siberia		5.90	7.00	6.00–8.00	5.60
Total					5.80

Sources: Aleksandrov, 'Typology', pp. 34, 37, 40 (1620s–40s, 1710, 1858, excl. Siberia);
Vodarskii, *Naseleniya Rossii v kontse XVII*, pp. 221–32 (my calculations, DM) (1678);
Tikhonov, *Pomeshchich'i*, p. 99 (*c.* 1710); Minenko, *Russkaya*, pp. 47, 76 (Siberia); Troinitskii,
Obshchii svod, vol. 1, pp. 20, 24 (my calculations, DM) (1897).

complex households in this period have been uncovered in the Northern Urals
region and Siberia.[9] (See Table 5.1.)

Although these trends towards large, complex peasant households occurred
in much of Russia, there were regional variations in household size and structure between the late seventeenth and late nineteenth centuries. A significant
proportion of households in the forest-heartland and Siberia remained relatively small and simple throughout this period. Data from the poll tax census
of 1762–63 for Yaroslavl' province, in the Central Non-Black Earth region,
indicate that average household size among the rural population (including
peasants of all categories) was 5.2 people, that just under half of all households
were complex, and that a quarter contained three generations. Nevertheless,

9 See Vodarskii, Ya. E., 'K voprosu o srednei chislennosti krest'yanskoi sem'i i naselennosti
dvora v Rossii v XVI–XVII vv.', in Beskrovnyi, L. G. (ed.), *Voprosy istorii khozyaistva i naseleniya
Rossii XVII v.* (Moscow, 1974), pp. 117–23; Baklanova, E. N., *Krest'yanskii dvor i obshchina na
russkom severe: konets XVII–nachalo XVIII v.* (Moscow, 1976), pp. 31–40; Vlasova, I. V., 'Sem'ya
i semeinye otnosheniya', in Aleksandrov, V. A. (ed.), *Na putyakh iz zemli Permskoi v Sibir'*
(Moscow, 1989), pp. 180–94; Minenko, *Russkaya*, pp. 42–76. See also Aleksandrov, 'Typology',
pp. 32–50.

three-quarters of rural households contained only one or two generations, and just over half were simple in structure. On the seigniorial estate of Baki, in Kostroma province in the same region, in the early nineteenth century there were a greater proportion of small, simple households. Their mean size was around five people, and only 11 per cent contained four or more adults.[10]

There were some rural communities in the forest-heartland where large and complex households prevailed. On the seigniorial estate of Sukhovarova, in Tver' province in the Central Non-Black Earth region, mean household size was high, but declined from 9.1 to 8.2 over the first half of the nineteenth century. The proportion of complex households was also very high, around 80–90 per cent, but had fallen slightly by the 1850s. Simple households rarely exceeded 10 per cent of the total. The size and structure of households was similar on the Gagarins' estate of Manuilovskoe, also in Tver' province, in the same period. Moreover, some appanage peasants in the forest-heartland lived in large, complex households. An investigation into 96 households in Vyatka province, in the Northern Urals region, in 1834 showed that their average size was just over nine people, and that 80 (83 per cent) were complex.[11]

In the forest-heartland as a whole, communities made up mostly of large, complex households were relatively unusual. The mean size of all households in Tver' province in 1859 was 7.3 people, and in other provinces of the Central Non-Black Earth region in the 1860s, between 6.2 and 6.9 people. Among appanage peasant households in the entire forest-heartland, the mean size was around six people. These small average sizes suggest large proportions of simple households.[12] Despite the increase in the average size and complexity of peasant households in the late seventeenth century, and the existence of islands of large, complex households on some seigniorial and appanage estates, small and simple households made up a substantial part of many village communities in the forest-heartland and Siberia between the late seventeenth and late nineteenth centuries.

In contrast, over the same period, a large proportion of peasant households in the steppe regions were large in size and complex in structure. Czap's work on the estate of Mishino, in Ryazan' province, enables us to look in detail at households of seigniorial peasants in the Central Black Earth region. Between 1782 and 1858, the average number of peasants per household in Mishino fluctuated between eight and ten. Up to three-quarters of households contained at

10 Mitterauer, M. and Kagan, A., 'Russian and central European family structures: A comparative view', *JFamH*, vol. 7 (1982), pp. 109–11 (I have combined 'extended' and 'complex' families as 'complex'); Melton, 'Household', pp. 568–9. See also Semevskii, V. I., 'Domashnii byt i nravy krest'yan vo vtoroi polovine XVIII v.' [II], *Ustoi* (1882), pt 2 (Feb.), pp. 68–71.
11 Czap, P., '"A large family: the peasant's greatest wealth": Serf households in Mishino, Russia, 1814–1858', in Wall, R. (ed.), *Family Forms*, pp. 146–9 (here and subsequently, I have combined Czap's figures for 'extended-family' and 'multiple-family' households as 'complex'); Bohac, R. D., *Family, Property, and Socioeconomic Mobility: Russian Peasants on Manuilovskoe Estate, 1810–1861*, unpublished PhD dissertation (University of Illinois, 1982), pp. 134–9, 172; *RGIA, f.* 515, *op.* 18, *d.* 165, *ll.* 369–86 *ob.*
12 Czap, 'A large family', pp. 146–9; Gorlanov, *Udel'nye*, p. 31 (my estimate, DM).

least nine people, and some as many as 20 or even 30. The large sizes were a result of complex structures. For most of the period, the proportion of complex households in Mishino varied between 80 and 90 per cent, but was slightly lower after 1831. Since some complex households were fraternal, the proportion with three or four generations was below that of all complex households, but never fell below half. Simple households were unusual in Mishino. Over the whole period 1782–1858, they averaged only 12 per cent of the total.

Examples of actual households in Mishino from a household inventory compiled in 1814 bring the data to life. The household of Ivan Mikhailov (Figure 5.1(a)) is a good example of a paternal, complex household. It contained three married couples, four generations and a total of ten people. Ivan, who was 65, lived with his 70-year-old wife, their son and daughter-in-law, grandson and granddaughter-in-law, and four young great-granddaughters. A fraternal, ҫomplex household, also of ten people, was headed by Dimitri Fedorov, a 53-year-old widower. His household (Figure 5.1(b)) comprised his unmarried teenage daughter, his son and daughter-in-law and their three-year-old girl, and also his younger brother and sister-in-law and their three children. One of the largest and most complex households was that of Tikhon Ignatev (Figure 5.1(c)). He lived under the same roof as his wife, their two married sons, two daughters-in-law and five grandchildren, an unmarried teenage son, plus his younger brother and sister-in-law and their five young children, and, in addition, his widowed sister-in-law with her newly married son and her unmarried daughter. Tikhon Ignatev was, thus, the head of a household containing 23 peasants. At the other end of the scale, the household of a 54-year-old widower named Sergei Vasilev is an example of a small, complex household (Figure 5.1(d)). He lived with his son and daughter-in-law and their three girls.[13]

This pattern of large, complex households was duplicated in Petrovskoe, another seigniorial estate, in neighbouring Tambov province. The average number of peasants in a household, the proportion of complex households, and the generational spread were all slightly lower than in Mishino, but were still high in comparison with the forest-heartland and Siberia. As in Mishino, moreover, there was a decline in the average size, complexity and generational spread of households in Petrovskoe by the 1850s. Large, and probably complex, households were also common among state and appanage peasants in the steppe regions in this period. The average state peasant household in Tambov and Voronezh provinces in the 1850s–60s contained around ten people. This was similar to the mean size of appanage peasant households in all the steppe regions in the first half of the nineteenth century.[14]

13 Czap, 'Perennial', pp. 10–12; *id.*, 'A large family', pp. 122–33; *id.*, 'Marriage and the peasant joint family in the era of serfdom', in Ransel, *Family*, pp. 118–21.
14 Hoch, *Serfdom*, pp. 61, 79–84, 89; Frierson, C. A., '*Razdel*: The peasant family divided', *RR*, vol. 46 (1987), pp. 43–4; Gorlanov, *Udel'nye*, p. 31.

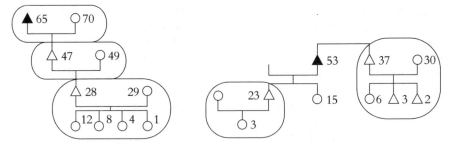

(a) Household of Ivan Mikhailov   (b) Household of Dimitri Fedorov
    (paternal complex household)   (fraternal complex household)

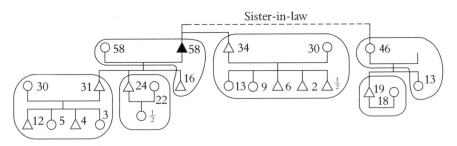

(c) Household of Tikhon Ignatev (very large complex household)

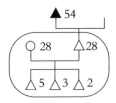

(d) Household of Sergei Vasilev (small complex household)

△ = male,   ○ = female,   ▲ = head of household   numbers = ages

Figure 5.1   Examples of households in Mishino in 1814 (from Czap, *A Large Family*, pp. 125, 126, 133; reproduced with permission of the author and Cambridge University Press)

The relatively minor short-term changes in the size and structure of households in villages in the central regions over the first half of the nineteenth century can be explained partly by 'demographic stress'. Temporary increases in the death rate and reductions in the birth rate, caused by famines, epidemics and the recruitment of many young men into the army in wartime, could quickly reduce large, complex households to small, simple households. The natural disasters and mass conscription during the Crimean War may explain the changes in Sukhovarova, Mishino and Petrovskoe in the 1850s. In the aftermath of disasters, however, some households would have been able to recover their previous size and structure quite quickly, for example by finding wives for their surviving sons and awaiting the arrival of children. On the other hand, the decline in average household size and increase in the numbers of simple households in the 1850s may have been the precursors of long-term trends.[15]

After the abolition of serfdom and other reforms of the 1860s–80s, there was a definite trend towards smaller and simpler households in the Central Black Earth region. Nevertheless, many peasants in the region continued to live in large and complex households in the late nineteenth century. Several historians have cited the study of 230 households in Voronezh province between 1887 and 1896 by the *zemstvo* statistician F. A. Shcherbina. The mean size of the households was 8.3 people, and two-thirds had complex structures. Although these findings are consistent with the prevailing size and structure of households in the region in the preceding period, therefore suggesting continuity, they need to be treated with caution. Shcherbina's sample was not representative of Voronezh province or the Central Black Earth region. According to data from the 1897 census, the average sizes of all households was only 6.5 people in Voronezh province and 6.3 in the region as a whole. There was a similar decline in average size of households in the other steppe regions in the late nineteenth century. The falling sizes were the result of declining proportions of complex households.

There was rather more continuity in the sizes and structures of peasant households before and after the 1860s in the forest-heartland. Another frequently cited work by a *zemstvo* statistician is D. N. Zhbankov's study of peasants in Kostroma province, in the Central Non-Black Earth region, published in 1891. It included a list of 61 households in four villages. The average size of these households was 5.1 (excluding migrant workers living in St Petersburg), or 6.2 (including the migrants). Thirty-three households, or 54 per cent, were simple in structure. These figures are similar to the village of Baki, also in Kostroma province, in the early nineteenth century (see above). The 1897 census revealed that the average size of peasant households in the Central Non-Black Earth region as a whole was 5.5 people.

As a result of the decline in the average size of peasant households in the Central Black Earth region after the 1860s, and the continuity in average sizes in the Central Non-Black Earth region, the regional variations in household sizes and structures between the steppe regions and the forest-heartland, which developed in the late seventeenth century, was much less pronounced by the end of the nineteenth century. According to data from the 1897 census,

15 See Czap, 'A large family', pp. 146–9; Hoch, *Serfdom*, pp. 79–84, 89. See also Ch. 1.

moreover, the average size of households throughout Russia was 5.8 people. It is significant that this was roughly the same as it had been in the early seventeenth century.[16] (See Table 5.1.)

The large, complex households that prevailed among peasants in the Central Black Earth region from the late seventeenth to the mid-nineteenth centuries cannot be dismissed as a minor regional deviation from a standard pattern of small, simple households. An increasingly large part of the Russian peasantry lived in the Central Black Earth region as a result of migration (see Ch. 2). Although the proportions of large, complex households in other regions and at other times were lower, moreover, they contained a greater proportion of the peasantry by virtue of their size. And small sizes did not always mean simple structures. The high death rates meant very large households were always likely to be rare. Thus, Aleksandrov's assertion that simple households predominated among Russian peasants in all regions from the sixteenth to the nineteenth centuries was far too sweeping. Much of his evidence was for the North-western and Northern regions and Siberia in the sixteenth and seventeenth centuries, and for the forest-heartland in the later period. He paid less attention to the Central Black Earth region in the eighteenth and first half of the nineteenth centuries, where large, complex households prevailed.

The disagreement between Aleksandrov and Czap cannot be reconciled simply with reference to changes over time and regional variations. All the discussion so far has concerned the structure of households at particular points in time based on 'snapshots' provided by individual censuses or household inventories. However, a census or inventory might have been compiled just before the marriage of an eldest son or birth of a first grandchild, or soon after the deaths of an older couple. As a result, a household which was about to become or had just ceased to be complex would be recorded as simple. In order to understand peasant household structures in more depth, it is necessary to adopt a dynamic approach that enables us to analyse how the structures of individual households developed over time. Dynamic analysis reveals more complicated patterns which challenge the idea that households in pre-industrial Europe can be divided into simple in the north-west of the continent and complex in the south and east. In large areas of western and central Europe, the main 'household system' was the 'stem family', in which one son continued to live with his father after he had married and started a family. On his father's death, this son inherited the household and its land. In the stem family system, therefore, the same household could be simple at one point in its life cycle and complex at another. As Czap was well aware, dynamic

---

16 Worobec, *Peasant Russia*, pp. 103–15; Shcherbina, F. A., *Krest'yanskie byudzhety* (Voronezh, 1900); Freeze, G. L., 'New scholarship on the Russian peasantry', *EHQ*, vol. 22 (1992), p. 607; Zhbankov, D. N., *Bab'ya storona* (Kostroma, 1891), pp. 103–10. Estimates of mean sizes in 1897 were calculated from census data on 'households connected by kinship' ('*khozyaistva svyazannye rodstvom*') for the entire population of Russia (as defined in Ch. 1). Troinitskii, *Obshchii svod*, vol. 1, pp. v–vi, 16, 20, 24.

analysis of household life cycles suggests ways of resolving the divergence between his and Aleksandrov's views on household structures in Russia.[17]

The life cycles of peasant households over time reflected the lives of their members. The main events in both were marriages, births, deaths and periodic divisions of some households. From the point of view of understanding household structures over time, or household systems, the most important factors were the marriage pattern and household divisions.

The marriage pattern

The predominant marriage pattern among the Russian peasantry in all regions and throughout the period covered by this book was near-universal and early marriage: a pattern that ensured high fertility. Marriage was central to the social and economic life of the Russian peasantry. Households were made up of a married couple or couples and their offspring, and each husband and wife pair usually formed a labour team (*tyaglo*), which was the basic unit of labour in the household economy and the village community. Each labour team was entitled to a share of the communal land. Almost all Russian peasants married. In Mishino, Ryazan' province, in the years 1782–1858, 95–100 per cent of all peasants aged 25–29 were or had been married. In Petrovskoe, Tambov province, in a similar period, women aged 20 to 40 'were rarely without husbands, and permanent celibacy was virtually unknown'. According to data on the whole rural population of Russia in 1897, the proportions of women and men who had ever been married by the age of 50 were 96 and 97 per cent respectively.[18]

Russian peasants also married early. Most, especially women, married when they were still quite young. A few peasants married in their early and mid-teens. For most of the period, women generally married between the ages of 16 and 18, and men slightly later, between 18 and 20.[19] There were regional variations in the age at marriage. Peasants married slightly later in the forest-heartland than the steppe regions. Among the rural population of Yaroslavl' province, in the Central Non-Black Earth region, around a third of all women

17 See Berkner, L. K., 'Rural family organization in Europe: A problem in comparative history', *PSN*, vol. 1 (1972), pp. 145–56; Hajnal, 'Two kinds', pp. 69–70. See also Czap, 'A large family', pp. 135–43; Worobec, *Peasant Russia*, p. 76.
18 Czap, 'Marriage', pp. 113–14; Hoch, *Serfdom*, pp. 76–7 (quotation); Coale, *Human Fertility*, p. 136; Tol'ts, 'Brachnost'', p. 140. (1897 data are for the European part of the Russian Empire.)
19 Smith, *Peasant Farming*, p. 81; Mironov, 'Traditsionnoe', pp. 91–2; Czap, 'Marriage', pp. 109–13; Hoch, *Serfdom*, pp. 76–7. On the basis of limited data on slaves in the sixteenth century, Hellie argued that fairly late marriage was the 'normal Russian pattern': Hellie, *Slavery*, pp. 437–42. For forceful rebuttals, see reviews by Mironov, B. N., *IS* (1984), no. 1, p. 202, and Crummey, R., *SR*, vol. 42 (1983), p. 686.

and half of all men aged 20–24 were not married at the time of the 1762–63 tax census. In Siberia in the eighteenth and nineteenth centuries, peasants tended to marry aged 20–22, but some were still single at 25. General patterns can be traced from the 1897 census. Among the rural female population, the proportion ever married was higher and the average age at marriage lower in the steppe regions than the forest-heartland. For example, the average age at marriage of rural women in the North-western region was 23–25, whereas in Ryazan', Voronezh and Saratov provinces, in the Central Black Earth and Lower-Volga regions, it was 18–19.5.[20]

The average age at marriage also changed over time. From data in parish registers for parts of Ryazan' province, Czap showed that the mean ages at marriage were 17.5 for women and 19 for men in the late eighteenth century, but had increased slightly to 18.2 for women and 20 for men by the 1850s. He also found a slight increase in the mean age at marriage over the same period on the estates of Mishino and Pokrovskoe in the same province. Nevertheless, he found that 95 per cent of all women marrying for the first time did so before their 21st birthday. Steven Hoch made similar findings concerning the low mean ages at first marriage (18.9 for women, 19.3 for men) in Petrovskoe, Tambov province, between 1813 and 1856. Rather than an upward trend, however, he saw short-term fluctuations as peasants postponed marriages in response to bad harvests, epidemics and mass wartime conscription.[21] By the end of the nineteenth century, however, there were indisputable increases in the mean ages at marriage. The abolition of serfdom and reforms of the other categories of peasants in the 1860s reduced pressure by landowners and officials on peasants to marry early (see below, pp. 168–9). Moreover, a growing number of men delayed marriage until they had spent a few years as migrant labourers or completed the much-reduced term of military service introduced in 1874. The age at which women married may have risen in response. In 1897, according to census data, the mean ages at first marriage for the rural population of the European part of the Russia Empire were 21.2 for women and 23.5 for men.[22] Despite the regional variations and changes over time, however, near-universal and early marriage prevailed among Russian peasants in all regions throughout the period between the early seventeenth and early twentieth centuries.

The marriage pattern among the Russian peasantry was similar to that of the largely peasant populations elsewhere in eastern Europe and, consequently, historical demographers have called it the 'Eastern European marriage pattern'.

20 Mitterauer and Kagan, 'Russian', pp. 117–20; Minenko, *Russkaya*, pp. 182–4; Worobec, *Peasant Russia*, pp. 125–8; Zverev, V. A., 'Brachnyi vozrast i kolichestvo detei u russkikh krest'yan Sibiri vo vtoroi polovine XIX–nachale XX v.', in Rusakova, L. M. and Minenko, N. A. (eds), *Kul'turno-bytovye protsessy u russkikh Sibiri XVIII–nachalo XX vv.* (Novosibirsk, 1985), p. 79. See also Chs 3 and 4.
21 Compare Czap, 'Marriage', pp. 109–13, and Hoch, *Serfdom*, pp. 76–7.
22 Coale, *Human Fertility*, p. 136; Engel, *Between*, pp. 37–40; Farnsworth, B., 'The Soldatka: Folklore and court record', *SR*, vol. 49 (1990), p. 71; Tol'ts, 'Brachnost'', p. 140; Worobec, *Peasant Russia*, pp. 125–8.

They have contrasted it with the prevailing marriage pattern in pre-industrial north-west Europe, where a significant proportion of people, around 10 per cent, never married, and those that did married later, often in their mid- and late twenties. Both European marriage patterns can be contrasted with the non-European pattern, in which many women married in their mid-teens, and fewer than 1 per cent never married.[23]

There was a direct connection between the 'Eastern European marriage pattern' and the complex household system in eastern Europe. When Russian peasants married, they went to live with one set of parents. In most cases, the bride moved in with her husband and lived under the authority of her parents-in-law in an enlarged, complex household. In a minority of cases, usually involving brides from families with no sons or adult males, the bridegroom moved in with his wife in order to secure the future of her natal household. This reversal of the usual custom was known as 'adoption' (*primachestvo*), and the son-in-law as a *primak* or *zyat'*. The custom of newly married couples living under the same roof as (usually) the husband's family meant that peasants could marry early since, unlike young couples in north-west Europe, they did not need to save until they could afford to set up a new household by themselves. Also in contrast to north-west Europe, Russian peasants did not have to wait until their parents died to inherit land as most Russian village communes allotted land to newly married couples. Moreover, given the high death rate, the fact that most Russian peasants married in their late teens or early twenties meant that multi-generational households could exist, as the parents of newlyweds were likely to be around 40 years old and, consequently, still alive. In Mishino, Czap concluded:

> Just as we do not find newly married couples living apart from their parents or other representatives of the parental generation, we also do not find a significant proportion of the elderly living apart from their children or kin of the offspring generation. Those parents about to start families and those who had completed theirs lived together in large households, headed by representatives of the older generations.[24]

* * *

Why did Russian peasants adopt a pattern of near-universal and early marriage? Some scholars have made a connection between the marriage pattern and the abundance of land in much of Russia before the nineteenth century.

23 Coale, *Human Fertility*, pp. 10, 21, 124–8, 136–44; Hajnal, J., 'European marriage patterns in perspective', in Glass, D. and Eversley, D. (eds), *Population in History* (London, 1965), pp. 101–43.
24 Czap, 'A large family', p. 132 (quotation); Aleksandrov, *Obychnoe*, pp. 198–206; Bohac, R. D., 'Peasant inheritance strategies in Russia', *JIH*, vol. 16 (1985), pp. 26, 36–9; Mitterauer and Kagan, 'Russian', p. 124; Worobec, *Peasant Russia*, pp. 57–62, 119–20. On adoptions of people who did not marry into households, see Ch. 6.

Conversely, the relative shortage of land in much of north-west Europe was a reason to delay marriage in order to restrict fertility and, hence, over-crowding.[25] More directly, in Russia it was in the interests of all parties in-volved – landowners (in the case of seigniorial peasants), officials responsible for state and appanage peasants, village communes and heads of peasant house-holds – to encourage all peasants to get married, and to do so young, in order to maximise the number of children that were born and, subsequently, the size of the labour force in each estate, village and household.

For landowners, the prevailing marriage pattern and resulting high fertility meant increasing the number of peasants they owned, the number of labour teams on their estates and, therefore, the amount of labour and other obliga-tions they could demand. The idea that serf owners interfered to enforce near-universal, early marriage has become a cliché in the literature on serfdom. Many historians have cited landowners' instructions to their estate managers ordering that all women were to be married by a certain age, often 17 or 18, and cases of landowners intervening to compel peasants to marry.[26] However, the number of landowners who paid such close attention to the daily lives of their peasants was relatively small (see Ch. 6). Moreover, near-universal and early marriage also prevailed among seigniorial peasants whose landowners allowed them more leeway, and among state and appanage peasants who were subject to less control. Therefore, actions by serf owners cannot solely, or even largely, explain the Russian peasantry's marriage pattern.

Village communes had a more immediate interest, and played a greater role, in peasants' lives than landowners. Communes were keen to encourage all peasants in their villages to marry early, because the resulting high birth rate would increase the numbers of peasants, and later labour teams, able to contribute to the communal burden of obligations and taxes to the landown-ing and ruling elites. To some extent, communes were acting in the interests, and on the instructions, of landowners and state officials. On the other hand, they also represented the interests of the heads of households who ran them (see Ch. 6). Communities encouraged younger peasants to marry early by pressure of public opinion. Unmarried adults were treated with disdain and considered to be exceptions, idlers and not 'real' peasants. Communities also promoted marriage by organising social occasions where young peasants could meet prospective partners (see below, p. 185).

The prevailing marriage pattern was also in the interests of heads of peasant households. The addition of daughters-in-law to their households, and the high fertility resulting from near-universal, early marriage, increased the size of their families and, in time, the labour forces at their disposal. Households needed large supplies of labour on hand to work in the fields at the peak times of agricultural work in the summer. In the mainly agricultural Central Black Earth region, it was reckoned that households needed two or more married

---

25 See Casey, J., *The History of the Family* (Oxford, 1989), pp. 127–8. See also Ch. 2.
26 See Semevskii, *Krest'yane*, vol. 1, pp. 302, 308–14; Aleksandrov, V. A., *Sel'skaya obshchina v Rossii (XVII–nachalo XIX v.)* (Moscow, 1976), pp. 303–9.

couples. In large households, moreover, some peasants could specialise in handicrafts or work as migrant labourers to earn money for the household purse (see Ch. 4).

Furthermore, early marriage was important in a society with a high death rate and low life expectancy. A marriage pattern that led to high birth rates was vital for self-preservation in rural Russia, with its very high levels of infant and childhood mortality, as it increased the chances that some children would reach adulthood (see Ch. 1). Early marriage was also an important way of trying to ensure households' labour capacity. In Mishino in the first half of the nineteenth century, peasants could expect to become parents when they were 18–20 years old, grandparents aged around 38–40, and great-grandparents in their mid-fifties. In a system of multi-generational, complex households, this meant that middle-aged peasants could rely on the younger generation of adults to do a large part of the manual labour, and that peasants who survived into old age could depend on peasants of working age in their households. Assuming generations of about 20 years, younger peasants reached their late teens, and began to take on a full share of work in the household economy and marry, at around the same time as their grandparents (if still living) were in their late fifties, and no longer able to make a large contribution to the work.

The system of communal and repartitional land tenure also encouraged heads of households to insist that their sons married, and did so as soon as possible. When households were enlarged by the creation of new labour teams by marriages, village communes granted them more land. In many cases, this extra land more than compensated for the increased share of the commune's obligations that larger households had to bear in return (see Ch. 6). The value of early marriage for households was summed up by the proverb: 'The earlier the marriage, the more profit for the house'. Heads of households, their wives and wider kin (as well as communes and landowners) also played important roles in encouraging younger peasants to marry early by helping them select partners, negotiating marriage contracts, and organising the ceremonies (see below, p. 185).[27]

The interests of the individual peasants who were getting married were of less importance than those of the heads of households, communes, landowners and officials. Most Russian peasants got married and did so early, therefore, because it met the needs of all these people and institutions to encourage a marriage pattern that created conditions for high fertility and large, complex households. The prevailing marriage pattern was not sufficient in itself to guarantee the predominance of complex households. For this it was also necessary to prevent married sons and younger brothers from leaving households headed by their fathers and elder brothers.

---

27 See Bushnell, J., 'Did serfowners control marriage? Orlov serfs and their neighbours, 1773–1861', *SR*, vol. 52 (1993), pp. 419–45; Czap, 'Marriage', pp. 115, 117, 132; Hoch, *Serfdom*, pp. 91, 93, 95, 119, 129; Mironov, 'Traditsionnoe', pp. 85–8; Smith, *Peasant Farming*, p. 81; Worobec, *Peasant Russia*, pp. 124, 126.

Two types of household divisions

Household divisions, along with marriages, were the most important events in the life cycles of peasant households and, together, were the main determinants of the prevailing household systems. Since the pattern of near-universal and early marriage was common throughout Russia, and endured for the whole period under consideration, variations in households structures can best be explained by different types of household divisions. The most important differences concerned the point in the lifetimes of individual peasants and life cycles of individual households that divisions took place. If all the sons, as well as the daughters, left their natal households to set up their own households when they got married, or shortly afterwards, then a system of simple households would predominate. On the other hand, if all sons brought their wives to live with their parents, and remained in their natal households until their fathers died, or even afterwards, then a complex household system would prevail. In the latter case, the only factor limiting the size and complexity of households was the death rate. The longer married peasants could be persuaded to remain in their parents' (or elder brothers') households, the larger the proportion of complex households. The two types of household divisions, before and after the death of the head, are usually called '*pre-mortem*' and '*post-mortem*' divisions.

Pre-mortem divisions were common in most of Russia until the mid-seventeenth century. Many sons left their parents and set up new, simple households on vacant land. Household divisions before the death of the head also predominated in Siberia throughout the period. In both cases, land was in plentiful supply. This meant that new households could easily find land to settle on, often near their parents' households. The absence or recent development of serfdom in Siberia and early seventeenth-century Russia was also important, as landowners did not, or not yet, restrict household divisions.[28]

A significant number of peasant households in the forest-heartland, including the Central Non-Black Earth region, continued to divide before the deaths of their heads in the 200 years after the mid-seventeenth century, in spite of the existence of serfdom. This was probably the case among the seigniorial peasants of Baki, Kostroma province, where small, simple households prevailed in the early nineteenth century (see above, p. 160). The practices in Baki may not have been typical in the forest-heartland. Most household divisions in the forest-heartland between the late seventeenth and mid-nineteenth centuries took place after their heads' deaths. Among church and seigniorial peasants in Vologda province, in the Northern region, in the late seventeenth and early eighteenth centuries, cases of sons leaving their natal households during their fathers' lifetimes were rare. Most household divisions were between brothers after their fathers' deaths. Partitions between co-resident cousins and uncles and nephews also featured prominently. *Post-mortem*

---

28 Aleksandrov, *Obychnoe*, pp. 61–2; Hoch, *Serfdom*, pp. 77, 79; Smith, *Peasant Farming*, p. 83; Minenko, *Russkaya*, pp. 49, 52–4, 57–8, 70–1, 75–6.

divisions also prevailed on the seigniorial estate of Manuilovskoe, Tver' province. Of 31 partitions in 1813–61, only five involved sons leaving their fathers' households.[29]

Post-mortem divisions overwhelmingly predominated among peasants in the Central Black Earth region, and probably also other steppe regions, between the late seventeenth and mid-nineteenth centuries. Partitions after the deaths of heads certainly prevailed on large seigniorial estates. In Mishino, Ryazan' province, between 1782 and 1858, only 18 out of 92 divisions (20 per cent) involved sons leaving their natal households during their fathers' lifetimes. Analysis of a smaller sample in Petrovskoe, Tambov province, showed that in only one partition out of 40 in 1813–27 and 1850–56 was a son leaving his father's household. Furthermore, in Mishino, three times as many peasants remained in their parents' households and succeeded to the headships on their fathers' deaths than became heads by breaking away and setting up new households. The mean age of peasants in Mishino who became heads of new households created by partitions was 47.75. This was 3.5 years older than the average age of peasants who succeeded to headships on the death of the old head. In Petrovskoe over a similar period, the equivalent ages were 40.8 and 38.5. Moreover, very few of those who broke away to establish new households were sons who had left their fathers. In many cases, they were the younger brothers of men who had succeeded to headships on their fathers' deaths. They broke away rather than submit to their elder brothers' authority. In many *post-mortem* partitions in Mishino and Petrovskoe, cousins separated from each other and nephews left their uncles' households. Thus, the vast majority of divisions in the two villages were *post-mortem*. The prevalence of large, complex households indicates that this was common throughout the Central Black Earth region.[30]

Not only did few sons break away from their natal households before their fathers' deaths, but many of the new households formed on partitions were complex rather than simple. In Mishino between 1782 and 1858, 92 households split, leading to the creation of 112 new households. Just over three-quarters of the new households were complex. Moreover, most simple households in Mishino were made up not of young married couples and young children, but families with older children that had broken away from complex households later in their life cycles and the lives of their heads. Some new households became complex within a few years. In Mishino, households usually partitioned only after the family units which broke away had themselves become complex, in other words, after the sons of household heads had married sons and, sometimes, even grandsons of their own.[31]

29 Aleksandrov, 'Typology', p. 46; Baklanova, *Krest'yanskii*, pp. 39, 165–6; Bohac, *Family*, pp. 141, 189, 194.
30 Czap, 'Perennial', pp. 17, 20–1; Hoch, *Serfdom*, pp. 84–7. See also Hajnal, 'Two kinds', pp. 86–7, 90.
31 Czap, 'Perennial', pp. 17–18; *id.*, 'A large family', p. 127. For similar cases in the Central Non-Black Earth region, see Melton, 'Proto-industrialization', p. 99; Bohac, *Family*, pp. 163–5.

The predominance of *post-mortem* partitions in much of Russia, and the complex household system it created, began to change after the end of serfdom and other reforms of the 1860s–80s. *Pre-mortem* partitions, in particular those between married sons and fathers, became more frequent. The change was accompanied by an increase in the numbers of all partitions. The changes were most marked, and happened most quickly, in the Central Non-Black Earth region. Local court records suggest that *pre-mortem* partitions made up around a third of the total in Yaroslavl' province in the 1870s. Similar changes occurred, but more slowly, in the Central Black Earth region. The records of courts and data collected by *zemstva* indicate that between 12 and 16 per cent of household divisions in Tambov and Voronezh provinces in the late nineteenth century took place before the death of the heads. The proportion of *pre-mortem* divisions and the numbers of all divisions in the Central Black Earth region increased further in the following decades.[32] These changes led to a growth in the proportion of small, simple households. This was a reversion to the practices and patterns that had prevailed in Russia before the mid-seventeenth century, and had survived in Siberia and, to a lesser extent, outlying parts of the forest-heartland in the intervening period.

The changes over time and regional variations, in particular between *pre-* and *post-mortem* divisions, raise two questions. First, why were household divisions, especially *pre-mortem* divisions, restricted in large parts of Russia between the mid-seventeenth and late nineteenth centuries? Second, why did partitions, notably *pre-mortem* partitions, become more frequent in the late nineteenth century? The answers to these questions are the keys to understanding the prevailing household systems among Russian peasants, and to resolving the divergent opinions of Aleksandrov and Czap on whether simple or complex households predominated.

* * *

In answer to the first question, the Russian state, landowners, village communes and heads of peasant households all acted to impede subordinate members of households, sons and younger brothers, from breaking away from their natal households to set up on their own. In the late eighteenth and first half of the nineteenth centuries, the state tried to restrict household divisions among state peasants. It required households that wanted to split to petition the authorities for authorisation. Under the terms of a decree of 1823, for example, permission would be granted only if the new households that would

---

32 Milogolova, I. N., 'Semeinye razdely v russkoi poreformennoi derevne', *VMU (I)* (1987), no. 6, pp. 37–8, 42–3; Frierson, '*Razdel*', pp. 37–9, 42–5; *id.*, 'Peasant family divisions and the commune', in *LCPCR*, pp. 308–11; Shanin, *Awkward*, pp. 31, 86–7. Worobec insisted that *post-mortem* partitions still predominated, especially in the Central Black Earth region: *Peasant Russia*, pp. 11–12, 78–9, 86–9, 92, 97–101, 220.

be formed contained a minimum of three or four labourers aged 15–60. The fact that the decree was repeated in the 1830s suggests that some households were dividing without permission. Nevertheless, the authorities did curtail divisions. Household partitions had been banned in some court villages in the eighteenth century.[33]

The actions by state and court peasant officials echoed measures taken by some noble landowners since the mid-seventeenth century. Prohibitions on household divisions were common in the eighteenth century. The Gagarins took steps to deter households from splitting on their estates in the early nineteenth century. In Manuilovskoe, Tver' province, they tried to achieve this by banning new households from erecting buildings on land designated for cultivation, and by delaying approval of communal resolutions allowing partitions. A new estate manager of Petrovskoe, in Tambov province, reported to the Gagarins' estate office in 1834 that he had 'strictly forbidden . . . the village elders to divide households at will without the permission of the estate management'. The ban was backed up by the threat of corporal punishment for men who set up their own households without authorisation.[34] Village communes also tried to restrain households from dividing unless they had very good reasons. Many looked 'upon requests for household division with a sceptical eye'. Heads of complex households also tried to prevent them breaking up.

State officials, landowners, communal elders and household heads all had similar reasons for discouraging divisions, especially *pre-mortem* divisions. Many of these reasons were similar to those which led the same people to encourage near-universal and early marriage (see above). *Post-mortem* partitions and the marriage pattern were both conducive to the existence, and predominance, of large, complex households. Such households were better able than small, simple units to support themselves, including young children and the very old who could not support themselves, and to meet their shares of the communal obligations to the landowners and the state. The practice of communal and redistributional land tenure also encouraged household heads to maintain large households as communes granted extra land allotments to larger units. It is significant that among Ukrainian peasants, who practised hereditary household land tenure, most sons left their fathers' households when they married. Furthermore, the concentration of peasants in larger households provided the labour necessary at peak times in the calendar of agricultural work in the summer. In outlying regions in the first stages of settlement, households needed large labour forces to establish new settlements and prepare virgin land for cultivation. A further reason why officials, landowners, communes and household heads tried to prevent *pre-mortem* partitions was that small,

33 Aleksandrov, *Obychnoe*, pp. 64–5; Druzhinin, *Gosudarstvennye*, vol. 1, p. 27; Minenko, *Russkaya*, pp. 57–60; Worobec, *Peasant Russia*, p. 86.
34 Bohac, 'Inheritance', pp. 29–31; Hoch, *Serfdom*, pp. 87–90 (quotation). See also Czap, 'A large family', pp. 122, 136, 149–50; Semevskii, *Krest'yane*, vol. 1, pp. 319–21.

simple households could easily be ruined if one adult died or was conscripted into the army.[35]

The forms of state obligations introduced in the seventeenth and early eighteenth centuries had an impact on the frequency and timing of household divisions, and the resulting sizes and structures of households. Many historians have attached great importance to the introduction of the household tax, in place of the land tax, between 1645–47 and 1678–79. Since all households were taxed at a flat rate, rather than varying amounts according to the area of land they cultivated, peasants and their communities could reduce their tax liability by living in larger households. The change in the unit of taxation prompted communes and heads of households to discourage household divisions and to encourage mergers. The prospect of having to pay the household tax also deterred sons and younger brothers who would otherwise have broken away. Although some larger households existed only on paper to fool the tax assessors, ample evidence has already been presented for an increase in the average size and complexity of peasant households in most regions in the second half of the seventeenth and early eighteenth centuries.[36]

It might be expected that the introduction of the poll tax by Peter the Great in 1718–24 would have reversed the trend, as there was no longer any fiscal advantage for peasants to live in larger households. Indeed, in the late eighteenth century some nobles blamed the substitution of the poll tax for the household tax for an increase in the numbers of *pre-mortem* divisions and a fall in the proportion of large, complex households on their estates. The other main obligation Peter imposed on the peasantry, recruitment into the army, also had the potential to persuade peasants that their best interests would be served by partitioning their households. Since many landowners and communes insisted that recruits be provided by larger households, because smaller households were unlikely to survive the loss of an adult male labourer, households with several adult males had an incentive to divide. Semevskii argued that the threat of recruitment did lead to household divisions in the late eighteenth century. However, the state, landowners and communes all took steps to prevent individual households from trying to stop their menfolk being conscripted in this way. Laws enacted in the 1820s and 30s banned state peasant households from dividing unless they had recently supplied a recruit. The estate administrations and communes on a number of seigniorial estates, for example Manuilovskoe, tried to enforce similar restrictions. Such measures met with mixed success. In Petrovskoe, the estate manager was unable to prevent an increase in household divisions in the 1850s, which may have been

35 Czap, 'A large family', pp. 105, 122, 136 (quotation); Aleksandrov, *Sel'skaya*, pp. 300–3; Bohac, 'Inheritance', p. 31; Frierson, '*Razdel*', pp. 42, 44; Hoch, *Serfdom*, pp. 91, 129–30; Melton, 'Proto-industrialization', pp. 98–9. On outlying regions, see Minenko, *Russkaya*, pp. 49, 54–7, 71–2; Vlasova, 'Sem'ya', pp. 179, 188. See also Chs 2, 4 and 6.
36 Aleksandrov, 'Typology', p. 36; Blum, *Lord and Peasant*, pp. 240, 277, 463; Shapiro, *Agrarnaya istoriya . . . XVII v.*, pp. 59–62, 66, 182; Vodarskii, *Naselenie Rossii v kontse XVII*, p. 47. Hellie overstated the case when he asserted that the household tax 'artificially created the famous Russian extended family': Hellie, *Slavery*, pp. 413, 419.

motivated by a desire to reduce the risk of losing a son or brother to the army during the Crimean War.[37]

Nevertheless, there is little evidence that, other than in exceptional circumstances, recruitment or the poll tax caused an increase in household divisions in general or *pre-mortem* divisions in particular. Landowners who thought more households were dividing were simply observing partitions that would have occurred in any case as part of normal household life cycles (see below, pp. 177–9). Moreover, any impetus towards divisions caused by Peter's twin burden of obligations was probably cancelled out by the impact of the increasing overall demands made by the landowning and ruling elites from the mid-seventeenth century. The high level of exploitation sometimes caused small households to go under, and compelled communes and households to strive to make the most efficient use of their labour resources. As far back as the 1650s–60s, when many peasants were drafted into tsar Alexis's army, peasants tried to maintain large households so that they could survive the loss of one or more men. In much of Russia in the following two centuries, communes and heads of households insisted that partitions were delayed until the new households that would be created contained sufficient adult labourers to meet their share of the communal burden and to support themselves without relying on the community. This usually meant *post-* rather than *pre-mortem* partitions.[38]

The impact of seigniorial obligations in delaying and hindering household divisions seems to have been most marked on estates where peasants served labour obligations (*barshchina*), for example Mishino and Petrovskoe in the Central Black Earth region. Moreover, the greater degree of control exercised by the estate administrations and communes on such estates made it more likely that they would succeed in preventing divisions. It is not surprising, therefore, that large, complex households predominated on these estates. In contrast, in Baki in the Central Non-Black Earth region, where most households were small and simple, the peasants paid dues (*obrok*) and seigniorial control was less rigid. Most state peasants paid dues, and there is evidence that their households partitioned earlier and more frequently and, thus, tended to be smaller and simpler, than those of seigniorial peasants.

The connection between the type and frequency of household partitions and the form of obligations may not be as clear cut. The main economic activity of the peasants in Mishino and Petrovskoe was labour-intensive arable farming, while many peasants in Baki engaged in non-agricultural activities that did not require households to maintain large labour forces. Moreover, compared with peasants who performed labour services and lived in the agricultural Central Black Earth region, peasants who paid dues and lived in the forest-heartland had more opportunities for migrant labour and, thus,

---

37 Vodarskii, 'K voprosu', p. 130; Semevskii, 'Domashnii' [II], p. 72; Hellie, R., 'The Petrine army', *CASS*, vol. 8 (1974), p. 249; Minenko, *Russkaya*, pp. 57–60, 64; Bohac, *Family*, pp. 166–7; Hoch, *Serfdom*, p. 156.
38 Aleksandrov, 'Typology', pp. 36–7, 46, 49, 51–2; Baklanova, *Krest'yanskii*, pp. 39, 99–102.

enjoyed greater independence from heads of households, communes and estate administrations. Melton argued that all these factors 'may have enabled young couples [in the more northerly region] to set up their own households free from parental control'. The tendency for state peasant households to divide more often, and live in smaller households, may simply reflect the fact that many lived in the forest-heartland and Siberia. Czap compared data on household sizes and found a 'higher degree of uniformity among mean household sizes of peasants of different categories within a region than among peasants of the same categories across regions'. Thus, the economic activities peasant households engaged in, which determined their labour needs, had more influence on the timing and frequency of partitions than the type of obligations they served, or the category they belonged to.[39]

Therefore, the main factors inhibiting household divisions, especially *pre-mortem* partitions, throughout Russia across the period from the mid-seventeenth to the mid-nineteenth centuries were the labour requirements of peasant agriculture, the high levels of exploitation by the landowning and ruling elites, and the degree of control this generated by the state, landowners, village communes and household heads.

* * *

The late nineteenth century, after the abolition of serfdom and other reforms, saw the start of a move away from *post-mortem* partitions and complex households. Throughout Russia, households began to divide more frequently, and a greater proportion split before the deaths of their heads. These changes were partly a result of the growth in non-agricultural work and wage labour, which were most marked in the Central Non-Black Earth region and elsewhere in the forest-heartland. These economic changes were partly responsible for the gradual development of a sense of individualism among younger peasants. Some sons earning wages resented having to pay towards the upkeep of their fathers' households, and demanded partitions so that they could become the masters of their own households. On the other hand, while they were away, migrant workers often left their wives and children with their parents, and the earnings they sent back helped to maintain large, complex households.[40] The military service reform of 1874 contributed to the increase in *pre-mortem* divisions. Before the Crimean War, in peacetime, every year around 1 per cent of the male peasant population was drafted into the army for long terms of service, from which most never returned. After 1874, a far larger proportion of peasants served for a maximum of six years, and then came back home. By

39 See Czap, 'A large family', p. 149; Hoch, *Serfdom*; Bohac, *Family*; Melton, 'Household', p. 569 (quotation). For comparisons with state peasants, see Czap, *op. cit.*, p. 148 (quotation); Vlasova, 'Sem'ya', pp. 186, 189, 192, 194.
40 Frierson, '*Razdel*', pp. 48–9; Johnson, R. E., 'Peasant and proletariat: Migration, family patterns, and regional loyalties', in *WRP*, pp. 84–7; Worobec, *Peasant Russia*, pp. 83–4, 105. See also Chs 4 and 9.

1900, around 20 per cent of adult male peasants had served in the army. When they returned home, some former soldiers no longer wanted to live in large, complex households, under the authority of their fathers or elder brothers, and broke away.[41]

The main reason for the increase in the number of partitions, and the tendency for more sons to break away before their fathers had died, was the abolition of serfdom and reforms of the other categories of peasants in the 1860s. The reforms ended the authority of noble landowners over the former seigniorial peasants, and reduced control by officials over state and appanage peasants. Moreover, the reforms broke the mutually reinforcing hierarchy of control, based on a conjunction of interests, that had stretched from heads of households, via communes, estate officials and landowners to the state authorities. It was this hierarchy of control which had helped maintain large and complex households. The greater powers to regulate partitions vested in village communal institutions after 1861 were not strong enough to counteract the centrifugal forces that existed inside large, complex households. Donald MacKenzie Wallace summed up a major cause of the break-up of large households in the 1860s–70s: 'The arbitrary rule of the Khozain [household head] was based on, and maintained by, the arbitrary rule of the proprietor, and both fell naturally together'. The government became so concerned about the increase in divisions, which it believed contributed to peasant impoverishment, that it enacted a law in 1886 to reinforce the control of communes, village elders and heads of household over partitions. The law had little effect. The increase in the number of all partitions, especially *pre-mortem* partitions, continued regardless.[42]

Two types of household life cycles

The two types of household divisions, *pre-* and *post-mortem*, did not affect just the proportions of simple and complex households in particular communities and regions at certain times. In combination with the marriage pattern, the two types of divisions led to two types of household life cycles: the 'phases of development' cycle and the 'perennial complex household' cycle.[43] The 'phases of development' cycle was a result of *pre-mortem* divisions and was, thus, widespread in most of Russia before the mid-seventeenth century and from the late nineteenth century. In the period in between it was common in Siberia and parts of the forest-heartland. This household life cycle was described by Alexander Chayanov. The size and structure of a household reflected the 'phases of development' of the dominant nuclear family unit within it. The best way to explain this life cycle is to describe a hypothetical example.

41 Worobec, *Peasant Russia*, pp. 90–2. See also Chs 3 and 9.
42 Wallace, *Russia*, vol. 1, p. 142; Frierson, '*Razdel*', p. 50; Worobec, *Peasant Russia*, pp. 87–97. On the 'conjunction of interests', see Hoch, *Serfdom*, p. 91. See also Ch. 6.
43 Bohac (*Family*, pp. 151–63) described several life cycles, but most are variations of the two main ones.

At the start of the first phase, the household consisted of a married couple, possibly with young children, which had just broken away from the husband's father's household. The new household got larger as more children were born and grew up. Nevertheless, throughout the first phase, the household remained simple in structure. The second phase began with the marriage of the first son, and the addition of his wife to the household. In due course, other sons married, brought their wives into the household, and the wives gave birth to children. The arrival of daughters-in-law cancelled out the departure of daughters, who married and moved into their husbands' natal households. During this second phase, therefore, the household was complex in structure. The start of the third phase was signalled by the departure of one of the sons with his wife and children. They broke away before the death of the head of the original household, in a *pre-mortem* partition, to set up their own, separate, simple household. In due course, other sons and their families left, also in *pre-mortem* divisions. At the end of the third phase, therefore, the original couple, now elderly, once again lived in a small household, either on their own in a simple household, or with one son who would succeed to the headship on his father's death. As the household went through the three phases, it had developed from a small, simple household into a large, complex household and then, finally, back to a smaller household with a simpler structure. Meanwhile, the new households that broke away from the original household before the father's death embarked on similar life cycles as they went through their 'phases of development'.[44]

The second type of life cycle, the 'perennial complex household' cycle, was a result of *post-mortem* divisions. It was, therefore, widespread in large parts of Russia from the late seventeenth to the late nineteenth century. It reached its most developed form on seigniorial estates in the Central Black Earth region, for example Mishino, in the eighteenth and first half of the nineteenth centuries. This life cycle was identified by Czap. Households conforming to this cycle were complex in structure throughout their existence. Under pressure from landowners, estate managers, communes and household heads, many large, complex households divided only when the new ones which were created were also complex. As a consequence, the different 'phases of development' of individual nuclear family units took place inside larger, complex households. This meant, in Czap's words:

Only low life expectancy, accidents of fertility, or a factor such as military service, prevented a married male peasant sharing a household with his parents and unmarried brothers for a period of ten or more years. Conversely, both partners in the original pair ... often died in a household containing all their surviving married sons. Because of this pattern, Mishino provided many instances of domestic groups which at the level of the ...

44 Chayanov, *Theory*, pp. 56–60. See also Confino, M., 'Russian customary law and the study of peasant mentalities', *RR*, vol. 44 (1985), p. 42; Czap, 'Perennial', p. 15.

178

household reflected two or all of the three phases of the developmental cycle simultaneously.

In Mishino, many households retained complex structures 'through a continuous sequence of generations', during which there was a turnover of heads and a partitioning off of new, complex households. The result was that Mishino (and other similar communities) contained many 'perennial complex households' with no beginning or end. Czap concluded: 'Of all the households found in Mishino at the end of the eighteenth century, excluding those later transferred . . . to another [village], 59 percent persisted continuously . . . as direct descent groups until 1858.'[45]

Thus, dynamic analysis of peasant households suggests that the key difference in structures was not between simple and complex households, but between two types of household life cycles: the 'phases of development' cycle and the 'perennial complex household' cycle. Since the pattern of near-universal, early marriage was common in Russia throughout the period, and most newly married couples spent at least the first part of their married lives in the household of one set of parents, the factor that determined households' life cycles was the point at which they divided: before or after the death of the head of household.

It is now possible to resolve the conflict between the conclusions of Aleksandrov and Czap outlined earlier. In communities and at times in which there were significant proportions of both simple and complex households, and in which households tended to divide before the death of the head of household, the predominant household life cycle was the 'phases of development' cycle. The figures on the proportions of different household structures, simple and complex, at certain fixed points in time in a given area merely reflected the percentages of households at particular phases of development at that time. The percentage of complex and simple households in a given community at different times could be quite different as a result of accidental demographic circumstances, without peasants having made any changes to their customary practices. The 'phases of development' household life cycle prevailed in most of Russia before the mid-seventeenth century and after the mid-nineteenth century, and in much of Siberia and outlying parts of the forest-heartland for the whole period. In contrast, in the Central Black Earth region in particular, but also in parts of other steppe regions and the forest-heartland between the late seventeenth and mid-nineteenth centuries, the high proportion of complex households and the custom of division after the death of their heads suggest that the 'perennial complex household' life cycle prevailed.

Furthermore, these two types of household life cycles can be reconciled into a single household system over time. In most regions of Russia and for most of the period under consideration, a majority of households were complex at *some* stages of their life cycles and, therefore, the complex household system

---

45 Czap, 'Perennial', pp. 15–18, 24 (he used the term 'perennial multiple family household').

was predominant among the Russian peasantry, i.e. the exact opposite of Aleksandrov's assertion that nuclear families were the norm and that more complex structures were temporary outgrowths. John Hajnal summed up the argument: 'The [complex] household system did not normally produce a situation where the majority of households were [complex] at any one time . . . However, under a [complex] household system, the majority of people were members of a [complex] household at some stage in their lives.'[46]

Succession of heads of households

Some 'perennial complex households' may have persisted for generations, but their heads, of course, did not. The death of household heads raised the question of who would succeed them. In complex households, moreover, the death of the old head often prompted the division of the household into two or more smaller households by surviving brothers. The head of a household was usually succeeded by the senior male, often the eldest son. In Mishino between 1782 and 1858, 58 per cent of deceased heads were succeeded by their sons, 8.2 per cent by their brothers, 6.4 per cent by their nephews, 5.8 per cent by their grandsons, and 1.7 per cent by adopted sons-in-law. The mean age at which men succeeded to headships on the death of the previous head in Mishino was 44.3. This was a little older than in Petrovskoe, where the average age was 38.5. On these two seigniorial estates, peasant men became heads of households about 20–25 years after they had married, and at around the same age at which they became grandfathers. On both estates, the over-whelming majority of male peasants in their 30s and between a third and a half of men in their 40s had not yet become household heads. By the time men were in their 50s, however, only 10 per cent were not heads of households. In comparison with other societies where simple households predominated, for example pre-industrial north-west Europe, the social maturity associated with heading a household came late to many Russian peasants.[47]

If there were no surviving adult males in a household, a woman could succeed. In Mishino between 1782 and 1858, 13.7 per cent of deceased heads were succeeded by their widows, who were, on average, 58.4 years old. There were isolated cases of daughters-in-law, sisters-in-law, sisters and nieces taking over household headships in Mishino. Female heads of households were not unusual in Russia. Rodney Bohac estimated that one-third of all households in Manuilovskoe, Tver' province, had a woman head at some point between 1813 and 1861. The numbers of female heads were higher than average, as many as 15 per cent, in wartime. During the Napoleonic Wars, when many men were conscripted into the army, some wives (and widows) acted as heads of households. More rarely, women took over headships from husbands who were still living in the village if the commune deemed them

46 Hajnal, 'Two kinds', p. 69 (he used the term 'joint household').
47 Bohac, 'Inheritance', p. 28; Czap, 'A large family', p. 137; *id.*, 'Perennial', pp. 20–1; Hoch, *Serfdom*, pp. 84, 87.

incompetent, for example as a result of drunkenness. Female household heads were fairly common later in the nineteenth century in parts of the Central Non-Black Earth region, for example Kostroma province, where many men were away for long periods working in cities.

Widows who headed households usually relinquished their position to their sons or other young male family members when they came of age. The few young women who headed small households with no adult males were in a very weak position, and had a hard job to survive the predations of their neighbours. However, Bohac argued that in Manuilovskoe some older female heads of more prosperous households, especially those with adult sons or married-in sons-in-law, 'might manage to be . . . secure, authoritative household head[s]'. He concluded: 'Such [successful] widows were rare, but their existence demonstrates that a few women, by dint of luck, property, strength of character, or some combination of these, managed to carve out some autonomy for themselves amid the patriarchy of the [village community].'[48] Nevertheless, most heads of households were men, a fact which reflected the patriarchal order of Russian peasant society.

Inheritance and division of household property

The death of a head of a household also raised the issue of the devolution of its property. However, inheritance on the death of household heads was less important in peasant Russia than in non-peasant Russia and many other societies, because the head of a Russian peasant household was not the sole owner of its property. Rather, he was the administrator of property that was owned jointly by all its members. This was enshrined in unwritten customary law and, later, in the statutes of 1861. In much of Russia from the early eighteenth century, moreover, the most important part of a household's property, its arable land, was held by village communes (see Ch. 6). Households had only use rights of the land, but these could be inherited. The property which most households had full ownership of included the buildings, the land they were built on and kitchen gardens, implements, livestock, stores of grain and personal possessions. Some households also owned land which they had purchased on top of their allotments from the commune. Although some wealthier peasants who engaged in non-agricultural activities began to think in terms of individual, personal property in the nineteenth century, it was not until the Stolypin land reforms of 1906–11 that Russian civil law recognised the heads of peasant households as the sole owners of their households' property, including the arable land.

Under joint ownership of household property, on the death of the head, all members were entitled to a share in a system of partible inheritance, which contrasted with primogeniture in the succession of new heads. Inheritance

---

48 Bohac, R. D., 'Widows and the Russian serf community', in Clements, *Russia's Women*, pp. 109–11 (quotations). See also Czap, 'Perennial', pp. 20–1; Engel, *Between*, pp. 53–4; Worobec, *Peasant Russia*, pp. 7, 45, 185, 194.

was usually patrilineal, i.e. it followed the male line. Thus, surviving sons, brothers, nephews, grandsons and, sometimes, marrying-in sons-in-law were all guaranteed part of the household property. Women were not totally excluded. In some parts of the Northern region before the mid-seventeenth century and in Siberia down to the nineteenth century, women could inherit household property, including land, from their fathers. Daughters' claims were strongest if there were no surviving sons. Peasant customs concerning inheritance, and property rights in general, made some allowance for women in most of Russia in the eighteenth and nineteenth centuries. On the death of their husbands, women retained control of their dowries and any personal property they had brought with them from their natal households when they married, including trousseaus purchased with the bride-price (see below, p. 188). In addition, throughout the period in many parts of Russia, widows received a 'portion' of around one-seventh of the household property. This was to support them, and to enable them to provide for their unmarried daughters. In many regions, widows could inherit more property, including land, but only as trustees until their sons grew up. Mostly, however, women depended on their menfolk when their husbands or fathers died.

The question of sharing out a household's property on the death of its head was not always immediate. In 'perennial complex households', most or all of the survivors continued to live together under the direction of the new head and kept the household's property intact. Indeed, many peasant practices and customs envisaged that this was the most likely possibility. It was certainly in the interests of the new head and his wife, the commune and, on seigniorial estates, the landowner. It entailed the least disruption to existing arrangements and was the best guarantee that households could continue supporting themselves and meeting their shares of the communal obligations. Inheritance on the death of a household head was important only if the survivors chose to divide the household and its property.[49]

The principles governing the distribution of the original household's property between new households created by divisions were similar to those guiding inheritance. As a general rule this meant partible inheritance down the male line. The head of each new household received a share. Property was often divided equally between sons or brothers. The son or brother who received the old house compensated the others. There were exceptions to the principle of equal shares. In parts of Siberia in the eighteenth and nineteenth centuries and the Central Non-Black Earth region in the late nineteenth century, some households allotted property according to individual peasants' contributions to the household's wealth. In addition, in large, complex households, more distant relatives of the old head, such as nephews and grandsons, often received smaller shares. If a household divided and shared out its property before the death of the head, then he exercised considerable authority over the distribution

---

49 Aleksandrov, *Obychnoe*, pp. 162–4, 244–53; Bohac, 'Inheritance', pp. 26–8; *id.*, 'Widows', pp. 100–1; Czap, 'Perennial', p. 7; Minenko, *Russkaya*, pp. 156–70; Shanin, *Awkward*, pp. 219–24; Smith, *Peasant Farming*, p. 82; Worobec, *Peasant Russia*, pp. 42–7, 62–75.

of the property. If a head 'retired', he tried to make sure that the son who was going to look after him and his wife in old age received a larger share. In the late nineteenth century, some elderly peasants drew up legal contracts to try to ensure their children would support them. Women did not receive property directly on household divisions, since it was usually shared between the new households rather than their individual members, and most new households had male heads. Women were entitled to keep their dowries and other 'women's property', however, and the distribution of property between households normally made allowance for the women who lived in them.

Village communes, guided by customary law, oversaw the distribution of property on household divisions, and aggrieved parties could appeal to them. Communal elders generally upheld the rights of the elderly to be maintained by their children, and decided other cases with the aim of ensuring that all households, including new ones formed by divisions, were capable of supporting themselves and meeting their obligations. The customs of joint household ownership of property and partible inheritance reflected at household level the practice of communal and repartitional tenure of the arable land that prevailed at village level.[50]

CUSTOMS AND RITUALS OF FAMILY LIFE

The customary and ritual life of Russian peasant families revolved around the stove (*pech'*), which was situated in one corner of the house, and the 'red corner' diagonally opposite. The stove provided heat to warm the house and for cooking. It was sometimes also the 'home' of the household's ancestral spirit (*domovoi*). Wherever it lived, peasants believed the spirit oversaw the running of the household and protected them from evil. In pre-Christian times, the images in the red corner may have represented the family's ancestors; but in later times, they were icons portraying the Christian God and some of the saints, to whom peasants prayed for protection from misfortune. Like agricultural festivals, the Russian peasantry's family customs and rituals contained a combination of beliefs and practices from the old, pagan religion and Orthodox Christianity.[51]

The main events in family life, and the practices that were followed, were marked by rituals and festivities. Family customs and rituals were central to the social and cultural life of Russian villages. They were also ways in which the older generation tried to ensure that younger peasants conformed to traditional practices, and passed them on to future generations.[52] The main events in the lives of peasants and their families were births, marriages and deaths.

50 Aleksandrov, *Obychnoe*, pp. 244–7; Bohac, 'Inheritance', pp. 26–9, 34–5; Czap, 'Perennial', p. 7; Frierson, 'Peasant', pp. 303–20; Minenko, *Russkaya*, pp. 156–70; Shanin, *Russia*, p. 70; Worobec, *Peasant Russia*, pp. 47–57. See also Ch. 6.
51 Matossian, 'Peasant', pp. 5–7, 19–20; Ivanits, *Russian Folk Belief*, pp. 51–9. See also Chs 4 and 9.
52 On the strong correlation between Russian folklore and actual demographic practices, see Mironov, 'Traditsionnoe'.

Birth customs

The birth rate was very high throughout Russia during the period covered by this book (see Ch. 1). The vast majority of births occurred to married peasant women in the relative security of their households. Illegitimate births were rare.[53] Once a young wife became pregnant, she could normally rely on the support of her female in-laws who she lived with. Nevertheless, expectant women were required to continue working, including manual labour in the household and the fields, sometimes even until the onset of labour pains. This undoubtedly added to the number of miscarriages. When birth was imminent, the family sent for the midwife (*babka-povitukha*), usually a middle-aged woman. Very few midwives had 'modern' medical training before the end of the nineteenth century, but they had practical experience and a wealth of customs to call upon to ease the arrival of the new baby into the world. They recited sayings, spells and prayers over the expectant mother, applied potions to her, and symbolically opened the gates of the yard and the doors and windows in the house. Midwives resorted to other customs, which would disturb modern practitioners, including walking women in labour around a table three times, steaming them inside the stove or bathhouse, or making them hang from the rafters. Once the babies were born, they were bound in swaddling clothes.

Russians believed that women who had just given birth, their babies, and anyone present during childbirth were 'impure'. Except in cases of very difficult births, no men, not even the father or the priest, were allowed to be present. As a result, 'childbirth was an exclusively female event', and an important area of peasant life in which women had sole responsibility. Midwives were among the few peasant women who enjoyed status in their communities outside their households.[54] The exclusion of men from births offers a curious contrast to the exclusion of women from the arable fields during sowing (see Ch. 4).

The occasion at which a newborn baby became accepted as a member of its household and village community, and acquired a name, was its christening. The church service, during which the baby was immersed in cold water, was followed by a ceremonial meal for the family, the godparents and the midwife. Christenings were low-key affairs. Peasants celebrated the birth of new children, especially sons, but were wary of expressing good wishes about the future of newly born children. This diffidence reflected the very high rates of infant and childhood mortality (see Ch. 1). For this reason, most babies were christened within two days of their birth.[55]

53 Ransel, D. L., 'Problems of measuring illegitimacy in prerevolutionary Russia', *JSocH*, vol. 16 (1982), pp. 111–27.
54 Fedorov, V. A., 'Mat' i ditya v Russkoi derevne (konets XIX–nachalo XX v.), *VMU (I)* (1994), no. 4, pp. 3–11; Levin, E., 'Childbirth in pre-Petrine Russia', in Clements, *Russia's Women*, pp. 44–59; Ramer, 'Childbirth', pp. 107–20; Semyonova, *Village Life*, pp. 8–14; Worobec, *Peasant Russia*, pp. 205–7.
55 Fedorov, 'Mat'', pp. 12–15; Semyonova, *Village Life*, pp. 15–17; Minenko, *Russkaya*, pp. 256–61. See also Ransel, D. L., 'Baptism in rural Russia', *History of the Family*, vol. 1 (1996), pp. 63–80.

Courtship and marriage customs

Marriage was central to the lives of Russian peasants, both male and female. An ethnographer working in Yaroslavl' province in the late nineteenth century was informed by a peasant: 'Among us an unmarried [man] is not considered a real peasant', and that bachelors were looked at 'partly with pity, like something that isn't whole, and partly with suspicion'. For female peasants too, marriage marked the point at which they became adults and full members of their communities. An ethnographer commenting on the very high incidence of marriage among Tambov peasants in the 1880s wrote 'only freaks and the morally depraved do not marry'.[56] There were few alternatives to married life. Male peasants who spent large parts of their lives as migrant labourers usually had wives in their home villages. The only significant exceptions were the small proportion of men drafted into the army for long terms of service before 1874 and their wives (*soldatki*), who were consequently denied a normal married life; a few Orthodox women who joined religious communities; and some Old Believer and sectarian women who refused to marry.[57]

In most peasant communities, the older generation helped arrange and supervise social occasions for young, unmarried peasants. At round dances (*khorovody*) and gatherings (*posidelki*), young peasants danced, sang folk songs, told and listened to tales, riddles, jokes and proverbs, or exchanged gossip. At other gatherings, young men and women worked together in a variety of tasks to help the whole village, for example repairing buildings or assisting households which had fallen on hard times. At other gatherings, it was the young women who worked, spinning, sewing or pickling vegetables, while the young men entertained them by singing and playing musical instruments. All these gatherings were expressly devised so that young men and women could become acquainted with prospective partners and show off their accomplishments, especially their proficiency at working. Some social occasions ended with young men and women pairing off. Bundling (lying together fully clothed) was common in parts of Russia. Sometimes young couples spent the night together in outbuildings. A double standard operated. Men who engaged in sex before marriage might be fined by the commune, but women who did so were often subjected to ritual humiliation. Taboos on pre-marital sex were relaxed in the late nineteenth century as the control of village communities over the younger generation lessened, and young peasants began to play greater roles in organising their social lives and choosing marriage partners.[58] Interestingly, in medieval times, young men and women had also had freer choice in whom they

---

56 Gromyko, *Traditsionnye*, p. 261 (quotation); Hoch, *Serfdom*, pp. 76–7 (quotation).
57 Farnsworth, 'Soldatka', pp. 58–73; Meehan-Waters, B., 'To save oneself: Russian peasant women and the development of women's religious communities in prerevolutionary Russia' in *RPW*, pp. 121–33; Glickman, 'Unusual circumstances', pp. 224–6.
58 See Gromyko, *Traditsionnye*, pp. 161–262; Worobec, *Peasant Russia*, pp. 128–42; Frank, S. P., '"Simple folk, savage customs?" Youth, sociability, and the dynamics of culture in rural Russia', *JSocH*, vol. 25, no. 4 (1991–92), pp. 711–36; Engel, B. A., 'Peasant morality and pre-marital relations in late 19th century Russia', *JSocH*, vol. 23 (1989–90), pp. 695–714.

married. This continued in some outlying areas in the eighteenth and nineteenth centuries. Most marriages among Siberian peasants in the nineteenth century were love matches, and some peasants eloped to defy their parents.[59]

For most of the period under consideration, especially in the central regions, the older generation maintained fairly strict control over young peasants in their households, and played a large role in deciding whom they married. Communes and, among seigniorial peasants, estate authorities also took an interest. This pattern of parental, communal and estate control over marriage seems to have been strongest on seigniorial estates in the eighteenth and first half of the nineteenth centuries. The older generation attached little significance to romance, beauty, attraction and, sometimes, the feelings of young peasants. Proverbs warned against being distracted by good looks: 'Choose between a wife who will pull the wagon and one who will ornament your yard'. In much of Russia, especially the central regions before the late nineteenth century, peasants expected brides to be virgins, but tolerated young couples who had sex once they were betrothed. Given the importance attached to fertility, some male peasants tried to make sure their prospective brides were capable of having children before agreeing to marry them. This was more common in Siberia. In some northern areas, moreover, unmarried mothers with sons had a good chance of marriage. The most important attributes peasants wanted in brides, however, were obedience, submissiveness, good health, diligence, and the strength and endurance to bear many children and carry out the heavy workload expected of young women.

Peasants looked for the equivalent qualities in prospective husbands for their daughters. They were suspicious of handsome men, and preferred responsibility, diligence, a capacity for hard work and, bearing in mind the ruinous consequences of drunkenness, sobriety. Parents also took account of the wealth and social status of the families of their daughters' suitors. They sought to marry them to prosperous households with high status in the village community. Marriages united not just two individuals, but two households. Kinship links were important in village politics. Overemphasis on the role of parents in choosing partners for their children may be misplaced. In the late nineteenth century, when young peasants had more freedom of choice, they tended to select their partners according to similar standards to those of their parents.[60]

Other factors affected peasants' choice of spouses. The Orthodox Church and local customs prohibited marrying relatives as distant as second cousins. Even people related by marriage and godparents were not allowed to marry. On the other hand, there were pressures that restricted the range of partners. Most peasants married other peasants who lived in or near their villages. Under serfdom, some landowners tried to ensure that their female peasants married

59 Pushkareva, N. L., 'Women in the medieval Russian family of the tenth through fifteenth centuries', in Clements, *Russia's Women*, p. 30; Minenko, *Russkaya*, pp. 203–10.
60 Czap, 'Marriage', p. 105; Engel, *Between*, pp. 17–19; Hoch, *Serfdom*, p. 102; Minenko, *Russkaya*, pp. 217–18; Semyonova, *Village Life*, pp. 63–4; Worobec, *Peasant Russia*, pp. 133–42. See also Ch. 6.

other peasants belonging to them, otherwise they risked losing not just a female peasant, but also her children. On occasions this aroused protests. Most land-owners allowed women to leave their estates to marry if they or their fiancés paid a departure fee. Some estate administrations even organised exchanges of brides between neighbouring villages belonging to different owners. After the end of serfdom, there were still social pressures to enforce endogamous rather than exogenous marriage. The young men of a village often adopted a 'pro-tective' attitude towards 'their' unmarried women, and were hostile to out-siders who tried to make their acquaintance. In parts of Siberia where villages were small and many of their inhabitants were related, however, peasants actively sought partners in other villages.[61]

Most peasants married partners close to them in age. There were excep-tions. Some households married boys to adult women in order to increase the number of labourers at their disposal. Widowers often preferred to marry younger women than widows nearer their own age. However, an informant on peasant life in Novgorod province in the late nineteenth century wrote: 'A lad marries – whom he chooses; a widower marries whoever will have him.'[62]

Peasants married at certain times of the year. Many of the functions at which young peasants socialised and met potential partners were held in the late summer and early autumn. They were followed by 'wedding seasons' after the harvest in October and November and, especially, between Christmas and Shrovetide in January and February. April and May were also fairly popular months for getting married. The timing of weddings was strongly influenced by the calendar of agricultural work and prohibitions by the Orthodox Church on marriages during major fasts. Most peasants got married in the lulls in agricultural work in the autumn and winter, while few married during the peak periods of field work. Thus, there were few weddings in the early spring (ploughing and sowing) and the summer (haymaking, harvesting, ploughing and sowing the fallow field). The impracticality of marrying in the early spring and late summer was reinforced by church bans on weddings during the Lent and Assumption fasts. The church also forbade weddings during St Philip's fast before Christmas.[63]

Russian peasants followed a series of rituals that led from the selection of partners to the wedding ceremonies. The women in households played a large role. The first stage was matchmaking. When, after making discreet enquir-ies, a young man's family had selected a potential bride, they sent matchmakers (*svakhi*) to her household. The matchmakers were usually married, female relatives of the suitor, often aunts and married sisters. When they arrived, the

---

61 Worobec, *Peasant Russia*, pp. 132, 149–50; Minenko, *Russkaya*, pp. 188–91, 194–202; Bushnell, 'Did', pp. 422–32, 441–5.
62 Glickman, 'Unusual circumstances', p. 225 (quotation); Smith, *Peasant Farming*, p. 81; Semevskii, 'Domashnii' [II], pp. 73–4; Minenko, *Russkaya*, pp. 184–7.
63 Kaiser, 'Seasonality', pp. 30–9; Worobec, *Peasant Russia*, pp. 130–1, 151–3. See also Chs 4, 8 and 9.

matchmakers spoke to the women first, and hinted at the purpose of their visit: 'We have a buyer, and you have the goods', or 'You have a daughter and we have a son'. If the female hosts wished to proceed, they sought the views of the father and the daughter. If they assented, the matchmakers and young woman's parents sat down to negotiate the terms of the marriage contract that sealed the betrothal. The contract included details of the gifts the bride and groom were to exchange, the compensation to be paid if one party backed out, the apportionment of the wedding costs and, most importantly, the dowry (*pridanoe*) and/or bride-price (*kladka*).[64]

A dowry, or trousseau, was property given to the bride by her family, and which remained her inalienable property throughout her marriage. A Russian peasant woman's dowry usually comprised a chest of clothes and linen, and sometimes also a spinning-wheel, some grain, a few domestic animals and money. A bride-price (or bridewealth) was property which was given to the bride's family by the groom's family in compensation for the loss of their daughter, her labour and reproductive powers. Bride-prices included clothes as well as money. (When a bride's family 'adopted' her husband, they paid a 'groomwealth'.) Russian bride-prices often contained an element of 'indirect dowry'. This was property given by the family of the groom to the family of the bride to cover the cost of her trousseau, and as a contribution towards the wedding expenses.

The existence or otherwise of dowries and bride-prices reveals a great deal about the importance of women, marriage and families in peasant life. The levels were set by negotiation between the two households. If the bride was of less 'worth', for example if she was weak, sickly, or had a reputation for engaging in pre-marital sex, then the bride-price would be reduced accordingly, or her family would give her a substantial dowry. Direct dowries alone were most common in parts of the Northern region of Russia, and in Ukraine, while the custom of bride-price predominated in most provinces of central and south-east Russia. Where both customs existed side-by-side, i.e. there was an exchange of property between the two households, the values of bride-prices normally exceeded those of dowries, and the 'purchase' element of bride-price ('true bride-price') was greater than that of indirect dowry. In short, most peasant marriages in Russia were accompanied by a transfer of property from the groom's household to the bride's that compensated for the relocation of its daughter to her husband's household.

Steven Hoch has linked the existence of true bride-price and village communes which shared out the land according to the sizes of households. He noted the geographical correlation between the two. The parts of the Northern region and Ukraine, where direct dowry prevailed and bride-prices were not paid, were regions where households held their land in hereditary, not communal, tenure. In these areas, the loss of a daughter did not have any impact on the

64 Czap, 'Marriage', pp. 103–4; Minenko, *Russkaya*, pp. 225–6; Semyonova, *Village Life*, pp. 63, 75–6; Worobec, *Peasant Russia*, pp. 132, 152, 154.

size of a household's landholdings. In large parts of Russia, however, where village communes repartitioned land on the basis of household size, the transfer of a daughter to her husband's household meant that the latter gained not just the labour and child-bearing potential of their new daughter-in-law, but was able also to form a new labour team, which was allocated land by the commune. Without compensation, households would have been reluctant to part with their daughters. Many households used the bride-prices received for their daughters to 'buy' wives for their sons. Thus, the practice of bride-price produced a fund that circulated around the households of a community, and encouraged universal, and early, marriage.[65]

Once the marriage contract had been agreed by the matchmakers and bride's family, the bargain was sealed by a ritual clasping of hands and drinking toasts in vodka. In some villages, marriage contracts were witnessed by communal officials or village priests. The agreement was now binding, and signified the betrothal of the young couple. Shortly afterwards, the groom and his family visited the bride's household for a formal 'inspection' of the bride, to make sure she was not disabled, sick or pregnant. The 'bride show' was followed by a feast and drink provided by the groom's family.[66]

On the morning of the wedding,[67] the groom's parents blessed him with an icon before he left in a wedding procession to his bride's household. The bride's relatives put up mock resistance, and had to be bought off with drink and money by the best man, before they would allow her to be taken to the church for the nuptial service (*venchanie*). The wedding party then proceeded to the groom's household, where the newly sanctified couple, the two families and members of the village community celebrated the rest of the secular part of the wedding (*svad'ba*). This was the point at which the bride first entered her husband's household. To symbolise her relocation from her natal to her married household, and her transfer from her father's to her husband's authority, the bride's father gave his new son-in-law a ceremonial lash. The culmination of the ceremony came when the newlyweds were led to a specially prepared nuptial bed to consummate their marriage. Although they were left in privacy, the fact of consummation and, until the late nineteenth century, proof of the bride's virginity, were matters of great interest to the assembled guests, who were eating, toasting and giving their blessing to the new couple in a wedding feast that lasted until dawn.

65 Hoch, *Serfdom*, pp. 95–102, 105. See also Worobec, *Peasant Russia*, pp. 63, 156–8; Minenko, *Russkaya*, p. 230. Some landowners tried to ban bride-prices, however, believing they discouraged marriages: Bushnell, 'Did', pp. 427–8.
66 Czap, 'Marriage', pp. 103–4; Semyonova, *Village Life*, pp. 76–9; Worobec, *Peasant Russia*, pp. 151, 154–6.
67 This account is based on sources for the European part of Russia in the late nineteenth century. See Semyonova, *Village Life*, pp. 79–94; Worobec, *Peasant Russia*, pp. 160–72; Benet, S. (ed.), *The Village of Viriatino: An Ethnographic Study of a Russian Village from before the Revolution to the Present* (New York, 1970), pp. 108–16. Marriage (and courtship) rituals were similar in earlier periods and Siberia: Pushkareva, 'Women', pp. 30–7; Semevskii, 'Domashnii' [II], pp. 100–7; Minenko, *Russkaya*, pp. 225–53. Some Siberian peasants, including Orthodox Christians as well as Old Believers and sectarians, did not marry in church: *ibid.*, pp. 221–4.

Marriage was not always a joyous time for the bride. She moved from the relative security of her parents' household to the uncertainty of married life in the household of a husband who may not have been her own choice. Her mother-in-law soon established her dominance over her, and assigned her a large share of household tasks. Many young peasant women approached married life with mixed feelings, with at least as much apprehension as anticipation of happiness and fulfilment. Prospective brides observed a period of ritual mourning between their betrothal and wedding, and expressed their feelings about the imminent loss of their 'maidenly freedom' and youth in traditional laments.[68]

Marriage among Russian peasants was usually for life. It was upheld by village communes and the Orthodox Church. Given the importance of marriage and households, widespread separation or divorce would have seriously undermined peasant life. In pre-Petrine Russia, however, the church had dissolved marriages on various grounds, including adultery, desertion and marital rape. But, from the mid-eighteenth century, the church restricted divorce. In the European part of Russia, very few peasant marriages ended other than in the death of one partner. Separation and common-law second marriages did take place in the freer atmosphere of Siberia, and became more widespread west of the Urals after around 1900.[69]

Death customs

Death was a regular visitor to Russian peasant households as mortality was high throughout the period under consideration. Death rates were highest among the very young and the old. Peasants who survived to adulthood, and escaped the periodic famines and epidemics, could expect to live into their fifties and sixties. Some survived into old age. Only in the late nineteenth century, however, did the overall level of mortality begin to fall. (See Ch. 1.)

Elderly and seriously ill peasants prepared to die by confessing their sins to a priest and taking the sacrament. Peasants approaching death made testaments asking the living to give them a Christian burial and to pray for the repose of their souls. After a peasant died, the body was lain on a bench in the red corner of the house with the head under the icons. The bereaved family then arranged for someone, often a spinster, to read the Psalter over the body, and made the arrangements for the funeral service and burial. Peasants considered dead bodies to be unclean and dangerous. The elderly women who washed and dressed bodies for burial disposed of the items they used very carefully. In a symbolic attempt to ensure that the souls of the deceased left their bodies and began their journey to the 'other world', women closed the

68 Worobec, *Peasant Russia*, pp. 119–20, 129–30, 158–9, 173.
69 See Freeze, G. L., 'Bringing order to the Russian family: Marriage and divorce in imperial Russia, 1760–1860', *JMH*, vol. 62 (1990), pp. 709–46; Levin, E., *Sex and Society in the World of the Orthodox Slavs, 900–1700* (Ithaca, NY, and London, 1989), pp. 114–26; Pushkareva, 'Women', p. 42; Minenko, *Russkaya*, pp. 137, 210–16; Worobec, *Peasant Russia*, pp. 197–8.

eyes and mouths of corpses. For the same reason, after the pall-bearers had collected corpses, family members closed the households' gates and tied them shut. These practices can be contrasted with the customs at births, when gates and doors were left open to ease the arrival of babies into this world (see above, p. 184). On the day of the funeral, the priest accompanied the coffin to the church for the requiem service, before the deceased was interred in the cemetery. The family sometimes hired women as mourners. After the burial, the family returned home for a wake.

Russian peasants often buried their dead with food, household tools and a few coins. This reflected their beliefs in the continued material existence of the body, and that the souls of the dead wandered the earth for 40 days before their judgement. Memorial services and commemorative feasts were held at intervals over the 40 days to assist souls' journeys from this world to the hereafter. By praying for the dead, moreover, peasants hoped to remove the threat of death from their lives, and to ensure that the deceased would inter-cede for the living in heaven. Russian peasants remembered their dead relat-ives and held associated rituals on several occasions during the year, including Yuletide, Shrovetide, *Radonitsa* (shortly after Easter), during Trinity or Green Yuletide week, and on St Dmitrii's Saturday at the end of October. These customs have been linked with the veneration of ancestors in the old, pagan religion.

Christine Worobec noted that Russian peasants identified death with women. The Psalter readers, body washers and mourners were often women, death was represented in Russian folklore as a woman with a scythe, and the Rus-sian word for death, *smert'*, is feminine. She argued that this 'represented the real world turned upside down. While on earth the patriarchy controlled and subordinated women, in the world beyond women were in control and took their revenge on the patriarchy by snuffing out life.'[70]

LIFE IN PEASANT HOUSEHOLDS

In between the rituals and ceremonies that marked the main events in the lives in peasant families, peasants got on with the more mundane aspects of life. Much time and energy was taken up by work. By custom, most tasks in the household and on the land were divided by gender. (See Ch. 4.) Child care was almost exclusively women's work. Young mothers resumed working in the household economy shortly after they gave birth, leaving their infants in the care of their mothers- and sisters-in-law. Indeed, young mothers were expected to return to work as quickly as possible. While women preferred daughters, fathers wanted sons. There was disappointment in households if

70 See Benet, *Viriatino*, pp. 122–4; Ivanits, *Russian Folk Belief*, pp. 5–12; Worobec, C. D., 'Death ritual among Russian and Ukrainian peasants: Linkages between the living and the dead', in Frank, S. P. and Steinberg, M. D. (eds), *Cultures in Flux: Lower-Class Values, Practices, and Resistance in Late Imperial Russia* (Princeton, NJ, 1994), pp. 11–33. Some Siberian peasants were buried without a church funeral: Minenko, *Russkaya*, pp. 262–3. See also Ch. 9.

the first-born child was a daughter. Sometimes fathers and grandparents did not express much regret if a baby girl died. Although it would be a misunderstanding of peasant attitudes to think of them as callous, the very high levels of infant and child mortality led them to develop a certain pragmatism and fatalism to the lives, and deaths, of young children. In the late nineteenth century, at the time of rapid population increase, rural doctors reported peasants' remarks such as: 'If the children do not die what will we do then? . . . Soon there will be no place to stand in the house.'[71]

Some historians of childhood have contended that the modern concepts of good mothering, parental affection, and childhood as a separate phase in human life were largely missing in pre-industrial societies. Patrick Dunn extended this view to Russia. He argued that, in the eighteenth and nineteenth centuries, Russian parents 'considered children and child rearing unimportant; children had to be cared for, but underlying that care was parental neglect, even hostility toward the children'. In contrast, Mary Matossian painted an idealised picture of childhood in Russian peasant households in the 1860s. Both views are too extreme. Russian peasant children had very different experiences from children in 'modern', urban societies, of course, but they still experienced childhood as a phase of life different from that of grown-ups. Russian peasant children often lived in crowded huts with several married couples, and quickly became aware of all aspects of adult life. They were expected to grow up quickly and do some work in their households while still fairly young. For peasants, children were an investment for the future, not a luxury, and were treated as such. This did not mean, however, that they lived in a world devoid of care and affection.[72] Peasant women did have maternal feelings towards their children, and expressed them in lullabies, for example: 'Slumber, Vasen'ka, Slumber, beloved, Go to sleep, precious. Sleep, dear child, Precious, golden child.'[73]

Children's upbringing centred on socialisation into the norms and values of peasant society and culture, including respect for their elders and the importance of hard, manual labour to support their households and communities. The men took part in this aspect of children's upbringing. In large, complex households, children were taught to work by their grandparents, aunts, uncles and cousins as well as their parents and siblings. Mothers and other women taught girls the tasks they would have to perform when they grew up and married. From an early age, girls helped their mothers in their daily work. Meanwhile, fathers and the other men taught boys all they needed to know, especially the skilled agricultural tasks in the fields which they would carry

71 Fedorov, 'Mat'', pp. 16–21; Frieden, 'Child care', pp. 246–7 (quotation); Ransel, 'Infant', pp. 113–23; Semyonova, *Village Life*, pp. 7–15, 95–6. See also Ch. 1.
72 See Dunn, P. P., '"That enemy is the baby": Childhood in imperial Russia', in Mause, L. de (ed.), *The History of Childhood* (New York, 1974), p. 385; Matossian, 'Peasant', pp. 20–4. See also Hoch, *Serfdom*, pp. 181–2; Semyonova, *Village Life*, pp. 25–7.
73 Martynova, A., 'Life of the pre-revolutionary village as reflected in popular lullabies', in Ransel, *Family*, p. 172.

out when they got older. Only towards the end of the nineteenth century did many peasant children receive some formal education, and then most who attended village schools did so for just two or three winters when their parents could spare them from their households and fields. In addition, like children in all societies, Russian peasant children played games, fought, ran around and got into mischief. Nevertheless, parents took care to prepare them for the arduous life they would face as adults.[74]

The households which peasant children grew up in were the settings for networks of relationships between their members. In most households, the head and his wife had the onerous task of reconciling the conflicting concerns of their family members in order that everyone pulled together in the interests of the whole household. The larger and more complex the household, the greater the likelihood of tensions and conflict. The chief axes of tension were between the female and male peasants, and the younger and older generations.

Russian peasant men gave the impression that their primary concern for their wives was for their labour. Some even equated their wives with their horses. In 1880 a peasant man told a researcher: 'A muzhik [male peasant] cannot survive long without both. If the housewife dies, you must find another. If the horse croaks, you must get another. To live on the land the muzhik must have a horse and a wife.'[75] Another feature of marital life among Russian peasants that attracted comment by educated observers was wife-beating. Olga Semenova-Tyan-Shanskaya, in her study of village life in Ryazan' province at the turn of the twentieth century, noted that men beat their wives if they discovered they were not virgins on their wedding night, if they refused to carry out their orders, or simply when the men were drunk. There were many proverbs on wife-beating, for example: 'The more you beat the old woman, the tastier the soup will be'. These suggest that peasant men believed they had the right to beat their wives. Some men were so callous that, according to Semenova, they were more worried if some household item got broken during a beating than whether they had done serious harm to their wives. The violence was not all one way. Some women beat their husbands. Semenova also noted that, even when they were calm and sober, most peasant men did not express their feelings for their wives, and that couples spent little time talking to each other. Observers of peasant life elsewhere in Russia, including Siberia, painted an equally grim picture of relations between husbands and wives. More recently, historian Eve Levin argued that the notion of romantic love, and the connection between marriage, love and sex, were absent among Orthodox Slavs before 1700. They were relatively new developments among nobles in the eighteenth and nineteenth centuries, moreover, and sometimes aroused suspicion among peasants.

74 Semyonova, *Village Life*, pp. 25–49; Worobec, *Peasant Russia*, pp. 122, 209–12; Minenko, *Russkaya*, pp. 117–22, 139–41; Eklof, B., *Russian Peasant Schools: Officialdom, Village Culture, and Popular Pedagogy, 1861–1914* (Berkeley, CA, and London, 1986).
75 Glickman, R. L., 'The peasant woman as healer', in Clements, *Russia's Women*, p. 149.

These observations suggest that married life in the modern, Western sense did not exist in rural Russia. Rather, relations between husbands and wives reflected the primarily economic function of marriage, and that peasants' main loyalty was to their households, not their spouses. The picture of callousness and brutality presented by educated outsiders, however, may to some extent have reflected the differences between the lives and ideas of the observers and observed, and has to be set against a folklore that contained many charms and incantations which peasants recited in the hope of ensuring a happy and loving married life. On the other hand, such charms may have reflected an ideal that was rarely attained. Nevertheless, it is not out of the question that, for much of the time and in the terms of their patriarchal culture, many peasant men kept their marriage vows to love, respect, defend and support their wives, and that many women loved, honoured and obeyed their husbands.[76]

Many young peasant wives lived for a number of years in the same houses as their fathers-in-law, usually the household heads. The close proximity of young women and middle-aged men who were not blood relatives sometimes gave rise to tensions. Some heads of households took advantage of their authority to sexually abuse their daughters-in-law. This seems to have been common in households where young, immature sons were married to adult women (see above, p. 187). Where this custom was widespread, it led to cycles of abuse in which humiliated sons in later life abused their daughters-in-law. The extent of this practice is hard to gauge. Household heads had such power over their families that many victims probably did not complain to their village communes or higher authorities. The fact that the Russian language contains a word (*snokhachestvo*) to describe a sexual relationship between a father-in-law and his daughter-in-law, however, suggests that it was widespread. Women whose husbands were conscripted into the army were also vulnerable to abuse, and liable to be overworked by their husband's families if they remained in their households.[77]

The lot of Russian peasant women in their husbands' households was often a difficult one that reflected the inferior position of women in peasant society overall. In spite of their considerable contributions to their households as labourers, home-makers, child-carers and mothers, peasant women were second-class members of a patriarchal society. The culture of the peasantry and the doctrines of the Russian Orthodox Church were deeply misogynous. The prevailing male attitude to women was expressed in numerous proverbs, such as: 'A hen is not a bird; a woman is not a person.' The Orthodox Church associated sexuality with the devil, and blamed women for tempting men into sin.[78]

---

76 Semyonova, *Village Life*, pp. 20–1, 101–3; Levin, *Sex*, p. 301. See also Minenko, *Russkaya*, pp. 123–38; Engel, *Between*, pp. 51–2; Worobec, *Peasant Russia*, pp. 178–90, 214–16.
77 See Engel, *Between*, pp. 20–1; Semevskii, 'Domashnii [II]', pp. 73–6; Smith, *Peasant Farming*, p. 81; Farnsworth, B., 'The litigious daughter-in-law', *SR*, vol. 45 (1986), pp. 49–64; *id.*, 'Soldatka'.
78 Dal', V. I., *Poslovitsy Russkogo Naroda: Sbornik*, 2 vols (Moscow, 1989 [reprint]), vol. 1, p. 308; Levin, *Sex*, pp. 45–59.

Rose Glickman argued that peasant women were 'subordinate, not just to one father or one husband, but to the entire male community', and that they were 'mute and powerless' in the face of relentless male domination. She went so far as to conclude that 'the patriarchal mentality was so deeply ingrained in peasant women as well as men that they never questioned what must have seemed to them a law of nature'. In contrast, most recent writers on Russian peasant women have stressed not just their oppression, but also how and to what extent they succeeded in carving out some living space for themselves inside the patriarchal order.

Some peasant women resisted male domination. Studies of peasant court cases in the nineteenth century provide evidence that some women, especially abused and oppressed wives, daughters-in-law and soldiers' wives, took active measures to protect their interests. Beatrice Farnsworth took the argument further than some when she concluded that 'peasant women in general . . . asserted and exercised rights, and instigated family and community change to a degree not hitherto recognised', and that the court cases she had examined 'represent the tip of an iceberg of discontent'. She may have overstated her case. Active resistance by women to the patriarchal order was hazardous. Only in a minority of cases did communities sympathise with women who had transgressed the patriarchal order. The usual punishment for women who refused to conform was exclusion from their households and communities and, thus, a precarious existence on the margins of peasant society. It is likely that the threat of exclusion partly explains why there was little active resistance by women.

Instead of resisting, most peasant women chose to accommodate to the patriarchy and, in return, gained some rewards. Women who conformed to the place men ordained for them were repaid, to some extent, with high dignity, and protection of this dignity. Male peasants defended the honour and reputations of their womenfolk against both physical and verbal assaults. Peasants who slandered women were punished. On occasions, peasant women sued successfully for redress in cases of rape. This is evidence not just that women had some status, but also that men were dishonoured if their wives or daughters were slandered or assaulted. The patriarchal culture, including customary law and the teachings of the Orthodox Church, compelled women to obey men, but also required certain conduct in men towards women. The church admonished men to take their wives' advice and to revere and care for them. Barbara Engel concluded 'a patriarchal order, at least in its ideal form . . . protected and looked after women, even as it constrained and sometimes oppressed them'. Moreover, the existence of spheres of life in which peasant women had the main responsibility, for example child care and the house and kitchen garden, meant that women spent much of their time away from men, and had control over these parts of their lives. That women played such a large role in arranging marriages, by acting as matchmakers, suggests that this was another important area in which they held real power in their households and communities. Women who accommodated to the patriarchal order probably did so also because it gave them and their families the best chance of survival in the harsh and uncertain conditions of rural Russia.[79]

The oppression peasant women were subjected to in the male-dominated society and culture of rural Russia did not necessarily mean that peasant women acted together in sisterhood. On the contrary, the relationship between daughters-in-law and mothers-in-law inside households was fraught with tensions and jealousies. For many peasant women, the marriage of their eldest son and the arrival of a daughter-in-law was the first chance they had had to dominate another adult. It seems that many took the opportunity to treat their daughters-in-law as harshly as they had been treated at the start of their married lives. Impressionistic evidence on intergenerational tensions and conflicts between the women in households is backed up by more concrete evidence from court cases in which daughters-in-law resorted to the law to protect themselves against oppressive mothers-in-law. Another female figure who attracted the hostility of young peasant women was the stepmother. As elsewhere, they were portrayed as evil, uncaring figures in Russian folklore.[80]

There were also intergenerational tensions between men in households. Sons were brought up to respect and obey their fathers, sentiments that were backed up by corporal punishment. As they approached and attained manhood, however, many sons felt the constraining influence of paternal authority in their households, and of the older generation in their communities. Hoch asserted that 'intergenerational antagonism was structurally endemic' in Petrovskoe. Some sons tried to resist attempts by their fathers to compel them to bear the brunt of manual labour in the household economy. Sons with earnings from migrant labour sometimes tried to keep all or part of the money for themselves, rather than hand it over to the household purse. The authority of fathers over their sons may have been greatest in the large, complex households on seigniorial estates in the eighteenth and first half of the nineteenth centuries, where heads of households were backed up not just by the village commune, but also by the estate management. Household heads had various means at their disposal to assert their authority. They could threaten to disinherit disobedient sons. The ultimate deterrent, until the reform of 1874, was the threat of sending recalcitrant sons as recruits to the army for the long term of service. Many contemporaries detected a decline in paternal authority over young men in the late nineteenth century. The abolition of serfdom, the military service reform and, in some regions, greater opportunities for outside earnings gave young men more scope to escape their fathers' authority. Some old peasants complained: 'The world now has completely disintegrated' and 'The eggs have started to teach the hen'.[81]

79 Glickman, 'Peasant women', pp. 55, 68 (quotations); Farnsworth, 'Litigious', pp. 102–3; Engel, *Between*, pp. 25–9, 239 (quotation); Pushkareva, 'Women'; Worobec, *Peasant Russia*, pp. 175–216.
80 Worobec, *Peasant Russia*, pp. 178, 204–6, 211; Minenko, *Russkaya*, pp. 154–6; Dunn, S. P., 'The family as reflected in Russian folklore', in Ransel, *Family*, pp. 153–70.
81 Hoch, *Serfdom*, pp. 131–2 (quotation); Minenko, *Russkaya*, pp. 148–51 (quotations); Worobec, *Peasant Russia*, pp. 211–14; Frank, 'Simple folk'. See also Ch. 6.

In spite of the tensions and conflicts within peasant households and the probable decline in patriarchal authority in the late nineteenth century, for most of the period under consideration and in most of Russia, peasant men managed to maintain their authority over the women, and the older generation kept the younger peasants in check. In almost all cases, moreover, the patriarchs who dominated their households and communities backed each other up. Only in exceptional circumstances did communes or higher authorities intervene in household affairs in support of the women or younger generation. For example, communes took action if a head was managing his household so badly or treating his family so harshly, often as a result of drunkenness, that his behaviour was undermining the economic viability or social stability of the household. Communes intervened because, given their collective responsibility for their obligations (see Ch. 6), the interests of the village community as a whole, as well as the individual household, were under threat.[82] A further, very important reason why the older generation were able to maintain control over the younger peasants in their households was that the latter knew that, in time, many of them would take over from their parents, and would then be in a position to impose their authority on their children. Thus, sons became heads of households and daughters-in-law became mothers-in-law, and the tensions, conflicts, discipline and accommodation continued from generation to generation.

CONCLUSION

The variations in the sizes and structures of Russian peasant households over time and by region were adaptations of the complex household system, which prevailed throughout much of Russia for most of the period under consideration. The differences, in particular the proportions of simple and complex households at points in time, reflected two types of household life cycles – the 'phases of development' and 'perennial complex household' cycles – inside this system. Which life cycle households experienced depended on whether they divided before or after the death of their heads.

Within the complex household system, Russian peasants adapted their strategies for organising their families to circumstances with the aims of securing their livelihoods in the present and continued existence in the future. In large areas of central Russia, especially on seigniorial estates in the Central Black Earth region in the eighteenth and first half of the nineteenth centuries, many peasants waited until the deaths of household heads before dividing their households. *Post-mortem* divisions ensured the predominance of large, complex households, some of which lasted for several generations as 'perennial' complex households. By maximising the labour force in individual households, peasants were better able to absorb the additional exploitation brought about by serfdom

---

82 Aleksandrov, *Sel'skaya*, pp. 294–8; Minenko, *Russkaya*, pp. 124–6, 148–52, 281–303; Worobec, *Peasant Russia*, pp. 45–6, 175, 213–14.

and the demands of the state that became especially severe from the reign of Peter the Great. The combined demands of the landowning and ruling elites remained very high throughout the ensuing century and a half. The prevalence of large, complex households, moreover, went some way to ensuring that households had sufficient adult labourers to support their members, including the very young, old and infirm.

Although labour needs were most pressing for peasant households in the central regions in the eighteenth and first half of the nineteenth centuries, households in all parts of Russia throughout the period were concerned to make the most effective use of their labour resources. The practice of delaying household partition until after the head's death, the key to maintaining large, complex households, spread outwards from the centre to more outlying areas. Nevertheless, *pre-mortem* household partitions prevailed before the late seventeenth and from the late nineteenth centuries, and in some outlying regions for the entire period. This suggests that, in these periods and regions, there were fewer constraints on households and less pressure on their labour capacity, but it does not indicate that these constraints and pressures were absent altogether.

The importance of households' labour requirements conditioned peasants' outlook. The attitudes of peasant men to women were a telling example of the extent to which they had been brutalised by the pressure they were under to meet their obligations and subsist. Some male peasants' views on the relative importance of their wives and their horses, their insistence that pregnant women carried on working until their labour pains began, and that new mothers resumed work as soon as possible after giving birth, indicate that men valued women's productive capacity in the household economy more highly than their reproductive capacity as mothers. While peasants were concerned to invest in the future by raising children, they were compelled by outside pressures to give precedence to the immediate labour needs of the household economy. The principal aim of the strategies pursued by peasants in their households, therefore, was to organise their labour resources in such a way as best ensured their livelihoods.

Several times in this and preceding chapters, reference has been made to village communes and their practice of periodically repartitioning the land between the households in their villages. Communes and their customs, including land tenure, are the subject of the next chapter.

CHAPTER 6

Communes

No institution in rural Russia has attracted so much attention, or been so widely misunderstood, as the village commune. Communes were the basic institutions of local government in Russian villages. Although run mostly by peasant elders, communes worked with the state and seigniorial authorities. They were guided by state decrees and landowners' instructions, as well as the peasants' unwritten customary law. Thus, communes linked the peasant households examined in the previous chapter with the ruling and landowning elites discussed in Chapter 3. Communal officials were responsible for a wide range of village affairs, including day-to-day administration, sharing out and collecting the obligations communities owed to their landowners and the state, and distributing the village' arable land between households. Communes directed the village economy, especially the three-field system of crop rotation. In addition, they made provision for villagers' welfare, and were responsible for law and order and for resolving disputes between their members.

Russian village communes are most famous for their functions concerning the land. In most Russian villages by the late eighteenth and early nineteenth centuries, arable land was held not by individual peasant households in hereditary tenure, but jointly by village communes. Communes distributed the land between households, and tried to ensure that all had shares that were roughly in conformance with their size and economic potential. Every few years, and this is the interesting part, many communes redistributed the land between households to take account of changes in their size.

Peasants acknowledged the significance of the commune by calling it the *mir:* a word that also means 'world'. The Russian state was aware of the commune's importance. By the mid-nineteenth century, senior officials had reached the conclusion that communes had uses beyond their administrative and fiscal functions. Since communes guaranteed their members access to land, officials believed that they inhibited the emergence of landless, impoverished proletarians, who would be unable to meet their obligations to the state and would threaten social stability. Village communes were assigned greater importance by the reforms of the 1860s. It was not only the Russian state that was keen on communes. The custom of periodic land redistribution led many Russian intellectuals to believe that Russian peasants were naturally cooperative and egalitarian. Some intellectuals thought that communes reflected the supposedly communal spirit of the Slavonic people. From the 1830s, these Slavophiles began to refer to the land-redistribution commune as the *obshchina*: a word derived from the Slavonic root meaning 'common'. In the late nineteenth century, some Populists took this idea further. They idealised the commune to the extent that some fervently believed it could serve as the basis for a new social order based on harmony and cooperation. Some thought the commune would allow Russia to leap straight from 'feudalism' to 'socialism', bypassing 'capitalism'. They wrote to Karl Marx, who entertained this notion towards the end of his life.[1]

Russian village communes attracted the attention of other foreigners. August von Haxthausen, the German baron who visited Russia in the 1840s, extolled the commune's virtues. He saw it as an organic institution that distinguished the Russian social order from that of western Europe, because it served as a bulwark against 'proletarianism' and the 'threat' of revolutionary social change.[2] On his arrival in Russia in the 1870s, Donald MacKenzie Wallace heard a great deal about the commune from intellectuals he met in St Petersburg. He left for the provinces with 'a great interest' in studying 'this wonderful institution'. He added: 'An institution which professes to solve satisfactorily the most difficult social problems of the future is not to be met with every day, even in Russia, which is specially rich in materials of study for the student of social science.'[3]

VILLAGE ADMINISTRATION

Throughout the period under consideration, most Russian peasants grouped their households in village communities. This was in contrast to the clusters of scattered farmsteads that had been the prevailing pattern of rural settlement in the medieval period. From the sixteenth century, most rural settlements were either villages (*sela*) or hamlets (*derevni*). The main distinction between them was that villages had churches, and were the centres of parishes that included the nearby hamlets. Villages were usually larger than hamlets. There were also differences in the sizes of rural settlements by region. In the north many contained only a few households. Villages were larger in the central regions and, on the open steppe in the south-east, contained as many as several hundred households. Early Russian settlers on the steppes had banded together for protection against nomadic raiders. The relative shortage of water sources to settle by was a more enduring reason why there were fewer, and larger, settlements in the south-east than in central and northern Russia. Villages differed in their layout. The most common, especially in the central regions, was a linear arrangement, in which households were grouped closely together along

1 See Grant, S. A., '*Obshchina* and *mir*', *SR*, vol. 35 (1976), pp. 636–51; Frierson, *Peasant Icons*, pp. 101–15; Marx, K. and Engels, F., *The Communist Manifesto* (Harmondsworth, 1967), p. 56 (preface to Russian edition of 1882).
2 Haxthausen, *Studies*, pp. 82–3, 292.
3 Wallace, *Russia*, vol. 1, pp. 179, 181.

the bank of a stream, river or lake, or a road. Whatever the layout, the most important point was that peasant households were located together, separate from and usually surrounded by the village's open fields, meadows, pastures and woodland.[4]

Russian villagers developed forms of communal administration to manage their affairs and relations with the outside world. On 'black' lands in the fifteenth and sixteenth centuries, several small settlements combined into township (*volost'*) communes. Members of each settlement attended the *volost'* assembly (*skhod*), which elected communal officials, including an elder and tax collector. From the sixteenth century, these communes underwent considerable changes as the Russian state granted vast areas of 'black' land to noble and ecclesiastical landowners. These landowners gradually established their authority over the communes on their lands, restricting the autonomy of communal assemblies and officials. Landowners' primary aims were to extract dues and labour from village communities. By the seventeenth century, landowners had broken up most of the old *volost'* communes in the Central Non-Black Earth region. They replaced them with smaller and weaker communes, which coincided with their estates.[5]

In the eighteenth and nineteenth centuries, over three-quarters of communes in the European part of Russia coincided with single villages. They were known as 'simple communes'. There were smaller numbers of 'split' and 'composite' communes. 'Split' communes contained only some of the households and part of the land in a village, and existed in villages which had more than one landowner. They were most common in the Central Non-Black Earth region. 'Composite' communes, like the old *volost'* communes, included several villages or a village and the surrounding hamlets. They were set up on large estates of several villages, and in the steppe regions where peasants left their villages to found 'daughter' settlements that remained part of the 'mother' communes.[6]

Historians of the commune have relied mainly on estate records, and have examined instructions sent by landowners to their managers, stewards and communes; reports from estate and communal officials back to the landowners; resolutions (*prigovory*) passed by communal assemblies; and petitions from peasants to their communes and landowners. More landowners' instructions and officials' reports were produced and have survived than communal resolutions. Most of the surviving records, moreover, are from the estates of large landowners who set up elaborate bureaucratic structures, some with head offices in Moscow, to run their domains. In villages on smaller estates,

---

4 See Matossian, 'Peasant', pp. 1–3; see also Ch. 2.
5 See Aleksandrov, V. A., 'Land reallotment in the peasant communes', in *LCPCR*, pp. 41–2; Blum, *Lord and Peasant*, pp. 24–5, 95–7, 504–10; Danilova, L. V., *Sel'skaya obshchina v srednevekovoi Rusi* (Moscow, 1994); Vdovina, L. N., *Krest'yanskaya obshchina i monastyr' v Tsentral'noi Rossii v pervoi polovine XVIII v.* (Moscow, 1988), p. 23.
6 Lewin, M., 'The *obshchina* and the village', in *LCPCR*, pp. 20–1; Gorskaya, *Krest'yanstvo*, p. 273; Channon, J., 'Regional variation in the commune: The case of Siberia', in *LCPCR*, pp. 69–70; Watters, F. M., 'The peasant and the village commune', in Vucinich, *Peasant*, p. 142.

and in most villages before the eighteenth century, much communal and estate business was conducted orally and generated no written records.[7]

Many landowners appointed managers (*upravlyayushchie*) and stewards or bailiffs (*prikazshchiki*) to administer their estates. They worked with officials from the village communes. Communes on lands belonging to monasteries, the state or the court had similar officials. The names, methods of appointment and duties of peasant functionaries varied from village to village. In most villages, there was a headman (*burmistr*), a tax-collector (*tseloval'nik*) and a clerk (*zemskii*), who was sometimes a sacristan from the parish church. Many villages also had elders (*starosty*), foremen (*starshina*) and selectmen (*vybornye*). They were assisted by overseers (*smotriteli*) and constables (*sotskie, pyatidesyatskie, desyatskie*). Most communes had a churchwarden (*tserkovnyi starosta*). Peasant functionaries were either appointed by the landowner, sometimes with the approval of the communal assembly (*skhod*), or elected by the assembly and confirmed in office by the estate management. Some peasant functionaries were paid by their landowners or were recompensed by having their seigniorial obligations reduced or waived. Others received payment from their communes, which raised taxes from their members for this purpose.[8]

There were wide variations in the distribution of duties and the balance of power between landowners and estate officials on the one hand, and village communes and peasant officials on the other. There were two extremes: estates on which landowners tried to run everything themselves, reducing communes to auxiliaries of their authority; and estates on which they left communes to manage themselves. In the late eighteenth century, for example, the magnate V.N. Samarin imposed a very strict regime on his extensive estates in central Russia. Communal assemblies could be called only by the headmen, who acted as intermediaries between the steward and the communes. Moreover, communal officials were expected to act as the landowner's agents and informers. Such strict regimes were rare, and few landowners attempted to eliminate communes altogether. More widespread were estates on which landowners (usually absentees) entrusted most administration to communes. Communal officials ran the villages, and reported back to the landowners, who retained overall control but did not interfere in the internal life of villages. Such landowners' interests did not extend much beyond the receipt of the obligations they demanded.

The administration of most seigniorial villages was shared between estate managers or stewards appointed by landowners, and peasant functionaries elected by communes. In the mid-seventeenth century, the boyar Boris Morozov ran his extensive estates in this fashion. Surviving documents show that Morozov's stewards wielded considerable authority in some areas, for

7 See Aleksandrov, *Sel'skoe*, pp. 44–6, 50–4, 117–18; Hoch, *Serfdom*, pp. 5–9; Melton, 'Enlightened', p. 676; Prokof'eva, *Krest'yanskaya*, pp. 16–19; Vdovina, *Krest'yanskaya*, pp. 26–33.
8 See Hoch, *Serfdom*, pp. 135, 165; Leonard, 'Landlords', pp. 121, 127–8; Mironov, 'Local government', pp. 170–95; Pushkarev, S. G., *Dictionary of Russian Historical Terms from the 11th Century to 1917* (New Haven, CT, 1970), pp. 6, 119, 147, 182.

example, managing the peasants' labour obligations (*barshchina*). In others, such as the distribution of land allotments between households and the administration of justice, the stewards' powers were limited by the participation of communal officials. Similar forms of mixed estate–communal administration were in operation throughout Russia in the eighteenth and first half of the nineteenth centuries on the estates of some of Russia's greatest landowners. Edgar Melton has argued that, from around 1750, a number of magnates tried to set up 'enlightened seigniorial' regimes by writing instructions that clearly defined their authority, and the functions, duties and responsibilities of communal officials.[9]

Landowners could, in theory, choose the way they ran their estates and the degree of self-government they allowed communes. But excessive regulation could be counter-productive. When he inherited his father's estates in the early nineteenth century, F. V. Samarin found them in a 'disordered' state and had to relax the rigid system of management (see above). The attempts to introduce 'enlightened' management in the late eighteenth century also met with difficulties and, by the 1830s, most had failed. In practice, many landowners saw the need to allow communes a role in estate administration, and consulted with peasant officials before making changes. Landowners realised that village elders had valuable knowledge of local conditions and customs. Some absentee landowners also saw that they could use communal officials as a counterweight to appointed managers, who might otherwise try to enrich themselves at the expense of both landowners and peasants. And the expense of hiring managers made it cheaper to rely on peasant officials.[10]

Communes on estates where administration was shared with seigniorial authorities appointed by absentee landowners may have had more control than the sources suggest since they have an in-built bias. It is extremely unlikely that landowners' instructions were implemented exactly as their authors intended. The reports landowners received from their estate and communal officials may not have been much more accurate, moreover, since these men would have been inclined to report what they thought the landowners wanted to read – that their instructions were being carried out – rather than the actual state of affairs. It is likely, therefore, that communes, or at least their peasant officials, had more leeway than is suggested by a straightforward reading of the sources.

In contrast, village communes and their peasant officials enjoyed little independence on small estates with resident landowners, who ran their domains themselves and thus knew a great deal about what was going on. In his study of seigniorial estates in the late eighteenth century, Michael Confino portrayed Russian landowners as miserly men who closely followed everything on their estates. This picture of petty squires (who made up the vast majority of all

9 Aleksandrov, *Sel'skaya*, pp. 55–111, 118–21, 128–42; Melton, 'Enlightened'. See also Baklanova, *Krest'yanskii*, pp. 138–44; Leonard, 'Landlords', p. 122.
10 See Aleksandrov, *Sel'skaya*, p. 64; Melton, 'Enlightened', pp. 702–8; Toumanoff, P., 'The development of the peasant commune in Russia', *JEcH*, vol. 41 (1981), p. 180.

noble landowners) living among their peasants and managing their estates contrasts with the image of absentee landowners (the minority) that is more common in the historical, and fictional, literature.[11]

Whether landowners lived on their estates, and could exercise direct control over the communes, depended largely on their state service commitments and the number of estates they owned. The principle that secular landowners had to serve the state was at the heart of the origins of serfdom (see Ch. 3). In the seventeenth century, however, many landowners served in military campaigns only in the summer, and large numbers evaded even this duty. In the early eighteenth century, Peter the Great enforced noble state service for life, and many nobles were compelled to leave their estates to serve. The nobility's service obligations were relaxed after Peter's death in 1725. In the 1730s, Empress Anna lowered the term of service to 25 years, so that 'the nobles can tend more closely to their . . . estates', and permitted one son to stay at home to manage their families' estates. Nevertheless, before the abolition of compulsory noble state service in 1762, most nobles did not live on their estates. The 'emancipation of the nobility' in 1762 did not lead nobles to abandon state service *en masse* and return to rural Russia. But an increasing number chose to live on their estates after a short period of service. More landowners moved to their estates after the provincial reform of 1775 and the 'Charter to the Nobility' of 1785 gave them more say in local affairs. Carol Leonard estimated that, in the 1780s and 90s, over half of all nobles resided on their estates. Peter Kolchin put the proportion in Saratov province in 1836 at one-third.[12]

Even if half of all noble landowners did live on their estates, this did not mean that half of all estates had a resident landowner, since many nobles owned several estates. A large proportion of the seigniorial peasantry belonged to a small number of magnates who owned numerous estates in several provinces. In the late 1640s, Boris Morozov owned over 10,000 peasant households on estates in 11 districts scattered throughout Russia. The seventh-largest serf owners in 1700, with nearly 4,500 households, were the Sheremetevs. By the 1850s, the Sheremetevs had become the richest noble family in Russia. In 1859, Count Sergei Dmitrievich Sheremetev owned almost 150,000 male peasants on estates in several regions. Other great magnate families, for example the Yusupovs, also acquired greater and more widely spread landholdings over the eighteenth and early nineteenth centuries.[13]

Ownership of land and peasants on this scale distanced communes from their owners. Extensive landownership did not mean large estates. Few individual estates contained more than 5,000 peasants, and larger estates were subdivided into separate villages.[14] In the early eighteenth century, 26 per cent of the

---

11 See Confino, *Domaines*, pp. 39–105; Crisp, *Studies*, p. 67; Kolchin, *Unfree Labor*, pp. 58–61.
12 Leonard, *Reform*, pp. 41, 45–6, 65–9 (quotation from p. 46); Kolchin, *Unfree Labor*, pp. 58–9.
13 Crummey, *Aristocrats*, pp. 112, 117–20; Vodarskii, Ya. E. and Shvatchenko, O. A., *Dvoryanstvo Rossii i ego krepostnye krest'yane XVII-pervaya polovina XVIII v.* (Moscow, 1989), pp. 34–7; Lieven, D., *The Aristocracy in Europe, 1815–1914* (Basingstoke and London, 1992), pp. 36–46.
14 Confino, *Domaines*, p. 117; Hoch, *Serfdom*, p. 3.

Russian seigniorial peasantry belonged to the tiny proportion of landowners who owned more than 500 male peasants. By the mid-nineteenth century, however, this had increased to 42 per cent. On the other hand, over the same period, the proportion of seigniorial peasants who belonged to the overwhelming majority of nobles who possessed 100 or fewer male peasants fell from 41 to 20 per cent.[15] This is significant because lesser landowners were most likely to own only one estate, and to live on it. Most magnates, in contrast, spent much of their time in Moscow, St Petersburg or abroad, and spent only the summer on one of their estates. Thus, although from the late eighteenth century, between a third and a half of noble landowners lived on their estates, a very large majority of villages did not have a resident landowner. Very few of the Sheremetevs' peasants ever came into contact with their owners, let alone had a Sheremetev for a neighbour.

Another factor which influenced the relative authority of landowners' administrations and peasants' communes was the type of obligations landowners demanded. Labour obligations (*barshchina*) required much greater supervision than dues (*obrok*) paid two or three times a year. Some landowners who demanded labour services tried to create strict regimes, but most relied on a combination of administration by appointed officials and communal self-government by peasants. Most landowners who demanded *obrok* allowed communes large degrees of autonomy, as long as they paid their dues. Some landowners used different systems of administration depending on the type of obligations they demanded. In the late seventeenth century, A. I. Bezobrazov personally supervised communes, or hired stewards to do so, on estates where he required his peasants to cultivate his demesnes. But he interfered little in communes from which he demanded dues. He handed their administration over to well-off peasants, who ran them in ways that were profitable for themselves and the landowner.[16] The proportion of communes obliged to serve labour obligations, thus coming under tighter control, grew from the late sixteenth century with the enserfment of the peasantry. In the last century of serfdom, the majority of seigniorial peasants performed *barshchina*, especially in the Central Black Earth region. (See Ch. 3.)

Recent research has cast doubt on the idea that there was a straightforward connection between the type of obligations and the degree of seigniorial or communal authority. It was possible for landowners to rely largely on peasant functionaries to enforce labour obligations. In his case study of the *barshchina* estate of Petrovskoe, in the Central Black Earth region in the first half of the nineteenth century, Steven Hoch has argued that there was a hierarchy of authority that extended from the Gagarins' estate office in Moscow, through the appointed bailiff on the estate, to the peasants who served as communal officials and heads of individual households. All these men supported each

15 Shepukova, N. M., 'Ob izmenenii razmerov dushevladeniya pomeshchikov Evropeiskoi Rossii v pervoi chertverti XVIII–pervoi polovine XIX vv.', *EAIVE 1963 g.* (Vilnius, 1964), pp. 388–419.
16 Aleksandrov, *Sel'skaya*, pp. 39, 55, 69–78, 112. See also Melton, 'Enlightened', pp. 677, 682.

others' authority, and had an interest in, and shared in the benefits from, enforcing seigniorial authority. The regime of 'social control' in Petrovskoe was strict because, rather than in spite, of the fact that it incorporated peasant communal officials. In the same period, on the estate of Baki in the Central Non-Black Earth region, where the peasants paid *obrok*, Melton has shown that Countess Lieven hired a manager to run her estate but, as in Petrovskoe, the communal officials had great authority.[17]

The degree of autonomy landowners allowed communes changed over time. The growth of labour obligations and landowners' authority from the late sixteenth century has already been noted. Changes can be detected on individual estates. At the beginning of the eighteenth century on the Shcherbatov's estates, stewards were responsible for the seigniorial economy, and communal officials for the peasants' economy. In the mid-eighteenth century, however, the two were combined and, by the start of the nineteenth century, the communal representatives had become silent participants in communal assemblies that were chaired by the steward and headman, both of whom had been appointed by the landowner.[18]

Among the seigniorial peasantry, therefore, the degree of autonomy enjoyed by communes varied from estate to estate, between regions, and over time. The factors affecting the balance of authority between landowners and communes also varied. In different villages at different times, the views of individual landowners, the presence or absence of the landowner, and the type of obligations all played a role.

The degree to which communes were responsible for administering villages also depended on the category the peasants belonged to. In general, communes of non-seigniorial peasants were in a similar position to communes on nobles' estates with more relaxed regimes and absentee landowners who demanded dues. The category that was closest to the seigniorial peasantry was the church peasantry. A case study of communes on the lands of the Joseph of Volokolamsk and Pafnut'ev-Borovsk monasteries in the first half of the eighteenth century suggests that they had a large measure of autonomy. After the secularisation of church land and peasants in 1762–64, moreover, many communes of former church peasants enjoyed considerable independence from the state.[19]

Throughout the eighteenth and first half of the nineteenth centuries, communes on state lands were left largely to run their own affairs. Emperor Paul reformed the administration of state villages in 1797, setting up *volost'* communes of several villages. But the measure did little more than acknowledge the reality of communal self-government. The state was an absentee landowner, demanded *obrok* from most of its peasants, and had neither the local officials nor the resources to oversee communes on its extensive domains. In 1837, on the eve of Kiselev's reforms, a government inspector in Vyatka province, in

17 Hoch, *Serfdom*; Melton, 'Household', pp. 559–85.
18 Aleksandrov, *Sel'skaya*, pp. 97–102.
19 Vdovina, *Krest'yanskaya*, pp. 42–3, 209–11.

the Northern Urals region, reported that state peasants were like a flock that has a shepherd 'but goes wherever it wants'. Even after the reforms, which imposed extra officials, functions and regulations on state peasant communes, they still operated much as they had done before.[20]

There were variations in the degrees of communal self-government between the groups that made up the state peasantry. The *volost'* communes of 'black' peasants in the Northern region enjoyed a great deal of independence long after the state had handed out most 'black' lands and peasants in the central regions to noble landowners and monasteries by the end of the sixteenth century. Over the seventeenth and eighteenth centuries, however, the state encroached on the freedom of the northern 'black' communes, gradually converting them into the lowest level of state administration to facilitate tax collection. Among the *odnodvortsy* along the old steppe frontier, communal administration emerged in the seventeenth century. The state imposed the duty to collect taxes on these communes in the late seventeenth and early eighteenth centuries. State peasants in Siberia, many of whom were migrants from the Northern region, began to set up *volost'* communes in the seventeenth century. From the early nineteenth century, largely for fiscal purposes, the state encouraged Siberian state peasants to form simple, village communes. Communes on court/appanage lands also had much autonomy, as long as they met their obligations.[21]

SHARING OUT COMMUNES' OBLIGATIONS

One of the most important functions of communes was sharing out their obligations to their landowners and the state between their member households. Estate and government officials interfered to varying degrees to ensure that communes met their obligations. More importantly, however, the members of many communes were held collectively responsible for obligations that were demanded, not from individual peasants or households, but from entire village communities. The principle of collective responsibility (*krugovaya poruka*) for obligations to the state dated back to medieval Russia. Communes were obliged to make sure that the total sum of their obligations was met, even if it meant some members paying the shares of defaulters. Many landowners, for example Boris Morozov and the Sheremetevs, enforced collective responsibility for seigniorial as well as state obligations. On the Sheremetevs' estate of Molodoi Tud, Tver' province, in 1788, the communal assembly had to collect an extra 73 kopeks from each unit of assessment, in addition to the 12 roubles 17 kopeks already collected, to make up for non-payment of *obrok* by 'defaulters and poor peasants'. State peasant communes were also held

20 See Mironov, 'Local government', pp. 177–88; Crisp, *Studies*, pp. 76–9, 82–3, 85–7; Haxthausen, *Studies*, p. 71. See also Ch. 3.
21 Gorskaya, *Krest'yanstvo*, pp. 141–2, 273, 340, 475; Shaw, D., 'Landholding and commune origins among the *odnodvortsy*', in *LCPCR*, pp. 106–14; Aleksandrov, V. A., 'Vozniknovenie sel'skoi obshchiny v Sibiri (XVII v.), *IS* (1987), no. 1, pp. 54–68; Okladnikov, *Krest'yanstvo Sibiri*, p. 297; Mironov, 'Local government', pp. 188–90.

collectively responsible for the payment of taxes and *obrok*, and providing recruits. From 1769, communal officials on state lands were liable to arrest if they failed to deliver their obligations. Collective responsibility meant, at least in theory, that the state and landowners could collect obligations from peasant communities without having to maintain officials in the villages.[22]

Within the principle of collective responsibility, communes apportioned their obligations between households. The main components of a commune's obligations were labour services and/or dues in cash or kind for landowners, and taxes and recruits for the state. Landowners who demanded *barshchina* set a figure of so many days' labour on the demesne from the whole commune. Communal and estate officials then divided up the labour obligations between the peasants. On some estates, they were guided by landowners' instructions. On the Kurakins' estates in Penza and Saratov provinces in the late eighteenth century, for example, communes took account of the economic potential of households, the amounts of land they held, and the ages of their members. In many communes, labour teams (*tyagla*) of husbands and wives were the main unit of assessment. The brunt of labour obligations was usually borne by males aged between around 18 and 55. Youths and older peasants performed lighter duties, while children and the elderly were exempt altogether. Some communal officials were freed from labour obligations, or worked as overseers rather than labourers. In the first half of the nineteenth century, when many landowners demanded that able-bodied peasants work three or even four days a week, peasants divided their time between the demesne and their own land in two main ways. Under the 'brother for brother' system, in a household with two adult males, one worked full-time on the landowner's land, while the other spent the whole week working on the household's land. In the other system, all the workers in a household spent three days working on each.[23]

Landowners who demanded *obrok* levied a total amount of cash or produce from entire communes. Some landowners left apportioning the *obrok* between households entirely in the hands of communal officials. Others prepared detailed instructions. The most common way in which communes and landowners shared out dues was according to individual household size, often measured in labour teams, the age structure of their members (the young and old usually paid less), and the amounts of land they held. Landowners and communes also took account of households' incomes from handicrafts, trade and migrant labour. Landowners such as the Sheremetevs were anxious not to miss any of their peasants' incomes that could be exploited. Their managers compiled detailed descriptions of their estates, including information on soil fertility, harvest yields, livestock numbers, windmills, markets and mineral resources,

22 Dewey, H. W. and Kleimola, A. M., 'From the kinship group to every man his brother's keeper: Collective responsibility in pre-Petrine Russia', *JGO*, vol. 30 (1982), pp. 321–35; Prokof'eva, *Krest'yanskaya*, p. 148 (quotation); Semevskii, *Krest'yane*, vol. 1, pp. 259–60.

23 Aleksandrov, *Sel'skaya*, pp. 206–8; Ignatovich, *Pomeshchich'i*, pp. 175, 178; Semevskii, *Krest'yane*, vol. 1, pp. 109–11.

as well as households' economic activities. Communes took account of households' incomes from non-agricultural activities in various ways. In the 'industrial village' of Velikoe Selo, Yaroslavl' province, Haxthausen noted that the commune divided obligations according to each household's landholdings. But, in order to take account of the fortunes that wealthier members had made in the textile trade, rich households were compelled to take on more land, and the corresponding *obrok*. They then leased land they could not or did not want to farm to other members for low rents that did not cover the dues. In Visena, Nizhnii Novgorod province, which was famous for its cobblers, the village elders assessed the wealth of all members and taxed them proportionately, according to a notional number of 'souls'. For example, a rich peasant had to pay for 30 souls, while a poor peasant for half a soul.[24]

Peter the Great set a figure for the amount of *obrok* to be collected from every male state peasant. However, state peasant communes shared out their *obrok* between households in similar ways to those used on private estates in order to bring households' dues into line with their ability to pay. In the 1840s, as part of Kiselev's reforms, the state peasants' *obrok* was replaced with a new land tax that took account of both the size and quality of the communal land.[25]

Communes of all categories of peasants were responsible for sharing out their obligations to the state, principally military recruitment and taxes. Landowners often gave communes greater independence in fulfilling their state obligations than seigniorial dues. Probably the most onerous state obligation was conscription, which began on a regular basis in 1705. Decrees on levies of recruits were concerned mainly with the numbers of men the armed forces needed, and stated only that the men selected should be of certain ages (between 17 and 35 from the late eighteenth century), above a minimum height, and without physical disabilities. Peter the Great expressed a preference for single men.

Many landowners laid down regulations for selecting recruits on their estates. Men were usually to be taken from either large, well-off households that contained several adult males and could cope with the loss of one, or from small, economically weak households, which made little contribution to the communal obligations. Landowners were anxious to protect economically viable, medium-sized households with two adult male workers, which would be seriously weakened if one was conscripted. Only a few landowners, for example V. N. Samarin, were personally involved in choosing which peasants were sent to the army. Most landowners, including magnates such as the Sheremetevs, left it largely to communes to select recruits. On many estates, communal officials chose candidates, presented lists of their names to communal assemblies for approval, and then sent the lists to the estate authorities or landowner to be ratified. Communal practices evolved as the numbers of recruits demanded increased over the eighteenth and nineteenth centuries. The convention of choosing bachelors soon fell into abeyance. Peasants from larger, better-off

24 Aleksandrov, *Sel'skaya*, pp. 207–16; Prokof'eva, *Krest'yanskaya*, pp. 139–47; Haxthausen, *Studies*, pp. 75–6, 111–13.
25 Crisp, *Studies*, pp. 73–4, 88–9.

households increasingly resisted communal and seigniorial policies which targeted them, and tried to pass the burden onto other households. In the late eighteenth century, many communes moved over to a system where all households, regardless of size, were liable to provide recruits. In some communes, all were required to send a son to the army in rotation. In others, the men of military age drew lots to decide who would serve.

The state played a greater role in choosing which state and appanage peasants served in the armed forces. In the first half of the nineteenth century, the state tried to enforce a system where peasant households on state and appanage lands supplied recruits in turn, with larger families at the top of the queue. In the 1830s and 40s, Kiselev took selection of recruits from the state peasantry out of the hands of communes, and introduced a lottery for all 20-year-old men to decide who served.

There were two other ways of meeting the recruitment obligation. Communes, and landowners, often chose to send men to the army as a punishment for persistent non-payment of their obligations or for antisocial behaviour. In 1788, the communal assembly in Molodoi Tud resolved: 'To send as recruits 71 men for neglecting their arable land, for non-payment of taxes, dubious characters, and landless peasants'. Hoch stressed that in Petrovskoe, in the first half of the nineteenth century, the commune's priority at recruit levies was 'to rid the estate of undesirables'. Another way to fulfil the obligation was to purchase substitutes or exemption certificates. These became common ways in which both entire communes and rich households escaped conscription.[26]

Communes also shared out their taxes between households. The systems of direct taxation had an important influence on the ways communes distributed the burden of all their financial obligations. Until the mid-seventeenth century, most communes shared out their taxes and other cash dues according to the amount of land households possessed. In the early eighteenth century, however, many communes began to apportion obligations according to the number of people in each household. The transition followed, and was probably caused by, the change in the tax base from land to people. Between 1645 and 1679, the state changed the unit of assessment of the main direct tax from the amount of land a household cultivated to the households themselves. After 1679, all households paid a flat-rate tax regardless of the size of their landholdings or the numbers of peasants they contained. With the introduction of the poll tax in 1719–24, the tax base was altered again, from households to male peasants. From 1724, all men were required to pay a uniform tax. Many landowners followed suit, and began to demand obligations according to the number of peasants in a commune rather than the amount of land they held.

The change in the tax base from land to people had an impact on the ways communes shared out all their obligations, including labour as well as money.

26 Aleksandrov, *Sel'skaya*, pp. 242–93; Bohac, R. D., 'The mir and the military draft', *SR*, vol. 47 (1988), pp. 652–66; Prokof'eva, *Krest'yanskaya*, pp. 151–7 (quotation from p. 152); Hoch, *Serfdom*, pp. 151–8 (quotation from p. 152); Melton, 'Enlightened', p. 700; Crisp, *Studies*, pp. 80, 90. See also Ch. 3.

This was reflected in a change in the meaning of the term '*tyaglo*'. The word, which literally meant 'burden', was originally used to describe a certain share of the commune's obligations and the corresponding area of land. In other words, households that held a particular amount of land had to pay a specific portion of the total obligations. By the mid-eighteenth century, after the introduction of the poll tax, *tyaglo* had also come to signify a labour team, often a husband and wife with a horse, in addition to the portion of the commune's obligations and share of the land assigned to the labour team. Each labour team, or *tyaglo*, in a commune had to fulfil the same amount of dues and services. Since the number of labour teams varied between households, communes continued to share out their total burden of obligations in accordance with households' resources and ability to pay. In practice, therefore, communes often shared out the poll tax not according to the number of male peasants in each household, but to the number of labour teams with a certain amount of land.[27]

In spite of the changes in the units of assessment for taxes and other obligations, communes among peasants of all categories adapted their existing practices to the imposition of new taxes and dues in order to maintain the basic principle of allocating obligations in line with households' resources. However, the change in the unit of assessment for the main direct tax from land to households, and then to male peasants, had major implications for the ways in which many communes shared out the village land.

LAND TENURE AND LAND USE

In return for the obligations that communes shared out between, and collected from, their member households, the state and landowners gave them the right to cultivate land to enable them to meet these obligations and support themselves.[28] From the mid- to late seventeenth century, every household in a commune had the right to a share of the communal land and, in return, had the duty to take on the commensurate portion of the commune's obligations. In some communes, peasants who were not fit for work, because of age or infirmity, and thus could not take on part of the communal obligations, were not entitled to land. When new households were formed, for example on the partition of old households, communes allocated them shares of the land and obligations. In the eighteenth and nineteenth centuries, however, many communes reallocated land not just when households divided, but also on a fairly regular basis to take account of changes in the size of existing households. Households that grew in size, for example when sons married and brought their wives to live with them, thereby creating extra labour teams, were allocated additional shares of the communal land. If there were no reserves of land, allotments were taken from households that had become smaller as a result of

27 See Aleksandrov, *Sel'skaya*, pp. 114, 204–19; Semevskii, *Krest'yane*, vol. 1, pp. 106–9; Shapiro, 'Perekhod', pp. 207–17; Dal', *Tolkovyi slovar'*, vol. 4, p. 454. See also Chs 3 and 5.
28 Some communes also bought or rented land: Vdovina, *Krest'yanskaya*, pp. 210–11; Watters, 'Peasant', pp. 147–50.

death or conscription. In this way, communes tried to ensure that households' allotments of land were in conformance with the number of labour teams they contained and, hence, their capacity to bear obligations and to support the peasants who lived in them.[29]

The origins of communal and repartitional tenure

Slavophiles such as I. D. Belyaev believed that village communes had existed in Russia since time immemorial, and had practised communal and repartitional land tenure since at least the fourteenth century. He wrote: 'The peasant commune [he used the nineteenth-century term *obshchina*] is a primordial Russian institution.'[30] In spite of the romantic views of Slavophiles and, a few decades later, some Populists, there is overwhelming evidence that communal and repartitional land tenure, and communes that practised it, had not existed since the distant past. Nor were they manifestations of some communal spirit innate in Slavonic people. Instead, they were more recent developments that had come about for more pragmatic reasons.

In the heyday of the old *volost'* communes in the fifteenth and sixteenth centuries, most peasant households throughout the forest-heartland had held their house and garden plots, arable land, and sometimes meadow land in individual household, hereditary tenure. The only lands that were held in common by communes were pastures, woodland and water resources. Land tenure seems to have been similar among communes on 'black' lands, and estates belonging to secular landowners, monasteries and the court.[31]

Over the following two centuries, however, the system of land tenure changed in villages in large parts of Russia. Most households continued to hold their houses and garden plots individually, but lost control of their plots of arable and meadow land to their communes. On some estates, even house and garden plots became subject to communal control. The change to communal tenure happened first in the Central Non-Black Earth region of the forest-heartland, and quickly spread to the Central Black Earth region. It also occurred first on seigniorial estates whose owners demanded *barshchina*. There was some antagonism between household and communal land tenure when communes whose peasants paid *obrok* moved towards communal tenure in the eighteenth century. Many peasants, especially on *obrok* estates, state lands and in the northern regions, retained the idea of household tenure as well as communal landholding. Some households continued to buy and sell plots of land as if they belonged to them. Household tenure survived longest on estates where handicrafts and trade (that did not involve farming the land) were more

29 See Atkinson, D., 'Egalitarianism and the commune', in *LCPCR*, pp. 8–9; Hoch, *Serfdom*, pp. 15–16.
30 Belyaev, I. D., *Krest'yane na Rusi*, 4th edn (Moscow, 1903) (first published 1860), pp. 31–3, 37–40, 77–8 (quotation from p. 56). See also Petrovich, 'Peasant', pp. 207–18.
31 See Baklanova, *Krest'yanskii*, pp. 130–3; Gorskaya, *Krest'yanstvo*, pp. 140–1, 273–4; Pushkarev, S. G., *Krest'yanskaya pozemel'no-peredel'naya obshchina v Rossii* (Newtonville, MA, 1976), pp. 5–7, 18–45, 149.

important than agriculture. Households on the Stroganovs' estates in the Northern Urals region still held their land individually in the early nineteenth century. They were unusual. By this time, communal land tenure was practised throughout much of Russia and among all categories of peasants.[32]

The practice of periodically repartitioning the land developed slightly later than communal tenure, and also spread from the Central Non-Black Earth region to the Central Black Earth region and, later, to more outlying regions. It also originated among communes of seigniorial peasants and then spread to other categories.[33] There were some cases of land redistribution as far back as the sixteenth century, but they were initially between adjoining settlements rather than between households within settlements. These were just the beginnings of the practice. Periodic redistribution of land by communes between households became widespread from the middle of the eighteenth century.[34] Setting aside for a while the belief of some Slavophiles and Populists that communalism and egalitarianism were innate in Russian or Slavonic peasant culture, historians have explained the origins of communal and repartitional land tenure with reference to population increase, the environment, and the ever-increasing demands of the ruling and landowning elites.

Many scholars have noted that communal tenure and land redistribution began in the densely populated central regions, and then spread to more outlying regions as their peasant populations got larger. When land was in abundance, for example in the forest-heartland in the sixteenth and seventeenth centuries and in border regions until the nineteenth century, households held their land in individual tenure. As the supply of land diminished because of increased population density, communes took control over the land. When the supply of untilled land that could be brought into cultivation by new or enlarged households ran out, communes were compelled to redistribute existing landholdings between households. One scholar who put forward this demographic interpretation was Alexander Kaufman at the end of the nineteenth century. He believed that contemporary Siberia, which was then being settled by Russian peasant migrants, represented 'living history' and could serve as a model for the changes in land tenure that had taken place earlier in the European part of Russia. Kaufman showed that communal and redistributional land tenure were gradually replacing household tenure first in western Siberia, and then further east, as population densities grew and the amount of vacant land fell. The resulting land shortages led to inequalities in the distribution of land between households that affected their ability to meet their obligations. The solution adopted by many communes was to repartition the land.[35]

32 Aleksandrov, *Sel'skaya*, pp. 181–7, 202, 227–37, 316–17; Baklanova, *Krest'yanskii*, pp. 130–8, 144–80; Pushkarev, *Krest'yanskaya*, 2nd pagn, p. 1; Vdovina, *Krest'yanskaya*, pp. 64–7, 78–90, 209.
33 See Atkinson, D., *The End of the Russian Land Commune, 1905–1930* (Stanford, CA, 1983), pp. 12–13; Robinson, *Rural Russia*, pp. 34–5.
34 See Aleksandrov, 'Land', p. 42; Gorskaya, *Krest'yanstvo*, pp. 274, 276, 337–9; Pushkarev, *Krest'yanskaya*, 2nd pagn, pp. 4–6, 16–17, 40; Semevskii, *Krest'yane*, vol. 1, pp. 102–6.
35 See Petrovich, 'Peasant', pp. 211–13, 216–17.

Although the demographic interpretation is compelling, Dorothy Atkinson has made a strong case against assigning it primary importance. She pointed out that communal and repartitional land tenure were absent, and household tenure predominated, in the Ukrainian provinces of Poltava and Chernigov. This was in spite of the fact that in the mid-nineteenth century they were more densely inhabited than neighbouring Russian provinces which had communal and repartitional tenure. She concluded that 'population growth was a necessary but insufficient cause of the development of communal redistributional practices'.[36]

Some scholars have argued that there was a relationship between the Russian environment and the development of communal and repartitional landholding. A. P. Shchapov, who was influenced by the environmental determinism that was fashionable in the nineteenth century, argued that the harsh natural conditions in much of Russia had contributed to a communal outlook among its peasants as they needed to collaborate to survive. In the forest-heartland in medieval times and later in Siberia, peasants combined in communes to carry out the arduous task of chopping down trees to clear land for agriculture. They then distributed plots between households according to their contributions to the joint effort. Because of the low fertility of the soil in much of the forest-heartland, especially the Northern region, communes regularly cleared new land and allocated new plots to households. Thus, the practice of communal reallocation of land, if not exchange between households, had a long history and can be attributed in part to the environment.[37]

While demographic and, to a lesser extent, environmental factors contributed to the evolution of the new form of land tenure, the most important reason why many Russian villages began to hold their land in common, and periodically to redistribute it between households, was the growing pressure of demands by landowners and the state. This argument was put forward forcibly by 'Westernisers' during the 1850s in a debate with the Slavophiles. Boris Chicherin attached much importance to Peter the Great's imposition of the poll tax. While Chicherin probably overstated the role of this particular tax, communal, and later repartitional, land tenure did develop at roughly the same time as the emergence and consolidation of the autocratic state and serfdom in Russia. And both the state and the landowners made increasing demands on peasant communities.[38]

Since obligations were demanded from entire communes, rather than individual households or peasants, and communes were held collectively responsible for their obligations, it was in communes' interests to make sure that all

36 Atkinson, *End*, pp. 13–14.
37 See Atkinson, 'Egalitarianism', pp. 7, 17; Aleksandrov, 'Land', p. 37; Milov, L. V., 'O prichinakh vozniknoveniya krepostnichestva v Rossii', *IS* (1985), no. 3, pp. 178–9. See also Ch. 4.
38 See Aleksandrov, *Sel'skaya*, pp. 15, 182, 187; Atkinson, *End*, pp. 6, 20–1; Pushkarev, *Krest'yanskaya*, pp. 3–7, 59; 2nd pagn, pp. 6–8, 16–17.

households had enough land to enable them to meet their share of the communal burden. The growing demands made on communes put them under ever-greater pressure to equate individual households' land allotments with their labour capacity and share of the communal obligations. If some households had insufficient land, but were capable of taking on a greater portion of the obligations because they had become larger, it made sense for communes to allot them more land. If they did not have any reserves, the additional allotments would have to be taken from other households that no longer had enough adults to cultivate them or to bear the corresponding share of obligations. The growth in the peasant population of Russia over the seventeenth and eighteenth centuries, which led to a reduction in the supply of vacant land around existing villages, made it more likely that when communes reassessed their members' allotments, land would have to be taken from some households and given to others.

Not only did communes' obligations increase over the seventeenth and eighteenth centuries, but the basis on which they were assessed was changed from land to people. The introduction of the household and then poll taxes in the late seventeenth and early eighteenth centuries had a major impact on the way communes shared out their land. When communes' taxes and other obligations came to be assessed on the basis of the number of households or male peasants, instead of the amount of land they farmed, communes had to pay more attention to sharing out their obligations and land between their members. This entailed periodic adjustments in households' landholdings as the need arose. Atkinson argued: 'Once the tax was fixed and equal for all individual households . . . [and, later, male peasants], the commune could no longer adjust the tax load in proportion to landholdings, but had to adjust landholdings in proportion to the tax.' Thus, over the seventeenth and eighteenth centuries, Russian village communes began allocating land to households according to the number of labour teams or males inside them, and periodically repartitioning the land to take account of changes.[39]

The connection between the origins of communal and repartitional land tenure and the taxes imposed by the Russian state and obligations demanded by Russian landowners becomes clearer when the practices of village communes in Russia are compared with those in the parts of east–central Europe annexed by the Russian state in the late seventeenth and eighteenth centuries. Most peasant households in Ukraine, Belorussia, Lithuania and the Baltic provinces held their land individually, and village communities did not repartition their land. It is very significant that the Russian state did not extend the poll tax to these areas until 1783 or later. Moreover, the local variants of serfdom, under which landowners demanded obligations from households according to the size of their land allotments, persisted after Russian annexation. A few

---

39 Atkinson, *End*, pp. 8–9 (quotation); *id.*, 'Egalitarianism', p. 9; Blum, *Lord and Peasant*, pp. 512–14, 526; Gorskaya, *Krest'yanstvo*, pp. 274, 337.

village communities in the empire's western borderlands did begin to hold their land communally and repartition it in the nineteenth century, but most continued with individual household land tenure.[40]

Communal and repartitional land tenure was also a form of avoiding or reducing risk: a factor behind many of the strategies adopted by Russian peasants to maintain their livelihoods. The practice of households holding several strips scattered around open fields, rather than one consolidated plot of land, was a common risk-averse strategy (see Ch. 4). The Russian practice of periodically redistributing the strips was a development of this practice. When strips were redistributed, households would gain and lose fertile strips of land as well as poor strips, and thus the risks of arable farming were regularly shared around. Since all members of village communities were jointly responsible for their obligations, moreover, there was an incentive for all households to ensure that others were not deprived of decent land.

Steven Hoch has put forward an argument to explain the origins of land redistribution that takes account of demographic and environmental factors and the exploitative social structure. He argued: 'Peasant goals in Russia were . . . to establish distributive mechanisms which reduced [the] risk in an uncertain environment and limited structurally the group most vulnerable to crisis by providing more equal access to [land].' He contrasted these goals with those of French peasants, most of whom were more interested in establishing 'freehold control over the land'. In France, and elsewhere in western and central Europe, peasants equated household size with land by moving people between households so that they had the labour resources to farm their land. Thus, if households had insufficient adults to cultivate their land, they hired labourers from other households and paid them wages, or arranged for young adults to work for them in return for board and lodging as live-in farm servants. In much of rural Russia, however, it was the other way round: it was the land, not the people, that moved around between households.[41]

Only a few Russian peasant households contained unrelated servants or labourers. Most that did were in the north of the forest-heartland in the seventeenth century. This was before the development of land-redistribution communes and the introduction of the poll tax. The only region where some Russian peasant households continued to have live-in servants after the poll tax was introduced was Siberia, where land redistribution developed only in the nineteenth century.[42] Instead of live-in servants, some peasant households in Russia 'adopted' a son-in-law if they were short of adult males (see Ch. 5). Another strategy that was closer to the system of live-in servants, and that was practised by Russian peasant households after the introduction of the

---

40 See Ignatovich, *Pomeshchich'i*, pp. 191–236; Kakhk, Yu. Yu., *'Ostzeiskii put'' perekhoda ot feodalizma k kapitalizmu: Krest'yane i pomeshchiki Estlyandii i Liflyandii v XVIII–pervoi polovine XIX veka* (Tallinn, 1988), pp. 130–42; Kula, W., *An Economic Theory of the Feudal System: Towards a Model of the Polish Economy, 1500–1800* (London and New York, 1976), pp. 49–51. See also Ch. 3.
41 Hoch, 'Serf Economy', p. 314; Mitterauer and Kagan, 'Russian', p. 126.
42 Shapiro, *Agrarnaya istoriya . . . XVII v.*, pp. 55–6; Baklanova, *Krest'yanskii*, p. 30; Vlasova, 'Sem'ya', pp. 182–3; Minenko, *Russkaya*, pp. 141–8.

poll tax, was 'adopting' peasants (known as *priemyshi*) from poorer households and using them as labourers. On a few seigniorial estates, landowners periodically moved peasants (*dol'niki*) between households, together with their shares of communal land and other property, in order to maintain a balance between households' labour and land resources. This practice was most common in Belorussia and in the adjoining province of Smolensk. It was rarer in more central parts of Russia. Thus, it may have reflected practices that evolved in regions annexed to the Russian state from the late seventeenth century.[43] Another way in which Russian peasants maintained a balance between their households' land and labour capacity was, of course, renting, buying and selling land. Some Russian peasants did this throughout the period under consideration, but in many regions in the eighteenth and nineteenth centuries, communal redistribution was much more important.[44]

Therefore, contrary to the beliefs of some Slavophile and Populist intellectuals, Russian village communes did not adopt the practice of land redistribution on account of some innate idea of egalitarianism, but because they saw it as the best way to make the most effective use of their land and human resources in order to ensure that their village communities, and the households that comprised them, were able to meet their obligations and subsist.

The Russian practice of periodically redistributing land between households to take account of changes in their size was fairly unusual, and contradicted Western ideas of private property, but was not unique. Jerome Blum found several examples throughout Europe of communities that held land jointly, and some that redistributed land. Few outside eastern Europe did so with the aims of equating allotments to household size or reducing inequalities. Many reserved the practice for meadows and pastures or repartitioned only marginal or waste land. Customs similar to Russian communal repartition existed in some non-European societies, for example caste segments in some Indian villages before the British enforced their ideas of land tenure, and groups of Mongol nomads, who reassigned grazing rights in particular pastures in line with changes in household size.[45]

In Russia, landowners and state officials recognised that communal and repartitional land tenure, and equalisation of allotments, not only assisted communes in fulfilling their existing obligations, but would also enable them to meet greater demands. Therefore, they actively encouraged communes to adopt these practices. In the mid-seventeenth century, before the introduction of the poll tax, Boris Morozov ordered stewards on his estates to divide the land equally between the peasants. In 1735 A. P. Volynskii instructed the village commune of Voronovo, on his estate near Moscow, to distribute the arable

43 See Ryabkov, 'Tormozyashchee', pp. 354–7.
44 See Chayanov, *Theory*, pp. 68, 132–3.
45 Blum, J., 'The European village as community', *Agricultural History*, vol. 45 (1971), pp. 171–4; Hryniuk, S., *Peasants with Promise: Ukrainians in Southeastern Galicia, 1880–1900* (Edmonton, 1991), pp. 117–18; Wolf, E., *Europe and the People without History* (Berkeley and Los Angeles, CA, 1982), p. 47; Seidenberg, S., 'The horsemen of Mongolia', in Carmichael, P., *Nomads* (London, 1991), p. 103.

land equally between households so that they could each pay an equal share of the village's taxes and seigniorial obligations. Many other landowners gave similar instructions to communes on their estates.[46]

There were differences in the development and practice of communal and repartitional land tenure between estates where peasants performed labour services and those where peasants paid dues. Landowners who required *barshchina* enforced communal repartition and equalisation of allotments earlier and more insistently than those who demanded *obrok*. The differences have been highlighted by case studies of individual estates. On the *barshchina* estate of Petrovskoe, Tambov province, in the first half of the nineteenth century, the commune repartitioned the arable land and labour obligations according to the number of *tyagla* in each household, thereby restricting economic differentiation between households. These practices were supported by the bailiff who was appointed by the Gagarins who owned the estate. In contrast, in the same period, on the *obrok* estate of Baki, Kostroma province, there were big differences in wealth between households. While the commune in Baki did practice land repartition, some households had more land than others, and a few had no arable land and had to live by working for richer peasants.

The reasons for these differences were straightforward. The capacity of most adult and able-bodied peasants to work for the landowner on the demesne was roughly the same, and they needed similar amounts of land to support themselves and their families. There was no reason, therefore, for landowners who demanded labour services to allow some households to become richer than others and to tolerate major inequalities. By enforcing rough equalisation of land allotments at a level sufficient for subsistence, moreover, landowners could take any 'surplus' land away from communes and add it to the demesne. Owners of *obrok* estates supported communal and redistributional tenure to make sure poorer households were not ruined and, thus, were able to pay their dues, but were less insistent on equalisation of allotments. Landowners who demanded *obrok* were content to tolerate a much greater degree of differentiation between households because they could demand higher dues from better-off peasants.[47]

The evidence presented so far has come mainly from communes on the estates of secular landowners. Communes of other categories of peasants also moved towards communal and redistributional land tenure. The transition seems to have taken place among church peasant communes at roughly the same time and for the same reasons as among seigniorial peasants. Vdovina's study of monastic estates in the first half of the eighteenth century strongly supports the view that repartitions became more common and widespread after the introduction of the poll tax. By the time church estates and peasants

46 Aleksandrov, *Sel'skaya*, pp. 56, 62–3; Blum, *Lord and Peasant*, p. 511; Pushkarev, *Krest'yanskaya*, 2nd pagn, pp. 7–14; Semevskii, *Krest'yane*, vol. 1, pp. 126–7.
47 Hoch, *Serfdom*, pp. 93–5, 104, 107, 124, 158; Melton, 'Household', pp. 564–9. See also Aleksandrov, *Sel'skaya*, pp. 238, 317, and Ch. 8.

were secularised in 1762–64, many communes had already adopted communal and repartitional land tenure.[48]

The state actively supported the extension of communal and repartitional landholding to other groups that made up the state peasantry. As on private estates, state peasant communes and some households saw advantages in these practices. The transition occurred later among state peasants than among seigniorial peasants, lasting well into the nineteenth century, as many lived in outlying regions.[49] The 'black' peasants of the Northern region stubbornly held on to household land tenure. Households treated their allotments as their own property, and regularly bought and sold them. The trade in land contributed to the growth of large disparities in the sizes of allotments between households in the same communes. The state became concerned that poorer households lacked the means to pay their taxes, and that the inequalities were socially divisive. In the 1750s the state tried to ban the trade in land. This was insufficient. Poorer peasants continued to complain about the inequitable distribution of land. Some state officials agreed. In 1785 the administrator in charge of the state peasantry in Archangel province reported 'justice demands that peasants who pay equal taxes should have equal shares in the land from which comes the wherewithal to pay the taxes'. At the end of the eighteenth century, the state ordered 'black' communes to share out some of their land equally and, in 1829, it compelled them to introduce repartition and equalisation of all their land. Better-off households opposed the change.[50]

Communal and repartitional land tenure was introduced by some communes of *odnodvortsy* on the old steppe frontier over the same period, and for similar reasons, following pressure from the state and complaints by poorer members. By 1850 about two-thirds of *odnodvortsy* villages held their land in communal tenure. Some wealthier households accepted the change because, although it meant losing some of their land, their obligations were reduced. Other better-off households resisted, and split away in order to retain household tenure.[51] State peasant communes in the Urals regions and Siberia also moved away from household tenure, under government pressure, in the nineteenth century.[52] Kiselev's reforms of the state peasantry of the 1830s and 40s retained communal and repartitional land tenure, although Kiselev believed the practices to be economically detrimental.[53] The spread of communal land tenure and periodic repartitions among court/appanage peasants began in the central regions in the seventeenth century, and became widespread in the

48 Gorskaya, *Krest'yanstvo*, p. 276; Vdovina, *Krest'yanskaya*, pp. 66–9, 119.
49 Aleksandrov, 'Land', p. 39; Blum, *Lord and Peasant*, p. 514.
50 Blum, *Lord and Peasant*, pp. 516–17 (quotation). See also Aleksandrov, 'Land', p. 40; Gorskaya, *Krest'yanstvo*, pp. 141, 340.
51 Blum, *Lord and Peasant*, pp. 518–19; Shaw, 'Landholding', pp. 115–19.
52 Vlasova, I. V., 'Obshchina i obychnoe pravo u russkikh krest'yan severnogo Priural'ya (XVII–XIX v.)', in Gromyko, M. M. and Listova, T. A. (eds), *Russkie: semeinyi i obshchestvennyi byt* (Moscow, 1989), pp. 27–30; Okladnikov, *Krest'yanstvo Sibiri*, p. 301.
53 Pushkarev, *Krest'yanskaya*, pp. 114–17.

eighteenth century. It developed in more outlying regions in the early nineteenth century, after pressure from the state and poorer households.[54]

Communal and repartitional land tenure spread from the central regions to the borderland in other ways. The idea that the custom emerged because Russian peasants were inherently communal and egalitarian was an intellectual construct of the nineteenth century (see above, pp. 199–200). Nevertheless, once these practices had become established for other, more pragmatic, reasons, they contributed to the emergence of egalitarian ideas among the Russian peasantry that took hold when they saw that they served their interests. Many peasant-migrants who moved to frontier regions, including Siberia, carried the ideas of communal and repartitional tenure with them as part of their 'cultural baggage'. When the need arose, they were prepared to introduce in outlying regions practices that had emerged much earlier in central Russia.[55]

Land repartitions

The general principles of land repartitions were similar in much of Russia. The communal arable land was usually divided into three fields around the village. Each field was further divided into sections (*yarusy*) according to soil fertility, the lie of the land, and the distance from the village. The sections were split into long, thin strips. Each strip in a given section was of roughly equal quality. Every household in the village had a number of strips that were widely scattered throughout various sections and in each of the three fields.

At a general, or 'black', repartition (*chernyi peredel*), all households returned their strips to the commune, which then repartitioned them between its members. Communes decided how many strips each household was entitled to in a number of ways. The most common among seigniorial peasants, especially those in the central regions who performed labour services, was by labour team (*tyaglo*). Many communes of seigniorial peasants who paid *obrok* and state peasants distributed land according to the number of male peasants in each household. During the nineteenth century, when land became scarcer in many regions as the population grew, communes developed new criteria for sharing out the land. Some assigned land according to the number of 'eaters' or 'consumers' in each household; others by the number of able-bodied adults ('workers' or 'producers'). Earnings from crafts and trade were taken into account in some villages. On some estates in the Central Non-Black Earth region in the first half of the nineteenth century, households' entitlements to land were gauged by the numbers of draught animals they owned. In regions where animal husbandry was important, for example Siberia, communes repartitioned meadow land according to how many cattle each household possessed. Once communes had determined how many strips of arable, or meadow, land

54 Gorskaya, *Krest'yanstvo*, p. 276; Semevskii, *Krest'yane*, vol. 2, pp. xii–xiii; Gorlanov, *Udel'nye*, pp. 20, 43.
55 See Atkinson, 'Egalitarianism', pp. 11–17; Pushkarev, *Krest'yanskaya*, p. 151; Gorskaya, *Krest'yanstvo*, pp. 273, 340–1; Channon, 'Regional', p. 69.

each household was due, they decided which strips households were to receive. In some villages, heads of households drew lots. In others, the members of communes simply agreed on, or more likely fought over, who got which strips.[56]

On some estates landowners laid down the procedures for land redistribution. In November 1855, for example, the Sheremetevs' estate office sent the following instructions to the estate of Molodoi Tud:

> In agreement with the master's estate manager, in every *vyt'* [an area of land][57] select 6 responsible peasants and order them: 1) to examine the household lists of peasants . . . [and] to determine the amount of communal land [to be allotted] to each peasant according to his family situation and means; 2) to declare the allocation of obligations . . . to the . . . commune, and then, in the spring of 1856 start to allot the land to the peasants . . . finishing . . . in the summer of 1856. And start to collect taxes according to the new distribution from 1857.[58]

There were wide variations in the frequency of 'black' repartitions. In the seventeenth century, communes that had adopted the practice carried out general repartitions rarely. In the eighteenth and first half of the nineteenth centuries, however, many communes carried out general repartitions every 12–15 years, after poll tax censuses. Since communes' tax liabilities were adjusted in line with population changes recorded in the censuses, it made sense to reapportion taxes and land allotments at the same time. In addition, communes sometimes repartitioned their land if large numbers of villagers had died during famines or epidemics, or had been conscripted in wartime. Under pressure from landowners, communes of seigniorial peasants on *barshchina* estates, especially in the central regions, carried out general repartitions more frequently than seigniorial communes who paid *obrok*, other categories of peasants, and communes in outlying regions such as Siberia.[59]

More frequent and widespread than 'black' reallocations of all the communal land involving every household were partial repartitions (*chastnye peredely, svalki-navalki, skidki-nakidki*). Communes regularly reallocated some strips to take account of fluctuations in the sizes of individual households, for example on the marriage of a son, the death of a head, or after household divisions. Partial repartitions often involved households whose members were related. Some communes never held general repartitions, and relied solely on partial

---

56 Haxthausen, *Studies*, pp. 79–80, 84; Prokof'eva, *Krest'yanskaya*, pp. 71–4; Semevskii, *Krest'yane*, vol. 1, pp. 109–19; Vdovina, *Krest'yanskaya*, pp. 72–87; Watters, 'Peasant', pp. 143–5; Bohac, *Family*, pp. 101–3; Ryabkov, 'Tormozyashchee', p. 359.
57 On the meanings of '*vyt'*', including links with '*tyaglo*', see Dal', *Tolkovyi slovar'*, vol. 1, p. 322; Semevskii, *Krest'yane*, vol. 1, p. 108.
58 Prokof'eva, *Krest'yanskaya*, pp. 92–3.
59 Gorskaya, *Krest'yanstvo*, p. 339; Aleksandrov, *Sel'skaya*, pp. 199–203; Semevskii, *Krest'yane*, vol. 1, pp. 120–2, 130; Pallot, J., 'The northern commune: Archangel Province in the late nineteenth century', in *LCPCR*, p. 59; Channon, 'Regional', p. 73.

redistributions to maintain a balance between their members' sizes and land allotments. This was the case in Petrovskoe, Tambov province, where over the first half of the nineteenth century the commune reallocated part of the land every year or two.[60] Although some recent research has suggested that land repartition may not have been as common, widespread or egalitarian as has sometimes been supposed, it was still a significant function of many communes in much of Russia in the eighteenth and nineteenth centuries, and was an important strategy adopted by many Russian peasant communities to maintain themselves and their ways of life.

Communal supervision of land use

Communes played a vital role in supervising the cultivation and use of their land. Communes directed the clearance of land from forest or steppe in the long-fallow systems used in earlier times and, later, in some outlying regions. In a large and expanding area of Russia, peasant households farmed strips of land in the communal open fields surrounding their villages under the three-field system of crop rotation (see Ch. 4) that required regulation by the commune. Communal tenure and regulation did not mean collective farming: households cultivated their strips of arable land individually. Nevertheless, every household had to sow and harvest the same crops in each field at the same time. Since the strips were very narrow, it would have been inadvisable for one household to plant one crop in one strip, while another household planted a different crop in an adjoining strip, because the likely outcome would have been a mixture of both crops. The custom of grazing livestock on stubble in the open fields after the harvest was another reason to enforce a common tillage system. Unless all households harvested their crops simultaneously, peasants whose crops were still ripening risked having them trampled and eaten by animals grazing on the stubble in neighbouring strips that had already been harvested.

Communal direction of compulsory crop rotation dates back to the introduction of the three-field rotation in parts of the forest-heartland in the sixteenth century. Indeed, Confino and other historians have argued that the emergence of the three-field system, the commune and serfdom at around the same time suggest that they were connected. The need to coordinate households' farming increased the role of the commune and, through the commune, enhanced the authority of the landowner. Communes and landowners had to coordinate general repartitions of land with the three-year cycles of crop rotation, and, since one field was left fallow each year, households had to be allotted equal numbers of strips in each of the three fields.[61]

60 Aleksandrov, *Sel'skaya*, p. 238; Channon, 'Regional', pp. 73–4; Pallot, 'Northern', pp. 60–1; Semevskii, *Krest'yane*, vol. 1, pp. 119–20; Hoch, *Serfdom*, p. 107.
61 See Confino, *Systèmes*, pp. 91–127; Atkinson, *End*, pp. 4, 14–17; Gorskaya, *Krest'yanstvo*, pp. 274, 276.

Village communes also managed the use of other land and natural resources, for example meadows, pastures, woodland and sources of water. Regulation of meadows and pastures was especially important in outlying regions such as Siberia where animal husbandry was a major part of the peasant economy. It was common practice for communes to partition, and repartition, meadow land between households, but pastures were normally held and used in common. In some villages, households had the right to graze a certain number of cattle on the village pasture. Many communes hired herders to tend the villagers' livestock, and some built communal byres to house them during the long winter months. Likewise, communes did not divide woodland between their members, but granted households rights to cut a certain amount of timber in a given period. Rivers and streams were important for water and fishing, and required regulation. In the village of Sorotskaya, in Archangel province in the Northern region, for example, the commune allocated positions for fishing on the riverbank and in mid-stream by lot until the 1850s and, in the second half of the nineteenth century, by annual auction.[62]

Many specialists have argued that Russian village communes' customs of land tenure and land use obstructed agricultural development. Blum asserted that redistributions of land and 'communal tillage' stifled 'any individual initiative that might have led to innovations and improvements'.[63] Such views were challenged by Wallace back in the 1870s and, more recently, by a number of historians. Households which improved their allotments, for example by using fertilisers, did not always lose out when land was repartitioned. In some villages, 'improvers' received compensation, or exchanged strips only with other 'improvers'. Elsewhere, prosperous households which had enriched their allotments prevented general repartitions so that they could keep their land. In spite of their reputation as tradition-bound and resistant to change, some communes initiated the introduction of new crops and crop rotations, for example clover in a four-field rotation, and organised drainage, irrigation and waste reclamation.[64] Practices similar to those of Russian communes in overseeing land use, directing crop rotations, and holding some land in common have been widespread throughout many parts of the world. These functions of Russian communes resembled those practised by village communities and manors in many areas of medieval and early modern Europe, including northwest Europe before the agricultural revolution. In pre-industrial Europe and other agricultural societies, including parts of southern Africa in the twentieth century, moreover, communal land tenure and communal control over land use have proved compatible with agricultural development.[65]

62 Atkinson, *End*, pp. 4, 17; Channon, 'Regional', pp. 70–1; Watters, 'Peasant', p. 143; Pallot, 'Northern', pp. 57–8.
63 Blum, *Lord and Peasant*, pp. 326–9, 337. See also Ch. 4.
64 Wallace, *Russia*, vol. 2, pp. 368–73; Kingston-Mann, 'Peasant communes', pp. 23–51; Worobec, C. D., 'The post-emancipation Russian peasant commune', in *LCPCR*, pp. 96–9; Bideleux, R., 'Agricultural advance under the Russian village commune system', *ibid.*, pp. 196–218.
65 See Rösener, *Peasantry*, pp. 22–3; Mingay, G. E. (ed.), *Arthur Young and his Times* (London, 1975), pp. 98–9; Low, A., *Agricultural Development in Southern Africa* (London, 1986), pp. 162–3.

Peasant attitudes to land ownership

The existence of communal and repartitional land tenure and communal supervision of land use in large parts of Russia in the eighteenth and nineteenth centuries led many contemporary observers and subsequent historians to conclude that Russian peasants had no concept of property in land in the Western legal sense. Moreover, peasants did not seem to recognise that, in Russian civil law, most of the land they cultivated was the property of noble landowners, the church (before 1762–64), the court or Appanage Department, or the state. The peasants' response to Ivan Yakushkin's proposal to free them from serfdom and rent them part of the land on the estate has often been quoted: 'We are yours, but the land is ours.' Many peasants, moreover, were reluctant to buy ('redeem') the land allocated to them after the abolition of serfdom in 1861. Russian peasants do seem to have had amorphous ideas about land ownership. Some apparently thought all land ultimately belonged to God or the tsar, but that they enjoyed the right to use it, because they and their forebears had cultivated it with their labour. From the mid-nineteenth century, when the land question was at the heart of reforms and discussions by officials and intellectuals, many peasants apparently believed, or hoped, that the tsar would grant them all the land in an all-Russian 'black repartition'.[66]

There is also evidence, however, that some peasants had a clear sense of the concept of land ownership and, in some cases, were prepared to pay for it. Laws enacted in 1803 and 1847 permitted seigniorial peasants to buy their land, and freedom, if their landowner was prepared to initiate the transaction or if the estates they lived on were auctioned to repay the owners' debts. Some peasants took advantage of these laws to buy their land and freedom. Throughout the period, some peasants rented and bought and sold land from other peasants in their own or neighbouring communities, or from other people. Moreover, in some areas, the practice of communal and redistributional land tenure had been imposed on reluctant peasants by the state (see above, pp. 219–20).

These contrasting attitudes among Russian peasants to land ownership can be explained partly by variations between regions and over time. Individual household land tenure, and a market in land between peasants, existed longest in the Northern region, where it lasted throughout the period under consideration. Peasants in areas where non-agricultural activities and market relations were well developed and widespread, for example the Central Non-Black Earth region, were used to trading in handicrafts and agricultural produce, and were often involved in wage labour. It was peasants in these areas who were more inclined to take advantage of laws allowing them to buy land, and did so prior to laws of 1801 and 1848 that expressly permitted peasants to own land.[67]

66 Yakushkin, *Zapiski*, p. 32; Emmons, T., 'The peasant and emancipation', in Vucinich, *Peasant*, pp. 52, 65; Engelgardt, *Letters*, pp. 228–38.
67 See Moon, *Russian Peasants*, pp. 80–112; Aleksandrov, *Obychnoe*, pp. 163–4; Bohac, *Family*, pp. 30–3. See also Ch. 3.

Population densities affected peasant attitudes to land. In regions and at times when land suitable for farming was plentiful, for example in the forest-heartland in the medieval period and some outlying regions into the nineteenth century, there was little need to buy and sell land. In such areas, land was, in reality, supplied by 'God' in abundance, and the only thing that mattered was who cleared and ploughed it. In regions with land shortages, for example in parts of central Russia by the nineteenth century, land was more valuable and peasants were prepared to pay to use or own it.

Peasants' attitudes to the concept of property in land were closely linked to the ways they held and used land, regardless of who had introduced the systems of land tenure and use, or why they had done so. In the nineteenth century in the central regions, where communes had held their arable land in communal tenure and periodically redistributed plots between households for several generations, many peasants had come to accept this form of tenure as long as it met their needs. Repartitions meant that land periodically circulated around the households in a village and, over time, each household cultivated a variety of strips in different parts of the open fields. The three-field system also involved the circulation of land around the village, as successive fields were sown with the winter or spring crops, or left fallow, in three-year cycles. These continual processes of circulation of land must have influenced the ways Russian peasants thought about who 'owned' it. The long-fallow systems of crop cultivation used in earlier times, and for longer in outlying areas, also entailed farming different areas of land on a regular or intermittent basis. It is possible that peasants came to think generally of land as something they were entitled to use and 'own', but did not attach the idea of 'ownership' to particular plots of land.[68]

In the revolution of 1917–21, when Russian peasants seized the opportunity to take over the land from private landowners and the state, most communities chose to seize and hold the land in common, and to share it out amongst themselves in a 'black repartition' throughout Russia.[69]

OTHER COMMUNAL FUNCTIONS

Russian village communes had other important functions. Communes were involved in several aspects of the village economy. On some estates, with the agreement of the landowner or estate authorities, communes were in charge of issuing passports to peasants who wanted to leave the village to work as migrant labourers.[70]

Many communes made some provision for the welfare of their members. Communes sometimes temporarily suspended or waived the obligations of weaker households, or lent them money. Communes organised assistance (*pomoch'*) for households that had fallen on hard times by arranging for some

68 See Sumner, *Survey*, pp. 21–3.
69 See Atkinson, *End*, pp. 170–85. See also Ch. 9.
70 Aleksandrov, *Sel'skaya*, pp. 70–4. See also Ch. 4.

villagers to help out with arduous tasks, or to cultivate land for families that lacked the labourers to do it for themselves. Households that received assistance rewarded their helpers with food and drink, especially vodka. More importantly, peasants who helped their neighbours earned the right to turn to the commune for assistance should they fall on hard times. Thus, *pomoch'* was a kind of mutual insurance policy. Communes were willing to help only some poor households. For example, they were prepared to help a family whose house and belongings had been destroyed by fire, a household in which the adults were ill, or a family whose father had died before his sons reached adulthood. Such households were worth helping because their hardship was temporary. The family that had been burned out could rebuild with assistance. The sick adults would probably get better. And the orphaned sons would grow up. In each case, the households' misfortune was short term and, in time, they would once again be economically viable and capable of making their contribution to the commune's obligations.

Communes were not prepared to provide a permanent 'safety net' for all poor families. They did not want to use valuable resources supporting households whose hardship seemed long term since they would become 'free riders'. Peasants were reluctant to assist households, moreover, if they thought that they would not be in a position to help them in return if they fell on hard times. Weaker households with little chance of ever supporting themselves and meeting their share of the village's obligations were sometimes allowed to go under. Sending a family's only adult male to the army, and marrying off or otherwise distributing the other members, was a fairly common way of ridding a village of a household that was a burden on its neighbours. Like land repartition, therefore, communal assistance was not a commitment to egalitarianism and communalism, but a strategy aimed at the long-term survival of the village community. In the last resort, destitute peasants had to rely on the Christian charity of their fellow villagers and beg for alms.[71]

Communes insured themselves against famine by maintaining reserve granaries. Most communes were reluctant to take this precaution unprompted, however, probably because they expected the state or their landowners to provide for them in times of dearth. Communal granaries did not become widespread until they were required by law in the first half of the nineteenth century. The state saw the maintenance of reserves in the villages as a way of insuring its tax receipts and avoiding being inundated with requests for assistance from landowners and communes after harvest failures.[72]

Maintaining law and order and dispensing justice in their villages were other communal duties. On seigniorial estates, these functions were shared between

71 Gromyko, *Traditsionnye*, pp. 31–64. See also Aleksandrov, *Sel'skaya*, pp. 225–6, 312; Atkinson, 'Egalitarianism', p. 13; Bohac, 'Widows', pp. 102–3; Hoch, *Serfdom*, p. 138; Smith and Christian, *Bread*, pp. 319–21; Lindenmeyr, *Poverty*, pp. 32, 41–3, 50–5. For an interpretation of the 'free-rider problem', based on self-interest of individuals rather than communities, see Popkin, S. L., *The Rational Peasant: The Political Economy of Rural Society in Vietnam* (Berkeley and Los Angeles, 1979), pp. 24–7, 255–7.
72 Haxthausen, *Studies*, p. 106; Hoch, *Serfdom*, p. 137; Pallot, 'Northern', p. 63. See also Ch. 3.

communal officials and the estate authorities. Communes in villages of all categories of peasants selected constables and watchmen. They kept an eye on outsiders who passed through their villages, especially fugitives, vagrants and deserters, and were supposed to apprehend anyone who illegally distilled spirits. Their main concern, however, was to protect the village people and their property. When necessary, constables carried out preliminary investigations to find the perpetrators of crimes. Enforcing law and order merged into administering justice. For minor offences, constables arrested miscreants and punished them on the spot. For more serious crimes, and to resolve disputes between villagers, communes had rudimentary courts and judicial procedures. Communal courts tried cases on the basis of customary law. On private estates, landowners' estate officials sat together with communal elders. Only very serious crimes, such as murder, or disputes with members of other communes were referred to higher, official courts. Communal courts handed down various punishments, including birching, fines and imprisonment. Communes sent serious offenders to serve in the army or to penal servitude in Siberia.[73]

Village communities also had less formal means of maintaining social control. Peasants who deviated from the norms of expected behaviour and threatened the economic viability of the community or the authority of the elders were subjected to 'rough' or 'popular' justice, known in Russian as *samosud*. Communities were particularly hostile to peasants who disobeyed the resolutions of communal assemblies, for example those concerning the cultivation of the village fields, peasants suspected of witchcraft, women who left husbands who mistreated them, and thieves, especially horse thieves. The loss of a horse was as great a blow to a household as the death of an able-bodied peasant. Communal assemblies met to discuss cases of peasants who had violated the norms of village life, and to decide on appropriate punishments. The main form of punishment was public shaming and humiliation. To take a typical example, a peasant who stole a goose from his neighbour in a village in Smolensk province in the late nineteenth century was paraded around the village three times with the goose hanging around his neck. After this ritual humiliation, he begged forgiveness and bought vodka for everyone in the village. Women who offended their communities were often stripped in public or tarred and feathered. Peasants who were suspected of more serious crimes, for example stealing horses, were beaten up or even lynched. The ultimate punishment for persistent offenders was to be expelled from the commune and, therefore, deprived of the right to land allotments and assistance in times of need.[74]

Communes were responsible for the upkeep of the parish church and clergy. On seigniorial estates, this duty was shared with landowners and estate

73 Gorskaya, *Krest'yanstvo*, pp. 278–9; Hoch, *Serfdom*, pp. 160–87; Mironov, 'Local government', pp. 170–3.
74 See Frank, S. P., 'Popular justice, community and culture among the Russian peasantry, 1870–1900', *RR*, vol. 46 (1987), pp. 239–66; Frierson, C. A., 'Crime and punishment in the Russian village . . . at the end of the nineteenth century', *SR*, vol. 46 (1987), pp. 55–69; Worobec, C. D., 'Horse thieves and peasant justice in post-emancipation imperial Russia', *JSocH*, vol. 21 (1987), pp. 281–93.

authorities. Until the eighteenth century, the borders of most communes and parishes were identical. Communes built and maintained churches on communal land, and selected and supported the clergy. The right of communes, and landowners, to choose their priests to be ordained by bishops demonstrated the extent of lay authority over parish churches. In the late seventeenth century, one bishop complained that 'the peasants are running the churches'. Gregory Freeze has argued that communes continued to control parishes, and retained the right to choose their own priests, until the end of the eighteenth century. In the early nineteenth century, the appointment of parish priests was taken over by the bishops. Parishioners were still largely responsible for supporting the parish clergy, however, through fees for rites and ceremonies, in particular christenings, weddings and funerals, and contributions to collections. Communes provided, and sometimes cultivated, land to support parish churches and clergy. Attempts by the higher church authorities in the first half of the nineteenth century to reduce priests' dependence on their parishioners were hampered by lack of money for stipends.[75]

Communes supervised the conduct of the households in their villages. Communes regulated household divisions, were involved in arranging marriages and bride-prices, and kept an eye on villagers' 'morals'. In most cases, communes supported the authority of the heads of households. The main concern of communes, as in so many other areas, was to ensure that their members were able to meet their share of the communal obligations and not become a burden on the community.[76]

Thus, village communes played a very large role in administering rural Russia throughout the period covered by this book, and were at the interface of the peasant world and the world of the landowning and ruling elites.

THE COMMUNE AND THE REFORMS OF THE NINETEENTH CENTURY

When the government embarked on major rural reforms in the mid-nineteenth century, including the abolition of serfdom, the future of the commune and its control over village land loomed large. Some 'enlightened bureaucrats' argued in favour of ending communal and repartitional land tenure as they believed it hindered economic development. Nevertheless, most officials recognised the expediency not just of retaining the commune but of strengthening it. The end of seigniorial authority in the villages in 1861, and the absence of the vast army of officials which would have been needed to replace it, left little option but to retain village communes as the lowest level of local government in rural Russia. The state had other reasons for keeping communes and their customary practices. Many senior officials, including reform-minded men such as Kiselev, accepted that communes were essential as guarantees of fiscal and social stability. Collective responsibility had long proved itself a cheap and

---

75 Freeze, *Russian Levites*, pp. 147–62 (quotation from p. 150); *id.*, *Parish Clergy*, pp. 29, 52–101.
76 See Aleksandrov, *Sel'skaya*, pp. 294–313; Hoch, *Serfdom*, pp. 91–132. See also Ch. 5.

effective way of making sure peasants met their obligations. Communal land tenure and periodic redistribution were believed to have two advantages. They ensured that peasants had the means to meet their obligations, and impeded the emergence of a landless, rootless proletariat which, the government feared, would make Russia liable to the sort of revolutions that had occurred in other parts of Europe in 1830 and 1848.[77]

The statutes abolishing serfdom in 1861 set up new 'village societies' (*sel'skie obshchestva*) of communities of peasants who had belonged to the same land-owner under serfdom. These new 'societies' contained entire villages, parts of villages or a number of villages. In the central regions, two-thirds were coterm-inous with the old village communes. In cases where they did not coincide, the old communes often continued alongside the new. Village societies were combined in townships (*volosti*), and both elected assemblies which, in turn, chose peasant officials who were responsible for administering the villages and working with the lowest level of the state provincial administration. Similar institutions were set up in villages of state and appanage peasants in the 1860s, replacing those established in the 1820s–40s. Communes' functions were not radically altered by the reforms of the 1860s. They were still responsible for sharing out and collecting taxes and obligations from their member house-holds. The principle of collective responsibility for all obligations, including the redemption payments for the land, was retained, as was communal and repartitional land tenure. Communes were permitted to change to household tenure only if there was a two-thirds majority in the communal assembly. Individual households could gain full ownership of their land, however, if they paid their full share of the redemption payments. Communes also con-tinued to carry out the other functions they had performed before 1861.[78]

In principle, communes enjoyed increased authority in the aftermath of the reforms of the 1860s. In practice, however, the removal of seigniorial author-ity was probably cancelled out by increasing interference from the growing state bureaucracy in rural areas. In the late nineteenth and early twentieth centuries, moreover, the main principles underpinning the continued role of communes in the villages were increasingly questioned in government circles. In 1893 the government tried to restrict the frequency of repartitions as it believed they were detrimental to agriculture. A decade later, in 1903, the government finally ended collective responsibility for taxes and redemption payments. The outbreak of rural revolution in 1905 seriously undermined the argument that communes were a force for social stability. The revolution finally con-vinced the authorities to take decisive action. The Stolypin land reforms of 1906–11 encouraged better-off peasants to break away from their communes and consolidate their landholdings in separate farms. The intention was to create a group of yeoman farmers who would be a force for stability. This, of

---

77 See Atkinson, *End*, pp. 22–3; Blum, *Lord and Peasant*, pp. 508–9; Crisp, *Studies*, p. 91; Mironov, 'Local government', pp. 182–90; Wallace, *Russia*, vol. 1, p. 210. See also Ch. 3.
78 Mironov, B., 'The Russian peasant commune after the reforms of the 1860s', *SR*, vol. 44 (1985), pp. 438–67; Worobec, *Peasant Russia*, pp. 17–22.

course, was the exact opposite of trying to achieve the same goal through rough levelling by equalising land allotments, which the state and many landowners had encouraged since the seventeenth century.[79]

VILLAGE POLITICS

Until quite recently, most historians put forward two conflicting interpretations of the balance of power in the politics of rural Russia. Many Russian historians writing in the late nineteenth and early twentieth centuries, and several Western historians writing later, stressed the authority of landowners and the state over village communes. This view, which was based largely on studies of large seigniorial *barshchina* estates from the mid-eighteenth century, allowed little room for independent initiative from communes or their members.[80] In contrast, a number of historians, especially Soviet scholars, emphasised the role of communes in standing up for the interests of their members. They cited numerous examples of communes organising protests against exploitation and oppression by landowners and state authorities. There is abundant evidence, moreover, for peasant solidarity in the name of the commune in the face of outsiders.[81]

Aleksandrov combined these two interpretations, and argued that communes were characterised by 'dualism'. On the one hand, the commune was an institution of 'feudal society'. By the eighteenth century, it had become a subordinate but important element of estate administration. Landowners were largely successful in using communes to maintain their authority over their peasants and to extract obligations from them. Communes were also involved in the administration of non-seigniorial villages on behalf of their owners. This side of the commune's 'dualism' included its administrative, fiscal and police functions in support of the existing order. On the other hand, Aleksandrov also argued that the commune was an organ of the peasantry that did not completely lose its autonomy under serfdom and state power. Landowners and state authorities had to rely on communes and consider their views. The commune, moreover, protected peasants' interests against landowners and the state, and supported the peasant economy and ways of life, which were enshrined in customary law. In short, communes facilitated the coexistence of the landowning and ruling elites and a subordinate peasantry.[82]

The chief weakness of all these views of the politics of rural Russia is that they allow little or no room for the existence of politics inside village communes, and ignore the importance of the relative power of different groups

79 See Atkinson, *End*, pp. 41–100. See also Ch. 9.
80 See Aleksandrov, *Sel'skaya*, pp. 9–15, 49; Crisp, *Studies*, pp. 66–70; Toumanoff, 'Development', p. 184.
81 See Gorskaya, *Krest'yanstvo*, p. 280; Aleksandrov, *Sel'skaya*, pp. 75, 125–7, 176; Baklanova, *Krest'yanskii*, pp. 188–90; Prokof'eva, *Krest'yanskaya*, pp. 185–209. See also Ch. 7.
82 Aleksandrov, *Sel'skaya*, pp. 314–15. His interpretation was anticipated by Ignatovich, *Pomeshchich'i*, pp. 187, 191. (I have expanded it to include the state and other non-seigniorial landowners.)

of peasants within their communities. Case studies of individual villages, such as Hoch's study of Petrovskoe and Melton's work in Baki, have presented more subtle accounts of power relations inside communities, and how communal institutions operated in practice. Rather than cooperation between peasants, however, these case studies have drawn attention to conflict. They have presented powerful evidence that Russian village communes were dominated by members of the older generation, or by factions of wealthier peasants whose power was based on kinship and patronage. The peasants who served as communal officials, and who ran the villages in conjunction with estate officials, usually came from these elites or supported them. Peasant elites used the power entrusted to them by landowners to oppress and exploit other peasants in pursuit of their own interests. Hoch emphasised the collusion between heads of households, communal elders and the landowner's bailiff, and went so far as to conclude that life in Petrovskoe 'was hostile, violent, vengeful, quarrelsome, fearful and vituperative'.[83]

Some communal functions that appear at first sight to have been exercised in the general interests of all their members seem, on closer examination, also or instead to have served the interests of generational or factional elites. In Hoch's interpretation of social control on the *barshchina* estate of Petrovskoe, the landowner's bailiff supported the authority of the heads of households over their extended families by refusing to allow the younger generation of married sons to break away and set up their own households. The commune, which was dominated by household heads, was supported by the bailiff in ensuring a reasonably equitable distribution of land in order to reduce conflicts between households. In return for the bailiff's support, the heads of households supported his authority, but in doing so ensured that their interests were served.

Peasant elites used the distribution of the communal obligations between households for their own benefit and to bolster their authority. In Petrovskoe, the household heads made sure that most of the communal labour obligations were performed by the younger generation of peasants in their households. Three-quarters of the labour services were carried out by the one-third of the village population which had reached adulthood but had not yet become heads of their own households. Until they attained this status, the middle generation of peasants aged between around 20 and 40 did most of the work but had no privileges in the commune or their households. In contrast, the heads of households enjoyed leisure, status and authority.[84]

Melton argued that the distribution of obligations was the issue which most often led to clashes between households or factions in a commune as each competed for better treatment from the communal and estate authorities. He also argued that the intensity of conflicts within communes was greater on estates where seigniorial control was weak, and there was significant economic

83 Hoch, *Serfdom*, pp. 133, 189 (quotation); Melton, 'Household', pp. 559–62.
84 Hoch, *Serfdom*, pp. 91–136, 158–9.

differentiation between households, than on estates where landowners maintained tighter control and there was greater equality. *Obrok* estates, such as Baki, were thus ripe for communal conflicts. The richest families were those that dominated the timber trade that was the main economic activity in the village. The wealthiest formed factions based on patronage networks. One of the factions controlled the commune. In the first decade of the nineteenth century, the daughter of one of the richest timber dealers, Vasili Voronin, was married to the communal clerk, Petr Ponamarev, who had great power because he was literate. Between them they were able to dominate communal affairs. The extent of the control of the communal oligarchs was such that Countess Lieven's estate manager, Ivan Oberuchev, felt it was in his best interests to cooperate with them.

The oligarchy kept itself in power by controlling the distribution of the commune's obligations, especially conscription. The ruling faction protected their own sons from the draft, and those of their kinsmen and households that worked for them in the timber trade. The burden of supplying recruits was born by peasants outside the patronage networks of the communal oligarchy. The oligarchy's power was such that it was able to undermine an attempt by an estate manager to remove the burden of conscription from the village. The manager introduced a progressive tax on the villagers to raise money to buy substitutes to send to the army in place of their sons. The ruling elite opposed the scheme since it removed one of the main means they used for dispensing patronage.[85]

Control over the distribution of obligations led to serious tensions between richer and more powerful peasants and the poorer and weaker members of their communities on many *obrok* estates. In Pavlovo, on the Sheremetevs' estates in Nizhnii Novgorod province where the peasants engaged in metal working, relations inside the commune degenerated to such an extent that poor peasants believed that the village elite had 'usurped the authority' of Count Sheremetev. The estate clerk complained to the landowner's estate office that the poor peasants 'consider all new directives as false laws issued by the rich peasants and not by the Count'. In 1800 tensions exploded over the selection of recruits. The communal assembly refused to ratify the list drawn up by the communal officials, and there was a full-scale riot against the peasant elite.[86]

Communal officials on other estates used the distribution of obligations to maintain their authority, and to take advantage of their positions to enrich themselves at the expense of the other members. On visiting his estate at Manuilovskoe in 1837, the landowner wrote: 'The draft duties were determined by some sort of calculation, that, in spite of all my desire and mental exercises, I could not master. I only knew that it worked to the profit of the village head and to the loss of the peasants.'[87] Peasants on several estates in Yaroslavl'

85 Melton, 'Household', pp. 560–78; *id.*, 'Enlightened', pp. 688–9. See also Bohac, 'Widows', pp. 102–3.
86 Melton, 'Enlightened', pp. 689–90.
87 Bohac, 'Mir', p. 652.

province complained to their landowners about headmen, elders and other communal officials acting without consulting their communes, taking rye from the reserve granaries, stealing from peasants, ploughing other peasants' land, and 'doing nothing'. Communal elders who enriched themselves at the expense of fellow-villagers were known as '*miroedy*' ('devourers of the commune'). On state lands, elders often collaborated with local officials to pass the burden of obligations, especially recruitment, onto other peasants.[88]

Communal repartitions of land are also open to reinterpretation. It was in the interests of peasant elites that all members of communes had enough land to enable them to pay their shares of the communal obligations. It was not in their interests, especially on *obrok* estates, to insist on an equitable distribution. Left to their own devices, some communes apportioned land as they wished. In Nikol'skoe, Yaroslavl' province, whose owner allowed communal self-government on his estates, communal records from the 1780s show no connection between the amount of land each household was allotted and the numbers of peasants they contained.[89] David Macey has gone further than many specialists in attacking the idea that the commune was 'the embodiment of some innate peasant egalitarianism'. He argued that land repartition was a 'conflict resolution mechanism': it was only by periodically repartitioning the land, which had been divided up into strips according to location, soil fertility, access to water, etc., that the commune could resolve the 'jealousies and conflicts within the village'.[90]

Communal elites sometimes came into conflict with poorer peasants and landowners over the provision of assistance. On occasions, 'enlightened seigniors' stepped in to compel communes to help needy peasants. In 1784 General Suvorov ordered the commune on his *obrok* estate in Penza province to help a poor, landless peasant rather than sending him to the army, which was the intention of the communal officials. Suvorov instructed the commune to find the peasant a wife, and to help the new household become viable by providing it with land, a house, cattle and a plough. Suvorov backed up his order by threatening to marry the poor peasant to the daughter of one of the rich peasants who dominated the commune.[91]

Communal officials often dispensed justice and enforced law and order in their own interests. Hoch has described a regime of 'punishment, fear, and control' in Petrovskoe that was maintained by the peasant functionaries and the bailiff. Heads of households cooperated with the bailiff in maintaining their authority over the younger generation by extensive use of corporal punishment. Recalcitrant peasants were also kept under control by the threat of being selected as recruits. In extreme cases, young adults who refused to submit to their elders were exiled to Siberia. The younger generation did not conform simply because of punishment or the threat of conscription and exile,

88 Leonard, 'Landlords', pp. 133–6; Crisp, *Studies*, p. 81.
89 Aleksandrov, *Sel'skaya*, p. 209.
90 Macey, D. A. J., 'The peasant commune and the Stolypin reforms', in *LCPCR*, pp. 220, 230.
91 Melton, 'Enlightened', p. 699.

but because they knew that in time, when they were middle-aged, they would have similar power over the younger generation in their village communities as well as in their households.[92]

Peasant elites operated in similar ways in church and state peasant communities. They manipulated communal assemblies into supporting their interests at the expense of poorer and weaker peasants. Government inspections of state peasant communes carried out in the 1830s, on the eve of Kiselev's reforms, uncovered widespread abuses. Inspectors reported that vodka flowed freely at the elections of communal officials as candidates tried to buy votes. Richer peasants did not always stand for election themselves, but supported poorer peasants on the understanding that they would favour them with lighter obligations if they won office.[93]

The social hierarchy in village communities was not just maintained by punishment, exploitation and bribery, but by socialisation. Respect for elders was an important part of peasant culture. It was reflected in proverbs such as 'The opinion of the older generation is always right' and 'Where there is age, there is also law.'[94] The composition of communal assemblies also reflected the authority of male peasants over female. Some women, usually widows, were recognised as heads of households and allowed to attend assemblies, but in only a few communes were women allowed to vote.[95]

Communal assemblies were renowned for their binding unanimity. This did not always represent consensus, however, but was often forced, and reflected the interests of elite peasants. Melton argued that, on seigniorial estates, large communal assemblies at which all households were represented were rare. More common were smaller assemblies attended either by elders and selectmen, or by heads of better-off and middling households. Such assemblies institutionalised the dominance of older or richer peasants. Assemblies attended by all members of communes, moreover, were often dominated by 'yellers and screamers' (*gorlany* and *krikuny*). These were rich peasants who intimidated the others, often with the aim of shifting the burden of obligations on to poorer peasants or allocating themselves more or better land.[96]

In the 1840s Haxthausen wrote approvingly that communes 'were not based on democratic equality among the members but on absolute authority, the "despotic power" . . . of the communal elders and, through them, of the group over its individual components'.[97] Three decades later, however, after the reforms of the 1860s and from a different perspective, Wallace enthused:

92 See Hoch, *Serfdom*, pp. 152–5, 160–86. See also Ch. 5.
93 Blum, *Lord and Peasant*, pp. 523–4; Crisp, *Studies*, p. 82; Vdovina, *Krest'yanskaya*, pp. 74–5; Smith and Christian, *Bread*, pp. 322–3.
94 See Gromyko, *Traditsionnye*, p. 94; Minenko, N. A., 'Stariki v russkoi krest'yanskoi obshchine zapadnoi Sibiri XVIII–pervoi polovine XIX v.', in Rusakova and Minenko, *Kul'turno-bytovye*, pp. 89–104; Dal', *Poslovitsy*, vol. 1, p. 309.
95 Bohac, 'Widows', p. 110; Glickman, R., 'Women and the peasant commune', in *LCPCR*, pp. 327–8. See also Ch. 5.
96 Melton, 'Household', p. 563. See also Mironov, 'Local government', pp. 175, 194–5.
97 Haxthausen, *Studies*, pp. 25–6 (Starr's introduction).

'Communes ... are capital specimens of representative Constitutional government of the extreme democratic type!'. He compared their 'constitutions' with the 'English type' of 'unwritten, traditional conceptions'. He noted that 'real authority resides in the Assembly, of which all Heads of Households are members', and that assemblies tried to reach unanimous decisions by acclamation, but accepted the results of votes on disagreements. He also observed that communal assemblies had become larger as most adult males attended, and that decisions were taken by 'noisy majorities'.[98]

Historians have been rather more sober in their judgements, and have expressed divergent opinions on whether communal assemblies did, as Wallace suggested, become more democratic and egalitarian after the 1860s. There was an increase in the numbers of households in many communities, as more married sons broke away from their fathers to set up on their own. This may have been a cause or a consequence of a reduction in the authority of the older generation in their households and communes. There were certainly greater tensions between the generations. Many younger men had more experience outside their villages as a result of the larger numbers who served in the army after the reform of 1874, and the growth in migrant wage labour. The increases in the numbers of young men with some formal education further contributed to a growing desire among the younger generation for greater independence from their fathers. By the early twentieth century, old men were regretting their loss of authority.[99]

There is also evidence that peasant women acquired a greater role in communal affairs in the late nineteenth century. At least in part, this was a result of the growing numbers of men who left their villages to work in urban areas. On the one hand, the workload of peasant women whose husbands were away for several months a year increased. On the other hand, the status of women was enhanced by the absence of their menfolk. The wives of migrants were more likely than other peasant women to be literate because of the need to keep in touch with their husbands and to deal with the local authorities. They also enjoyed a better standard of living, and tended to be 'independent, self-reliant, and self-assured, and to know "the value of their labor and themselves"'. Migrants' wives in some communities were granted a voice, and a vote, in village assemblies when their husbands were away. This was ratified in Russian law in 1890. Some parts of the Central Non-Black Earth region, where male migrant labour was widespread, became known as 'women's kingdoms' on account of the numerical preponderance and relative power of women.[100]

Other specialists have maintained that communes were still dominated by old, wealthy, male peasants in the late nineteenth century. This was the view Olga Semenova expressed in her study of a peasant community in Ryazan'

98 Wallace, *Russia*, vol. 1, pp. 192–6.
99 Wallace, *Russia*, vol. 2, pp. 358–60; Zyryanov, *Krest'yanskaya*, pp. 243–50. See also Chs 3, 4 and 5.
100 Engel, *Between*, pp. 34–63 (quotation from p. 51).

province, in the Central Black Earth region, at the turn of the twentieth century. She noted that peasants complained that they needed to have relatives, or money to buy vodka, to gain the support of the commune. Relations between peasant households within village communities seem, thus, to have been marked by 'complex lines of solidarity and hostility'.[101] The main axes of tensions within village communities were similar to those inside households (see Ch. 5), and pitted younger peasants against the older generation, poorer peasants against richer villagers, women against men and, in addition, factions based on networks of kinship and patronage against other groups. In much the same way as peasant communities elsewhere in the world, therefore, Russian villages were riven by conflicts as well as a degree of cooperation.

CONCLUSION

The enthusiasm among some nineteenth-century intellectuals for Russian village communes and their seemingly egalitarian practices concerning the land was largely misplaced. Recent scholarship has brought the commune down from the heights of abstraction to more prosaic reality. Communes served as forums for village politics of a mundane and distinctly unharmonious kind. They did not always represent the interests of all their members, but could act as the tool of the older generation or factions of richer peasants within villages, who dominated them and took advantage of their positions to enhance their authority over other peasants.

Nevertheless, to some extent, peasant households did pull together to work for the subsistence of their communities. No-one benefited if a number of households went under. Periodic land redistribution emerged largely as a pragmatic response to the increasing demands by the state and landowners among seigniorial peasants in the central regions of Russia over the seventeenth and eighteenth centuries. It later spread to peasants of other categories and to some more outlying regions. Communal and repartitional land tenure enabled communities to make the most effective use of their land and labour resources. It was, thus, another strategy developed by peasants to ensure the livelihoods of their households and communities in the face of population increase, the harsh environment, and the demands of the landowning and ruling elites. Russian village communes could also serve as forces for cohesion among their members when they felt threatened by outsiders. On occasions, communes overcame the differences between their members, and represented the interests of entire village communities in their dealings with the elites that oppressed and exploited them.

101 Semyonova, *Village Life*, pp. 164–5, 117 (notes by Ransel). See also Gromyko, *Traditsionnye*, pp. 93–6.

CHAPTER 7

Protest

The most dramatic cases of protest by Russian peasants against the landowning and ruling elites, before the rural revolutions of 1905–07 and 1917–21, were four great revolts led by cossacks in the seventeenth and eighteenth centuries. Most important, from the point of view of peasant involvement, were the revolts led by Stepan ('Sten'ka') Razin in 1670–71 and Emelyan Pugachev in 1773–74. Before, between, and especially after the four revolts, Russian peasants took part in more limited forms of protest against oppression and exploitation, including flight to the borderlands; small-scale 'disturbances', in which groups of peasants tried to extract concessions from landowners or state authorities; and 'everyday resistance', such as under-fulfilment of obligations, lying, and other 'weapons of the weak'.[1] This chapter starts with a discussion of the causes of peasant protest, but the largest part is devoted to an analysis of the four main forms of protest (revolt, flight, 'disturbances' and 'everyday resistance'). Particular attention is paid to the timing and geographical location of the different forms of protest, as well as their causes, the aims of the participants, and the consequences. The objectives and achievements of peasants who protested are discussed in the final section of the chapter.

CAUSES AND OPPORTUNITIES

The causes of peasant protest against the landowning and ruling elites in Russia can be divided into two categories: particular or immediate grievances, and general or underlying discontent. Inseparable from the causes are the circumstances which created opportunities for peasants to resist.

Peasant protests were often sparked off by particular grievances. Increases in existing demands by landowners and the state and the introduction of new types of obligations were common catalysts. One of the most frequent reasons for increases in state obligations, and protests against them, was Russia's regular and expensive wars. Much of the cost was borne by the peasantry through higher taxation, and most of the soldiers were conscripted from the peasantry. Peasants who paid dues (*obrok*) disliked being transferred to labour services

---

1 See Kolchin, *Unfree Labour*, p. 241. See also Scott, J. C., *Weapons of the Weak: Everyday Forms of Peasant Resistance* (New Haven, CT, and London, 1985).

(*barshchina*), as the change entailed greater supervision and, sometimes, reductions in their land allotments by landowners to create or enlarge their demesnes. Any attempts to take land from peasants provoked a hostile reaction. Peasants also protested against harsh treatment by landowners or officials. Changes of landowner, as a result of inheritance or purchase, were often occasions for protests by peasants, who were concerned that their new owners might alter existing arrangements or increase their obligations. For the same reason, reforms by the state, even those which aimed to improve conditions for peasants, regularly provoked resistance. Seigniorial and state authorities who tried to interfere with peasants' traditional agricultural methods often met with stubborn opposition. This was not because peasants were mindlessly resistant to change, but because they feared that the 'innovations' might fail, threatening their subsistence, or that they would have to work harder for the benefit only of their exploiters. (See Ch. 4.)

Natural disasters, especially harvest failures, were all too frequent causes of distress and could lead to protests. For many peasants, the real burden of obligations was caused not so much by the amounts landowners and state officials demanded, but by inflexibility in times of hardship. In years when the harvest was good or earnings from non-agricultural activities were high, peasant households and communities could hand over quite large proportions of their surplus product and income without adversely affecting their subsistence or productive capacity. If the harvest was poor or other earnings low, however, households and communities might not have a surplus, and any demands would seriously threaten their subsistence. Peasants who had fallen on hard times expected, and sometimes protested if they did not get, aid from the seigniorial and state authorities, or at least temporary reductions in or suspensions of their obligations. Above all, peasants resisted anything that threatened to upset the strategies they had developed at household and village levels to ensure their subsistence and livelihoods.

Underlying these particular grievances were more general factors. Many Russian peasants undoubtedly resented the restrictions on their freedom of movement and the demands for obligations made by landowners and the state. It is probable that the discontent they aroused was strongest at times when they were relatively new and steadily increasing, and when peasant communities and households were still in the process of developing strategies to deal with them. Thus, in the central regions of Russia, peasant hostility to enserfment and the growth in restrictions and demands by the autocratic state was probably greatest in the second half of the sixteenth and the seventeenth centuries. Underlying grievances continued throughout the servile period, however, especially among seigniorial peasants required to perform labour obligations. Peasant resistance to enserfment and the growing demands made by the state continued in more outlying regions of Russia after the mid-seventeenth century, as the power of the landowning and ruling elites spread outwards from the centre in the train of peasant migration (see Chs 2 and 3). Seigniorial peasants whose forebears had been 'free' state peasants particularly resented the yoke of serfdom.[2]

There was a cultural dimension to general discontent. Russian peasants, and other members of the lower orders, became increasingly alienated by the growing 'westernisation' of the state and elites, which led to a 'cultural gulf' in Russian society. The cultural reformation of the elites began in the seventeenth century, but was given greater impetus by Peter the Great (1682–1725). He transformed and secularised the image of the ruler from 'Orthodox tsar' to a more distant 'Sovereign Emperor', and replaced the old capital of Moscow in central Russia with the new imperial capital of St Petersburg in the far north-west. Initially under pressure from Peter, many nobles, including officials and army officers, remodelled their customs, education, dress and houses on those of the social elites of north-west Europe. During the eighteenth century, many adopted western European languages, especially French, in place of Russian. With the exception of men conscripted into the army, cultural westernisation spread to the mass of the population very slowly, if at all, before the late nineteenth century. The cultural reformation of the state and elites also spread more slowly to outlying regions, where it provoked much hostility among the lower orders, not least because many Russians who lived there were Old Believers, who had rejected the reforms of the rites and ceremonies of the Russian Orthodox Church made by Patriarch Nikon in the 1650s, and who clung tenaciously to other old, Muscovite ways. The cultural transformation of the ruling and landowning elites was not complete. Many older traditions, including an ethos of paternalism, lived on, coexisting with newer, Western ways.[3]

The existence of both particular and general grievances among the Russian peasantry did not always lead to protests. One of the most striking features of the history of peasant protest in servile Russia is not how much active resistance there was, but how little. Part of the reason for this was that peasant communities were not always united against outside exploitation, but divided amongst themselves (see Ch. 6). Most Russian peasants, moreover, were fully aware that the balance of power and violence lay squarely in the hands of the authorities, who were in a position to deal with almost any outbreaks of open resistance or revolt.

An important precondition for open peasant protests, therefore, was not just causes of discontent but opportunities to resist. Opportunities for protest and revolt were greater in more outlying regions, further from the centre, where

---

2 See Kakhk, Yu. Yu. and Ligi, Kh. M., 'O svyazi mezhdu antifeodal'nymi vystupleniyami krest'yan i ikh polozheniem', *IS* (1976), no. 2, pp. 82–97; Usenko, O. G., 'Povod v narodnykh vystuplenniyakh XVII–pervoi polovine XIX veka v Rossii', *VMU (I)* (1992), no. 1, pp. 39–50; Kolchin, *Unfree Labour*, pp. 302–13; Fedorov, V. A., *Krest'yanskoe dvizhenie v Tsentral'noi Rossii 1800–1860* (Moscow, 1980), pp. 41–78. See also Scott, *Moral Economy*.
3 See Cherniavsky, *Tsar*, pp. 72–95; *id.*, 'The Old Believers and the new religion', *SR*, vol. 25 (1966), pp. 1–39; Raeff, M., *The Origins of the Russian Intelligentsia: The Eighteenth Century Nobility* (New York, 1966).

state control was relatively weak. Furthermore, countless thousands of peasants who lived within reach of frontier areas took the opportunity to flee there to escape oppression and exploitation. Opportunities were also provided by temporary weaknesses in the authority of the state and landowners, for example when Russia was involved in wars, as much of the army, which could otherwise have been used to put down rebellious peasants, was away fighting external enemies. Additional opportunities for peasants to protest were created by divisions within the landowning and ruling elites. The most striking example is the civil wars of the 'Time of Troubles' of 1598–1613 (see below). In later periods, discussion and implementation of rural reforms, especially if some officials and landowners opposed them, also created opportunities which were exploited by discontented peasants. Information about impending reforms or other opportunities for peasants to improve their position also sparked off peasant unrest, especially if peasants could claim some support from sections of the ruling elites.[4] The greater propensity of peasants in right-bank Ukraine than in Russia to rebel can be explained partly in this way. The Ukrainian peasants' Polish landowners were often at odds or in conflict with the Polish king (before the partitions of Poland of 1772–95) or the Russian authorities (after the partitions), thus providing peasants with regular opportunities to protest and revolt.[5]

FORMS

There were four main forms of peasant protest in Russia. The most extreme, and rarest, was open revolt, but more common were limited forms such as flight, disturbances known as '*volneniya*', and 'everyday resistance'. The form of protest peasants chose reflected not just the intensity of their grievances, but the opportunities open to them. Aware of the balance of force against them, peasants were usually concerned to make their protest while trying to minimise or avert the risk of provoking a violent reaction. Thus, peasants only very rarely resorted to violence, and usually put forward what they believed to be, or could present as, legitimate demands within the existing social order. The following discussion of the main forms of protest considers the nature and scale of protests, their causes and the opportunities which allowed peasants to act, their objectives and the consequences.

The four great revolts

The four great revolts were led by the cossacks Ivan Bolotnikov in 1606–07, Stepan Razin in 1670–71, Kondratii Bulavin in 1707–08, and Emelyan Pugachev

---

4 See Moon, *Russian Peasants*.
5 See Moon, D., 'Memories of the cossack era, the Haidamak movement, and the Koliivshchyna in right-bank Ukrainian peasant unrest in 1848', in Isayevych, Ya. and Hrytsak, Ya. (eds), *Druhii mizhnarodnii konhres Ukrainstiv. L'viv, 22–28 serpnya 1993 r. Dopovidi i povidomlennya. Istoriya,* pt I (L'viv, 1994), pp. 166–71.

in 1773–74. Each leader attracted much support, including some peasants, and put together motley rebel armies in the borderlands which, with the exception of Bulavin's, moved towards the centre of Russia. All the revolts resulted in thousands of deaths on both sides and destruction of much property. The leaders, also except for Bulavin, tried to legitimise their revolts by claiming to rebel 'in the name of the tsar' against the ruler's 'evil advisers', officials and nobles. Pugachev claimed that he was the late Emperor Peter III. The revolts had some early successes, but many of the rebels were inexperienced, poorly armed and ill-suited to fighting the Russian army. All four revolts ended in defeat. Most Soviet historians and a few of their Western counterparts tried to impose order on the chaos by categorising the revolts as 'peasant wars' which, they argued, were caused by and directed at serfdom and autocracy (or 'feudalism'). Several scholars have compared them with revolts in other pre-industrial societies.[6] However, both the nature and objectives of the Russian revolts are open to question, and the chaos which surrounded them hampers simple categorisation.

Origins and participants
Bolotnikov's revolt of 1606–07 was part of the civil wars of the Time of Troubles, when various factions, including members of both elites and lower orders, struggled for power and influence after the death of Ivan the Terrible's only surviving son and heir, Fedor, in 1598. Bolotnikov was a cossack and former slave. His rebel army included some peasants, mainly from the south-west of the Central Black Earth region. Most of the rebels, however, were cossacks, slaves and townsmen, and also included some nobles. The rebel army, like other factions during the Time of Troubles, fought in the name of a pretender who claimed to be another son of Ivan the Terrible, Dmitrii, who had in reality died in suspicious circumstances in 1591. The first 'false Dmitrii' had managed to seize the throne and rule for a year in 1605–06. The Time of Troubles lasted until after the election of Michael Romanov as tsar in 1613.[7]

The last three revolts are better seen as 'frontier rebellions' by sections of the population, albeit mainly the lower orders, of the borderlands.[8] All three were led by Don Cossacks, and had their origins in disputes between cossack hosts and the Russian state, and between rank and file cossacks and cossack

---

6 See Avrich, P., *Russian Rebels, 1600–1800* (New York, 1972); Buganov, V. I., *Krest'yanskie voiny v Rossii XVII–XVIII vv.* (Moscow, 1976).

7 See Perrie, M., *Pretenders and Popular Monarchism in Early Modern Russia: The False Tsars of the Time of Troubles* (Cambridge, 1995); Stanislavskii, A. L., *Grazhdanskaya voina v Rossii XVII v.: Kazachestvo na perelome istorii* (Moscow, 1990); Dunning, C., 'R. G. Skrynnikov, the Time of Troubles, and the "First Peasant War" in Russia', *RR*, vol. 50 (1991), pp. 71–81; Danning, Ch., 'Byla li v Rossii v nachale XVII veka krest'yanskaya voina?', *VI* (1994), no. 9, pp. 21–34.

8 Nol'te, G.-G., 'Russkie "krest'yanskie voiny" kak vosstaniya okrain', *VI* (1994), no. 11, pp. 31–8. See also Khodarkovsky, M., 'The Stepan Razin uprising: Was it a "peasant war"?', *JGO*, vol. 42 (1994), pp. 1–19; Alexander, J. T., *Emperor of the Cossacks: Pugachev and the Frontier Jacquerie of 1773–1775* (Lawrence, KN, 1973), esp. pp. 185–7, 206–20; Madariaga, *Russia*, pp. 239–55, 268–73, esp. pp. 270–3; Raeff, M., 'Pugachev's rebellion', in *id.*, *Political Ideas and Institutions in Imperial Russia* (Boulder, CO, 1994), pp. 234–67, esp. p. 254.

officers. At issue was the decline in the cossacks' traditional autonomy and privileges as the state extended its power and demands to the steppe frontier where they lived. The Razin and Bulavin revolts began as rebellions by rank-and-file Don Cossacks and recently arrived fugitive peasants. The Pugachev revolt broke out among disaffected Yaik Cossacks in the Southern Urals region.[9] Although many cossacks were of peasant descent and, from the mid-eighteenth century, many rank-and-file cossacks became more like militarised state peasants, it is inaccurate to see cossack participation in and leadership of the revolts as surrogate peasant participation and leadership. Cossacks were a distinct social group from peasants, and their interests clashed as often as they coincided.[10]

The last three revolts involved people from a variety of other groups in the southern and eastern borderlands. Inhabitants of the towns seized by Razin along the lower and middle Volga were prominent among his supporters. Pugachev had less urban support, but his army included many industrial serfs who worked in the mines, foundries and factories of the Urals. Large numbers of Finnic and Turkic peoples of the Volga basin joined Razin's revolt, and many Bashkirs and other non-Russians supported Pugachev. Members of the social elites of some non-Russian peoples participated in the revolts, but hardly any members of the Russian social elites took part in the last three revolts. Many of the Russians who took part in the last three revolts were Old Believers.[11]

Russian peasants were, thus, only one group among several involved in the revolts, and usually a minority. Bulavin's revolt was mainly a cossack affair, but there were outbreaks of peasant unrest in parts of the Central Black Earth region adjoining the Don Cossack territory. Russian peasants took part in large numbers only in the Razin and Pugachev revolts. Razin's advance up the Volga in the summer of 1670 sparked off widespread peasant revolts throughout much of the Mid-Volga region and the extreme south-east and east of the Central Non-Black Earth and Central Black Earth regions. In the final stage of his revolt in the summer of 1774, Pugachev moved into the Mid-Volga region, took Kazan', but was immediately routed by a government army. The rebel leader and the remains of his forces fled south through the territory to the west of the Volga, igniting peasant revolts on a slightly smaller scale than in 1670 in the Mid- and Lower-Volga regions and the south-easternmost part of the Central Black Earth region. However, when Bolotnikov's, Razin's and

9 See Avrich, *Russian Rebels*, pp. 59–69, 147–55, 180–3, 187–90; Khodarkovsky, 'Stepan Razin', pp. 4–7; Pavlenko, N. I., 'K voprosu o roli donskogo kazachestva v krest'yanskikh voinakh', in Tikhvinskii, S. L. (ed.), *Sotsial'no-ekonomicheskoe razvitie Rossii* (Moscow, 1986), pp. 62–75; Longworth, P., 'Peasant leadership and the Pugachev revolt', *JPS*, vol. 2 (1974–75), pp. 183–5.
10 See Yaresh, L., 'The "Peasant Wars" in Soviet historiography', *ASEER*, vol. 16 (1957), p. 244; Stanislavskii, *Grazhdanskaya*, esp. pp. 44, 124, 247; Khodarkovsky, 'Stepan Razin', pp. 4–5. See also Ch. 1.
11 See Avrich, *Russian Rebels*, pp. 23–5, 31–2, 40, 74–6, 80, 88–91, 99–100, 145–7, 156–61, 196–203, 216–17, 230–1; Khodarkovsky, 'Stepan Razin', pp. 11–16; Solov'ev, V. M., 'K voprosu ob uchastii gorodskogo naseleniya v krest'yanskoi voiny pod predvoditel'stvom S. T. Razina', *IS* (1982), no. 2, pp. 143–50; Bodger, A., 'Nationalities in history: Soviet historiography and the Pugačëvščina', *JGO*, vol. 39 (1991), pp. 561–81.

Pugachev's rebel armies moved towards the central regions, where most Russian peasants lived and where serfdom had been established first, in spite of the fears of some landowners and officials and murmurs of discontent among some peasants, the mass of the Russian peasantry did not rise up. None of the revolts sparked off a massive peasant revolt against serfdom and the autocracy in the forest-heartland of Russia.[12]

Causes and opportunities
Peasants who took part in the revolts usually had specific grievances. During the final stage of the Pugachev revolt, for example, trouble was widespread on estates where peasants had recently been converted from *obrok* to *barshchina*, or where landowners had recently raised their obligations. The average level of seigniorial obligations throughout Russia seems to have increased in the mid-eighteenth century, on the eve of Pugachev's revolt.[13] In addition, all four revolts took place at times of acute stress, mainly as a result of wars, which had led to higher demands for taxes and conscripts. The Bolotnikov revolt took place during the civil wars of the Time of Troubles, the Razin revolt shortly after the end of the Thirteen Years' War (1654–67), the Bulavin revolt at the height of the Great Northern War (1700–21), and the Pugachev revolt towards the end of the Russo-Turkish War of 1768–74.

The underlying causes of peasant participation in the revolts are suggested by their location. All the areas where large numbers of peasants took part were in the southern and south-eastern borderlands, in particular the Mid-Volga, Lower-Volga and Don, and Southern Urals regions, and the extreme south-eastern areas of the Central Black Earth and Central Non-Black Earth regions. At the time of the revolts, these borderlands were still being settled. Serfdom and other constraints and demands were relatively new, and thus seemed most onerous. Many of the peasants in these regions, moreover, were migrants or fugitives who had left the central regions to escape serfdom and growing exploitation. The rebels were especially hostile to landowners and officials in Western, rather than Muscovite, clothes.[14]

The wars which contributed to the outbreak of revolts by increasing peasants' burdens led also to temporary weakening of state power, thus creating both discontent and opportunities to revolt. That the state was weakened during the Time of Troubles is self evident. Wars affected the power of the state at the time of the other revolts. After the Thirteen Years' War (1654–67), tsar Alexis disbanded part of his army, as he lacked the means to maintain it, and so did not have forces to hand to send against Razin's rebels. As a result of the Great Northern War (1700–21) and Russo-Turkish War (1768–74), large parts

12 See Avrich, *Russian Rebels*, pp. 5, 89–90, 102, 119, 158, 173–4, 224–38; Nol'te, 'Russkie'; Pavlenko, 'K voprosu', pp. 68–74; Hart, J., 'Razin's second coming: Pugachev's rebellion in the Middle Volga region, July–August 1774', in Bartlett, R. P. *et al.* (eds), *Russia and World of the Eighteenth Century* (Columbus, OH, 1988), pp. 506–20.
13 See Avrich, *Russian Rebels*, pp. 226, 291 n. 85; Mironov, 'Consequences', pp. 468–9. See also Ch. 3.
14 See Avrich, *Russian Rebels*, pp. 134, 146, 221.

of the regular army were away at the front when Bulavin's and Pugachev's revolts began.[15]

Opportunities for revolts to break out and gather momentum were greatest in outlying areas, where the state was still relatively weak. It is a reflection of the geographical expansion of Russian state power over the seventeenth and eighteenth centuries that each successive revolt began further from Moscow than the previous one. Bolotnikov's revolt began on the border with Poland, then only about 300 miles south-west of Moscow. Razin's and Bulavin's revolts broke out on the Don, around twice that distance from the centre of power. The last revolt, Pugachev's, started in what is now north-west Kazakhstan, about 650 miles south-east of Moscow and over 1,000 miles from St Petersburg. The weakness of state power in the borderlands can be contrasted with its strength in the centre. Each rebel army was heavily defeated by government forces when it approached central Russia. Pugachev was crushed at Kazan', 400 miles east of Moscow; Razin was defeated a little further down the Volga at Simbirsk; and Bulavin never left the Lower Don and Volga region. Only Bolotnikov reached Moscow, but only as a result of the anarchy of the Time of Troubles, and did not take the capital.[16] Opportunities for *peasants* to rebel were created not only by wars and the weakness of state power in the border-lands, but also by the fact that in each case the revolts had broken out earlier among cossacks and other groups of people. Peasants joined the Razin, Bulavin and Pugachev revolts in the later parts, when the authorities were already overstretched dealing with their initial stages.

Objectives

All four rebel leaders issued proclamations in which they made various prom-ises in attempts to mobilise support. Bolotnikov promised property and noble status to slaves and the poor of Moscow if they murdered their masters and rich merchants. Two years later, the second 'false Dmitrii' promised peasants and slaves their masters' property and wives if they joined him.[17] When Razin advanced up the Volga in 1670, he sent out emissaries with 'seditious letters', addressed to 'all the common people', in which he proclaimed he was going to the Russian heartland to establish the cossack way of life 'so that all men will be equal'. He called on '[w]hoever wants to serve God and the sovereign, and the great host, and Stepan Timofeevich [Razin]' to help eliminate the 'traitors' and 'bloodsuckers' of peasant communes. In 1708, Bulavin sent out 'incendiary leaflets' to peasants in areas near the Don Cossack territory exhort-ing them to 'annihilate the boyars, Germans and profiteers' and to 'plough for themselves'.[18]

---

15 See Avrich, *Russian Rebels*, pp. 1, 53, 134–5, 182, 240; Keep, *Soldiers*, pp. 80–7; Raeff, 'Pugachev's rebellion', p. 234.
16 See Nol'te, 'Russkie'; Perrie, *Pretenders*, pp. 109–30; Alexander, J. T., *Autocratic Politics in a National Crisis: The Imperial Russian Government and Pugachev's Revolt, 1773–1775* (Bloomington, IN, and London, 1969).
17 Perrie, *Pretenders*, pp. 63, 87–90, 125–8, 171–3, 189–90.
18 Avrich, *Russian Rebels*, pp. 89 (quotation), 156–8; Khodarkovsky, 'Stepan Razin', pp. 12–13.

The most prolific writer (or, as he was illiterate, dictator) of proclamations was Pugachev. In the name of 'the Sovereign Emperor Peter III', he made promises to different groups of people to gain their support, backed up by threats for those who refused. His first decrees, in the autumn of 1773, were addressed mainly to cossacks and non-Russian peoples. In the winter of 1773–74, when revolt moved into the Urals where there were many industrial serfs, Pugachev promised to postpone, reduce or abolish the poll tax and levies of conscripts, and to lower the prices of salt and vodka.[19] In the summer of 1774, when Pugachev and his rebel army arrived in the Mid-Volga region, they found themselves for the first time in an area where there were large numbers of agricultural peasants on seigniorial estates. Pugachev adapted his decrees accordingly. The most radical were issued in the towns of Saransk and Penza, in the Mid-Volga region, on 28 and 31 July 1774, when the rebels were fleeing south after their defeat at Kazan'. The decrees proclaimed:

We grant to all who formerly belonged to the peasantry, in subjection to the landowners, the status of faithful subjects of our own crown, and We reward them with the ancient cross and prayers, heads and beards, with freedom and liberty and eternal cossackdom, without demanding recruit levies, the poll tax and other monetary dues, and with possession of the land, with forests, hayfields, fisheries and salt lakes, without payment or dues . . . and we free all them from the taxes and oppressions formerly imposed on the peasants . . . by the nobles and the bribe-taking judges . . . . And we wish you the salvation of your souls and a peaceful life on earth, for which we endured . . . a wandering exile and not a few misfortunes from the aforementioned villainous nobles . . . We command . . . those who formerly were nobles on their . . . estates, those opponents of our power and disturbers of the Empire and destroyers of the peasantry [are to be] caught, punished and hanged, and treated in the same way as they, having no Christianity in them, treated you, peasants. On the extermination of [these] opponents and villainous nobles, everyone can enjoy a quiet and peaceful life, which will last forever.[20]

The rebel leaders' promises reflected only what they thought peasants wanted in return for their support, and thus cannot be taken as statements of Russian peasants' actual objectives. To some extent, however, peasants' objectives can be inferred from their responses to the proclamations. In each case, rebel leaders' appeals prompted some peasants to rise in revolt. Before we can try to understand the objectives of these peasants, however, we need to consider why some peasants were willing to believe in the pretenders and were prepared to act on the basis of rebel proclamations.

19 See Alexander, *Emperor*, pp. 59–123; Avrich, *Russian Rebels*, pp. 191–203.
20 See Perrie, M., '"Class ideology" or "social psychology"? Russian peasant consciousness in the Pugachev revolt', unpublished paper presented to Conference 'Peasant Culture and Consciousness', Bellagio, Italy, January 1990. (Cited with author's permission. I have made minor changes to the translation.)

One of the most striking features of the four revolts was that they were aimed not against the tsars, but their 'villainous' advisers, the evil boyars, nobles and officials. With the exception of Bulavin, all the leaders claimed to be rebelling in the name of a pretender to the throne. Pretenders were quite common in seventeenth- and eighteenth-century Russia, and also appeared periodically in other pre-industrial societies. Russia after the end of the old ruling dynasty in 1598 proved very fertile ground for the succession of men who claimed that Ivan the Terrible's son Dmitrii had not died, that he was Dmitrii, and had come back to recover his throne from the boyars who had tried to do away with him and usurp his birthright. It was in the name of 'tsar Dmitrii' that Bolotnikov led his rebel army to Moscow in 1606. In 1670 Razin included in his entourage a false tsarevich Alexis, who he claimed was tsar Alexis's eldest son who had, in reality, died suddenly a few months earlier. Razin announced that the tsarevich had managed to escape from boyars who had tried to kill him, and that he, Razin, had been ordered by the tsar to lead a revolt against the traitors. Bolder was Pugachev's claim to be Peter III. The real Peter III had reigned for only a few months in 1762, before being deposed, succeeded by his wife, Catherine the Great, and killed. The story Pugachev told the Yaik Cossacks in 1772 was typical of pretenders' explanations for their reappearances. He claimed that he had escaped his murderers, spent the intervening years wandering abroad, before returning to Russia, where he had seen the sufferings of the common people at the hands of the nobles and officials. He now intended to go to St Petersburg, send Catherine to a nunnery, reclaim his throne, and deliver his subjects from oppression.

In spite of the improbability of an enlightened, German-born prince having a reputation as a 'just tsar' and being seen by Russian peasants as their benefactor, there were good reasons why the real Peter III could have appeared in this light. During his short reign he had carried out a series of acts which favoured peasants or appeared to do so. His controversial withdrawal of Russia from the Seven Years' War ensured that there was no levy of recruits that year, or for several years to come. He abolished compulsory state service for nobles altogether. It has been argued that some peasants saw this as a precursor to the abolition of serfdom. Since the state had originally bound peasants to nobles' estates in return for nobles serving the state, then it followed that if nobles were no longer obliged to serve, then peasants should no longer have obligations to the nobles. There is little evidence, however, that peasants actually thought along these lines. But peasants did understand some of Peter III's other measures as beneficial. He relaxed restrictions on Old Believers, many of whom were peasants, and allowed schismatics who had fled abroad to return. He banned merchants from buying peasants to work in factories and mines. Most importantly from the peasant point of view, he secularised church land and peasants, thus converting church peasants to state peasants, reduced their dues, and gave them the titles to their land. When Peter III disappeared suddenly in June 1762, and was succeeded by his wife who promptly reversed his decree on secularisation, it was only a short step in the popular imagination to a belief that Peter III had been deposed by nobles and officials to stop him converting the nobles' peasants to state peasants, i.e. abolishing serfdom. Therefore, Peter III was an 'appropriate prototype' for a 'just tsar', and Pugachev was the only one of many 'willing actors' who posed as Peter III.[21]

It is hard to accept at face value that many Russian peasants really did believe Pugachev was who he claimed to be. However, Pugachev tried to live up to his imposture. He issued proclamations and decrees in the name of Peter III, and set up his own court which aped that in St Petersburg. Moreover, most of Pugachev's peasant supporters never actually saw or met him, and so had no way of verifying his claim at first hand. There were, however, innumerable reasons for doubt, news of which probably spread just as quickly as information about his claim and promises. Pugachev was a crude, cossack deserter who bore little resemblance to the portrayal of Peter III on official documents, seals and coins, and he could not read or write Russian, let alone German. He seriously undermined his claim by marrying a local cossack woman while Peter III's wife, Catherine, was still alive. The release of Pugachev's real wife and children from prison in Kazan' in July 1774 almost sent the whole edifice of pretence crashing to the ground. Nevertheless, many Russian peasants were prepared to place their hopes in crude adventurers, like Pugachev and his predecessors, who told fantastic stories and led revolts.

Belief in pretenders was ambiguous. Peasants and others who rebelled in the names of pretenders created a world of suspended reality that lasted until the harsh truths of the real world returned and their belief was exposed as fantasy. While reality was in suspense and the belief lasted, it can be seen as a legitimising devise used by rebels to try to justify and give legal sanction to actions they would otherwise not have risked taking. The belief was a licence for them to act as they wished. Thus, the actions of peasant-rebels in the name of pretenders may give clues to their objectives.[22]

The best evidence for the objectives of peasant-rebels in the unreal world of revolts in the name of pretenders is to be found in their responses to Razin's and Pugachev's proclamations. In 1670, many Russian peasants in the Mid-Volga region and parts of adjoining regions responded to Razin's appeals. They attacked, plundered and burnt the property of landowners, monasteries and officials, and destroyed documents, such as title deeds to estates and tax registers, which recorded the power of landowners and the state to exploit them. Some peasants killed their landowners, but more handed them over to rebel cossacks to be dealt with. Many nobles and officials fled in fear of their lives. Pugachev's arrival in the Volga basin in the summer of 1774 and his dramatic proclamations were followed by peasant revolts in much of the

21 See Longworth, P., 'The pretender phenomenon in eighteenth-century Russia', *P & P*, no. 66 (1975), pp. 61–84; Perrie, *Pretenders*, pp. 1–6, 239–46; Avrich, *Russian Rebels*, pp. 94–5, 139–42, 176, 183–91 (contrary to Avrich's claim, Peter III did not lower the salt tax; this was done by Catherine: see Ch. 3); Raeff, 'Pugachev's rebellion', pp. 239–40, 244–5.
22 See Avrich, *Russian Rebels*, pp. 228–9; Field, D., *Rebels in the Name of the Tsar* (Boston, MA, and London, 1989; 1st edn 1976), pp. 208–14; Madariaga, *Russia*, p. 240. On Pugachev's attempts to live up to his pretence, see Longworth, 'Leadership', pp. 187–93.

region. Some peasants left their villages to join Pugachev's army. Others formed
rebel bands, arming themselves with pitchforks and scythes. They roamed the
countryside, ransacking landowners' property, burning documents, and sometimes slaughtering nobles and officials who had not already fled. Most peasants remained in their villages. Some called on the rebels to come and deal
with landowners and stewards who had earned their hatred. Other peasants
seized their landowners and estate officials and sent them to the rebels for
summary justice. Three hundred landowners who had been handed over by
peasants were executed in Saransk during the three days Pugachev and his
army were camped outside the town. There were similar scenes at other rebel
encampments. In some villages, peasants took matters into their own hands,
beating up or killing their owners and estate managers as well as looting their
property.

The destruction and murder were not all indiscriminate. In both 1670 and
1774, some peasants distinguished between 'bad' landowners who had treated
them harshly, whom they singled out to be killed, and 'good' landowners
who had treated them well, whom they spared. On an estate in Saratov province in 1774, peasants saved the lives of the family of the *philosophe* Alexander
Radishchev (who was away at the time) by hiding them from the rebels.
Nevertheless, during the final stage of the Pugachev revolt, around 1,000
nobles, officials, army officers and clergy, including women and children, were
killed by rebels, many in a brutal manner. Most were hanged, bludgeoned to
death, shot, stabbed or beheaded. Many women were raped before they were
murdered.[23]

During the revolts there was a thin dividing line between social protest,
on the one hand, and brigandage and vengeance, on the other. During all four
revolts, the rebel armies, including peasants, degenerated into bands of looters
in captured towns and estates. Some peasants took the opportunity provided
by revolts to settle long-standing grievances by punishing or killing cruel and
exploitative landowners and estate officials. The fact that many peasants were
reluctant to take matters into their own hands, preferring to await the arrival
of the rebels or hand 'miscreant' landowners over to the insurgents, suggests
a degree of caution or risk avoidance. In the event of the restoration of law
and order – and the return of reality – the peasants' hands would be clean, and
they could blame the murders on the rebels.

But the objectives of peasant participants in the revolts were not simply
seizure and destruction of property and murderous revenge against selected
members of the social elites. The attacks on 'bad' landowners who had
oppressed, exploited and mistreated their peasants, taken together with the
cases in which peasants spared or protected 'good' landowners, suggest that

23 Avrich, *Russian Rebels*, pp. 89–93, 102, 119, 224–38; Alexander, *Emperor*, pp. 161–77, 184–5.
Excluding those killed during the Pugachev revolt, a few hundred landowners and stewards were
murdered by peasants between the 1760s and 1850s (Semevskii, *Krest'yane*, vol. 1, pp. 413–18;
Ignatovich, *Pomeshchich'i*, 2nd edn [1910], p. 256), but these numbers have to be seen in the
context of the enormous size of the population.

some peasants may have been content simply with landowners who demanded lighter obligations and treated them well. Thus, the objectives of some peasants who took part in the revolts may have been limited to redress of particular grievances and an amelioration of their condition inside the existing order, including even the continuation of serfdom, but under 'good masters'.

This does not mean that some peasants who took part in the four great revolts did not have broader objectives. An Old Believer factory serf from the Urals who was captured during the Pugachev revolt told the authorities:

> Who Pugachev was did not trouble us, nor did we even care to know. We rose in order to come out on top and to take the place of those who had tormented us. We wanted to be masters and to choose our own faith . . . Had we won, we would have had our own tsar and occupied whatever rank and station we desired.

Such views were less common among peasants than among cossacks. As well as his other pronouncements, Pugachev spoke of making Yaitsk, the Yaik Cossacks' capital, the capital of Russia, and the Yaik Cossacks the new elite. In 1670 Razin had told his followers that he intended to march on Moscow, destroy the boyars, bring freedom to the 'common people', and establish the cossack way of life throughout Russia. These ideas conjure up an image of a 'world turned upside down', in which the hierarchical social system was left unchanged, but some people improved their positions within it. In other words, some rebels, including some peasants, did have broader objectives. They wished to replace the 'masters', and live off the labour of others in the same way as the old 'masters' had done.[24]

Some historians have maintained that the rebels were fighting to realise higher objectives outside the existing social and political order. Some Soviet historians, guided more by Marxist–Leninist ideology than by the evidence, asserted that the four 'peasant wars' had the revolutionary objective of overthrowing the existing 'feudal' order and preparing the way for 'capitalism'.[25] A little less implausibly, other historians argued that the rebels aimed to realise a vision of a new, utopian social order based on an idealised version of cossack self-government under a 'just tsar' who cared for his people. 'Freedom' (*volya*) would be obtained by eliminating the hated nobles and officials, who stood

---

24 See Avrich, *Russian Rebels*, pp. 89, 231–2 (quotation), 292; Khodarkovsky, 'Stepan Razin', pp. 12–13; Perrie, *Pretenders*, pp. 246, 249; Ryndzyunskii, P. G. and Rakhmatullin, M. A., 'Nekotorye itogi izucheniya Krest'yanskoi voiny 1773–1775 gg.', *IS* (1972), no. 2, pp. 82–5; Solov'ev, V. M., 'Aktual'nye voprosy izucheniya narodnykh dvizhenii', *IS* (1991), no. 3, pp. 137–9.
25 See Buganov, V. I., 'Ob ideologii uchastnikov krest'yanskikh voin v Rossii', *VI* (1974), no. 1, pp. 44–60; Indova, E. I., Preobrazhenskii, A. A. and Tikhonov, Yu. A., 'Lozungi i trebovaniya uchastnikov krest'yanskikh voin v Rossii XVII–XVIII vv.', in Cherepnin, L. V. (ed.), *Krest'yanskie voiny v Rossii* (Moscow, 1974), pp. 239–69; Mavrodin, V. V., 'Ideologiya vosstavshikh', in *id.* (ed.), *Krest'yanskaya voina v Rossii v 1773–1775 gg.: Vosstanie Pugacheva*, 3 vols (Leningrad, 1961–70), vol. 2, pp. 413–43. Other Soviet historians challenged this view: see Ryndzyunskii and Rakhmatullin, 'Nekotorye', pp. 82–5.

between the tsar and his people, abolishing serfdom, and creating a society based on equality rather than hierarchy.[26]

This view drew on the work of the Soviet folklorist K. V. Chistov. He addressed the question of the peasants' objectives by interpreting the stories about the pretenders as 'popular socio-utopian legends' about 'returning deliverer tsars'. He argued that they represented the hopes and ideals of the Russian peasantry, and served as a radical, secular 'ideology' for popular revolts in the name of a 'returning deliverer tsar'. He traced the origins of the 'legends' to the end of the sixteenth century, and argued that they existed until the mid-nineteenth century, i.e. for the duration of serfdom. Chistov examined the stories about the false Dmitriis and later pretenders, including the false Peter IIIs, and identified several common features: the 'tsar-deliverer' intends to carry out social reforms, but is dethroned by the evil boyars who intend to kill him; the 'deliverer' manages to escape, sometimes miraculously, but has to hide or wander the land for several years before returning and revealing himself to the people; in spite of opposition from the boyars and the ruling tsar, the 'tsar-deliverer' regains the throne, rewards his supporters, punishes the traitor-boyars, and carries out reforms, including abolishing serfdom. One of the implications of Chistov's argument was that the ideals expressed in the 'legends' created an environment in which pretenders could emerge and gain popular support because they embodied the aspirations of the common people. In other words, it was the 'legends' that came first, not the pretenders.[27]

Maureen Perrie has questioned Chistov's view. She argued that the 'legends' about the false Dmitriis during the Time of Troubles simply reflected the stories the pretenders made up to explain their 'escapes' from death and re-appearances. She discovered that some of the stories Chistov cited about the false Dmitriis were current only among literate people outside Russia, and cannot be seen as evidence for the existence of 'popular socio-utopian legends' about 'returning deliverers' among the Russian peasantry in the early seventeenth century. Moreover, Perrie has also pointed out that, in contrast to the folklores of several European societies, the Russian folk tradition did not contain stories about 'sleeping kings' who would return to save their people. There was no equivalent of King Arthur in Russian folklore. Thus, Perrie has turned Chistov's interpretation on its head, and argued that it was the pretenders who came first, not the 'legends'.[28]

Is Perrie's criticism of Chistov's view valid for the 250 years after the Time of Troubles? There is much similarity between the Peter III 'variant' of Chistov's 'popular legends' and the story Pugachev made up to explain 'his'

26 See Avrich, *Russian Rebels*, pp. 46–7, 117, 173, 249–50, 256–7, 321–2; Longworth, P., 'The Pugachev revolt: The last great cossack peasant rising', in Landsberger, H. A. (ed.), *Rural Protest: Peasant Movements and Social Change* (London, 1974), pp. 220–30, 241–3.
27 Chistov, K. V., *Russkie narodnye sotsial'no-utopicheskie legendy XVII–XIX vv.* (Moscow, 1967), pp. 24–236, esp. pp. 30–2.
28 Perrie, *Pretenders*, pp. 4, 35–7, 42, 64–9, 111–12, 241, 245.

escape from Catherine's supporters in 1762 (see above, p. 246). Moreover, parts of Pugachev's story were repeated in some of his proclamations and, thus, brought to a larger audience. Pugachev's claim, and similar stories told by earlier, false Peter III's, thus seem to have predated and prompted the spread of the stories about the return of Peter III.[29]

While Chistov's 'popular socio-utopian legends' about 'returning tsar-deliverers' may not have existed separately from actual pretenders for most if not all of the seventeenth and eighteenth centuries, it is possible that the periodic appearance of pretenders who told similar stories contributed to the creation of a new tradition. A good example is the rumours which spread about the Grand Duke Constantine after 1825. His renunciation of the throne on the death of Alexander I in 1825, and the abortive Decembrist revolt by aristocratic officers during the interregnum, led to rumours that Constantine had been deposed by the officers because he intended to grant the peasants freedom from serfdom. These stories spread immediately, before the appearance of a pretender, but did not provoke any revolts in Constantine's name.[30] The fact that rumours about Constantine and the earlier pretenders were told and retold by peasants suggests that they had some sympathy with their contents. It is likely, moreover, that they embellished the stories with their own ideas and aspirations. Even though Russian peasants did not invent the stories, or the idea of 'returning deliverer tsars', in all probability many were familiar with the idea of a ruler who had been deprived of the throne somehow returning and enacting major reforms in their favour. Some may even have hoped that this would happen.[31]

What is the significance of the stories about 'returning deliverer-tsars' for elucidating peasants' objectives? Chistov argued that the 'legends' were part of a tradition of *secular* radicalism among the Russian peasantry, and implied that they could be taken at face value as expressions of peasants' objectives. Other historians, however, especially non-Soviet specialists, have drawn attention to obvious parallels between the stories and Christian beliefs in the second coming of Christ and the establishment of the Millennium (see Revelation, 20: 1–5). Many Old Believers, some of whom supported Razin and who were more prominent among Bulavin's and Pugachev's followers, identified Peter the Great (or his father Alexis) with AntiChrist, and believed the end of the world was nigh. Perrie suggested, moreover, that there were magical overtones to the apparent 'resurrections' of men who were supposed to be dead, as they echo a contemporary popular belief in Russia that sorcerers could raise themselves from the grave.[32] Such beliefs may seem incredible to people

---

29 See Perrie, *Pretenders*, p. 250.
30 See Rakhmatullin, M. A., 'Legenda o Konstantine v narodnykh tolkakh a slukhakh 1825–1858 gg.', in Yanin, V. L. (ed.), *Feodalizm v Rossii* (Moscow, 1987), pp. 298–308.
31 On rumours, see Moon, *Russian Peasants*, esp. pp. 165–75.
32 See Solov'ev, 'Aktual'nye', pp. 138–9, 141; Siegelbaum, L. H., 'Peasant disorders and the myth of the tsar: Russian variations on a millenarian theme', *Journal of Religious History*, vol. 10 (1979), pp. 223–35; Cherniavsky, 'Old Believers', pp. 13–33; Perrie, *Pretenders*, pp. 64–9, 111–12, 245–6.

educated in the rational, 'modern' intellectual world. They would have seemed more tangible in the mental world of Russian peasants before the twentieth century, a world almost untouched by the ideas generated by the Scientific Revolution and the Enlightenment. Nevertheless, it is probable that stories about former rulers rising from the dead, returning and ushering in a utopian social order rang true for Russian peasants only in another world, the miraculous and magical supernatural world of hopes and dreams, which peasants were all too well aware was separate from the real world in which they lived, worked, and continued to be oppressed.

Consequences

There were examples of successful revolts involving peasants in some pre-industrial societies. In most cases, such as early modern China, the elites were either very weak, or divided amongst themselves with the peasant-rebels allied to one faction. The long-term consequences of such victorious revolts, however, were often simply the replacement of the old elite with a new one, and the continued existence of a hierarchical social structure, or the return of such a structure after a short interlude.[33] Some historians have suggested that the Russian revolts led by Razin and Pugachev might have won if they had advanced on Moscow at the start of their risings. This seems improbable. Over the seventeenth and eighteenth centuries the growing might of the Russian state and its armed forces made the prospect of a successful popular revolt, in the borderlands as well as the heartland, increasingly unlikely. A popular revolt in which the poor and weak triumphed over the rich and powerful was not, and was never likely to be, achieved in tsarist Russia prior to the twentieth century. Instead, those who took part in the four great revolts of the seventeenth and eighteenth centuries faced the bitter consequences of defeat. All four leaders were executed or killed. The authorities carried out merciless campaigns of retribution against the populations of insurgent areas. After Razin's defeat, punitive forces razed entire villages in the Mid-Volga region and executed their inhabitants. Eye-witnesses described the gruesome sight of captured rebels hanging from gibbets on rafts floating down the Volga as examples to others. There were similar reprisals after Pugachev's defeat.[34]

Peasant participation in the four revolts was also counterproductive in the long term. The revolts led to the reinforcement, rather than weakening, of the existing social order. In March 1607, at the end of Bolotnikov's revolt, tsar Vasilii Shuiskii increased landowners' control over their peasants by extending the period during which they could recover fugitives from five to 15 years. The state continued to intensify serfdom. Richard Hellie asserted that the Bolotnikov revolt and Moscow riots of 1648 led to an 'alliance' between the state and landowners, which was cemented by the completion of the enserfment of the peasantry by provisions of the 1649 Law Code. Hellie went on

---

33 Solov'ev, 'Aktual'nye', pp. 137–8; Scott, *Weapons*, pp. xv–xvi.
34 See Avrich, *Russian Rebels*, pp. 43–4, 103–15, 167–72, 239–45; Solov'ev, 'Aktual'nye', p. 136.

to argue that the Razin and Bulavin revolts further strengthened the alliance between all noble landowners and the state against the threat from below.[35] The Pugachev revolt of 1773–74 reinforced the coalition between state and nobles. Catherine secured it with her 'Charter to the Nobility' of 1785, which confirmed their rights and privileges. The revolt spurred the empress to speed up her provincial reform. The reform, announced in November 1775, increased state control over the provinces, reducing the chance of a revolt similar to Pugachev's breaking out and taking hold again.[36] The defeat of Pugachev's revolt was followed by the completion of the long-standing state policy of 'harnessing' the cossack hosts. The state ensured the loyalty of cossack officers by raising their status to that of Russian nobles in the 1780s, while allowing the position of rank-and-file cossacks to decline. Less reliable hosts, for example the Zaporizhzhian Cossacks of southern Ukraine, were disbanded. Cossacks later became staunch supporters of the Russian state, depriving potential future popular revolts of possible leaders.[37]

The response of the government and landowners to the revolts was not confined to repression, but included some limited concessions. On 17 March 1775 Catherine issued a proclamation, to mark the end of the war with Turkey the previous summer, in which she bestowed various 'favours' on her subjects. She ended some minor taxes, wrote off some arrears, granted amnesties to some army deserters and fugitive peasants, and released some prisoners. She laid down that seigniorial peasants who had been freed by their owners could not be re-enserfed. In addition, she granted a general pardon to all participants in the Pugachev revolt who had not already been punished, ordered all investigations to cease, and commuted outstanding death sentences to penal servitude. She justified the concessions by attributing the participation of many people in the revolt to 'stupidity, ignorance or superstition', rather than treachery. There were further measures. The provincial reform of 1775 contained provisions for estates of landowners who mistreated or made excessive demands on their peasants to be taken into trusteeship (see Ch. 3). Catherine's main reaction to the Pugachev revolt, however, was to try to forget about it. She consigned the revolt to 'eternal oblivion'. Furthermore, Boris Mironov has detected a decline in the real level of seigniorial peasants' *obrok* after the 1770s, and speculated that landowners may have been persuaded to reduce their demands by the revolt.[38]

Not all the empress's concessions in her proclamation can be attributed to a desire to prevent a repetition of the Pugachev revolt. Many would have been forthcoming anyway, because it was the custom for rulers to grant 'favours' at the end of wars. Some of the measures, moreover, were consistent with a

---

35 Hellie, *Enserfment*, pp. 108, 329 nn. 34 and 35, 138–42, 246–9, 381 n. 110. *Cf.* Koretskii, *Formirovanie*, p. 369.
36 See Alexander, *Autocratic*, pp. 227–45, 251; Madariaga, *Russia*, pp. 277–303.
37 Longworth, *Cossacks*, pp. 178–80, 224–35, 242.
38 *PSZ*, 1, vol. XX, pp. 82–6, no. 14275 (17 March 1775); Alexander, *Emperor*, pp. 197–9; Mironov, 'Consequences', p. 469.

general trend in legislation in eighteenth-century Russia aimed at 'protecting' the mass of the population (see Ch. 3). Nevertheless, all the concessions Catherine granted in 1775 were fairly trivial in comparison with the scale of the revolt, the demands of some of the participants, and the extent of the repression.

No concessions had been forthcoming after the previous revolts. Thus, Russian peasants lost far more than they gained from the participation of some of their numbers in the four great revolts. This reality was reflected in folklore. Although there was a large body of folklore which presented 'Sten'ka' Razin as a popular hero (see below, pp. 278–9), Vladimir Solov'ev has drawn attention to some folk songs and tales which were hostile towards Razin. He argued that this reflected a view among many Russians that violent revolt was futile and only made the position of the people worse, and that injustice was better than disorder.[39]

In the borderlands after 1774, and in the central regions throughout the servile period, most Russian peasants preferred, or had little choice in accepting, some degree of accommodation with the state and seigniorial authorities. There was no revolt involving Russian peasants on anything approaching the scale of the Pugachev revolt until the rural revolutions of 1905–07 and 1917–21. This did not mean that Russian peasants accepted their lot and bore it with fatalistic submission. Peasants continued to protest against the landowning and ruling elites after 1774, as they had done between the four revolts, but most resorted to non-violent and sometimes non-confrontation forms of protest, which were less likely to provoke a massive reaction by the authorities, and more likely to lead to some improvement in their lives.

Flight

The second main form of peasant protest was flight. From the end of the sixteenth century, most Russian peasants were bound to the land and banned from moving without permission. The authorities backed up these bans by measures to find, punish and return fugitives to their previous homes and owners (see Ch. 3). Nevertheless, peasants continued to move illegally throughout the following three centuries.

Causes and origins

Peasants had various motives for fleeing their homes. Some flight was local and short-term. This was common throughout Russia, including both central and outlying regions, and over the entire period. Individual peasants ran off and hid for a while, often in forests near their villages, to avoid punishment, registration in the tax censuses, or recruitment. Other fugitive peasants, including whole families and even entire village communities, fled greater distances,

---

39 Solov'ev, V. M., 'Russkaya fol'klornaya traditsiya o Razinskom vostanii', *VMU (I)* (1995), no. 5, pp. 19–29. *Cf.* Longworth, P., 'The subversive legend of Sten'ka Razin', *Rossiya/Russia: Studi i ricerche a cura di Vittorio Strada*, no. 2 (1975), pp. 17–40.

and were gone for longer periods if not permanently.[40] This sort of flight was part of the larger process of peasant migration, legal and illegal, to the border-lands discussed in Chapter 2. Some idea of the scale of peasant flight can be gauged from the poll tax censuses. Between 1719 and 1727, around 200,000 male peasants were absent from their places of residence, and in 1727–41, 327,046 were 'in flight'. This was around 5 per cent of the total taxable population.[41]

There were regional patterns in the origins of peasant flight. Like authorised migrants, fugitives left the 'old borderlands' of Russia, where ever greater restrictions and obligations were imposed on peasants by the expansion of state control, seigniorial landownership and serfdom from the central regions. Growing population put pressure on the land resources of the old borderlands as well as central Russia. From the mid-sixteenth century into the eighteenth century, there were constant streams of illegal migrants from the peripheries of the forest-heartland and the north-western parts of the Central Black Earth and Mid-Volga regions. With the further expansion of state and seigniorial exploitation, the origins of most peasant flight moved to more outlying regions. In the eighteenth and nineteenth centuries, many fugitives fled from the south and east of the Central Black-Earth and Mid-Volga regions, and from parts of the Lower-Volga and Don and Southern Urals regions and western Siberia.[42]

Most runaway peasants had particular reasons to leave their villages. Peasants fled the estates of exploitative and harsh landowners. Increases in peasants' obligations, reductions in land allotments, and excessive punishment were com-mon motives.[43] Many peasants fled in wartime to escape the state's demands for additional taxes and recruits.[44] Poor harvests and the threat of famine also compelled peasants to move off, especially if the estate or local authorities were unwilling or unable to offer them assistance.[45] After the schism in the Russian Orthodox Church in the 1660s, many Old Believers and members of religious sects fled the central regions to escape persecution.[46] Opportunities for peasants to flee were created by lax enforcement of the restrictions on peasant movement in the areas they fled from, the existence of places where fugitive peasants could hide or avoid being caught, for example forests and the greater anonymity of towns, and the proximity of border areas where state

40 See Kozlova, *Pobegi*, pp. 56–9; Snezhnevskii, V. I., 'K istorii pobegov krepostnykh v poslednei chetverti XVIII i v XIX stoletiyakh', in *Nizhegorodskii sbornik*, vol. X (1890), pp. 522–3, 548, 550; Ignatovich, *Pomeshchich'i*, pp. 303–4.
41 Alefirenko, P. K., *Krest'yanskoe dvizhenie i krest'yanskii vopros v Rossii v 30–50-kh godakh XVIII v.* (Moscow, 1958), p. 95; Kabuzan, *Narodonaselenie*, pp. 170–1.
42 See Blum, *Lord and Peasant*, pp. 157–63; Koretskii, *Zakreposhchenie*, pp. 235–6, 267–9; id., *Formirovanie*, pp. 83–4; Kozlova, *Pobegi*, pp. 37–43, 48; Alefirenko, *Krest'yanskoe*, pp. 97–100; Rakhmatullin, M. A., *Krest'yanskoe dvizhenie v velikorusskikh guberniyakh v 1826–1857 gg.* (Moscow, 1990), pp. 73–7.
43 See Kozlova, *Pobegi*, pp. 57–60; Semevskii, *Krest'yane*, vol. 1, pp. 395–6; Snezhnevskii, 'K istorii', pp. 519–22; Okun', S. B. (ed.), *Krest'yanskoe dvizhenie v Rossii v 1850–1856 gg.: Sbornik dokumentov* (Moscow, 1962), p. 605.
44 See Smirnova, T. I., 'Pobegi krest'yan nakanune vystupleniya S. T. Razina', *VI* (1956), no. 6, pp. 129–31; Alexander, *Emperor*, p. 165.
45 See Koretskii, *Zakreposhchenie*, pp. 267–9; Moon, *Russian Peasants*, pp. 41–6.
46 Cherniavsky, 'Old Believers', p. 4.

control was weak and fugitives could also escape detection. Sometimes local populations and officials in frontier areas connived with fugitive peasants, allowing them to stay instead of handing them over to the authorities to be returned to their previous homes (see below, pp. 259, 261).

Objectives and destinations

Flight was a result not just of 'push' causes inducing peasants to flee their homes, but also of 'pull' causes attracting them to other places. Many fugitive peasants had fairly clear ideas about their destinations. In the sixteenth and seventeenth centuries, many peasants moved from the estates of one land-owner to another if they thought they could get a better deal, for example lower obligations, more land, and assistance in times of dearth (see Ch. 3). Many fugitives sought wage labour in the ports along the river Volga and Black Sea coast, and in industrial cities, including Moscow and St Petersburg.[47] The main destinations of fugitive peasants, however, were the outlying regions of Russia. Peasants moved from the old to the new borderlands. From the late sixteenth century until well into the eighteenth century, fugitives moved to the Mid-Volga and Central Black Earth regions, especially the south-eastern parts, and further afield to the Lower-Volga and Don and Urals regions and to Siberia. From the early eighteenth century, however, peasants began to flee from some of these areas, to escape the expansion of state authority and serf-dom, and moved further afield to the open steppes along the lower reaches of the Don and Volga rivers and to the north of the Black Sea and the Caucasus Mountains. Peasants also fled across the Urals to Siberia, and beyond to the Kazakh steppe and Altai Mountains. Until the first partition of Poland in 1772, many peasants fled from the North-western region of Russia across the Polish border.[48]

Most peasants who moved to outlying regions aimed to build better, freer and more secure lives for their families in areas where they hoped the restrictions and demands of the state and landowners would be less onerous, or non-existent, and there would be more land to farm. Thus, the objectives of many fugitive peasants seem to have been limited to escaping from particular griev-ances and to making some improvement in their lives, while continuing to live as peasant farmers. Fugitives who aimed to work as wage labourers also had limited objectives. Even though some fugitive seigniorial peasants sought to escape from serfdom by registering as state peasants or townspeople, the statuses they aspired to were still part of the lower orders of Russian society. The objectives of all these fugitives were inside, and did not fundamentally

---

47 See Kozlova, *Pobegi*, pp. 33–5, 48–9, 111–27; Snezhnevskii, 'K istorii', pp. 533–4; Rakhmatullin, *Krest'yanskoe*, pp. 70–1. On migrant labour see Ch. 4.
48 See Koretskii, *Zakreposhchenie*, pp. 235–6, 267–9; id., *Formirovanie*, pp. 83–4; Kozlova, *Pobegi*, pp. 30–2, 44–51; Alefirenko, *Krest'yanskoe*, pp. 96–100, 107–11; Semevskii, *Krest'yane*, vol. 1, pp. 399–408; Ignatovich, I. I., *Krest'yanskoe dvizhenie v Rossii v pervoi chetverti XIX v.* (Moscow, 1963), pp. 443–7; Rakhmatullin, *Krest'yanskoe*, pp. 71–7; Mamsik, T. S., *Krest'yanskoe dvizhenie v Sibiri: vtoraya chetvert' XIX v.* (Novosibirsk, 1987), pp. 79–97; Treadgold, *Great*, pp. 25–6, 30, 71–2.

challenge, the existing social order. Indeed, the state wanted to settle its frontiers with Russian peasants (see Ch. 2).

Some fugitive peasants had higher objectives, which were on the fringes of the existing order. Large numbers of peasants fled to the cossack hosts along the southern and south-eastern frontiers. Several cossack hosts, including those of the Don, the north Caucasus, and Zaporizhzhia, had long traditions of admitting fugitive peasants from central Russia and Ukraine. Some fugitives were granted cossack status. On occasions, the Russian authorities sanctioned the conversion of peasants into cossacks. But, for most of the time, they made ever more insistent demands that cossacks hand over fugitive peasants to be returned to their owners.[49] A rough guide to the scale of peasant flight to the cossack hosts is the rapid increase in the numbers of cossacks. Between the 1720s and 1860, the number of male Don Cossacks (the largest host) increased from 29,000 to 304,000. A tenfold increase in under a century and a half, well above the average rate of natural growth of the total Russian population, can be explained only by the continued admission of new members, including runaway peasants.[50]

The initial attraction of cossackdom to fugitive peasants was not the possibility of land which they could cultivate free from the demands of landowners and the state. For a long time, well into the eighteenth century, cossack hosts banned farming in their territories, as they associated farming with peasants, and peasants with serfdom and oppression, which were anathema to them. Rather, fugitive peasants were drawn by the cossacks' freer lifestyle, with its tradition of raiding and exemption from taxation. Fugitives were also attracted by the chance to share in the subsidies the cossack hosts received from the Russian state in return for defending the steppe frontier. For a long time, cossackdom offered fugitive peasants the prospect of a radical improvement in their lives, even a 'world turned upside down', in which they would be part of a privileged elite, which did not pay taxes and was supported partly by state subsidies. In marked contrast to their previous lives, therefore, runaway peasants who managed to join the cossacks lived at the expense of others, mostly peasants, who paid the taxes which funded the subsidies. Cossack status was not an option for more than a minority of Russian peasants, however, and increasingly only for a small number of the fugitives who reached the hosts. It was also a possibility which was disappearing with the decline of the cossack way of life. In any case, cossackdom was never a viable alternative for the mass of the Russian population.[51]

The cossack elites became increasingly concerned that allowing ever greater numbers of fugitive peasants to join them would not only exacerbate the tensions with the Russian authorities, who wanted them to return runaways, but lead to a reduction of their shares of the subsidies they received from Moscow. Cossack officers began to keep larger amounts of the subsidies for

49 See Longworth, *Cossacks*, pp. 126–8, 177–8.
50 Kabuzan, *Izmeneniya*, p. 70 (1720s); *MGSR*, Krasnov, *Zemlya Voiska Donskogo*, p. 201 (1860).
51 See Stanislavskii, *Grazhdanskaya*, esp. p. 44; Avrich, *Russian Rebels*, pp. 65–6.

themselves, generating tensions within the hosts as lower-ranking cossacks and new arrivals insisted on receiving part. In 1666, on the eve of the Razin revolt, a Don Cossack named Vasilii Us led a party of several hundred poor cossacks and peasants up the Don towards Moscow. They intended to ask tsar Alexis to take them into service in return for a subsidy. As the party approached Tula, however, it dispersed on news that a detachment of troops had been sent against it.[52] In subsequent decades, lower-ranking cossacks and new arrivals failed to persuade the cossack elites to share the subsidy with them. Nevertheless, cossack hosts continued to attract fugitive peasants even as the cossack officers became more like the noble landowners in the areas the runaways had fled from and as the cossacks' freer way of life was eroded by the state. (See above, p. 253.)

Other fugitive peasants may have had higher objectives, outside the existing social order. The folklorist Chistov claimed to have identified another genre of 'popular socio-utopian legends' about 'far-off lands'. Russian peasants, he claimed, fervently believed they would find freedom, justice and expanses of vacant, fertile earth in distant locations. Some 'legends' described apparently imaginary lands, such as 'Belovod'e' ('White Water'). Others spoke of real places: 'the new line' (the fortified lines along Russia's south-eastern frontiers); the river Dar'ya (the Syr and Amur Dar'ya rivers in central Asia); Anapa (a fortress on the north-east coast of the Black Sea). Chistov maintained that these 'legends' played an important role in enticing peasants to flee their homes and, to a large extent, were expressions of their hopes and ideals, which they projected onto distant lands. They became 'distant but bright lights on their horizon . . . a colourful mirage, which called and led them, forced them to sever centuries-old roots binding them to the land that had been tilled by their forebears.' In other words, Chistov argued that the 'legends' came first, not the 'far-off lands'.[53]

Chistov's interpretation of 'legends' about 'far-off lands' is liable to similar objections to those levelled at his views on 'legends' about 'returning deliverer tsars' (see above, pp. 250–2). Contrary to the impression created by Chistov, the general themes of many 'legends' were reasonably accurate descriptions of the situation in some of Russia's borderlands, and were thus based on reality rather than myth. State and seigniorial oppression and exploitation were less severe in the borderlands than in the central regions. Land was in greater supply and more fertile in the steppe zone than in the more densely populated and less productive forest-heartland. (See Chs 2 and 3.) More specifically, several of Chistov's 'legends' were not legends at all, but information which had reached peasants about current government policies encouraging the settlement

52 Avrich, *Russian Rebels*, pp. 65–6.
53 Chistov, *Russkie*, pp. 237–326 (quotations from p. 317). For similar views, see Kleyankin, A. V., 'S Volgi-na legendarnuyu "Reku Dar'yu"', *VI* (1971), no. 6, p. 149; Mordovtsev, D. L., *Nakanune voli* (St Petersburg, 1889), p. 23. Although Chistov was concerned with secular utopias, there are obvious parallels with the biblical 'promised land' flowing with 'milk and honey' (Exodus, 3: 8).

of certain frontier areas in return for privileges, including grants of land, loans, and exemptions from taxation and recruitment (see Ch. 2). In addition, the local authorities in some border areas were sometimes prepared to turn a blind eye to the illegal status of fugitive seigniorial peasants, and permitted them to settle. At certain times and in some places, the central authorities went along with this violation of the usual principle of returning fugitives. At other times and in other areas they did not, but the disagreement between local and central authorities created opportunities for fugitives to take advantage of. Thus, there were genuine possibilities for fugitive peasants who managed to reach particular frontier areas at certain times.

'Legends' about the possibility of free settlement along the 'river Dar'ya' in the mid-1820s seem to have been sparked off by the fact that, under the terms of a decree of 23 February 1823, a number of fugitive seigniorial peasants were exiled to Siberia (admittedly, a long way from the Syr and Amur Dar'ya rivers) instead of being sent home. News of this reached several villages in the Mid-Volga region in 1825, and was a contributory cause of the flight of several thousand peasants. Over 3,000 peasants were caught in Orenburg province, in the Southern Urals region, and were punished before being sent back. The decree was subsequently repealed. More specifically, the 'legends' concerning 'Anapa' in the 1830s were garbled versions of the policy of encouraging migration to the north-east coast of the Black Sea, where Anapa was located. Controversially, local authorities were permitted to allow fugitive seigniorial peasants to settle. The result was a wave of flights, mostly from Voronezh province in the south-east of the Central Black Earth region. Half a century later, in the 1880s, rumours spread that the tsar was offering land to peasants who moved to Siberia at precisely the time when the state did change its policy from hindering to encouraging peasant migration to Siberia, and was providing settlers with land and other assistance. Peasants received information about state settlement policy and the prospects of being accepted by local authorities in frontier areas from a variety of sources, for example migrant workers returning from border areas, emissaries from local officials in sparsely populated areas seeking labourers, and peasants who had fled earlier, managed to settle, and then returned to collect their families and fellow-villagers. Many peasants made careful preparations before setting out. They sent scouts to check that there was substance to the information they had received, and bought fake documents and passports.[54]

Most Russian peasants were too pragmatic to abandon their homes for an uncertain future simply in response to vague 'legends' about 'far-off lands'. The reality behind many of Chistov's 'legends' suggests that his interpretation can be turned on its head. It was real 'far-off lands' which presented genuine opportunities for fugitives to settle that came first, not the 'legends'. It is doubtful, moreover, that many fugitives had very high expectations about what

---

54 Compare Chistov, *Russkie*, pp. 305, 309–10, 316–17; Kleyankin, 'S Volgi', pp. 149–53, and Moon, *Russian Peasants*, pp. 23–61; Coquin, *La Sibérie*, pp. 411–20.

they could expect to find when they reached their destinations. In all likelihood, the objectives of many fugitives were no more than an improvement in their peasant lifestyles, inside the existing social order but further from the centre of power.

The only fugitive peasants in Russia who seem to have fitted Chistov's interpretation, and had objectives which transcended the existing order, were some religious dissenters. From the 1660s many fled from persecution to distant regions, for example the far north, the Urals, Siberia and the steppe frontier. Once dissenters had arrived in remote areas, many tried to establish utopian communities where they aimed to live according to their ideals in peace and harmony and supported by their own labour. More extreme sectarians carried on moving to ever more remote areas. In southern Siberia in the eighteenth and nineteenth centuries, groups of sectarians set off to find their 'promised land', which they called 'Belovod'e' ('White Water'). They established several communities in the Altai mountains, beyond the fortified line that marked the limit of Russian control.[55]

Some sectarians' searches took them much further. In 1877, when the explorer Nikolai Przheval'skii reached Lob Nor (a lake over 500 miles south of the Altai mountains in Chinese central Asia), he was amazed to learn from local inhabitants that a party of around 100 Russian sectarians had arrived there in 1861. They had taken Lob Nor for 'Belovod'e', and tried to establish a community. The environmental conditions were so harsh, however, that they had been unable to farm the land and had left. More remarkably, Donald Rayfield has pointed out that the word 'Lob' is cognate with an Indo-European root meaning white, and that 'Nor' is Mongol for lake. Thus, 'Lob Nor' really does mean 'White Water'. Some archaeologists who have examined mummified bodies found in the area have concluded that earlier inhabitants of the region were of Indo-European stock. It is also possible that this community was well known far beyond central Asia since it was on one of the routes of the Silk Road linking Asia and Europe. Nevertheless, even if this was the original 'White Water', how it came to be transformed into a promised land for Russian religious sectarians centuries later is likely to remain a mystery.[56]

Consequences

The consequences of peasant flight were mixed. Although less confrontational than revolts, flight still provoked a hostile response from the authorities. Indeed, one of the reasons the Russian state had banned peasant movement

---

55 Chistov, *Russkie*, pp. 239–89; Mamsik, T. S., *Pobegi kak sotsial'noe yavleniya: pripisnaya derevnya Zapadnoi Sibiri v 40–90-e gg XVIII v.* (Novosibirsk, 1978), pp. 6–21, 85–114; *id.*, *Krest'yanskoe*, pp. 178–205. See also Field, D., 'A far-off abode of work and pure pleasures' [review of Klibanov, A. I., *Narodnaya sotsial'naya utopiya v Rossii*], *RR*, vol. 39 (1980), pp. 348–58.
56 See Rayfield, D., *The Dream of Lhasa: The Life of Nikolay Przhevalsky, Explorer of Central Asia* (London, 1976), p. 98; Allen, T. B., 'The Silk Road's lost world', *NGM*, vol. 183, no. 3 (1996), pp. 44–51.

and enserfed a large part of the peasantry was the departure of many peasants from the lands of gentry cavalrymen to the estates of magnates and from the forest-heartland to the steppe frontier in the late sixteenth and early seventeenth centuries. (See Ch. 3.)

The scale of peasant flight was so large, and the economic and strategic advantages for the state in settling the borderlands so great, however, that the authorities regularly violated the principle that runaways were to be caught and returned. In some cases, the central authorities had little choice but to accept a *fait accompli*, and allow runaways to remain in frontier areas. In others, local authorities and cossacks connived with illegal migrants and permitted them to settle. One of the most striking examples took place in the mid-eighteenth century. The Russian government tried to lure fugitives who had fled across the border to Poland to return home by offering them pardons, permission to settle in villages belonging to the state or the court (i.e. not noble landowners), and temporary exemptions from taxes and recruitment. Contrary to the government's intentions, but all too predictably, some seigniorial peasants fled to Poland and then promptly turned around, went back, and presented themselves to the Russian authorities to claim the privileges for returnees, including freedom from serfdom. The government put a stop to this practice by banishing peasants who tried to use the law in this way to eastern Siberia.[57] The government was happier to allow some peasants to take advantage of its laws. In late eighteenth and early nineteenth centuries, many religious dissenters were sent to southern Ukraine and Transcaucasia. Others who followed voluntarily were allowed to remain.[58]

The lives of fugitive peasants were often difficult. Some became outlaws. Banditry was common in many parts of Russia in the seventeenth century, and remained a serious problem for the authorities along the lower Volga, the steppe frontier and other outlying areas until well into the nineteenth century. Brigands (*haidamaki*) were more widespread in Ukraine. Many fugitive peasants drifted to Russia's towns and cities, and eked out a meagre living on the fringes of the law. Hundreds of vagrants, including fugitive peasants, were expelled from St Petersburg after the Decembrist revolt in 1825.[59] Other fugitives found work in factories, in workshops or on the land. Many of the runaway peasants who reached cossack territories in the eighteenth and early nineteenth centuries ended up working as labourers on cossacks' farms. Fugitive peasants were often at the mercy of the people they worked for. Unscrupulous employers took advantage of their illegal status. In the early nineteenth century, a rich peasant in Nizhnii Novgorod province was found to be harbouring fugitives and using them as labourers on his land. He paid them

57 Belyavskii, *Krest'yanskii*, pp. 41–2.
58 Ismail-Zade, D. I., *Russkoe krest'yanstvo v Zakavkaz'e: 30-e gody XIX–nachalo XX v.* (Moscow, 1982), pp. 34–8.
59 See Keep, J., 'Bandits and the law in Muscovy', *SEER*, vol. 35 (1956–57), pp. 201–22; Eeckhaute, D., 'Les brigands en Russie du XVIIe au XIXe siècle', *RHMC*, vol. 12 (1965), pp. 161–202; Monas, S., *The Third Section* (Cambridge, MA, 1961), p. 49.

nothing, fed them only with bread (and occasionally vodka), and even built huts with underground exits and places to hide them in case the authorities searched his property. Many fugitive peasants simply ended up being re-enserfed by new owners, sometimes with more land than they had farmed before. Fugitive peasants who failed to attain even a limited improvement in their lives sometimes ran away again or returned home.[60]

In contrast, many fugitive peasants did find fewer restrictions, more land and greater opportunities in the borderlands. Although it is impossible to prove, probably the majority succeeded in establishing themselves and building new lives. Like all migrants, unauthorised or authorised, fugitive peasants had to work hard to overcome problems created by environmental conditions which were often unfamiliar and sometimes unsuited to their customary farming methods. They also had to deal with the hostility of some native peoples. Fugitive peasants who fled to Russia's borderlands could attain the freer way of life they sought only while frontier areas remote from state control still existed. Throughout Russia's 'new' borderlands, including cossack lands, the ever-growing tentacles of state control reached out to put an end to fugitives' newly found freedoms. From the late eighteenth century, the possibilities for escaping the control and demands of the Russian state by fleeing further south and east were diminishing as the frontiers of the Russian Empire moved ever further from the central regions and even the old borderlands. Soon there would be nowhere left to run to. (See Ch. 2.)

Peasant flight was more common in the earlier part of the period and in the borderlands. There is, thus, a rough similarity in the periodisation and geographical location of peasant flight and the four great revolts. However, peasant flight from outlying regions continued long after the end of the Pugachev revolt in 1774. Peasants who lived in the central regions, a long way from the areas where the revolts took place, were also remote from borderlands to which they could flee with any possibility of reaching their destination. Therefore, most Russian peasants in the central regions, and in larger parts of Russia in the latter part of the servile period, resorted to more limited forms of protest than revolt or flight.[61]

Disturbances (volneniya)

Many peasant protests have been classified as 'disturbances' (*volneniya*), in which groups of peasants confronted seigniorial and/or state authorities. These 'disturbances' were one of the most common forms of peasant protest in

60 See Chekmenev, S. A., 'Razvitie khutorskogo khozyaistva na Kubani i Stavropol'e v kontse XVIII–pervoi polovine XIX v.', *EAIVE 1966 g.* (Tallinn, 1971), pp. 298–309; Snezhnevskii, 'K istorii', pp. 534–7.
61 See Rakhmatullin, *Krest'yanskoe*, p. 80; Snezhnevskii, 'K istorii', pp. 589–92. *Cf.* Ryndzyunskii, P. G., 'K izucheniyu', p. 211.

Russia, especially in the central regions and in the last century of serfdom. One of their more striking features was the peasants' reluctance to use violence in case they provoked a more violent response from the authorities.[62]

Peter Kolchin has shown that many disturbances followed a fairly typical pattern. Most disturbances were collective protests, usually by a village or a group of villages. The role of village communes and their elders in organising disturbances has led many historians to stress the importance of communal solidarity in Russian peasant resistance. Kolchin contrasted the communal nature of peasant protest in Russia with individual resistance by slaves in the American south. However, the issue is not as clear cut. Since Russian village communes also served as the lowest level of seigniorial and state administration, their elders had mixed loyalties, and many used their positions to their own advantage and to the detriment of the rest of the peasants. Some peasants protested against communal elders who they thought to be siding with the landowners or state authorities. In such cases, one of the first actions by peasants in many disturbances was to elect new elders. An analysis of the ages of the 'leaders' of a sample of disturbances in the years 1826 to 1857 showed that younger peasants became increasingly prominent over this period. This suggests that older peasants, the traditional village elites, may have been losing their ability to maintain control over the younger generation. The role of peasant women in disturbances is harder to gauge. This is partly because village affairs were by custom largely a male preserve, and partly because the officials who reported on peasant unrest tended to concentrate only on the peasant 'leaders', who were usually male, and referred to the rest of the peasants as a 'crowd'. Research on peasant women in disturbances after 1861 has shown that they did play significant roles.[63]

Many disturbances started when a group of peasants made a particular demand to the estate management, landowner or local officials, or submitted a petition to higher authorities, for example an absentee landowner, the provincial or central authorities, or even the tsar. Peasant communities chose representatives to travel to provincial capitals or St Petersburg to present their petitions, and collected money to meet their expenses.[64] The grievances peasants articulated almost always concerned specific issues. Peasants complained if they felt the seigniorial or state authorities were demanding excessive obligations from them or denying them access to sufficient land, or if they had taken land away

62 The following section is based mostly on Kolchin, *Unfree Labour*, pp. 257–65, 272–7, 296–301, 303–13; Moon, *Russian Peasants*, pp. 17–22, 62–112. See also Koretskii, *Zakreposhchenie*, pp. 235–300; Alefirenko, *Krest'yanskoe*, pp. 136–50; Semevskii, *Krest'yane*, vol. 1, pp. 419–56; vol. 2, pp. 107–9, 155–8, 220–36; Rubinshtein, N. L., 'Krest'yanskoe dvizhenie v Rossii vo vtoroi polovine XVIII v.', *VI* (1956), no. 11, pp. 34–40, 45–51.
63 See Kolchin, *Unfree Labour*, pp. 269–78, 471 n. 34; Prokof'eva, *Krest'yanskaya*, pp. 200–9; Rakhmatullin, M. A., 'Vozrastnoi sostav vozhakov krest'yanskogo dvizheniya v Rossii (1826–1857 gg.)', *IS* (1984), no. 6, pp. 139–49; Engel, B. A., 'Women, men, and the languages of peasant resistance, 1870–1907', in Frank and Steinberg, *Cultures*, pp. 34–53. On intra-communal and household frictions in Russia, see Chs 5 and 6.
64 On the ambiguous legal status of peasant petitions, see Moon, *Russian Peasants*, p. 64.

from them, were treating them harshly or subjecting them to cruel punishments, or refusing to assist them in times of hardship. Arbitrary behaviour by local officials and neighbouring landowners was a frequent grievance among state peasants. Many petitions by seigniorial peasants claimed that their owners did not have the legal right to own them. The arrival of new landowners or estate managers sparked off disturbances if peasants were concerned that they would depart from accepted practices, demand higher obligations, or introduce other changes which they feared would adversely affect their condition. State reforms often provoked unrest, for example the disturbances that followed the reforms of the appanage and state peasants in the 1820s–40s, including the 'riots' against compulsory potato cultivation.[65]

Peasants sometimes backed up or legitimised the demands in their petitions by citing particular laws, including misunderstandings or misinterpretations, or occasionally biblical texts. Since relatively few peasants were literate and had access to legal documents, they sought help in writing petitions from people who could read and write, for example literate peasants who worked as communal or estate scribes, church readers, lower-ranking parish clergymen, petty clerks in the local administration, demobilised soldiers and migrant workers. These were usually people of limited means with some formal education who were seeking to supplement their incomes. Some had no qualms about taking advantage of peasants' illiteracy for profit.[66]

Russian peasants took advantage of whatever opportunities presented themselves to put forward their grievances. In 1766 Catherine the Great called on sections of the population, including state peasants, to send petitions and deputies to her Legislative Commission. Many state peasants made full use of this chance to present their grievances. On the few occasions when rulers visited the provinces, peasants deluged them with petitions. During Catherine's trip down the Volga in 1767 she was given several hundred petitions, some by seigniorial peasants. Government inspectors, who were sent out periodically to assess the quality of local administration, were also swamped with peasant petitions.[67]

Peasants protested when they perceived that the landowning and ruling elites were temporarily weak and when the demands made on them were very high, for example in wartime when peasants' underlying grievances were exacerbated by additional demands for taxes and recruits. The level of peasant

---

65 See Gorlanov, *Udel'nye*, pp. 80–90; Druzhinin, *Gosudarstvennye*, vol. 2, pp. 456–524. See also Chs 3 and 4.
66 See Indova, E. I. (ed.) *Krest'yanskie chelobitnye XVII v.* (St Petersburg, 1994); Raskin, D. I., 'Ispol'zovanie zakonodatel'nykh aktov v krest'yanskikh chelobitnykh serediny XVIII v.', *IS* (1979), no. 4, pp. 179–92; Kamkin, A. V., 'Pravosoznanie gosudarstvennykh krest'yan vtoroi poloviny XVIII v.', *IS* (1987), no. 2, pp. 163–73; Moon, *Russian Peasants*, pp. 8–10, 14–17, 88–106; Pomeranz, W. E., 'Justice from underground: The history of underground *Advokatura*', *RR*, vol. 52 (1993), pp. 321–40. For peasants citing scripture, see Okun', *Krest'yanskoe*, pp. 361, 646 n. 382.
67 See Freeze, G., *From Supplication to Revolution: A Documentary Social History of Imperial Russia* (New York and Oxford, 1988), pp. 11–13, 75–84; Alexander, J. T., *Catherine the Great* (Oxford and New York, 1989), p. 111; *RGIA, ff.* 1375–6, 1379–81, 1383–4, 1387.

unrest rose during Napoleon's invasion of Russia in 1812. There were serious outbreaks during the Crimean War (1853–56), when hundreds of peasants tried to volunteer for short-term service in temporary militias, apparently in the belief that they could thus attain exemption from the much longer and hated term of regular military service, and freedom from serfdom.[68] Divisions within the landowning and ruling elites created opportunities for peasants to protest. In 1819–20 a dispute between the state authorities and the elite cossack land-owners of the Don, over the latter's right to own peasants, came out into the open and precipitated a wave of peasant protests.[69] In 1859 news leaked out that members of the central and local authorities were divided over the actions of many tax farmers and tavern keepers in selling vodka of lower quality and at higher prices than were required by law. The result was hundreds of riots against taverns by peasants who felt they had official support.[70]

At the heart of many disturbances were concerns among peasants that their subsistence or ways of life were being threatened by elite outsiders, or that landowners and officials were not treating them in the ways they expected. In most cases, however, peasants' demands were restricted to redress of particu-lar grievances and some amelioration in their condition. Very few peasants challenged the existing social order. Seigniorial peasants seeking freedom from serfdom did not demand the abolition of the entire institution. Most asked only to be converted to state peasants, who enjoyed greater freedom and lighter obligations but were still members of the lower orders.

Peasants involved in disturbances often refused to perform labour services or pay obligations while they were waiting for answers to their petitions or demands. In disputes involving a change of landowner, seigniorial peasants frequently refused to acknowledge the authority of the new owner until the case had been settled. Work stoppages were common, and quite effective, at peak times of the agricultural calendar. A prolonged suspension of work on seigniorial land at harvest time gave peasants some leverage as it was poten-tially very damaging to the landowner's economy.

Stewards, landowners or local officials responsible for villages where peas-ants were 'insubordinate' called on the local police if they were unable to settle disputes themselves. This was usually the point at which the documentation of disturbances begins, thus allowing historians to follow the authorities' ver-sions of the events that followed and their attempts to uncover the causes of the unrest. The first official to arrive at the scene was normally a local police official. His usual course of action was to summon the insubordinate peasants to an outdoor meeting, sometimes in the churchyard, and to try to persuade them to submit to authority and resume meeting their obligations. Exhorta-tions were backed up with threats of punishment. Parish priests were often called to admonish disobedient peasants. Some quoted the passages from the

68 See Valk, S. N. (ed.), *Krest'yanskoe dvizhenie v 1796–1825 gg.: Sbornik dokumentov* (Moscow, 1961), pp. 18–20, 280–310, 856–61; Moon, *Russian Peasants*, pp. 113–64.
69 Ignatovich, *Krest'yanskoe dvizhenie na Donu*.
70 Christian, *'Living Water'*, pp. 324–48.

New Testament in which Christ instructed people to obey the secular authorities and 'render unto Caesar what was Caesar's' (Matthew, 22: 21).[71]

If peasants continued to resist, representatives of ever-higher levels of officialdom travelled to the village to harangue the disobedient peasants and demand that they submit or face severe punishment. Villages where serious disturbances were taking place were often visited successively by more police officials, district and provincial marshals of the nobility, provincial governors, and staff officers of the corps of gendarmes. In the most serious cases, aides-de-camp were sent from St Petersburg on the orders of the tsar. The reports written by these officials speak of large, sullen crowds of 'stubborn' peasants refusing to listen to reason and exhortations to submit, rejecting negative replies to their petitions or complaints, and insisting that it was they who were in the right. Some peasants refused to accept that the officials who came to their villages were who they claimed to be, or that rejections of their petitions were genuine. This suspicion was in large part a result of peasants' experiences of the corruption and arbitrariness of local officials, and the extent to which the latter acted in the interests of the local nobles by whom some were elected.[72]

In extreme cases, officials tried to intimidate peasants into submission by sending for detachments of soldiers or, in outlying regions, cossacks. Insubordinate peasants were threatened with corporal punishment, arrest and trial. If these threats were not sufficient, then the authorities seized the peasants they believed to be the 'instigators' or ringleaders, and had them flogged in front of the others to encourage them to give up their protest. This was the stage when some disturbances dissolved into violence. Police reports describe how peasants used makeshift weapons against detachments of soldiers or officials, and how soldiers were 'compelled' to open fire 'in self-defence' on crowds of unruly peasants. The inevitable result in such cases was that peasants were killed or badly wounded. There were some massacres. One of the most serious was at Maslov Kut, in Stavropol' province in the north Caucasus, in 1853. The peasants of the settlement refused to accept their servile status, and demanded that they be returned to the state peasantry. After repeated exhortations had failed to persuade a crowd of over 2,000 to abandon their protest and disperse, the provincial governor, Major-General Volotskii, ordered a battery of artillery to open fire. Over 100 peasants were killed, and twice that number wounded.[73] This was exceptional, however, and most disturbances ended more peacefully.

After many disturbances the alleged instigators, ringleaders, peasants who had submitted petitions, and others adjudged to have played major roles in inciting the unrest and resisting the authorities were arrested and put on trial. The most common sentences handed down included corporal punishment, ranging from flogging to running the gauntlet between ranks of 500 men, terms of imprisonment, sometimes in penal labour battalions, exile to Siberia,

---

71 See Freeze, *Russian Levites*, pp. 179–83; Okun', *Krest'yanskoe*, p. 358.
72 See Moon, *Russian Peasants*, pp. 18–19, 187 nn. 51, 52; Ignatovich, *Pomeshchich'i*, pp. 60–7.
73 Okun', *Krest'yanskoe*, pp. 364–6, 647 n. 388.

and enlistment in the army. In the aftermath of more serious disturbances, detachments of troops were quartered in villages to make sure peasants kept their promises to obey the authorities, and to punish them by making them pay for the soldiers' upkeep.[74]

Disturbances did not always result only in repression and punishment, but sometimes led to concessions by landowners and the state. In 1851 peasants on an estate in Penza province owned by the statesman P. D. Kiselev complained about the tyrannical behaviour of the steward, who had overworked and beaten them, taken some of their livestock, and raped several young peasant women. After a protracted disturbance, for which several peasants were punished, Kiselev dismissed the steward and reorganised the estate management. This was just one of many examples of minor gains made by peasants who confronted their landowners or estate officials. The state authorities increasingly went to some lengths to investigate the causes of disturbances, and to find out whether they had been provoked by 'abuses of seigniorial authority'. On occasions, for example during a wave of unrest in 1826, the government ordered provincial authorities to maintain vigilance over the behaviour of landowners and estate managers. The authorities acted against some landowners, who were deemed to have been responsible for causing disorders, by taking their estates into 'trusteeship'. Some landowners were tried and punished. (See Ch. 3.) Peasant unrest was one factor which persuaded some senior officials to consider regulating relations between landowners and peasants. In 1853, after the massacre at Maslov Kut, Minister for Internal Affairs D. G. Bibikov ordered provincial authorities to enforce as law the recommendation made in 1797 by Emperor Paul that nobles limit labour services to three days a week (see Ch. 3).[75]

In the first half of the nineteenth century, the government bodies responsible for the administration of the appanage and state peasants took action against some local officials who were discovered to have provoked disorders by extorting money from peasants or otherwise taking advantage of their position for personal gain. For example, four appanage peasants in Kazan' province complained that a local official named Krasnov had taken bribes from them to protect their sons from being enlisted in the army in 1827. But, they claimed, because they had not paid him the full sums he demanded, he had deliberately selected their sons as recruits the following year. After a lengthy investigation, and in spite of his denials, Krasnov was dismissed. But the complainants' sons were not returned from the army. Other officials were dismissed after appanage peasants complained that they had extorted money from them. During the reforms of the state peasantry in the 1830s–40s, Kiselev, in his capacity as Minister for State Domains, worked to improve the calibre of local officials.

74 See Fedorov, *Krest'yanskoe*, pp. 120–1; Ignatovich, I. I., 'Krest'yanskie volneniya', in *VR*, vol. III, pp. 51–2.
75 See Semevskii, *Krest'yane*, vol. 1, pp. 213–28; *id.*, *Krest'yanskii vopros*, vol. 2, pp. 573–5; Kolchin, *Unfree Labour*, pp. 259–65, 296–301; Fedorov, *Krest'yanskoe*, pp. 121–5; Rakhmatullin, *Krest'yanskoe*, pp. 167–87; Okun', *Krest'yanskoe*, pp. 386, 649–50 n. 403.

Many who had abused their authority, and provoked peasant discontent, were dismissed.[76]

The authorities took account of some views expressed by peasants in disturbances. Peasant unrest during famines, especially those of 1821–22 and 1833–34, helped persuade the government to enact measures to improve the provision of famine relief. In 1841–42 Kiselev opposed the idea of compulsory communal tillage to stock reserve granaries in state peasant communities on the grounds that it was contrary to the peasants' customs and thus 'inconvenient and dangerous'. He was aware that the recent introduction of communal tillage for this purpose among appanage peasants had provoked much resistance.[77] The wide-scale peasant protests in 1858–59 against the adulterated and expensive vodka sold in many taverns prompted some officials to put pressure on tax farmers and tavern keepers to sell spirits at the strengths and prices required by law. The protests further convinced members of the government of the necessity of abolishing the whole system of tax farming.[78]

Daniel Field has suggested that there was a large element of ritual in the behaviour of the protagonists during many disturbances. Peasants insisted that their complaints were legitimate and had been sent through the correct channels. They often supported their claims with resolutions passed by the village commune as well as references to laws and sometimes the Bible. Insubordinate peasants usually insisted on the total unity of the village community, expressed in the aphorism 'The commune is a great person' ('*Mir – velik chelovek*'). The officials involved in 'restoring order' also indulged in ritualised behaviour, which was based on the common idea among elite Russians that peasants were usually loyal and submissive, but on account of their ignorance, simplicity and gullibility, were easily led astray. Thus, they tried to persuade peasants to submit by insisting that they had been deluded by 'evil-minded people', and tried to find 'instigators' from the margins of or outside the village community to be punished. It is likely that many peasants went along with this notion as it enabled them to minimise the consequences of their actions. At the end of many disturbances, officials were content to accept 'open-hearted expressions of regret' and promises of submission by the majority of peasants, and the necessity of punishing only a handful of alleged instigators. Sometimes parish priests held services where the peasants confessed their error, asked for their sins to be forgiven, and promised to obey lawful authority. Many officials also demanded that peasants sign or make their mark on statements promising to obey. Disturbances often ended with a tacit agreement between the two sides to end the impasse. Officials were satisfied, because they could report that they had done their job and restored order. Estate authorities were satisfied,

---

76 See *RGIA, f.* 515, *op.* 18, *d.* 128, *ll.* 1–9 *ob.*, 28–31, 62 (see also *dd.* 11, 15, 16); Druzhinin, *Gosudarstvennye*, vol. 2, pp. 91–101; Adams, 'Reforms', pp. 29–32.
77 Ignatovich, I. I., *Bor'ba krest'yan za osvobozhdenie* (Leningrad and Moscow, 1924), pp. 113–88, esp. pp. 152–4; Druzhinin, *Gosudarstvennye*, vol. 2, pp. 48–9; Gorlanov, *Udel'nye*, pp. 22–3, 80, 83; *RGIA, f.* 515, *op.* 18, *d.* 165. See also Ch. 3.
78 Christian, *'Living Water'*, pp. 286–352.

because the peasants had submitted. And, in some cases, peasants were also satisfied because they had made their point, most had not endured severe punishment, and they had sometimes won small concessions.[79]

Disturbances after which the state and seigniorial authorities made some concessions to peasants were probably more common in the last century of serfdom than in the preceding period, but there is no doubt that they were greatly outnumbered by confrontations in which peasants gained nothing or suffered as a result of their protests. Even when concessions were made, the peasants' 'ringleaders' were still punished. This was probably to remind them that the balance of power still lay in the hands of the landowning and ruling elites, and as a warning against challenging authority in the future. The authorities made limited concessions in order to maintain the existing order by taking action against a few landowners and officials who had neglected or violated their 'obligations' towards peasants in their charge, or by taking some account of peasants' subsistence and other basic needs. Nevertheless, 'disturbances' served as a crude mechanism by which peasants and the landowning and ruling elites in Russia tried to resolve by negotiation some of the disagreements between them within the existing social order.

Everyday resistance

The fourth main form of peasant protest in Russia was 'everyday resistance'. Of all the forms of protest, this was the hardest to detect (by contemporary landowners and officials as well as historians), the most limited, the least confrontational, the most difficult to prevent, and the one in which peasants' objectives were the lowest. But for all these reasons, it was probably also the most successful. Many peasants, as a matter of course, tried to get away with reducing the restrictions and demands made on them by the landowning and ruling elites while, at the same time, trying to avoid detection and a hostile reaction. This form of protest seems to have been most common in the central regions of Russia and in the latter part of the servile period: in places and at times when the degrees of seigniorial and state control were greatest, and opportunities for more open forms of protest most limited.

Common forms of everyday resistance included theft and vandalism of estate property, poaching game, allowing livestock to graze on seigniorial pasture or woodland (there is even a word for this in Russian, *potrava*), and illegal timber cutting in seigniorial or state woodland (which also has its own word, *porubka*). If they could get away with it, peasants turned up late for their labour obligations and left early, kept the best labourers to work on their own land, and did not overstrain themselves. This attitude was summed up in several proverbs, for example 'to work as if on the landowners' land' ('*rabotat' slovno na barshchine*'). Landowners countered wilful poor work on the demesne

---

79 See Field, D. [review of Okun', S. B. and Sivkov, K. V. (eds), *Krest'yanskoe dvizhenie v Rossii v 1857–mae 1861 gg.* (Moscow, 1963)], *Kritika*, vol. III, no. 3 (1967), pp. 34–55.

by stricter supervision and requiring peasants to complete certain tasks rather than work for so many days.[80]

Peasants tried to reduce or evade their financial obligations by various expedients. The most common and simplest were under- or non-payment of *obrok* and taxes for as long as they could get away with, and constant requests to be permitted to pay less than they were supposed to and at a later date. Peasant households and communities ran up enormous arrears in their monetary dues to landowners and the state. Attempts to evade cash dues were common when the levels of household production and incomes had been reduced, for example by bad harvests, and when landowners and the state were demanding higher obligations. Many peasants managed to avoid paying some of their taxes during Russia's regular and onerous wars. Peasants tried to reduce or avoid their monetary dues at other times, and rich as well as poor peasants did so, suggesting that opportunities to pay less were as important as specific causes.[81]

Peasants showed much ingenuity in reducing their taxes. Until the mid-seventeenth century, when the main direct tax was assessed by the area of land peasants cultivated, many cut their tax liability by farming less land. Others cultivated plots in forest clearings, and hid them from the authorities or bribed them to turn a blind eye. Partly to overcome this problem, the land tax was replaced by a flat-rate tax on each household in 1645–79. Many peasants responded to the change by combining into larger households or postponing splitting into smaller ones to reduce the amount of tax per head they had to pay. One of the reasons Peter the Great moved to a poll tax near the end of his reign was to combat these tax-avoidance strategies. He was not completely successful. It took several attempts, and threats of drastic punishments, to compile a fairly accurate register of those eligible to pay the tax. And in 1724, the first year poll tax was collected, there was a shortfall of up to 25 per cent of the expected revenue. This was partly due to harvest failures, widespread outbreaks of disease, and the impoverishment of much of the population as a result of Peter's earlier massive demands to finance his wars. Some, but not all, of the shortfall was collected later. The reintroduction of the assessment of appanage and state peasants' obligations by the size of their land allotments in the late eighteenth and early nineteenth centuries was accompanied by a return to the practice of concealing cultivated land from the authorities.[82]

Peasants resorted to 'everyday resistance' against other obligations demanded by the state. Peasants went to great lengths to prevent themselves and members of their households from being recruited into the army. Richer peasants bribed recruitment officers or bought substitutes. Young men hid in woods

80 See Bohac, R. D., 'Everyday forms of resistance: Serf opposition to gentry exactions, 1800–1861', in *PECPER*, pp. 236–60; Rakhmatullin, *Krest'yanskoe*, pp. 60–6; Dal', *Tolkovyi slovar'*, vol. 3, pp. 324, 358; Ignatovich, *Pomeshchich'i*, pp. 160–1. On landowners' attempts to reduce shirking, see Ch. 3.

81 See Rakhmatullin, *Krest'yanskoe*, pp. 63–4; Neupokoev, *Gosudarstvennye*, pp. 76–9; Koretskii, *Zakreposhchenie*, pp. 248–9; Fedorov, *Pomeshchich'i*, pp. 242–5.

82 See Shapiro, *Agrarnaya istoriya . . . XVII v.*, pp. 180–3; Anisimov, *Podatnaya*, pp. 264–7; Gorlanov, *Udel'nye*, pp. 46, 73–9. See Chs 3 and 5.

when levies were being raised, feigned illness or disability, or even cut off their trigger fingers to make them unfit for service. In an attempt to stamp out self-mutilation, recruits without the requisite number of fingers were sent to labour battalions.[83] Peasants resisted the state monopoly on the production and sale of alcoholic drinks, an important source of revenue, by brewing and distilling their own beverages. In spite of the authorities' efforts to enforce the monopoly, some peasants continued to distil 'moonshine' (*samogon*) well into the eighteenth century and after.[84]

Peasants tried to cover up for petty acts of protest by lying, dissembling and feigning ignorance and stupidity. These were also useful 'weapons of the weak' for peasants involved in other forms of protest. Many fugitives realised that they could not be returned to their previous homes if they did not reveal where they were from, or claimed to have forgotten. As a result, there was a special category of fugitives who could not remember their names or places of origin ('*nepomnyashchii rodstva*'). The authorities combatted this strategy by sending many such fugitives to the army or penal servitude.[85] Peasants who appeared before police investigations behaved in a similar manner. Donald MacKenzie Wallace concluded:

> the . . . majority of . . . peasants, when dealing with the authorities, consider the most patent and barefaced falsehoods as a means of self-defence . . . [W]hen a muzhik is implicated in a criminal affair, and a preliminary investigation is being made, he probably begins by constructing an elaborate story to explain the facts and exculpate himself. The story may be a tissue of self-evident falsehoods from beginning to end, but he defends it valiantly as long as possible. When he perceives that the position which he has taken up is utterly untenable, he declares openly that all he has said is false, and that he wishes to make a new declaration. This second declaration may have the same fate as the former one, and then he proposes a third.[86]

A related strategy was 'false compliance' with the symbols and laws of the ruling elite. In his influential and thought-provoking study of peasant protest in the second half of the nineteenth century, Field suggested that Russian peasants' protestations of allegedly 'naive' faith in the tsar may have been a more conscious tactic to try to reduce punishment for rebellion by manipulating official 'myths' of peasant monarchism. In a similar manner Russian peasants often 'misunderstood' items of legislation to be in their favour, and then tried to act on the basis of their interpretations to attain certain objectives under a cloak of legality. There is clearly a connection, moreover, between this sort of behaviour and that of peasants who joined the revolts led by or in the name of pretenders.[87]

---

83 See Bohac, 'Mir', pp. 652–66; Wirtschafter, *From Serf*, pp. 18–19. See also Ch. 3.
84 Christian, '*Living Water*', pp. 28–9.
85 Moon, *Russian Peasants*, pp. 26, 39–40.
86 Wallace, *Russia*, vol. 1, p. 327.
87 See Field, *Rebels*, pp. 209–12; Moon, *Russian Peasants*.

The objectives of peasants involved in everyday resistance were mostly limited to small reductions in the restrictions and demands imposed on them, in other words, smoothing down the sharp edges of oppression and exploitation to make their daily lives a bit less arduous. In particular, peasants wanted the demands made on them by outsiders to be flexible and to be adjusted in line with changes in their ability to pay, in particular those caused by bad harvests.

One of the problems in trying to assess the consequences of 'everyday resistance' is that much successful protest of this type escaped detection. The most successful everyday resistance would, by definition, have left little trace in the documentary record. To draw conclusions from silences in the written sources is rather problematic. To the extent that low-level protests were discovered and successful efforts to counteract them were made by the landowning and ruling elites, then they can be seen to have failed. However, the constant efforts by landowners and state officials to try to deal with the wide variety of strategies of everyday resistance provides evidence for the persistence of low-level protest, and that it achieved some marginal successes. That Russian peasants managed to frustrate the state's attempts to extract as much revenue as it wanted from them can be gauged from the high level of arrears peasants accumulated, the periodic changes in the main direct tax, and the regular occasions, often on the accession of a new ruler, at the end of wars, and during and after famines, when rulers wrote off tax arrears and postponed or cancelled levies of recruits. Evidence from the records of nobles' estates, moreover, suggests that peasants managed to establish some control over how much their landowners were able to take from them in dues and labour services.[88]

OBJECTIVES AND ACHIEVEMENTS

The objectives of all four main forms of peasant protest in servile Russia can be considered on different levels. At the first and lowest level, peasants aimed to resolve particular grievances and achieve some improvement in their condition, but without challenging the existing social and political order. Peasants insisted that the obligations demanded from them by the landowning and ruling elites were in conformance with their productive capacity, and were reduced, postponed or waived altogether in times of hardship. They insisted that landowners and the state offered them assistance when they needed it, in particular when the harvest failed; that they were provided with sufficient land to cultivate to support themselves and meet their obligations; that they were not subjected to excessive punishment; and that outside authorities did

---

88 See Hoch and Augustine, 'Tax censuses', p. 423; Dement'ev, E. I., 'Russkaya derevnya posle otechestvennoi voine 1812 g.', *IZ*, vol. 116 (1988), pp. 301–12; Fedorov, *Pomeshchich'i*, pp. 242–5; Neupokoev, *Gosudarstvennye*, pp. 76–80; Brooks, E. W., 'Reform in the Russian Army, 1856–1861', *SR*, vol. 43 (1984), pp. 63–82.

not upset the strategies they adopted in their households and communities to ensure their subsistence and livelihoods.

At this lowest level, therefore, peasants' objectives were limited to insisting that landowners and officials were 'good masters' who took account of their needs, and that rulers were '*batyushka*-tsars' who cared for the welfare of 'their peasants'. These objectives were limited to demands that elites acted in keeping with the paternalism many professed, and which, from the late eighteenth century, the state made some efforts to enforce. That relations between dependent 'clients' and elite 'patrons' have been marked by mutual obligations, as well as exploitation, has been the subject of much discussion in works on pre-industrial societies. The idea, or rather ideal, of reciprocity as a 'right', which was expected by the lower orders, has been developed by E. P. Thompson and James Scott in their seminal works on 'moral economies' in England in the early stages of industrialisation in the eighteenth century, and in south-east Asia as it came under colonial rule in the nineteenth and twentieth centuries.[89] It may be that many Russian peasants were prepared to meet their obligations to their landowners and the state as long as the latter fulfilled their 'obligations' to them. In Scott's words: 'Most subordinate classes are . . . far less interested in changing the larger structures of the state and the law than in what Hobsbawm has . . . called "working the system . . . to their minimum disadvantage".'[90]

The objectives of some of the peasants who took part in the four great revolts and who fled from their homes seem to have been restricted to this lowest level. But limited objectives were most common among peasants involved in 'disturbances' and 'everyday resistance', especially in the central regions of Russia and in the latter part of the servile period. Nevertheless, many Russian landowners and government officials were concerned that peasant protests were based on deeper underlying grievances, and had correspondingly higher objectives. In the first half of the nineteenth century, many members of the elites were worried that peasants aimed to overthrow serfdom by violent revolt from below. To some extent, however, this concern was based on fears of a repetition of the Pugachev revolt, rather than the actual level of peasant unrest or the aims peasants were putting forward. Heightened concerns about the prospect of revolts led some officials and landowners to exaggerate the scale of protests, especially in the last decade of serfdom.[91]

Peasants involved in some protests aimed to achieve a much more radical improvement in their position, but one which was still within the existing social order. These peasants wanted to turn the tables, become oppressors and exploiters themselves, and live at the expense of others in a 'world turned upside down'. This was clearly the aim of some peasants who took part in the

89 Thompson, 'Moral economy'; Scott, *Moral Economy*, esp. pp. 7, 32–3, 41, 45, 52, 157–92.
90 Scott, *Weapons*, p. xv. See also Ch. 3.
91 See Christian, '*Living Water*', pp. 321–4; Moon, *Russian Peasants*, pp. 63–4, 67–8; Nifontov, A. S., 'Statistika krest'yanskogo dvizheniya v Rossii 50-kh gg. XIX v.', in *Voprosy istorii sel'skogo khozyaistva, krest'yanstva i revolyutsionnogo dvizheniya v Rossii* (Moscow, 1961), pp. 186–8.

four great revolts in the hope of victory, and of some who fled to cossack hosts with the aim of abandoning the drudgery of agricultural labour for the less arduous and better-remunerated life of cossacks guarding the steppe frontier in return for subsidies from the tsars.

This higher-level objective was in keeping with the norms of Russian peasant society, and was not restricted to turning the tables on nobles and officials. The whole system of hierarchy in peasant households and communities involved some peasants, usually the older generation of male peasants or an elite faction, living in relative ease by passing the main burdens of work and obligations onto the younger generation of male peasants and their wives or subordinate groups. This objective was neatly summed up by Alexander Engel'gardt in 1881: 'Every peasant, if the circumstances are favourable, will exploit everyone else in the most splendid fashion, it is all the same whether it be a peasant or a lord, he will squeeze the juice out of him, will exploit his need.'[92] This higher-level objective implies an apparent belief among many Russian peasants that individuals could improve their position only at the expense of others, that there was little chance of all peasants improving their position simultaneously, or of the abolition of the existing social order and the establishment of a new order without oppression and exploitation. The idea that some people can get larger shares of the pie than others, but that the whole pie cannot get bigger (or be replaced by a new pie), has been detected by specialists on other peasant societies.[93]

These two levels of objectives, lower and higher, to some extent reflected the division in the causes of peasant protest into particular grievances and general factors made near the start of this chapter. Particular grievances prompted peasants to resolve them inside the existing order. More general discontent led some peasants to try to attain a radical change in their status, but still within the social order. The two levels of objectives also coincided partly with the forms of protest. The objectives of some peasants who took part in the four great revolts and some who fled to the frontiers were at the higher of the two levels. Most, if not all, peasants who confronted the authorities in 'disturbances' or opted for non-confrontational 'everyday resistance' had lower-level objectives, aimed solely at the redress of specific complaints. In addition, the objectives of seigniorial peasants were often more limited than those of state peasants. Many peasants who lived on nobles' estates sought simply transfer to the state peasantry. There is also some correlation between the two levels of objectives and the timing and geography of peasant protest in Russia. Peasants who protested in the earlier part of the servile period or in the borderlands for a longer period tended to have higher objectives than those of peasant-protesters in the central regions of Russia and in a larger area in the later part of the period. This suggests that peasants were more inclined to try to end or

---

92 Engelgardt, *Letters*, p. 223. See also Chs 5 and 6.
93 Foster, G. M., 'Peasant society and the image of the limited good', *American Anthropologist*, vol. 67 (1965), pp. 293–315.

substantially reduce exploitation and oppression when they were relatively new and increasing.

The most important factor determining the level of objectives of protesting peasants, however, was the opportunities open to them. For most peasants in central Russia, especially in the last century of serfdom, there was very little chance of attaining anything more than some limited concessions or slight improvements in their condition through limited and non-violent forms of protest. To have tried to achieve higher objectives by more confrontational and violent protests would, in all likelihood, have been doomed to failure and counterproductive.[94]

Some peasants involved in protests in servile Russia may have had even higher objectives, which were outside the existing social and political order and would have required its abolition to be realised. This third and highest level was a utopian vision of an ideal society based on equality, without obligations, with an abundance of land and, in some cases, under the benevolent authority of a 'just' tsar. The best evidence to support the idea that some Russian peasant protests aimed to create a utopian society comes from the views and actions of some religious dissenters who sought to establish ideal communities near or beyond the frontiers of the Russian state. It is harder to find much firm evidence that these views were the objectives of protests by other Russian peasants. When some of the other evidence that does seem to support this idea is subjected to closer scrutiny, moreover, much of it tends to evaporate.

The proclamations issued by the leaders of the great revolts, especially Pugachev, seem at first to support the idea that peasants aimed to create utopian societies, until it is remembered that the rebel leaders were not peasants, and that their promises were designed to attract supporters rather than serve as 'programmes' for a future society. Some of the more fanciful elements of peasants' alleged hopes for a better life in 'legendary' 'far-off lands' may have been added, consciously or unconsciously, by writers such as Chistov.[95] Some historians have argued that the facts that rebel peasants professed faith in the tsar and claimed to be rebelling in his name, and that many peasants sent petitions to the ruler in the hope of attaining justice, are evidence for a naive and idealistic peasant faith in the tsar. The type of monarchism that emerges when the evidence is examined more carefully, however, is manipulative and pragmatic rather than naive and utopian. Field has argued that peasants claimed to be rebelling in the name of the tsar in the hope of reducing the consequences for their actions by giving them a cloak of legitimacy. In a similar vein, peasants sent petitions to the rulers, not out of some naive belief that the tsars were on their side, but because they were the highest level of

---

94 See Moon, *Russian Peasants*, pp. 2–4, 165–81. See also Litvak, B. G., *Krest'yanskoe dvizhenie v Rossii v 1775–1904 gg.* (Moscow, 1989), pp. 151–2, 179–91; *cf.* Ryndzyunskii, P. G., 'O nekotorykh spornykh voprosov istorii krest'yanskogo dvizheniya v Rossii', *VI* (1987), no. 8, pp. 79–88.
95 See Chistov, *Russkie*, pp. 237–326. See also Mordovtsev, *Nakanune*, p. 23.

authority they could appeal to, and probably the only one likely to be above corruption. From the late eighteenth century, moreover, the small steps taken by Russia's rulers to offer peasants some degree of protection suggested that they might judge in favour of peasants against nobles and officials who were in breach of the law.[96]

Part of the problem in trying to find evidence for the idea that some Russian peasant protests were directed at creating an ideal society outside the existing order is that some people who have written about the Russian peasantry, including Populist intellectuals in late nineteenth-century Russia and a few subsequent historians, seem to have projected their own visions for a future just society onto the peasants. The result was an idealised misunderstanding of the aims of peasant protest which, in many ways, were similar to the persistent misinterpretations of other features of Russian peasant society, most notably communal and repartitional land tenure. Many apparently egalitarian features of Russian peasant life were not based on an abstract notion of equality for its own sake, but on the need to cooperate in order to subsist and ensure their livelihoods (see Ch. 6). The objectives of most Russian peasant protests were equally pragmatic and, for the most part, based on a realistic assessment of the circumstances.

The more limited the objectives of peasant protest, and the more limited and less violent the forms of protest, the more likely peasants were to achieve some of their goals. Throughout the servile period, some Russian peasants managed to achieve redress of particular grievances and reductions in the burdens imposed on them. The persistence and level of peasant arrears is evidence for the partial success of strategies of non- and under-payment. From around the mid-eighteenth century, moreover, concerns in the central government for the consequences both for revenues and for the social stability of completely unrestricted power over peasants by landowners and local officials compelled them to take some action against the worst excesses of corruption, extortion and 'abuses of authority'. Soviet historians overstated the causal connection between peasant unrest and reforms which made some concessions to peasants, for example the secularisation of the church peasants in 1762–64, the 1797 recommendation that landowners demand no more than three days' labour a week, and the reforms of the state peasants in the 1830s–40s.[97] To argue that there was no connection, however, would be to go too far in the other direction. For similar reasons, the state made some provision for peasants' subsistence needs. If landowners and officials were not able or not prepared to feed peasants in times of dearth, moreover, they had little choice but to allow peasants to leave their villages to fend for themselves.[98] Thus, in

---

96 See Field, *Rebels*, pp. 1–29; Moon, *Russian Peasants*, pp. 72–3, 80, 95, 98–100, 112, 126, 142, 152, 156–7, 163–4, 174, 176.
97 See Abramova, I. L., 'Politika samoderzhaviya v otnoshenii chastnovladel'cheskikh krest'yan v 1796–1801 gg.', *VMU (I)* (1989), no. 4, pp. 47–59; Okun' and Paina, 'Ukaz', pp. 283–99; Druzhinin, *Gosudarstvennye*, vol. 1, pp. 102–9, 207–44.
98 See Koretskii, *Formirovanie*, pp. 71, 78–9; Moon, *Russian Peasants*, p. 42.

marked contrast to the consequences of open revolt with ambitious aims, limited forms of protest with low-level objectives did achieve some results.

Apart from a few exceptional cases, therefore, most protests by Russian peasants did not have higher objectives of creating a vision of a utopian society outside the existing social and political order. This does not mean that most peasants accepted the oppressive and exploitative social system in servile Russia with equanimity and passive fatalism, nor that they had no ideas about how their lives could be better. The gap between the limited possibilities of what was attainable through minor acts of protest and what they might have wished for in an ideal world was filled by a rich and imaginative cultural life, which found expression in religion and folklore.

Only a small minority of Russian peasants had a good understanding of Orthodox Christian theology, but many had a grasp of some of the main ideas, in particular the assurance of eternal life in the kingdom of heaven for those who observed the teachings of the church, took the sacraments, and avoided mortal sin. The Christian heaven was not simply a utopia outside and above the oppressive social order in tsarist Russia, but had elements of a 'world turned upside down'. The evangelist Matthew reported Christ's statement that in the Kingdom of God 'many that are first shall be last and the last shall be first' (Matthew, 19: 30).

Some Populists in late nineteenth-century Russia thought that religious observance led most Russian peasants to resign themselves to wait passively until they reached heaven to receive their reward for toil and obedience in this world. Populists believed that, together with peasants' faith in the tsars, religion was one of the reasons why they were reluctant to be won over to the cause of revolutionary social and political change on earth. It is possible, however, that it was the sort of changes proposed by these educated outsiders, and the impractical ways they proposed to achieve them, that persuaded many peasants that the solace of religion and hope in the tsar was preferable to the harsh repression that would undoubtedly follow any rash and ill-conceived acts of protest.

Religion, like monarchism, could be a double-edged sword in the hands, or minds, of Russian peasants. The people who rejected the reforms of the Russian Orthodox Church in the mid-seventeenth century also rejected the secular authority which supported them. As many as 15–20 per cent of the population, mainly peasants, became Old Believers. Some later became members of radical religious sects. Over time, the state and official church gradually relaxed persecution of dissenters but, throughout the period, a small but significant part of the Russian peasantry was in conflict with the official church and state. Many historians, starting with the Populist A. P. Shchapov in the 1850s and subsequently most Soviet historians, argued that the motives of peasants who adhered to the Old Belief were as much social and political as religious, and that they were using religion as an opportunity for protest against the secular as well as the religious authorities. Although these scholars may have taken the argument too far, the participation of many dissenters in revolts and flight to the frontier and beyond does suggest a connection between religious and social protest. For most peasants, however, both Orthodox and dissenter, it is likely that religion did offer them not so much the opportunity to resist secular authority, but some hope in divine protection against drought, famine, disease and the trials and uncertainties of peasant life on earth, and the prospect of a better life in another world.[99]

Folklore contains further clues to what Russian peasants might have wanted in an ideal world. Russian folklore may not have had a tradition of 'returning deliverer tsars', but it did contain images of 'good tsars' who supported the common people against the 'evil boyars'. Tales and songs in the Russian folk tradition suggest that peasants looked back to an imaginary golden age when a 'good tsar' sat on the throne. The 'good tsars' who feature most frequently by name in Russian folklore are Ivan the Terrible and Peter the Great. In reality, these two rulers had done a great deal to worsen the lot of the peasantry through their parts in the origins and consolidation of serfdom and their heavy demands for taxes and conscripts. Both tsars had also, however, acted against the interests of the boyars and nobles. It may have been these actions, or garbled recollections of them, which helped endear Ivan and Peter to later generations of peasants.[100]

The 'good tsars' of Russian folklore sometimes came to the aid of 'humble heroes' who were in dispute with 'rich or powerful protagonists', for example boyars, who were trying to cheat them. The tsar in tales of this type acted as 'just judges' and 'benevolent figures of authority'. They usually settled disagreements in favour of the humble heroes and punished their opponents. In some tales the tsar ordered the two to exchange clothes, symbolising that they had swapped places in the social hierarchy. Landowners and boyars were portrayed in many tales as dull and slow as well as grasping. Thus, they were easily outsmarted by clever and quick-witted, but poor and humble, characters. Moreover, humble heroes did not always need the help of a benevolent tsar. This suggests that the desired self-image of many members of the lower orders was canny and sharp tricksters.[101]

Another character in Russian folklore who stood up for the mass of the population against their oppressors was the 'rebel hero', especially 'Sten'ka' Razin. Many, but significantly not all, folk songs and tales portrayed Razin as a popular hero. The folkloric Sten'ka was endowed with magical powers, which enabled him to outsmart and defeat the authorities. He was invulnerable

99 See Treadgold, D. W., 'The peasant and religion', in Vucinich, *Peasant*; Crummey, R. O., 'Old Belief as popular religion', *SR*, vol. 52 (1994), pp. 700–12; Chulos, C. J., 'Revolution and grassroots re-evaluation of Russian Orthodoxy: Parish clergy and peasants in Voronezh province, 1905–17', in Pallot, *Transforming Peasants*, pp. 90–112; Engelstein, L., 'Rebels of the soul: Peasant self-fashioning in a religious key', *RH*, vol. 23 (1996), pp. 197–213; Field, D., 'Peasants and propagandists in the Russian movement to the people of 1874', *JMH*, vol. 59 (1987), pp. 415–38.
100 See Perrie, M., *The Image of Ivan the Terrible in Russian Folklore* (Cambridge, 1987); Riasanovsky, N., *The Image of Peter the Great in Russian Literature and Thought* (New York and Oxford, 1985), pp. 74–85.
101 See Perrie, M., 'Folklore as evidence of peasant *mentalité*', *RR*, vol. 48 (1989), pp. 125–31, 137, 141.

to bullets; he could go around without being seen or heard; he could kill men with an unloaded gun and capture cities by magic. Chains could not bind him; prisons could not hold him; torture could not break him. In one tale, Sten'ka escaped from prison by drawing a boat on the wall of his cell and sailing away; in another he turned himself into a fly and flew through the air. Longworth maintained that the folklore about Sten'ka Razin was 'subversive', and that many peasants were wary about repeating songs and tales to ethnographers in case it got them into trouble. For this reason, in some folk tales and songs Sten'ka Razin was alluded to in a 'secret language' as a 'raven' or 'the sun', and referred to in metaphors, for example: 'Rise, rise, O red sun, And warm us poor people.' Unlike the 'good tsars' of Russian folklore, Razin was depicted as a Christ-like figure who would rise again and return to save the people from oppression. A century after Razin's revolt, some people apparently believed that Pugachev, who was born in the same village on the Don, was the second coming of Razin. A smaller body of folklore grew up around Pugachev. In 1833, when Alexander Pushkin visited areas where Pugachev's revolt had taken place, he found that memories and tales about the events and the rebel leader were still very much alive among old people he met.[102]

What do these aspects of popular culture tell us about the objectives of peasant protest in servile Russia? What, in Perrie's words, was the 'relationship of *mentalité* to action'? Drawing mainly on oral culture in eighteenth-century France, Robert Darnton argued that 'tricksterism' in folk tales suggested a strategy by which 'little people' could cope with 'a cruel and capricious world'. Indeed, the cunning heroes of some Russian tales parallel the tactics of 'everyday resistance' in real life. Some scholars have been too ready to find in 'just rulers' and 'bandits' in folk culture evidence for a popular radicalism which served as 'guiding myths' for protest. For many peasants in many societies, including Russia, the prospects of attaining anything approaching the aims which seem to be suggested by their folklore were very remote. The negative image of the real Razin in some tales reflected popular awareness of the serious consequences of open revolt (see above, pp. 252–4). Folkloric rebels and good tsars, as well as the periodic rumours about 'returning deliverers', were not part of a radical and subversive ideology, but were simply stories. They were part of the rich oral culture of the Russian peasantry, which livened up the drudgery of work in their households and fields. These stories enabled peasants to vent pent-up frustrations, and to have imaginary revenge against their oppressors. To some extent, the function of these aspects of oral culture was simply escapism, similar to another common feature of Russian peasants' culture: the oblivion attained by drinking large quantities of vodka.[103]

In the end, serfdom was abolished and the other ways in which the landowning and ruling elites exploited the Russian peasantry were reformed by

102 Longworth, 'Subversive', pp. 17–40 (quotation on p. 21); Solov'ev, 'Russkaya'; Ovchinnikov, R. V., *Nad 'Pugachevskimi' stranitsami Pushkina* (Moscow, 1985), pp. 4, 130.
103 See Perrie, 'Folklore', pp. 126, 142; Darnton, R., *The Great Cat Massacre and Other Episodes in French Cultural History* (London, 1984), pp. 59–67; Madariaga, *Russia*, p. 240.

action from above, by tsars Alexander II and III, in the 1860s–80s. The roles played by peasant protest, and elites' perceptions and fears of peasant unrest, in the decisions to enact the reforms have been and will continue to be the subject of much debate. Whatever the part played by peasant protest, however, the reforms were not designed to, and did not, resolve all the grievances or meet all the aspirations of the Russian peasantry. Indeed, many peasants protested against the terms of the abolition of serfdom in 1861. Most of the unrest in 1861 took the form of 'disturbances'. In the village of Bezdna, Kazan' province, however, the disturbances ended in a massacre of at least 60 or 70 peasants when troops fired on a crowd who stubbornly insisted on an interpretation of the statutes closer to their hopes than their real meaning.[104]

* * *

Russian peasants continued to have major grievances in the decades after the reforms of the 1860s, most notably their continuing subordinate status and the growing problem of 'land hunger'. The latter was especially common among former seigniorial peasants and many peasants in the central regions regardless of their previous categories. Russian peasants continued to protest throughout the post-reform decades. Their main objective was to gain access to more land.[105]

When the opportunities arose in 1905 and 1917, as a result of acute national crises created by defeats in wars, divisions within the elites, and revolts against the authorities by many sections of the population, Russian peasants once again took mass, open direct action against the landowners and the state. In contrast to the four great revolts of the seventeenth and eighteenth centuries, which had broken out in similar circumstances, the peasant revolts which started in 1905 and 1917 were not confined to the borderlands, but took place all over Russia. Moreover, both the forms and objectives of peasant protests escalated as the wider revolutions, involving other groups in society, struck at the heart of state power. Peasants seized land, burned manor houses, and drove landowners from the villages. The peasant uprisings which began in 1905 were suppressed by 1907. In 1917, however, the downfall of the monarchy in February–March 1917 and the growing revolutionary crisis created the chance for a full-scale peasant revolution throughout Russia. (See Ch. 9.)

CONCLUSION

The peasant revolts of 1905 and 1917 played a large part in the end of the old regime in rural Russia. In the preceding three centuries, however, open revolts by peasants had prevented major social and political change by provoking the landowning and ruling elites to consolidate their power over the peasantry.

---

104 See Emmons, 'Peasant'; Field, *Rebels*, pp. 31–111. See also Ch. 3.
105 See Anfimov, *Ekonomicheskoe*, esp. pp. 201–2.

This consolidation took place first in the central regions and then in the borderlands, where many peasants who had previously fled to escape growing oppression were once again brought under control. For much of the servile period and in much of Russia, therefore, peasant protest was restricted to limited and mostly non-violent 'disturbances' and 'everyday resistance'. Although peasants dreamed of wider changes or even ideal societies, most confined their objectives to limited improvements in their lives and minor concessions to redress specific grievances as they tried to carve out some living space inside the oppressive and exploitative social order.

These limited forms of protest with limited aims were part of a larger political process involving not only peasants against elites, but also, on occasions, some peasants against the older generation of peasants or dominant factions in their villages, as well as the central state authorities against some local officials and landowners. Sometimes, especially in the last decades of serfdom, the central authorities took action against local officials and landowners who had 'abused' their authority over peasants, with negative consequences for both the peasants, who suffered at their hands, and the central government, which lost revenue that had been syphoned off by corrupt and exploitative officials and landowners, and faced the prospect of potentially harmful peasant unrest. This wider political process in rural Russia did not, as Soviet historians maintained, constitute a 'peasant movement' which undermined the existing order, but to some extent served as a crude mechanism for dealing with and sometimes resolving disputes between many of the parties involved, including peasants. Limited protest enabled many peasants to mitigate some of the worst excesses of exploitation. Limited protest with limited objectives was, thus, another strategy which assisted Russian peasants in their wider goal of trying to ensure their subsistence and livelihoods.

CHAPTER 8

Consumption

Subsistence was the underlying aim of the various strategies adopted by peasant households and communities throughout much of Russia between the early seventeenth and early twentieth centuries. Peasants tried to make the most effective use of the resources at their disposal, principally labour and land, to try to ensure that they produced sufficient to support themselves, and to meet the irreducible demands of the landowning and ruling elites. Peasants had varying degrees of success in their efforts to subsist, leading to differences in levels of consumption among the population of rural Russia. At the macro-level, there were differences in peasants' standards of living over time, in both the short and long terms, and variations between peasants in different regions. There were also disparities at the micro-level, between households in the same communities. In addition, individual households experienced changes in their living standards over time.

All attempts to measure Russian peasants' levels of consumption have been fraught with difficulties. Historians and other investigators have disagreed over the reliability and comparability of the available data, and the most appropriate methodological and theoretical approaches to adopt to them. Attempts have been made to assess peasant living standards at the macro-level of large populations and the micro-level of individual households. 'Snapshots' of the relative prosperity of households at fixed points in time have shown varying degrees of 'differentiation' inside village communities. More interestingly, and controversially, attempts have been made to measure changes in the relative wealth of households over time. At the centre of such ventures has been the debate between adherents of Lenin and Alexander Chayanov. They argued, respectively, for the primary importance of households' relationship to the developing 'capitalist mode of production', and the numbers and ages of their members. Writing in the 1870s, Donald MacKenzie Wallace expressed another, more intractable problem:

> The rural life, and in general the economic organization, of Russia is so peculiar . . . that even the fullest data regarding the quantity of land enjoyed by the peasantry, the amount of dues paid for it, the productivity of the soil, [and] the price of grain . . . would convey to an Englishman's mind no clear conception of the peasants' actual condition.[1]

1 Wallace, *Russia*, vol. 2, p. 345.

Nevertheless, it is possible to examine ways in which scholars have assessed the levels of consumption of Russia's peasants, and the conclusions they have reached.

IMPOVERISHMENT OR PROSPERITY?

Many Russian peasants remembered only the hard times. Again quoting Wallace: 'The village annals [of Ivanovka, Novgorod province] contained no important events except bad harvests, cattle-plagues, and destructive fires, with which the inhabitants seem to have been periodically visited from time immemorial. If good harvests were ever experienced, they must have faded from popular recollection.'[2] This gloomy view has found much support from historians. Many scholars working in the West prior to the 1980s, together with most Soviet historians, argued that throughout the centuries covered by this book the majority of Russian peasants had low standards of living, and that many were impoverished. For the period before the abolition of serfdom in 1861, this negative view stressed the high and rising levels of exploitation, as landowners demanded more labour or dues from their peasants, and the small and decreasing sizes of peasants' allotments, as many landowners allegedly took land from them to augment their demesnes. The demands on peasants made by the state also increased. The high and growing exactions of the landowning and ruling elites were contrasted with the low and stagnant levels of productivity of traditional peasant agriculture, which were exacerbated by regular bad harvests. Russian peasants' struggles to eke out a living were intensified by the harsh environmental conditions they lived in. Most Soviet historians asserted that the condition of the majority of peasants, especially the poorest, was miserable, and that this was one facet of a 'crisis of the feudal-serf economy' in the decades prior to 1861. Conditions on many noble estates were so bad, it was maintained, that they led to declining numbers of seigniorial peasants in the first half of the nineteenth century. State and appanage peasants may have been slightly better off, but they too endured a struggle to survive.

The abolition of serfdom, in this view, worsened the peasants' plight. The reforms of the appanage and state peasants were only slightly more favourable. As a result of the reforms of the 1860s, all Russian peasants were burdened with high redemption payments for the land they were permitted to purchase, on top of high taxes. Many peasants ran up large arrears as they were unable to meet their obligations. The freed serfs, moreover, lost part of the land they had previously cultivated for themselves. The rapid growth in the rural population in the late nineteenth century aggravated the 'land hunger'. Nevertheless, most village communes persisted with 'backward' agricultural techniques, which did not yield enough, it was alleged, to feed the ever-increasing numbers of mouths. The peasants' farming methods made the situation even worse

2 Wallace, *Russia*, vol. 1, pp. 56–7.

by exhausting the soil. Regardless of the growing poverty in the villages, it was long maintained – notably by Alexander Gerschenkron – that the tsarist government used revenue raised by taxing the peasantry to finance industrialisation, and that it continued to export grain to pay for industrial development even when there was insufficient for domestic consumption. A few peasants managed to enrich themselves, but the majority faced a constant battle against destitution. The 1891–92 famine and the rural revolutions that broke out in 1905 and 1917 were seen as the inevitable outcome of a 'crisis of Russian agriculture'.[3]

This picture of peasant immiseration in the centuries before and the decades after the reforms of the 1860s is too grim to be plausible. The Soviet scholar Alexander Shapiro noted the absurdity of the implication in the work of many of his colleagues that peasant living standards were continually declining. At a conference in 1959 he remarked:

> There is a paradox. A researcher investigates the condition of peasants in the early feudal period. Their condition is already so bad that it cannot get any worse. They are literally dying out. But then, later on, their condition gets even worse; in the 15th century, even worse, in the 16th, 17th, 18th, 19th centuries, worse, worse, and worse. Thus it goes on right up to the Great October Socialist Revolution [of 1917] . . . [P]easants' living standards are elastic and can decline, but surely they cannot do so indefinitely. How did they exist? I think the time has come . . . to study more seriously the condition of the peasants . . . I do not think anything terrible will happen if . . . we reach the conclusion that in some period [the peasants'] condition . . . got better.[4]

A number of scholars, especially some Western historians over the last two decades, have shown that Shapiro's scepticism was well founded. Many elements of the alleged 'crisis of the feudal-serf economy' between the late eighteenth century and 1861, including deteriorating peasant living standards, have been challenged. One of the problems with the contention that landowners' demands were increasing while the sizes of peasants' land allotments were declining is that it relies to a large extent on a comparison of data from the 'General Land Survey' of the late eighteenth century and the 'Descriptions of Seigniorial Estates' drawn up by landowners in 1858–59. Aside from problems of comparing figures from different sources, there are doubts over the accuracy of the 'Descriptions'. Many landowners seem deliberately to have overstated the level of obligations they demanded from their peasants in the hope of maximising any compensation they would receive for their loss at the impending abolition of serfdom. They also appear to have understated

---

3 See, for example, Koval'chenko, *Russkoe*; Druzhinin, N. M., *Russkaya derevnya na perelome, 1861–1881 gg.* (Moscow, 1978); Robinson, *Rural Russia*, pp. 36–44, 94–116; Gerschenkron, A., 'Agrarian policies and industrialization: Russia, 1861–1917', *Cambridge Economic History of Europe*, vol. 6, pt 2 (Cambridge, 1965), pp. 706–800. See also Chs 3 and 4.
4 Shapiro, A. L. [discussion], *EAIVE 1958 g.* (Tallinn, 1959), p. 221.

the sizes of their peasants' allotments with the aim of reducing the amounts of land that would be assigned to peasants by the reform. Other sources, in particular the 'Regulatory Charters' produced soon after abolition and which are widely believed to be more accurate, paint a less gloomy picture of the seigniorial peasants' lot in the last years of serfdom. The low figures for crop yields often cited as evidence for economic crisis and peasant poverty in the first half of the nineteenth century were also taken from sources (provincial governors' annual reports) whose accuracy has been doubted. Moreover, the argument that the enserfed peasantry was 'dying out' as a result of increasing exploitation and declining living standards has been refuted. The fall in the relative and absolute sizes of the seigniorial peasant population in the last few decades before 1861 was due largely to transfers to the state peasantry and other social estates.[5]

Interpretations of peasant living standards under serfdom have rightly focused on the impact of exploitation, but have often done so at the expense of other aspects of the dependent relationship between seigniorial peasants and their owners. Looking back to the era of serfdom, which had ended shortly before he arrived in Russia, Wallace noted that 'the condition of serfs under [an enlightened, rational and humane] proprietor . . . was much more enviable than that of the majority of English agricultural labourers'. He added that Russian serfs had had a house, a garden plot, livestock, a share of the communal arable land, implements, and obligations for their lords, but temporary assistance in times of difficulty.[6] While this view is impressionistic, and ignores the condition of serfs under harsh and exploitative landowners, it serves as a corrective to the belief that serfdom had only negative consequences for the material welfare of enserfed peasants.

The further notion that peasant living standards deteriorated after the end of serfdom in 1861, during a 'crisis of Russian agriculture' in the late nineteenth century, has been questioned by revisionist historians in a debate that has been raging since the late 1970s.[7] Many aspects of the 'crisis' argument have been challenged. While the burden of obligations on the freed serfs seems to have increased in the period of 'temporary obligation' that followed the reform, once peasants began to 'redeem' their land, the payments they made were lower. The extent of the arrears peasants accumulated has often been used as evidence for declining living standards. This argument rests on the assumption that peasants ran up arrears because they were too poor to meet their payments. Closer investigation suggests that peasants paid their redemption payments, and other direct taxes, when they could afford to do so, but did not pay when they were unable to, thereby bringing their obligations into line with their ability to pay and putting their subsistence needs first. It is also

5 See Chs 3 and 4.
6 Wallace, *Russia*, vol. 1, pp. 258–9. See also Ch. 3.
7 The debate was sparked off by Simms, J. Y., 'The crisis of Russian agriculture at the end of the nineteenth century: A different view', *SR*, vol. 36 (1977), pp. 377–98. See also Hoch, 'On good numbers'; Wheatcroft, 'Crises'; and Chs 3 and 4.

likely that peasants did not pay if they thought they could get away with it. The state lacked the means to compel all peasants to make their payments in full. Instead, it periodically rescheduled payments and wrote off some arrears. Nevertheless, peasants paid 95 per cent of the total amount of redemption payments they were required to. A shortfall of 5 per cent was what the legislators had anticipated, and made allowance for in their calculations.

It is possible that reforms by the tsarist government in the nineteenth century may have had positive effects on peasant living standards. Steven Hoch has put forward the provocative argument that, by the 1880s, the land settlement set in train by the reform of 1861 had reduced the amount of their incomes or the product of their labour that former seigniorial peasants had to hand over in return for their land. The reform 'produced direct, measurable benefits to the formerly servile peasantry', which 'help explain the observed [i.e. declining] mortality trends'. If Hoch is right, then the abolition of serfdom led in time to an improvement in the material condition of the former serfs, which contributed to the acceleration in the growth of the peasant population in the late nineteenth century. It has also been suggested that Kiselev's reforms of the 1830s–40s made more land available to state peasants, in return for proportionately lower obligations, and that this led to improved nutrition, greater prosperity and population increase in state villages.[8]

The abolition of the poll tax in the 1880s and the move towards increased or new indirect taxes on goods of mass consumption – for example vodka, tea, sugar, cotton cloth, tobacco, matches and kerosene – has been seen as a major hardship for peasants. Indirect taxes, especially on necessities, are most burdensome for the poorest sections of the population. Against this, it has been argued that a disproportionate amount of revenue from indirect taxes came from urban rather than rural inhabitants, and that peasants were readily able to find substitutes for the taxed items, for example *samogon* ('moonshine') for vodka, *kvas* (see below, p. 289) for tea, honey in place of sugar, and homespun linen instead of factory-made cotton. Peasants had managed for centuries without tobacco, matches and kerosene (for oil lamps), and did so again when they could not afford them. Moreover, the tax on salt, which was a necessity and was hard to replace, had been abolished in 1881. Since many peasants found temporary work in towns and cities, however, they were among the urban consumers who made up a significant part of the market for taxed consumer goods. Together with the poorest peasants in the villages, moreover, they were least able to find substitutes for essential taxed goods. But the growing revenues from taxes on consumer goods suggest that among the population as a whole, including peasants, consumption of these goods was increasing. Figures on the *per capita* output of consumer goods confirm this trend.

There is no doubt that the land settlement of 1861 deprived many freed serfs of part of the land they had farmed for themselves under serfdom. The losses were greatest in more fertile regions. There is also no doubt that land

8 Hoch, 'On good numbers', pp. 70–5; Adams, 'Reforms', pp. 37–8.

hunger was a serious and growing problem, especially in the more densely populated central regions of Russia. Nevertheless, many peasants found solutions. They rented and bought land on top of their allotment land. Rising rents and prices for land in the late nineteenth century are evidence that there were peasants who could pay more, as well as for increasing demand for land. From 1883 many peasants bought land with help from the state Peasant Land Bank set up for that purpose. Growing numbers of peasants resorted to the long-standing tradition of migrating to the outlying regions to find new land to cultivate. From the 1880s the government gave some assistance to migrants. Extensification of production was not the only solution. There was also some intensification. Village communes and their customary practices were not always barriers to agricultural 'improvement'. Some communes supported or organised changes in techniques and crops.

Land shortages, rural over-population and under-employment led ever-larger numbers of peasants to leave their villages in search of wage labour to support themselves and their families. The increasing supply of labour was met by growing demand for labourers to work on commercially run farms and in the new and expanding industries in Russia's growing towns and cities. Many peasants benefited from opportunities to work in industry. The conditions they lived and worked in were often very bad, but the extra earnings migrant labourers sent back to the villages supplemented their families' incomes from farming, and thus made it possible for many households to remain on the land, subsist, and preserve their ways of life.

Gerschenkron's thesis, that the government financed industrialisation at the expense of the peasantry by diverting resources from agriculture through high taxes and by exporting grain needed for domestic consumption, has been largely refuted by economic historians in recent years. Resources were transferred from peasant agriculture to industry, but mostly by non-budgetary mechanisms, including growing rural demand for industrial output. Grain exports did increase faster than grain output between 1884 and 1904, but there were no mechanisms by which the government could force peasants *en masse* to part with grain they needed for subsistence. Rather, the changes in the whole system of taxation by Finance Minister Bunge in the 1880s shifted the burden away from the peasantry. To the extent that industrialisation was financed from taxation, it was the urban population and the commercial and industrial sectors of the economy that paid for it, not peasants who remained in their villages and engaged primarily in agriculture. Moreover, there was substantial, if uneven, growth and development in the agricultural sector of the economy as well as the industrial. On average, both output and domestic consumption of agricultural produce, including grain, increased faster than the population in late tsarist Russia.[9]

9 Compare Gerschenkron, 'Agrarian policies'; and Wheatcroft, 'Crises', pp. 131–6; Harrison, M., 'The peasantry and industrialisation', in Davies, *From Tsarism*, pp. 104–7; Plaggenborg, S., 'Tax policy and the question of peasant poverty in tsarist Russia 1881–1905', *CMR*, vol. 36 (1995), pp. 53–69. See also Chs 3 and 4.

In the revisionist interpretation, therefore, there was no mass impoverishment among the entire population of rural Russia in the decades after 1861. It cannot be denied that there were periods of hardship, nor that there were areas where peasants were worse off than others. There is also no doubt that some peasants fared better while others lost out. But the existence of some cases of rural poverty does not add up to a general 'crisis of Russian agriculture', including declining living standards for the peasantry as a whole, during the whole period between the mid-nineteenth and the early twentieth centuries.

Debates about the living standards of Russian peasants throughout the period covered by this book, including the pre-reform period, are still in progress. Problems over the availability and reliability of sources make resolutions in the near future unlikely. To the extent that some degrees of consensus are emerging, they are tending away from 'crisis' interpretations and towards more favourable views of the average living standards among most Russian peasants. One way to move beyond the debates is to turn to one element of peasant consumption. The most important, from the perspective of subsistence, was diet.

DIET

Russian peasants' basic diet[10] was summed up in the saying '*shchi da kasha pishcha nasha*' ('cabbage soup and porridge/gruel is our food'). Peasants grew the grain for porridge and cabbage for soup in their arable fields and kitchen gardens. The livestock most peasants kept supplied them with meat, fat, dairy produce and eggs. Peasants also gathered and hunted. Fruits, berries, mushrooms, nuts and honey were collected in forests. Some peasants hunted for small game and caught fish. Many peasants also bought some provisions. Buying food was most important in areas where peasants specialised in non-agricultural activities, such as parts of the forest-heartland from the mid-eighteenth century. In the late nineteenth century, as the rural economy became more commercialised, increasing numbers of peasants relied more heavily on food they had bought rather than produced for themselves. Both peasant men and women worked in their household economies to produce food, but preparing meals and preserving food was the task of women. They cooked food on top of or inside the stoves that also provided heat for peasants' houses.[11] A diet based largely on grain, vegetables and some animal produce was similar to that of many peasants elsewhere in pre-industrial Europe. Peasants in other parts of the world also relied on cereals, including rice, as their staple food.[12]

10 The following section relies heavily on Smith and Christian, *Bread*; and Smith, *Peasant Farming*, esp. pp. 33–5, 39, 44–6, 57–76, 88. See also Ch. 4.
11 On stoves, see Tempest, S., 'Stovelore in Russian folklife', in Glants and Toomre, *Food*, pp. 1–14.
12 For comparative perspectives, see Montanari, M., *The Culture of Food* (Oxford, 1994), esp. pp. 30–3, 47–51, 73–8, 100–7, 152–3; Blum, *End*, pp. 183–9.

Grain made up at least two-thirds, by both weight and calories, of the food consumed by most Russian peasants. The importance of grain began to fall only in the second half of the nineteenth century, when many peasants started to eat more potatoes instead. The main cereal crop peasants grew for human consumption was rye. It was celebrated in Russian folklore as 'mother rye' ('*rozh' matushka*') and 'rye – the provider of mother's milk' ('*rzhitsa kormilitsa*'). Barley was important in more northerly areas. In the south-eastern steppe regions, wheat became widespread in the eighteenth century. Wheat was considered a luxury, however, and peasants usually grew it for sale rather than consumption. Peasants also grew buckwheat and millet for their own consumption, and oats for themselves as well as fodder for their livestock.

Peasants ate grain in a number of ways. Whole grain or pounded groats, usually buckwheat, barley, millet or oats, were boiled to make porridge or gruel (*kasha*). Grain ground into flour was baked into bread. Traditional Russian rye bread made from soured dough was dark, heavy, aromatic, very filling and nutritious. No meal was complete without it, and Russian peasants treated bread with great reverence. Peasants also used flour to make noodles (*lapsha*), pancakes (*blini*), ravioli (*pel'meni*), pies and pastries (*pirogi*), both savoury and sweet. Grain was the main ingredient in the peasants' main drink, *kvas*: a sort of light or small beer made from malted grain, grain meal or bread. *Kvas* was safer to drink than water as it was boiled during preparation and the small amount of alcohol it contained served as an antiseptic.

After grain, the most important element of Russian peasants' diet was vegetables, especially cabbage, cucumbers, onions, garlic, carrots, beetroots, turnips, radishes, peas and beans. Since fresh vegetables were available for only short periods of the year, peasant women preserved large quantities, usually by pickling them in brine. For much of the year, pickled cabbage, cucumbers and beetroot made up a large part of peasants' diet. Pickled or fresh, vegetables were made into soups, which were usually the main course at midday meals. In much of Russia, especially the central regions, cabbage soup (*shchi*) was so common that it can be considered the Russian national dish. Further south and in Ukraine, beetroot soup (*borshch*) filled the same role. Peasants also ate vegetables boiled and as fillings in pies.

Animal produce made up part of peasants' diet. Meat, dairy produce and eggs were provided by the cows, sheep, goats, pigs, chickens and geese that many peasants kept. Wildfowl and other small game were additions to peasants' diets. Peasants added butter, sour cream, cottage cheese and animal fat to porridges and soups to make them more substantial. They also ate meat in pies. Russian peasants seem to have preferred animal fat to meat. Many scholars have agreed that meat was a luxury that most Russian peasants ate only on feast days. R. E. F. Smith maintained that the shortage of Russian names for meat dishes 'may reflect the lack of meat in the national diet'. In contrast, in his study of Petrovskoe in Tambov province in the first half of the nineteenth century, Hoch noted that prices for meat, poultry and eggs were low in the Central Black Earth region. He argued that 'some form of meat was certainly available weekly, if not daily'. While meat was more widely available in the south-east of the Central Black Earth region where Petrovskoe was situated, Hoch does not seem to have taken full account of the large number of days of fasting and abstinence, around 180 a year, in the calendar of the Russian Orthodox Church. Many peasants observed the church's bans on the consumption of meat, or all animal produce, on these days.[13] On some fast days Orthodox believers were permitted to eat fish. Peasants ate fish on other days, especially in areas in the vicinity of rivers, lakes and seas where they were readily available. Fish soup (*ukha*) appeared on peasants' meal tables in some regions. Throughout Russia, peasants preserved fish for their own consumption and for sale. It was easy to freeze fish in the winter, and fish were preserved by smoking, salting and drying throughout the year.

The fruits, berries and mushrooms which peasants gathered in woodland near their villages were used in pies and pastries. Berries were added to *kvas* for flavour. Like most foodstuffs, especially those available for only limited parts of the year, the fruits of the forest were preserved for consumption or sale at other times. Strings of dried mushrooms were a common sight in peasants' houses and at village markets. The main preservative used for fruit and berries was another product of the forest, honey from wild bees. The only items in their diet that most Russian peasants regularly bought, rather than produced or gathered for themselves, were salt, which was the most important preservative, and vodka, which was an essential accompaniment to peasants' festivals.

The basic elements of the peasant diet were similar throughout much of Russia and remained reasonably constant over time. There were some additions. Russian peasants slowly overcame their initial suspicion of potatoes in the 1840s and 50s, when a series of bad grain harvests demonstrated their value as a substitute for cereals. By the late nineteenth century this import from the New World made up a significant part of peasants' diet as potatoes partly supplanted other root vegetables and *kasha*. Other nineteenth-century additions included items that most peasants were not able to produce but had to buy. Sugar began to take over from honey as a preservative and sweetener, and tea started to edge out *kvas* as the main beverage. Both, however, remained luxuries.

Probably the most striking feature of the everyday diet of the Russian peasantry was its monotony: bread, porridges, soups and vegetables, supplemented by relatively small amounts of animal produce. On some fast days, peasants added vegetable oil, instead of animal fat and dairy produce, to their porridges and soups. On the strictest fast days even vegetable oil was forbidden. The frugality of the food peasants ate during fasts and the monotony of their diet on ordinary days contrast with the richer and more varied fare they

---

13 Compare Smith, *Peasant Farming*, p. 70 (quotation); Smith and Christian, *Bread*, pp. 251–2, 260–6; Frierson, 'Forced hunger', pp. 60–1 (on Engel'gardt); and Hoch, *Serfdom*, p. 48. See also Heretz, L., 'The practice and significance of fasting in Russian peasant culture at the turn of the [20th] century', in Glants and Toomre, *Food*, pp. 67–80.

consumed on the holidays and festivals that marked the cycle of agricultural work, the main events in family life, and the principal religious feasts. Peasants' festive tables were covered with meat and fish dishes, pies, pastries and pancakes, savoury and sweet, and other delicacies. Equally important were the alcoholic drinks, in particular vodka, with which peasants washed down their food and drank toasts.[14]

In spite of its tedium, the day-to-day diet of Russian peasants was well balanced by modern nutritional standards. It contained all the main types of food that humans require: carbohydrates, proteins, fats and oils, vitamins and essential minerals. Russian peasants were well aware of the types and quantities of food they needed. In the 1880s, based on his close observations of the peasants he lived among in Smolensk province, Alexander Engel'gardt concluded:

> People know *exactly how much you earn on a particular food, what type of food is necessary for what kind of work.* If, on a diet consisting of cabbage soup, pork and buckwheat gruel [*kasha*] with animal fat, you can carry in a certain time, say, a cubic fathom of earth, then if you replace buckwheat gruel with barley gruel you will carry less, say 7/8 of a cubic fathom, while on potatoes you carry even less, say 3/4 of a cubic fathom . . . This is all perfectly well known to a navvy or a woodchopper, so that, once they know the price of food and the wages available, they can calculate precisely which food is most economical.[15]

For much of the time, many Russian peasants seem also to have had sufficient to eat. Hoch has argued that, in the first half of the nineteenth century, the peasants of Petrovskoe (admittedly in the fertile province of Tambov) enjoyed 'relative, if tenuous, prosperity'.[16] In other regions and especially in years of dearth, however, Russian peasants were less well fed and suffered from shortages (see below, pp. 296–8).

Accounts by foreigners who visited Russia in the eighteenth and nineteenth centuries suggest that the diet of Russian peasants was at least as good, in both quality and quantity, as that of peasants and labourers in central and western Europe. William Coxe, an Englishman who travelled widely in northern and eastern Europe in the 1770s and 80s, noted that Russian peasants had 'plenty of wholesome food', were 'well clothed, [and] comfortably lodged'. Martha Wilmot, an Irishwoman who was in Russia from 1803 to 1808, wrote during a visit to Princess Dashkova's estate in Kaluga province: 'those who imagine the Russ [*sic*] peasantry sunk in sloth and misery imagine a strange falsehood. Wou'd to God our Paddys . . . were half as well clothed or fed the year round

14 On festive diets, see Smith and Christian, *Bread*, pp. 79–81, 251–2, 293, 316–17; Semyonova, *Village Life*, pp. 110–14; and on fast diets, Heretz, 'Practice'.
15 Smith and Christian, *Bread*, pp. 257–8, 261, 286–7, 327 (quotation). See also Frierson, 'Forced hunger', pp. 54–7.
16 Hoch, *Serfdom*, pp. 50–1, 64 (quotation). For an optimistic estimate of peasant food consumption in 1788, see Blanchard, *Russia's Age of Silver*, pp. 238–45. This favourable view may also be valid for serf workers. See Esper, 'Condition'.

as are the Russians.' An English sea captain named John Cochrane, who undertook a long tour of Russia and Siberia in the early 1820s, made a similar observation: 'I have no hesitation . . . in saying, that the condition of the peasantry here is far superior to that class in Ireland. In Russia, provisions are plentiful, good and cheap; while in Ireland they are scanty, poor, and dear . . .' Other travellers remarked that peasants they encountered in Russia were better fed, as well as dressed and housed, than villagers in parts of France, Italy and elsewhere. The views of foreigners are, of course, only anecdotal evidence. If Russian peasants did eat better than Irish peasants, it may be more of a comment on deprivation in rural Ireland than on affluence in rural Russia. Some travellers may have been misled by the hospitality they received into thinking that Russian peasants ate well, and ate meat dishes, on most days. It would be easy, moreover, to present quotations from other travellers' accounts on the poverty they found in Russian villages.[17]

Firmer evidence for the relative prosperity of some Russian peasants has been presented by some historians. Ian Blanchard estimated that, in the late eighteenth and early nineteenth centuries, Russia's *per capita* national income was only 5–15 per cent lower than those of contemporary England and France. Hoch calculated that, excluding years of crisis, 'the peasants of Petrovskoe were . . . better nourished than their French and Belgian counterparts at the turn of the nineteenth century and certainly had a better diet than most persons living in developing countries today'.[18]

VARIATIONS IN CONSUMPTION

Inside this general picture of apparent well-being, Russian peasants' levels of consumption varied over time, in both the long and short term, and between regions. The various categories of peasants (especially seigniorial and state peasants) and the strata (rich, middle and poor) which many specialists have divided peasants into also fared differently.

Changes over time

Some long-term trends in the levels of consumption of the Russian peasantry can be identified, although there are few hard data for the period before the mid-nineteenth century. In the late sixteenth century, many Russian peasants suffered a marked downturn in their condition, and serious hardship. The causes

17 Blanchard, *Russia's Age of Silver*, p. 283 (Coxe); Madariaga, I. de, *Catherine the Great* (New Haven, CT, and London, 1990), p. 153 (Wilmot); Pipes, *Russia*, p. 151 (Cochrane). On the contradictory nature of travellers' accounts on Russia and elsewhere, see Madariaga, *Russia*, pp. 551–2; Blum, *End*, pp. 192–3. Less favourable assessments of Russian peasant living standards by foreigners were made in times of famine: Rösener, *Peasantry*, p. 150.
18 Blanchard, *Russia's Age of Silver*, p. 282; Hoch, *Serfdom*, p. 50.

were both natural factors, such as climatic fluctuations leading to bad harvests, and human actions, in particular Ivan the Terrible's 'terror' (*oprichnina*) and long wars. The Englishman Giles Fletcher, and other foreigners who visited Russia in the late sixteenth century, commented on the symptoms of economic decline and distress they witnessed. The depopulation of much of the forest-heartland, as many peasants migrated to the steppe regions, attracted much attention. The peasants' plight was worsened by the development of serfdom and other restrictions and demands on the mass of the rural population. Despite the consolidation of serfdom over the first half of the seventeenth century, many Russian peasants seem to have benefited from a general economic recovery that began in the 1620s.[19] The poor harvests and high levels of exploitation during the reign of Peter the Great contributed to a downturn in peasant living standards during the late seventeenth and early eighteenth centuries.[20]

Both quantitative and impressionistic evidence suggest that average material living standards of many Russian peasants improved over the rest of the eighteenth century. There was a steady increase in agricultural production, especially from the middle of the century. Most of the increase was due to the growth in the area of land cultivated which, in turn, was largely a consequence of the expansion of peasant settlement and arable farming to the fertile southeastern parts of the forested steppe and, further afield, to the open steppe. The gradual improvement in the climate as the 'little ice age' came to an end contributed to better harvests. The increase in production was partly cancelled out by the continued growth in levels of exploitation. But by the mid-eighteenth century, the various strategies peasants had devised to make the most effective use of their resources to support themselves and meet their obligations (discussed in the preceding chapters) were in operation throughout large parts of Russia, especially the central regions. Many of the foreign travellers who wrote that Russian peasants were reasonably well fed visited Russia in the late eighteenth and early nineteenth centuries. Although many peasants may not have been aware of it at the time, the whole 'pie' was getting bigger, not just the 'pieces' taken by the elites. It is possible, however, that the improvement in average living standards tailed off in the early nineteenth century, leaving them at similar levels until the middle of the century.[21]

Reasonably reliable figures for the consumption of agricultural produce in rural Russia are available from the 1850s, thus making possible more precise assessments of peasant subsistence. The Russian government estimated that, on average, a person needed around 300 kg of grain a year to subsist. This is the equivalent of approximately 2,500 calories a day, which is in line with modern estimates by the World Health Organisation of the average calorific

19 See Blum, *Lord and Peasant*, pp. 152–65, 235; Shapiro, A. L., *Agrarnaya istoriya Severo-Zapada Rossii XVI v.: Novgorodskie pyatiny* (Leningrad, 1974), pp. 267–99.
20 See Anisimov, *Podatnaya*, pp. 274–82.
21 On trends in exploitation and production, see Chs 3 and 4.

intake necessary for people to live. Adult males engaged in hard, manual labour, however, need rather more calories, around 3,900–4,000 a day.[22]

For most of the late nineteenth and early twentieth centuries, especially the period 1885–1913, grain production increased faster than the population in the European part of the Russian Empire. Boris Mironov estimated that average annual consumption of grain and potatoes per person among the rural population in the European provinces of the empire was 285 kg in the 1850s. It fell slightly, to 262 kg, in the 1870s and 1880s, but rose to 359 kg by 1913. Since grain and potatoes made up around 80 per cent of peasant food intake, these figures indicate that the harvests in late tsarist Russia largely met the subsistence needs of the peasantry. The figures are, of course, averages and they conceal genuine difficulties in some years and certain areas. For other parts of the period and in some regions, however, there were large marketable surpluses. The increasing trade in grain and other agricultural produce had important consequences for peasant consumption. Most of the surpluses were sold inside Russia. As a result of the growing regional specialisation in the rural economy, which had developed from the mid-eighteenth century, many peasants in the forest-heartland relied partly on shipments of surplus grain from the fertile black earth regions to the south.[23]

Russian peasants may have been consuming more grain and potatoes but, on average, they had been eating less meat and dairy produce since the mid-eighteenth century. In this regard, the diet of Russian peasants was following a trend that had begun among rural inhabitants of western and central Europe in the sixteenth century. Declining meat consumption in rural Russia was most marked in the central regions, where the growing population put greatest pressure on the land. The result was an increase in arable farming at the expense of animal husbandry, because growing grain produces more calories per acre than raising livestock. Mironov estimated that the numbers of peasant cattle fell by 29 per cent per person in the European part of the Empire between 1870 and 1913. As a result, there was a corresponding decline in consumption of meat and dairy produce by peasants.[24]

In spite of the decline in the amounts of meat and dairy produce eaten by Russian peasants, according to Mironov, they consumed an average of 2,952 calories a day in the years 1896–1904. Children, the elderly, and women of all ages ate less than average. Adult male peasants had an average daily intake of 4,133 calories. This gave them sufficient energy for the hard, physical labour

22 Smith and Christian, *Bread*, p. 330; Mironov, B. N., 'Diet, health, and stature of the Russian population from the mid-nineteenth century to the beginning of the twentieth century', in Komlos, J. (ed.), *The Biological Standard of Living on Three Continents* (Boulder, CO, 1995), p. 64.

23 Mironov, 'Diet', pp. 68–72 (Mironov made allowance for grain set aside for seed, export, urban consumption, and purposes other than food, e.g. distilling, and for the growing consumption of potatoes by converting them to the equivalent of grain at a ratio of 3:1). See also Gregory, 'Grain marketings', pp. 146–52; Nifontov, *Zernovoe*, pp. 124–5, 140–1, 198–207, 219, 286–95; Wheatcroft, 'Crises', pp. 137–8; and Ch. 4.

24 Rubinshtein, *Sel'skoe*, p. 401; Wheatcroft, 'Crises', pp. 142–4; Mironov, 'Diet', pp. 69–70. See also Blum, *End*, pp. 186–7. On the debate over livestock holdings, see Ch. 4.

necessary to cultivate their land and carry out other work to support their households.[25]

* * *

The long-term trends, which for large parts of the period seem to have been moving in the direction of higher levels of food consumption *per capita*, concealed short-term, cyclical and haphazard changes. It was these more immediate changes that would have been most apparent to peasants, and had the most tangible impact on their lives. David Christian has analysed two main short-term trends in peasant food consumption: seasonal variations over the course of a year, and year-by-year fluctuations depending on the size of the harvest.[26]

The cycle of the seasons and the agricultural year had a significant impact on peasants' diet. There was also some correlation between the availability of food and the main fasts in the calendar of the Russian Orthodox Church. In the late summer and autumn, peasants had not only the most to eat, but also the best quality and the greatest variety of food. Grain was in abundance once the harvest had been brought in. The months of August, September and October were also the time when peasant households had the largest supplies of fresh vegetables from their garden plots, and when there was a profusion of berries and mushrooms to be gathered in the woods. By the end of the summer, peasants' livestock had been grazing out of doors for several months, and were at their fattest. As a result, there was usually plenty of milk to be drunk, made into butter, cottage cheese and soured dairy produce. This was also the time when peasants had the largest amounts of meat to eat as they slaughtered many of their animals in the autumn. The alternative was to set aside substantial amounts of fodder to feed them over the long winter months. The early autumn was also, of course, the time when peasants celebrated the harvest. At the heart of the festivities were feasting on the fruits of their labours and the inevitable bouts of drinking.

Over the long, cold winter months, peasants' meals gradually contained less fresh food and a narrower range of victuals, but the quantities they ate were still fairly generous. St Philip's fast in the weeks before Christmas marked the start of the downturn in the quantity and quality of the food peasants had to eat. In most years, grain from the harvest was still in plentiful supply throughout the winter. But the fresh vegetables, fruit, meat and dairy produce that had been eaten in the autumn were replaced by pickled, brined, salted, dried and soured foodstuffs. Preserved foods were not as nutritious as their fresh equivalents, but were far better than nothing, and added welcome variety and taste to the growing monotony of peasants' meals.

As the months passed from the previous year's harvest, the reserves of grain and preserved foods that households had laid in steadily diminished.

25 Mironov, 'Diet', p. 71.
26 Smith and Christian, *Bread*, p. 331.

The quality and variety of what was left also declined. The low point often coincided with the onset of spring and the start of the new agricultural year. Livestock were also at their lowest ebb as supplies of fodder were running out. The first green shoots in the pastures were anxiously awaited by peasants and their beasts. It was probably no coincidence that spring was the time of the two main fasts in the Orthodox Church calendar, Lent and SS Peter and Paul, which were preceded and interrupted by feasting on remaining food at Shrovetide, Easter and the other festivals of spring. The worst was usually over by early summer. The first vegetables were ready to be picked; mushrooms, wild herbs and other edible plants began to appear around villages and in the woods. Once the cattle were put out to pasture, milk again became available. However, grain sometimes began to run short. Occasionally, peasants anticipated the harvest by reaping some grain before it was ripe. Once the main harvest had been gathered in, the seasonal cycle of abundance and scarcity began again.

The impact of the seasonal variations in the quantity, quality and range of foodstuffs peasants had to eat varied depending on their level of prosperity. Poorer peasants suffered worst as their reserves ran low in the spring, forcing them to borrow from village usurers ('kulaks'), beg from neighbours, resort to substitutes (see below), or do without bread altogether for a few weeks. Sometimes, poor peasants had to sell newly harvested grain at low prices in the autumn to repay their debts and pay their taxes and other dues, but then had to buy grain to eat at far higher prices in the spring. Year-by-year fluctuations in the size of the harvest affected the magnitude of seasonal changes in the diet of all peasants, rich and poor.[27]

The haphazard cycle of good and bad harvests led to the most striking variations over time in the levels of peasant food consumption. In good years, when the harvest was bountiful, most peasants prospered. There was plenty of grain for the variety of foods, not just bread, made from flour and groats. Peasants fed grain to their livestock, fattening them up, and thus increasing the availability of dairy produce and meat for human consumption. Surplus grain and animal produce were sold to meet cash dues to landowners and the state, to pay off arrears and debts that had been run up in bad years, and to buy a few luxuries. Any grain still left over could be held in reserve in case of poor harvests in subsequent years, or distilled into *samogon*. Contrary to the impression created by some writers, good harvests were not rare events in most of Russia in the period under consideration.

In sharp contrast, when harvests were bad or failed altogether, many peasants suffered serious hardship. Bad harvests led to food shortages, high prices and, in exceptionally poor years, widespread hunger and famine. High prices affected peasants differently. Those with grain to sell gained from the extra money they earned, while peasants who needed to buy grain were at a

---

27 See Smith and Christian, *Bread*, pp. 335–8, 344; Frierson, 'Forced hunger', pp. 52–4; Heretz, 'Practice'; Druzhinin, *Gosudarstvennye*, vol. 1, pp. 382–3.

disadvantage, especially if they had little to sell to raise the money they needed. In the worst years, most peasants had to buy grain and suffered the consequences of high prices, food shortages and hunger. Before the twentieth century, the main causes of crop failures and famines were climatic rather than human or institutional. To some extent, moreover, the landowning and ruling elites in tsarist Russia took steps to 'protect' peasants from hunger. Starving peasants repeatedly demanded assistance from their landowners and state officials. The most frequent responses were reductions, postponements or simply waiving of obligations. In the late eighteenth and nineteenth centuries, when reserve granaries and funds were set up, loans or grants of grain and cash alleviated some distressed peasants in years when harvests were poor. In the worst years, however, the 'protection' afforded by elites was not enough to avert disaster. Hungry peasants sometimes resorted to violence to seize grain. Others left their villages, with or without permission, in search of food and work, or simply begged from anyone who had some food, even dried crusts, to give them.

Peasants tried to overcome food shortages in other ways. They sold livestock to raise money to buy food, or slaughtered and ate their animals to stave off hunger and save on animal fodder, which could then be used for human consumption. They killed and ate whatever animals and birds they could find, including dogs, cats and vermin. Peasants used substitutes, 'famine foods', to eke out or replace their meagre stocks of grain. Some substitutes, such as distillery waste, bran, chaff and flax seeds, were less nutritious than grain flour but contained some nourishment. Others were indigestible or even harmful. Famished peasants made bread, or what had to serve as bread, from mixtures containing dried and powdered straw, acorns, pine and fir cones. Leaves from an assortment of plants, including root vegetables, nettles, goosefoot and pigweed were somehow mixed in or used to make soups. In desperate conditions, peasants were driven to eat bark, leaves from trees, hay, moss and even soil and animal dung. There were occasional reports of cannibalism. The bodies of those who had already died sometimes seemed the last hope for those still clinging to life. In the depths of the worst subsistence crises there were even reports of parents, driven mad by hunger, murdering and eating children they could no longer feed to try to save themselves.[28]

Crop failures and food shortages were all too regular occurrences in rural Russia, but it is possible that their frequency has sometimes been exaggerated. The common assertion that there was one bad year out of three does not stand up to scrutiny. One bad year per decade seems more likely. Some periods and regions were hit more severely than others. Towards the end of the period covered by this book, the years 1889–92 and 1905–08 were marked by

28 See Smith, *Peasant Farming*, pp. 145–7; Smith and Christian, *Bread*, pp. 109–12, 190, 196, 200, 338–51; Moon, *Russian Peasants*, pp. 41–6. For harrowing accounts of famines in the 1830s, see Hoch, *Serfdom*, pp. 49–54; Indova, E. I., *Krepostnoe khozyaistvo v nachale XIX v.: po materialam votchinnogo arkhiva Vorontsovykh* (Moscow, 1955), pp. 164–6. On bad harvests in contexts of population, protection, production and protest see Chs 1, 3, 4 and 8.

short-term troughs in grain production *per capita*, including the famine of 1891–92. Sharp downturns in the food supply were usually temporary. Notwithstanding the horrors of hunger and starvation, two or three good harvests in succession cancelled out most of the consequences of all but the worst subsistence crises. They could not, however, remove from peasants' minds the fear of crop failure that had such a profound impact on their attitudes and the strategies they devised to try to ensure their subsistence.[29]

Besides bad harvests, peasants' living standards were also hit by other periodic crises. Epidemics of plague and cholera, as well as other infectious diseases, led to the sudden deaths of many peasants. The weakest, the very old and young, suffered most. From a purely economic point of view (setting aside the emotional loss and grief), the loss of people who were not able to make much of a contribution to the work of peasant households may have had a beneficial impact on living standards. The deaths of able-bodied adults, however, could plunge the survivors into destitution.[30] The emergencies that had the most harmful impact on peasant living standards after bad harvests and epidemics were wars. The increases in conscription in wartime took away from villages not just large numbers of young adult men who did most of the work in the fields, but also many of the horses which provided the main draught power. Russia's regular involvement in major wars hit the productive capacity and, therefore, levels of consumption of peasant households and communities. Peasants suffered most in areas where hostilities took place. Smolensk province was plundered by Napoleon's army in 1812.[31]

Regional variations

There were also variations in peasant consumption between regions. The economic crises that adversely affected peasant living standards in the late sixteenth and early seventeenth centuries were confined mostly to the forest-heartland. Many of the substantial numbers of peasants who migrated to the forested steppe in these decades enjoyed higher living standards once they had established themselves on the more fertile land.[32] This was part of a general pattern of regional variations in peasant living standards throughout the period under consideration. For the most part, peasants who lived in or migrated to outlying regions were better off than those in central Russia. With the growth in population and expansion of peasant settlement over the centuries, peasants had to move ever further from the centre to gain the advantages

---

29 See Blum, *Lord and Peasant*, p. 329; Hoch, 'Famine'; Simms, 'Economic impact'; Wheatcroft, 'Crises', pp. 133–6, 144, 146. On the periodisation of bad harvests throughout the period covered by this book, see Chs 1 and 4.
30 On disease, see Ch. 1.
31 Dement'ev, 'Russkaya'; Ryabkov, 'Tormozyashchee', p. 353. See also Chs 1 and 3.
32 See Blum, *Lord and Peasant*, p. 236; and Ch. 2.

of life in the borderlands. For most of the eighteenth and nineteenth centuries, the relatively low population densities in the regions of the open steppes to the south-east, the coniferous forest belt in the north, and Siberia in the east meant that peasants in these areas had access to more land than their counterparts in the central regions. Much of the land in the steppe regions was fertile and productive black earth. Although ploughing up new land was hard work, virgin land, including non-black earth, was more productive than soil that had been tilled for generations. Moreover, serfdom was either weakly developed or did not exist in some border areas. The state sometimes granted immunities or reductions in obligations for peasants who settled in frontier areas. The distance of outlying regions from the centre was also a factor, since it gave peasants more leeway in running their lives with only limited interference and demands from the landowning and ruling elites.[33]

The peasants of Petrovskoe in Tambov province, who according to Hoch were relatively prosperous in most years in the first half of the nineteenth century, had the advantage of living in the extreme south-east of the Central Black Earth region, on the border of the forested steppe and open steppe. There was still a lot of unsettled land in this area at the end of the eighteenth century. The well-being of the peasants of Petrovskoe is not surprising as the soil they cultivated was very fertile, and they had more than adequate allotments of land.[34] In spite of Hoch's comments to the contrary, however, the material standard of living of Petrovskoe's peasants may not have been typical of the Central Black Earth region as a whole. It is likely that they were better off than many peasants in more crowded parts of the region to the north-west that had been settled and farmed since the seventeenth century and had less fertile soil. Peasants who lived in the more hospitable parts of Siberia also enjoyed relatively high living standards. In 1856, Peter Semenov (later Semenov-Tyan-Shanskii) was 'startled' by the well-being of the peasants he saw in western Siberia. He compared their condition favourably with that of enserfed peasants in the Central Black Earth region in European Russia. Semenov was better able than foreign travellers to comment accurately on rural living standards. He was a leading member of the Imperial Russian Geographical Society, which collected statistics on social and economic conditions in Russia and, as a nobleman, he owned estates inhabited by peasants in Ryazan' province in the north of the Central Black Earth region.[35]

There were differences in the content as well as the quantities of food eaten by peasants in more outlying regions of Russia. The most striking contrast was that meat and dairy produce made up a larger part of the peasant diet than in more central regions. This was because there was more land for pastures and meadows to feed livestock. Hoch may have slightly overstated the importance of meat in peasants' diet in Petrovskoe in the first half of the nineteenth

33 See Chs 2–4.
34 See Hoch, *Serfdom*, pp. 12–13, 23–8.
35 Lincoln, *Semenov*, p. 24.

century, but peasants in more outlying areas did eat more meat. Semenov noted that in western Siberia in 1856: 'Meat dishes, including beef and veal, domestic fowl and wild game, as well as fish, were a part of the peasants' daily diet.' There is no doubt, however, that raising livestock remained an important part of the peasant economy on and beyond the fringes of the forested steppe for longer than in the north-west of the Central Black Earth region and elsewhere in central Russia. It remained important in Siberia throughout the nineteenth century.[36]

There were also factors in some outlying areas that had adverse effects on peasant food consumption. Harvests were more variable in the open steppe regions than in central Russia because the rainfall was less reliable. As many as one in five harvests in the open steppe were less than two-thirds the average size in the second half of the nineteenth century. It was in these regions that the famines of the nineteenth (and twentieth) centuries were worst. In good years, however, the fertile black earth of the open steppes yielded bountiful harvests. In remote parts of the Northern region and Siberia, where the conditions were very near the margins for successful grain cultivation, slight variations in the climate, in particular late frosts, could ruin the chance of a good harvest. Regional shortages of food were exacerbated by the difficulty and expense entailed in moving grain from areas where there was a surplus. Until the rapid expansion of the railway network after the 1850s, the transport infrastructure of Russia was not able to move enough food quickly to areas suffering shortages. As the famine of 1891–92 in the Volga regions demonstrated, however, the railways that existed by the end of the nineteenth century were still not adequate to avert the consequences of major regional crop failures.[37]

The existence of occasional problems in some outlying regions does not refute the general argument that peasants who lived in border areas tended to have higher standards of living than those in the centre. While there was no general all-Russian agricultural 'crisis' in the late nineteenth century, parts of the central regions were certainly poorer than the borderlands. Grain production *per capita* increased in Russia as a whole in the late nineteenth and early twentieth centuries, but declined slightly in the Central Black Earth region. As a result, there were pockets of real poverty among the peasant population, and it was this region that suffered most from over-population and land hunger. In contrast, it was in the peripheral regions, including western Siberia, southern Ukraine and the non-Russian western borderlands, that agriculture was most developed, and where peasants enjoyed the highest living standards in late tsarist Russia.[38]

36 Hoch, *Serfdom*, pp. 45–8; Lincoln, *Semenov*, p. 24 (quotation). See also Rubinshtein, *Sel'skoe*, pp. 253, 289, 324; and Ch. 4.
37 See Smith and Christian, *Bread*, pp. 341–5. See also Chs 2 and 4.
38 See Bushnell, J., 'Peasant economy and peasant revolution at the turn of the century: Neither immiseration nor autonomy', *RR*, vol. 46 (1988), pp. 78–9; Nifontov, *Zernovoe*, pp. 276, 286; Wheatcroft, 'Crises', pp. 138–42, 146; Gatrell, *Tsarist Economy*, pp. 39–40, 139–40.

Differences between categories and strata of peasants

Living standards differed between the categories that made up the Russian peasantry before the reforms of the 1860s. Of the two largest categories, state and seigniorial peasants, it is often stated that state peasants enjoyed higher standards of living as they had lower obligations and larger allotments of land. On the other hand, some state peasant communities suffered from the depredations of neighbouring noble landowners who seized parts of their land. The condition of the state peasants seems to have improved, however, after Kiselev's reforms of the 1830s and 40s. In his study of state and seigniorial peasant agriculture in the years 1842–61 in the Ukrainian province of Khar'kov (which adjoined the Central Black Earth region of Russia), Zack Deal concluded that the *per capita* output of peasants in the two categories was similar, but that the lighter obligations of the state peasants meant that they had larger surpluses. As a result, in comparison with their neighbours on noble estates, state peasants farmed less intensively and devoted more resources to animal husbandry. State peasants grew more grain for fodder, and left more of their land unsown to use as meadows and pasture. In addition, state peasants invested more of their resources in non-agricultural activities. All told, state peasants in Khar'kov province in these years enjoyed both higher standards of living and more leisure than their neighbours on seigniorial estates.

The disparity between state and seigniorial peasants may not have been quite as clear cut. The form of obligations peasants had to their landowners, either the state or nobles, also had an impact on their material well-being. Most state peasants in Russia for most of the period under consideration paid obligations in cash (*obrok*). Many seigniorial peasants also paid *obrok* to their landowners. The rest of the seigniorial peasantry, however, were compelled to perform labour obligations (*barshchina*) on their landowners' demesne. This form of obligation was more onerous and harder to avoid than monetary dues. But labour services did have the advantage that they shared the risks of farming between peasants and landowners. Both suffered if the harvest failed. Peasants who paid dues had to petition for their obligations to be reduced in years of dearth. State peasants may have been generally better off than seigniorial peasants on account of where they lived. The majority lived in more outlying regions of Russia (see Ch. 3), where all peasants seem to have been more prosperous. A large part of the seigniorial peasantry was concentrated in the more crowded central regions, where conditions were often less favourable. It would be a mistake to over-generalise about the relative prosperity of the two main categories of peasants. The surveys of state lands conducted in the 1830s, prior to Kiselev's reforms, uncovered cases of serious poverty among some state peasants. In the late nineteenth century, however, it is generally accepted that former state peasants were better off than former seigniorial peasants, since the latter, on average, received less land and had to pay more for it.[39]

39 See Blum, *Lord and Peasant*, pp. 475–93; Deal, *Serf*, p. 388; Druzhinin, *Gosudarstvennye*, vol. 1, esp. pp. 472–5. See also Ch. 3.

Many specialists have divided peasant societies into three strata: rich, middle and poor. The size of each category, obviously, depends on how they are defined. By many criteria and estimates, 'middle peasants' were the largest stratum among the Russian peasantry in the nineteenth century.[40] The numbers of rich households were the smallest. Some rich peasants in Russia were called 'kulaks', a pejorative term which means 'fists' and referred to their alleged tight-fistedness in lending money to their poorer neighbours at high rates of interest. It was not until the Soviet period, however, that rich peasants who hired labourers were branded 'kulaks' by the authorities.[41]

Mironov estimated average levels of food consumption among peasants in each stratum in the mid-nineteenth century. Middle peasants consumed, on average, more than the 3,900–4,000 calories per day reckoned to be the minimum necessary for people engaged in hard agricultural labour. Average food consumption in poor households did not give their members the energy they needed to cultivate their land. The situation was similar in the late nineteenth century. Mironov estimated the average daily consumption among adult male peasants in the three strata as follows: poor peasants (who he put at nearly 30 per cent of the entire peasantry), 3,182 calories; middle peasants, 4,500 calories; rich peasants, 5,662 calories. If these estimates are accurate, then the only way adult males in poor households could have had sufficient to eat would have been at the expense of other members of their families. Since many Russian peasants earned parts of their income from non-agricultural activities, a number of which were less arduous than agricultural labour, and since work in the fields was interrupted by regular holidays and confined to a maximum of six months a year, then for several months large numbers of adult male peasants may have been able to subsist and work on less than 3,900–4,000 calories.

There were also variations in the balance of the diets of peasants in the three strata. Mironov estimated that, in the mid-nineteenth century, rich peasants got 31 per cent of their calorific intake from meat and dairy produce, while poor peasants obtained only 19 per cent. Grain, potatoes and vegetables made up a larger part of the diet of peasants in poor households than that of their wealthier neighbours. Rich peasants, moreover, were able to maintain a balanced and varied diet for their members throughout the year, and usually had the resources to survive years of dearth. In contrast, it was poor peasants who experienced the greatest hardships in the spring and after bad harvests.[42]

All the ways of examining levels of consumption discussed so far have been at the macro-level of averages for large populations. Another approach is to move down to the micro-level, and to consider the living standards of the basic units of peasant society: individual households.

40 See, for example, Shanin, *Russia*, pp. 94–102.
41 See Shanin, *Russia*, pp. 156–8; Frierson, *Peasant Icons*, pp. 139–40.
42 Mironov, 'Diet', pp. 71–2. All Mironov's figures are for the European part of the Russian Empire. See also Smith and Christian, *Bread*, pp. 352–5.

Peasant households were units of consumption as well as of production and reproduction, and family dwelling places. Levels of consumption, or living standards, varied between households in the same communities, and the standards of living of individual households changed over time. Many scholars who have investigated the Russian peasant economy in the late nineteenth and early twentieth centuries have relied on data collected by *zemstvo* statisticians and other specialists. Measuring the levels of consumption of peasant households in the period before the 1870s and 80s is very difficult, since all the necessary data are not available. The relative wealth of individual peasant households in the preceding centuries has been gauged in a number of ways, including analysis of the sizes of their land allotments or the area they sowed, the numbers of horses and other livestock they owned, the volume of agricultural output and handicraft goods they produced, wages earned by their members, and the amounts they paid in obligations and taxes.[43]

Although the concept and value of dividing peasant societies into rich, middle and poor has been questioned, it is a useful way to measure 'differentiation' in consumption, as well as other indices of prosperity, between households at fixed points in time. Most specialists have noted a strong positive correlation between household wealth and size. The more prosperous households in a community were usually bigger, with more able-bodied adults, larger land allotments and more livestock, than poorer households. What specialists have disagreed about has been the reasons for such inequalities and their permanence. Individual households that were poor at one point in time were sometimes middle or even rich several years later. On the other hand, the fortunes of some rich households declined. The two best-known theories put forward to explain changes over time in the relative prosperity of peasant households are those of Lenin and Chayanov.[44]

The theories of Lenin and Chayanov

In the 1890s, as part of his study *The Development of Capitalism in Russia*, Lenin investigated the rural economy. His main source was *zemstvo* data on the productive resources, economic activities and expenditure of peasant households in 13 provinces. He argued that capitalism was developing in rural Russia, and that it was leading to the disintegration of the peasantry and the village commune. He claimed that the Russian peasantry was becoming stratified into two distinct 'classes': small numbers of rich peasants, who constituted a 'rural bourgeoisie'; and large and growing numbers of poor peasants,

---

43 Merl ('Socio-economic', pp. 63–4) has pointed out, however, that ownership of the means of production by peasant households was not necessarily a good guide to economic well-being.
44 Both theories are also relevant to peasant households' productive activities and the larger economic systems of which they were a part. Indeed, one of Chayanov's main concerns was to integrate production and consumption in a 'theory of peasant economy'. See Ch. 4.

who made up a 'rural proletariat'. The 'rural bourgeoisie' were motivated by the desire to make profits from selling agricultural and other produce at the market. To this end, they accumulated the means of production, in particular land and horses, and increasingly relied on hired labour. 'Rural proletarians', on the other hand, did not have enough land and other resources to support themselves, and had to work as wage labourers for rural entrepreneurs from the rich peasantry (as well as landowners and industrialists). Lenin believed that the 'middle peasantry', previously the largest stratum, was disappearing. A few were becoming rural entrepreneurs, but most were declining towards the mass of impoverished wage labourers. Lenin concluded, or rather asserted, 'we have shown . . . that the peasantry have completely split up into two opposite groups'.[45]

Lenin was arguing against the Populists, who believed that capitalism was not developing in the Russian countryside, that the Russian peasantry and the village commune were not disintegrating, and that differences in prosperity between peasant households were a result of differences in their size and the corresponding amounts of land they were allotted by their communes. A more sophisticated rebuttal of Lenin's 'class analysis' of rural differentiation was put forward by Chayanov in the 1910s and 20s. One of the problems with Lenin's work was that it was based on data that were essentially static. He had examined inequalities between households only at fixed points in time. The data available to Lenin did not permit dynamic analysis that took account of changes over time in the economic status of individual households. 'Dynamic studies', which traced the fate of individual households over time, had been carried out by the early twentieth century and were available to Chayanov.

Chayanov built on the Populists' belief that capitalism was not developing in rural Russia, and argued that peasants' economic behaviour was different from that of capitalist entrepreneurs. Peasants were not motivated by profits, he argued, but by the subsistence needs of their households. According to Chayanov's theory, the main determinant of a peasant household's standard of living was its size and composition which, in turn, were a result of the 'phase of development' it was at in its life cycle (see Ch. 5). To take a hypothetical example: a small household, comprising a married couple and their young children with one share of allotment land from the commune, was relatively poor. As the sons grew up, married, and brought their wives to live with them in their parents' household, it was allotted additional land by the commune, and became both larger and more prosperous. When the married sons broke away and set up on their own, taking with them their families, shares of the household's land and other property, however, then one large and wealthy household was replaced by two or three smaller and poorer ones. In time, as they embarked on their life cycles, the new households set up by

---

45 See Lenin, 'Development', pp. 70–187 (quotation from p. 187). See also Ellis, *Peasant Economics*, pp. 51–6; Gatrell, P., 'Historians and peasants: Studies of medieval England in a Russian context', *P & P*, no. 96 (1982), pp. 38–43.

sons grew in size, acquired more land, and became wealthier, and so on for generations.

The important factor was not just the number of peasants in a household, but the ratio of 'consumers' to 'workers': the 'dependency ratio' (see Ch. 4). A household containing several young children and old people, who were unable to work but needed to be fed, and relatively few able-bodied youths and adults, had a high dependency ratio. The 'workers' in such a household would have to work very hard to support all its members ('self-exploitation'). All the members of such a household would have only low standards of living. On the other hand, the 'workers' in a household with relatively few non-working members would not have to work as hard, would therefore enjoy more leisure, and be better off. In other words, peasants' *per capita* income was inversely proportional to the dependency ratio of their households. In any one community at any one time, some households were becoming more prosperous, while others were getting poorer. Several years later, however, some of the households which had been getting richer might have been experiencing a decline in their fortunes, and vice versa. 'Dynamic studies' of household wealth showed that, over the course of their lifetimes, individual peasants could live successively in poor, middle and rich households, or the other way round, depending on the 'phase of development' in their households' life cycle and the resulting dependency ratio. The general trend of changes in the wealth of peasant households in a community, moreover, was egalitarian, towards levelling rather than polarisation.[46]

To sum up, in Lenin's theory socio-economic differentiation between peasant households was permanent, was leading towards the polarisation of the peasantry into a small class of rich entrepreneurs and a large class of poor labourers, and was a result of the development of capitalism. In Chayanov's theory, differences in peasant households' living standards were temporary, possibly cyclical, tended towards levelling, and did not reflect any fundamental changes in the nature of the rural economy. (See Table 8.1.)

Lenin's and Chayanov's theories are best seen as models or hypotheses, against which to test empirical data on the relative prosperity of actual peasant households.[47] The following subsections will consider some of the evidence for differentiation and socio-economic mobility among peasant households at different times and in different regions.

The forest-heartland before the late seventeenth century
In the sixteenth and most of the seventeenth centuries in the forest-heartland of Russia (where most Russian peasants lived), there were disparities between the wealth of peasant households in many communities. As in later periods, relatively prosperous households tended to be larger than their less well-off neighbours. Some Soviet historians argued that capitalism was starting to

46 See Chayanov, *Theory*, pp. 53–89; Ellis, *Peasant Economics*, pp. 109–21; Gatrell, 'Historians', pp. 43–9; Shanin, *Awkward*, pp. 45–80, 101–9.
47 See Shanin, *Russia*, pp. 164–5.

TABLE 8.1

DIFFERENTIATION OF PEASANT HOUSEHOLDS

(hypothetical examples)

(a) Lenin's model

Peasant households by stratum	1890	1900	Net change
Poor	300	650	350 (+)
Middle	600	200	400 (−)
Rich	100	150	50 (+)

(b) Chayanov's model

Peasant households by stratum	1900	1910		
		Poor	Middle	Rich
Poor	650	300	250	100
Middle	200	50	100	50
Rich	150	50	50	50
All		400	400	200

Source: Based on Gatrell, 'Historians and peasants', pp. 38, 46.

emerge in the economy of rural Russia at this time. This conclusion was based on dogma rather than hard evidence. The agricultural sector of the economy was overwhelmingly natural in the sixteenth and seventeenth centuries, and the proportion of peasant households' output they put on the market was very small. The main mechanisms for transferring agricultural produce from peasant producers to the small minority of the population not engaged in farming were obligations in labour, kind or cash to landowners and the state. Earnings from trade contributed to the prosperity of a few richer peasant households, but were not central to their budgets, and cannot explain all the differences in the wealth between households in the forest-heartland at that time.

It is far more likely that demographic factors played a large role in determining the relative wealth of peasant households in pre-Petrine Muscovy. The prevailing patterns of early and near-universal marriage and household partitions before the death of household heads meant that the average size of households was fairly small, five to six people, and many went through a series of 'phases of development'. The custom of dividing property between household members led to the periodic dissolution of larger and wealthier households and the creation of new units that were initially smaller and poorer but had the potential to grow in size and wealth. Chayanov's model depended on the ability of households to get more land as their numbers grew. In this early period, most held their land in household tenure. Nevertheless, many households were able to increase the amounts of land they cultivated to support growing numbers. In all but the most densely populated central areas, some uncultivated or abandoned land was available. Sons often set up new homesteads on new land when they broke away from their fathers. Some households rented or bought extra land from their neighbours or landowners if they needed more. Chayanov's model may, therefore, help explain some differences in wealth between households, and changes over time, in the forest-heartland over two centuries before the time he was writing about.

The forest-heartland of Russia prior to the late seventeenth century was not simply a patchwork of Chayanovian peasant family farms. There were also more permanent patterns of differentiation that depended on factors other than household demography. In many village communities there were relatively small numbers of labourers (*bobyli*) with little or no land, who supported themselves mainly by working for richer peasants, who thus maintained their relative prosperity at the expense of others. A number of labourers lived in the households they worked for. Some of these landless labourers were younger peasants or new arrivals in a settlement, who went on to marry, acquire land, and set up their own households. Therefore, the status of these landless labourers was temporary, in contrast to that of the permanent class of 'rural proletarians' Lenin believed existed in late nineteenth-century Russia. There were other landless labourers in the earlier period, however, who retained their lowly status and relative poverty throughout their lives.[48] Another category of poor peasants in parts of the forest-heartland before the seventeenth century was share-croppers (*polovniki*). Many rented land from richer peasants (or merchants, landowners or monasteries), and handed over (usually) half of the grain they harvested from this land in payment. Share-cropping was another way in which richer peasants with large amounts of land could maintain their status by taking advantage of poorer neighbours. Instead of hiring them to cultivate their land, they leased part of it to them in return for half the crop. The high proportion they had to hand over gave most share-croppers little chance to improve their position.[49]

Some differences in the relative prosperity of peasants and households in this early period may, therefore, have been long lasting. The system of assessing obligations and taxes before the second half of the seventeenth century – by the amount of land households held – meant that there was little reason for village elders, landowners or state officials to insist that all peasants in a community were allotted land (see Chs 3 and 6).

Although better-off peasants sold some of their produce at local markets, it is probable that production for sale was not the chief reason why they

48 See Smith, *Peasant Farming*, esp. pp. 80–3, 95, 135, 180–2, 187, 221; Gorskaya, *Krest'yanstvo*, pp. 337–8; Kopanev, *Istoriya*, pp. 140–2; Nazarov, V. D. and Tikhonov, Yu. A., 'Krest'yanskii i bobyl'skii dvor v svetskikh vladeniyakh tsental'nykh uezdov pervoi poloviny XVII v.', *IS* (1977), no. 4, pp. 152–62. See also Chs 3, 5 and 6.
49 See Blum, *Lord and Peasant*, pp. 484–5; Semevskii, *Krest'yane*, vol. 2, pp. 700–21; Shapiro, *Russkoe krest'yanstvo*, pp. 215–23.

hired labourers or let out part of their land to share-croppers. Leisure and status in their communities may have been more important in a society where subsistence was the main motive for production and the market was only weakly developed. The socio-economic structure of villages in the forest-heartland of Russia before the late seventeenth century contained elements of what could be described as permanent differentiation without capitalism.[50] Most differences in wealth between peasant households in the forest-heartland in this earlier period, however, were probably temporary, and in all likelihood conformed to Chayanov's life-cycle model.

Outlying regions after the seventeenth century
There were substantial differences in the relative prosperity of peasant households in some more outlying regions of Russia after the seventeenth century. In her study of Russian peasant households in western Siberia in the eighteenth and first half of the nineteenth centuries, Soviet scholar N. A. Minenko discovered a strong correlation between the size of families, the areas of land they sowed, the numbers of horses they possessed, and their prosperity in comparison with other households. Minenko included a ritual quotation from Lenin on the importance of wage labour in prosperous households, but provided little evidence to support this view. There was a similar pattern in differences in land-holding between peasant households in parts of the Northern region in the eighteenth century. In both western Siberia and the Northern region in this period, substantial proportions of peasant households, 10–20 per cent or higher, had no land or livestock. Although the published data do not allow the fates of individual households to be traced over time, it is possible that at least some of the differences in prosperity were a result of temporary household demographic factors. Many households in both regions were small in size and simple in structure, because sons usually broke away from their fathers' households in *pre-mortem* partitions. Consequently, individual households grew and then fell in size over their life cycles, and experienced corresponding changes in their living standards. Some of the households without land or livestock may simply have been at a stage when they were small and poor, but had the potential to improve their status. Some, moreover, engaged in non-agricultural activities, and so did not need land or animals to maintain reasonable standards of living.[51]

Other households without land or livestock, however, may have been poor and unable to escape poverty. Some were trapped in share-cropping agreements. This practice persisted in parts of the northern regions long after it had died out in the rest of the forest-heartland by the seventeenth century. The number of share-croppers in the northern regions was quite small, however,

50 See Shapiro, A. L., 'Ob opasnosti modernizatsii ekonomicheskoi istorii russkogo krest'yanstva XVII–pervoi poloviny XVIII v.', *EAIVE 1959 g.* (1961), pp. 52–68. *Cf.* Preobrazhenskii, *Krest'yanstvo*, pp. 173–93.
51 See Minenko, *Russkaya*, pp. 77–107; Baklanova, *Krest'yanskii*, pp. 10–83, 192–3; Semevskii, *Krest'yane*, vol. 2, pp. 619–20, 660–6. See also Ch. 5.

and fell from around 15,000 householders in the 1740s to a little over 5,000 by 1795.[52] Similar differences in wealth between peasant households also endured along the old steppe frontier in the south-east. A small number of *odnodvortsy* (descendants of military servitors) continued to own a few serfs for over a century after they had been demoted to state peasants in 1719. As the economic as well as social fortunes of the *odnodvortsy* declined further, the condition of their serfs, who never numbered more than around 30,000–40,000 of both sexes, also deteriorated.[53]

The non-Russian western borderlands and beyond

There were also significant differences in the relative prosperity of peasant households in the non-Russian western borderlands of the empire annexed after 1650. In most of these areas, peasant households held their land in individual tenure, and their obligations and taxes were assessed according to the size of their land-holdings or the number of draught animals they owned. These practices continued long after Russian annexation. In many village communities in the western borderlands, households were subdivided into a hierarchy of categories from relatively prosperous families with relatively large holdings of land and livestock, at one extreme, to landless and horseless labourers at the other.[54]

Many village communities elsewhere in pre-industrial Europe were also stratified between different gradations of households. Excluding gentry, they included yeomen, husbandmen, small-holders, cottagers and labourers. Households with more land than they could farm with the labour of their own members often hired day labourers or took in farm servants. In part, such practices were a result of local marriage patterns and inheritance customs that were different from those in Russia. In much of pre-industrial central and north-west Europe, people tended to marry late, between 25 and 30, and a substantial minority never married. In some areas, moreover, land was not shared between all sons, but passed on intact to one under impartible inheritance in a system of stem families. Many of the day labourers and live-in farm servants in such areas were single young men and women who were not eligible to inherit land. Many were trying to save up enough money to marry and set up their own households. Some disinherited children from poorer families never succeeded in doing so, and remained poor and unmarried throughout their lives. Many wealthier families arranged for their younger sons to serve apprenticeships, so that they could learn a trade or craft, and earn enough to marry. The custom of impartible inheritance enabled prosperous families to pass on all their land and much of their other wealth intact, thereby creating relatively long-lasting social and economic hierarchies in village communities. Many German agricultural settlers who moved to Russia in the eighteenth century

---

52 Semevskii, *Krest'yane*, vol. 2, pp. 700–17; Shapiro, *Russkoe krest'yanstvo*, p. 215.
53 See Pallot and Shaw, *Landscape*, pp. 42, 46–8; Semevskii, *Krest'yane*, vol. 2, pp. 770–4.
54 See Blum, *Lord and Peasant*, pp. 461, 532–3; Druzhinin, *Gosudarstvennye*, vol. 1, pp. 332–4, 438–72; Ignatovich, *Pomeshchich'i*, pp. 191–2, 223–36; Kakhk, *Ostzeiskii put'*, pp. 98–117.

practised impartible inheritance, with similar results for the socio-economic profile of their communities.[55]

The practices of late and restricted marriage (leading to low fertility), impartible inheritance and labour mobility that evolved in parts of central and northwest Europe in the period before industrialisation were partly responses to the problem of trying to support their populations at reasonable standards of living in the face of growing scarcities of land. In many areas these practices resulted in long-term inequalities in the distribution of wealth between households. In much of Russia, however, the relative abundance of land until rather later put little pressure on peasants to alter their practices of near-universal and early marriage (with consequent high fertility) and partible inheritance. When growing population and increasing demands by the landowning and ruling elites began to put more pressure on Russian peasants, especially in the central regions from the mid-seventeenth century, the solutions adopted were different from those in many other parts of Europe, and had different consequences for the distribution of wealth between the members of village communities.

The central regions (mid-seventeenth to late-nineteenth centuries)
In central Russia, especially in the period between the mid-seventeenth and mid-eighteenth centuries, many peasant households and village communities developed a number of practices with the aim of making the most efficient use of their resources – especially labour and land – in order to support themselves and meet their obligations, but without fundamentally altering the relatively low levels of technology and capital investment in the rural economy. Throughout the central regions, landless labourers and share-croppers had been largely eliminated by the end of the seventeenth century as village communes allotted them shares of the land, and the communities' burden of obligations. The same aim of bringing households' land and labour resources into conformance, in order to make the most effective use of both, was achieved by the introduction of communal and repartitional land tenure, and communal assistance for households that were temporarily unable to support themselves. Effective use of labour was also achieved by restricting household divisions and compelling the younger generation of adults to continue to live with one set of parents in large, complex households. For the most part, these strategies were supported by heads of peasant households, communal elders, estate managers, landowners and state officials. All were intent on maintaining the viability of peasant households and communities. The result of these strategies was that resources and wealth were more evenly distributed between peasant households than in the preceding period, or in many other parts of Europe. Thus, these strategies served as 'levelling mechanisms'. This was levelling based on pragmatism, however, not idealism.[56]

55 See Blum, *End*, pp. 95–115; Rösener, *Peasantry*, pp. 36–8, 152–6; Overton, *Agricultural Revolution*, pp. 36–43; Casey, *History*, pp. 116–45; Hajnal, 'Two kinds', pp. 70–1, 92–9; Löwe, H.-D., 'Differentiation in Russian peasant society, 1880–1905', in *LCPCR*, p. 166. See also Chs 5 and 6.
56 See Chs 3–6.

Levelling was most marked on seigniorial estates where peasants engaged mainly in agriculture and performed labour obligations in the Central Black Earth region between the mid-eighteenth century and the end of serfdom in 1861. In his study of the estate of Mishino, in Ryazan' province, Peter Czap identified a substantial number of peasant households that remained large in size and complex in structure throughout the decades from the 1780s to the 1850s. The village commune and estate steward maintained a fairly even distribution of resources between households. In 1822, there was an average of 0.41 horses per person in Mishino. Out of 130 households, only three did not own a horse, and only one had more than one horse per person. Land was also evenly divided between the labour teams that made up households. Czap concluded that the 'commune and/or the estate administration achieved a high degree of success in controlling [the distribution of horses and land,] and in this way enforced their own criteria for a minimum standard of living among all the households on the estate'.[57]

Edgar Melton analysed the social structure of a similar estate in the Central Black Earth region, Rastorg in Kursk province, in the context of the debate between the Leninist and Chayanovian models. He demonstrated that the small proportion (13 per cent) of households in Rastorg who were unable to meet their obligations, as reported by the estate steward in 1806, were poor because they were small in size and had relatively few able-bodied adults. For example, the households headed by Vasilii and Samson Lisoi were poor because they had split before their father's death, creating two weak households out of one potentially strong one. Zakhar Ermakov and his wife were struggling because they had six children aged 14 or younger. Since they had three teenaged sons, however, their household had the potential to become larger and more prosperous in the space of only a few years. The average size of the 23 poor households on the estate was 5.1, whereas the other 153 households contained, on average, 9.8 people. Melton's study of Rastorg strongly suggests that, when levelling mechanisms did not work, it was Chayanovian patterns of differentiation that emerged.[58]

There were also many communities in the Central Non-Black Earth region where the evolution of significant, and permanent, differences in the relative wealth of peasant households was limited. Because craft production, trade, wage labour and commercial agriculture were relatively well developed in this region, many Soviet specialists were anxious to find evidence for Leninist differentiation of the peasantry into a few rich entrepreneurs and a mass of poor labourers.[59] Other Soviet historians, however, accepted that capitalist polarisation of the peasantry was not taking place on a wide scale in the Central

57 Czap, 'Perennial', pp. 18–19. See also Hoch, *Serfdom*, pp. 104–17, 127–32, 187–9.
58 Melton, 'Proto-industrialization', pp. 94–104. Some Soviet historians claimed, with little evidence, to have detected 'class differentiation' in the Central Black Earth region in this period: Druzhinin, *Gosudarstvennye*, vol. 1, pp. 407–8, 415–16.
59 See Druzhinin, *Gosudarstvennye*, vol. 1, pp. 398–400; Preobrazhenskii, *Krest'yanstvo*, pp. 379–404.

Non-Black Earth region prior to the late nineteenth century. They noted the slow and uneven pace in the formation of capitalist relations in the region, and the effectiveness of practices adopted by many landowners and communes to promote levelling rather than differentiation between peasant households. As in the Central Black Earth region, such practices were most effective on estates where the peasants' main activity was agriculture and they performed labour services. N. A. Bogoroditskaya discovered little evidence of differentiation and polarisation between peasant households on the estates of the Orlov-Davydov family in Nizhnii Novgorod province in the first half of the nineteenth century. The peasants' main economic activity was agriculture, but most peasants paid dues (*obrok*) rather than performed labour services. Compared with the other estates discussed here, there were more poor households and wider fluctuations over time in the proportions in each strata. Some rich households produced surpluses of farm produce which they sold. But with the exception of two wealthy households who ran carting businesses, there was little use of hired labour.[60]

Rodney Bohac's case study of 'family, property, and socioeconomic mobility' in Manuilovskoe, in Tver' province, in the same period also examined a seigniorial estate in the Central Non-Black Earth region where the peasants engaged largely in agriculture (supplemented by crafts, trade and migrant wage labour) and paid dues. He discovered quite large differences in prosperity between households on the estate, but no trend towards greater stratification over time. His study is of particular interest, however, because he traced the fate of individual households over time. At risk of over-simplifying his subtle distinctions between several types of household life cycles, he showed that households which were able to retain complex structures and large sizes for prolonged periods (Czap's 'perennial' complex households) were better off than those which went through a series of 'phases of development' and were, thus, simple in structure and small in size for significant parts of their life cycles. Bohac's analysis also showed that dependency ratios played a role in determining household wealth and socio-economic mobility.[61]

The limited degrees of progressive differentiation among much of the peasant population of the central regions of Russia in the eighteenth and first half of the nineteenth centuries suggest that the 'development of capitalism' had not made much headway, and that the various strategies adopted by many peasant households, communes, estate managers, landowners and officials reduced socio-economic differentiation. Poor households were given some support to prevent them from going under, and opportunities for richer households to become more prosperous were restricted. If there was conflict between richer and poorer households over these strategies, seigniorial and state authorities often backed the poorer peasants. An important determinant of the relative

60 Bogoroditskaya, N. A., 'Rassloenie krest'yan v Simbileiskoi imenii Nizhegorodskogo uezda v pervoi polovine XIX v.', *EAIVE 1965 g.* (Moscow, 1970), pp. 265–79. See also Ryabkov, 'Tormozyashchee'.
61 Bohac, *Family*.

prosperity of peasant households was their size. In villages where communes periodically redistributed the land and in which household divisions were restricted, differences in the relative wealth of most individual families were relatively narrow. In parts of the Central Non-Black Earth region where more households broke up before the death of their heads, creating more smaller units, disparities in wealth between households depended to a large extent on the stages in their life cycles they had reached. Thus, differences in the prosperity of peasant households in many communities in central Russia between the mid-seventeenth and late nineteenth centuries are better explained by Chayanov's model.

Outlying regions from the mid-eighteenth century
Starting in the mid-eighteenth century, some of the strategies that had developed in central Russia, in particular communal and repartitional land tenure and restrictions on household divisions, spread outwards to some parts of the more outlying regions. The strategies also became more common among state peasants, partly as a result of pressure from the state (see Chs 5 and 6). The status of the some of the poorest peasants in outlying regions was addressed by the government in the middle decades of the nineteenth century. In 1827 state officials acted to protect the remaining share-croppers in the Northern region, who numbered around 3,000, from excessive exploitation. They were then settled on state lands and incorporated into the state peasantry.[62] The anomaly of some *odnodvortsy* along the old steppe frontier owning serfs was ended between 1842 and 1858. The Ministry of State Domains bought up the roughly 8,000 serfs who still belonged to *odnodvorsty*, and converted them to state peasants.[63] As a result of these measures, permanent institutional disparities in the socio-economic status of households in some rural communities were ended, and there were improvements in the living standards of peasants who had formerly been at the very bottom of the hierarchy.

Industrial villages (late eighteenth to late nineteenth centuries)
Not all the evidence on the distribution of resources and wealth between peasant households in Russia prior to the late nineteenth century provides more support for Chayanov's model than Lenin's. In some villages in the Central Non-Black Earth region and parts of adjoining regions there were trends towards more permanent differentiation, and polarisation. They were most marked in villages where handicrafts, trade and wage labour played a large part in the local economy. Peasants in such villages were heavily involved in the market. They sold their craft produce and labour, and bought the raw materials they required for cottage industry and the food they needed to eat. Some peasants grew 'industrial' crops, such as flax and hemp, and fruit and vegetables primarily for sale. Market-orientated economic activities were more

62 Semevskii, *Krest'yane*, vol. 2, p. 718. *Cf.* Blum, *Lord and Peasant*, pp. 484–5.
63 Hoch and Augustine, 'Tax censuses', pp. 410, 412.

common among peasants who paid dues, and who lived in the hinterland of large cities and in 'industrial' villages, such as Ivanovo in Vladimir province. (See Ch. 4.)

Two other industrial villages, where peasants paid dues, Baki in Kostroma province and Mstera in Vladimir province, were the subjects of case studies by Melton. Many households in Baki engaged in subsistence agriculture, but the main economic activity was lumbering and the timber trade. Sixteen wealthy timber traders bought lumber from some local peasants, and hired others to load it onto barges and take it downstream for sale. In 1813 the estate manager drew up an inventory of most of the households in Baki. He ranked two households as 'well to do' and ten as 'industrious'. They contained most of the timber merchants, and comprised 10 per cent of the households on the estate. The richest peasant, Andreyan Osokin, had capital of around 50,000 roubles and employed around 200 peasants. Seventy-five households (60 per cent) were classed as 'middle' or 'lower-middle'. They had diversified economies involving agriculture and varying combinations of crafts, trade and wage labour for the timber merchants. The middle-ranking households had an average of 5.6 members, compared with an estate mean of 5.02. The average dependency ratio of middle households, 1:1, was also favourable. 'Lower-middle' households were a little smaller, with 5.2 members, and had a less favourable average dependency ratio of 1:1.26. The 34 'poor' households (27 per cent) were much smaller, with an average of only 3.6 members and a mean dependency ratio of 1:1.8. Nearly half had no arable land, and most relied heavily on menial wage labour, working on the land of middle peasants or as domestic servants for richer households.[64]

The industrial village of Mstera was well known for its icon painters, but also had three linen mills. Many peasant households engaged in market gardening, but otherwise agriculture was of little importance. Production of icons, linen, and fruit and vegetables for sale, and the purchase of raw materials and food, meant that the market played a large role in the village economy. Melton divided the 307 out of 365 households in Mstera in 1859 for which he had data into rich, middle and poor strata according to their annual incomes. The average annual household income was 567 roubles. Twenty-nine out of the 307 households (9.4 per cent) had annual incomes over 1,000 roubles and were 'rich'. The richest, the Golyshevs, earned 7,500 roubles. They ran an illustrating business, put out work to cottage workers, and had just opened a lithography workshop. The Golyshevs sold their prints and broadsheets at their shop in Mstera and, via pedlars, throughout Russia. Most of the other rich households were wholesale food merchants. In the village, 182 households (59 per cent of those for which data exist) had incomes between 100 and 1,000 roubles and were ranked as 'middle-level'. The wealthiest households in this stratum were those of the icon masters, who ran workshops and hired a few workers. The poorest households in the village, a little under half

64 Melton, 'Household', pp. 564–9, 582 n. 73.

the total, depended on wage labour and piecework for the icon masters and Golyshevs, and on money earned from selling garden produce. The existence of a workhouse and soup kitchen in Mstera indicates that some of the peasants were not always able to support themselves without assistance.[65]

Melton's studies of the social structure of Baki and Mstera provide examples of two extremes of wealth among peasant households: wealthy businessmen who hired labour and produced goods for sale, and poor wage labourers who depended mainly on what they could earn by working for better-off peasants. The big differences in income and wealth between households in Baki and Mstera had come about as a result of the development of non-agricultural activities and market forces, and the ability of some peasants to exploit others. Although the data do not allow the fates of individual households to be traced over time, Melton's findings provide some support for Lenin's model of 'class differentiation'. There seems to have been little change in the social structure of Mstera in the decades after 1859, however, suggesting that the differentiation was relatively static and not part of a trend towards greater polarisation. Melton contrasted the social structure of Mstera with the agricultural estate of Rastorg (see above, p. 311), where Chayanov's model seemed more appropriate. However, the majority of households in Mstera and Baki, as well as Rastorg, were in the 'middle' stratum.[66]

Many Soviet historians were quick to draw attention to the similarity between the social structure of some 'industrial villages' in the Central Non-Black Earth region in the last decades before 1861 and the trend towards polarisation which Lenin claimed to have identified on a wider scale in rural Russia in the following decades. V. A. Fedorov, for example, pointed to the case in Ivanovo of the Grachevs, rich serf-entrepreneurs, who bought serfs to work in their mills in the name of the Sheremetevs who owned them. Rich peasant families such as the Grachevs maintained their wealth and status from generation to generation.[67]

The economy and pattern of differentiation between households in industrial settlements such as Ivanovo, Mstera and Baki were not unusual in the forest-heartland of Russia in the last century of serfdom. But wealthy industrialists and poor wage labourers were peasants only in their legal social category. They did not conform to definitions of 'peasants' put forward by most specialists (see Ch. 1). Lenin, after all, was tracing (or predicting) the demise of peasant society. It should be remembered, however, that the vast majority of peasants in the forest-heartland in this period still relied mainly on agriculture, and were involved in market-orientated activities only to limited degrees. Trends in the relative prosperity of most peasant households, moreover, bore little resemblance to the model of progressive polarisation put forward by Lenin. Together with most of the rest of Russia, the main patterns in the distribution

65 Melton, 'Proto-industrialization', pp. 72, 81–92.
66 Melton, 'Proto-industrialization', pp. 89–92; *id.*, 'Household', pp. 566–8.
67 Fedorov, *Pomeshchich'i*, pp. 236–8, 250–4. See also Preobrazhenskii, *Krest'yanstvo*, pp. 392–6; and Ch. 4.

of wealth between peasant households in the Central Non-Black Earth region as a whole between the late eighteenth and late nineteenth centuries were still closer to those described by Chayanov.

Russia in the late nineteenth and early twentieth centuries
The real test for the rival models of Lenin and Chayanov is rural Russia in the late nineteenth and early twentieth centuries, since this was the society they were studying. The far greater availability of data for this period, more-over, provides more evidence with which to test their theories. Most Soviet scholars followed Lenin's mode of analysis, and reached conclusions that broadly supported those in his 1899 book *The Development of Capitalism in Russia*. A typical example is I. D. Koval'chenko's study of a sample of peas-ant household budgets from three provinces in the Central Black Earth and Mid-Volga regions of Russia (and Khar'kov province in Ukraine) in the early twentieth century. He focused on household size, wage labour (both labour hired by households to cultivate their land, and wages earned by household members working for others), expenditure on productive resources (labour, land, horses, implements, etc.), volume of production for sale, and gross and net income. Koval'chenko's conclusions stressed the extent to which capital-ism had developed in the rural economy and 'the rise of a small stratum of prosperous households and the ruin of a mass of poor households . . .'.[68] Such interpretations did not find favour with all Soviet historians. In the late 1950s A. M. Anfimov argued that, in much of the Russian countryside at the turn of the twentieth century, practices reminiscent of seigniorial obligations under serfdom, such as peasants renting land from nobles by working for them (*otrabotka*) or handing over a share of the harvest, were more important than 'capitalist' wage labour. As a result, he maintained, the development of cap-italism in parts of rural Russia was restricted, and the polarisation of the peasantry into two conflicting 'classes' was limited.[69]

Indeed, within a decade of the publication of *The Development of Capitalism*, Lenin himself had modified his trenchant assertion on the polarisation of the peasantry. What changed his mind was the rural revolution of 1905–07, dur-ing which members of peasant communities all over Russia had acted together against noble landowners and state officials. This striking evidence for the continued cohesion of peasant communities meant that Lenin's earlier view on the disintegration of the peasantry into two conflicting classes was untenable. Lenin admitted that his earlier conclusion was overstated, but did not abandon his general argument about the eventual polarisation of the peasantry. Set-ting aside limitations in the data available to Lenin in the 1890s and 1900s, the

---

68 Koval'chenko, I. D., 'The Peasant economy in central Russia in the late 19th and early 20th century', in *AOCI*, pp. 455–75. Freeze ('New scholarship', p. 608) pointed to shortcomings in this article.
69 See Anfimov, A. M., 'K voprosu o kharaktere agrarnogo stroya evropeiskoi Rossii v nachale XX v.', *IZ*, vol. 65 (1959), pp. 119–62. Anfimov later 'recanted': *Krest'yanskoe*, p. 7. See also Shanin, *Russia*, pp. 150–65.

principal problem with his 'class analysis' was that he was describing what he wanted to see happen for political reasons. Lenin wanted the Russian peasantry to disintegrate into a small rural bourgeoisie and large rural proletariat so that the latter would struggle against the rural bourgeoisie and join the tiny urban and industrial working class in Russia in a 'socialist revolution' under the leadership of his 'vanguard party'.[70]

The debate over the socio-economic structure of peasant communities in late nineteenth- and early twentieth-century Russia was revived among Western scholars in the 1960s and 1970s. Teodor Shanin sought to explain peasant cohesion not just in 1905–07, but also during the revolution of 1917–21 and in the 1920s. He drew on and developed both the data and methodologies of *zemstvo* statisticians and other contemporary Russian specialists. He made particular use of 'dynamic studies' that traced changes over time in the fortunes of individual households. Shanin stressed the importance of a wider range of factors than household demography, but noted the trends for larger and richer households to partition into less well-off smaller family units, and for some smaller and poorer households to get both larger and more prosperous. Other weaker and poorer households disappeared, by merging with other households, migrating, or becoming extinct through the departures and deaths of their members. Shanin also argued that there were few landless wage labourers in rural Russia at this time, and that most were young men and women who had not yet married. Wage labour was, therefore, a temporary experience for some peasants at a particular point in their lives. Permanent or 'proletarian' wage labour among poor peasants who had no other ways of supporting themselves was rare. Shanin concluded that patterns of socio-economic mobility in peasant communities in late tsarist Russia were 'multi-directional' and possibly 'cyclical'. The main tendencies, he argued, were levelling and cohesion rather than polarisation and conflict.[71]

Shanin's work, and that of the Russian specialists he drew on, including Chayanov, has been sharply criticised.[72] Other Western scholars who followed Shanin's lead took account of these criticisms, and tried to make allowances for shortcomings in the available evidence. Investigations into data from a number of provinces as well as detailed case studies of smaller samples have suggested that changes over time in the distribution of resources between peasant households tended in the direction of levelling rather than polarisation. Significant roles in limiting long-term differentiation between rich and poor households were played by communal land redistribution and changes in the demographic structure of households, in particular the periodic partition of larger, and richer, households. Levelling trends and the importance

70 Lenin, V. I., 'The agrarian programme of social democracy in the first Russian revolution, 1905–1907', *Collected Works*, vol. 13 (Moscow, 1972), pp. 217–429. See also Service, R., *Lenin: A Political Life*, 3 vols (Basingstoke and London, 1985–94), vol. 1, pp. 69–70, 164, 228 n. 56.
71 Shanin, *Awkward*; id., *Russia*, pp. 95–101, 117–18, 151–5.
72 One of the strongest critics was Mark Harrison: see 'Resource allocation and agrarian class formation: The problem of social mobility among Russian peasant households, 1880–1930', *JPS*, vol. 4 (1977), pp. 127–61.

of household life cycles have been detected in predominantly agricultural provinces, such as Voronezh in the Central Black Earth region. It is noteworthy, however, that they have also been shown to be important in areas such as Kostroma province in the Central Non-Black Earth region, where non-agricultural activities, including wage labour in factories, were widespread. There was also little socio-economic differentiation in relatively economically developed Yaroslavl' province in the same region.[73] 'Capitalist polarisation' between peasant households, along the lines described by Lenin, was relatively unusual in late tsarist Russia. It was restricted largely to some parts of the Central Non-Black Earth region, including industrial villages and poorer areas such as Tver' province, and to outlying regions of the Russian Empire, in particular southern Ukraine, where the agricultural economy was more developed, the use of wage labour (including migrants from the central regions) was more common, and the proximity of the Black Sea ports gave relatively easy access to large markets.[74]

Beyond Lenin and Chayanov

The theoretical models put forward by Lenin and Chayanov have done great service in suggesting lines of enquiry and stimulating further research. But neither model has been fully supported by the evidence, or remained unscathed in the debates over socio-economic mobility in Russian peasant communities. Nevertheless, case studies of the distribution of wealth between peasant households over the entire period covered by this book have provided, on balance, more support for Chayanov's model based on household life cycles than for Lenin's theory concerning households' relationship to the developing 'capitalist mode of production'. Above all, for most of the period and in much of Russia, the majority of peasant households were neither substantially richer nor poorer than most other households in their communities. Extremes of wealth and poverty were usually transitory rather than permanent: Russian peasant communities did not become polarised into a small, prosperous rural 'bourgeoisie' and a large, impoverished rural 'proletariat', but were made up mainly of households in the 'middle' stratum. The two theories are not mutually exclusive. Lenin's model is supported by some evidence, mostly from the nineteenth and early twentieth centuries, from a few economically 'developed' communities and regions, where peasant households specialised in non-agricultural

73 See Löwe, 'Differentiation', pp. 165–95; Merl, 'Socio-economic', pp. 47–54, 63; Wilbur, E. M., 'Peasant poverty in theory and practice: A view from Russia's "impoverished center" at the end of the nineteenth century', in *PECPER*, pp. 101–27; Johnson, R. E., 'Family life-cycles and economic stratification: A case-study in rural Russia' [Kostroma], *JSocH*, vol. 30 (1997), pp. 705–31; Ekonomakis, E. G., 'Patterns of migration and settlement in prerevolutionary St Petersburg: Peasants from Iaroslavl and Tver provinces', *RR*, vol. 56 (1997), pp. 20–1. Field's sophisticated analyses of stratification (*AOCI*, pp. 477–505; *LCPCR*, pp. 143–64) did not consider changes over time.
74 See Ekonomakis, 'Patterns', pp. 16–18; Lenin, 'Development', pp. 70–85; Gatrell, *Tsarist Economy*, pp. 128–40.

activities or growing crops or raising livestock primarily for sale. In such communities, buying and selling handicraft and factory produce, raw materials, foodstuffs and labour played a more important part in economic life than in the majority of villages, where peasant households' consumption needs remained the main motive for production.

Specialists who followed the pioneering work of Lenin and Chayanov have pointed to limitations in both theories. Lenin exaggerated the 'development of capitalism' in rural Russia, and its role in creating permanent and growing inequalities in village communities. He failed to appreciate the temporary nature of many disparities in wealth, and ignored the fact that members of rich as well as poor households worked as wage labourers. On the other hand, Chayanov's model overstated the importance of household demographic structures. His model did not fully allow for the growing importance of non-agricultural activities and markets in produce and labour in the rural economy. Both Chayanov and Lenin neglected other causes of prosperity and poverty in peasant households. More recent specialists have emphasised a wider range of factors, and interaction between them, in leading to differentiation and socio-economic mobility in Russian peasant communities.

The forms and levels of exploitation imposed on Russia's peasants reduced the validity of both models for the two centuries or so before the 1860s. The high levels of exploitation which peasant households were subjected to by the ruling and landowning elites inhibited the development of markets, since a large part of peasants' production was expropriated rather than sold. Some peasant households did employ wage labour under serfdom, but many used it to carry out their labour obligations, not for commodity production. In response to exploitation, many village communities and peasant households – either of their own accord, or in collaboration with or under pressure from landowners and state officials – adopted strategies that promoted levelling in the distribution of resources. Some noble landowners intervened to insist that rich households assisted poorer households on their estates. Many households were maintained at levels that allowed subsistence and the ability to meet their obligations. The emergence of strata of rich and poor households was impeded in large parts of rural Russia in the period preceding that which was Lenin's and Chayanov's main concern. Moreover, the degrees of differentiation that had existed in many village communities before the late seventeenth century were greatly reduced. Thus, the conditions for Leninist differentiation and polarisation of peasant communities were largely absent from much of rural Russia before the 1860s. To the extent that household life cycles were subsumed in large, complex households containing two or more nuclear family units, however, Chayanov's model was not directly relevant either.

Exploitation, the limited degrees of market formation, and the existence of levelling mechanisms in village communities in large parts of Russia, especially the central regions, did not prevent the emergence of some relatively long-lasting disparities in wealth between peasant households in the eighteenth and nineteenth centuries. A number of recent case studies of rural communities in the central regions have shown that minorities of relatively prosperous and poor households, typically around 10–15 per cent of each, retained their socio-economic status for periods of a few decades.[75] These, and other less extreme, differences in prosperity between households have been explained by a range of factors.

Misfortune and natural disasters affected households differently. Small and poor households were often unable to cope with the loss of any of their adult members, or their livestock, to disease, or with the destruction of their wooden homesteads by fire. Nor did they have reserves to fall back on if the harvest failed. Poor households could not always rely on assistance from their communes, especially if whole villages had been afflicted by disasters or if they were not deemed to have the potential to recover. In contrast, many richer households had the resources, including labour, horses and reserves of grain, to help them survive all but the most devastating misfortunes and disasters.[76]

Other resources, besides the labour of household members and allotments from communal land, were very important in determining the ability of peasant households to improve or maintain their standards of living. Small and poor households were not always able to escape poverty simply by waiting for children to be born and grow up, and for communes to allocate them more land. Moreover, labourers were not sufficient to cultivate new allotments of land. Poor households also needed ploughs and other implements, horses or oxen to pull them, stocks of seed to sow, and (in non-black earth regions) the livestock to produce enough manure to fertilise the land. Some poor households who lacked the resources to cultivate the land allotted to them by the commune leased it to richer households that did. In contrast, the richest peasant households sometimes had accumulated wealth, in the forms of livestock, grain reserves and implements, or the money to buy them. This enabled them to take on more land and cultivate it. Richer households were also able to get extra labour by hiring it or by adopting sons if they lacked their own. The advantages of accumulated wealth meant that not all larger households were condemned to lose their relative prosperity if their labour resources declined for biological or demographic reasons. A few richer households were 'capitalists', for example the well-known but unusual examples of peasant entrepreneurs in Ivanovo and other 'industrial villages'. By no means all such richer households were potentially members of a capitalist bourgeoisie. It is likely that many were motivated less by the desire to make profits by producing goods for sale, than by the aim of maintaining their higher levels of consumption, guaranteeing their security, and enjoying some leisure and status in their communities.

---

75 See Bohac, *Family*, pp. 6, 128–9, 252; Melton, 'Proto-industrialization', pp. 87–9; *id.*, 'Household', pp. 566–8; Merl, 'Socio-economic', p. 64; Wilbur, 'Poverty', pp. 111–21; Johnson, 'Family', pp. 723–5.
76 See Bohac, *Family*, p. 252; Johnson, 'Family', pp. 724–6; Wilbur, 'Poverty', pp. 111–15. See also Ch. 6.

Thus, ownership of, or access to, all the means of production, not just labour and land, were vitally important if poor households were to improve their socio-economic status as they embarked on their life cycles. Accumulated wealth enabled small minorities of richer households to retain their relative prosperity in spite of changes in the numbers of able-bodied labourers they contained. Bohac concluded that 'although both household size and structural changes affected socioeconomic movement on Manuilovskoe estate [between 1810 and 1861] . . . , material resources [especially horses and grain stocks] were the most critical variable in explaining . . . patterns of household mobility'.[77]

Accumulating labour, land, livestock, implements, stocks of grain, raw materials, money and other resources was of little use unless the members of peasant households had the necessary skills and ability to make effective use of them. Basic agricultural skills were passed on from generation to generation. 'Improved' farming techniques, and the additional resources they needed, had to be acquired, as did handicraft skills and the business acumen necessary for commerce. Literacy and numeracy were also valuable skills that were necessary for many non-agricultural occupations. The ability to assimilate new ideas, and to learn from experience, were valuable assets that some peasants were able to use to improve the status of their households.[78] Good management by households' heads was essential if they were to prosper. Bad management, especially by heads who had succumbed to drink, was an all too frequent cause of hardship and poverty. Prosperous households were able to maintain their wealth and status by making good matches for their children, by adopting sons-in-law or sons if they had no male children of their own, and by careful regulation of household partitions, the distribution of property between the new households and the younger generation. Bohac paid particular attention to 'inheritance strategies' in his study of Manuilovskoe. He noted that households did not always enforce the custom of partible inheritance if economic conditions or household welfare demanded otherwise.[79]

Another way in which a few households were able to retain their prosperity was by taking part in village politics with the aim of controlling the commune and, therefore, its role in distributing land and obligations between households. In Baki, Kostroma province, factions of richer households dominated the commune and used it to further their interests. The prosperous timber dealers in the village gave preferential treatment to themselves and their 'clients' (especially households that provided them with labourers) at the expense of poorer and weaker households. The crucial issue was the selection of recruits. The estate managers elected by the peasants in Manuilovskoe in the years 1810–61 often came from the wealthiest households. Elections were accompanied by conflicts over social and economic issues. On at least one occasion,

77 Bohac, *Family*, pp. 7 (quotation), 94–105. See also Gatrell, *Tsarist Economy*, pp. 82–3.
78 See Bohac, *Family*, pp. 112, 245–6. See also Ch. 4.
79 Bohac, *Family*, pp. 183–220, 252, 269; *id.*, 'Inheritance'. See also Wilbur, 'Poverty', pp. 116, 119–20, 123; Worobec, *Peasant Russia*, pp. 44–6, 218–19; and Ch. 5.

in 1830, the landowner intervened to ensure the election of a less well-off manager. The relative weight of the voices of 'rich' and 'middle' peasant households varied from village to village. Village politics undoubtedly played a role in influencing the distribution of wealth between households, but this was just one of a number of factors that, together, affected the relative prosperity of peasant households in communities all over Russia.[80]

In Chayanov's model, household size and structure were the major determinants of wealth. But the ability of richer households to gain control over village communes, together with the advantages of accumulated wealth, the acquisition of skills, good management, and the use of inheritance strategies meant that some households that had become more prosperous on account of their size were able to maintain their wealth and numbers in the medium or even long term. They often did so, moreover, at the expense of poorer and weaker households, which were never able to increase their size or improve their standard of living. Thus, households could be wealthy because they were large, but they could also be large because they were wealthy.[81] Relatively stable patterns of differentiation, with small proportions of households at the extreme ends of the scale for decades, existed in many communities throughout Russia over the whole period under consideration. In many cases, however, their existence had little to do with 'capitalism'.

A further objection to Lenin's and Chayanov's models is that both ignored socio-economic differentiation between peasants inside households. Although the interests of households in their entireties usually took precedence over those of individual members, the people who normally took the important decisions about the allocation of resources inside households were their heads, most of whom were middle-aged men. The decisions they took, like those of their fathers before them, tended to favour the older generation over young adults and children, and men over women. In purely material terms, young adult men probably consumed more food than other members of their families, but they needed all the calories they could get in order to carry out most of the hard manual labour on which they all depended. The younger generation of adult women also worked extremely hard in the household economy, in addition to bearing and bringing up the children, but it is unlikely that they received much material compensation.

As in so many aspects of the social and economic history of the Russian peasantry before the late nineteenth century, shortages of data hinder attempts to test these hypotheses about socio-economic differentiation between peasants inside households. In some large and complex households, individual family units cooked and ate separately. This may have enabled the heads of households to exert control over subordinate younger couples by controlling the amounts of food they were allocated. The ways in which assets were distributed when households divided possibly suggest how wealth was shared out

---

80 Bohac, *Family*, pp. 273–5; Melton, 'Household'. See also Fedorov, *Pomeshchich'i*, p. 252; and Ch. 6.
81 See Gatrell, 'Historians', p. 49; Johnson, 'Family', p. 722.

inside them. Younger men, especially nephews rather than sons of household heads, inherited less than other beneficiaries. Women retained some property rights, but ultimately depended on their husbands, fathers or brothers.[82]

What was at stake inside peasant households was not just levels of consumption of food, clothing and other goods, nor the distribution and division of labour, but less tangible matters such as leisure, status and respect. Who rose first in the morning to bake the bread and milk the cow (young women), who slept closest to the stove in winter (the household head and his wife), who sat opposite the icon corner at the meal table and dipped his spoon into the communal soup pot first (the household head) were every bit as important in influencing and signifying the individual peasants' quality of life as more easily quantifiable aspects of consumption.

CONCLUSION

Trying to convey a clear conception of the actual condition of the Russian peasantry is still as difficult as Wallace found over a century ago. Nevertheless, historians have made considerable progress in collecting and interpreting large quantities of data on peasant consumption. One of the most important achievements has been the recognition that 'peasantry' is not a synonym for 'poverty' and 'destitution'. Over a generation ago, Shapiro criticised the work of many Soviet historians on the grounds that, taken together, their findings suggested that the condition of the Russian peasantry was in continual decline for several centuries until 1917. A more plausible answer to the question about peasant living standards is not just that in some periods they got better, but that distinctions need to be made between long- and short-term trends, between different regions of Russia, categories of peasants, households, and individuals within households.

Russian peasants were better off in some periods and in some regions than others. Certain categories fared better than others. But throughout Russia for the entire period under consideration, the living standards of individual peasants, and changes in them, were affected by a whole host of factors, including their age, gender and position in their families. Peasant living standards were affected by the size and structure of their households, the standing of their households in their village communities, decisions taken by household heads and communal elders, the demands of their landowners and the state authorities for obligations, and the amounts of land and degree of protection they granted in return. Also important were random fluctuations in the harvest and the effects of disease, and opportunities created in the economy at local and national levels. Peasants' levels of consumption were influenced by most or all of these factors at any one time. Some pulled in different directions and

82 See Bohac, *Family*, pp. 184–6, 286; Harrison, 'Resource', pp. 150–1. See also Ellis, *Peasant Economics*, pp. 171–95. On the importance of gender and age in households and communities, see Chs 5 and 6.

cancelled each other out. If several pulled in one direction at once, peasants could experience extremes of relative prosperity or poverty.

To move from the particular to the general, and taking the Russian peasantry as a whole across the entire period between the early seventeenth and the early twentieth centuries, it is likely that most peasants were able to maintain at least adequate levels of consumption more often than not. The best evidence for this is the substantial growth in the peasant population in Russia over these centuries (see Ch. 1). However, the relationship between levels of consumption and population increase is not straightforward, as demographic trends are the result of the interplay of a number of factors, including disease as well as nutrition. Nevertheless, to the extent that population increase was a result of peasants maintaining satisfactory levels of consumption, it was not just chance. Rather, it was a consequence of the relative success of the various strategies peasant households and communities devised and adopted in order to give them the best chances of ensuring their subsistence and livelihoods.

This tentative conclusion does not deny the squalid conditions many Russian peasants lived in, their harsh lives, the uncertainty caused by the prospect of periodic harvest failures, nor the extent to which they were exploited. Neither is this an argument that the majority of Russian peasants were prosperous. Rather, the point is to stress the endurance of Russian peasants' society and economy, which was a result of the rationality of their economic decision making in their own terms, and in the contexts of the environmental conditions they lived in and their lowly status in Russian society. Russian peasants supported not only themselves but also the elites of Russian society and the Russian state with the obligations they served, the dues and taxes they paid, and the military conscripts they provided. It was on the back of the society and economy of the Russian peasantry, moreover, that the tsarist state expanded far beyond the original forest-heartland and created a vast Eurasian empire in the centuries after the 1550s.

CHAPTER 9

Continuity

The history of the Russian peasantry between 1600 and 1930 was marked by elements of continuity and change. Until the turn of the twentieth century it was the former that prevailed. The most striking continuity was the endurance of Russian peasant society. Throughout the entire period under consideration, peasants made up the overwhelming majority (at least 80 per cent) of the population of Russia. Indeed, it was not until 1959 that the urban population of Russia (RSFSR) exceeded the number of rural inhabitants. This milestone had been passed in England in 1851. Many parts of the less developed world, however, were still predominantly rural in the late twentieth century.[1] The basic features of Russian peasant society, which were similar in many respects to those of other peasantries in other places, also endured between the early seventeenth century and the turn of the twentieth century. The Russian peasantry was and remained a subordinate and exploited group of people, most of whom relied largely but not solely on household-based agriculture to support themselves and to meet the obligations demanded from them by the landowning and ruling elites of Russian society.

The Russian peasantry's ways of life evolved during the period under consideration in processes of interaction with a number of factors, some of which changed over time, and over all of which peasants had only limited control. The most important were the size and growth of the peasant population, especially in relation to the amounts of land available for cultivation, the natural environments peasants lived in, and the forms and levels of exploitation they were subjected to. From the late nineteenth century, moreover, Russian peasants were affected by, and took part in, social, economic and cultural changes associated with 'modernisation'.

* * *

The peasant population in Russia grew substantially over the whole period, especially from the mid-eighteenth century, and most rapidly in the late

1 Andrle, V., *A Social History of Twentieth-Century Russia* (London, 1994), p. 235; Waller, P. J., *Town, City, and Nation: England, 1850–1914* (Oxford and New York, 1983), p. 1; Keyfitz and Flieger, *World Population*, pp. 107, 109, 203. On definitions of urban, see Rowland, R. H., 'Urbanization and migration data in Russian and Soviet censuses', in Clem, R. S. (ed.), *Research Guide to the Russian and Soviet Censuses* (Ithaca, NY, and London, 1986), pp. 114–16; Waller, *op. cit.*, pp. 1–8; Keyfitz and Flieger, *op. cit.*, pp. 9–10. On the proportions of various populations engaged in agriculture at different times, see Introduction.

nineteenth century. A major reason for the growing numbers was the high birth rate resulting from near-universal and early marriage. Most peasant women were married for the majority of their child-bearing years. Russian peasants promoted high birth rates for a number of reasons. There was an abundance of land available for cultivation by the growing numbers of peasants in most of Russia prior to the end of the eighteenth century, but only in more outlying regions, including the open steppes to the south-east and Siberia, in the following century. Over the nineteenth century, moreover, there were increasing opportunities for non-agricultural work. The complex household system and the practice of communal land redistribution also encouraged early marriage and high fertility. Another reason why Russian peasants wanted to have large numbers of children was the very high death rates, especially infant and childhood mortality, which they were powerless to reduce. As a result of the unhygienic conditions and customs of village life and environmental factors, endemic diseases, periodic epidemics and bad harvests posed constant and recurring threats to the inhabitants of households and communities. Only at the end of the nineteenth century did death rates start to decline.[2]

The environmental conditions in Russia had a significant impact on the ways peasants organised their lives. Peasants had little or no control over the *natural* fertility of the soil or the climate, both of which were so critical for agriculture. One way in which Russian peasants could change the natural environment they lived in was by migrating. From the late sixteenth century, countless millions moved from the forest-heartland, across the Oka river, to the more fertile, black earth, steppe regions to the south and east, and beyond the Ural mountains to Siberia. The natural environment of the forested-steppe belt (including much of the Central Black Earth and Mid-Volga regions) was well suited to peasant farming. By the early nineteenth century, the regions of the forested-steppe had replaced those of the mixed-forest belt (mostly the Central Non-Black Earth and North-western regions) as the centre of gravity of Russian peasant settlement. Between the late seventeenth century and the turn of the twentieth century, a large majority of Russian peasants lived in the four central regions of the mixed-forest and forested-steppe belts. Ever larger numbers, however, migrated from these regions to more outlying areas of the expanding Russian state, including the open steppes and Siberia. Fewer peasants migrated to the northern regions of the forest-heartland.

Peasants also altered the environments they lived in without migrating. They did this by exploiting the natural resources around their villages, above all by preparing land for cultivation by removing, and sometimes burning, the natural vegetation. Unbeknown to the peasants, however, by chopping down large swathes of forest and clearing vast areas of steppe grasses they were creating problems for future generations. The climate of the fertile steppe regions became drier and the rainfall less reliable, increasing the risk of poor

---

2 For fuller discussion of many of the points covered in this chapter, and references, see earlier chapters.

harvests. The loss of natural vegetation contributed to soil erosion, which also adversely affected agricultural production. The application of fertilisers, mostly animal manure, was not sufficient to compensate for the growing harm done to the soils in much of Russia by peasant agriculture.

A third major factor that affected the ways of life of the Russian peasantry was exploitation. Landowners (nobles until 1861, the church until 1762–64, the tsars' families and the state) extracted obligations from peasants on their domains. The institution of serfdom, under which very roughly half the peasantry was bound to nobles' estates, originated in the forest-heartland in the late sixteenth century, and later spread to many other areas west of the Urals. Serfdom was consolidated in law in 1649. Similar restrictions were imposed on other categories of peasants. Landowners demanded obligations in the forms of labour and dues in cash or kind. All peasants had obligations to the state, which were streamlined by Peter the Great into annual levies of recruits for the army from 1705 and the poll tax from 1724. Peasant communities were jointly responsible for their obligations until 1903. Indirect taxes on vodka and other goods were a further drain on peasant households' budgets.

The level of exploitation by landowners and the state combined was very high. For much of the period under consideration, especially from the mid-eighteenth to the mid-nineteenth centuries, it is likely that Russian peasants were compelled to hand over around half of the product of their labour. Russian peasants' obligations were probably a little lower in the earlier and later parts of the period under consideration. There were also short-term trends. The demands of the state increased during Russia's regular wars, but fell after the cessation of hostilities. The wars of Peter the Great, and other conflicts of the eighteenth and nineteenth centuries, were especially burdensome for the Russian peasantry. The level of exploitation also varied by region. Peasants' obligations were higher in the central regions of Russia than in more outlying areas.

Distinctions between the central and outlying regions of Russia, and between the forest-heartland and the more fertile black earth regions, are essential for an understanding of the various practices and customs that made up the ways of life of the Russian peasantry in the period from the early seventeenth century to the turn of the twentieth century.

* * *

In order to support their growing numbers, cope with the environmental conditions they lived in, and meet the demands of the landowning and ruling elites, Russia's peasants developed a series of strategies to ensure their subsistence and livelihoods. Some strategies were devised in collaboration with members of the elites, many of whom recognised that their own interests were served by taking some account of the basic needs of 'their' peasants. But the extent to which many landowners and state officials devolved the day-to-day running of village communities onto the elites of peasant society gave heads of peasant households and village elders the leeway to devise their own ways to manage their affairs.

The motives behind all aspects of Russian peasants' ways of life should not be reduced to a struggle for survival in a harsh and uncertain world. Nor should the views of some nineteenth-century Russian intellectuals, who idealised peasant villages as model egalitarian communities, be believed. Like members of all human societies, Russian peasants were motivated by passions, jealousies, desire for power over others, and selfish concerns for themselves, their families and associates. Given the conditions they lived in, however, including joint responsibility for their obligations, the interests of individual peasants and households were often best served by trying to ensure at least the subsistence of the households and village communities of which they were part, rather than trying to seek their own advantage at the expense of ruining others. Life in Russian peasant villages could be nasty, brutish and quarrelsome, but these were moderated by an awareness that some degree of communalism was in the interests of all their members.

The most important strategies peasants developed involved their productive activities, the practices they adopted to organise and manage their labour and land at household and village levels, and the ways in which they tried to establish some control over the demands made by elites through protest and accommodation. In many cases, peasants' strategies did not aim to maximise the production and productive capacity of their households and communities, nor to extract maximum concessions from elites. Rather, they aimed to reduce the risk of failure and destitution. 'Risk aversion' and the 'subsistence ethic' strongly influenced the practices and customs of Russian peasants' ways of life. That peasants cooperated in households and villages does not mean that there was no conflict between them, nor that peasants were unaware of, and did not try to deal with, the problem posed by 'free-riders' trying to take advantage of their neighbours.

Some nineteenth-century Russian intellectuals perceived a number of the peasantry's strategies, especially large complex households and communal land redistribution, to be long-standing and even defining features of Russian peasant society. In fact, these and other practices originated among peasants who lived on seigniorial and church land in the central regions of Russia between the mid-sixteenth and early eighteenth centuries. Before turning to these strategies, it is worth looking at those they replaced.

* * *

The practices and customs employed by Russian peasants before the mid-seventeenth century in the forest-heartland (where most Russian peasants lived at that time) were appropriate to population densities and levels of exploitation that were generally lower than those in much of central Russia in subsequent centuries. Some of these earlier strategies continued to be used by peasants in more outlying areas, where population densities and levels of exploitation remained relatively low, in the eighteenth and nineteenth centuries.

In much of the forest-heartland before the seventeenth century, peasants relied heavily on arable farming, and used two-field crop rotations or long-fallow systems. Such methods of cultivation, that made very extensive use of the land, were also common for much of the eighteenth and nineteenth centuries in many outlying parts of Russia and Siberia where land remained in plentiful supply. In addition to arable farming, many peasants in the forest-heartland before the mid-seventeenth century kept large numbers of livestock. The importance of animal husbandry persisted in more outlying regions in subsequent centuries. Again, human population density is part of the explanation. Rearing animals requires several times as much land to produce the same quantity of food for human consumption, measured in calories, as growing grain. Peasants in the forest-heartland in the earlier period engaged in hunting and gathering in the vast woodlands that covered most of central and northern Russia. Peasants also produced handicraft goods. Some peasants were involved in small-scale trade, but the peasant economy in central Russia in this earlier period was geared overwhelmingly towards subsistence and self-sufficiency.

Many peasant households in the forest-heartland prior to the mid-seventeenth century contained nuclear families and were small in size and simple in structure. Most sons left their parents' households and set up their own homesteads when or shortly after they married and started their own families. Thus, young male peasants usually left their natal households before the deaths of their fathers. Most young women left their parents' households to live with their husbands. There were also large proportions of small, simple peasant households in many outlying areas throughout the seventeenth, eighteenth and nineteenth centuries. There were important exceptions. Peasants in some frontier regions in the early stages of settlement lived in large households in order to provide them with the labour necessary to clear and cultivate virgin land. The prevalence of small and simple households in the earlier period suggests that heads of households could see no reason to prevent their sons from breaking away, or had no strong authority to support them in keeping the younger generation of adults under control in their households.

In village communities in the forest-heartland before the late seventeenth century, and in most outlying regions until well into the nineteenth century, arable land was usually held in individual, household tenure. Peasant households passed on their arable land to the next generation by sharing it out between their heirs in a system of partible inheritance. The low population densities and levels of exploitation, in comparison with central Russia in the eighteenth and most of the nineteenth centuries, go some way to explaining the existence of household land tenure in the preceding period, and its survival in the borderlands. However, some village communities in these regions and in these periods did hold woodland, pastures and sometimes meadows in common.

Peasants who protested against the landowning and ruling elites in the forest-heartland before the late seventeenth century, and for around a century or more afterwards in some outlying regions, were prepared to use extreme methods, including mass, open direct action. Moreover, many peasants resorting to extreme and violent forms of protest had radical objectives. Peasants fled in large numbers from the forest-heartland, where serfdom was emerging, to seek better and freer lives in the borderlands, but from the late seventeenth and early eighteenth centuries, large-scale peasant flight continued only from peripheral parts of the central regions (the 'old' borderlands) and from regions even further from the centre of state and seigniorial power.

The four great revolts (Ch. 7) involving peasants (and other people) took place in the seventeenth and eighteenth centuries and were increasingly restricted to the borderlands. Only Bolotnikov's rebel army in 1606–07, which included few peasants, reached Moscow. Serious peasant unrest at the time of the Bulavin revolt of 1707–08 was confined to the south of the Central Black Earth region. In 1670, there was a mass peasant *jacquerie* in large parts of the Mid-Volga region and some adjoining areas of the central regions in the final stage of the Razin revolt. In comparison, and in spite of the high levels of violence involved, the peasant revolts in the last phase of the Pugachev revolt in 1774 were further from the centre of Russia, posed less of a challenge to the social order and the state, and were suppressed more quickly. This is not to understate the ferocity of the peasants who murdered their landowners in the Volga basin in the summer of 1774, but to contrast the scale and extent of the violence with that which had taken place a little closer to Moscow around a century earlier in 1670.

* * *

Peasants who lived in the central regions of Russia during the period between the late sixteenth and early eighteenth centuries adapted, and in some cases altered, the practices that had been employed earlier by their forebears. In their place, they devised other strategies to ensure their subsistence and livelihood, in particular the three-field crop rotation, large and complex households, and communal and repartitional land tenure. In addition, peasants increasingly resorted to more limited forms of protest. The timing and location of the origins of these strategies strongly suggests that they were devised in response to the growing restrictions and demands on peasants made by the landowning and ruling elites, including serfdom and the state's demands for taxes and recruits, that took place in the central regions of Russia over this period. A little later, the growing peasant population began to put pressure on the amounts of land available for cultivation in parts of central Russia. The constraints and opportunities offered by the natural environment influenced both the strategies peasants devised and variations between regions.

Some of the strategies that had evolved in the central regions of Russia by the early eighteenth century made up a way of life that came to be celebrated by some Slavophiles and Populists in the nineteenth century as the archetypal way of life of the Russian peasantry. The practices and customs of peasants in central Russia also attracted the attention of western Europeans, including August von Haxthausen and Donald MacKenzie Wallace. Even Karl Marx took an interest in the Russian peasant commune towards the end of his life. Moreover, these strategies were studied by Russian historians, geographers, economists, ethnographers and other specialists, many of whose works are cited in this book.

The main productive strategy adopted by Russian peasants in the central regions from the sixteenth and seventeenth centuries was the three-field system of crop rotation for growing grain. The arable land around villages was divided into three open fields, each of which was used in turn for the winter and spring cereals before being left fallow for a year. This was a smaller proportion of fallow than under the two-field and long-fallow systems it supplanted. The three-field system was overseen by village communes, but the fields were divided into strips, and cultivated by individual households using the labour of family members, fairly simple implements, and horses for draught power. Once the three-field rotation had been adopted, if peasants needed to produce more grain, whenever and wherever possible, they ploughed up and cultivated more land using their customary methods, i.e. by extensification rather than intensification of production.

Between the late seventeenth and late nineteenth centuries, many Russian peasants needed to increase agricultural production to meet higher obligations and to support larger numbers of people. The relationship between increases in production and population growth was not just one way. Peasants grew more grain to feed more mouths; and higher output contributed to growth in their numbers. In addition to cultivating grain, many peasants kept some livestock for meat and dairy produce (as well as the draught power and manure necessary for grain cultivation), grew vegetables and other crops in their garden plots, and engaged in handicraft production, trade and migrant wage labour.

Russian peasants were disinclined to maximise their production and incomes. Many were averse to the drudgery of the extra labour entailed, at the cost of leisure, because opportunities to sell surplus produce at the market and the range of goods available for them to buy were fairly limited. The likelihood that most of any increases in production would be taken away by the ruling and landowning elites was an added disincentive. For many Russian peasants, moreover, producing sufficient food to subsist was more important than taking a chance on innovations, such as new crops or techniques, that might result in higher production, but also might fail. Relying on tried and trusted crops and techniques were risk-averse strategies. Another way of reducing risk was diversification. Households engaged in different types of farming, and both agricultural and non-agricultural activities, in line with the common-sense logic of not putting all their eggs in one basket.

Non-agricultural pursuits were more important in the forest-heartland, where the soils and climate were less suitable for farming than the black earth and

longer growing season of the steppes. From the mid-eighteenth century, a
degree of regional specialisation developed between the black earth regions,
where agriculture remained predominant, and the forest-heartland, where peasants devoted more time and resources to handicrafts. The growth in specialisation by region led to an expansion of inter-regional trade, which meant that
production for sale became a more important, if still secondary, motive for
peasants' economic ventures. The growth in the market created more opportunities for peasants to make a living, or to supplement farming, by trade and
wage labour. Edgar Melton, who compared an agricultural village in the
Central Black Earth region and a 'proto-industrial' village in the Central Non-
Black Earth region in the nineteenth century, concluded: 'Russian peasants did
not all inhabit the same economic universe.'[3] There were, thus, two fairly
distinct peasant ways of life in the central regions from the mid-eighteenth
century. 'Proto-industry' remained a minority activity, however, even in the
Central Non-Black Earth region in the nineteenth century. Overall, the agricultural way of life predominated among the Russian peasantry.

The needs of the peasant economy influenced the strategies peasants
developed at household and village levels to organise their two main resources:
labour and land. Heads of peasant households insisted on near-universal and
early marriage to ensure high birth rates and, thus, many children and grandchildren to work in the household economy when they grew up, and to support their elders in old age. From the late seventeenth century in the central
regions, especially the Central Black Earth region, many household heads
prevented their sons from breaking away and setting up their own households
when they reached adulthood, married and had children of their own. Instead,
many adult sons continued to live with their parents until, and sometimes
after, their fathers had died. If grown-up sons felt constrained by their fathers,
the position of their wives, who lived with their husbands under the authority of their parents-in-law, was even more restricted. The prevalence of *post-
mortem* household divisions in much of central Russia from the late seventeenth
to the late nineteenth centuries meant that many peasant communities contained substantial proportions of large, complex households, comprising more
than one married couple and at least two generations. In contrast, the earlier
practice of *pre-mortem* partitions had led to the prevalence of small, simple
households containing nuclear families.

The complex household system which predominated in much of central
Russia for around two centuries was an effective way of organising labour
resources for agriculture. Peasant farming required large amounts of intensive
labour at peak times in the calendar of field work. Large and complex households were also welfare institutions as they contained sufficient able-bodied
adults to support the old, young and infirm who could not support themselves.
In addition, the system of complex households was a way of reducing risk.
Larger households with several adults and married couples were better able

3 Melton, 'Proto-industrialization', p. 71.

332

than small households with only one married couple to withstand the loss of one or more adults to disease, famine or as recruits to the army. There were regional variations in household practices. *Post-mortem* partitions and large, complex households were less widespread in parts of the forest-heartland, where agriculture was less important than other economic activities.

In central Russia, especially the Central Black Earth region, village communes devised new strategies to manage their land during the seventeenth and early eighteenth centuries. Many communes began to hold their arable land in communal tenure and, later, started periodically to redistribute the strips of arable between households. Households that had decreased in size since the previous distribution lost some of their strips, while households that had got larger were allocated more. The practice of communal and repartitional land tenure is one of the best known but least understood features of Russian peasant society. Dorothy Atkinson concluded that 'the conditions of rural life gave rise to a social concept of egalitarianism, not as a "Utopian illusion" . . . but as a practical and culturally conditioned adjustment to limited resources'.[4]

Village communes carried out other important functions. They directed the three-field system of crop rotation. There was some coincidence between the existence of the three-field system and communal land tenure, but there was no reason why the system could not operate without communal land-holding. In parts of pre-industrial Europe households held their arable land individually but cultivated it under the three-field system directed by manorial courts or other local bodies. In much of central Russia from the late seventeenth century, communal elders – who were heads of their own households – strongly upheld the authority of household heads in their communities over the younger generation. Communes supported the prevailing marriage pattern and restrictions on household divisions that, together, led to the predominance of large and complex households. Furthermore, communes mediated in disputes between households, and organised assistance for those that had temporarily fallen on hard times but stood a good chance of recovery. Many activities of village communes were motivated by the need to ensure the livelihoods of their communities and most, if not always all, of their members.

The last main area of strategies developed by Russian peasants in the central regions in the seventeenth and eighteenth centuries were limited forms of protest against the landowning and ruling elites. The main ways in which peasants in central Russia from this time protested were non-violent and ritualised confrontations, or 'disturbances', and less confrontational tactics of 'everyday resistance', for example shoddy work, failing to pay dues and taxes in full and on time, and misunderstanding orders. Peasants resorted to these 'weapons of the weak' with the aim of attaining some limited concessions, for example reductions in their obligations or assistance in times of dearth. To some extent, landowners and state authorities were prepared to make

4 Atkinson, 'Egalitarianism', p. 11.

concessions in the interests of continuing to extract obligations from the peasants and maintaining the social order.

Limited forms of protest with limited aims were another risk-averse strategy. For most of the period between the mid-seventeenth and the end of the nineteenth centuries, most Russian peasants, especially in the central regions, were well aware that the balance of force lay squarely in the hands of the ruling and landowning elites. Moreover, the extent to which some members of the elites of peasant society had been co-opted into enforcing the oppression and exploitation of the rest of the peasantry (see below) further restricted the opportunities for peasants to protest. Therefore, many peasants tried to attain only some amelioration in their condition or redress of particular grievances through limited and non-violent forms of protest. Most peasants saw no sense in risking everything, including their lives, by attempting to gain a more radical improvement in their status, or the near-impossible goal of overthrowing the entire hierarchical and exploitative social system, through violent revolts that were almost certainly doomed to fail.

* * *

Some of these strategies of production, household and communal organisation and protest gradually spread from the central regions, where they had developed over the late sixteenth, seventeenth and early eighteenth centuries. During the eighteenth and nineteenth centuries, strategies similar to those described above were adopted by some Russian peasants who moved to or already lived in more outlying regions, such as parts of the south-eastern steppe regions, northern areas of the forest-heartland, and Siberia. Some peasants in these areas began to employ such practices in response partly to the growth in their numbers (due to immigration and natural increase), and partly to the geographical expansion of seigniorial landownership, serfdom and state exploitation which accompanied peasant migration from the central regions. The strategies also spread from seigniorial and church peasants to other categories, in particular the state peasants who made up much of the rural population of the borderlands.

The availability of more land in outlying regions enabled generations of Russian peasant-migrants to recreate features of their lives in their previous homes throughout many parts of a vast and expanding territory. Peasant-migrants had to adapt their traditional practices to the differing circumstances they encountered, especially the environmental conditions, in the areas they settled. For example, peasants in different regions grew different crops. Wheat became widespread in the warmer south-east, but barley was more suitable in the harsher climate of the north and Siberia. Oxen replaced horses as the main draught animals in areas with heavy black earth. For the most part, however, elements of continuity between their old and new lives were greater than those of change among peasant migrants from the centre.[5]

5 See Moon, 'Peasant migration'.

Although many of the practices and customs that had evolved among peasants in the central regions by the early eighteenth century could be adapted to suit different conditions, their diffusion was by no means complete throughout the whole territory of Russia. Some strategies, such as the three-field system and communal and repartitional land tenure, were adopted very late in a number of areas, for example only in the late nineteenth century in parts of Siberia. Some of the strategies were never employed in some areas, especially those most remote and with environments most distinct from central Russia. In far-flung regions peasants persisted with other strategies, for example extensive cultivation rather than the three-field rotation.

* * *

Throughout Russia, the various strategies that made up peasants' ways of life were enforced by heads of households and elders of village communes, who backed them up by communal justice, public shaming and corporal punishment. However, these were not always sufficient. The interests of households and communities in their entireties or, more accurately, of the older generation or dominant factions of peasants in villages, never succeeded in completely eliminating the interests and desires of individual peasants, especially the younger generation of adults, both women and men. For much of the period from the mid-seventeenth century until the reforms of the 1860s, heads of households and communal elders found some coincidence of interests with estate managers appointed by noble landowners, the landowners themselves, and local and central state officials. All had a common interest in maintaining their status and authority by passing the burden of obligations onto the younger generation of able-bodied, adult peasants. Those people in the villages who were responsible for sharing out communities' obligations and land between households, and between peasants inside households, had powerful levers to maintain their control. Peasants who challenged the authority of elite members of their communities and households risked being compelled to bear a larger part of the obligations or being denied access to the best land.

The ultimate threat was exclusion from their communities and loss of the entitlements to land and protection that went with membership. From 1760 village communities and landowners were permitted to exile peasants to Siberia without trial. The state had long used exile as a way of ridding central Russia of people who refused to conform. Tens of thousands of peasants were banished to the sleeping land east of the Urals. Another form of exclusion from village communities, and one of the strongest weapons in the hands of the communal elders, estate managers and local officials, was the system of military conscription introduced by Peter the Great in 1705. In most years, communities had to supply a specified number of recruits, who served for life until 1793 and for 25 years from then until the reforms of the 1850s to '70s. Village elders, estate managers and officials had a degree of control over the selection of recruits. This greatly assisted them in maintaining control over

335

households which would not, or could not, meet their share of their communities' obligations. It also gave them power over young men who threatened their authority. Those who did not pull their weight or dissented risked being sent to the army.

Many younger peasants, women as well as men, accepted their subordinate status in their households and communities without the need for drastic punishments or threats of exclusion. Younger peasants knew that, when they became middle-aged, many of them would occupy the positions of authority held by their parents and the older generation. In time, they would have the opportunity to wield control over their sons and daughters-in-law and the younger peasants in their households and communities. Christine Worobec has suggested that one reason why many peasant women accommodated to male domination was because 'they believed that the fate of their families was tied to the maintenance of the patriarchal system'.[6] Furthermore, many peasants supported the practices enforced in their families and villages since they recognised that they ensured their subsistence and livelihoods.

* * *

The strategies developed by Russian peasants in the central regions, some of which spread later to parts of more outlying regions, were to a large extent responses to the development of serfdom and state exploitation from the late sixteenth and seventeenth centuries, and the increased levels of obligations that lasted until the abolition of serfdom in 1861 and other reforms of the 1860s–80s. The systems of direct taxation, the household tax introduced in 1678–79 and the poll tax in 1719–24, had a particular impact. They go some way to explaining strategies adopted by peasants in Russia, especially the complex household system and communal and repartitional land tenure. These practices differed from those employed by peasants in the non-Russian western borderlands of the empire annexed after the mid-seventeenth century. These regions retained their old systems of taxation, and serfdom, until at least the late eighteenth century, and most of the local peasants continued to live in small, simple households and hold their land in household tenure. The differences between the practices of Russian peasants and those of their counterparts in Lithuania, Belorussia and Ukraine strongly suggest that some features of the ways of life of Russian peasants, in particular the household system and land tenure, were a result of interaction between peasants and the Russian state over the late seventeenth and early eighteenth centuries.

The degrees of exploitation and social control in Russia were highest in communities of peasants who performed labour services on seigniorial estates in the central regions, and parts of adjoining regions, in the second half of the eighteenth and first half of the nineteenth centuries. Some of these communities have been the subjects of micro-studies, for example Peter Czap's work

6 Worobec, *Peasant Russia*, p. 219.

on Mishino in Ryazan' province and Steven Hoch's on Petrovskoe in Tambov province, both in the Central Black Earth region. It was on estates such as these that the strategies and the ways they were enforced, as described above, were most developed: the three-field system of grain cultivation; the predominance of large, complex households maintained by heads who prevented their married sons from breaking away during their lifetimes; communal and repartitional land tenure; the subordination of the younger generation of peasants to household heads and village elders; and limited forms of protest, in particular 'everyday resistance'. These strategies were ways of organising the resources of peasant households and communities most effectively to ensure both the peasants' livelihoods and the ability of the landowning and ruling elites to extract large parts of the product of their labour.

*   *   *

The strategies that made up peasants' ways of life became enshrined in the norms of unwritten customary law. This was part of the rich and varied culture of the Russian peasantry. Peasant households and communities held rituals, celebrations and festivities to commemorate the main events in the cycles of their economic and social lives, in particular the stages of work in the fields from ploughing to harvesting, and the rites of passage in peasants' lives, especially courtship and marriage. The ceremonies served to celebrate these important events, to enforce the overall strategies of which they were part, and to pass them on to subsequent generations. Peasant children saw both the practices and customs that were followed, and their importance in the lives of their families and communities. Children were also socialised into peasant culture by the older generation, especially their grandparents, through folk tales, songs and proverbs. In all these ways, peasant children were brought up to respect their elders and the customs they followed.

Agricultural practices and customs in Russia, as in many pre-industrial societies, were a central part of the ritual year.[7] Many of the rituals and festivals were connected with old, pagan fertility rites. However, the calendar of the Russian Orthodox Church was superimposed on the pagan ritual calendar in the sixteenth century, at around the same time as some of the strategies discussed above started to emerge. The pagan and Christian calendars began in midwinter. The pagan Yuletide (*Svyatki*) and Christian Christmas (*Rozhdestvo*) roughly coincided with each other and with the winter solstice. Peasants celebrated the midwinter festival by attending church services and singing carols (*kolyadki*), followed by the customary drinking and overeating. The ritual foods included whole-grain porridge (*kut'ya*). A few weeks later, peasants celebrated the week-long festival of Shrovetide (*Maslenitsa*) with mock fights, sledging,

7 This section is based on Ivanits, *Russian Folk Belief*, esp. pp. 5–12; Matossian, 'Peasant', pp. 31–9; Minenko, N. A., *Kul'tura russkikh krest'yan Zaural'ya: XVIII-pervaya polovina XIX v.* (Moscow, 1991), pp. 201–10; Smith and Christian, *Bread*, pp. 97–100, 138–9; Höwe, J. E., *The Peasant Mode of Production: as Exemplified by the Russian Obshchina-Mir* (Tampere, 1991), pp. 40–52.

lighting bonfires, burning straw dummies and riding around the village on horseback bearing flaming torches. Most important were the feasts, which included pancakes (*bliny*), and were accompanied by drink. The carnival mood of Shrovetide was followed by the Christian fast of Lent, which lasted for 40 days until Easter.

The fact that the Christian Easter was a moveable feast created problems in a ritual year centred on farming. Christian holidays which depended on the date of Easter, and thus varied from year to year, could not be used to mark the timing of particular tasks in the agricultural year. This may explain the survival of the pre-Christian festival of the 'Welcoming of Spring'. It was held at the time of the spring equinox, which occurred between Shrovetide and Easter. Peasant women greeted the spring by baking pastries in the shape of birds, whose return from more temperate climes heralded the arrival of warmer weather, and also the start of work in the arable fields: ploughing, harrowing and sowing. Some of the rituals to welcome the spring were moved to nearby Christian holidays. Palm Sunday (*Verbnoe voskresen'e*) was marked by church services at which priests blessed branches of willow. They symbolised both the palm branches, with which people had welcomed Jesus to Jerusalem shortly before his death (John, 12: 13), and the arrival of spring. Willow is one of the first plants to break into bud in Russia. It was around this time that peasants in much of Russia drove their livestock out of their winter stalls and onto the new spring pastures.

The Orthodox Church struggled to keep its most important feast, Easter (*Paskha*), free from the remnants of pagan festivals of spring. On Easter Sunday, peasants attended church services to celebrate the resurrection of Christ. But they also observed rituals that had survived or been adapted from pre-Christian customs. They prepared and ate a cottage cheese cake (also called *paskha*), sweet bread (*kulich*) and, of course, painted eggs. All were symbols of fertility, rebirth and new life. Happily for the church these themes were largely in keeping with the meaning of the resurrection. Less appropriate was the pagan feast of *Radunitsa*, during St Thomas's week in the second week after Easter, when peasants took food to the graveyards for their deceased forebears.

Seven or eight weeks after Easter was Trinity or *Rusal'naya* week, also known as Green Yuletide (*Zelenye Svyatki*). This was the main festival at which Russian peasants celebrated the advent of new, green vegetation in the spring. They decorated their houses and villages with branches from birch trees. Girls adorned themselves with birch garlands. Peasants also welcomed, and then banished, *Rusalka* (the female water spirit) by making dolls in her image and ripping them apart in the fields. As usual, food and drink played a large part in the celebrations. The final festival of the first half of the year was John the Baptist's (Ivan Kupalo) day, on 24 June. This roughly coincided with the summer solstice. Peasants celebrated midsummer's day by lighting and jumping through bonfires, ritual bathing, decorating trees, making and destroying dolls, holding mock funerals, and the customary eating and drinking. In parts of Russia in the nineteenth century, the rituals of John the Baptist day were held a few days later, on 29 June, the feast of St Peter.

Most of the rituals and festivals between the winter and summer solstices anticipated or celebrated the end of winter, the return of the sun, the thaw, the arrival of spring, and the reappearance of vegetation after nature had lain dormant for several months under snow and ice. The overriding themes of all the festivals of spring were fertility, rebirth and hope for a bountiful harvest. The veneration of ancestors has also been connected with the idea of rebirth. The festivities in the first half of the ritual year were mere interruptions in the gathering pace of labour in the fields. St Peter's day signalled the start of haymaking, which lasted around three weeks, and was quickly followed by the harvest. These were the most arduous weeks of agricultural labour, and were known as the '*strada*', or 'suffering'.

In October, when the months of hard work on the land were over and the crops had been safely gathered in, came one of the biggest celebrations: the harvest festival. Peasants gave thanks for the harvest at lengthy church services, and then spent the rest of the holiday eating enormous feasts, singing, dancing, merrymaking, entertaining relatives and neighbours, and, above all, drinking themselves to oblivion. Peasants who were exhausted from weeks of backbreaking toil did not forget, however, that the annual cycle of agricultural labour would start again in a few months' time, when winter once again gave way to spring. Some parts of the harvest festivities linked that year's harvest with the next, and expressed the hope for another successful year.

Many peasant rituals, ceremonies and supernatural patrons had elements from both Orthodox Christianity and pagan beliefs based on fertility. It has long been common to label Russian peasants' religious practices and beliefs 'dual faith' (*dvoeverie*), and to emphasise conflict between the Christian and pagan aspects. Soviet scholars argued that Christianity had been imposed by the ruling elites, and that Russian peasants had struggled to retain some of their pagan rituals. The view that many calendar customs in early modern Britain had pagan origins has recently been attacked by Ronald Hutton. He argued that the idea of 'pagan survivals' from the remote past in Britain was invented by scholars in the eighteenth and nineteenth centuries. Practices long held to be pagan in origin were, he maintained, remnants of late medieval, pre-Reformation Christianity that persisted in secular, popular culture.[8] This argument is not applicable to the Russian ritual year, not least because Russia did not experience a reformation during which many rituals were banned by the established church. The changes in the rites and ceremonies of the Russian Orthodox Church in the 1650s and 60s were far less extensive. In addition, Russia remained 'pagan' far longer than Britain. It was converted to Christianity only in the late tenth century, four centuries after the reintroduction of Christianity to Britain. In Russia, moreover, Christianity took a long time to spread from the urban elites to the peasants. Eve Levin has argued that the

8 Hutton, *Stations*, pp. vii–viii, xi, 408–19.

combination of pagan and Christian elements in Russian peasants' beliefs is better understood as 'a folk version of Christianity' which drew 'on both pagan and Christian concepts'.[9]

Aspects of Russian peasants' culture, both secular and religious (regardless of the belief system they came from), served to interpret the wider world peasants lived in, and their position in it. Peasant culture sought to explain misfortunes and disasters with reference to malevolent supernatural forces, and offered various means of protection by appealing to benevolent other-worldly patrons. Folklore contained images of how peasants saw themselves, and how they hoped members of the elites would behave towards them. In addition, village culture provided peasants with regular opportunities for escape from the drudgery of hard work and the uncertainties of a life dependent on environmental and human forces that were largely beyond their ability to control. Popular religion offered solace in the after-life. The fantastic world of folk tales and songs conjured up imaginary, and unattainable, worlds of boundless wealth and good fortune. The bouts of heavy drinking that accompanied most festivities gave a more prosaic, and temporary, escape from the harsh realities of peasant life.

* * *

The strategies that originated in central Russia between the late sixteenth and early eighteenth centuries, and the cultural practices in which many were enshrined, continued in many areas throughout the eighteenth and nineteenth and into the twentieth centuries. The persistence of the peasantry's ways of life created a sense of timelessness and stability in Russian peasant society and culture. In the long term, reference points for measuring the passage of time and recalling incidents in peasants' lives were provided by memorable events, such as the founding of their villages, changes of landowner, accessions of new tsars, or other random events such as harvest failures, epidemics and wars. In between such irregular occurrences, and in the short term, changes in the world the peasants made often appeared to be cyclical or haphazard fluctuations. Time in peasant Russia was marked by the endless cycle of the seasons and the continual process of the replacement of one generation by the next.[10]

The rhythm of the seasons determined the cyclical calendar of agricultural work, in particular ploughing, sowing and harvesting, that lasted from early

---

9 Levin, E., '*Dvoeverie* and popular religion', in Batalden, S. K. (ed.), *Seeking God: The Recovery of Religious Identity in Orthodox Russia, Ukraine, and Georgia* (DeKalb, IL, 1993), pp. 31–52. See also Chulos, C. J., 'Myths of the pious or pagan peasant in post-emancipation central Russia (Voronezh Province), *RH*, vol. 22 (1995), pp. 181–216.
10 Some writers have contrasted 'cyclical' and 'ritualized' time in pre-industrial societies with modern 'linear' time. See Höwe, *Peasant*, pp. 40–52; and Thompson, E. P., 'Time, work-discipline and industrial capitalism', *Customs*, pp. 352–403. Kathleen Parthé identified various 'kinds of "time"' including 'cyclical' and 'generational' time, that operated in the *literary* works of the village writers of the 1950s–70s: *Russian Village Prose: The Radiant Past* (Princeton, NJ, 1992), pp. 48–63.

spring into the autumn. Also from the late spring to the autumn, peasants pastured their animals out of doors. During the long winter months they kept them indoors and fed them on hay they had mown the previous summer. As has already been noted, the agricultural calendar and some older pagan festivals coincided partly with those of the Russian Orthodox Church. Holidays and rituals – agricultural, pagan and Christian – punctuated the cycle of labour on the land. They provided relief from hard work, but also indicated the timing of particular tasks, such as sowing the arable fields and haymaking.

Agricultural output varied from year to year as a result of random fluctuations in the harvest and the health and fertility of peasants' livestock. In both cases, the levels of production were largely dependent on environmental factors mostly outside peasants' powers to control. Agricultural work in the spring and summer alternated with non-agricultural activities in the autumn and winter. Many peasants spent the long winter months engaged in handicraft production. Some left their villages in search of seasonal wage labour in the slack months in the calendar of field work, but came back in the summer for haymaking and harvesting. Other migrant labourers left for longer periods, before eventually returning home.

The passage of time in the lives of peasant households also seemed cyclical. Peasants did not always know their precise ages in years,[11] but measured people's journey through their lives in various stages from birth, through infancy, childhood, youth, adulthood, marriage, parenthood, maturity and old age. Death could come at any stage. The life paths of individuals combined to create life cycles of smaller households based on nuclear families. They expanded as the children grew up and married, and then contracted when they left their parental homes to set up their own homesteads. Life cycles of nuclear family units were subsumed in larger, more complex households. Peasant marriage customs generated further cycles as brides moved from their parents' to their husbands' households, and as the bride-prices paid by grooms' families circulated in the opposite direction. All households that survived for several generations had a succession of heads as older patriarchs died and were succeeded by, usually, their sons or younger brothers.

The social lives of village communities over time were marked by the passing of generations of elders or factions that dominated them. Communal direction of land tenure and land use created more cycles: the periodic distribution and redistribution of strips of arable land; and the three-course rotation of winter crop, spring crop, fallow in each of the three fields that continued for year upon year. Interaction between village communities and seigniorial and state authorities was also cyclical in the sense that it was marked by continual processes of protest and accommodation.

All these elements combined to produce haphazard and cyclical fluctuations in the levels of consumption and welfare of individual communities,

11 See Kaiser, D. H. and Engel, P., 'Time- and age-awareness in early modern Russia', *CSSH*, vol. 35 (1993), pp. 824–39; Rowney, D. K. and Stockwell, E. G., 'The Russian census of 1897: Some observations on the age data', *SR*, vol. 37 (1978), pp. 217–27.

households and peasants. The spring and early summer months could be times of shortage and hardship, while the period immediately after the harvest and the slaughter of livestock in the autumn was usually marked by abundance and prosperity. In some years, peasant households' earnings were high from both their agricultural and non-agricultural activities. In other years, success in one area compensated for failure in others. In the worst years, failure in all economic pursuits led to poverty and destitution. With a couple of good harvests in succession, however, the losses in lean years could quickly be made up. Larger households with high proportions of able-bodied adults to dependants, large allotments of land and high earnings from other activities were generally better off than smaller, less fortunate, households that had lower ratios of 'workers' to 'consumers', less land and lower earnings. A few years later, however, the positions might be reversed. Some larger households might have got smaller and poorer as a result of the death of some of their members, the departure of young married men and their families, leading to an increase in their 'dependency ratios' and the loss of part of their land. Some smaller households, however, might have become more prosperous as sons grew up, married, thus providing more able-bodied adults, and were allocated more land by the commune. Many peasant households in Russia experienced cycles of relative affluence and poverty, which at least in part were a consequence of changes in their size and structure over time.

The cyclical and random patterns of change in rural Russia, together with peasants' largely pre-industrial perceptions of time as cyclical rather than linear, their oral culture that enshrined and perpetuated the practices and customs of their ways of life, and the persistence for several generations of the strategies they adopted to ensure their subsistence and livelihoods, created a sense of timelessness that was apparent to peasants, contemporary observers and some historians. This sense of timelessness was, however, at best misleading and at worst inaccurate.

Three examples of Russian peasants adapting and changing the practices and customs of their ways of life have already been discussed. Peasants changed the ways they lived and worked in the central regions between the late sixteenth and early eighteenth centuries. In particular, many adopted the three-field crop rotation, the complex household system, communal and redistributional land tenure, and limited forms of protest. Peasant-migrants to more outlying regions adapted the practices they were familiar with in their original homes, or adopted new ones, as and when necessary. From the mid-eighteenth century, moreover, peasants who remained in the central regions made some adaptations to the ways they organised their lives. There was some degree of regional specialisation and interregional trade between the largely agricultural black earth regions and the less fertile forest-heartland, where non-agricultural activities became more important. In each of these three examples, peasants were responding to such factors as the growing pace of population increase, with resulting pressure on the land, and high and increasing demands for obligations by the landowning and ruling elites. In all cases, peasants took account of the natural environments they lived in.

* * *

Towards the end of the period under consideration, Russian peasants had to adapt and alter their customary practices and ways of life to cope with further changes. The abolition of serfdom in 1861, other reforms of the 1860s–80s, rapid population growth, improvements in transport, urbanisation, industrialisation, the growth of a national market and cultural changes all contributed to wider processes, sometimes called 'modernisation', that gradually and from low starting points began to gather pace in the last decades before the collapse of tsarist Russia in 1917. It is inaccurate, however, to speak simply of the 'modernisation' of the Russian peasantry by forces from outside the villages. The processes of change were not just one-way. Peasants took part in and shaped the changes just as much as they themselves were altered in the process. Rather than undermining aspects of the peasants' ways of life, moreover, at least in the short term, some of the changes taking place in late tsarist Russia reinforced peasant strategies and customs that had evolved earlier for other reasons.[12]

The terms of the abolition of serfdom of 1861 and the reforms of the appanage and state peasants enacted at around the same time left largely unchanged and unchallenged the rural economy and the peasants' basic units of social organisation, households and communes. In fact, the scope and authority of peasant self-government at village level was reinforced by the reforms. The reforms did not fundamentally alter Russian peasant society, but changed the relationship between peasant society and the ruling and landowning elites. The noble landowners were largely removed as intermediaries between the former seigniorial peasantry and the state. The reforms also set in process mechanisms, spread over several decades, to enable peasants to secure control over their land by purchase ('redemption'). The result was to reinforce, rather than weaken, peasants' existing legal ties to the land. The practice of communal and repartitional tenure of arable land was supported by the statutes of the 1860s. The increasing pressure on the land that resulted from the rapidly growing rural population, moreover, made it even more important that village communities made the most effective use of their land by maintaining a balance between households' land allotments and labour resources.

The greater opportunities for wage labour caused by the growth of urban centres and the development of industry gave a new lease of life to the system of large and complex households at the very time when the growing rural population was forcing peasants off the land. The construction of a national

12 For fuller discussion of points in the next few paragraphs (in comparison with contemporary France), see Moon, 'Citizens'.

network of railways after the 1850s greatly facilitated the geographical mobility of peasants in search of work, in rural as well as urban areas. By late nineteenth century, large numbers of peasants, especially young men and women, left their households and villages to work in towns or cities. They were employed in a variety of occupations, including factory work in the growing industrial sector of the Russian economy. Many found only menial, unskilled jobs, and had to live and work in overcrowded, insanitary and dangerous conditions. Women fared worst. Most female migrants worked in poorly paid, unskilled positions. Far more were employed as domestic servants than in factories. Economic necessity compelled some to turn to prostitution.[13]

While they were away, migrant-workers drew on peasant customs forming *arteli* (associations) of *zemlyaki* (peasants from the same or neighbouring villages). They lived and worked together, and provided networks of support for new arrivals from their villages or districts. Despite living in towns and cities for periods of time, however, many male migrant workers adhered to the customary peasant pattern of early and near-universal marriage. Many left their wives and children in their parents' households while they were away, and sent home part of their wages to support them. John Bushnell concluded: 'The tenacity with which peasants held on to their traditional social and economic practices [at the turn of the twentieth century] may have had something to do with the increasing availability of by-employment, of migrant or short-term urban labor, of outlets for handicraft production.'[14] Furthermore, probably a majority of migrant-workers intended to, and did, return home to their villages permanently after a few years. The aim of many was to make their fortunes in urban areas and then return home to live as rich peasants.[15]

Peasants also accommodated to the military service reform of 1874. As a result of the reform, far larger numbers of young men left their villages to serve for much shorter terms, six years at most, than under the Petrine system of recruitment. Moreover, nobles as well as peasants were liable to conscription. The Minister of War, Dmitrii Milyutin, hoped his measure would turn the army into the 'school of the nation'. His hope was not realised. Instead, peasant-conscripts seem to have 'peasantised' the reformed army. Peasant-conscripts were disorientated by their first few months in the army, during which it was impressed on them that they had to 'speak, look, turn and move with military precision'. Once basic training was completed, however, soldiers spent most of their time working to support their regiments' economies. Regiments tried to grow and cook their own food and make their own uniforms. Some soldiers were sent to work as labourers in the civilian economy to earn money for the regimental coffers. Officers used soldiers as servants.

13 See Bradley, J., *Muzhik and Muscovite: Urbanization in Late Imperial Russia* (Berkeley, CA, 1985); Engel, *Between*; Johnson, R. E., *Peasant and Proletarian: The Working Class of Moscow in the Late Nineteenth Century* (Leicester, 1979).
14 Bushnell, 'Peasant economy', p. 82.
15 See Bater, J. H., 'Transience, residential persistence, and mobility in Moscow and St Petersburg, 1900–1914', *SR*, vol. 39 (1980), pp. 239–54; Friedgut, T. H., *Iuzovka and Revolution: Life and Work in Russia's Donbass, 1869–1924* (Princeton, NJ, 1989), p. 216.

Like migrant-workers, peasant-soldiers ran their lives through *arteli* of *zemlyaki*. Life in the reformed army for many peasant-soldiers replicated their experiences in their villages or as migrant labourers to such an extent that Bushnell concluded: 'it is scarcely credible that military service could have done much to reshape peasant mentality', and that 'the world of the Russian soldier bore a strong resemblance to the world of the Russian peasant'.[16]

Many Russian peasants became aware of the need for some education over the second half of the nineteenth century, but met this need without undermining their culture. While the written word had always played a part in village life, it increasingly encroached on rural Russia in the wake of the reforms of the 1860s, and as more complex relationships, such as renting land and dealing with middlemen, played a larger part in the peasant economy. Migrants working in towns and cities needed basic literacy and numeracy skills to do some types of work, and to keep in touch with their families in the villages and send back part of their earnings. The *volost'* courts set up for peasants after 1861 used written documents at the heart of their procedures.[17] Peasants in the villages in Ryazan' province, in the Central Black Earth region, studied by Olga Semenova at the turn of the twentieth century, remarked of a young peasant: 'He'll be better paid if he can read and write'; 'In Moscow it is more important than here to know reading and writing, and you are judged by your knowledge of it'; and 'It is harder to cheat a literate person'.[18]

Russian peasants recognised the value of literacy and numeracy before the Russian state was prepared to pay for village schools. Until the 1890s the main initiative for building schools and hiring teachers in rural areas came from the peasants. Once district and provincial councils (*zemstva*) and the central Ministry of Popular Education began to take over the provision of primary education in the villages, many peasants were anxious to limit their children's involvement. Many parents took their children out of school after only two winters, once they had grasped the basic skills of reading, writing and arithmetic but before they had completed the curriculum. Only a very small proportion of peasant children went on to secondary schools. Peasant parents were worried that their children would be socialised into the culture of educated Russia, and would cease, or refuse, to be useful members of their households and communities. Parents were also concerned that educated children would leave the villages and not support them in their old age. Ben Eklof acknowledged that peasants seem to have anticipated the findings of modern specialists on literacy and education. He concluded: 'Peasants recognized that their children had to learn how to read, write, and count in order to survive in a world increasingly crowded with written documents, but they had no use for

16 Bushnell, J., *Mutiny amid Repression: Russian Soldiers in the Revolution of 1905–1906* (Bloomington, IN, 1985), pp. 1–23; *id.*, 'Peasants in uniform: The tsarist army as a peasant society', in *WRP*, pp. 101–14.
17 See Brooks, J., *When Russia Learned to Read: Literacy and Popular Culture, 1861–1917* (Princeton, NJ, 1985), pp. 3–34; Burbank, J., 'A question of dignity: Peasant legal culture in late imperial Russia', *C & C*, vol. 10 (1995), pp. 391–404.
18 Semyonova, *Village Life*, pp. 44–5.

the cultural baggage that accompanied basic instruction. Educators wanted to civilize the peasant; villagers wanted to produce children in their own image.'[19] In the short term, it was the peasants who were more successful in this struggle for the hearts and minds of village children.

Peasant culture was also sufficiently adaptable to accommodate new fashions, materials and artifacts that reached the villages as a result of the growing contacts with towns, cities and industries. Olga Semenova recorded that peasants who worked in Moscow returned to the villages with 'city clothes', including peaked caps, and wore boots instead of bast footwear. Younger peasants were starting to smoke cigarettes rather than pipes, and many peasants began to carry wallets to keep their money in. Returning migrant workers also brought back accordions, which increasingly replaced more traditional instruments such as balalaikas, for providing music at village festivities. Richer peasants acquired samovars, an urban luxury, to boil water for tea, another recent arrival in the villages. Peasant craftsmen used new images from urban and industrial life, for example scenes from St Petersburg and paddle steamers, but incorporated them into traditional forms of peasant art together with older images. Peasant women's dowries started to contain cash and manufactured cloth, rather than homespun fabrics.[20]

At least in the short term, therefore, peasants in late nineteenth-century Russia were able to preserve many aspects of their social, economic and cultural practices by adapting them to some of the changes in the wider world that were touching on the lives of ever-larger numbers of rural inhabitants. The Russian peasantry remained a distinct, and still largely separate, part of the population of Russia at the turn of the twentieth century.

* * *

Russia's peasants were not able to absorb and assimilate all the changes taking place in late tsarist Russia without at least sowing the seeds for long-term changes in their customs and ways of life. The peasants' by now traditional three-field system of crop rotation came under increasing pressure from the growing population in many parts of central Russia. Some peasants began to adopt more intensive crop rotations and grew potatoes, which produced more calories per acre than grain. Many reduced the numbers of animals they kept, because they did not have sufficient pasture and meadow land to support them. Many peasants devoted more time and resources to crafts, trade and wage labour to support their households.

Other peasant strategies changed or began to disappear as the reforms of the 1860s–80s greatly altered the ways peasants were exploited. By the late nineteenth century, moreover, the overall level of exploitation was lower than it

---

19 Eklof, *Russian Peasant Schools*, esp. pp. 70–119, 471–82 (quotation from p. 476).
20 Semyonova, *Village Life*, pp. 37, 55, 141–2, 146; Smith and Christian, *Bread*, pp. 236–45, 356; Netting, A., 'Images and ideas in Russian peasant art', in *WRP*, pp. 169–88; Worobec, *Peasant Russia*, p. 158.

had been under serfdom and in the years immediately after 1861. An important consequence was a reduction in the degree of hierarchical control over, and within, Russian peasant society. The aspects of the Russian peasantry's most distinctive strategies that fell away most sharply were those that involved the subordination of the younger generation to their parents in their households and to the older generation in their villages. A slight decline can also be detected in the authority of men over women. There were long-term changes in peasant family customs. The average ages at marriage rose slightly. Young adults were allowed more freedom in choosing their marriage partners. Communities showed greater tolerance of pre-marital sex. Most importantly, growing numbers of young adults broke away from their parents' households before their fathers' deaths. The result was an increase in the numbers and proportions of small, simple family units in place of the large, complex households that had prevailed in much of central Russia over the preceding two centuries.

The decrease in the authority of the older generation of peasants that allowed these changes to take place can be attributed to a number of factors. Older peasants lost some of the means their predecessors had used to maintain their control over the younger men and women in their households and villages. The abolition of serfdom in 1861 broke the coincidence of interests, and mutual support, between heads of peasant households and village elders, on the one hand, and estate authorities, landowners and state officials on the other. Household heads and elders were left more to their own devices to maintain control over the younger generation.

The increase in migrant wage labour meant that more young peasants had sources of income that were independent of their parents' households, and spent more time away from their families and villages than previous generations. While they were away, many migrant workers experienced the very different and more dynamic world of Russia's growing industrial cities. Many younger male peasants began to feel less bound by the customs of village life, more independent and, consequently, more determined than their fathers and grandfathers to be their own bosses in their own households. Many male migrant workers were content to leave their wives and children in their parents' large and complex households while they were away. On their return to their villages, however, many broke away from their fathers' households and set up on their own. The impact of migrant labour seems to have been greater on peasant women than on men. Many women who migrated from the villages to work in towns and cities adopted the predominant marriage pattern of the urban population: they married later than their mothers or sisters who had stayed in the villages had done, and a larger proportion never married. The departure of large numbers of men from villages had an impact on the peasant women who were left behind. They acquired greater self-assurance and higher living standards, were more likely to be able to read and write, and gained more control over their lives in their households and villages while their husbands, fathers and brothers were away.

The military service reform of 1874 lessened the authority of the older generation of peasants over young men. Under the previous system, which had been in operation since 1705, the threat of being sent to the army for very long terms of service had been a strong deterrent to non-conformist behaviour. With the reduction of the maximum term of service to six years in 1874, however, conscription no longer amounted to a long sentence to penal servitude from which most never returned. Most importantly, village elders no longer had any control over who was sent to the army. Recruits were selected by ballot from all eligible men aged 20. Military service not only ceased to be a means by which the older generation maintained control, moreover, but became a force for change in intergenerational relations in village communities. Most conscripts now came home at the end of their military service. After their experiences of life outside their villages, many were reluctant to submit to the authority of their fathers and village elders, and demanded the right to break away from their fathers' households and set up on their own.

Another change that peasants had accommodated to in the short term, but that posed a threat to the authority of heads of households and village elders over the younger generation in the long term, was the expansion of schooling. Initially, parents had succeeded in limiting the impact of formal education on their children's attitudes. By the end of the nineteenth century, however, the ability to read and write marked out a substantial and growing proportion of the younger generation from their elders. According to crude data on literacy in rural areas from the 1897 census, 41.8 per cent of males aged 10–19 and 37.1 per cent of those aged 20–29 were literate. In contrast, only 26.8 per cent of males aged 40–49, 20.4 per cent aged 50–59, and 16.6 per cent aged 60–69 could read and write. Literacy rates among rural women were around a quarter of those for men, but differences between age cohorts were similar. The gulf between an increasingly literate and schooled younger generation and a largely illiterate and unschooled older generation widened after 1897.[21] The ability to read gave many younger peasants greater opportunities than their parents and grandparents to discover and assimilate information from sources outside the largely oral culture of the villages that contradicted the norms of peasant life or presented alternative lifestyles. Peasants who could read and write were more likely to work in towns and cities than those who could not. Some migrant-workers learned to read while they were away from their villages. In time, by the early twentieth century, peasants were not just learning to read, but began to learn from reading.[22]

The increasing pace of social, economic and cultural changes in late tsarist Russia, and the wider variety of experiences open to younger peasant women and men who participated in them, could not but have had a profound impact

---

21 Mironov, B. N., 'Literacy in Russia, 1797–1917. Obtaining new historical information through the application of retrospective predictive methods', *SSH*, vol. 25, no. 3 (1986–87), p. 100.
22 Compare Brooks, *When*, and Eklof, *Russian Peasant Schools*, esp. p. 481. Eklof has slightly modified his earlier view that peasants were not yet learning from reading at this time. See Moon, *Russian Peasants*, p. 185 n. 11.

on the peasants' ways of life in rural Russia. The decline in the power of traditional village authority figures, especially heads of households and village elders, and the decay of the system of large, complex households, did not necessarily mean that Russian peasant society itself was in decline. Rather, the extent to which Russian peasants were able to adapt to these and other changes is evidence for the resilience of their ways of life in the changing world around them. The basic structure of peasant economic and social organisation in households and village communities persisted. But this resilience was only short term. Peasant society could adapt only so far without changing itself or being changed out of recognition. As more peasants gained experiences that radically differed from or challenged the norms of village life, the prospect was opened for the eventual transformation, and decline, of Russian peasant society.

The pace of the decline of the more traditional ways of life of the Russian peasantry was limited by the fact that the young men and women who were least prepared to accept them left the villages permanently to make new lives in urban Russia. The numbers that did so in the late nineteenth and early twentieth centuries were relatively low, however, in comparison with the vast peasant population that remained in the villages. Young peasant women seem to have become more estranged than men from the patriarchal society and culture of the villages as a result of education and opportunities to work in urban areas. An inspector of one of the provincial midwifery schools reported that many female graduates

> no longer like to live in the countryside, and don't remove their city clothes. They go very unwillingly to visit peasants in their simple carts, and sometimes even refuse. They are so alienated from the peasants, and the latter from them, that the peasants almost never turn to them for help, continuing as before to use simple, untrained women.[23]

Barbara Engel noted that only a small minority of peasant women moved permanently to cities, but concluded: 'The growth of a capitalist wage economy and its urban setting offered an attractive alternative to the village for some spinsters, young widows, and, perhaps most of all, discontented wives. These, the most marginal women in the village, could earn a living in the city, while its relative anonymity enabled them to forge a new life for themselves.'[24]

In contrast, the far larger numbers of female and male peasants who returned to their home villages after a period working away, or who never left, were those who were more content to conform to the customs and traditions of peasant life. Many younger adult peasants were satisfied by the greater freedom offered by the prospect of setting up their own households, independent of the older generation, when or shortly after they married partners of their own choice. The decay of the system of large, complex households, caused by the increase in *pre-mortem* partitions, led to an increase in the numbers and

23 Ramer, 'Childbirth', pp. 111–12.
24 Engel, *Between*, p. 239.

proportions of small, simple households that went through 'phases of development' as they grew and then contracted. One result was greater differentiation in wealth between households. To the extent that differences were caused by household life cycles, they were only short term. But the growth in non-agricultural pursuits, wage labour and the commercialisation of the rural economy began to lead to greater and more permanent socio-economic differentiation between households in some communities. The slow and patchy growth in differentiation inside the peasantry at the turn of the twentieth century should not be overstated. Nor was the peasantry, as Lenin hoped, dividing into a small 'rural bourgeoisie' and a large 'rural proletariat'.

The decade after 1905 saw further evidence that the old social order in rural Russia was being challenged. Growing numbers of younger male peasants expressed their antipathy to authority, both inside and outside their villages, by antisocial and disruptive behaviour. Gangs of young men got drunk, hurled obscenities, sang bawdy songs in public places, and played loud music on their accordions late at night, vandalised and stole property, fought amongst themselves and attacked passers-by. They also engaged in more serious crimes, including violent assaults, rape and murder. Their most common targets were members of their parents' generation, village elders, Stolypin 'separators' (see below), parish clergy, policemen, officials, educated people and nobles. Contemporaries branded such behaviour 'hooliganism', and blamed it on the 'pernicious' influence of towns, where law and order was also under threat from young, lower-class men. Many rural 'hooligans' were indeed labourers who spent part of the year working in factories in urban areas. To some extent, therefore, increasing contacts between Russia's peasants and its growing urban and industrial centres were weakening traditional structures of rural authority.[25]

In spite of the existence of internal tensions, and the increasing pace of change in the larger society in which they lived, cohesion was more apparent than division among the Russian peasantry in the early twentieth century. For the most part, Russia's peasants still had more common interests with their fellow villagers than with outsiders. This was demonstrated when many peasants joined in the revolution that had broken out in urban Russia in 1905.[26]

Towards the end of the revolution of 1905–07 the tsarist government tried to foment division among peasant communities. Peter Stolypin's land reforms of 1906–11 permitted peasants to leave their village communes and consolidate and enclose their land separately from that of their neighbours. Stolypin aimed to promote the interests of relatively prosperous yeoman farmers, whom he hoped would become a force for social stability in rural Russia. The implementation of the reforms was accompanied by conflict and disorder as

---

25 See Weissman, N. B., 'Rural crime in tsarist Russia: The question of hooliganism 1905–1914', *SR*, vol. 37 (1978), pp. 228–40; and Neuberger, J., *Hooliganism: Crime, Culture, and Power in St. Petersburg* (Berkeley, CA, 1993).
26 See Perrie, M. P., 'The Russian peasant movement of 1905–1907', *P & P*, no. 57 (1972), pp. 123–55; Shanin, T., *Russia, 1905–07: Revolution as a Moment of Truth* (Basingstoke and London, 1986).

many peasants tried to prevent some of their neighbours from leaving their communes. Only a small minority of peasant households in the Russian provinces of the empire had separated from their communes by 1917, when the collapse of tsarist Russia put a premature end to the reform. In contrast to the abolition of serfdom and reforms of the other categories of peasants in the 1860s, however, the aim of Stolypin's reforms was to transform Russian peasant society and the rural economy. The possible long-term results, had revolution not broken out in 1917, remain one of the great counterfactual questions of Russian history. In the short term, however, Judith Pallot has noted the 'relative resilience' of the commune to attack and its 'flexibility in the face of the change'.[27]

To some extent, and setting aside for a moment the long-term results of state intervention and sustained urbanisation and industrialisation, many of the changes that took place inside peasant society in the last decades of tsarist Russia can be seen as adaptations of older strategies or the development of new practices that were part of the evolution of new peasant ways of life. Some of the strategies adopted by peasants in late tsarist Russia, moreover, were not new, but reversions to older practices that had been widespread in the forest-heartland before the late seventeenth century, and had survived longer in some outlying regions. There were striking similarities between the sizes and structures of peasant households in these three periods/regions. In all three, many households were small in size and simple in structure because married sons separated from their parents' households and set up on their own before, rather than after, their fathers' deaths. A possible explanation for the similarity in practices is the levels of exploitation and resulting degrees of social control by the ruling and landowning elites over the peasantry as a whole, and by the older generation of peasants over young adults. These were all greatest in the central regions of Russia between the late seventeenth and late nineteenth centuries. In this context, the predominance of large and complex households, caused by restrictions on married sons leaving their fathers' households, can be seen as responses to high levels of exploitation.

There were also some similarities in the forms and aims of peasant protest against the landowning and ruling elites in late nineteenth- and early twentieth-century Russia, in the forest-heartland before the late seventeenth century, and for at least part of the intervening period in some borderlands. Rather than restrict themselves largely to limited, non-violent and even non-confrontational forms of protest with limited objectives, some peasants in these three periods/regions were prepared to use more extreme forms of mass and open protest to try to attain more radical objectives. Peasants fled in large numbers from the forest-heartland in search of greater freedom in the borderlands until the late seventeenth and early eighteenth centuries. Large numbers of peasants once again fled central Russia for the borderlands, especially Siberia, in the late

---

27 Pallot and Shaw, *Landscape*, p. 192. For a different view, see Macey, D. A. J., '"A wager on history": The Stolypin agrarian reforms as process', in Pallot, *Transforming Peasants*, pp. 149–73.

nineteenth century, before mass migration was authorised by the government in the 1880s. This time, peasants were escaping the pressure of population increase on their ways of life, rather than growing exploitation and enserfment. More striking is the similarity between peasant participation in the four great revolts of the seventeenth and eighteenth centuries and the involvement of large numbers of peasants throughout Russia in the revolutions of 1905–07 and 1917–21. In both cases, peasants joined in uprisings that had begun earlier among other groups of people.

The return to mass direct action with radical aims, after almost a century and a half in which few Russian peasants – especially in the central regions – had resorted to open and violent protest to try to attain radical aims, can be attributed to the broader changes taking place in late tsarist Russia. This is not the place for a detailed analysis of the origins of the revolutions and peasant participation in them, but some remarks can be made on possible reasons for the dramatic change in the forms and aims of peasant protest in early twentieth-century Russia. Since the late nineteenth century, there had been an increase in both immediate and underlying grievances among the peasantry. Peasants were struggling to adapt their practices and customs to changes taking place in Russian society as a whole. The old view among historians of declining living standards among the mass of the peasantry in late tsarist Russia is no longer tenable. Nevertheless, the pressure of population increase on the land probably cancelled out part of any gain from the decline in the level of exploitation after the reforms of the 1860s–80s. Land hunger was most acute in the densely populated Central Black Earth region. Throughout the decades after 1861, many peasants seem to have expected, and demanded, that the authorities enact a major redistribution of all the land that remained in the possession of nobles, the state and other non-peasants. Their hopes were frustrated.

Another reason for peasant participation in the revolutions of the early twentieth century was the emergence of opportunities to revolt with a chance of attaining some of their goals. The pace of change in late tsarist Russia had created not just discontent and a decline in traditional authority in peasant communities, but had led to similar developments in Russian society as a whole. There was increasing disquiet and protest by many different groups in Russia, most notably the emerging middle classes and urban workers. The ruling elites were divided over how to deal with the social consequences, including growing disaffection, of the economic 'modernisation' they were anxious to promote in the interests of maintaining Russia's status as a world power. Some senior officials advocated concessions and reforms to appease the growing social discontent, while hardliners insisted on repression and retrenchment.[28]

More immediately, the authority of the ruling elites suffered serious blows as a consequence of Russia's disastrous military defeats by Japan in 1904–05

28 See Wcislo, *Reforming*.

and by Germany in the First World War by 1917. On both occasions, military defeat and the stresses of modern war, on top of existing strains within society, sparked off revolutions in the cities that subsequently spread to the villages when peasants saw opportunities to take advantage of the situations for their own ends. The tsarist regime weathered the revolution of 1905–07 but collapsed in February–March 1917. Members of the elites, in particular generals in the army, persuaded Nicholas II to abdicate against a background of rising social discontent on the streets of the imperial capital culminating in the mutiny by some soldiers of the Petrograd garrison. A recent historian of the 1917 revolution, Christopher Read, has argued that 'it is essential to bear in mind that it was not the social revolution that brought about the collapse of the Russian state, but the collapse of the state [in February–March 1917] that facilitated the social revolution'.[29]

In 1917, as in 1905, Russian peasants saw their chance and joined the revolution. Many peasants understood the abdication of the tsar and the downfall of the old regime to mean the end of large-scale private landownership. Over the summer and autumn of 1917 peasants began to tire of waiting for the Provisional Government to enact a land reform. Some began to take matters into their own hands, seizing land from nobles, driving them from their estates, and burning down manor houses. In October 1917, one of Lenin's first acts after the Bolsheviks had seized power was to issue the 'Decree on Land'. The Bolsheviks had little support in rural Russia and gave peasants what they wanted: a nationwide 'black repartition' (*chernyi peredel*) of all the land. The scale of peasant land seizures increased after the decree.[30]

Peasants who took part in the revolutions, in 1905–07 as well as 1917–21, drew on the traditions of Russian peasant society. The institution that played the largest part in organising peasant participation was not one of the new radical political parties, such as the peasant-orientated Socialist Revolutionaries, but the venerable village commune. In 1917–18 it was village communes that directed the land seizures. Communes also compelled those who had separated under the terms of Stolypin's reforms to return to the fold. The distribution of the seized land between households was directed by communes on similar principles to those which guided the partition, and repartition, of village land in normal times. In another throwback to the past, the descendants of seigniorial peasants took over the land of the nobles who had owned their forebears on the principle: 'Ours was the lord, ours is the land.'[31]

29 Read, C., *From Tsar to Soviets: The Russian People and their Revolution, 1917–1921* (London, 1996), p. 45.
30 See Gill, G. J., *Peasants and Government in the Russian Revolution* (London, 1979); Perrie, M. P., 'The peasants', in Service, R. (ed.), *Society and Politics in the Russian Revolution* (Basingstoke and London, 1992), pp. 12–34; Channon, J., 'The Bolsheviks and the peasantry: The land question during the first eight months of Soviet rule', *SEER*, vol. 66 (1988), pp. 593–624; Read, *From Tsar*, pp. 101–20, 228–32.
31 Figes, O., *Peasant Russia, Civil War: The Volga Countryside in Revolution (1917–1921)* (Oxford, 1989), p. 50.

In 1917–18 around 50 million *desyatiny* of land in Russia (RSFSR) that had previously belonged to nobles, the tsars' family and the state passed into peasant hands. When the figures are examined in detail and disaggregated, however, the results appear less impressive. Most was not arable land but forests. A large part of the land peasants acquired was in more outlying regions, such as the Lower Volga and Don. In the Central Black Earth region, where land hunger was most acute, peasants gained an average of only 0.25–0.5 *desyatiny* per person, an increase of around 28 per cent of their existing holdings. Moreover, a large part of the land seized had been rented by peasants before the revolution. Nevertheless, they no longer had to pay the rents, and their debts to the Peasant Land Bank were cancelled.[32] The agrarian revolution of 1917–18 was the last example of the traditional Russian peasant practice of trying to maintain their ways of life by extensification rather than intensification of production.

The causes, forms and aims of peasant participation in the revolutions of the early twentieth century were further examples of the adaptability of the Russian peasantry to changes in the world they lived in, and of their ability to take advantage of opportunities that arose. By taking part in and weathering the revolutions, moreover, Russian peasant society outlived the tsarist state with which its fate had been so closely intertwined since the sixteenth century.

The Russian peasantry's victory in the agrarian revolution of 1917–18 was short lived. After 1917, the peasantry came up against a ruling Communist Party (as the Bolsheviks called their party from 1918) which was committed to the elimination of small-scale, household-based, peasant agriculture and its replacement with large-scale, collectivised farming. The Party was intent on building 'socialism' in the new Soviet Union by speeding up the existing processes of urbanisation and industrialisation that had already spelled the end of peasant societies elsewhere in Europe. In other words, the Party aimed to eliminate the Russian peasantry. It had few qualms over the means it used to this end. The scene was set for the Russian peasantry's last struggle, and its eventual demise in the aftermath of Stalin's forced collectivisation of agriculture launched in 1929–30.

CONCLUSION

Decisive change and decline were the main themes in the history of the Russian peasantry in the twentieth century. Throughout the preceding epoch which is the main subject of this book, however, the history of Russian peasant society was marked by broad continuities, both in the ways peasants organised their lives and in their position in Russian society. Russian peasants were rational and creative actors in their world and in their dealings with outsiders. They ensured the survival of their society into the twentieth century by devising,

---

32 See Atkinson, *End*, pp. 179–83; Shanin, *Awkward*, pp. 153–4.

adopting and, when necessary, modifying or changing a variety of strategies to ensure their subsistence and livelihoods. They did this both by themselves and in conjunction with members of the landowning and ruling elites. The strategies peasants employed thus made up viable, flexible and enduring ways of life. The main reason why the world the peasants made endured so long, therefore, was its ability to adapt to change.

CHAPTER 10

Change

The world the peasants made in Russia survived well into the twentieth century only to fall victim to Stalin's forced collectivisation of agriculture after 1929. In the light of the horrors that followed, the middle years of the 1920s seem an 'Indian summer' in rural Russia. The Communist Party and institutions of Soviet power were still quite weak in the villages, where the bulk of the Russian population still lived. Until the end of the decade, the Party and state had neither the strength nor the will to implement their long-term goal of eliminating small-scale peasant farming and replacing it with large-scale, collectivised agriculture as part of an industrialised, 'socialist' economy. For much of the 1920s Russia's peasants were left largely to their own devices with relatively limited or intermittent interference from outside.

The Communist Party's problems in rural Russia had been clearly demonstrated during the Civil War that had broken out a few months after the Party seized power in October 1917. During the Civil War the Party assumed central control over the economy and tried to mobilise the resources of the territory it held. Millions of peasant men were conscripted into the Red Army. In order to feed the army and the cities, the Party tried to extract surplus produce from rich peasants (whom it branded 'kulaks') by organising committees of poor peasants (*Kombedy*) in the hope of provoking 'class struggle' in the villages. The attempt failed because Lenin's 'class analysis' of socio-economic differentiation inside the peasantry was incorrect (see Ch. 8). Many peasant communities overcame their internal differences and united against this attempt by outsiders to take away their grain. The Party resorted to forced requisitions. The economic policies of the Civil War were known as 'War Communism'. For many Communists, they were not just emergency measures on account of the war, but an attempt to advance rapidly towards 'communism'. In reality, the excesses of War Communism seriously undermined the economy, especially the rural sector, and led to a breakdown in trade between agriculture and industry.

War Communism turned many peasants against the new regime that, in October 1917, had sanctioned and encouraged their land seizures and, during the Civil War, had seemed marginally preferable to the 'Whites', whom many peasants feared would return the land to the landowners. Nevertheless, many peasants resisted the forced grain requisitions and other demands by concealing their reserves, selling them on the black market, and reducing the areas of land they cultivated. Peasants also resisted conscription into the Red Army and the often arbitrary and corrupt conduct of local Party and Soviet officials. Some resorted to more active opposition. Bands of peasants known as 'Greens', including deserters from both Red and White armies, waged guerilla warfare against both sides. Peasant resistance was most marked, and most violent, in the Lower-Volga and Don and Southern Urals regions, the south-east of the Central Black Earth region, especially Tambov and Voronezh provinces, and in Ukraine. As in previous centuries, therefore, the most serious peasant resistance took place in outlying regions where central control was relatively weak. Some of these areas contained large cossack populations, whose ancestors had taken part in the great revolts of the seventeenth and eighteenth centuries. These regions were also the chief grain-growing areas under Soviet control and thus the main targets of requisitioning. In 1920, when Red victory seemed assured, a number of armed peasant revolts broke out against Soviet power. The most serious was led by an independent Socialist Revolutionary, Alexander Antonov, in Tambov province. The regime's response was harsh repression and reprisals, but also reform.[1]

In March 1921 the Party abandoned War Communism and introduced the New Economic Policy (NEP). Under NEP, small-scale peasant farming, private light industry and private internal trade were permitted to coexist with state-controlled heavy industry and foreign trade. Grain requisitioning was replaced by a fixed tax in kind. In 1924, when the currency had been stabilised, the tax in kind was converted into money. NEP was a retreat from War Communism and a major concession to the peasantry.[2] But the change in policy came too late to avert the massive famine of 1921–22, which was caused largely by the excesses of grain requisitioning during the Civil War. In the Soviet Union as a whole, including a large part of Ukraine, around five million people died of hunger and disease. These deaths were on top of the millions who had died during the Civil War and the First World War. The majority of the dead in the years 1914–22, both military and civilian, were either peasants or of peasant origin.[3]

In the years after 1922, the Russian peasantry gradually recovered from the catastrophic effects of world war, revolutions, civil war, requisitioning and famine. Under NEP there was a resurgence of the traditional rural institutions – peasant households and village communes – as well as other elements of the

1 See Figes, *Peasant Russia*; Graziosi, A., *The Great Soviet Peasant War: Bolsheviks and Peasants, 1917–1933* (Cambridge, MA, 1996), pp. 16–37; Osipova, T., 'Peasant rebellions: Origins, scope, dynamics, and consequences', in Brovkin, V. N. (ed.), *The Bolsheviks in Russian Society: The Revolution and the Civil Wars* (New Haven, CT, and London, 1997), pp. 154–76; DuGarm, D., 'Peasant wars in Tambov Province', *ibid.*, pp. 177–98.
2 On War Communism and NEP, see Nove, A., *An Economic History of the USSR, 1917–1991*, 3rd edn (Harmondsworth, 1992), pp. 39–114.
3 See Graziosi, *Great*, pp. 38–9; Wheatcroft and Davies, 'Population', pp. 62–4; Wehner, M., 'Golod 1921–1922 gg. v Samarskoi gubernii i reaktsii sovetskogo pravitel'stva', *CMR*, vol. 38 (1997), pp. 223–42.

Russian peasantry's customary ways of life. Most communities in the central regions continued to hold their arable land in communal and repartitional tenure, and still cultivated it under the three-field system. By 1926–27 agricultural output had returned to its pre-1914 level. But all was not well in the villages of Russia. The crippling human losses of 1914–22 had hit young men most of all. Women outnumbered men in rural Russia throughout the 1920s. Wartime conscription had also taken millions of horses from the villages to serve in the tsarist, Red and White armies. The resulting shortages of labour and draught power posed major constraints on agricultural output that had still not been overcome by the late 1920s.[4]

COLLECTIVISATION

Many members of the Communist Party were unhappy with the 'retreat' to NEP in 1921. Only a few, such as Nikolai Bukharin, believed that small-scale peasant farming and private trade, combined with taxation and a degree of price fixing, could generate the resources necessary to transform the still largely traditional, rural and agricultural Russia of the 1920s into the modern, urban, industrial and 'socialist' society they aimed to build. Throughout the 1920s the Soviet government had difficulties in meeting its needs for agricultural produce. Attempts to intervene in the market to give preference to industry over agriculture and, in 1927–29, to seize grain by force only exacerbated the problems. As they had done during the Civil War, peasants reacted by withholding produce from sale, selling grain at higher prices on the black market, and cutting back the areas they sowed. Impatience in the Party over the resumption of the 'socialist offensive' was reflected in power struggles inside the leadership. In 1928–29, when Stalin completed his victory over his main rivals, NEP was abandoned and the Party leadership committed itself to rapid, centrally planned industrialisation and the collectivisation of agriculture. The Party wanted to guarantee, and increase, its procurements of agricultural produce, and transfer resources from agriculture to assist industrial development and the 'construction of socialism'.[5]

Lynne Viola has recently described collectivisation as an attempt to control and extract tribute from the peasantry, 'an all-out attack against the peasantry, its culture, and way of life'.[6] In the first wave of forced collectivisation in the winter of 1929–30 and the early spring of 1930, Party officials and workers ('25,000ers') who were sent out from the cities cajoled and coerced peasants to join the new collective farms (*kolkhozy*). The collectivisers also attacked village churches and clergy, and implemented 'dekulakisation'. Richer peasants,

4 See Wheatcroft and Davies, 'Population', pp. 64–7; *id.*, 'Agriculture', in Davies, *Economic Transformation*, pp. 111–12; Fitzpatrick, S., *Stalin's Peasants: Resistance and Survival in the Russian Village after Collectivization* (New York and Oxford, 1994), pp. 19–47.
5 See Davies, R. W., *The Socialist Offensive: The Collectivisation of Soviet Agriculture, 1929–30* (Basingstoke and London, 1980), pp. 1–146.
6 Viola, *Peasant Rebels*, p. [vii]. The following account is based largely on Viola's book (see Moon, D., 'Peasant rebels under Stalin' [review article], *RevR*, vol. 11 [1998], pp. 74–8).

and many others who resisted, were branded 'kulaks'. Their property was confiscated and they were deported. Many 'kulaks' also lost their lives. Peasants who joined the collective farms, either under duress or voluntarily, also lost most of their property to the new *kolkhozy*. Their households' strips of arable land and horses were handed over. In some villages, collectivised peasants were also forced to give up their other livestock, implements, garden plots, houses, and sometimes even their furniture, pots and pans, clothes and other belongings.

The assault on the peasantry sparked off rumours in rural Russia. There were five main themes: Soviet power and the collective farm as AntiChrist and portents of the end of the world; impending retribution against peasants who joined the collective farms; imminent invasion by foreign armies, which would kill peasants who had entered the *kolkhozy* and then disband them; the 'godless nature of Communism and moral abominations of the new collective farm order', including the socialisation of women and children; and the collective farm system as a 'second serfdom'. The rumours expressed the peasants' fears, and according to Viola served as a 'subversive ideology' and ensured village cohesion.

Peasants resorted to various strategies as a first line of defence. Many sold their livestock, grain reserves, implements and other property. Others slaughtered and ate their animals, distilled their grain into *samogon* (moonshine), and destroyed their belongings. Some did so as a protest against the socialisation of property, thinking it better than handing their goods over to the collective farms. Others deliberately impoverished themselves to avoid being branded 'kulaks'. They clearly felt that 'self-dekulakisation' was preferable to the horrors of the official policy. Some justified selling or killing their horses by telling officials they would not be needed on the collective farms because 'Soviet power' would provide them with tractors. As well as covering their tracks by dissembling, peasants resorted to other traditional forms of protest. Millions, including many 'self-dekulakised' peasants, fled their villages. Some travelled to eastern parts of the Soviet Union. Larger numbers moved to towns and cities in search of work. Tens of thousands of peasants petitioned the central authorities. Many petitioners were careful to use the appropriate 'Sovietese', but it is very unlikely that any had faith in Stalin. Most peasants held Stalin directly and personally responsible for collectivisation and the ensuing chaos and disaster.

When more passive forms of resistance failed, peasants resorted to mass, open protests and violence. They did so in spite of the power of the Soviet state and its armed forces, which many peasants had witnessed at first hand only a decade earlier during the Civil War. Peasants tried to intimidate 'activists' among their own numbers and officials with threats of violence and acts of 'terror'. According to official statistics, in 1930 alone, 1,198 peasant activists and officials were murdered and five times that number assaulted. The other common form of terror was the 'red rooster': arson. There were thousands of cases of the property of peasant activists, officials and collective farms being burned down. The conflict was intensified by thousands of 'disturbances' in the winter of 1929–30 and early spring of 1930. Peasants disrupted meetings held to organise collective farms. Large crowds of peasants, including women and children as well as men bearing scythes and pitchforks, tried to scare the collectivisers into leaving them alone. Peasants rioted in last-ditch attempts to prevent the formation of collective farms, or to disband those already set up; to stop the socialisation of their belongings, or to recover property which had already been taken; to free 'kulaks' awaiting expulsion; and to defend their churches against closure and priests from deportation or worse. The authorities used armed force to put down some revolts, leading to countless deaths.

Resistance to collectivisation was strongest in the Mid-Volga and Lower-Volga and Don regions, including the north Caucasus, and in Ukraine. The authorities also met much opposition in parts of the Central Black Earth region, Siberia and central Asia. Peasant resistance was strongest in similar areas to the locations of peasant rebellions during the Civil War and the great revolts of the seventeenth and eighteenth centuries. As in 1918–21, moreover, the most serious protests were in the main grain-growing areas, where the authorities concentrated their efforts and used most coercion.

There were tensions between peasants inside villages as well as protests by peasants united against collectivisation. Much of the violence was directed at peasants who entered the *kolkhozy* voluntarily. Some younger men, especially veterans of the Red Army and those who had worked in cities, joined the collective farms in the hope of escaping the authority of their fathers and the older generation. A few women welcomed collectivisation as a way of escaping the patriarchal authority of their husbands and fathers. Village activists included poorer peasants, who saw the chance to end the dominance of richer peasants. The Soviet authorities and, subsequently, most Soviet historians attributed the violence against peasant activists and supporters of collectivisation to 'kulaks'. This is easily refuted. Even in the official figures, which overstated the numbers of 'kulaks', they were alleged to have been responsible for only half the acts of 'terror' in 1930. In a more subtle analysis of intra-village relations in Siberia during collectivisation and dekulakisation, James Hughes has argued that the Party succeeded initially in creating some support for the policies among 'poor' and 'middle' peasants.[7]

Most recent works on collectivisation, such as Viola's, have emphasised the collective nature of peasant protests against policies which were being imposed by outsiders by force, and which threatened the ways of life of *all* peasants. This argument can be illustrated by the important role played by peasant women in the resistance. Women were active in protests against policies which adversely affected the areas of life that were traditionally their 'domains', for example the socialisation of domestic livestock and household grain stocks. Women were also active in protests directed at the whole

---

7 Hughes, J, *Stalinism in a Russian Province: A Study of Collectivization and Dekulakization in Siberia* (Basingstoke and London, 1996).

policy of collectivisation. Viola argued that peasant women manipulated official images of them as irrational '*baby*' ('hags') prone to spontaneous outbursts of hysteria in order to make more direct challenges to the policy than men would have been allowed to get away with.

In the winter of 1929–30 peasant resistance to collectivisation and dekulakisation prompted the authorities to implement the policies more quickly. In March 1930, however, Stalin called a halt. In a typical example of 'double-speak', he wrote an article entitled 'Dizzy with Success'. He blamed the 'excesses' that had caused the resistance on local officials who had got carried away with their 'success' in implementing collectivisation. Stalin was worried that the mass peasant defiance would disrupt the spring sowing and thus lead to food shortages. He was also worried that the protests could escalate into a massive revolt, with damaging consequences for the regime. Peasants responded to the retreat with glee. Many told disheartened officials that the Party was on 'their side', and that they had 'won'. The retreat sparked off more protests and mass departures from the *kolkhozy*. The peasants' joy was short lived. The retreat proved to be temporary, and the drive for all-out collectivisation was resumed later in 1930. It was carried out at a less immoderate pace than in the hectic months of the winter and early spring of 1929–30. The collectivisation of agriculture in the Soviet Union was completed over the following few years.

The new collectivised order did create unprecedented opportunities for some rural inhabitants. Despite opposition from both men and women, some rural women worked as tractor drivers. A few, for example Pasha Angelina, were celebrated in official propaganda and became famous. A small minority of women worked in rural occupations that required specialised education, for example as agronomists, veterinary surgeons and farm accountants. A few women served as chairs of collective farms and local soviets. A few rural women moved to urban areas where they attained professional and managerial positions. The most dramatic example was probably that of Polina Osipenko. Although from a poor peasant family, she trained as a pilot and, emulating Amelia Earhart, set several world records for long-distance aviation in the 1930s.[8]

Nevertheless, the achievements of a few cannot conceal the fate of the vast majority. Collectivisation was a decisive point in the centuries-old history of the Russian peasantry. It destroyed many elements of their ways of life, including some that were among the defining features of peasant societies. Households ceased to be the principal units of social and economic organisation among rural Russians. The other main institution in rural Russia, the village commune (the *mir*), was abolished by decree in July 1930. Many of the *kolkhozy* set up in early 1930, at least on paper, were gigantic and included several villages. In addition, strip farming was ended, the open fields enclosed,

8 Manning, R. T., 'Women in the Soviet countryside on the eve of World War II, 1935–1940', in *RPW*, pp. 206–35.

and the three-field system of crop rotation finally brought to an end in the large parts of Russia where it was still in operation.

Over the 1930s collective farmers were able to extract some very limited concessions in the organisation and structure of collective farms. A few aspects of the peasants' ways of life revived. The gigantic collective farms were broken up into smaller farms, many of which coincided with pre-collectivised communes and villages. Households resumed some of their former significance. 'Brigades', the main units of labourers in the collective fields, were often based on groups of households. With some restrictions, collective farmers were permitted to leave their *kolkhozy* to work in towns and cities to help support their households. The more extreme versions of collective farms, in which most property had been 'socialised', were downgraded. Households regained some limited property rights. They were allowed to own their houses and their contents. They were also permitted to have garden plots, and to keep some livestock, including a cow as well as smaller domestic animals and fowl. But there were limitations on the sizes of 'private plots' and what they could be used for. At first, collective farmers were allowed to use their plots only to help support themselves by providing them with vegetables, including potatoes, fruit, dairy produce, eggs and such like. From 1932, however, collective farmers were permitted to trade in the produce of their private plots. Thus, some limited private trade in agricultural produce was allowed to exist within the centrally planned, 'socialist' economy of the Soviet Union.

The most important restrictions on households of collective farmers were retained. They were not permitted to have plots of arable land where they could grow grain, nor were they allowed to own horses, which were still the main draught power in rural Russia. Thus, collective farm households were not in a position to maintain a balanced economy, including arable farming as well as cultivating their garden plots, keeping a few animals, and earning some money outside their villages. Households were not able to support themselves independently of the collective farms, but had to rely on them for bread and meagre wages in return for cultivating the collective fields. The only traditional 'peasant family farms' in Russia after 1930 were the diminishing numbers of independent peasants (*'edinolichniki'*), who refused to join the *kolkhozy*. They were subjected to increasing restrictions, and had largely disappeared by the end of the 1930s as most either entered the collective farms, left the villages, or died.[9]

In some ways collective farming was similar to serfdom. Both were means by which the ruling elites extracted a large part of the product of the labour of the rural population. Some villagers who attacked the collective farms as a 'second serfdom' equated work in the collective fields with labour obligations on seigniorial estates. In a number of crucial respects, however, collectivised agriculture was different. Serfdom had been imposed on top of a peasant

---

9 See Davies, R. W., *The Soviet Collective Farm, 1929–1930* (Basingstoke and London, 1980); Fitzpatrick, *Stalin's Peasants*, esp. pp. 103–97.

society and economy which already existed and, with some adaptations, continued to exist during and after the servile period. Under serfdom, Russia's peasants had allotments of arable land and took most of the major decisions concerning their economic production and social organisation at household and village levels. Russian 'serfs' were 'peasants' in the ways that specialists have defined them (see Ch. 1).

Collective farming went further than serfdom. Rural Russians lost their arable land to the collective farms. The major decisions were taken away from households and village communities and put in the hands of collective farm chairmen, many of whom (at least in the first half of the 1930s) came from outside the villages. Farm chairmen acted on the directives of their political superiors: the Communist Party leadership at local and central levels. Edicts from on high included detailed 'sowing plans' that often took little account of local conditions or the needs of the collective farmers. Very few noble landowners had told their serfs what to sow or how to farm the land, and most that tried to soon desisted. Unlike serfdom, therefore, collectivised agriculture was incompatible with the continued existence of a peasant society. Collective farmers were not 'peasants'.

The collectivisation of agriculture not only spelled the end of peasant society in Russia, but led directly to a catastrophic fall in the numbers of Russians who lived in rural areas and worked on the land. The campaign to 'eliminate kulaks as a class' resulted in the disappearance from the villages of enormous numbers of peasants. Throughout the entire Soviet Union in the years 1930–33, between 2 and 2.5 million 'kulaks' were exiled within the regions they lived in, and over 2.1 million were deported to labour camps or 'special settlements' in remote parts of the Soviet Union. Several hundred thousand died on the way to their places of exile and in the appalling conditions they had to live in after they arrived. Unknown numbers were executed. There was a second wave of 'dekulakisation' in 1937–39, when additional tens or hundreds of thousands of 'kulaks' were deported or executed. In 1932–33, between the waves of dekulakisation, large parts of the Soviet Union were hit by a devastating famine. The main cause was the continued extraction of grain by the Soviet state from a demoralised rural population, in spite of repeated warnings from collective farm chairmen and local officials that there was insufficient grain left in the villages to feed their inhabitants. More conservative estimates suggest that famine deaths amounted to between five and seven million. Ukrainians and Kazakhs suffered worst, but the famine also struck Russian villages, especially in the Volga regions and the north Caucasus.[10]

In addition to the vast numbers of peasants who were deported, executed or died of starvation and disease, millions more fled the villages to escape collectivisation, 'dekulakisation' and famine. Many moved to the towns and

10 See Davies, *Soviet History*, pp. 162–4, 170–1; Wheatcroft and Davies, 'Population', pp. 67–77; Graziosi, *Great*, pp. 58–70; Conquest, R., *The Harvest of Sorrow: Soviet Collectivisation and the Terror Famine* (London, 1986).

cities. The urbanisation of Russia that had accompanied the increased pace of industrialisation since the 1880s continued more quickly under Soviet centrally planned economic development. In the Soviet Union as a whole, in the years of the first five-year plan alone (1928–32), around 12 million people left the villages for urban areas. Many of the migrants found work on construction sites or in the new industries. Large-scale migration to towns and cities continued after 1932, despite the reintroduction in that year of controls on the movement of rural inhabitants. Between 1926 and 1939, a total of 18.5 million people moved from rural to urban areas. Most harmful for the future of rural Russia, the majority of those who left were young men and women.[11]

In the words of Sheila Fitzpatrick, 'the typical Russian village in the 1930s was hungry, drab, depopulated, and demoralized'. Village communities and households disintegrated in the aftermath of collectivisation. The average size of households in rural Russia fell from around five people in the late 1920s to between 3.9 and 4.4 ten years later. In spite of their small size, many were not simple households containing two parents and their unmarried children, but often comprised assorted conglomerations of people, not all of whom were even related. The enormous numbers of deaths and deportations and the departure of large numbers of young men and women had very damaging effects on rural family life. Children were left without parents, elderly people without children, and wives without husbands. The number of divorces increased, but formal terminations of marriages were far exceeded by the numbers of men who deserted their wives and left the villages for good. Eligible men were in such short supply that the custom of grooms' households paying bride-prices was reversed. Households began to pay men to marry their daughters. Some men took advantage, married several women in succession, and abandoned their pregnant brides. The depopulation of the villages and decay in traditional family life contributed to a sharp fall in the birth rate. In the late 1930s the birth rate in rural Russia was only 32 per thousand. This was two-thirds of the level it had been at the start of the century.

The breakdown of the customary ways of life and culture in Russia's villages was accompanied by growing crime rates and an intensification of intra-village conflicts. The increase in the late 1930s in the numbers of local collective farm chairmen, in place of outsiders, worsened the friction. Villagers fought to attain managerial positions, and to use them or influence those that held them, to serve their interests at the expense of their neighbours. Although manipulated from above, the 'purges' of the late 1930s enabled some collective farmers to exact revenge on farm managers and local officials by denouncing them to the authorities.[12]

---

11 See Wheatcroft and Davies, 'Population', p. 69; Fitzpatrick, *Stalin's Peasants*, pp. 80–102; Hoffman, D. L., *Peasant Metropolis: Social Identities in Moscow, 1929–1941* (Ithaca, NY, 1994). Internal passports, which permitted their holders to move, were revived in December 1932, but not issued to collective farmers until 1974: Matthews, *Passport*.
12 See Fitzpatrick, *Stalin's Peasants*, pp. 204–312 (quotation from p. 262).

The removal of a few individuals did not reverse the dramatic changes of the previous decade that had witnessed the end of the world the peasants had made in Russia.

AFTERMATH

It is difficult to conceive how the situation in rural Russia could have got worse, but in June 1941 the Soviet Union was invaded by the German army on the orders of Hitler. The western borderlands, especially Belorussia and Ukraine, suffered most, but large parts of central Russia were also occupied. German forces reached the outskirts of Leningrad in the north, Moscow in the centre and Stalingrad on the lower Volga. The invaders reached the north Caucasus in 1942. The hopes expressed by many peasants in 1930 that collectivisation would be reversed by foreign invaders were dashed. The Germans treated the rural population even more brutally than the Soviet authorities had done in the 1930s. The war increased the hardships of the entire Soviet population, not just the large numbers who lived under German occupation. Millions of men were conscripted. Nearly two-thirds of the men who served in the Soviet armed forces in 1941–45 came from the rural population. Most never returned. The standard estimate of the total human losses, military and civilian, of the Soviet Union during the 'Great Patriotic War' is 27 million. The impact of these catastrophic losses was exacerbated in rural areas because the existing imbalance between the numbers of men and women increased still further. Among the war dead, men outnumbered women by almost 3:1. Moreover, many men from the rural population who served in the army and survived the war settled in urban areas after they had been demobilised. As a result, in 1950, women made up 65 per cent of able-bodied collective farm workers.[13]

Much of the immense human cost of the Soviet Union's victory over Germany was thus paid by the rural population. Rural Russians paid this price, moreover, before they had recovered from collectivisation and the famine of the early 1930s. During the Second World War, on his visit to Moscow in August 1942, Winston Churchill asked Stalin if 'the stresses of this war [had] been as bad . . . as carrying through the policy of the Collective Farms'. Stalin replied: 'Oh no, the Collective Farm policy was a terrible struggle', adding that the struggle with the 'kulaks' had been 'all very bad and difficult, but [he maintained] necessary'.[14] The sufferings of rural inhabitants continued after 1945. In 1946–47 large parts of the central and south-eastern Soviet Union were hit by another famine. The harvest was very poor in 1946 on account of

13 See Barber, J. and Harrison, M., *The Home Front, 1941–1945: A Social and Economic History of the USSR in World War II* (London and New York, 1991), pp. 39–42, 59–62, 84–5, 99–104, 187–8, 217; Dallin, A., *German Rule in Russia, 1941–1945* (London, 1957), pp. 320–72; Dodge, N. D. and Feshbach, M., 'The role of women in Soviet agriculture', in *RPW*, p. 241.
14 Churchill, W. S., *The Second World War*, vol. 4, *The Hinge of Fate* (London, 1951), pp. 447–8.

a drought, but the authorities continued to extract grain from farms without regard to the subsistence needs of their inhabitants. Around two million died.[15] The only positive effects of the war on Russian villagers were some relaxations in the collective farm system. Collective farmers were allowed to increase the size of their private plots at the expense of collective fields. Many farmers earned large profits from selling produce from their plots at high prices to the urban population. But these gains were wiped out in a currency reform after the end of the war. Furthermore, the wartime relaxations were soon reversed. Tighter control over collective farmers was resumed. Private plots were cut back and the land returned to the collective fields. Subsequent changes were also detrimental to collective farmers and what was left of the traditional, rural ways of life. The sizes of private plots were further restricted, collective farms based on old villages and communes were amalgamated into giant *kolkhozy*, and more farm managers were appointed from outside the villages.

From the mid-1950s, under Khrushchev, there were a number of changes which, to some extent, benefited the rural population. The government raised the prices it paid for agricultural produce and, hence, the wages paid to collective farmers. The permitted sizes of private plots were increased. Investment in agriculture was given greater priority. Some of the money went towards extensification of agriculture during Khrushchev's 'virgin lands campaign' of the 1950s. Around 300,000 Russians and Ukrainians moved south and east, and ploughed up almost 89 million acres of untilled or abandoned land in south-east European Russia, southern Siberia and northern Kazakhstan. Other money was used for intensification of farming. Soviet factories turned out more tractors, combine harvesters and other agricultural machinery. The chemical industry produced more non-organic fertilisers, herbicides and pesticides. By the 1960s and 70s, moreover, amenities such as piped water, gas and mains electricity became more common in the villages. Collective farms improved the provision of social and welfare services, including health care and schools. Some villagers acquired consumer goods and luxuries, for example fridges and motorbikes. The accordions which had arrived in Russian villages in the late nineteenth century were superseded by gramophones and wireless sets.

At a more basic level, other post-war trends had harmful consequences for agriculture and the old ways of life in rural Russia. None of the reforms solved the many problems inherent in collectivised farming. Mechanisation, the growing use of chemicals, and careless farming techniques did increasing damage to the environment, leading to more serious problems in later decades. The steady decline in the rural population continued. As in previous decades, it was the younger generation, especially the men, who left. The population of rural Russia, and the workforce of the collective farms, was increasingly middle-aged or elderly, and female. Millions of young men sought work in towns and cities after completing their compulsory military service. Many other young people, women as well as men, moved to towns and cities

15 Zima, V. F., *Golod v SSSR 1946–7 gg.* (Moscow, 1996).

to enter colleges of further or higher education and stayed on after they completed their courses. Many found work in industry, others in white-collar jobs. Few returned to the villages.[16]

Some villagers put rather more distance between themselves and their rural origins. In 1961, a man born 27 years earlier in the village of Klushino, on a collective farm 150 miles north-east of Smolensk, was launched into orbit in a capsule on top of a Soviet rocket. Yuri Gagarin, the first man in space, was born a Russian peasant.[17] A couple of years after Gagarin became the first cosmonaut, however, Soviet collectivised agriculture failed to produce enough to feed the population, and the Soviet Union had to start importing food from 'capitalist' countries.[18]

By the late twentieth century Russia had become a predominantly urban society. Since 1959 the majority of the population had lived in towns and cities rather than villages. Despite its many problems, urban Russia in the last few decades of the twentieth century was a modern, industrial and developed society. For most Russians, and people around the world, the word '*Mir*' no longer meant 'village commune' but was the name of the Soviet/Russian space station orbiting the earth. The decreasing proportion of Russians who still lived in the villages and worked on the land, around 20 per cent in the 1980s, were left on the margins of the society of which, for centuries, their forebears had been a central and by far the largest part.

Gorbachev's economic reforms of the late 1980s, and the end of Communist Party rule and the Soviet Union itself in 1991, offered the prospect of an end to the collective farm system. The 'law of the peasant farm' of November 1990 permitted collective farmers in Russia to take a share of the collective land, machinery and other property, and to leave to set up on their own. Subsequent laws provided for the privatisation and break-up of collective farms. But the de-collectivisation and privatisation of agriculture in post-Soviet Russia were less successful than measures enacted in the People's Republic of China from 1978 to dismantle its collective farms. Moreover, during the 1990s, Russian private farmers had nothing even approaching the levels of government support available in North America and the European Union. Although family farmers in China, the USA and EU experienced many difficulties in the late twentieth century, the problems facing their counterparts in Russia were much greater.

Like many peasants who tried to break away from their communes under Stolypin's reforms in the early part of the century, the 'separators' of the 1990s faced obstruction. Some *kolkhoz* chairmen allocated them poor land and damaged machinery. Farmers who broke away faced high costs. Agricultural

16 See Nove, *Economic History*, pp. 303–13, 336–48, 372–82; Libert, B., *The Environmental Heritage of Soviet Agriculture* (Wallingford, 1995); Dodge and Feshbach, 'Role', pp. 236–70; Bridger, S., 'Soviet rural women: Employment and family life', in *RPW*, pp. 271–93.
17 See Doran, J. and Bizony, P., *Starman: The Truth behind the Legend of Yuri Gagarin* (London, 1998).
18 Nove, *Economic History*, pp. 372–7.

equipment, seed, fertilisers, and the credit to buy them with, were very expensive, while the prices farmers could get for their produce were relatively low. Government assistance fell a long way short of promises. Russian private farmers were in no position to compete with importers of food from Western states, whose governments afforded their farmers far more protection against the uncertainties of the global market. Many of Russia's new 'peasant farmers' went out of business. In early 1996 there were only 280,000 'peasant farms' in Russia. They contained only 5 per cent of the arable land, and less than 1 per cent of the total population. The majority of the small and demoralised rural population of post-Soviet Russia in the 1990s were unwilling to give up the very basic safety net and rudimentary welfare provisions provided by the collective farms. In a final twist to the tragic history of rural Russia in the twentieth century, most villagers were reluctant to take the risk of leaving the collective farms that their parents and grandparents had fought so hard to resist in the 1930s.[19]

CONCLUSION

By the late twentieth century, remnants of the traditional ways of life of Russia's peasants continued to exist in only a few remote parts of northern Russia and Siberia, and in the recollections of older villagers who could remember the times before collectivisation and Soviet power. Reflections of the peasantry's old ways of life, with varying degrees of distortion, can be found in the works of historians (such as this book), artifacts preserved in folk museums, collections of folklore, and the nostalgic literary works of the 'village writers' (*derevenshchiki*) of the 1950s–70s.[20]

The often tragic experiences of Russian peasants in the years of Soviet power, and the pitiful legacy of their ways of life in the 1990s, should not prompt the romanticisation of Russian peasant society before 1930 or 1917.[21] The world the peasants lost was not idyllic. In many ways it resembled rural societies in less developed countries outside Europe in the twentieth century. Most Russian peasants throughout the main period covered by this book lived in cramped and often squalid conditions. They did not have access to what people living in the developed world in the late twentieth century took for granted as basic amenities, such as constant availability of water fit for drinking, reliable supplies of food and effective health care. All Russian peasants lived at the mercy of the elements and environmental conditions of which

19 See Butterfield, J., Kuznetsov, M. and Sazonov, S., 'Peasant farming in Russia', *JPS*, vol. 23, no. 4 (1996), pp. 79–105; Wegren, S. K., 'The politics of private farming in Russia', *JPS*, vol. 23, no. 4 (1996), pp. 106–40. See also Powell, S. G., *Agricultural Reform in China: From Communes to Commodity Economy, 1978–1990* (Manchester and New York, 1992); Rösener, *Peasantry*, pp. 206–14.
20 See Kovalev, E. M. (comp.), *Golosa krest'yan: Sel'skaya Rossiya XX veka v krest'yanskikh memuarakh* (Moscow, 1996); Hilton, *Russian Folk Art*; Reeder, R. (ed. and trans.), *Russian Folk Lyrics* (Bloomington, IN, 1993); Parthé, *Village Prose*.
21 For a recent romanticised view, see Gromyko, M. M., *Mir russkoi derevni* (Moscow, 1991).

they had only partial understanding, and over which they had little control. Death was ever present in Russian villages. It took people of all ages, not just mostly the old, and sometimes struck with little warning. Most notable from a modern perspective, and no doubt most harrowing for peasants at the time, was the fact that around half of all peasant children died before they were five years old.

Those who survived to adulthood led difficult lives. Peasant women and young men were largely kept in the places ordained for them in a patriarchal social order, which was enforced by middle-aged male heads of households and male village elders in a system of day-to-day subjugation that replicated the oppression of all Russia's peasants by the ruling and landowning elites who lived at their expense. Violence, including by men against women, was almost routine. Peasant labour, both domestic work by women in their households and agricultural work by men and women on the land, was often dirty, arduous and monotonous, and must have seemed interminable. It was interrupted only by periodic agricultural, family and church festivals, and the bouts of heavy drinking that accompanied them. The respite from agricultural labour afforded by the long Russian winter was cancelled out by the intense discomfort of whole families being cooped up together, sometimes with livestock, in the stifling atmosphere of their smoke-filled and ill-lit wooden huts for months on end. The dramatic and sudden arrival of spring in Russia was a mixed blessing as it signalled the onset of another cycle of back-breaking labour in the fields.

Nevertheless, the terrible experiences of Russian peasants in the twentieth century surpassed anything that had happened to their forebears. The decades after 1917 saw decisive changes in the villages, most imposed from outside, which led to the demise of Russian peasant society. Some of the changes, for example those caused by industrialisation and urbanisation, can be traced back to the late nineteenth century, and were similar to long-term trends that had led to the decline of peasant societies elsewhere in the developed world. Others, in particular collectivisation, were peculiar to those parts of the globe that came under Communist rule. Centrally planned economic development greatly accelerated the pace of social and economic change in the Soviet Union but had catastrophic consequences for Russia's peasants. The traditional ways of life in rural Russia were, of course, no longer viable in the middle and later decades of the twentieth century. What is most striking about the end of the world the peasants made in Russia, however, was the speed, brutality and suffering that accompanied its passing.

Guide to further reading

This selective list includes mostly works in English, and favours recent studies. Books and articles that appeared too late to be considered in the text are indicated by an asterisk. (See 'Abbreviations used in notes' where necessary.)

INTRODUCTION

For surveys of the historical literature on European peasantries, see *Scott, T. (ed.), *The Peasantries of Europe from the Fourteenth to the Eighteenth Century* (London and New York, 1998) (organised by country or region); Rösener, W., *The Peasantry of Europe* (Oxford, 1994) (organised thematically). See also Le Roy Ladurie, E., 'Peasants', in *NCMH*, vol. 13, pp. 115–63. For interdisciplinary 'peasant studies' literature, much of which concerns Asia, Africa, and South and Central America in the twentieth century, see Shanin, T. (ed.), *Peasants and Peasant Societies: Selected Readings*, 2nd edn (Harmondsworth, 1988); Ellis, F., *Peasant Economics: Farm Households and Agrarian Development*, 2nd edn (Cambridge, 1993).

The standard work on the Russian peasantry before 1861 is still Blum, J., *Lord and Peasant in Russia from the Ninth to the Nineteenth Century* (Princeton, NJ, 1961). For a new, admirably concise, survey, see *Melton, E., 'The Russian peasantries, 1450–1860', in Scott, *Peasantries of Europe*, pp. 227–65. Recent work is surveyed in Bartlett, R., 'The peasantry and serfdom in the time of Peter the Great', in Cross, A. (ed.), *Russia in the Reign of Peter the Great: Old and New Perspectives*, 2 parts (Cambridge, 1998), pt 1, pp. 53–63; Channon, J., 'From muzhik to kolkhoznik: Some recent Western and Soviet studies of peasants in late imperial and early Soviet Russia', *SEER*, vol. 70 (1992), pp. 127–39; Eklof, B., 'Ways of seeing: Recent Anglo-American studies of the Russian peasant (1861–1914)', *JGO*, vol. 34 (1988), pp. 57–79; Moon, D., 'Agriculture and peasants, industry and workers, political parties and revolution', *EHQ*, vol. 22 (1992), pp. 597–604; *id.*, 'Recent books on the Russian peasantry', *HJ*, vol. 35 (1992), pp. 953–8; *id.*, 'Women in rural Russia from the tenth to the twentieth centuries', *C & C*, vol. 12 (1997), pp. 129–38.

CHAPTER 1: POPULATION

The peasant population at the end of the nineteenth century is examined in Moon, D., 'Estimating the peasant population of late imperial Russia from the 1897 census', *EAS*, vol. 48 (1996), pp. 141–53; Shanin, T., *Russia as a 'Developing Society'* (Basingstoke and London, 1986), pp. 57–65, 93–102. See also Clem, R. S. (ed.), *Research Guide to the Russian and Soviet Censuses* (Ithaca, NY, and London, 1986). Data from earlier censuses (in tables) are in Kabuzan, V. M., *Izmeneniya v razmeshchenii naseleniya Rossii v XVIII–pervoi polovine XIX v.* (Moscow, 1971).

For surveys of Russian demographic history, see Czap, P., 'Russian history from a demographic perspective', in Kosinski, L. A. (ed.), *Demographic Developments in Eastern Europe* (New York and London, 1977), pp. 120–37; Ransel, D. L., 'Recent Soviet studies in demographic history', *RR*, vol. 40 (1981), pp. 143–57. Sophisticated Western works include Coale, A. *et al.*, *Human Fertility in Russia since the Nineteenth Century* (Princeton, NJ, 1979); Blum, A. and Troitskaja, I., 'La mortalité en Russie aux XVIIIe et XIXe siècles: Estimations locales·à partir des *Revizzi*', *Population*, vol. 51 (1996), pp. 303–28; Hoch, S. L., 'Famine, disease, and mortality patterns in the parish of Borshevka, 1830–1912', *Population Studies*, vol. 52, no. 3 (1998). (See also 'Households' below.)

For comparative and theoretical works, see Wrigley, E. A., *Population and History* (London, 1969); Dupâquier, J., 'Population', in *NCMH*, vol. 13, pp. 80–114; Anderson, M., *Population Change in North-Western Europe, 1750–1850* (Basingstoke and London, 1988); Schofield, R. *et al.* (eds), *The Decline of Mortality in Europe* (Oxford, 1991).

CHAPTER 2: ENVIRONMENT

The issues in this chapter are discussed in more detail in Moon, D., 'Peasant migration and the settlement of Russia's frontiers, 1550–1897', *HJ*, vol. 40 (1997), pp. 859–93. Interactions between Russians and their environments are analysed by historical geographers in Bater, J. H. and French, R. A. (eds), *Studies in Russian Historical Geography*, 2 vols (London, 1983); and Pallot, J. and Shaw, D. J. B., *Landscape and Settlement in Romanov Russia, 1613–1917* (Oxford, 1990).

Peasant migration, including interactions with environments and native peoples, are also discussed in Barrett, T. M., 'Lines of uncertainty: The frontiers of the north Caucasus', *SR*, vol. 54 (1995), pp. 578–601; Goryushkin, L., 'Migration, settlement and the rural economy of Siberia, 1861–1914', in Wood, A. (ed.), *The History of Siberia* (London and New York, 1991), pp. 140–57; Hellie, R. (ed.), *The Frontier in Russian History* (*Russian History*, vol. 19 [1992]); Khodarkovsky, M., *Where Two Worlds Met: The Russian State and the Kalmyk Nomads, 1600–1771* (Ithaca, NY, 1992); Sunderland, W., 'Peasants on the move: State peasant resettlement in imperial Russia, 1805–1830s', *RR*, vol. 52 (1993), pp. 472–85; *id.*, 'Russians into Yakuts? "Going native" and problems of Russian national identity in the Siberian north, 1870s–1914', *SR*, vol. 55 (1996), pp. 806–25; Treadgold, D. W., *The Great Siberian Migration: Government and Peasant in Resettlement from Emancipation to the First World War* (Princeton, NJ, 1957).

For comparative perspectives, see Crosby, A. J., *Ecological Imperialism: The Biological Expansion of Europe, 900–1900* (Cambridge, 1986); Jones, E. L., 'The environment and the economy', in *NCMH*, vol. 13, pp. 15–42; McNeill, W. H., *Europe's Steppe Frontier, 1500–1800* (Chicago and London, 1964); Simmons, I. G., *Environmental History* (Oxford, 1993).

CHAPTER 3: EXPLOITATION

Exploitation is one of the main themes of Blum, J., *Lord and Peasant*. The persistence of serfdom is considered in Moon, D., 'Reassessing Russian serfdom', *EHQ*, vol. 26 (1996), pp. 483–526.

On the origins of serfdom, see Culpepper, J. M., 'The legislative origins of peasant bondage in Muscovy', *FOG*, vol. 14 (1969), pp. 162–237; and Hellie, R., *Enserfment and Military Change in Muscovy* (Chicago and London, 1971). For historiographical surveys, see Petrovich, M. B., 'The peasant in nineteenth-century historiography', in Vucinich, W. S. (ed.), *The Peasant in Nineteenth-Century Russia* (Stanford, CA, 1968), pp. 218–30; Worobec, C. D., 'Contemporary historians on the Muscovite peasantry', *CSP*, vol. 23 (1981), pp. 315–27. Smith, R. E. F., *The Enserfment of the Russian Peasantry* (Cambridge, 1968) is a collection of documents in translation.

On military service, see Keep, J. L. H., *Soldiers of the Tsar: Army and Society in Russia, 1462–1874* (Oxford, 1985); and Wirtschafter, E. K., *From Serf to Russian Soldier* (Princeton, NJ, 1990). On taxation, see Kahan, A., *The Plow, the Hammer and the Knout: An Economic History of Eighteenth-Century Russia* (Chicago and London, 1985), pp. 319–49; and Christian, D., *'Living Water': Vodka and Russian Society on the Eve of Emancipation* (Oxford, 1990).

Studies of the abolition of serfdom include Emmons, T., *The Russian Landed Gentry and the Peasant Emancipation of 1861* (Cambridge, 1968); Field, D., *The End of Serfdom: Nobility and Bureaucracy in Russia, 1855–1861* (Cambridge, MA, and London, 1976); Zaionchkovsky, P. A., *The Abolition of Serfdom in Russia*, S. Wobst (ed. and trans.) (Gulf Breeze, FL, 1978); Zakharova, L. G., 'Autocracy and the abolition of serfdom in Russia, 1856–1861', *SSH*, vol. 26, no. 2 (1987). Moon, D., *The Abolition of Serfdom in Russia in 1861* is in preparation. For documents, see Vernadsky, G., *A Source Book for Russian History from Early Times to 1917*, 3 vols (New Haven, CT, and London, 1972), vol. 3, pp. 589–605. On other reforms, see Eklof, B. *et al.* (eds), *Russia's Great Reforms, 1855–1881* (Bloomington, IN, 1994).

For comparative perspectives, see Blum, J., 'The rise of serfdom in Eastern Europe', *AHR*, vol. 62 (1957), pp. 807–36; *id.*, *The End of the Old Order in Rural Europe* (Princeton, NJ, 1978); Bush, M. L. (ed.), *Serfdom and Slavery: Studies in Legal Bondage* (London and New York, 1996); Kolchin, P., *Unfree Labor: American Slavery and Russian Serfdom* (Cambridge, MA, and London, 1987).

CHAPTER 4: PRODUCTION

General books on Russian economic history include Crisp, O., *Studies in the Russian Economy before 1914* (London, 1976); Kahan, *The Plow, the Hammer and the Knout*; Gatrell, P., *The Tsarist Economy, 1850–1917* (London, 1986); Gregory, P., *Before Command: An Economic History of Russia from Emancipation to the First Five-Year Plan* (Princeton, NJ, 1994). Several essays in Bater and French, *Studies in Russian Historical Geography*, and Pallot and Shaw, *Landscape and Settlement*, are also relevant.

For major works on Russian agriculture, see Smith, R. E. F., *The Origins of Farming in Russia* (Paris and The Hague, 1959); *id.*, *Peasant Farming in Muscovy* (Cambridge, 1977); Confino, M., *Systèmes Agraires et Progrès Agricole: l'Assolement Triennal en Russie aux XVIIIe–XIXe Siècles* (Paris and The Hague, 1969). Pavlovsky, G., *Agricultural Russia on the Eve of Revolution* (London, 1930) is a detailed study by a former official of the tsarist Ministry of Agriculture.

On handicrafts, trade and wage labour, see Melton, E., 'Proto-industrialization, serf agriculture and agrarian social structure: Two estates in nineteenth-century Russia', *P & P*, no. 115 (1987), pp. 73–87; Rudolph, R. L., 'Agricultural structure and proto-industrialization in Russia: Economic development with unfree labour', *JEcH*, vol. 45 (1985), pp. 47–69; Engel, B. A., *Between the Fields and the City: Women, Work and Family in Russia, 1861–1914* (Cambridge, 1994); *Burds, J., *Peasant Dreams and Market Politics: Labor Migration and the Russian Village, 1861–1905* (Pittsburgh, PA, 1998).

A selection of agricultural implements, handicraft tools and produce are in the State Museum of Ethnography in St Petersburg. See Shangina, I. I., *Russkie sel'sko-khozyaistvennye orudiya XIX–XX vv.: Katalog kollektsii* (Leningrad, 1981).

For theoretical and comparative perspectives, see Ashton, T. H. and Philpin, C. H. E. (eds), *The Brenner Debate: Agrarian Class Structure and Economic Development in Pre-Industrial Europe* (Cambridge, 1985); Baron, S., 'The transition from feudalism to capitalism in Russia', *AHR*, vol. 77 (1972), pp. 715–29; Chayanov, A. V., *The Theory of Peasant Economy* (Manchester, 1986); Ellis, *Peasant Economics*; Overton, M., *Agricultural Revolution in England* (Cambridge, 1996).

CHAPTER 5: HOUSEHOLDS

One of the pioneers of modern Western scholarship on Russian peasant households and families was Peter Czap: see his 'Marriage and the peasant joint family in the era of serfdom', in Ransel, D. L. (ed.), *The Family in Imperial Russia* (Urbana and Chicago, IL, 1978), pp. 103–23; '"A large family: the peasant's greatest wealth": Serf households in Mishino, Russia, 1814–1858', in Wall, R. (ed.), *Family Forms in Historic Europe* (Cambridge, 1983), pp. 105–51; 'The perennial multiple family household, Mishino, Russia 1782–1858', *JFamH*, vol. 7, no. 1 (1982), pp. 5–26. Other important works on households under serfdom include Bohac, R. D., *Family, Property, and Socioeconomic Mobility:*

Russian Peasants on Manuilovskoe Estate, 1810–1861, unpublished PhD dissertation (University of Illinois, 1982); *id.*, 'Peasant inheritance strategies in Russia', *JIH*, vol. 16 (1985), pp. 23–42; 'Widows and the Russian serf community', in Clements, B. E. *et al.* (eds), *Russia's Women: Accommodation, Resistance, Transformation* (Berkeley and Los Angeles, CA, 1991), pp. 95–112; Bushnell, J., 'Did serfowners control marriage? Orlov serfs and their neighbours, 1773–1861', *SR*, vol. 52 (1993), pp. 419–45; Hoch, S. L., *Serfdom and Social Control: Petrovskoe, a Village in Tambov* (Chicago, 1986), pp. 65–132. Some Soviet research was summarised in Aleksandrov, V. A., 'Typology of the Russian peasant family in the feudal epoch', *SSH*, vol. 21, no. 2 (1982), pp. 26–62.

On the period after 1861, see Farnsworth, B., 'The litigious daughter-in-law', *SR*, vol. 45 (1986), pp. 49–64; Frierson, C. A., '*Razdel*: The peasant family divided', *RR*, vol. 46 (1987), pp. 35–51; Ransel, D. L., 'Infant-care cultures in the Russian empire', in Clements, *Russia's Women*, pp. 113–32; Worobec, C. D., *Peasant Russia: Family and Community in the Post-Emancipation Period* (Princeton, NJ, 1991).

For comparative perspectives, see Mitterauer, M. and Kagan, A., 'Russian and central European family structures', *JFamH*, vol. 7 (1982), pp. 103–31; Laslett, P., *Household and Family in Past Time* (Cambridge, 1972); Wall, *Family Forms*; Anderson, M., *Approaches to the History of the Western Family, 1500–1914* (Basingstoke and London, 1980); Casey, J., *The History of the Family* (Oxford, 1989).

CHAPTER 6: COMMUNES

Essays by many major specialists are in Bartlett, R. P. (ed.), *Land Commune and Peasant Community in Russia: Communal Forms in Imperial and Early Soviet Society* (Basingstoke and London, 1990). Atkinson, D., *The End of the Russian Land Commune, 1905–1930* (Stanford, CA, 1983) also surveys, in less detail, the origins and development of the commune. The functions and workings of communes in the nineteenth and early twentieth centuries are examined in Mironov, B. N., 'Local government in Russia in the first half of the nineteenth century', *JGO*, vol. 42 (1994), pp. 161–201; *id.*, 'The Russian peasant commune after the reforms of the 1860s', *SR*, vol. 44 (1985), pp. 438–67; Pallot and Shaw, *Landscape and Settlement*, pp. 136–63; Anfimov, A. M. and Zyrianov, P. N., 'Elements of the evolution of the Russian peasant commune in the post-reform period (1861–1914), *SSH*, vol. 21, no. 3 (1982–83), pp. 68–96; Anfimov, 'On the history of the Russian peasantry at the beginning of the twentieth century', *RR*, vol. 51 (1992), pp. 396–407. See also *Pallot, J., *Land Reform in Russia 1906–1917: Peasant Responses to Stolypin's Project of Rural Transformation* (Oxford, 1999).

Of particular interest are micro-studies of village communities under serfdom: Bohac, R. D., 'The Mir and the military draft', *SR*, vol. 47 (1988), pp. 652–66; *id.*, 'Widows and the Russian serf community', in Clements,

Russia's Women (Manuilovskoe, Tver' province); Hoch, *Serfdom and Social Control*, pp. 91–190 (Petrovskoe, Tambov province); Melton, E., 'Household economies and communal conflicts on a Russian serf estate, 1800–1817', *JSocH*, vol. 26 (1993), pp. 559–85; **id.*, *The Other Serfdom: Economy and Community on an Obrok Estate in Russia, 1800–1836*, forthcoming (Baki, Kostroma province). Some landowners' instructions to communal officials and stewards are in Vernadsky, *Source Book*, vol. 2, pp. 441–9.

For comparative perspectives, see Blum, J., 'The European village as community', *Agricultural History*, vol. 45 (1971), pp. 157–78; *id.*, 'The internal structure and polity of the European village community from the 15th to the 19th century', *JMH*, vol. 43 (1971), pp. 541–76; Scribner, R. W., 'Communalism: Universal category or ideological construct?', *HJ*, vol. 37 (1994), pp. 199–207. See also Sabean, D., *Power in the Blood: Popular Culture and Village Discourse in Early Modern Germany* (Cambridge, 1984); Ooms, H., *Tokugawa Village Practice: Class, Status, Power, Law* (Berkeley and Los Angeles, CA, 1996).

CHAPTER 7: PROTEST

Avrich, P., *Russian Rebels, 1600–1800* (New York, 1972) is a general account of the four great revolts. For critical surveys of the Soviet literature, see Yaresh, L., 'The "Peasant Wars" in Soviet historiography', *ASEER*, vol. 16 (1957), pp. 241–59; Alexander, J. T., 'Recent Soviet historiography on the Pugachev revolt', *CSS*, vol. 4 (1970), pp. 602–17. On individual revolts, see Dunning, C., 'R. G. Skrynnikov, the Time of Troubles, and the "First Peasant War" in Russia', *RR*, vol. 50 (1991), pp. 71–81; Khodarkovsky, M., 'The Stepan Razin uprising: Was it a "Peasant War"?', *JGO*, vol. 42 (1994), pp. 1–19; Alexander, J. T., *Emperor of the Cossacks: Pugachev and the Frontier Jacquerie of 1773–1775* (Lawrence, KN, 1973).

Other forms of protest are discussed in Bohac, R. D., 'Everyday forms of resistance: Serf opposition to gentry exactions, 1800–1861', in *PECPER*, pp. 236–60; Christian, *'Living Water'*, pp. 286–352; Kolchin, *Unfree Labor*, pp. 241–357; Moon, D., *Russian Peasants and Tsarist Legislation on the Eve of Reform: Interaction between Peasants and Officialdom, 1825–1855* (Basingstoke and London, 1992).

Popular monarchism and pretenders are examined in Perrie, M., *Pretenders and Popular Monarchism in Early Modern Russia: The False Tsars of the Time of Troubles* (Cambridge, 1995); Longworth, P., 'The pretender phenomenon in eighteenth-century Russia', *P & P*, no. 66 (1975), pp. 61–84; Field, D., *Rebels in the Name of the Tsar* (Boston, MA, and London, 1989).

For comparative perspectives, see Bercé, Y.-M., *Revolt and Revolution in Early Modern Europe* (Manchester and New York, 1987); Landsberger, H. A. (ed.), *Rural Protest: Peasant Movements and Social Change* (London, 1974); Mousnier, R., *Peasant Uprisings in Seventeenth-Century France, Russia and China* (New York, 1970); Scott, J. C., *The Moral Economy of the Peasant: Rebellion and Subsistence in South East Asia* (New Haven, CT, and London, 1976); *id.*, *Weapons of the Weak: Everyday Forms of Peasant Resistance* (New Haven, CT, and London, 1985).

CHAPTER 8: CONSUMPTION

On diet and food consumption, see Smith, R. E. F. and Christian, D., *Bread and Salt: A Social and Economic History of Food and Drink in Russia* (Cambridge, 1984) (an invaluable overview); Hoch, *Serfdom and Social Control*, pp. 15–64 (a case study); Gregory, P., 'Grain marketings and peasant consumption in Russia, 1885–1913', *EEH*, vol. 17 (1980), pp. 135–64. The debate over living standards after 1861 is assessed in Gregory, *Before Command*, pp. 37–54; Hoch, S. L., '"On good numbers and bad": Malthus, population trends and peasant standard of living in late imperial Russia', *SR*, vol. 53 (1994), pp. 41–75; Wheatcroft, S. G., 'Crises and the condition of the peasantry in late imperial Russia', in *PECPER*, pp. 128–72.

For case studies of differentiation and socio-economic mobility, see Melton, 'Proto-industrialization, serf agriculture and agrarian social structure', *P & P*, no. 115 (1987); Bohac, *Family, Property, and Socioeconomic Mobility*; Wilbur, E. M., 'Peasant poverty in theory and practice: A view from Russia's "impoverished center" at the end of the nineteenth century', in *PECPER*, pp. 101–27; Johnson, R. E., 'Family life-cycles and economic stratification: A case-study in rural Russia', *JSocH*, vol. 30 (1997), pp. 705–31.

For theoretical and comparative perspectives (in addition to works cited above under 'Production'), see Gatrell, P., 'Historians and peasants: Studies of medieval England in a Russian context', *P & P*, no. 96 (1982), pp. 22–50; Shanin, T., *The Awkward Class: Political Sociology of Peasantry in a Developing Society, Russia 1910–1925* (Oxford, 1972); Arnold, D., *Famine: Social Crisis and Historical Change* (Oxford, 1988); Crafts, N., 'Some dimensions of the "quality of life" during the British industrial revolution', *EcHR*, vol. 50 (1997), pp. 617–39.

CHAPTERS 9 AND 10: CONTINUITY AND CHANGE

(This section concentrates on the 1860s to the 1930s.) For a long time the standard book on the peasantry in late imperial Russia was Robinson, G. T., *Rural Russia under the Old Regime* (Berkeley and Los Angeles, 1932). Few books span the revolution of 1917, but see Volin, L., *A Century of Russian Agriculture: From Alexander II to Khrushchev* (Cambridge, MA, and London, 1970); Yaney, G., *The Urge to Mobilize: Agrarian Reform in Russia, 1861–1930* (Urbana and Chicago, IL, and London, 1982); Schmemann, S. [an American journalist], *Echoes of a Native Land: Two Centuries of a Russian Village* (London, 1997).

For broadly representative collections of essays by many of the major specialists, see Eklof, B. and Frank, S. P. (eds), *The World of the Russian*

Peasant: Post-Emancipation Culture and Society (Boston, MA, and London, 1990); Farnsworth, B. and Viola, L. (eds), *Russian Peasant Women* (Oxford, 1992); Bartlett, *Land Commune and Peasant Community in Russia*; Kingston-Mann, E. and Mixter, T. (eds), *Peasant Economy, Culture, and Politics of European Russia, 1800–1921* (Princeton, NJ, 1991); Frank, S. P. and Steinberg, M. D. (eds), *Cultures in Flux: Lower-Class Values, Practices, and Resistance in Late Imperial Russia* (Princeton, NJ, 1994); Pallot, J. (ed.), *Transforming Peasants: Society, State and the Peasantry, 1861–1930* (Basingstoke and London, 1998).

A few works by contemporary Russian writers are available in English: Engelgardt, A. N., *Letters from the Countryside, 1872–1887*, C. A. Frierson (ed. and trans.) (New York and Oxford, 1993); Semyonova-Tian-Shanskaia, O., *Village Life in Late Tsarist Russia*, D. L. Ransel (ed.), M. Levine (trans.) (Bloomington, IN, 1993); Stepniak, *The Russian Peasantry* (London, 1905).

Developments in rural Russia in the late nineteenth and early twentieth centuries are compared with contemporary France in Moon, D., 'Peasants into Russian citizens? A comparative perspective', *RevR*, vol. 9 (1996), pp. 43–81. (The Russian Peasantry in the period 1881–1991 will be examined in a companion volume currently in preparation by another author.)

Glossary

appanage peasants (*udel'nye*) peasants living on land of tsars' families (1797–1860s) (see also court peasants)

artel' (-i) association(s) (especially migrant workers and soldiers)

baba (-y) female peasant(s) (peasant term)

barshchina labour services (under serfdom)

batyushka little father (peasant form of address to priests, nobles, tsars)

black-ploughing peasants (*chernososhnye*) part of state peasantry (see below)

bobyli landless labourers

bol'shak male head of household

boyar aristocrat, wealthy landowner in Muscovite Russia

chernyi peredel black repartition (of land)

chernozem black earth

church peasants (*tserkovnye*) peasants living on land of Russian Orthodox Church (to 1762–64)

court peasants (*dvortsovye*) peasants living on land of tsars' families (to 1797)

derevnya (-i) hamlet(s)

Descriptions of Seigniorial Estates (*Opisaniya pomeshchich'ikh imenii*) documents compiled by landowners in 1858–59 on eve of abolition of serfdom

desyatina (-y) 2.7 acres or 1.09 hectares

district (*uezd*) subdivision of province

dvor household

household tax tax paid by peasant households (1646–1723)

izba peasant house

kasha porridge or gruel

kholopstvo slavery (to 1723)

kladka bride-price

kolkhoz (-y) collective farm(s) (in Soviet Union)

kosulya (-i) 'improved' wooden plough(s)

krugovaya poruka collective responsibility

kvas slightly alcoholic drink made from malted grain, grain meal or bread

mir village commune (peasant term)

muzhik (-i) male peasant(s) (peasant term)

obrok dues in cash or kind

obshchina term for village commune devised by intellectuals in the 1830s

odnodvortsy 'single homesteaders', descendants of military servitors on steppe frontier, part of state peasantry from 1719 (see below)

otkhodnik (-i) migrant wage labourer(s)

plug 'true' plough

poll tax tax paid by male members of lower orders (peasants and towns-people) (1724–1883/1899)

polovnik (-i) share-cropper(s)

pomeshchik (-i) noble landowner(s)

pomoch' mutual assistance

pridanoe dowry or trousseau

province (*guberniya*) main geographical subdivision of Russian state, *c.* 1708–1920s

Regulatory Charters (*Ustavnye gramoty*) documents drawn up in 1861–63 recording land allotments of freed serfs and dues and services owed to landowners in return

saban Tatar plough adopted by some Russian peasants

samogon illegally distilled spirits, 'moonshine'

seigniorial peasants (serfs) (*pomeshchich'i*) peasants bound to estates of nobles

sel'skie obshchestva village societies (set up in 1861)

selo (-a) village(s)

serfdom institution under which peasants were bound to landed estates of nobles

serfs see seigniorial peasants

sokha traditional Russian wooden plough

soslovie (-ya) social estate(s) or legal category/ies in tsarist Russia, e.g. peasantry, nobility, clergy

soul tax see poll tax

sovkhoz (-y) state farm(s) (in Soviet Union)

starosta elder

state peasants (*kazennye, gosudarstvennye*) peasants living on land belonging to state

steppe grasslands or prairies in south-east Russia and Siberia

taiga coniferous forest in northern Russia and Siberia

tyaglo (-a) labour team(s) (usually husband and wife); amount(s) of obligations born by team(s); area(s) of land allotted to team(s)

volnenie (-ya) disturbance(s)

volost' (-i) township(s) or group(s) of villages

zemlyaki peasants from the same or neighbouring villages

zemstvo (-a) elected district/provincial council(s) set up from 1864

Index of authors cited

Only full references are given.

Subject index

abolition of serfdom, *see* serfdom, abolition of

Adams, Bruce 101

adopted sons-in-law 167, 188, 216

agriculture 120–43, 329, 331, 334, 337–41, 346, 361–2, 366
- animal husbandry 11, 15, 61, 91, 119, 139–42, 147, 223, 294, 295, 296, 300, 301, 329
- arable farming 14–15, 45, 61, 91, 119, 120, 121–39, 141–2, 151, 222, 293, 294, 296–8, 300, 329
- comparisons 1–2, 132, 133, 134, 223
- implements 123, 125, 128–9, 130, 131, 144, 145, 248, 360
- 'improvement' of 1–2, 107, 108, 126, 129, 130–1, 223, 287
- rituals and ceremonies 123–4, 125, 140, 291, 295, 337–40
- *see also* commercial farmers/farming, crop yields, field grass husbandry, flax, hemp, potatoes, rye, slash-and-burn farming, three field system, vegetables

Aksakov, Sergei 49

Aleksandrov, V.A. 158, 164, 172, 179, 230

Alexander I (reigned 1801–25) 91, 100, 108, 251

Alexander II (reigned 1855–81) 4, 110

Alexis (reigned 1645–76) 175, 251

aliens (*inorodtsy*) 14, 19

Altai Mountains 37, 48, 256

Anfimov, A.M. 316

Anisimov, E.V. 81

Anna (reigned 1730–40) 204

appanage peasants, *see* court/appanage peasants

appanage peasants, reforms of 93, 106, 107, 112–13, 130, 131, 142–3, 229, 264, 267–8

arable farming, *see* agriculture

armed forces/army 14, 22, 65, 69, 82–4, 85–6, 88, 110, 113, 241, 243, 265, 344–5
- *see also* conscription, wars

ascribed peasants 78

Atkinson, Dorothy 214, 215, 333

auctions law (1847) 109

aviation 361

Baki, Kostroma province 8, 160, 163, 170, 175, 206, 218, 231–2, 314, 315, 321

Baltic peoples, region 16, 18, 58, 108, 130, 215

banditry 261, 279

barshchina, *see* labour services

Bashkirs 19, 46, 60–1, 106

Belorussia, Belorussians 3, 16, 18, 19, 58, 71, 106, 112, 215, 217

Belyaev, I.D. 212

Bezdna, Kazan' province 280

Bibikov, D.G. 267

billeting obligation 85–6

birth customs 184

birth rates 23–5, 30–2, 34–5, 58–9, 165, 326, 332, 364

black earth, *see* soils and soil fertility

'black' land and peasants 103, 201, 207, 212, 219

'black repartition' 220, 224, 353

Blanchard, Ian 292

Blum, Jerome 7, 9, 126, 127, 134, 137, 217, 223

Bogoroditskaya, N.A. 312